Seeing Ourselves

SEEING OURSELVES

Third Edition

*Classic, Contemporary,
and Cross-Cultural
Readings in Sociology*

Edited by

JOHN J. MACIONIS
Kenyon College

NIJOLE V. BENOKRAITIS
University of Baltimore

PRENTICE HALL
Englewood Cliffs, New Jersey 07632

Library of Congress Cataloging-in-Publication Data

Seeing ourselves : classic, contemporary, and cross-cultural readings
   in sociology / edited by John J. Macionis, Nijole V. Benokraitis. —
   3rd ed.
      p.   cm.
   Includes bibliographical references.
   ISBN 0–13–101130–8
   1. Sociology.   I. Macionis, John J.   II. Benokraitis, Nijole
V. (Nijole Vaicaitis).
HM51.M165 1995
301—dc20   94-6822
                                                      CIP

Acquisitions editor: Nancy Roberts
Editorial/production supervision and interior design: Joan Stone
Cover designer: Lorraine Bello
Production coordinator: Mary Ann Gloriande
Editorial assistant: Pat Naturale

 © 1995, 1992, 1989 by Prentice-Hall, Inc.
A Simon & Schuster Company
Englewood Cliffs, New Jersey 07632

Printed in the United States of America

10 9 8 7 6 5 4 3 2

ISBN 0-13-101130-8

PRENTICE-HALL INTERNATIONAL (UK) LIMITED, *London*
PRENTICE-HALL OF AUSTRALIA PTY. LIMITED, *Sydney*
PRENTICE-HALL CANADA INC., *Toronto*
PRENTICE-HALL HISPANOAMERICANA, S.A., *Mexico*
PRENTICE-HALL OF INDIA PRIVATE LIMITED, *New Delhi*
PRENTICE-HALL OF JAPAN, INC., *Tokyo*
SIMON & SCHUSTER ASIA PTE. LTD., *Singapore*
EDITORA PRENTICE-HALL DO BRASIL, LTDA., *Rio de Janeiro*

CONTENTS

v

SEX AND GENDER

AGING AND THE ELDERLY

THE ECONOMY AND WORK

POLITICS, GOVERNMENT, AND THE MILITARY

FAMILY

SOCIAL CHANGE AND MODERNITY

PREFACE

Beginning the study of human society is an exciting experience. It transforms the ways we understand the surrounding world so that we end up seeing ourselves in a new way. This extraordinary collection of readings is designed to make the discovery of sociology, and its application to the investigation of our own society and others around the world, rich and rewarding.

This anthology presents the very best of sociological thought, including the work of the discipline's pioneers as well as that of men and women conducting today's cutting-edge research or raising significant questions about human society. It provides excellent reading material for a number of courses, including introductory sociology, social problems, cultural anthropology, social theory, social stratification, American studies, women's studies, and marriage and the family.

THE THREE C'S: CLASSIC, CONTEMPORARY, AND CROSS-CULTURAL

The third edition of *Seeing Ourselves,* the most popular reader in the discipline, has more outstanding scholarship than ever before—seventy-five selections that represent the breadth and depth of sociology. This unique anthology is not only extensive; it also systematically weaves together three different kinds of selections. For each general topic typically covered in a sociology course, three types of articles are included: *classic, contemporary,* and *cross-cultural.*

Classic articles—twenty-nine in all—are sociological statements of recognized importance and lasting significance. Included here are the ideas of sociology's founders and shapers—including Emile Durkheim, Karl Marx, Max Weber, Georg

Simmel, Ferdinand Toennies, as well as Margaret Mead, W. E. B. Du Bois, Louis Wirth, George Herbert Mead, and Charles Horton Cooley. Also found here are more recent contributions by Jessie Bernard, Robert Merton, Erving Goffman, Peter Berger, Kingsley Davis and Wilbert Moore, C. Wright Mills, Talcott Parsons, Leslie White, and Jo Freeman.

Of course, we recognize that not everyone will agree about precisely which selections warrant the term "classic." We hope, however, that instructors will be pleased to see the work of so many outstanding men and women—carefully edited with students in mind—available in a single, affordable source.

Twenty-four *contemporary* selections focus on current sociological issues, controversies, and applications. These articles show sociologists at work and demonstrate the importance of ongoing research. They make for stimulating reading and offer thought-provoking insights about ourselves and the surrounding world. Among the contemporary selections in *Seeing Ourselves* are Shulamit Reinharz on feminist research, Dianne Herman pointing out the cultural roots of sexual violence, William Bennett's contention that the United States is entering a period of cultural decline, Deborah Tannen's view of why the two sexes often talk past each other, Sally Helgesen on the competitive edge women bring to the corporate world, Robert Reich's investigation of the domestic consequences of the global economy, William Julius Wilson's account of the ghetto underclass, William O'Hare's profile of affluent Latinos, Naomi Wolf on the "beauty myth," Stephanie Riger's research on sexual harassment, Betty Friedan's views on aging, James Woods on homosexuality in the workplace, Catharine MacKinnon's analysis of pornography as a power issue, Norval Glenn's argument that the trend in the United States is for people to put their individual interests ahead of loyalty to their families, Gerald Jaynes and Robin Williams' comparative look at the health of black people and white people in the United States, Lester Brown's survey of the state of the world's environment, and Robert

Bellah's thoughts about the difficulty of finding a sense of meaningful participation in modern society.

The twenty-two *cross-cultural* selections offer sociological insights about the striking cultural diversity of our world. Included are well-known works such as "The Nacirema" by Horace Miner, "India's Sacred Cow" by Marvin Harris, and "The Amish: A Small Society" by John Hostetler. Other articles explore issues and problems including how race and class affect socialization, ways in which advertising depicts people of various backgrounds, differences between Japanese corporations and their U.S. counterparts, global patterns of crime, the staggering burden of African poverty, varying cultural attitudes toward homosexuality, traditional arranged marriage in India, Islam's view of women, academic achievement among Southeast Asian immigrants, how the AIDS epidemic is ravaging other continents, and the plight of indigenous peoples worldwide. Cross-cultural selections broaden students' understanding of other cultures as well as stimulate critical thinking about our own society.

ORGANIZATION OF THE READER

This reader parallels the chapter sequence common to textbooks used in introductory sociology. Of course, instructors can easily and effectively use these articles in a host of other courses, just as teachers can assign articles in whatever order they wish. For each of the twenty-two general topics, a cluster of three or four articles is presented, including at least one classic, at least one contemporary, and at least one cross-cultural selection. The expansive coverage that these seventy-five articles provides ensures that instructors can choose readings well suited to their own courses.

The first grouping of articles describes the distinctive sociological perspective, brings to life the promise and pitfalls of sociological research, and demonstrates the discipline's applications to a variety of issues. The selections that follow focus on key concepts: culture, society, socialization, social interaction, groups and organizations, and deviance. The focus then turns to various dimensions of social inequality, with attention to class, race and ethnicity, gender, and aging. The major social institutions are covered next, including the economy and work; politics, government, and the military; family; religion; education; and health and medicine. The final sets of articles explore dimensions of global transformation—including population growth, urbanization, the natural environment, social movements, and social change.

A NOTE ON LANGUAGE

All readings are presented in their original form; the editors have not altered any author's language. Readers should be aware that some of the older selections—especially the classics—use male pronouns rather than more contemporary gender-neutral terminology, and one article employs the term "Negro." We have not changed the language in any article, wishing not to violate the historical authenticity of any document. We urge faculty and students, with the original articles in hand, to consider the significance of changing language in their analysis of the author's ideas.

TEACHING FEATURES

This reader has two features that enhance the learning of students. First, a brief introduction, preceding each selection, presents the essential argument and highlights important issues to keep in mind while completing the reading. Second, each article is followed by "Critical-Thinking Questions," which develop the significance of the reading, help students evaluate their own learning, and stimulate class discussion.

INSTRUCTOR'S MANUAL WITH TEST QUESTIONS

Prentice Hall now offers with *Seeing Ourselves* an Instructor's Manual, prepared by Leda A. Thompson. For each selection, the Instructor's Manual provides a summary of the article's arguments and conclusions, eight multiple-choice questions (with answers), and several essay questions. The multiple-choice questions are also available on computer disk for users of IBM and Macintosh personal computers.

CHANGES TO THE THIRD EDITION

We are grateful to our colleagues at hundreds of colleges and universities who have made *Seeing Ourselves* a part of their courses. Energized by this unparalleled reception, the editors have produced the strongest edition yet—one that includes more articles and better material. Here are the key changes:

1. **Thirty-one new articles** appear in the third edition, bringing the total to seventy-five. We have added eight new *classics* to this revision, including work by Toennies ("Gemeinschaft and Gesellschaft"), Durkheim ("Anomy and Modern Life"), Simmel ("The Dyad and the Triad"), Margaret Mead ("Sex and Temperament in Three Primitive Societies"), and Robert Merton ("Manifest and Latent Functions"). Twenty-three new *contemporary* and *crosscultural* selections reflect new developments in the field of sociology (such as Shulamit Reinharz's "Feminist Research Methods" and Deborah Tanne's sociolinguistic "You Just Don't Understand: Women and Men in Conversation"), as well as changes in the United States (William Bennett's "The Decline of U.S. Society") and the larger world (Jack Mendelsohn's "Arms Control and the New World Order").

2. **New coverage of the natural environment** is represented by Rachel Carson's classic ("Silent Spring"), Lester Brown's contemporary survey ("The State of the World's Natural Environment"), and Alan Durning's global call to action ("Supporting Indigenous Peoples").

3. **A new ordering of "institutional" articles** presents the Economy and Work cluster first since, in most people's minds, the economy is the most influential social institution. Next appear institutional articles focusing on politics, government, and the military; family; religion; education; and health and medicine.

4. **The third edition continues its emphasis on diversity.** In *Seeing Ourselves,* "diversity" means various points of view on important issues. Moreover, the new lineup contains even more selections from scholars (especially women, African Americans, and Latinos) whose contributions are often overlooked.

In all, the third edition of *Seeing Ourselves* better conveys sociology's diversity of viewpoints and methodologies as it captures the fascinating complexity of the social world.

As in the past, we invite faculty and students to share their thoughts and reactions to this reader. Write to John Macionis at the Department of Anthropology-Sociology, Olof Palme House, Kenyon College, Gambier, Ohio 43022-9623 or to Nijole Benokraitis at the Department of Sociology, University of Baltimore, 1420 North Charles Street, Baltimore, Maryland 21201-5779. Internet addresses for electronic mail are MACIONIS@KENYON.EDU and NBENOKRAITIS@UBMAIL.UBALT.EDU

First, the relationship between writers and publishers is a distinctive mix of friendship, disciplinary collegiality, creative tension, and a common commitment to doing the best job possible. For her unwavering support from the outset, we wish to express our gratitude to Nancy Roberts, editor-in-chief at Prentice Hall. Robert Thoresen, senior sales representative for Prentice Hall, provided valuable suggestions as the plan for this book took form. Skillful editorial review was provided by Amy Marsh Macionis, who, along with Sharon Duchesne, carefully completed the time-consuming task of securing permission to reprint material.

A number of other colleagues offered comments on the plan for this reader and suggested material to be included: E. Keith Bramlett, University of North Carolina at Asheville; Polly A. Fassinger, Concordia College; Sam Marullo, Georgetown University; Harland Prechel, Texas A & M University; Anne Szopa, I. U. East; and Henry A. Walker, Cornell University.

Finally, John Macionis and Nijole Benokraitis dedicate this edition of *Seeing Ourselves* to the men, women, and children of Lithuania who are valiantly struggling to create for themselves a society with many of the virtues that too many of us take for granted. We salute our ancestors and relatives for their determination, courage, and unflagging spirit despite fifty years of oppression.

ACKNOWLEDGMENTS

The editors are grateful to a number of colleagues for their assistance in the preparation of this reader.

Classic

1

The Promise of Sociology

C. Wright Mills

To C. Wright Mills, the sociological imagination *is a special way to engage the world. To think sociologically is to realize that what we experience as* personal problems *are often widely shared by others like ourselves. Thus many personal problems are actually* social issues. *For Mills, one of sociology's most outspoken activists, the sociological imagination encouraged collective action to change the world in some way.*

Nowadays men often feel that their private lives are a series of traps. They sense that within their everyday worlds, they cannot overcome their troubles, and in this feeling, they are often quite correct: What ordinary men are directly aware of and what they try to do are bounded by the private orbits in which they live; their visions and their powers are limited to the close-up scenes of job, family, neighborhood; in other milieux, they move vicariously and remain spectators. And the more aware

SOURCE: *The Sociological Imagination* by C. Wright Mills. Copyright © 1959 by Oxford University Press, Inc.; renewed 1987 by Yaraslava Mills, pp. 1–6. Reprinted by permission of the publisher.

they become, however vaguely, of ambitions and of threats which transcend their immediate locales, the more trapped they seem to feel.

Underlying this sense of being trapped are seemingly impersonal changes in the very structure of continent-wide societies. The facts of contemporary history are also facts about the success and the failure of individual men and women. When a society is industrialized, a peasant becomes a worker; a feudal lord is liquidated or becomes a businessman. When classes rise or fall, a man is employed or unemployed; when the rate of investment goes up or down, a man takes new heart or goes broke. When wars happen, an insurance salesman becomes a rocket launcher; a store clerk, a radar man; a wife lives alone; a child grows up without a father. Neither the life of an individual nor the history of a society can be understood without understanding both.

Yet men do not usually define the troubles they endure in terms of historical change and institutional contradiction. The well-being they enjoy, they do not usually impute to the big ups and downs of the societies in which they live. Seldom aware of the intricate connection between the patterns of their own lives and the course of world history, ordinary men do not usually know what this connection means for the kinds of men they are becoming and for the kinds of history-making in which they might take part. They do not possess the quality of mind essential to grasp the interplay of man and society, of biography and history, of self and world. They cannot cope with their personal troubles in such ways as to control the structural transformations that usually lie behind them.

Surely it is no wonder. In what period have so many men been so totally exposed at so fast a pace to such earthquakes of change? That Americans have not known such catastrophic changes as have the men and women of other societies is due to historical facts that are now quickly becoming "merely history." The history that now affects every man is world history. Within this scene and this period, in the course of a single generation, one-sixth of mankind is transformed from all that is feudal and backward into all that is modern, advanced, and fearful. Political colonies are freed; new and less visible forms of imperialism installed. Revolutions occur; men feel the intimate grip of new kinds of authority. Totalitarian societies rise, and are smashed to bits—or succeed fabulously. After two centuries of ascendancy, capitalism is shown up as only one way to make society into an industrial apparatus. After two centuries of hope, even formal democracy is restricted to a quite small portion of mankind. Everywhere in the underdeveloped world, ancient ways of life are broken up and vague expectations become urgent demands. Everywhere in the overdeveloped world, the means of authority and of violence become total in scope and bureaucratic in form. Humanity itself now lies before us, the super-nation at either pole concentrating its most coordinated and massive efforts upon the preparation of World War Three.

The very shaping of history now outpaces the ability of men to orient themselves in accordance with cherished values. And which values? Even when they do not panic, men often sense that older ways of feeling and thinking have collapsed and that newer beginnings are ambiguous to the point of moral stasis. Is it any wonder that ordinary men feel they cannot cope with the larger worlds with which they are so suddenly confronted? That they cannot understand the meaning of their epoch for their own lives? That—in defense of selfhood—they become morally insensible, trying to remain altogether private men? Is it any wonder that they come to be possessed by a sense of the trap?

It is not only information that they need—in this Age of Fact, information often dominates their attention and overwhelms their capacities to assimilate it. It is not only the skills of reason that they need—although their struggles to acquire these often exhaust their limited moral energy.

What they need, and what they feel they need, is a quality of mind that will help them to use information and to develop reason in order to achieve lucid summations of what is going on in the world and of what may be happening within themselves. It is this quality, I am going to contend, that journalists and scholars, artists and publics, scientists and editors are coming to expect of what may be called the sociological imagination.

The sociological imagination enables its possessor to understand the larger historical scene in terms of its meaning for the inner life and the external career of a variety of individuals. It enables him to take into account how individuals, in the welter of their daily experience, often become falsely conscious of their social positions. Within that welter, the framework of modern society is sought, and within that framework the psychologies of a variety of men and women are formulated. By such means the personal uneasiness of individuals is focused upon explicit troubles and the indifference of publics is transformed into involvement with public issues.

The first fruit of this imagination—and the first lesson of the social science that embodies it—is the idea that the individual can understand his own experience and gauge his own fate only by locating himself within his period, that he can know his own chances in life by becoming aware of those of all individuals in his circumstances. In many ways it is a terrible lesson; in many ways a magnificent one. We do not know the limits of man's capacities for supreme effort or willing degradation, for agony or glee, for pleasurable brutality or the sweetness of reason. But in our time we have come to know that the limits of "human nature" are frighteningly broad. We have come to know that every individual lives, from one generation to the next, in some society; that he lives out a biography, and that he lives it out within some historical sequence. By the fact of his living he contributes, however minutely, to the shaping of this society and to the course of its history, even as he is made by society and by its historical push and shove.

The sociological imagination enables us to grasp history and biography and the relations between the two within society. That is its task and its promise. To recognize this task and this promise is the mark of the classic social analyst. It is characteristic of Herbert Spencer—turgid, polysyllabic, comprehensive; of E. A. Ross—graceful, muckraking, upright; of Auguste Comte and Emile Durkheim; of the intricate and subtle Karl Mannheim. It is the quality of all that is intellectually excellent in Karl Marx; it is the clue to Thorstein Veblen's brilliant and ironic insight, to Joseph Schumpeter's many-sided constructions of reality; it is the basis of the psychological sweep of W. E. H. Lecky no less than of the profundity and clarity of Max Weber. And it is the signal of what is best in contemporary studies of man and society.

No social study that does not come back to the problems of biography, of history, and of their intersections within a society has completed its intellectual journey. Whatever the specific problems of the classic social analysts, however limited or however broad the features of social reality they have examined, those who have been imaginatively aware of the promise of their work have consistently asked three sorts of questions:

(1) What is the structure of this particular society as a whole? What are its essential components, and how are they related to one another? How does it differ from other varieties of social order? Within it, what is the meaning of any particular feature for its continuance and for its change?

(2) Where does this society stand in human history? What are the mechanics by which it is changing? What is its place within and its meaning for the development of humanity as a whole? How does any particular feature we are examining affect, and how is it affected by, the historical period in which it moves? And this period—what are its essential features? How does it differ from other periods? What are its characteristic ways of history-making?

(3) What varieties of men and women now prevail in this society and in this period? And what varieties are coming to prevail? In what ways are they selected and formed, liberated and repressed, made sensitive and blunted? What kinds of "human nature" are revealed in the conduct and character we observe in this society in this period? And what is the meaning for "human nature" of each and every feature of the society we are examining?

Whether the point of interest is a great power state or a minor literary mood, a family, a prison, a creed—these are the kinds of questions the best social analysts have asked. They are the intellectual pivots of classic studies of man in society—and they are the questions inevitably raised by any mind possessing the sociological imagination. For that imagination is the capacity to shift from one perspective to another—from the political to the psychological; from examination of a single family to comparative assessment of the national budgets of the world; from the theological school to the military establishment; from considerations of an oil industry to studies of contemporary poetry. It is the capacity to range from the most impersonal and remote transformations to the most intimate features of the human self—and to see the relations between the two. Back of its use there is always the urge to know the social and historical meaning of the individual in the society and in the period in which he has his quality and his being.

That, in brief, is why it is by means of the sociological imagination that men now hope to grasp what is going on in the world, and to understand what is happening in themselves as minute points of the intersections of biography and history within society. In large part, contemporary man's self-conscious view of himself as at least an outsider, if not a permanent stranger, rests upon an absorbed realization of social relativity and of the transformative power of history. The sociological imagination is the most fruitful form of this self-consciousness. By its use men whose mentalities have swept only a series of limited orbits often come to feel as if suddenly awakened in a house with which they had only supposed themselves to be familiar. Correctly or incorrectly, they often come to feel that they can now provide themselves with adequate summations, cohesive assessments, comprehensive orientations. Older decisions that once appeared sound now seem to them products of a mind unaccountably dense. Their capacity for astonishment is made lively again. They acquire a new way of thinking, they experience a transvaluation of values: In a word, by their reflection and by their sensibility, they realize the cultural meaning of the social sciences.

Perhaps the most fruitful distinction with which the sociological imagination works is between "the personal troubles of milieu" and "the public issues of social structure." This distinction is an essential tool of the sociological imagination and a feature of all classic work in social science.

Troubles occur within the character of the individual and within the range of his immediate relations with others; they have to do with his self and with those limited areas of social life of which he is directly and personally aware. Accordingly, the statement and the resolution of troubles properly lie within the individual as a biographical entity and within the scope of his immediate milieu—the social setting that is directly open to his personal experience and to some extent his willful activity. A trouble is a private matter: Values cherished by an individual are felt by him to be threatened.

Issues have to do with matters that transcend these local environments of the individual and the range of his inner life. They have to do with the organization of many such milieux into the institutions of an historical society as a whole, with the ways in which various milieux overlap and interpenetrate to form the larger structure of social and historical life. An issue is a public matter: Some value cherished by publics is felt to be threatened. Often there is a debate about what that value really is and about what it is that really threatens it. This debate is often without focus if only because it is the very nature of an issue, unlike even widespread trouble, that it cannot very well be defined in terms of the immediate and everyday environments of ordinary men. An issue, in fact, often involves a crisis in institutional arrangements, and often too it involves what Marxists call "contradictions" or "antagonisms."

In these terms, consider unemployment. When, in a city of 100,000, only one man is unemployed, that is his personal trouble, and for its relief we properly look to the character of the man, his skills, and his immediate opportunities. But when in a nation of 50 million employees, 15 million men are unemployed, that is an issue, and we may not hope to find its solution within the range of opportunities open to any one individual. The very structure of opportunities has collapsed. Both the correct statement of the problem and the range of possible solutions require us to consider the economic and political institutions of the society, and not merely the personal situation and character of a scatter of individuals.

Consider war. The personal problem of war, when it occurs, may be how to survive it or how to die in it with honor; how to make money out of it; how to climb into the higher safety of the military apparatus; or how to contribute to the war's termination. In short, according to one's values, to find a set of milieux and within it to survive the war or make one's death in it meaningful. But the structural issues of war have to do with its causes;

with what types of men it throws up into command; with its effects upon economic and political, family and religious institutions, with the unorganized irresponsibility of a world of nation-states.

Consider marriage. Inside a marriage a man and a woman may experience personal troubles, but when the divorce rate during the first four years of marriage is 250 out of every 1,000 attempts, this is an indication of a structural issue having to do with the institutions of marriage and the family and other institutions that bear upon them.

Or consider the metropolis—the horrible, beautiful, ugly, magnificent sprawl of the great city. For many upper-class people, the personal solution to "the problem of the city" is to have an apartment with private garage under it in the heart of the city and, forty miles out, a house by Henry Hill, garden by Garrett Eckbo, on a hundred acres of private land. In these two controlled environments—with a small staff at each end and a private helicopter connection—most people could solve many of the problems of personal milieux caused by the facts of the city. But all this, however splendid, does not solve the public issues that the structural fact of the city poses. What should be done with this wonderful monstrosity? Break it up into scattered units, combining residence and work? Refurbish it as it stands? Or, after evacuation, dynamite it and build new cities according to new plans in new places? What should those plans be? And who is to decide and to accomplish whatever choice is made? These are structural issues; to confront them and to solve them requires us to consider political and economic issues that affect innumerable milieux.

Insofar as an economy is so arranged that slumps occur, the problem of unemployment becomes incapable of personal solution. Insofar as war is inherent in the nation-state system and in the uneven industrialization of the world, the ordinary individual in his restricted milieu will be powerless—with or without psychiatric aid—to solve the troubles this system or lack of system imposes upon him. Insofar as the family as an institution turns women into darling little slaves and men into their chief providers and unweaned dependents, the problem of a satisfactory marriage remains incapable of purely private solution. Insofar as the overdeveloped megalopolis and the overdeveloped automobile are built-in features of the overdeveloped society, the issues of urban living will not be solved by personal ingenuity and private wealth.

What we experience in various and specific milieux, I have noted, is often caused by structural changes. Accordingly, to understand the changes of many personal milieux we are required to look beyond them. And the number and variety of such structural changes increase as the institutions within which we live become more embracing and more intricately connected with one another. To be aware of the idea of social structure and to use it with sensibility is to be capable of tracing such linkages among a great variety of milieux. To be able to do that is to possess the sociological imagination. . . .

CRITICAL-THINKING QUESTIONS

1. Why do people in the United States tend to think of the operation of society in personal terms?

2. What are the practical benefits of the sociological perspective? Are there liabilities?

3. What does Mills have in mind in suggesting that by developing the sociological imagination we learn to assemble facts *into social analysis?*

THE SOCIOLOGICAL PERSPECTIVE

Classic

2

Invitation to Sociology

Peter L. Berger

Using the sociological perspective changes how we perceive the surrounding world, and even ourselves. Peter Berger compares thinking sociologically to entering a new and unfamiliar society—one in which "things are no longer what they seem." This article should lead you to rethink your social world, so that you become aware of truths that you may never before have realized.

. . . It can be said that the first wisdom of sociology is this—things are not what they seem. This too is a deceptively simple statement. It ceases to be simple after a while. Social reality turns out to have many layers of meaning. The discovery of each new layer changes the perception of the whole.

Anthropologists use the term "culture shock" to describe the impact of a totally new culture upon a newcomer. In an extreme instance such shock will be experienced by the Western explorer who is told, halfway through dinner, that he is eating the nice old lady he had been chatting with the previous day—a shock with predictable physiological if not moral consequences. Most explorers no longer encounter cannibalism in their travels today. However, the first encounters with polygamy or with puberty rites or even with the way some nations drive their automobiles can be quite a shock to an American visitor. With the shock may go not only disapproval or disgust but a sense of excitement that things can *really* be that different from what they are at home. To some extent, at least, this is the excitement of any first travel abroad. The experience of sociological discovery could be described as "culture shock" minus geographical

SOURCE: *Invitation to Sociology* by Peter L. Berger. Copyright © 1963 by Peter L. Berger. Reprinted with permission of Doubleday, a division of Bantam, Doubleday, Dell Publishing Group, Inc.

displacement. In other words, the sociologist travels at home—with shocking results. He is unlikely to find that he is eating a nice old lady for dinner. But the discovery, for instance, that his own church has considerable money invested in the missile industry or that a few blocks from his home there are people who engage in cultic orgies may not be drastically different in emotional impact. Yet we would not want to imply that sociological discoveries are always or even usually outrageous to moral sentiment. Not at all. What they have in common with exploration in distant lands, however, is the sudden illumination of new and unsuspected facets of human existence in society. This is the excitement and, as we shall try to show later, the humanistic justification of sociology.

People who like to avoid shocking discoveries, who prefer to believe that society is just what they were taught in Sunday school, who like the safety of the rules and the maxims of what Alfred Schuetz has called the "world-taken-for-granted," should stay away from sociology. People who feel no temptation before closed doors, who have no curiosity about human beings, who are content to admire scenery without wondering about the people who live in those houses on the other side of that river, should probably also stay away from sociology. They will find it unpleasant or, at any rate, unrewarding. People who are interested in human beings only if they can change, convert, or reform them should also be warned, for they will find sociology much less useful than they hoped. And people whose interest is mainly in their own conceptual constructions will do just as well to turn to the study of little white mice. Sociology will be satisfying, in the long run, only to those who can think of nothing more entrancing than to watch men and to understand things human. . . .

To ask sociological questions, then, presupposes that one is interested in looking some distance beyond the commonly accepted or officially defined goals of human actions. It presupposes a certain awareness that human events have different levels of meaning, some of which are hidden from the consciousness of everyday life. It may even presuppose a measure of suspicion about the way in which human events are officially inter-

preted by the authorities, be they political, juridical, or religious in character. If one is willing to go as far as that, it would seem evident that not all historical circumstances are equally favorable for the development of sociological perspective.

It would appear plausible, in consequence, that sociological thought would have the best chance to develop in historical circumstances marked by severe jolts to the self-conception, especially the official and authoritative and generally accepted self-conception of a culture. It is only in such circumstances that perceptive men are likely to be motivated to think beyond the assertions of this self-conception and, as a result, question the authorities. . . .

Sociological perspective can then be understood in terms of such phrases as "seeing through," "looking behind," very much as such phrases would be employed in common speech—"seeing through his game," "looking behind the scenes"—in other words, "being up on all the tricks."

. . . We could think of this in terms of a common experience of people living in large cities. One of the fascinations of a large city is the immense variety of human activities taking place behind the seemingly anonymous and endlessly undifferentiated rows of houses. A person who lives in such a city will time and again experience surprise or even shock as he discovers the strange pursuits that some men engage in quite unobtrusively in houses that, from the outside, look like all the others on a certain street. Having had this experience once or twice, one will repeatedly find oneself walking down a street, perhaps late in the evening, and wondering what may be going on under the bright lights showing through a line of drawn curtains. An ordinary family engaged in pleasant talk with guests? A scene of desperation amid illness or death? Or a scene of debauched pleasures? Perhaps a strange cult or a dangerous conspiracy? The facades of the houses cannot tell us, proclaiming nothing but an architectural conformity to the tastes of some group or class that may not even inhabit the street any longer. The social mysteries lie behind the facades. The wish to penetrate to these mysteries is an analogon to sociological curiosity. In some cities that are suddenly struck by calamity this wish may be abruptly realized. Those who have experienced wartime bombings know of the sudden encounters with unsuspected (and sometimes unimaginable) fellow tenants in the air-raid shelter of one's apartment building. Or they can recollect the startling morning sight of a house hit by a bomb during the night, neatly sliced in half, the facade torn away and the previously hidden interior mercilessly revealed in the daylight. But in most cities that one may normally live in, the facades must be penetrated by one's own inquisitive intrusions. Similarly, there are historical situations in which the facades of society are violently torn apart and all but the most incurious are forced to see that there was a reality behind the facades all along. Usually this does not happen, and the facades continue to confront us with seemingly rocklike permanence. The perception of the reality behind the facades then demands a considerable intellectual effort.

A few examples of the way in which sociology "looks behind" the facades of social structures might serve to make our argument clearer. Take, for instance, the political organization of a community. If one wants to find out how a modern American city is governed, it is very easy to get the official information about this subject. The city will have a charter, operating under the laws of the state. With some advice from informed individuals, one may look up various statutes that define the constitution of the city. Thus one may find out that this particular community has a city-manager form of administration, or that party affiliations do not appear on the ballot in municipal elections, or that the city government participates in a regional water district. In similar fashion, with the help of some newspaper reading, one may find out the officially recognized political problems of the community. One may read that the city plans to annex a certain suburban area, or that there has been a change in the zoning ordinances to facilitate industrial development in another area, or even that one of the members of the city council has been accused of using his office for personal gain. All such matters still occur on the, as it were, visible,

official, or public level of political life. However, it would be an exceedingly naive person who would believe that this kind of information gives him a rounded picture of the political reality of that community. The sociologist will want to know above all the constituency of the "informal power structure" (as it has been called by Floyd Hunter, an American sociologist interested in such studies), which is a configuration of men and their power that cannot be found in any statutes, and probably cannot be read about in the newspapers. The political scientist or the legal expert might find it very interesting to compare the city charter with the constitutions of other similar communities. The sociologist will be far more concerned with discovering the way in which powerful vested interests influence or even control the actions of officials elected under the charter. These vested interests will not be found in city hall, but rather in the executive suites of corporations that may not even be located in that community, in the private mansions of a handful of powerful men, perhaps in the offices of certain labor unions, or even, in some instances, in the headquarters of criminal organizations. When the sociologist concerns himself with power, he will "look behind" the official mechanisms that are supposed to regulate power in the community. This does not necessarily mean that he will regard the official mechanisms as totally ineffective or their legal definition as totally illusionary. But at the very least he will insist that there is another level of reality to be investigated in the particular system of power. In some cases he might conclude that to look for real power in the publicly recognized places is quite delusional. . . .

Let us take one further example. In Western countries, and especially in America, it is assumed that men and women marry because they are in love. There is a broadly based popular mythology about the character of love as a violent, irresistible emotion that strikes where it will, a mystery that is the goal of most young people and often of the not-so-young as well. As soon as one investigates, however, which people actually marry each other, one finds that the lightning-shaft of Cupid seems to be guided rather strongly within very definite channels of class, income, education, [and] racial and religious background. If one then investigates a little further into the behavior that is engaged in prior to marriage under the rather misleading euphemism of "courtship," one finds channels of interaction that are often rigid to the point of ritual. The suspicion begins to dawn on one that, most of the time, it is not so much the emotion of love that creates a certain kind of relationship, but that carefully predefined and often planned relationships eventually generate the desired emotion. In other words, when certain conditions are met or have been constructed, one allows oneself "to fall in love." The sociologist investigating our patterns of "courtship" and marriage soon discovers a complex web of motives related in many ways to the entire institutional structure within which an individual lives his life—class, career, economic ambition, aspirations of power and prestige. The miracle of love now begins to look somewhat synthetic. Again, this need not mean in any given instance that the sociologist will declare the romantic interpretation to be an illusion. But, once more, he will look beyond the immediately given and publicly approved interpretations. . . .

We would contend, then, that there is a debunking motif inherent in sociological consciousness. The sociologist will be driven time and again, by the very logic of his discipline, to debunk the social systems he is studying. This unmasking tendency need not necessarily be due to the sociologist's temperament or inclinations. Indeed, it may happen that the sociologist, who as an individual may be of a conciliatory disposition and quite disinclined to disturb the comfortable assumptions on which he rests his own social existence, is nevertheless compelled by what he is doing to fly in the face of what those around him take for granted. In other words, we would contend that the roots of the debunking motif in sociology are not psychological but methodological. The sociological frame of reference, with its built-in procedure of looking for levels of reality other than those given in the official interpretations of society, carries with it a logical imperative to unmask the pretensions and the propaganda by which men cloak their actions with each other. This unmasking imperative is one of the characteristics of sociology particularly at home in the temper of the modern era. . . .

CRITICAL-THINKING QUESTIONS

1. How can we explain the fact that people within any society tend to take their own way of life for granted?

2. What does Berger think is the justification for studying sociology?

3. What is involved in sociological "debunking"? How are others likely to respond to sociological insights?

THE SOCIOLOGICAL PERSPECTIVE

Contemporary

3

Womanspeak and Manspeak: Sex Differences and Sexism in Communication, Verbal and Nonverbal

Nancy Henley, Mykol Hamilton, and Barrie Thorne*†

One way in which society shapes our lives involves gender, *the social significance of being female or male. This article explores the power of society to shape the everyday lives of women and men. The authors argue that language itself confers privileges and power to males. They suggest, too, that male dominance and female deference are evident in countless familiar patterns.*

A woman starts to speak but stops when a man begins to talk at the same time; two men find that a simple conversation is escalating into full-scale competition; a junior high school girl finds it hard

* We would like to acknowledge the influence of Cheris Kramarae on this paper, through her writing and other collaboration with us.

† There are many studies which could not be cited here because of space limitations; for further information on any of the topics mentioned in this chapter, see the comprehensive annotated bibliography in Thorne, Kramarae, and Henley (1983).

to relate to her schoolbooks, which are phrased in the terminology of a male culture and refer to people as "men"; a woman finds that when she uses the gestures men use for attention and influence, she is responded to sexually; a female college student from an all-girl high school finds a touch or glance from males in class intimidating.

What is happening here? First, there are differences between female and male speech styles, and the sexes are often spoken about in different ways. Male nonverbal communication also has certain elements and effects that distinguish it from its female counterpart. Moreover, females and males move in a context of sexual inequality and strongly differentiated behavioral expectations. Because interaction with others always involves communication of some sort, verbal and nonverbal, it is through communication that much of our pattern of sexist interaction is learned and perpetuated. . . .

Language has been used in the past, and is still used, to dehumanize a people into submission; it both reflects and shapes the culture in which it is embedded.

THE SEXIST BIAS OF ENGLISH

Sexism in the English language takes three main forms: It ignores; it defines; it deprecates.

Ignoring

Most of us are familiar with ways in which our language ignores females. The paramount example of this is the masculine "generic," which has traditionally been used to include women as well as men. We are taught to use *he* to refer to someone whose sex is unspecified, as in the sentence, "Each entrant should do his best." We are told that using *they* in such a case ("Everyone may now take their seat") is ungrammatical; yet Bodine (1975) reports that prior to the eighteenth century, *they* was widely used in this way. Grammarians who insist that we use *he* for numerical agreement with the antecedent overlook the disagreement in gender such usage may entail. Current grammars condemn "he or she" as clumsy, and the singular "they" as inaccurate, but expect pupils to achieve both elegance of expression and accuracy by referring to women as *he*. Despite the best efforts of grammarians, however, singular *they* has long been common in informal conversation and is becoming more frequent even in formal speech and writing.

Many people who claim they are referring to both females and males when they use the word *he* switch to the feminine pronoun when they speak of someone in a traditionally feminine occupation, such as homemaker or schoolteacher or nurse, raising questions about the inclusion of females in the masculine pronoun. Although compared to specific masculine reference the masculine "generic"

occurs infrequently, it has a high occurrence in many of our lives; MacKay estimates that highly educated Americans are exposed to it a million times in their lifetimes. . . .

Defining

Language both reflects and helps maintain women's secondary status in our society, by defining her and her "place." Man's power to define through naming is illustrated in the tradition of a woman's losing her own name, and taking her husband's, when she marries; the children of the marriage also have their father's name, showing that they too are his possessions. The view of females as possessions is further evidenced in the common practice of applying female names and pronouns to material possessions such as cars ("Fill 'er up!"), machines, and ships. . . .

The fact that our language generally ignores women also means that when it does take note of them, it often defines their status. Thus "lady doctor," "lady judge," "lady professor," "lady pilot" all indicate exceptions to the rule of finding males in these occupations. Expressions like "male nurse" are much less common, because many more occupations are typed as male and because fewer men choose to enter female-typed occupations than vice versa. Even in cases in which a particular field is female-typed, males who enter it often have a term of their own, with greater prestige, such as *chef* or *couturier*. Of course, patterns of usage subtly reinforce our occupational stereotypes; and deeper undertones further reinforce stereotypes concerning propriety and competency. . . .

Deprecating

The deprecation of women in the English language can be seen in the connotations and meanings of words applied to male and female things. The very word *virtue* comes from an old root meaning *man;* to be *virtuous* is, literally, to be "manly." Different adjectives are applied to the actions or productions of the different sexes: Women's work may be referred to as *pretty* or *nice;* men's work will more often elicit adjectives like *masterful, brilliant.* While words such as *king, prince, lord, father* have all maintained their elevated meanings, the similar words *queen, madam,* and *dame* have acquired debased meanings.

A woman's sex is treated as if it were the most salient characteristic of her being; this is not the case for males. This discrepancy is the basis for much of the defining of women, and it underlies much of the accompanying deprecation. Sexual insult is applied overwhelmingly to women; Stanley (1977), in researching terms for sexual promiscuity, found 220 terms for a sexually promiscuous woman but only 22 terms for a sexually promiscuous man. Furthermore, trivialization accompanies many terms applied to females. . . . The feminine endings *-ess* and *-ette,* and the female prefix *lady,* are added to many words which are not really male-specific. Thus we have the trivialized terms *poetess, authoress, aviatrix, majorette, usherette.* Male sports teams are given names of strength and ferocity: "Rams," "Bears," "Jets." Women's sports teams often have cute names like "Rayettes," "Rockettes." As Alleen Nilsen (1972) has put it,

The chicken metaphor tells the whole story of a girl's life. In her youth she is a *chick,* then she marries and begins feeling *cooped up,* so she goes to *hen parties* where she *cackles* with her friends. Then she has her *brood* and begins to *henpeck* her husband. Finally she turns into an *old biddy.* (p. 109)

. . . Recent research on conversational interaction reflects the attempt to conceptualize language not in terms of isolated variables nor as an abstract code, but within contexts of use, looking at features of conversation within the give-and-take of actual talk. Pamela Fishman (1983) analyzed recurring patterns in many samples of the household conversations of three heterosexual couples. Although the women tried more often than the men to initiate conversations, the women succeeded less often because of minimal responses from their male companions. In contrast, the women pursued topics the men raised, asked more questions, and did more verbal supportwork than the men. Fishman concluded that the conversations were under male control, but were mainly produced by female work.

SELF-DISCLOSURE

Self-disclosure is another variable that involves language but goes beyond it. Research studies have found that women disclose more personal information to others than men do. Subordinates (in work situations) are also more likely to self-disclose than superiors. People in positions of power are required to reveal little about themselves, yet typically know much about the lives of others—perhaps the ultimate exemplar of this principle is the fictional Big Brother.

According to the research of Jack Sattel (1983), men exercise and maintain power over women by withholding self-disclosure. An institutional example of this use of power is the psychiatrist (usually male), to whom much is disclosed (by a predominantly female clientele), but who classically maintains a reserved and detached attitude, revealing little or nothing of himself. Nonemotionality is the "cool" of the professional, the executive, the poker player, the street-wise operator. Smart men—those in power, those who manipulate others—maintain unruffled exteriors. . . .

NONVERBAL COMMUNICATION

Although we are taught to think of communication in terms of spoken and written language, nonverbal communication has much more impact on our actions and reactions than does verbal. One psychological study concluded, on the basis of a laboratory study, that nonverbal messages carry over four times the weight of verbal messages when both are used in interaction. Yet, there is much ignorance and confusion surrounding the subtler nonverbal form, which renders it a perfect avenue for the unconscious manipulation of others. Nonverbal behavior is of particular importance for women, because their socialization to docility and passivity makes them likely targets for subtle forms of social control, and their close contact with men—for example as wives and secretaries—entails frequent verbal and nonverbal interaction with those in power. Additionally, women have been found to be more sensitive than men to nonverbal cues, perhaps because their survival depends upon it. (Blacks have also been shown to be better than whites at interpreting nonverbal signals.) . . .

Demeanor

Persons of higher status have certain privileges of demeanor that their subordinates do not: The boss can put his feet on the desk and loosen his tie, but workers must be more careful in their behavior. Also, the boss had better not put her feet on the desk; women are restricted in their demeanor. Goffman (1967) observed that in hospital staff meetings, the doctors (usually male, and always of high status) had the privilege of swearing, changing the topic of conversation, and sitting in undignified positions. They could lounge on the (mostly female) nurses' counter and initiate joking sessions. Attendants and nurses, of lower status, had to be more circumspect in their demeanor. Women are also denied privileges of swearing and sitting in the undignified positions allowed to men; in fact, women are explicitly required to be more cautious than men by all standards, including the well-known double one. This requirement of propriety is similar to women's use of more proper speech forms, but the requirement for nonverbal behavior is much more compelling.

Body tension is another sex-differentiated aspect of demeanor. In laboratory studies of conversation, communicators are more relaxed with lower-status addressees than with higher-status ones, and they are more relaxed with females than with males. Also, males are generally more relaxed than females; females' somewhat tenser postures are said to convey submissive attitudes (Mehrabian 1972).

Use of Space

Women's general bodily demeanor must be restrained and restricted; their femininity is gauged, in fact, by how little space they take up, while masculinity is judged by males' expansiveness and the strength of their flamboyant gestures. Males control both greater territory and greater personal space, a situation associated with dominance and high status in both human beings and animals. Both field and laboratory studies have found that people tend to approach females more closely than males, to seat themselves closer to females and otherwise intrude on their territory, and to cut across their paths. In the larger aspect of space, women are also less likely to have their own room or other private space in the home.

Looking and Staring—Eye Contact

Eye contact is greatly influenced by sex. It has been repeatedly found that in interactions, women look more at the other person than men do and maintain mutual eye contact longer. . . . Other writers have observed that rather than stare, women tend more than men to avert the gaze, especially when stared at by men. Public staring, clothing designed to reveal the contours of the body, and public advertising, which lavishly flashes women across billboards and through magazines, all make females a highly visible sex. Visual information about women is readily available, just as their personal information is available through greater self-disclosure.

Smiling

The smile is women's badge of appeasement. . . . Women engage in more smiling than men do, whether they are truly happy or not. Research has confirmed this. Erving Goffman (1979) analyzed the depiction of gender in U.S. print advertising and concluded that women's smiles are ritualistic mollifiers; women smile more, and more expansively, than men. The smile is a requirement of women's social position and is used as a gesture of submission. . . . The smile is generally thought to signal to an aggressor that the subordinate individual intends no harm. In many women, and in other subordinate persons, smiling has reached the status of a nervous habit.

Touching

Touching is another gesture of dominance, and cuddling to the touch is its corresponding gesture of submission. Touching is reportedly used by primates to maintain a dominance order, and it is likely that it is used by human beings in the same way. Just as the boss can put a hand on the worker, the master on the servant, the teacher on the student, the business executive on the secretary, so men more frequently put their hands on women, despite a folk mythology to the contrary. . . . Much of this touching goes unnoticed because it is expected and taken for granted, as when men steer women across the street, through doorways, around corners, into elevators, and so on. The male doctor or lawyer who holds his female client's hand overlong, and the male boss who puts his hand on the female secretary's arm or shoulder when giving her instructions, are easily recognizable examples of such everyday touching of women by men. There is also the more obtrusive touching: the "pawing" by sexually aggressive males; the pinching of waitresses and female office and factory workers; and the totally unexpected and unwelcomed tactual familiarity women are subjected to from complete strangers on the street.

Many interpret this pattern of greater touching by males as a reflection of sexual interest and of a greater level of sexuality among men than women. This explanation, first of all, ignores the fact that touching is a status and dominance signal for human and animal groups. . . . It also ignores the findings of sexual research, which give us no reason to expect any greater sexual drive in males than in females. Rather, males in our culture have more freedom and encouragement to express their sexuality, and they are also accorded more freedom to touch others. Touching carries the connotation of possession when used with objects, and the wholesale touching of women carries the message that women are community property. . . .

Intimacy and Status in Nonverbal Gestures

There is another side to touching, one which is much better understood: Touching symbolizes friendship and intimacy. To speak of the power dimension of touching is not to rule out the intimacy dimension. A particular touch may have both components and more, but it is the *pattern* of touching between two individuals that tells us most about their relationship. When touching is symmetrical—that is, when both parties have equal touching privileges—it conveys information about the *intimacy* dimension of the relationship: Much touching indicates closeness, and little touching indicates distance. When one party is free to touch the other but not vice versa, we gain information about the *status,* or power, dimension: The person with greater touching privileges is of higher status or has more power. Even when there is mutual touching between two people, it is most likely to be initiated by the higher-status person; e.g., in a dating relationship it is usually the male who first puts an arm around the female or begins holding hands.

Gestures of Dominance and Submission

We have named several gestures of dominance (invasion of personal space, touching, staring) and of submission (allowing oneself to be touched, averting the eyes, and smiling). Pointing may be interpreted as another gesture of dominance, and the corresponding submissive action is to stop talking or acting. In conversation, interruption often functions as a gesture of dominance, and allowing interruption signifies submission. Often mock play between males and females also carries strong physical overtones of dominance: the man squeezing the woman too hard, "pretending" to twist her arm, playfully lifting her and tossing her from man to man, chasing, catching, and spanking her. This type of "play" is also frequently used to control children and to maintain a status hierarchy among male teenagers.

BREAKING THE MOLD—A FIRST STEP

Women can reverse these nonverbal interaction patterns with probably greater effect than can be achieved through deliberate efforts to alter speech patterns. Women can stop smiling unless they are happy, stop lowering their eyes, stop getting out of men's way on the street, and stop letting themselves be interrupted. They can stare people in the eye, be more relaxed in demeanor (when they realize it is more a reflection of status than of morality), and touch when they feel it is appropriate. Men can likewise become aware of what they are signifying nonverbally. They can restrain their invasions of personal space, touching (if it is not mutual), and interrupting. They may also benefit by losing their cool and feeling free to display their more tender emotions. Males and females who have responsibility for socializing the next generation—that is, parents and teachers particularly—should be especially aware of what they are teaching children about dominance, power, and privilege through nonverbal communication.

CRITICAL-THINKING QUESTIONS

1. In what ways does the English language "ignore," "define,'" and "deprecate" females? How does the language present males?

2. How do everyday gestures contain statements about power differences? In what ways do people—typically males—indicate that they are "in charge"? What are some gestures that people— usually females—use?

3. What are some of the authors' suggestions about changing gender-based patterns of interaction?

REFERENCES

BODINE, A. 1975. Androcentrism in prescriptive grammar: Singular "they," sex-indefinite "he," and "he or she." *Lang. in Soc.,* 4:129–46.

FISHMAN, P. 1983. Interaction: The work women do. In *Language, gender and society,* ed. B. Thorne, C. Kramarae, & N. Henley. Rowley, MA: Newbury House.

GOFFMAN, E. 1967. The nature of deferences and demeanor. In *Interaction ritual* (pp. 47–95), by E. Goffman. New York: Anchor.

GOFFMAN, E. 1979. *Gender advertisements.* New York: Harper & Row.

MACKAY, D. G. 1983. Prescriptive grammar and the pronoun problem. In *Language, gender and society,* ed. B. Thorne, C. Kramarae, & N. Henley. Rowley, MA: Newbury House.

MEHRABIAN, A. 1972. *Nonverbal communication.* Chicago: Aldine Atherton.

NILSEN, A. P. 1972. Sexism in English: A feminist view. In *Female Studies VI* (pp. 102–9), ed. N. Hoffman, C. Secor, & A. Tinsley. Old Westbury, NY: Feminist Press.

SATTEL, J. 1983. Men, inexpressiveness, and power. In *Language, gender and society,* ed. B. Thorne, C. Kramarae, & N. Henley. Rowley, MA: Newbury House.

STANLEY, J. P. 1977. Paradigmatic woman: The prostitute. In *Papers in language variation* (pp. 303–21), ed. B. Shores & C. P. Hines. University, AL: University of Alabama Press.

4

Body Ritual Among the Nacirema

Horace Miner

Most people take their life for granted; when they think about society at all, it is usually viewed as both natural and good. To help us step back from our society, anthropologist Horace Miner describes the Nacirema, a peculiar people living in North America (whose lives should strike you as familiar). Miner's intellectual sleight-of-hand illustrates how the sociological perspective involves detachment, so that everyday life becomes something new and unusual.

The anthropologist has become so familiar with the diversity of ways in which different peoples behave in similar situations that he is not apt to be surprised by even the most exotic customs. In fact, if all of the logically possible combinations of behavior have not been found somewhere in the world, he is apt to suspect that they must be present in some yet undescribed tribe. This point has, in fact, been expressed with respect to clan organization by Murdock (1949: 71). In this light, the magical beliefs and practices of the Nacirema pre-

sent such unusual aspects that it seems desirable to describe them as an example of the extremes to which human behavior can go.

Professor Linton first brought the ritual of the Nacirema to the attention of anthropologists twenty years ago (1936: 326), but the culture of this people is still very poorly understood. They are a North American group living in the territory between the Canadian Cree, the Yaqui and Tarahumare of Mexico, and the Carib and Arawak of the Antilles. Little is known of their origin, although tradition states that they came from the east. According to Nacirema mythology, their nation was originated by a culture hero, Notgnihsaw, who is otherwise known for two great feats of strength—

SOURCE: "Body Ritual Among the Nacirema," by Horace Miner. Reproduced by permission of the American Anthropological Association from *American Anthropologist,* vol. 58, no. 3, 1956. Not for further reproduction.

the throwing of a piece of wampum across the river Pa-To-Mac and the chopping down of a cherry tree in which the Spirit of Truth resided.

Nacirema culture is characterized by a highly developed market economy which has evolved in a rich natural habitat. While much of the people's time is devoted to economic pursuits, a large part of the fruits of these labors and a considerable portion of the day are spent in ritual activity. The focus of this activity is the human body, the appearance and health of which loom as a dominant concern in the ethos of the people. While such concern is certainly not unusual, its ceremonial aspects and associated philosophy are unique.

The fundamental belief underlying the whole system appears to be that the human body is ugly and that its natural tendency is to debility and disease. Incarcerated in such a body, man's only hope is to avert these characteristics through the use of the powerful influences of ritual and ceremony. Every household has one or more shrines devoted to this purpose. The more powerful individuals in this society have several shrines in their houses, and, in fact, the opulence of a house is often referred to in terms of the number of such ritual centers it possesses. Most houses are of wattle and daub construction, but the shrine rooms of the more wealthy are walled with stone. Poorer families imitate the rich by applying pottery plaques to their shrine walls.

While each family has at least one such shrine, the rituals associated with it are not family ceremonies but are private and secret. The rites are normally only discussed with children, and then only during the period when they are being initiated into these mysteries. I was able, however, to establish sufficient rapport with the natives to examine these shrines and to have the rituals described to me.

The focal point of the shrine is a box or chest which is built into the wall. In this chest are kept the many charms and magical potions without which no native believes he could live. These preparations are secured from a variety of specialized practitioners. The most powerful of these are the medicine men, whose assistance must be rewarded with substantial gifts. However, the medicine men do not provide the curative potions for their clients, but decide what the ingredients should be and then write them down in an ancient and secret language. This writing is understood only by the medicine men and by the herbalists who, for another gift, provide the required charm.

The charm is not disposed of after it has served its purpose, but is placed in the charm-box of the household shrine. As these magical materials are specific for certain ills, and the real or imagined maladies of the people are many, the charm-box is usually full to overflowing. The magical packets are so numerous that people forget what their purposes were and fear to use them again. While the natives are very vague on this point, we can only assume that the idea in retaining all the old magical materials is that their presence in the charm-box, before which the body rituals are conducted, will in some way protect the worshipper.

Beneath the charm-box is a small font. Each day every member of the family, in succession, enters the shrine room, bows his head before the charm-box, mingles different sorts of holy water in the font, and proceeds with a brief rite of ablution. The holy waters are secured from the Water Temple of the community, where the priests conduct elaborate ceremonies to make the liquid ritually pure.

In the hierarchy of magical practitioners, and below the medicine men in prestige, are specialists whose designation is best translated "holy-mouth-men." The Nacirema have an almost pathological horror of and fascination with the mouth, the condition of which is believed to have a supernatural influence on all social relationships. Were it not for the rituals of the mouth, they believe that their teeth would fall out, their gums bleed, their jaws shrink, their friends desert them, and their lovers reject them. They also believe that a strong relationship exists between oral and moral characteristics. For example, there is a ritual ablution of the mouth for children which is supposed to improve their moral fiber.

The daily body ritual performed by everyone includes a mouth-rite. Despite the fact that these people are so punctilious about care of the mouth, this rite involves a practice which strikes the uninitiated stranger as revolting. It was reported to me that the ritual consists of inserting a small bundle of hog hairs into the mouth, along with certain magical powders, and then moving the bundle in a highly formalized series of gestures.

In addition to the private mouth-rite, the people seek out a holy-mouth-man once or twice a year. These practitioners have an impressive set of paraphernalia, consisting of a variety of augers, awls, probes, and prods. The use of these objects in the exorcism of the evils of the mouth involves almost unbelievable ritual torture of the client. The holy-mouth-man opens the client's mouth and, using the above-mentioned tools, enlarges any holes which decay may have created in the teeth. Magical materials are put into these holes. If there are no naturally occurring holes in the teeth, large sections of one or more teeth are gouged out so that the supernatural substance can be applied. In the client's view, the purpose of these ministrations is to arrest decay and to draw friends. The extremely sacred and traditional character of the rite is evident in the fact that the natives return to the holy-mouth-man year after year, despite the fact that their teeth continue to decay.

It is to be hoped that, when a thorough study of the Nacirema is made, there will be careful inquiry into the personality structure of these people. One has but to watch the gleam in the eye of a holy-mouth-man, as he jabs an awl into an exposed nerve, to suspect that a certain amount of sadism is involved. If this can be established, a very interesting pattern emerges, for most of the population shows definite masochistic tendencies. It was to these that Professor Linton referred in discussing a distinctive part of the daily body ritual which is performed only by men. This part of the rite involves scraping and lacerating the surface of the face with a sharp instrument. Special women's rites are performed only four times during each lunar month, but what they lack in frequency is made up in barbarity. As part of this ceremony, women bake their heads in small ovens for about an hour. The theoretically interesting point is that what seems to be a preponderantly masochistic people have developed sadistic specialists.

The medicine men have an imposing temple, or

latipso, in every community of any size. The more elaborate ceremonies required to treat very sick patients can only be performed at this temple. These ceremonies involve not only the thaumaturge but a permanent group of vestal maidens who move sedately about the temple chambers in distinctive costume and headdress.

The *latipso* ceremonies are so harsh that it is phenomenal that a fair proportion of the really sick natives who enter the temple ever recover. Small children whose indoctrination is still incomplete have been known to resist attempts to take them to the temple because "that is where you go to die." Despite this fact, sick adults are not only willing but eager to undergo the protracted ritual purification, if they can afford to do so. No matter how ill the supplicant or how grave the emergency, the guardians of many temples will not admit a client if he cannot give a rich gift to the custodian. Even after one has gained admission and survived the ceremonies, the guardians will not permit the neophyte to leave until he makes still another gift.

The supplicant entering the temple is first stripped of all his or her clothes. In everyday life the Nacirema avoids exposure of his body and its natural functions. Bathing and excretory acts are performed only in the secrecy of the household shrine, where they are ritualized as part of the body-rites. Psychological shock results from the fact that body secrecy is suddenly lost upon entry into the *latipso*. A man, whose own wife has never seen him in an excretory act, suddenly finds himself naked and assisted by a vestal maiden while he performs his natural functions into a sacred vessel. This sort of ceremonial treatment is necessitated by the fact that the excreta are used by a diviner to ascertain the course and nature of the client's sickness. Female clients, on the other hand, find their naked bodies are subjected to the scrutiny, manipulation, and prodding of the medicine men.

Few supplicants in the temple are well enough to do anything but lie on their hard beds. The daily ceremonies, like the rites of the holy-mouth-men, involve discomfort and torture. With ritual precision, the vestals awaken their miserable charges each dawn and roll them about on their beds of pain while performing ablutions, in the formal movements of which the maidens are highly trained. At other times they insert magic wands in the supplicant's mouth or force him to eat substances which are supposed to be healing. From time to time the medicine men come to their clients and jab magically treated needles into their flesh. The fact that these temple ceremonies may not cure, and may even kill, the neophyte, in no way decreases the people's faith in the medicine men.

There remains one other kind of practitioner, known as a "listener." This witch-doctor has the power to exorcise the devils that lodge in the heads of people who have been bewitched. The Nacirema believe that parents bewitch their own children. Mothers are particularly suspected of putting a curse on children while teaching them the secret body rituals. The counter-magic of the witch-doctor is unusual in its lack of ritual. The patient simply tells the "listener" all his troubles and fears, beginning with the earliest difficulties he can remember. The memory displayed by the Nacirema in these exorcism sessions is truly remarkable. It is not uncommon for the patient to bemoan the rejection he felt upon being weaned as a babe, and a few individuals even see their troubles going back to the traumatic effects of their own birth.

In conclusion, mention must be made of certain practices which have their base in native esthetics but which depend upon the pervasive aversion to the natural body and its functions. There are ritual fasts to make fat people thin and ceremonial feasts to make thin people fat. Still other rites are used to make women's breasts larger if they are small, and smaller if they are large. General dissatisfaction with breast shape is symbolized in the fact that the ideal form is virtually outside the range of human variation. A few women afflicted with almost inhuman hypermammary development are so idolized that they make a handsome living by simply going from village to village and permitting the natives to stare at them for a fee.

Reference has already been made to the fact that excretory functions are ritualized, routinized, and relegated to secrecy. Natural reproductive functions are similarly distorted. Intercourse is taboo as a topic and scheduled as an act. Efforts are made to avoid pregnancy by the use of magical materials or by limiting intercourse to certain phases of the moon. Conception is actually very infrequent. When pregnant, women dress so as to hide their condition. Parturition takes place in secret, without friends or relatives to assist, and the majority of women do not nurse their infants.

Our review of the ritual life of the Nacirema has certainly shown them to be a magic-ridden people. It is hard to understand how they have managed to exist so long under the burdens which they have imposed upon themselves. But even such exotic customs as these take on real meaning when they are viewed with the insight provided by Malinowski when he wrote (1948: 70):

Looking from far and above, from our high places of safety in the developed civilization, it is easy to see all the crudity and irrelevance of magic. But without its power and guidance early man could not have mastered his practical difficulties as he has done, nor could man have advanced to the higher stages of civilization.

CRITICAL-THINKING QUESTIONS

1. Did you understand that Miner is describing the "American"—"Nacirema" spelled backwards? Why do we not recognize this right away?
2. Using Miner's approach, describe a baseball game, an auction, shoppers in a supermarket, or a college classroom.
3. What do we gain from being able to "step back" from our way of life as Miner has done here?

REFERENCES

LINTON, R. 1936. *The study of man.* New York: Appleton-Century.

MALINOWSKI, B. 1948. *Magic, science and religion.* Glencoe, IL: Free Press.

MURDOCK, G. P. 1949. *Social structure.* New York: Macmillan.

SOCIOLOGICAL RESEARCH

Classic

5

The Case for Value-Free Sociology

Max Weber

The following is part of a lecture given in 1918 at Germany's Munich University by Max Weber, one of sociology's pioneers. Weber lived in politically turbulent times, in which the government and other organizations were demanding that university faculty teach the "right" ideas. Weber responded to these pressures by encouraging everyone to be politically involved as citizens; yet, he maintained that the teachers and scholars should prize dispassionate analysis rather than political advocacy. This selection stimulates critical thinking about the mix of fact and value that is found in all sociological research.

Let us consider the disciplines close to me: sociology, history, economics, political science, and those types of cultural philosophy that make it their task to interpret the sciences. It is said, and I agree, that politics is out of place in the lecture-room. It does not belong there on the part of the students. . . . Neither does [it] belong in the lecture-room on the part of the [instructors], and

when the [instructor] is scientifically concerned with politics, it belongs there least of all.

To take a practical stand is one thing, and to analyze political structures and party positions is another. When speaking in a political meeting about democracy, one does not hide one's personal standpoint; indeed, to come out clearly and take a stand is one's damned duty. The words one uses in such a meeting are not means of scientific analysis but means of canvassing votes and winning over others. They are not plowshares to loosen the soil of contemplative thought; they are swords against the enemies: Such words are weapons. It

SOURCE: *From Max Weber: Essays in Sociology,* ed. and trans. H. H. Gerth and C. Wright Mills. Copyright © 1946 by Oxford University Press, Inc., renewed 1973 by H. H. Gerth. Reprinted with permission.

would be an outrage, however, to use words in this fashion in a lecture or in the lecture-room. If, for instance, "democracy" is under discussion, one considers its various forms, analyzes them in the way they function, determines what results for the conditions of life the one form has as compared with the other. Then one confronts the forms of democracy with nondemocratic forms of political order and endeavors to come to a position where the student may find the point from which, in terms of his ultimate ideals, he can take a stand. But the true teacher will beware of imposing from the platform any political position upon the student, whether it is expressed or suggested. "To let the facts speak for themselves" is the most unfair way of putting over a political position to the student.

Why should we abstain from doing this? I state in advance that some highly esteemed colleagues are of the opinion that it is not possible to carry through this self-restraint and that, even if it were possible, it would be a whim to avoid declaring oneself. Now one cannot demonstrate scientifically what the duty of an academic teacher is. One can only demand of the teacher that he have the intellectual integrity to see that it is one thing to state facts, to determine mathematical or logical relations or the internal structure of cultural values, while it is another thing to answer questions of the *value* of culture and its individual contents and the question of how one should act in the cultural community and in political associations. These are quite heterogeneous problems. If he asks further why he should not deal with both types of problems in the lecture-room, the answer is: because the prophet and the demagogue do not belong on the academic platform.

To the prophet and the demagogue, it is said: "Go your ways out into the streets and speak openly to the world," that is, speak where criticism is possible. In the lecture-room we stand opposite our audience, and it has to remain silent. I deem it irresponsible to exploit the circumstance that for the sake of their career the students have to attend a teacher's course while there is nobody present to

oppose him with criticism. The task of the teacher is to serve the students with his knowledge and scientific experience and not to imprint upon them his personal political views. It is certainly possible that the individual teacher will not entirely succeed in eliminating his personal sympathies. He is then exposed to the sharpest criticism in the forum of his own conscience. And this deficiency does not prove anything; other errors are also possible, for instance, erroneous statements of fact, and yet they prove nothing against the duty of searching for the truth. I also reject this in the very interest of science. I am ready to prove from the works of our historians that whenever the man of science introduces his personal value judgment, a full understanding of the facts *ceases*. . . .

The primary task of a useful teacher is to teach his students to recognize "inconvenient" facts—I mean facts that are inconvenient for their party opinions. And for every party opinion there are facts that are extremely inconvenient, for my own opinion no less than for others. I believe the teacher accomplishes more than a mere intellectual task if he compels his audience to accustom itself to the existence of such facts. I would be so immodest as even to apply the expression "moral achievement," though perhaps this may sound too grandiose for something that should go without saying.

CRITICAL-THINKING QUESTIONS

1. Why does Weber seek to set the campus apart from society as an "ivory tower"?

2. How is the classroom a distinctive setting in terms of political neutrality? If instructors cannot be entirely free from value positions, why should they strive to point out "inconvenient facts" to their students?

3. Do you see arguments for instructors presenting passionate advocacy of issues that are of great political and moral significance?

SOCIOLOGICAL RESEARCH

Contemporary

6

Feminist Research Methods

Shulamit Reinharz

How do various feminist research methods differ from conventional methods of scientific investigation? In this selection, Shulamit Reinharz identifies the methods feminist researchers actually use and explains why they use them. She also considers the role men can play in feminist research.

. . . I am not interested in telling feminists what methods to use. Instead, I believe a fresh approach is needed that begins with the question: What is the *range* of methods feminist researchers use? I accept Mary Daly and C. Wright Mills' idea that we think of method not as "the codification of procedures" but rather as "information about . . . actual ways of working."[1] I therefore treat the question "What is feminist research?" as an empirical problem. My approach requires listening to the voices of feminist researchers at work[2] and accepting their diversity.

DEFINING "FEMINIST"

To use this approach means that I have to define

feminism. A conversation among members of the Mud Flower Collective, a group of U.S. Christian feminist theologians, illustrates the difficulty of this task.

MARY: I think it's simply the struggle against sexism.
CARTER: I agree, but I'd have to add that this involves a stubborn insistence, a refusal to compromise the well-being of women.
KATE: For me it doesn't have anything to do with women; it's the commitment to end white supremacy, male domination, and economic exploitation.
ADA: For me feminism and feminist are different. Only the person can say if she's feminist; but feminism has to do with understanding sexism as the paradigm of all oppression. And I

SOURCE: *Feminist Methods in Social Research* by Shulamit Reinharz. Copyright © 1992 by Oxford University Press, Inc., pp. 5–6, 10–16. Reprinted by permission of the publisher.

agree with the refusal to compromise women's welfare—both women's rights and women's well-being.

BEV: I'd have to say that it begins in a woman's assertion of her power. It's not, in the first instance, a theory, but a very personal act.

BESS: For me it always has to be preceded by the word Black, and it means the creation of inclusivity and mutuality, which involves struggle against what I call the trinity of sexism, racism, and classism. . . .

NANCY: I believe it begins with the "experiencing of your experience" and that it means insisting on the well-being of women, all women, which is why racism must be examined in any feminist analysis.[3]

In addition to these differences, there are also traditional distinctions among liberal, radical, and socialist/Marxist feminism, each with its distinctive explanation of the origins of sexism and suggestions to overcome it. Differences in the definition of feminism exist among people of different classes, races, generations,[4] and sexual orientations. Differences among feminists exist around specific issues such as sadomasochism and pornography.[5] Differences exist between academic and activist feminists as well. Sometimes people who do not want to be labeled "feminist" are given the label anyhow. Conversely, some people who want to be acknowledged as feminist are not.[6] That these differences exist is fortunate because the lack of orthodoxy allows for freedom of thought and action.[7]

My solution to the practical problem of a working definition is to use people's self-definition. Thus, this book is guided by three straightforward definitions of feminist research methods:

1. Feminist research methods are methods used in research projects by people who identify themselves as feminist or as part of the women's movement.
2. Feminist research methods are methods used in research published in journals that publish only feminist research, or in books[8] that identify themselves as such.
3. Feminist research methods are methods used in re-

search that has received awards from organizations that give awards to people who do feminist research. . . .

HISTORICAL ROOTS

I believe the materials examined in this book represent a significant step in women's history. During the so-called first wave[9] of the women's movement in the United States,[10] for example, women struggled for *the right to be educated.*[11] In the so-called second wave, women strove for additional goals related to education: *the right to criticize* the accepted body of knowledge, *the right to create* knowledge, and *the right to be educators* and educational administrators. Regarding these hard-earned rights, Canadian sociologist Dorothy Smith says, "The women's movement has given us a sense of our right to have women's interests represented in sociology, rather than just receiving as authoritative the interests traditionally represented in a sociology put together by men."[12]

At first, the very act of discovering sexism in scholarship was revolutionary. That discovery clarified the mission of feminist scholarship and made it possible to demonstrate to suspicious non-feminists that there was a problem to be addressed. Elizabeth Minnich, a leader in curricular reform in the United States, expressed this well in 1977:

To a stunning extent, the interests of one half of the human race have not been thought about through history: Men have not thought about them, and women have been kept ignorant. . . . If we adopt uncritically the framework, the tools, the scholarship created overwhelmingly by and for men, we have already excluded ourselves. . . . We are being forced to try to discover new intellectual constructs because many of those we have don't fit our experience and were never intended. to.[13]

Discussion of "solutions" to these problems occurred first in small workshops, lectures, study groups, and articles in newsletters—a kind of underground,[14] as Canadian researcher Jill Vickers pointed out, noting that feminists were both "conducting 'proper' research for disciplinary consumption . . . and have created an underground in which the norms of feminist research have emerged." The underground came into existence

"Since most have endured a rigorous disciplinary 'education' in orthodox method," making "the sort of open discussions of the newly emerging principles of feminist method" that are necessary "for logical and normative reconstruction" rare. Only in passing or in meetings of the underground was there explicit "convergence of individual feminists' ideas about method."[15]

Many people innovated on their own, trying to find ways of doing research that did not imitate the problems they had discovered. At the same time they hoped to avoid rejecting their disciplinary canon altogether. As in revolutionary struggles, feminist critics of the dominant culture fused their criticism and downplayed their differences. The title of an early (1975), famous anthology by U.S. feminist sociologists Marcia Millman and Rosabeth Kanter, *Another Voice,* for example, implies that its numerous contributors spoke in a single voice. Today, a book about the same topic would necessarily refer to voice*s*.

When the "second" feminist wave began to surge through academia and new rights were beginning to be asserted, it was radical simply to study women. For example, in the early 1970s when Jessie Bernard wrote that "practically all sociology to date has been a sociology of the male world,"[16] a person might call her method "feminist" merely by virtue of the fact that she was studying women. Later in 1978, however, when Mary Daly argued that the very concern with methodology was a reflection of patriarchy,[17] the definition of feminist research became more complicated. Was our very concern with methods reactionary?

When Jeanne Gross and bell hooks claimed in 1984 that academic feminism is part of white culture, feminist research became defined for some as part of *the problem,* rather than *the solution.*[18] bell hooks' harsh critique of white women's research efforts proclaimed that "even though they may be sincerely concerned about racism, their methodology suggests they are not yet free of the type of paternalism endemic to white supremacist ideology."[19] This accusation continues to this day, as Cheryl Townsend Gilkes explains in a recent article showing how white feminist scholarship ignores the church, "the most important social settings that Black people control."[20] Does our concern with feminist methods make us blind to issues of racism? As a white woman, I feel it is my responsibility to learn as much as possible about racial diversity and interracial attempts at mutual understanding[21] to avoid feeding into the type of research that bell hooks and Cheryl Gilkes reject.

One course I teach at Brandeis University, "Women and Intellectual Work," is devoted to locating and studying the work of neglected, historical female sociologists in order to challenge the male-hegemonic history of this field.[22] In this context, I have uncovered examples of early feminist scholars' interest in questions of methodology.[23] The relation between feminism and methodology has been a long-standing feature of women's attempts to change the status quo. It is not a new concern.

From the start feminists have recognized the need to reform research practices. A case in point is nineteenth-century British sociologist Harriet Martineau,[24] who believed that observers typically misunderstood the societies they studied. The problem, as she saw it, was that observers compared other societies with their own.[25] That point was echoed in the writing of feminist critics of the late 1970s who pointed out that male researchers misunderstood women because they compared women to men.

Similarly, Ida B. Wells, a Black nineteenth-century U.S. woman who published analyses of lynchings and led the fight against them, had strong convictions about methods. She believed that the most "reputable" sources must be used so that the conclusions could not be contested by those in power. She wrote:

For a number of years the *Chicago Tribune,* admittedly one of the leading journals of America, has made a specialty of the compilation of statistics touching upon lynching. The data compiled by that journal and published to the world January 1st, 1894, up to the present time has not been disputed. In order to be safe from the charge of exaggeration, the incidents hereinafter reported have been confined to those vouched for by the *Tribune.*[26]

Drawing on such material, illustrating how a

particular method was used by nineteenth- or early twentieth-century feminist researchers,[27] I include a section on "historical roots" at the outset of most chapters of this book. This inclusion also reflects the significance of historical figures in raising the consciousness of contemporary women. The following comment by Celia Eckhardt concerning Frances Wright (1795–1852) is not uncommon: "It was Fanny Wright, in fact, who turned me in middle age into a feminist—both by way of the positions she argued so forcefully and because of the way she was treated in the United States of America."[28] Just as historical feminist figures permeate the consciousness of contemporary feminists, historic methodological ideas underpin current debates on feminist methodology.

ONGOING QUESTIONS AND QUESTS

Just as there was a diverse set of views about educating women during the "first" wave of the women's movement, there are diverse views today about the knowledge feminists wish to produce. Starting in the underground and now aboveground, feminists are engaged in an ongoing discussion about feminist methodology. Does it exist? Should it exist? What is it? Are there different types? Is there a female or feminist cognitive style that could inform an alternative method? Is feminist disciplinary research a contradiction in terms given that for the most part the disciplines still reject the politics of feminism and still deny that they themselves are political? Does academia depoliticize feminism? Is feminist methodology more methodology and less feminism? British psychologist Celia Kitzinger answers this way:

For me, being both a feminist and a psychologist means to be responsible to other feminists for my psychology, and, equally to be responsible to other psychologists for my feminism. To remain identified with each group, I need to be able to offer something positive to each. To feminism I offer my analysis of the dangers of psychobabble invading the women's movement, and my "insider" knowledge of a patriarchal discipline.... To psychology I offer my analyses of the role of rhetoric within the social sciences, a radical and social constructionist perspective as an alternative to positivist–empiricist approaches, and my "insider" knowledge of lesbianism and feminism.... While rejecting the label

"feminist psychologist" as a contradiction in terms, I am passionate in my commitment both to feminism and to psychology. The intellectual excitement and the practical impact of my research and teaching are lodged in the space created by this contradiction—and the challenge of contradiction seems infinitely more creative than the comfort of compromise![29]

Clearly, she is engaged passionately in the contradictions of her identity rather than being debilitated by them.

Judith Lorber, former editor of *Gender & Society*, a major U.S. feminist sociological journal, answers the ongoing questions in a strikingly different way. Although acknowledging that women's realities are different from men's, she doubts that "a special way of doing research—feminist methodology—is the only way women's realities can be tapped and understood" and she questions "whether feminist methodologies are unique to feminists." She does not accept the claim that

feminist methods were different from masculinist methods.... While I do not think that feminist methodology is unique, I think feminists do uniquely contribute to social science by seeing patterns and interrelationships and causes and effects and implications of questions that nonfeminists have not seen and still do not see.[30]

Some feminists argue that there is no special affinity between feminism and a particular research method. Others support interpretive, qualitative research methods; advocate positivist, "objective" methods; or value combining the two. Some imply "use what works," others "use what you know," and others "use what will convince." How can we do research without perpetuating the very problems we have identified? Is it enough to make women visible? Are certain techniques more appropriate than others for feminist research?

A NOTE ABOUT MEN

Some men (and some women) are hostile to the idea of feminist research,[31] while other men label themselves feminist and their research "feminist research." The feminist community is divided about men's roles as feminists. Psychologist Nancy Henley argues against anti-male feelings, writing that "being pro-woman and anti-male supremacy does not necessarily mean being anti-man."[32] Others such as Mary Daly claim that men can support feminism but cannot *be* feminists because they lack women's experience:

Male authors who are now claiming that they can write accurately "about women" give away the level of their comprehension by the use of this expression. The new consciousness of women is not mere "knowledge about," but an emotional-intellectual-volitional rebirth.[33]

Men, on the other hand, have pointed out the oppressive nature of being excluded by women. For example, U.S. male sociologist Terry Kandal wrote:

Feminist critical discourse has raised the epistemological question of whether one must be a woman in order to contribute to an authentic sociology of or for women. Obviously, having written this book, my answer is: not necessarily. Although a man cannot experience what it means to be a woman, this does not preclude making a contribution to the sociology of women. William James' distinction between "knowing" and "knowing about" is apropos. Oppression seems to me to have transgender aspects, which those who have experienced it can communicate.[34]

Those feminists who disagree with the exclusion of men point to the excellence of some feminist research conducted by men.[35] In Del Martin's view, for example, Detroit Police Department Commander James Bannon's sociological study of domestic social conflict "shows a high degree of feminist consciousness and a keen awareness of the victim's predicament that is generally lacking in police attitudes."[36] She suggests that feminists differentiate among men.

Men who study problems faced by women sometimes present themselves as closely aligned with the victims. For example, Edward Donnerstein, Daniel Linz, and Steven Penrod concluded their study of pornography by explaining that they

attempted to approach the topic of violence against women in the media as objectively as possible. But as men, husbands, significant others, and fathers . . . we are personally and morally deeply offended by many of the media depictions of women we have described in this book. We have undertaken our investigations both because we are intellectually curious about the effects of exposure to pornography and other images of women in

the media, and because we are concerned about the negative impact of these materials on the members of our society—particularly our fellow male members. Our . . . hope is that in the end the truth revealed through good science will prevail and the public will be convinced that these images not only demean those portrayed but also those who view them.[37]

Some feminists distrust the intentions of people who are "intellectually curious" rather than passionately angry about the idea of pornography. But pornography, to continue this example, is a topic on which there are also differences within the feminist community itself!

Men who conduct what they call "feminist research" are a minority in a minority and thus report being under special scrutiny. Richard Evans described

historians and archivists . . . in East and West Germany [who] were unable to clearly conceal their surprise that [he] had chosen to study feminism, and some of them clearly thought [he] would have done better to have picked a subject that was more central to the concerns of the historical profession in general and to have left feminism to women. At the same time, [his] research aroused a good deal of interest in supporters of the Women's Liberation movement, and it naturally brought [him] into contact with many of them. These two influences forced [him] to embark on a more general consideration of women's history, the reason for its neglect, and the problems involved in researching and writing it.[38]

Men might not be aware that women conducting feminist research or research about feminism are likely to receive the same ambivalent reaction from nonfeminists.

Another reaction from the wider public is an assumption that male researchers who study topics such as masculinity and the sociology of gender are homosexual. Clive Pearson wrote:

The point of course, is not whether I am or even what the categorisation means for gay people in sociology, but that it was automatically assumed that a heterosexual man would not have a research interest in male practice. My research is concentrated on the responses to the Women's Movement of men in "men's groups" and the impact of the Women's Movement on left political groupings, but my position within sociology, as defined by many of my male colleagues, has led me to attempt to open up the positions and practices of men in sociology.[39]

In an opposite vein, U.S. psychologist Michelle Fine points out that men are not victimized when they study feminists or women. Rather they are viewed as *greater* authorities than the people about whom they speak:

those who study injustice are often ascribed more objectivity, credibility, and respect. When men discuss feminist scholarship, it is' taken more seriously than when women do. When whites study the Black family the work may be viewed as less "biased" than when Black scholars pursue the same areas. . . . But if a Black social scientist studies white people, one might expect the resulting analyses to be considered the "Black perspective."[40]

My use of the criterion of self-definition provided me with a straightforward approach to these conundra. I include the work of men who call themselves feminist in a research publication. Since I have found so few instances, I suspect the closer men come to understanding feminism, the more reluctant they are to take the label. Nevertheless, it seems important to examine the specific instances where it occurs.

CRITICAL-THINKING QUESTIONS

1. What is feminism? Can men be feminists? Must women be feminists?
2. What is feminist research? How much consensus is there on what is meant by feminist research methods?
3. Does feminism merely modify the focus of scientific research, or does it transform science in a basic way?

NOTES

1. C. Wright Mills, *The Sociological Imagination* (New York: Oxford University Press, 1959), p. 195. There is irony in mentioning Mills in this regard, since Mills worked as a coauthor with his wives (Dorothy James and Ruth Harper), yet it is he who is considered author. See Irving Louis Horowitz, *C. Wright Mills: An American Utopian* (New York: The Free Press, 1983), esp. pp. 71–72, 79.

2. See Judith Rollins, *Between Women: Domestics and Their Employers* (Philadelphia, PA: Temple University Press, 1985), p. 17, for a discussion of this approach.

3. The Mud Flower Collective, *God's Fierce Whimsy: Christian Feminism and Theological Education* (New York: The Pilgrim Press, 1985), pp. 14–15.

4. Barbara Macdonald with Cynthia Rich, *Look Me in the Eye: Old Women, Aging and Ageism* (San Francisco: Spinsters, Ink, 1983).

5. Robin Ruth Linden, Darlene Pagano, Diana Russell, and Susan Star, eds., *Against Sadomasochism: A Radical Feminist Analysis* (San Francisco: Frog in the Well Press, 1982); and Mary Roth Walsh, ed., *The Psychology of Women: Ongoing Debates* (New Haven, CT: Yale University Press, 1987).

6. Ruth Levitas, "Feminism and Human Nature," in *Politics and Human Nature,* ed. Ian Forbes and Steve Smith (New York: St. Martin's Press, 1983).

7. Foreword in Arlyn Diamond and Lee Edwards, eds., *The Authority of Experience: Essays in Feminist Criticism* (Amherst, MA: University of Massachusetts Press, 1977).

8. Inquiries concerning feminist methodology that examine articles and not books reach the conclusion that feminist research does not deviate much from androcentric standards. See Richard T. Walsh, "Where Is the Research Relationship in Feminist Psychology Research?," paper presented at the Annual Meeting of the American Psychological Association, 1987; and M. Brinton Lykes and Abigail Stewart, "Evaluating the Feminist Challenge to Research in Personality and Social Psychology, 1963–1983," *Psychology of Women Quarterly,* 10, no. 4 (1986), 393–412. Monographs afford feminists greater control than do journal articles. For this reason it was essential to not confine my study to journals. See also Dale Spender, "The Gatekeepers: A Feminist Critique of Academic Publishing," in *Doing Feminist Research,* ed. Helen Roberts (London: Routledge & Kegan Paul, 1981). For a discussion of the barriers to publishing books see *Gatekeeping: The Denial, Dismissal and Distortion of Women,* ed. Dale Spender and Lynne Spender, a special issue of *Women's Studies International Forum,* 1983, 6(5).

9. The terms "first- and second-waves" make invisible all the feminist work that occurred in between. See Leila Rupp and Verta Taylor, *Surviving in the Doldrums: The American Women's Rights Movements, 1945 to the 1960s* (Columbus, OH: Ohio State University Press, 1990).

10. See Jessie Bernard, *The Female World from a Global Perspective* (Bloomington, IN: Indiana University Press, 1987) for a discussion of the importance of recognizing differences between women's struggles in the United States as compared with other countries, and for her discussion of the importance of not using the word "American" as an adjective equivalent to United States.

11. See Louise Michele Newman, ed., *Men's Ideas/Women's Realities* (New York: Pergamon, 1985); Rosalind Rosenberg, *Beyond Separate Spheres: Intellectual Roots of Modern Feminism* (New Haven, CT: Yale University Press, 1982); Barbara Miller Solomon, *In the Company of Education Women: A History of Women and Higher Education in America* (New Haven, CT: Yale University Press, 1985); and Janet Sayers, *Biological Politics* (London: Tavistock, 1982).

12. Dorothy E. Smith, "Women's Perspective as a Radical Critique of Sociology," *Sociological Inquiry,* 44, no. 1 (1974), 7–13, esp. p. 7.

13. Elizabeth Minnich, "Discussion," *The Scholar and the Feminist IV: Connecting Theory, Practice, and Values,* a conference sponsored by The Barnard College Women's Center, April 1977, p. 53.

14. The underground may consist of women's studies classroom discussions and feminist organization newsletter articles.

15. Jill McCalla Vickers, "Memoirs of an Ontological Exile: The Methodological Rebellions of Feminist Research," in *Feminism in Canada,* ed. Geraldine Finn and Angela Miles (Montreal: Black Rose Books, 1982), pp. 27–46, esp. p. 32.

16. Jessie Bernard, "My Four Revolutions: An Autobiographical History of the ASA," *American Journal of Sociology,* 78, no. 4 (1973), 773–91.

17. See Mary Daly, *Gyn/Ecology: The Metaethics of Radical Feminism* (Boston: Beacon Press, 1978).

18. Jeanne Gross, "Feminist Ethics from a Marxist Perspective," *Radical Religion,* 3, no. 2 (1977), 52–56; quoted in bell hooks, *Feminist Theory: From Margin to Center* (Boston: South End Press, 1984), pp. 26–27.

19. Op. cit., p. 12.

20. Cheryl Townsend Gilkes, "The Roles of Church and Community Mothers: Ambivalent American Sexism or Fragmented African Familyhood?" *Journal of Feminist Studies in Religion,* 2, no. 1 (1986), 41–59, esp. p. 57.

21. Becky Thompson, "Raisins and Smiles for Me and My Sister: A Feminist Theory of Eating Problems, Trauma, and Recovery in Women's Lives," doctoral dissertation, Department of Sociology, Brandeis University, 1990.

22. Mary Jo Deegan, "Transcending a Patriarchal Past: Teaching the History of Women in Sociology," *Teaching Sociology,* 16 (1988), 141–50.

23. Shulamit Reinharz, "Teaching the History of Women in Sociology; or Dorothy Swaine Thomas, Wasn't She the Woman Married to William I.?," *The American Sociologist,* 20, no. 1 (1989), 87–94; Shulamit Reinharz and Ellen Stone, eds., *Looking at Invisible Women* (Washington, D.C.: University Press of America, 1992); Kathleen E. Grady, "Sex Bias in Research Design," *Psychology of Women Quarterly,* 5, no. 4 (1981), 628–36.

24. Valerie Pichanik, *Harriet Martineau: The Woman and Her Work, 1802–1876* (Ann Arbor, MI: University of Michigan Press, 1980); Gayle Yates, ed., *Harriet Martineau on Women* (New Brunswick, NJ: Rutgers University Press, 1985).

25. Michael R. Hill, ed., Harriet Martineau, *How to Observe Morals and Manners* (1836) (New Brunswick, NJ: Transaction Books, 1989).

26. Ida B. Wells, *A Red Record: Tabulated Statistics and Alleged Causes of Lynchings in the United States, 1892–1893–1894* (reprint, Salem, NH: Ayer Company, 1987), p. 15.

27. See Debra Kaufman and Barbara Richardson, *Achievement and Women: Challenging the Assumptions* (New York: The Free Press, 1982), for another example of how contemporary feminist research questions are embedded in an historical context.

28. Celia Eckhardt, "Fanny Wright: The Woman Who Made the Myth" (paper presented at Conference on "Autobiographies, Biographies and Life Histories of Women: Interdisciplinary Perspectives," University of Minnesota, May 23, 1986), p. 1.

29. Celia Kitzinger, "Resisting the Discipline," in *The Practice of Psychology by Feminists,* ed. Erica Burman (London: Sage, 1990), pp. 26–27.

30. Judith Lorber, "From the Editor," *Gender & Society,* 2, no. 1 (1988), 5–8.

31. Joseph Adelson, "Androgyny Advocates Pose a Threat to Scientific Objectivity," *Behavior Today,* 11, no. 11 (1980), 1–3; and Joseph Adelson and Carolyn Sherif, "Resolved: Division 35 of A.P.A. Is/Is Not a Scholarly Disaster Area," *Behavior Today,* June 2, 1980, p. 3.

32. Nancy Henley, *Body Politics: Power, Sex, and Nonverbal Communication* (Englewood Cliffs, NJ: Prentice-Hall, 1977), p. viii.

33. Mary Daly, *Beyond God the Father* (Boston: Beacon Press, 1973), p. 200, fn. 9.

34. Terry Kandal, *The Woman Question in Classical Sociological Theory* (Miami: Florida International University Press, 1988), p. xiv.

35. Carol Ehrlich considers the following to be excellent feminist research done by men: Joel Aronoff and William Crano, "A Re-examination of the Cross-Cultural Principles of Task Segregation and Sex Role Differentiation in the Family," *American Sociological Review,* 40 (1975), 12–20; Howard Ehrlich, "Selected Differences in the Life Chances of Men and Women in the United States" (Baltimore, MD: Research Group One, Report no. 13); and Dean Knudsen, "The Declining Status of Women: Popular Myths and the Failure of Functionalist Thought," *Social Forces,* 48 (Dec. 1969), 183–93. See also Martin Meissner, "The Reproduction of Women's Domination in Organizational Communication," University of British Columbia (unpublished manuscript). For a defense of men's study of women, see Aileen S. Kraditor's foreword in Ronald Hogeland, ed., *Women and Womanhood in America* (Lexington, MA: D. C. Heath, 1973).

36. Del Martin, *Battered Wives* (New York: Simon & Schuster, 1976), p. xviii.

37. Edward Donnerstein, Daniel Linz, and Steven Penrod, *The Question of Pornography: Research Findings and Policy Implications* (New York: The Free Press, 1987), p. 196.

38. Richard J. Evans, preface to *The Feminists: Women's Emancipation Movements in Europe, America, and Australasia 1840–1920* (New York: Barnes and Noble, 1977).

39. Clive Pearson, "Some Problems in Talking about Men," in *Looking Back: Some Papers from the BSA 'Gender & Society' Conference,* ed. Sue Webb and Clive Pearson, in *Studies in Sexual Politics,* ed. Liz Stanley and Sue Scott (University of Manchester, Department of Sociology, 1984), pp. 46–59, esp. p. 48.

40. Michelle Fine, "Contextualizing the Study of Social Injustice," *Advances in Applied Social Psychology,* ed. Michael Saks and Leonard Saxe (Hillsdale, NJ: Erlbaum, 1985), pp. 103–26.

7

Applying U.S. Ethics to Research in South Africa

Ivy N. Goduka

Doing cross-cultural research can be both difficult and dangerous. In this selection, Ivy Go-duka explains that political constraints in countries such as South Africa present the researcher with ethical and methodological problems as well as the potential of physical harm. She ar-gues that the ethical guidelines required of researchers in the United States and other West-ern countries are simply not relevant in "authoritarian societies."

I am a black South African. I was born and grew up in Herschel in the homeland of the Transkei. Recently I completed a Ph.D. in the College of Hu-man Ecology at Michigan State University, and for my dissertation I conducted field research (Go-duka 1987) on black children in three black resi-dential areas in South Africa: Herschel; the resettlement of Thornhill, in the homeland of the Ciskei; and white-owned farm areas in Queens-town and in Zastron. In the process of conducting

that research I became acutely aware of the con-tradictions inherent in any attempt to apply ethical codes designed in the relatively liberal, economi-cally stable, politically "safe," and literate soci-eties of North America and Europe to research practices in an authoritarian context such as South Africa.

This paper illustrates the disjunctures created when ethical codes designed in one cultural and political context are applied to a quite different one. I draw upon my background as a black South African and my graduate training at Michigan State University. Because I was trained in the United States, and because my research project

SOURCE: "Ethics and Politics of Field Research in South Africa," by Ivy N. Goduka, *Social Problems,* vol. 37, no. 3, August 1990, pp. 329–40. Copyright © 1990 by the Society for the Study of Social Problems. Reprinted with permission.

was funded by the National Science Foundation, I was obligated to abide by the ethical guidelines of the American Sociological Association (1988). I will first describe the political and cultural contexts in South Africa, contrast these with the political and cultural contexts in the United States, and examine the implications of these contexts for research. In an effort to bridge the differences between these two contexts, I will discuss my research topic, its origins, purpose, methods, and data collection procedures. I will then explore the limitations of informed consent and prohibitions against covert research when applied to an authoritarian context such as South Africa.

RESEARCH CONTEXTS

South Africa

South Africa is an authoritarian society that gives little or no state protection of individual rights, particularly for blacks. This lack of protection results from the system of apartheid, a policy of rigid racial discrimination that has existed in South Africa since 1948. Many laws and acts have been passed by the South African government that serve to entrench and legalize apartheid. These laws include population registration, land reservation, education, and job reservation acts. These laws and acts deny blacks in South Africa the right to vote and serve to keep them landless, powerless, and lacking in all the basic resources necessary for survival. Because they lack basic resources, blacks are not only illiterate and poverty-stricken but also ignorant, vulnerable, and powerless to make decisions and choices directly affecting their own lives, particularly those regarding family issues. . . .

Living conditions for blacks in the white-owned farm areas are also very poor. Workers, including children, are housed in large unfurnished sheds with no internal walls or beds. Families live in corrugated iron huts. There is usually no internal water, and there is a general lack of sanitation. Farm life is characterized by what Nasson (1984) calls acute squalor, chronic poverty, and almost total lack of alternative employment opportunities.

Farm laborers, and their children who grow up working on the farm, learn to be dependent on white farmers for jobs, food, and housing. Thus, under apartheid, black families not only live under impoverished conditions, they are disenfranchised and prevented from making basic individual decisions about family affairs.

The United States

In contrast to the authoritarian South African context, the laws of the United States are founded on respect for the rights of the individual regardless of race. This respect for individual rights is also emphasized and required in research, particularly in the ethical and legal imperative of informed consent (Lidz et al. 1984). The state laws regulating informed consent are deeply rooted in the individualistic tradition of the English common law and have been adopted and used in the American legal system. . . .

The guidelines professionally specified for sociologists are outlined by the American Sociological Association (ASA 1988). I followed these ethical guidelines in my research in South Africa. These guidelines are offered as applicable to research on human subjects irrespective of disciplinary area, and illustrate ethical codes current in the various human sciences. They are based on nine major principles (American Sociological Association 1988:4–5). In this paper, only those guidelines that relate to deception and informed consent are cited.

In abridged form, these ASA guidelines are: (1) Sociologists must not knowingly use their professional roles as covers to obtain information for fraudulent or covert purpose. (2) Sociologists must take culturally appropriate steps to secure informed consent and to avoid invasion of privacy. Special actions may be necessary where the individuals studied are illiterate, of very low social status, and/or unfamiliar with social research. (3) Study design and information-gathering techniques should conform to regulations protecting the rights of human subjects, irrespective of source of funding, as outlined by the American Association of University Professors in "Regulations governing research on human subjects" (Academe 1981).

It is clear that the ASA document covers a fair number of specific and somewhat general principles regarding the protection of the research participants. In order to ascertain that researchers in the United States abide by the guidelines on informed consent, universities have attempted to aid researchers and protect the welfare of human subjects in a variety of ways. Consequently, universities have instituted human subjects research review committees that must approve of the ethics of a specific procedure before the research may be conducted. . . .

The University Committee on Research Involving Human Subjects (UCRIHS) at Michigan State University, where I was studying at the time of this research, did not require a signed consent form prior to starting fieldwork. However, Michigan State's UCRIHS reviewed my proposal to ensure that the rights and welfare of the subjects were not violated. Although the proposal as a whole met all the standards and requirements of social research, because of the committee's strong emphasis on informed consent, that section had to be revised twice before the proposal was approved. The National Science Foundation, which provided funding for this research, also required a copy of the informed consent form prior to approving the application for funding. The consent form I used as required by UCRIHS at Michigan State University reads as follows:

Parent/Guardian's Name: _____. I freely give consent for my child and I to take part in this study. I understand that my child and I are free to discontinue our participation in the study at any time. My participation and my child's participation in the study does not guarantee any beneficial results to me and to my child. I understand that, at my request, I can receive additional explanation of the study after my participation is completed, and that the results of the study will be treated in strict confidence and we will remain anonymous. Within these restrictions, results of the study will be made available to me at my request (Goduka 1987:260).

At the end of the consent form, the subject is required to attach her/his signature and date it. This document is legally binding on the researcher. It emphasizes individuals over collectivities, and contractual relations between the researcher and the subjects; it assumes the legalistic rights of the subjects, as well as the right to make choices and have control over one's life. As I will illustrate by my discussion of the problems I encountered while attempting to apply the ASA guidelines in my research, the political and cultural conditions that gave rise to the development of such professional codes of research ethics in the United States simply do not exist in South Africa.

BRIDGING TWO CULTURES

The Research Project: Methods and Procedures

My research project, which ultimately came to be titled "Behavioral Development of Black South African Children: an Ecological Approach" (Goduka 1987), originated from my own childhood experience in Herschel, in the homeland of the Transkei, and a concern for how black children grow and develop in the rural areas of South Africa under apartheid. Thus, the study's purpose was to examine the physical growth and behavioral development of black elementary school children in South Africa from an ecosystem perspective. A number of selected ecological factors, namely, the area of residence, the type of family structure, parent's socio-economic status, family mobility, and the home environment, were examined as these might modify the nutritional status and the socio-emotional and cognitive development of children.

The sample included 300 children and their parents or guardians from the Xhosa ethnic group. I selected a sub-sample of one hundred children from each of the three areas studied (homeland of the Transkei; resettlement of Thornhill; and white-owned farms). Before children were tested and parents were interviewed, I gave each child who was in the sample a letter explaining the purpose of the research, and a copy of the consent form that the parents were to fill out and give to the child to return to school the following day. Both the letter and a copy of the consent form were first written in English and then translated into Xhosa, a language spoken by the subjects. About one-half (52 percent) of the parents or guardians filled out the consent forms and returned them to school via their children the next day. My assistants and I made home visits to the other half of the sample to explain the purpose of the study and request that the parent or guardian fill out the informed consent form.

A team of three researchers (two research assistants from the homeland of the Transkei whom I had hired, and myself) assessed children at school for cognitive and social-emotional development. We also took measures of physical growth (height, weight, and head circumference). The assessment and measuring of children took place at school. In most cases testing was done during recess, in other cases it took place after school. The three of us made home visits to observe parent-child interaction and home conditions, and to administer a questionnaire to the parent or guardian of each child in order to obtain demographic data. . . .

Ethics and Access

A major problem for me in doing this particular project arose out of my position as a black South African: how to gain access to white-owned farm areas. On the basis of the Group Area's Act, black families may live, work, and move freely only in the homeland and resettlement areas. Similarly, whites, coloreds, and Asians may live only in their designated areas. To live and work in urban areas and on white-owned farms, blacks are required by law to obtain a pass (identification document) and work permit from the white government. The same laws applied to me and my research assistants when conducting research on white-owned farm areas. Unlike the homeland and the resettlement areas, the farm areas are directly under the control of the Pretoria regime, as are the schools in white-owned areas. Therefore, as black South Africans we had to obtain permission from Pretoria in order to gain entry into the schools in these areas and to interview farm laborers.

While preparing my research proposal, I had to decide whether I would do covert research or be completely open and honest about my project's purpose. The latter, in all probability, would have caused the South African, as well as the Transkeian and Ciskeian governments to refuse me access to the schools and homes. Realizing these difficulties, I decided to use the same strategies that other social scientists have used when dealing with the South African government.

While doing research in South Africa, van den Berghe (1968:185–86) concluded "I decided that I should have no scruples in deceiving the government and that the paramount consideration in my dealings with the state would be to minimize obstacles to my research without compromising my principles." When he applied for a South African visa, he decided that it would be unwise to reveal the real purpose of his study, which was to look at race relations. Instead he stated that he was a social scientist interested in "the spectacular economic development of South Africa" (1988:185–86). He also refused certain customary white privileges, and decided to break some laws that he considered iniquitous or that exposed his non-white friends to embarrassment.

In order to gain access to these research sites, I chose van den Berghe's strategy. For instance, I phrased the title of the study in a way that would not be alarming to the government of South Africa, the school administrators, or the subjects. My research was designed to study black children under apartheid and originally was titled "Behavioral Development of Black South African Children Under Apartheid." After I alerted my guidance committee to problems I would encounter with this title, the committee allowed me to change it. The committee also was afraid that the government of South Africa would view this title as challenging the status quo, and would not allow me access to areas where blacks live. Consequently, I changed the title to "Behavioral Development of Black South African Children: An Ecological Approach" (Goduka 1987). This was a less threatening yet all-inclusive title that would save me from the possibility of refused access or even possibly going to jail. The human ecological framework used in this study also helped in phrasing a title acceptable to the government of South Africa. It was acceptable because it sounded like social science jargon and thus apolitical.

Gaining access to the homeland of the Transkei and the resettlement of Thornhill was easy both because these are "independent" areas assigned to blacks and because we were black and from one of these areas. However, I had to go personally to Pretoria for an interview before the government gave us the approval to enter the white-owned farm areas. Because I am a native of South Africa, I know and understand how the government operates, I knew how to manipulate the system to obtain what I wanted. The first strategy that I devised was to secure the assistance of a white liberal South African who would have credibility for the Pretoria white minority government. I asked my major professor, who was also the director of the study at Michigan State University, to request in writing that the Deputy Director of the National Institute of Personnel Research (NIPR) in Johannesburg supervise my work while I collected data in South Africa. (I had worked for the NIPR before coming to study at Michigan State. The Deputy Director, who is an opponent of apartheid, had been my supervisor at the institute.) After he expressed his willingness to supervise the research, his name was given in the letter to the school administrators and parents or guardians. In addition, administrators and parents or guardians were given his telephone number at the institute and were instructed to call him if they had further questions about the project.

An interview with the chief school administrator in Pretoria, which lasted two to three hours, did not give weight to my case primarily because of the color of my skin and the fact that I am a woman. What overcame this deficiency, however, was a telephone conversation between the chief school inspector and the Deputy Director of the NIPR. The latter was then asked to write a letter explaining who I was. In the letter he added: "Her university has appointed me as a supervisor of her fieldwork in South Africa. I would be grateful if you could give her the assistance that she seeks

with a view to completing fieldwork of her Ph.D. research" (Goduka 1987:261e).

Thus, I had to use the NIPR to get into the schools on white-owned farms. I knew the NIPR had more credibility in the eyes of the government than my committee members, who were thousands of miles away in the United States. Telephone calls to and fro would have been a waste of time and money. However, under normal circumstances, i.e., without the imposition of economic sanctions upon the South African government by the Reagan administration, a call from the United States probably would have carried more weight than the NIPR.

Getting approval from Pretoria made entry to some farm areas easier; however, in other areas we were totally refused entry. The white Boer farmers knew their word was final, and that their treatment of "Kaffirs" or "niggers" (as they referred to us) would not jeopardize their situation. The white farmers have the complete support of the government since they vote for the president, and the economy of South Africa is dependent on what they produce.

Another access problem we had concerned driving around the white-owned farms in the evenings. Because of the political turmoil, marked by extreme tension between blacks and whites, 1986 was a bad year to be in South Africa. Some of the interviews and observations in the farm areas were scheduled in the evening, after the laborers were off work. On several occasions we were stopped on the road because of a road-block and would be late for interviews, or end up missing interview appointments. We were asked to produce passes, or identification cards, by white police officers. Failure to do so on the spot led many travellers to be taken away and locked in jail. We were fortunate that we knew the law and were prepared in that respect. Our bags were searched, and the research material would be tossed all over in the trunk. All this was done out of spite: "Die Kaffirs dink hulle is slim"—"these niggers think they are smart. Who are you to do research?" as one officer commented, laughing sarcastically. We would spend hours being interrogated by young, ignorant, white police officers. Some interviews had to be cancelled because of the state of emergency and declared curfews.

Going back to the homeland after interviews was another problem. Although trust and rapport were established and maintained to some extent with teachers, school children, and parents, we found that villagers, particularly high school students, were suspicious. Not only were we viewed as "outsiders," because the rented car we were using had a Johannesburg registration, but also we were occasionally stopped by villagers for interrogation, and were accused of collaborating with the Pretoria government. The problems we encountered, therefore, came not only from the white establishment but also from some blacks. Having been out of the country for five years, I was viewed as a stranger, especially to young children. However, the presence of the two local teachers who were my research assistants made a great difference. Thus, while conducting research in South Africa was a traumatic experience for me, familiarity with the policy of apartheid and knowing what to expect made the situation somewhat less traumatic. Nonetheless, my conscience has since been bothering me. I do not know to what degree I may have violated ethical codes in the process of meeting the practical need of access, and what penalty I could be made to pay for doing so.

Ethics and Dissemination of Findings

Another major concern I had was how to disseminate the findings to the research participants or to the authorities if they so desired. Although the informed consent the parents had signed stated that "the results of the study will be made available to me at my request," I knew that since I was dealing with an illiterate group, the meaning of the consent form would not be understood. Since no promises were made in writing to the authorities, I decided to send copies of the dissertation to only a few universities in the homelands. For my safety, I did not send a copy to Pretoria. However, suppose the government of Pretoria had forced me to make a written promise to send findings as a con-

dition to obtaining approval to enter white-owned farm areas? If I had signed a contract in order to get what I wanted, then refused to deliver for fear of my safety—would this be regarded as a "criminal act" by the ASA, and would I be made to confess my "sins"? I am not in a position to answer these questions and will leave them up to the Association. However, below I offer a few suggestions that might help alleviate difficulties when scientists transplant ethical codes to authoritarian contexts.

DISCUSSION

. . . To date, very little work has been done either by professional organizations or by individuals to address the special ethical considerations of conducting research in an authoritarian society. Little information has been published about problems involved in undertaking research in repressive societies such as South Africa, the People's Republic of China, the Middle East, the Soviet Union, and various Latin American countries. The lack of such reports may be motivated by the fear (on the part of the researchers and the funding agencies) that the governments of these countries might then make it hard for outsiders to conduct research.

Mosher's (1985) report on his experiences in the People's Republic of China is one rare example. In his thought-provoking and controversial book, *Journey to the Forbidden China*, Mosher relates how he was told by Chinese officials that, despite his stamped travel permit, he had entered a restricted region—and must confess to having willfully violated the People's Republic of China's Travel Regulations for Foreigners. Although he managed to extricate himself from this predicament, this led to his abrupt departure from the PRC and, even worse, to the charge of espionage that the Chinese officials leveled against him.

Certain social scientists have addressed covert research in general rather than research which relates specifically to repressive societies. For example, Bulmer (1982) points out that the researcher may be entitled, and indeed compelled, to adopt covert methods. He maintains that the social scientist is justified in using such measures where necessary in order to achieve the higher objective of scientific truth. Bulmer's argument ties to the context of repressive societies and can be extended to the South African situation. Galliher (1982:159–60) also addresses this issue:

The question is how much honor is proper for the sociologist in studying the membership and organization of what he considers an essentially dishonorable, morally outrageous, and destructive enterprise? Is not the failure of sociology to uncover corrupt, illegitimate, covert practices of government or industry because of the supposed prohibition of professions tantamount to supporting such practices?

Although Galliher is referring to doing research directly on the powerful (government and industry), one can also conduct research among the oppressed with the intention of exposing those in power.

Appelbaum, Lidz, and Meisel (1987) suggest that discussions of informed consent in medical settings must be supplemented by hands-on training. They propose that students be taught "how to communicate information, facilitate patient participation, and handle questions of impaired competency and voluntariness" (Appelbaum, Lidz, and Meisel 1987:265–66). As my discussion of my own research project has illustrated, securing truly informed consent is just as problematic (if not more so) for researchers doing fieldwork in authoritarian and/or impoverished societies as it is for medical practitioners. Universities should prepare prospective researchers for what lies ahead in the field. The training and guidance that graduate students currently receive about informed consent and what it entails is insufficient. It barely covers the applicability and relevance of informed consent in closed societies.

A major part of graduate training should emphasize that ethical codes designed in one context may not apply across cultures, and/or across time. Ethical codes designed in the relatively liberal, economically stable, politically "safe," and literate societies of North America and Europe are irrelevant to research practices in an authoritarian context such as South Africa. Furthermore, it should be emphasized that some ethical codes that applied in the 1950s may not be applicable in the 1990s. The training should also stress that informed consent is fundamentally limited and limiting. As the guidelines regarding informed consent stand at present, it is only suited for use by middle class social scientists for studying middle class populations, or business contractors who fulfill the requirement of knowledgeability, voluntary participation, and competent choice.

Western academic institutions should also study what guidelines work in which places, under what conditions, and for whom, before sending their students to other countries to conduct research. They should consult black South African scholars who are in the United States or abroad to strategize ways for doing research in that country. There is, further, a need for scientists in Africa to Africanize research to meet the needs of Africans, rather than to adopt Anglo- and Euro-centric ethics and methods of research.

Finally, any professional code is useful only as a guideline or as a moral pathfinder sensitizing students, researchers, and supervisors to ethical elements prior, during, and after the project (Punch 1986). When major decisions are to be made, the responsibility should rest with the individual investigator, who presumably is cognizant of the professional codes, the politics, and the culture under which the subjects live. Most important, professional associations must examine the relevance of informed consent in authoritarian societies. I suggest that the research codes include a guideline that reads: "When one conducts research in an authoritarian society, covert research may be necessary in order to expose the powerful." Is this too much of a risk for such associations to take?

CRITICAL-THINKING QUESTIONS

1. From a researcher's perspective, why is South Africa an "authoritarian society"?

2. In the United States, how do state laws and uni-

versity guidelines try to protect the rights of the people who are studied?

3. What were the ethical problems that Goduka encountered? How did she resolve them?

4. Goduka shows that ethical guidelines are not universal but culturally bound. Do you think that ethical guidelines should be changed to facilitate or accommodate cross-cultural research?

REFERENCES

ACADEME. 1981. Regulations Governing Research on Human Subjects: Academic Freedom and the Institutional Review Board. December, 358–70.

AMERICAN SOCIOLOGICAL ASSOCIATION. 1988. Proposed Revisions to Code of Ethics. Washington, D.C.: American Sociological Association.

APPELBAUM, P. S., C. W. LIDZ, and A. MEISEL. 1987. *Informed consent: Legal theory and clinical practice.* New York: Oxford University Press.

BULMER, M. 1982. *Social research ethics.* New York: Holmes and Meier.

GALLIHER, J. F. 1982. The protection of human subjects: A re-examination of the professional code of ethics. In *Social research ethics* (pp. 159–60), ed. M. Bulmer. New York: Holmes and Meier.

GODUKA, I. N. 1987. Behavioral development of black South African children: An ecological approach. Ph.D. diss., Michigan State University.

LIDZ, C. W., A. MEISEL, E. ZERUBAVEL, M. CARTER, R. M. SESTAK, and L. H. ROTH. 1984. *Informed consent: Study of decisionmaking in psychiatry.* New York: The Guilford Press.

MOSHER, S. W. 1985. *Journey to the forbidden China.* New York: The Free Press.

NASSON, B. 1984. Bitter harvest: Farm schooling for black South Africans. Second Carnegie Inquiry into Poverty and Development in Southern Africa (Paper no. 97). Rondebosch, Cape Town, School of Economics.

PUNCH, M. 1986. The politics and ethics of fieldwork. London: Sage.

VAN DEN BERGHE, P. R. 1968. Research in South Africa: The story of my experiences with tyranny. In *Ethics, politics, and social research* (pp. 185–86), ed. G. Sjoberg. Cambridge: Schenkman.

CULTURE

Classic

8

Symbol: The Basic Element of Culture

Leslie A. White

Leslie A. White, a noted anthropologist, argues in this selection that the key to human existence is the ability to use symbols. While all animals are capable of complex behavior, only humanity depends on symbolic activity. This is the special power that underlies our autonomy as the only creatures who live according to meanings we set for ourselves. Thus symbols convert our animal species into humanity, in the process transforming social behavior into true civilization.

. . . All human behavior originates in the use of symbols. It was the symbol which transformed our anthropoid ancestors into men and made them human. All civilizations have been generated, and are perpetuated, only by the use of symbols. It is the symbol which transforms an infant of *Homo sapiens* into a human being; deaf mutes who grow up without the use of symbols are not human beings.

SOURCE: Excerpt from "The Symbol: The Origin and the Basis of Human Behavior," by Leslie A. White in *The Science of Culture*. Copyright © 1949 Leslie A. White. Renewal copyright © 1976 by Crocker National Bank. Reprinted by permission of Farrar, Straus and Giroux, Inc.

All human behavior consists of, or is dependent upon, the use of symbols. Human behavior is symbolic behavior; symbolic behavior is human behavior. The symbol is the universe of humanity. . . .

That there are numerous and impressive similarities between the behavior of man and that of ape is fairly obvious; it is quite possible that chimpanzees and gorillas in zoos have noted and appreciated them. Fairly apparent, too, are man's behavioral similarities to many other kinds of animals. Almost as obvious, but not easy to define, is a difference in behavior which distinguishes man from all other living creatures. I say "obvious" because it is quite apparent to the common man that the nonhuman animals with which he is familiar do not and cannot enter, and participate in, the world in which he, as a human being, lives. It is impossible for a dog, horse, bird, or even an ape, to have *any* understanding of the meaning of the sign of the cross to a Christian, or of the fact that black (white among the Chinese) is the color of mourning. No chimpanzee or laboratory rat can appreciate the difference between Holy water and distilled water, or grasp the meaning of *Tuesday, 3*, or *sin.* No animal save man can distinguish a cousin from an uncle, or a cross cousin from a parallel cousin. Only man can commit the crime of incest or adultery; only he can remember the Sabbath and keep it Holy. It is not, as we well know, that the lower animals can do these things but to a lesser degree than ourselves; they cannot perform these acts of appreciation and distinction *at all.* It is, as Descartes said long ago, "not only that the brutes have less Reason than man, but that they have none at all.". . .

A symbol may be defined as a thing the value or meaning of which is bestowed upon it by those who use it. I say "thing" because a symbol may have any kind of physical form; it may have the form of a material object, a color, a sound, an odor, a motion of an object, a taste.

The meaning, or value, of a symbol is in no instance derived from or determined by properties intrinsic in its physical form: The color appropriate to mourning may be yellow, green, or any other color; purple need not be the color of royalty; among the Manchu rulers of China it was yellow. . . . The meaning of symbols is derived from and determined by the organisms who use them; meaning is bestowed by human organisms upon physical things or events which thereupon become symbols. Symbols "have their signification," to use John Locke's phrase, "from the arbitrary imposition of men."

All symbols must have a physical form otherwise they could not enter our experience. . . . But the meaning of a symbol cannot be discovered by mere sensory examination of its physical form.

One cannot tell by looking at an *x* in an algebraic equation what it stands for; one cannot ascertain with the ears alone the symbolic value of the phonetic compound *si;* one cannot tell merely by weighing a pig how much gold he will exchange for; one cannot tell from the wave length of a color whether it stands for courage or cowardice, "stop" or "go"; nor can one discover the spirit in a fetish by any amount of physical or chemical examination. The meaning of a symbol can be grasped only by nonsensory, symbolic means. . . .

Thus Darwin says: "That which distinguishes man from the lower animals is not the understanding of articulate sounds, for as everyone knows, dogs understand many words and sentences."[1]. . .

The man differs from the dog—and all other creatures—in that *he can and does play an active role in determining what value the vocal stimulus is to have, and the dog cannot.* The dog does not and cannot play an active part in determining the value of the vocal stimulus. Whether he is to roll over or go fetch at a given stimulus, or whether the stimulus for roll over be one combination of sounds or another is a matter in which the dog has nothing whatever to "say." He plays a purely passive role and can do nothing else. He learns the meaning of a vocal command just as his salivary glands may learn to respond to the sound of a bell. But man plays an active role and thus becomes a creator: Let *x* equal three pounds of coal and it does equal three pounds of coal; let removal of the hat in a house of worship indicate respect and it becomes so. This creative faculty, that of freely, actively, and arbitrarily bestowing value upon things, is one of the most commonplace as well as *the* most important characteristic of man. Children employ it freely in their play: "Let's pretend that this rock is a wolf.". . .

All culture (civilization) depends upon the symbol. It was the exercise of the symbolic faculty that brought culture into existence, and it is the use of symbols that makes the perpetuation of culture possible. Without the symbol there would be no culture, and man would be merely an animal, not a human being.

Articulate speech is the most important form of symbolic expression. Remove speech from culture and what would remain? Let us see.

Without articulate speech we would have no *human* social organization. Families we might have, but this form of organization is not peculiar to man; it is not *per se,* human. But we would have no prohibitions of incest, no rules prescribing exogamy and endogamy, polygamy or monogamy. How could marriage with a cross cousin be prescribed, marriage with a parallel cousin proscribed, without articulate speech? How could rules which prohibit plural mates possessed simultaneously but permit them if possessed one at a time, exist without speech?

Without speech we would have no political, economic, ecclesiastic, or military organization; no codes of etiquette or ethics; no laws; no science, theology, or literature; no games or music, except on an ape level. Rituals and ceremonial paraphernalia would be meaningless without articulate speech. Indeed, without articulate speech we would be all but toolless: We would have only the occasional and insignificant use of the tool such as we find today among the higher apes, for it was articulate speech that transformed the nonprogressive tool-using of the ape into the progressive, cumulative tool-using of man, the human being.

In short, without symbolic communication in some form, we would have no culture. "In the Word was the beginning" of culture—and its perpetuation also.

To be sure, with all his culture man is still an animal and strives for the same ends that all other living creatures strive for: the preservation of the individual and the perpetuation of the [species]. In concrete terms these ends are food, shelter from the elements, defense from enemies, health, and offspring. The fact that man strives for these ends just as all other animals do has, no doubt, led many to declare that there is "no fundamental difference between the behavior of man and of other creatures." But man does differ, not in *ends* but in *means.* Man's means are cultural means: Culture is simply the human animal's way of living. And, since these means, culture, are dependent upon a faculty possessed by man alone, the ability to use symbols, the difference between the behavior of man and of all other creatures is not merely great, but basic and fundamental.

The behavior of man is of two distinct kinds: symbolic and nonsymbolic. Man yawns, stretches, coughs, scratches himself, cries out in pain, shrinks with fear, "bristles" with anger, and so on. Nonsymbolic behavior of this sort is not peculiar to man; he shares it not only with the other primates but with many other animal species as well. But man communicates with his fellows with articulate speech, uses amulets, confesses sins, makes laws, observes codes of etiquette, explains his dreams, classifies his relatives in designated categories, and so on. This kind of behavior is unique; only man is capable of it; it is peculiar to man because it consists of, or is dependent upon, the use of symbols. The nonsymbolic behavior of *Homo sapiens* is the behavior of man the animal; the symbolic behavior is that of man the human being. It is the symbol which has transformed man from a mere animal to a human animal. . . .

The infant of the species *Homo sapiens* becomes human only when and as he exercises his symbol faculty. Only through articulate speech—not necessarily vocal—can he enter the world of human beings and take part in their affairs. The questions asked earlier may be repeated now. How could a growing child know and appreciate such things as social organization, ethics, etiquette, ritual, science, religion, art, and games without symbolic communication? The answer is of course that he could know nothing of these things and have no appreciation of them at all. . . .

Children who have been cut off from human intercourse for years by blindness and deafness but who have eventually effected communication with their fellows on a symbolic level are exceedingly illuminating. The case of Helen Keller is exceptionally instructive. . . .

Helen Keller was rendered blind and deaf at an early age by illness. She grew up as a child without symbolic contact with anyone. Descriptions of her at the age of seven, the time at which her teacher, Miss Sullivan, came to her home, disclosed no *human* attributes of Helen's behavior at all. She was a headstrong, undisciplined, and unruly little animal.

Within a day or so after her arrival at the Keller home, Miss Sullivan taught Helen her first word, spelling it into her hand. But this word was merely a sign, not a symbol. A week later Helen knew several words but, as Miss Sullivan reports, she had "no idea how to use them or that everything has a name." Within three weeks Helen knew eighteen nouns and three verbs. But she was still on the level of signs; she still had no notion "that everything has a name."

Helen confused the word signs for "mug" and "water" because, apparently, both were associated with drinking. Miss Sullivan made a few attempts to clear up this confusion but without success. One morning, however, about a month after Miss Sullivan's arrival, the two went out to the pump in the garden. What happened then is best told in their own words:

I made Helen hold her mug under the spout while I pumped. As the cold water gushed forth, filling the mug, I spelled "w-a-t-e-r" into Helen's free hand. The word coming so close upon the sensation of cold water rushing over her hand seemed to startle her. She dropped the mug and stood as one transfixed. A new light came into her face. She spelled "water" several times. Then she dropped on the ground and asked for its name and pointed to the pump and the trellis, and suddenly turning round she asked for my name. . . . *In a few hours she had added thirty new words to her vocabulary.*

But these words were now more than mere signs as they are to a dog and as they had been to Helen up to then. They were *symbols*. Helen had at last grasped and turned the key that admitted her for the first time to a new universe: the world of human beings. Helen describes this marvelous experience herself:

We walked down the path to the well-house, attracted by the fragrance of the honeysuckle with which it was covered. Someone was drawing water and my teacher placed my hand under the spout. As the cool stream gushed over one hand she spelled into the other the word *water,* first slowly, then rapidly. I stood still, my whole

attention fixed upon the motion of her fingers. Suddenly I felt a misty consciousness as of something forgotten—a thrill of returning thought; and somehow *the mystery of language was revealed to me.* I knew then that "w-a-t-e-r" meant the wonderful cool something that was flowing over my hand. That living word awakened my soul, gave it light, hope, joy, set if free!

Helen was transformed on the instant by this experience. Miss Sullivan had managed to touch Helen's symbol mechanism and set it in motion. Helen, on her part, grasped the external world with this mechanism that had lain dormant and inert all these years, sealed in dark and silent isolation by eyes that could not see and ears that heard not. But now she had crossed the boundary and entered a new land. Henceforth the progress would be rapid.

"I left the well-house," Helen reports, "eager to learn. Everything had a name, and each name gave birth to a new thought. As we returned to the house every object which I touched seemed to quiver with life. That was because I saw everything with the strange new sight that had come to me."

Helen became humanized rapidly. "I see an improvement in Helen from day to day," Miss Sullivan wrote in her diary, "*almost from hour to hour.* Everything must have a name now. . . . She drops the signs and pantomime she used before as soon as she has words to supply their place. . . . We notice her face grows more expressive each day. . . ."

A more eloquent and convincing account of the significance of symbols and of the great gulf between the human mind and that of minds without symbols could hardly be imagined.

The natural processes of biologic evolution brought into existence in man, and man alone, a new and distinctive ability; the ability to use symbols. The most important form of symbolic expression is articulate speech. Articulate speech means communication of ideas; communication means preservation—tradition—and preservation means accumulation and progress. The emergence of the faculty of symboling has resulted in the genesis of a new order of phenomena: an extrasomatic, cultural order. All civilizations are born of, and are perpetuated by, the use of symbols. A culture, or civilization, is but a particular kind of form which the biologic, life-perpetuating activities of a particular animal, man, assume.

Human behavior is symbolic behavior; if it is not symbolic, it is not human. The infant of the genus *Homo* becomes a human being only as he is introduced into and participates in that order of phenomena which is culture. And the key to this world and the means of participation in it is—the symbol.

CRITICAL-THINKING QUESTIONS

1. Why does White argue that a deaf mute unable to communicate symbolically is not fully human?

What opposing argument might be made? What position would White take in the pro-choice versus pro-life abortion controversy?

2. Because the reality we experience is based on a particular system of symbols, how do we tend to view members of other cultures? What special efforts are needed to overcome the tendency to treat people of different cultures as less worthy than we are?

3. How did gaining the capacity to use symbols transform Helen Keller? How did this ability alter her capacity for further learning?

NOTE

1. Charles Darwin, *The Descent of Man,* chap. 3.

CULTURE

Classic

9

Manifest and Latent Functions

Robert A. Merton

Robert Merton made a major contribution to structural-functional theory by pointing out that social patterns have both manifest and latent functions. Manifest functions are those consequences that are familiar, planned, and generally recognized. Latent functions, on the other hand, are unfamiliar, unplanned, and widely overlooked. For this reason, Merton argued, comprehending latent functions is a special responsibility of sociologists. Merton illustrates this process by offering observation about the pattern of conspicuous consumption.

. . . Armed with the concept of latent function, the sociologist extends his inquiry in those very directions which promise most for the theoretic development of the discipline. He examines the familiar (or planned) social practice to ascertain the latent, and hence generally unrecognized, functions (as well, of course, as the manifest functions). He considers, for example, the conse-

SOURCE: *Social Theory and Social Structure* revised and enlarged edition by Robert K. Merton. Copyright © 1967, 1968 by Robert K. Merton. Reprinted with permission of The Free Press, Macmillan Publishing Company, a Member of Paramount Publishing.

quences of the new wage plan for, say, the trade union in which the workers are organized or the consequences of a propaganda program, not only for increasing its avowed purpose of stirring up patriotic fervor, but also for making large numbers of people reluctant to speak their minds when they differ with official policies, *etc*. In short, it is suggested that the *distinctive* intellectual contributions of the sociologist are found primarily in the study of unintended consequences (among which are latent functions) of social practices, as well as in the study of anticipated consequences (among which are manifest functions).

[Illustration:] The Pattern of Conspicuous Consumption. The manifest purpose of buying consumption goods is, of course, the satisfaction of the needs for which these goods are explicitly designed. Thus, automobiles are obviously intended to provide a certain kind of transportation; candles, to provide light; choice articles of food to provide sustenance; rare art products to provide aesthetic pleasure. Since these products *do* have these uses, it was largely assumed that these encompass the range of socially significant functions. Veblen indeed suggests that this was ordinarily the prevailing view (in the pre-Veblenian era, of course): "The end of acquisition and accumulation is conventionally held to be the consumption of the goods accumulated. . . . This is at least felt to be the economically legitimate end of acquisition, *which alone it is incumbent on the theory to take account of.*"[1]

However, says Veblen in effect, as sociologists we must go on to consider the latent functions of acquisition, accumulation, and consumption, and these latent functions are remote indeed from the manifest functions. "But, it is only when taken in a sense far removed from its naive meaning [*i.e.* manifest function] that the consumption of goods can be said to afford the incentive from which accumulation invariably proceeds." And among these latent functions, which help explain the persistence and the social location of the pattern of conspicuous consumption, is [the fact that] . . . it results in a *heightening or reaffirmation of social status.*

The Veblenian paradox is that people buy expensive goods not so much because they are superior but because they are expensive. For it is the latent equation ("costliness = mark of higher social status") which he singles out in his functional analysis, rather than the manifest equation ("costliness = excellence of the goods"). Not that he denies manifest functions *any* place in buttressing the pattern of conspicuous consumption. These, too, are operative. . . . *It is only that these direct, manifest functions do not fully account for the prevailing patterns of consumption. Otherwise put, if the latent functions of status-enhancement or status-reaffirmation were removed from the patterns of conspicuous consumption, these patterns would undergo severe changes of a sort which the "conventional" economist could not foresee.*

CRITICAL-THINKING QUESTIONS

1. Why, according to Merton, is the study of latent functions one of the important tasks of sociologists?
2. Distinguish between the manifest and latent functions of owning designer clothing, a fine car, or a large home.
3. According to Thorstein Veblen, whom Merton cites in his analysis, does the higher cost of various goods typically attest to their higher quality? Why or why not?
4. Identify some of the manifest and latent functions of (a) a primary school spelling bee, (b) sports, and (c) attending college.

NOTE

1. Thorstein Veblen, *Theory of the Leisure Class* (1899) (New York: Vanguard Press, 1928), p. 25.

10

The Rape Culture

Dianne F. Herman

Culture is vital in the human species, but some cultural patterns are destructive. Dianne Herman argues that, by linking sexuality and violence, the United States is a "rape culture" that undermines healthy relationships. Although "date rape" has always existed, it has only recently been seen, by social scientists and practitioners, as a form of violence. However, many young adults—including college students—still view date rape as a "normal" part of dating.

When Susan Griffin wrote,"I have never been free of the fear of rape," she touched a responsive chord in most women.[1] Every woman knows the fear of being alone at home late at night or the terror that strikes her when she receives an obscene telephone call. She knows also of the "mini-rapes"—the pinch in the crowded bus, the wolf whistle from a passing car, the stare of a man looking at her bust during a conversation. Griffin has

argued, "Rape is a kind of terrorism which severely limits the freedom of women and makes women dependent on men."[2]

Women live their lives according to a rape schedule. . . .

Because of the aggressive–passive, dominant–submissive, me-Tarzan–you-Jane nature of the relationship between the sexes in our culture, there is a close association between violence and sexuality. Words that are slang sexual terms, for example, frequently accompany assaultive behavior or gestures. "Fuck you" is meant as a brutal attack in verbal terms. In the popular culture, "James Bond alternately whips out his revolver and his

SOURCE: "The Rape Culture," by Dianne F. Herman, in *Women: A Feminist Perspective,* 3d ed., ed. Jo Freeman (Mountain View, CA: Mayfield, 1984). Copyright © 1984 by Dianne Herman. Reprinted with permission.

cock, and though there is no known connection between the skills of a gun-fighter and love-making, pacifism seems suspiciously effeminate."[3] The imagery of sexual relations between males and females in books, songs, advertising, and films is frequently that of a sadomasochistic relationship thinly veiled by a romantic facade. Thus, it is very difficult in our society to differentiate rape from "normal" heterosexual relations. Indeed our culture can be characterized as a rape culture because the image of heterosexual intercourse is based on a rape model of sexuality.

LEGAL DEFINITIONS OF RAPE

If healthy heterosexuality were characterized by loving, warm, and reciprocally satisfying actions, then rape could be defined as sex without consent, therefore involving either domination or violence. Instead, rape is legally defined as sexual intercourse by a male with a female, *other than his wife*, without the consent of the woman and effected by force, duress, intimidation, or deception as to the nature of the act. The spousal exemption in the law, which still remains in effect in most states, means that a husband cannot be guilty of raping his wife, even if he forces intercourse against her will. The implication of this loophole is that *violent, unwanted* sex does not necessarily define rape. Instead, rape is *illegal* sex—that is, sexual assault by a man who has no legal rights over the woman. In other words, in the law's eyes, violence in legal sexual intercourse is permissible, but sexual relations with a woman who is not one's property is not.

From their inception, rape laws have been established not to protect women, but to protect women's property value for men.

Society's view of rape was purely a matter of economics—of assets and liabilities. When a married woman was raped, her husband was wronged, not her. If she was unmarried, her father suffered since his investment depreciated. It was the monetary value of a woman which determined the gravity of the crime. Because she had no personal rights under the law, her own emotions simply didn't matter.[4] Because rape meant that precious merchandise was irreparably damaged, the severity of the punishment was dependent on whether the victim was a virgin. In some virgin rapes, biblical law ordered that the rapist marry the victim, since she was now devalued property.[5] The social status of the victim was also important, as a woman of higher social status was more valuable. . . .

Due to pressure from feminist groups, the legal definition of rape has been broadened in many states over the last decade.[6] Evidentiary rules requiring corroboration, cautionary instructions, psychiatric examinations, and prior sexual history have been eliminated or revised in most states. A survey of 151 criminal-justice professionals in Florida, Michigan, and Georgia found that these types of reforms in rape-law legislation have received widespread acceptance and approval. "Further, the findings suggest that law reform need not generate the confusion, uncertainty, or antagonism predicted by some early analysts."[7]

Some jurisdictions have established categories of sexual offenses that allow for sex-neutral assaults, taking into account that men and children, as well as women, can be victims. Others have allowed prosecution when sexual assaults include acts other than penetration of the vagina by the penis, such as sodomy or oral copulation. The latest struggle has been to remove the spousal exemption in the laws, so that husbands are not immune to prosecution for rape by their wives. Each of these changes reflects an evolving understanding that rape laws should not be in existence to regulate control of virginal female bodies for sole ownership by one man; rather, rape should be defined as a sexual assault and crime of violence by one person against another.[8]

HOW COMMON IS RAPE?

There was a steady increase in the rape rate between the mid-sixties and 1980, when it leveled off. In 1964, 11.2 rapes and attempted rapes were reported nationally per 100,000 inhabitants. That figure climbed to 26.1 reports per 100,000 by

1974, and, in the 1980s, has fluctuated between 33.5 and 37.9.[9] Since male victims rarely report rape, this means that, in 1987, 73 of every 100,000 females in the United States reported that they were victims of rape or attempted rape.[10]

These statistics are based on *reported* rapes. Victimization surveys indicate that for every reported rape, an additional one to three rapes have occurred but have not been reported.[11] Diana E. H. Russell's 1978 study of 930 San Francisco women found that 44 percent reported at least one completed or attempted rape.[12] Only 8 percent, or less than one in twelve, of the total number of incidents were ever reported to the police. Using Russell's findings, the actual incidence of rape is twenty-four times higher than FBI statistics indicate.

In addition, a woman is probably less safe from rape in this country than she is in any other developed nation. The United States has one of the highest rape rates in the world.[13] In 1984, the United States had 35.7 rapes per 100,000 people. The Bureau of Justice Statistics found European nations had an average of 5.4 rapes per 100,000 inhabitants in that same year.[14]

VICTIMS OF RAPE

Many myths surround the crime of rape, but perhaps most common are those that imply that the victim was responsible for her own victimization. Projecting the blame on the woman is accomplished by portraying her as a seductress. The conventional scenario is one of a man who is sexually aroused by an attractive, flirtatious woman. But the image of the rape victim as seductive and enticing is at odds with reality. Rapes have been committed on females as young as 6 months and as old as 93 years. Most victims tend to be very young. In one study in Philadelphia of reported rapes in 1958 and 1960, 20 percent of the victims were between 10 and 14 years of age; another 25 percent were between 15 and 19.[15] According to data compiled in 1974 by Women Organized Against Rape,

41 percent of rape victims seen in hospital emergency rooms in Philadelphia were 16 or younger. The category with the highest frequency of victims was the range between 13 and 16 years of age.[16] A comprehensive review of the literature on rape victimization published in 1979 noted that the high-risk ages are adolescents (aged 13 to 17) and young adults (aged 18 to 24).[17] In 1985, The National Crime Survey, based on findings from a continuous survey of a representative sample of housing units across the United States, reported that the rape rate is highest for those white women between ages 16 and 19, and for those black women between ages 25 and 34.[18]

. . . Rape is a crime commonly committed by an assailant who is known to the victim. Even in cases where women do report to the police, victim and offender are frequently acquainted. In a study of 146 persons admitted to the emergency room of Boston City Hospital during a one-year period from 1972 to 1973 with a complaint of rape, 102 of these rapes were reported to police. Forty of these victims who reported the assault knew their assailant.[19] Burgess and Holmstrom believe that victims who know their rapists are less apt to report the crime. Their study found that victims who reported rapes by assailants known to them had more difficulty establishing their credibility than did victims raped by strangers, and these cases had a higher likelihood of dropping out of the criminal-justice system.[20] . . .

In 1982, *Ms.* magazine reported a series of studies on college campuses confirming that, even given new and more liberal attitudes about premarital sex and women's liberation, date rape and other forms of acquaintance rape may be reaching epidemic proportions in higher education. In some cases, women have even been assaulted by men ostensibly acting as protective escorts to prevent rape.[21] A 1985 study of over 600 college students found that three-quarters of the women and more than one-half of the men disclosed an experience of sexual aggression on a date. Nearly 15 percent of the women and 7 percent of the men said that intercourse had taken place against the woman's will.[22] The victim and offender had most likely known each other almost one year before the sexual assault. Date rape occurred most frequently when the man initiated the date, when he drove to and from and paid for the date, when drinking took place, and when the couple found themselves alone either in a car or indoors. In these instances, it appears that college men may feel they have license to rape.

In explaining date rape, one set of authors have stated,

women are often seen as legitimate objects of sexual aggression. Rape can be viewed as the logical extension of a cultural perspective that defines men as possessors of women. The American dating system, in particular, places females in the position of sexual objects purchased by men. Women are groomed to compete for men who will shower them with attention and favors, men are socialized to expect sexual reward (or at least to try for that reward) for their attention to women. This perspective presents the woman as a legitimate object of victimization: If a man is unable to seduce a woman, and yet has provided her with certain attention and gifts, then he has a right to expect sexual payment. Only the situation of rape by a total stranger escapes the influence of this reasoning. In any other case, if a woman knows her attacker even slightly, she is likely to be perceived as a legitimate victim of a justified aggressor.[23]

The tendency to dismiss rape allegations when victim and offender know each other has contributed to the silence that surrounds marital rape. Finkelhor and Yllo in their study of marital rape found that only one textbook on marriage and the family of the thirty-one they surveyed mentioned rape or anything related to sexual assault in marriage.[24] These authors cite studies that indicate that at least 10 percent of all married women questioned on this topic report that their husbands have used physical force or threats to have sex with them.[25] Marital rape may be the most common form of sexual assault: More than two times as many of the women interviewed had been raped by husbands as had been raped by strangers.[26] . . . Husbands' desires to frighten, humiliate, punish, degrade, dominate, and control their spouses were found to be the most common motivations for the

sexual assaults. In their 1980–81 study of Boston area mothers, Finkelhor and Yllo found that about half of the marital rape victims were also battered.[27] Many cases were uncovered in which wives were tortured through sadistic sexual assaults involving objects. Many more were humiliated by being forced to engage in distasteful or unusual sexual practices. One-quarter of the victims in their survey were sexually attacked in the presence of others—usually their children.[28] Many times, the rape was the final violent act in a series of physical and emotional abuses or the payback when a woman filed for separation or divorce. Sadly, many women suffer years of abuse thinking that the assaults are caused by their failure to be good wives or feeling that they have no way out and that this is the lot of the married woman. Too often, their husbands justify their attacks on their wives by blaming the wives for causing their loss of control, or by saying that they are entitled to treat their spouses any way they choose.

Because rape so frequently involves people who know each other, most rapists and their victims are of the same race and age group. In 1985, approximately 80 percent of all rapes and attempted rapes were intraracial.[29] One reason that the myth that rapes are interracial dies hard is that cases of this type frequently receive the most publicity. In a study of rape in Philadelphia, researchers discovered that the two major newspapers, when they reported on rape cases, mentioned mainly interracial offenses. Intraracial rapes were only occasionally mentioned.[30] Gary LaFree examined the effect of race in the handling of 881 sexual assaults in a large midwestern city. He found that black males who assaulted white women received more serious charges, longer sentences, and more severe punishment in terms of executed sentences and incarceration in the state penitentiary.[31] Although black women are three times more likely to be raped than are white women, rape is least prosecuted if the victim is black.[32] The rape of poor, black women is not an offense against men of power.

WHY MEN RAPE

. . . One of the most surprising findings of studies on rape is that the rapist is normal in personality, appearance, intelligence, behavior, and sexual drive.[33] Empirical research has repeatedly failed to find a consistent pattern of personality type or character disorder that reliably discriminates the rapist from the nonrapist. According to Amir, the only significant psychological difference between the rapist and the normal, well-adjusted male appears to be the greater tendency of the former to express rage and violence. But this finding probably tends to overemphasize the aggressive personality characteristics of rapists, since generally only imprisoned rapists have been studied. Those few rapists who are sentenced to prison tend to be the more obviously violent offenders. In fact, studies by some researchers have found one type of rapist who is fairly meek and mild-mannered.[34] What is clear is that the rapist is not an exotic freak. Rather, rape evolves out of a situation in which "normal" males feel a need to prove themselves to be "men" by displaying dominance over females.

In our society, men demonstrate their competence as people by being "masculine." Part of this definition of masculinity involves a contempt for anything feminine or for females in general. Reported rapes, in fact, are frequently associated with some form of ridicule and sexual humiliation, such as urination on the victim, anal intercourse, fellatio, and ejaculation in the victim's face and hair. Insertion into the woman's vagina of broomsticks, bottles, and other phallic objects is not an uncommon coup de grace.[35] The overvaluing of toughness expresses itself in a disregard for anything associated with fragility. In the rapist's view, his assertion of maleness is automatically tied to a violent repudiation of anything feminine.

Most rapes are not spontaneous acts in which the rapist had no prior intent to commit rape but was overcome by the sexual provocations of his victim. Statistics compiled from reported rapes show that the overwhelming majority are planned. In one study, 71 percent of all reported rapes were prearranged, and another 11 percent were partially planned. Only 18 percent were impulsive acts.[36] Planning is most common in cases of group rape. Even when the rapist is acting alone, a majority of the rapes involves some manipulations on the part of the offender to place his victim in a vulnerable situation that he can exploit. . . .

Most convicted rapists tend to project the blame on others, particularly the victim. Schultz found that the sex offender is twice as likely to insist on his innocence as is the general offender.[37] "In two-thirds of the cases one hears, 'I'm here on a phoney beef,' or 'I might have been a little rough with her but she was asking for it,' or 'I might have done it but I was too drunk to remember.' "[38] They also rationalize the act by labeling their victims "bad" women. Some rapists excuse and deny their crime by portraying the victim as a woman of questionable sexual reputation or as a person who has placed herself in a compromising position, thus "getting what she deserved."[39] . . .

American culture produces rapists when it encourages the socialization of men to subscribe to values of control and dominance, callousness and competitiveness, and anger and aggression, and when it discourages the expression by men of vulnerability, sharing, and cooperation. In the end, it is not only the women who become the victims of these men, but also the offenders themselves, who suffer. These men lose the ability to satisfy needs for nurturance, love, and belonging, and their anger and frustration from this loss expresses itself in acts of violence and abuse against others. The tragedy for our society is that we produce so many of these hardened men.

SOCIETY'S RESPONSE TO RAPE

. . . The police have considerable discretion in determining whether a crime has been committed. In 1976, according to a study by the FBI, 19 percent of all forcible rapes reported to the police were unfounded.[40] *Unfounding* simply means that the police decide there is no basis for prosecution. . . .

According to many studies, one of the most frequent causes of unfounding rape is a prior relationship between the participants. In the Philadelphia study, 43 percent of all date rapes were unfounded. The police, according to the researcher, seemed to be more concerned that the victim had "assumed the risk" than they were with the fact that she had not given consent to intercourse.[41]

Another common reason police unfound cases is the apparent lack of force in the rape situation. The extent of injuries seems to be even more important in the decision to unfound than is whether the offender had a weapon.[42] There is no requirement that a male businessperson must either forcibly resist when mugged or forfeit protection under the law. But proof of rape, both to the police and in court, is often required to take the form of proof of resistance, substantiated by the extent of injuries suffered by the victim. Yet local police departments frequently advise women not to resist if faced with the possibility of rape.

In a confusion partially of their own making, local police precincts point out contradictory messages: They "unfound" a rape case because, by the rule of their own male logic, the woman did not show normal resistance; they report on an especially brutal rape case and announce to the press that the multiple stab wounds were the work of an assailant who was enraged because the woman resisted.[43]

The victim is told that if she was raped it was because she did not resist enough. But if she fights back and is raped and otherwise assaulted, police blame her again for bringing about her own injuries because of her resistance. . . .

One reason physicians are reluctant to diagnose injuries as caused by a sexual assault is due to their reluctance to have to give up their valuable time to testify on behalf of the prosecution. In the early seventies, the District of Columbia newspapers reported that doctors of D.C. General Hospital were intentionally giving negative medical reports of rape victims so they would not be called to court. In one case that reached the appeals court, the doctor had reported absolutely no injuries even though police photographs showed bruises and scratches on the victim's face. As a result, the trial court dismissed the rape charges and the defendants were

only found guilty of assault with intent to commit rape.[44]

For many women, the experience of having their account of the events scrutinized, mocked, or discounted continues in the courtroom. Women have often said that they felt as though they, not the defendants, were the persons on trial. According to Burgess and Holmstrom, "Going to court, for the victim, is as much of a crisis as the actual rape itself."[45] They quote one victim shortly after she appeared in district court: "I felt like crying. I felt abused. I didn't like the questions the defense was asking. I felt accused—guilty 'til proven innocent. I thought the defense lawyer made it a big joke."[46] They relate how one twelve-year-old girl had a psychotic breakdown during the preliminary court process.[47]

The victim, by taking the case to court, incurs extensive costs, both psychological and financial. Expecting to testify just once, she is likely to have to repeat her story at the hearing for probable cause, to the grand jury, and in superior-court sessions. To convey the discomfort of such a process, feminists have recommended that individuals imagine having to tell an audience all the details of their last sexual experience. In addition to exposing themselves to public scrutiny, rape victims may be subject to harassment from the friends or family of the perpetrator.

Financially, the time away from work nearly always stretches beyond expectations. According to Burgess and Holmstrom, the victims they accompanied to court were often forced to sit three to four hours in the courthouse, only to be told that the case had been continued. After they and their witnesses had taken time off from work and, in some cases, traveled great distances, they were less than enthusiastic about the idea of seeing justice done.[48] Wood has said, "Due to the traumatic experience which a victim must go through in order to attempt to secure the attacker's successful prosecution, it is amazing any rape cases come to trial."[49]

Even if the victim is resilient enough to pursue her case, she may encounter prejudicial attitudes from judges and juries. . . . Shirley Feldman-Summers and Karen Lindner investigated the perceptions of victims by juries and found that, as the respectability of the victim decreased, the jury's belief that the victim was responsible for the rape increased.[50] In a sense, juries have created an extralegal defense. If the complainant somehow "assumed the risk" of rape, juries will commonly find the defendant guilty of some lesser crime or will acquit him altogether.[51] "A seventeen-year-old girl was raped during a beer-drinking party. The jury probably acquitted, according to the judge, because they thought the girl asked for what she got."[52] In one case, according to Medea and Thompson, "a woman who responded with 'fuck off' when approached lost her case because 'fuck' is a sexually exciting word."[53] If the victim knew the offender previously, especially as an intimate, juries will be reluctant to convict.

In one case of "savage rape," the victim's jaw was fractured in two places. The jury nevertheless acquitted because it found that there may have been sexual relations on previous occasions, and the parties had been drinking on the night of the incident.[54]

. . . Despite attempts to educate the public about the dynamics of rape, myths still persist. Martha Burt, in a study of almost 600 Minnesota residents, found that most believed that "Any healthy woman can resist a rapist." "In the majority of rapes, the victim was promiscuous or had a bad reputation." "If a girl engages in necking or petting and she lets things get out of hand, it is her fault if her partner forces sex on her." "One reason that women falsely report a rape is that they frequently have a need to call attention to themselves." Burt found that rapists also subscribed to these myths in attempts to excuse and rationalize their behavior.[55] The implication of her study is that the general population's attitudes toward women who are raped is very similar to the rapist's view of his victim.

During the 1986–87 school year, a survey was taken of over 1500 sixth to ninth graders who attended the Rhode Island Rape Crisis Center's assault-awareness program in schools across the state. The results of the survey strongly indicated that even the next generation of Americans tends

to blame the victim of sexual assault. For example, 50 percent of the students said a woman who walks alone at night and dresses seductively is asking to be raped. In addition, most of the students surveyed accepted sexually assaultive behavior as normal. Fifty-one percent of the boys and 41 percent of the girls stated that a man has a right to force a woman to kiss him if he has spent "a lot of money" on her. Sixty-five percent of the boys and 57 percent of the girls in junior high schools said it is acceptable for a man to force a woman to have sex if they have been dating for more than six months. Eighty-seven percent of the boys and 79 percent of the girls approved of rape if the couple were married. Interestingly, 20 percent of the girls and 6 percent of the boys taking the survey disclosed that they had been sexually abused.[56]

In cases of rape, judges, juries, police, prosecutors, and the general public frequently attribute blame and responsibility to the victim for her own victimization. Unfortunately, these negative responses are often compounded by reactions from family and friends. Encounters with parents, relatives, friends, and spouses many times involve either anger at the victim for being foolish enough to get raped or expressions of embarrassment and shame that family members will suffer as a result of the attack. . . .

THE RAPE CULTURE

. . . As long as sex in our society is construed as a dirty, low, and violent act involving domination of a male over a female, rape will remain a common occurrence. The erotization of male dominance means that whenever women are in a subordinate position to men, the likelihood for sexual assault is great. We are beginning to see that rape is not the only way in which women are sexually victimized, and that other forms of sexual exploitation of women are rampant in our society.[57] Feminists have raised our consciousness about rape by developing rape crisis centers and other programs to assist victims and their families, by reforming laws and challenging politicians, by training professionals in medicine and in the criminal-justice system, and by educating women and the general public on the subject. They are also enlightening us about pornography; sexual harassment on the job and in higher education; sexual exploitation in doctor, dentist, and therapist relations with patients; and sexual assault in the family, such as incest and rape in marriage.

Rape is the logical outcome if men act according to the "masculine mystique" and women act according to the "feminine mystique." But rape does not have to occur. Its presence is an indication of how widely held are traditional views of appropriate male and female behavior, and of how strongly enforced these views are. Our society is a rape culture because it fosters and encourages rape by teaching males and females that it is natural and normal for sexual relations to involve aggressive behavior on the part of males. To end rape, people must be able to envision a relationship between the sexes that involves sharing, warmth, and equality, and to bring about a social system in which those values are fostered.

CRITICAL-THINKING QUESTIONS

1. According to Herman, what is the link between sexuality and violence in U.S. culture? Why is it sometimes difficult to differentiate rape from normal heterosexual relations in our culture?

2. Why does date rape occur? What about marital rape?

3. How do rapists rationalize their behavior? How does our society respond to rape?

NOTES

1. Susan Griffin, "Rape: The All-American Crime," *Ramparts,* 10 (Sept. 1971), 26.

2. Ibid., 35.

3. Ibid., 27.

4. Carol V. Horos, *Rape* (New Canaan, CT: Tobey Publishing Co., 1974), p. 4.

5. Ibid., p. 5.

6. Rosemarie Tong, *Women, Sex and the Law* (Totowa, NJ: Rowman & Allanheld, 1984), pp. 90–123.

7. Barbara E. Smith and Jane Roberts Chapman, "Rape Law Reform Legislation: Practitioner's Perceptions of the Effectiveness of Specific Provisions," *Response,* 10 (1987), 8.

8. Tong, op. cit., pp. 90–123.

9. *Forcible Rape: An Analysis of Legal Issues,* 2. Table I reports the rape rate for each year from 1960 to 1975. Figures for subsequent years can be found in *Uniform Crime Reports: Crime in the United States* (Federal Bureau of Investigation, U.S. Department of Justice, Washington, D.C.) for each year.

10. 1987 *Uniform Crime Reports for the United States* (Washington, DC: U.S. Department of Justice, 1987), 14.

11. Duncan Chappell, "Forcible Rape and the Criminal Justice System: Surveying Present Practices and Reporting Future Trends," in *Sexual Assault,* ed. Marcia J. Walker and Stanley L. Brodsky (Lexington, MA: Lexington Books, 1976), p. 22. Annual surveys by the federal government report that from 1973 to 1986, between 41 and 61 percent of all rapes and attempted rapes were reported to the police. Bureau of Criminal Justice Statistics Bulletin, *Criminal Victimization—1986,* Table 5, p. 4. However, the National Institute of Law Enforcement and Criminal Justice reported in *Forcible Rape: Final Project Report,* March 1978, that "the *actual* number of rapes in the United States is approximately four times the reported number" (p. 15).

12. Diana E. H. Russell, *Sexual Exploitation* (Beverly Hills, CA: Sage Publications, 1984), pp. 35–36.

13. Diana Scully and Joseph Marolla, " 'Riding the Bull at Gilley's': Convicted Rapists Described the Rewards of Rape," *Social Problems,* 32 (Feb. 1985), 252.

14. *International Crime Rates* NCJ-110776 (Special Report by the Bureau of Justice Statistics), May 1988, Table 1, p. 2.

15. Menachem Amir, *Patterns in Forcible Rape* (Chicago: University of Chicago Press, 1971), p. 341

16. Women Organized Against Rape, *W.O.A.R. Data* (Philadelphia: mimeo., 1975), p. 1.

17. Russell, op. cit., p. 79.

18. U.S. Department of Justice, Bureau of Justice Statistics, *Criminal Victimization in the United States, 1985,* NCJ-104273, May 1987, Table 9, p. 18.

19. Lynda Lytle Holmstrom and Ann Wolbert Burgess, *The Victim of Rape* (New Brunswick, NJ: Transaction, 1983), p. xxi.

20. Ibid.

21. Karen Barrett, "Date Rape, a Campus Epidemic?" *Ms.,* 11 (Sept. 1982), 130.

22. "Date Rape: Familiar Strangers," *Psychology Today* (July 1987), p. 10.

23. Susan H. Klemmack and David L. Klemmack, "The Social Definition of Rape," in *Sexual Assault,* ed. Marcia J. Walker and Stanley L. Brodsky (Lexington, MA: Lexington Books, 1976), p. 136.

24. David Finkelhor and Kersti Yllo, *License to Rape, Sexual Abuse of Wives* (New York: Holt, Rinehart and Winston, 1985), p. 6.

25. Ibid., pp. 6–7.

26. Ibid., p. 8.

27. Ibid., pp. 22, 113.

28. Ibid., p. 133.

29. *Criminal Victimization—1985,* Table 37, p. 39.

30. Comment, "Police Discretion and the Judgment that a Crime Has Been Committed—Rape in Philadelphia," *University of Pennsylvania Law Review,* 117 (1968), 318.

31. Gary D. LaFree, "The Effect of Sexual Stratification by Race on Official Reactions to Rape," *Amer. Soc. Rev.,* 45 (1980), p. 842.

32. *Criminal Victimization—1985,* Table 7, p. 17.

33. Menachem Amir, *Patterns in Forcible Rape* (Chicago: University of Chicago Press, 1971), p. 314. See also Benjamin Karpman, *The Sexual Offender and His Offenses* (New York: Julian Press, 1954), pp. 38–39.

34. See, for example, Camille E. LeGrand, "Rape and Rape Laws: Sexism in Society and Law," *California Law Review,* 61 (1973), 922; and Marray L. Cohen, Ralph Garofalo, Richard Boucher, and Theoharis Seghorn, "The Psychology of Rapists," *Seminars in Psychiatry,* 3 (Aug. 1971), 317.

35. Brownmiller, op. cit., p. 195.

36. Amir, op. cit., p. 334.

37. Leroy Schultz, "Interviewing the Sex Offender's Victim," *J. of Criminal Law, Criminology and Police Science,* 50 (Jan./Feb. 1960), 451.

38. R. J. McCaldon, "Rape," *Canadian J. of Corrections,* 9 (Jan. 1967), 47.

39. Scully and Marolla, "Convicted Rapists' Motive," 542.

40. *1976 Uniform Crime Reports,* 16.

41. Comment, "Police Discretion," 304.

42. See, for example, Duncan Chappell et al., "Forcible Rape: A Comparative Study of Offenses Known to the Police in Boston and Los Angeles," in *Studies in the Sociology of Sex,* ed. James M. Henslin (New York: Appleton-Century-Crofts, 1971), p. 180.

43. Ibid., p. 291.

44. Janet Bode, *Fighting Back* (New York: Macmillan, 1987), pp. 130–31; *United States v. Benn* 476 F. 2d. 1127, 1133 (1973).

45. Ann Wolbert Burgess and Lynda Lytle Holmstrom, *Rape: Victims of Crisis* (Bowie, MD: Robert Brady Co., 1974), p. 197.

46. Ibid.

47. Ibid., p. 211.

48. Ibid., p. 200.

49. Pamela Lakes Wood, "The Victim in a Forcible Rape Case: A Feminist View," *American Criminal Law Review,* 7 (1973), 335.

50. Shirley Feldman-Summers and Karen Lindner, "Perceptions of Victims and Defendants in Criminal Assault Cases," *Criminal Justice and Behavior,* 3 (1976), 327.

51. Note, "The Rape Corroboration Requirement: Repeal Not Reform," *Yale Law Journal,* 81 (1972), 1379.

52. Wood, "Forcible," 341–42.

53. Andrea Medea and Kathleen Thompson, *Against Rape* (New York: Farrar, Straus and Giroux, 1974), p. 121.

54. Wood, op. cit., 344–45.

55. Martha R. Burt, "Cultural Myths and Supports for Rape," *J. of Personality and Social Psych.,* 38 (1980), 855.

56. Jacqueline J. Kikuchi, "What Do Adolescents Know and Think about Sexual Abuse?" (paper presented at the National Symposium on Child Victimization, Anaheim, Calif., April 27–30, 1988).

57. See, for example, Lin Farley, *Sexual Shakedown* (New York: Warner Books, 1978); Kathleen Barry, *Female Sexual Slavery* (New York: Avon Books, 1979); Andrea Dworkin, *Pornography: Men Possessing Women* (New York: Putnam, 1981).

11

India's Sacred Cow

Marvin Harris

Anthropologist Marvin Harris uses the approach of cultural ecology to investigate how exotic and seemingly inexplicable cultural patterns may turn out to be everyday strategies for human survival in a particular natural environment. In this article, he offers his own favorite example: Why do people in India—many of whom are hungry—refuse to eat beef from the "sacred cows" that are found most everywhere?

Whenever I get into discussions about the influence of practical and mundane factors on lifestyles, someone is sure to say, "But what about all those cows the hungry peasants in India refuse to eat?" The picture of a ragged farmer starving to death alongside a big fat cow conveys a reassuring sense of mystery to Western observers. In countless learned and popular allusions, it confirms our deepest conviction about how people with inscrutable Oriental minds ought to act. It is comforting to know—somewhat like "there will

always be an England"—that in India spiritual values are more precious than life itself. And at the same time it makes us feel sad. How can we ever hope to understand people so different from ourselves? Westerners find the idea that there might be a practical explanation for Hindu love of cow more upsetting than Hindus do. The sacred cow—how else can I say it?—is one of our favorite sacred cows.

Hindus venerate cows because cows are the symbol of everything that is alive. As Mary is to Christians the mother of God, the cow to Hindus is the mother of life. So there is no greater sacrilege for a Hindu than killing a cow. Even the taking of human life lacks the symbolic meaning, the unutterable defilement, that is evoked by cow slaughter.

According to many experts, cow worship is the number one cause of India's hunger and poverty. Some Western-trained agronomists say that the taboo against cow slaughter is keeping one hundred million "useless" animals alive. They claim that cow worship lowers the efficiency of agriculture because the useless animals contribute neither milk nor meat while competing for croplands and foodstuff with useful animals and hungry human beings. . . .

It does seem that there are enormous numbers of surplus, useless, and uneconomic animals, and that this situation is a direct result of irrational Hindu doctrines. Tourists on their way through Delhi, Calcutta, Madras, Bombay, and other Indian cities are astonished at the liberties enjoyed by stray cattle. The animals wander through the streets, browse off the stalls in the market place, break into private gardens, defecate all over the sidewalks, and snarl traffic by pausing to chew their cuds in the middle of busy intersections. In the countryside, the cattle congregate on the shoulders of every highway and spend much of their time taking leisurely walks down the railroad tracks.

To Western observers familiar with modern industrial techniques of agriculture and stock raising, cow love seems senseless, even suicidal. The efficiency expert yearns to get his hands on all those useless animals and ship them off to a proper fate. And yet one finds certain inconsistencies in the condemnation of cow love. When I began to wonder if there might be a practical explanation for the sacred cow, I came across an intriguing government report. It said that India had too many cows but too few oxen. With so many cows around, how could there be a shortage of oxen? Oxen and male water buffalo are the principal source of traction for plowing India's fields. For each farm of ten acres or less, one pair of oxen or water buffalo is considered adequate. A little arithmetic shows that as far as plowing is concerned, there is indeed a shortage rather than a surplus of animals. India has 60 million farms, but only 80

million traction animals. If each farm had its quota of two oxen or two water buffalo, there ought to be 120 million traction animals—that is, 40 million more than are actually available.

The shortage may not be quite so bad since some farmers rent or borrow oxen from their neighbors. But the sharing of plow animals often proves impractical. Plowing must be coordinated with the monsoon rains, and by the time one farm has been plowed, the optimum moment for plowing another may already have passed. Also, after plowing is over, a farmer still needs his own pair of oxen to pull his oxcart, the mainstay of the bulk transport throughout rural India. Quite possibly private ownership of farms, livestock, plows, and oxcarts lowers the efficiency of Indian agriculture, but this, I soon realized, was not caused by cow love.

The shortage of draft animals is a terrible threat that hangs over most of India's peasant families. When an ox falls sick a poor farmer is in danger of losing his farm. If he has no replacement for it, he will have to borrow money at usurious rates. Millions of rural households have in fact lost all or part of their holdings and have gone into sharecropping or day labor as a result of such debts. Every year hundreds of thousands of destitute farmers end up migrating to the cities, which already teem with unemployed and homeless persons.

The Indian farmer who can't replace his sick or deceased ox is in much the same situation as an American farmer who can neither replace nor repair his broken tractor. But there is an important difference: Tractors are made by factories, but oxen are made by cows. A farmer who owns a cow owns a factory for making oxen. With or without cow love, this is a good reason for him not to be too anxious to sell his cow to the slaughterhouse. One also begins to see why Indian farmers might be willing to tolerate cows that give only 500 pounds of milk per year. If the main economic function of the zebu cow is to breed male traction animals, then there's no point in comparing her with specialized American dairy animals, whose main function is to produce milk. Still, the milk produced by zebu cows plays an important role in meeting the nutritional needs of many poor families. Even small amounts of milk products can improve the health of people who are forced to subsist on the edge of starvation.

Agriculture is part of a vast system of human and natural relationships. To judge isolated portions of this "ecosystem" in terms that are relevant to the conduct of American agribusiness leads to some very strange impressions. Cattle figure in the Indian ecosystem in ways that are easily overlooked or demeaned by observers from industrialized, high-energy societies. In the United States, chemicals have almost completely replaced animal manure as the principal source of farm fertilizer. American farmers stopped using manure when they began to plow with tractors rather than mules or horses. Since tractors excrete poisons rather than fertilizers, a commitment to large-scale machine farming is almost of necessity a commitment to the use of chemical fertilizers. And around the world today there has in fact grown up a vast integrated petrochemical-tractor-truck industrial complex that produces farm machinery, motorized transport, oil and gasoline, and chemical fertilizers and pesticides upon which new high-yield production techniques depend.

For better or worse, most of India's farmers cannot participate in this complex, not because they worship their cows, but because they can't afford to buy tractors. Like other underdeveloped nations, India can't build factories that are competitive with the facilities of the industrialized nations nor pay for large quantities of imported industrial products. To convert from animals and manure to tractors and petrochemicals would require the investment of incredible amounts of capital. Moreover, the inevitable effect of substituting costly machines for cheap animals is to reduce the number of people who can earn their living from agriculture and to force a corresponding increase in the size of the average farm. We know that the development of large-scale agribusiness in the United States has meant the virtual destruction of the small family farm. Less than 5 percent of U.S. families now live on farms, as compared with 60 percent about a hundred years ago. If agribusiness

were to develop along similar lines in India, jobs and housing would soon have to be found for a quarter of a billion displaced peasants.

Since the suffering caused by unemployment and homelessness in India's cities is already intolerable, an additional massive build-up of the urban population can only lead to unprecedented upheavals and catastrophes.

With this alternative in view, it becomes easier to understand low-energy, small-scale, animal-based systems. As I have already pointed out, cows and oxen provide low-energy substitutes for tractors and tractor factories. They also should be credited with carrying out the functions of a petrochemical industry. India's cattle annually excrete about 700 million tons of recoverable manure. Approximately half of this total is used as fertilizer, while most of the remainder is burned to provide heat for cooking. The annual quantity of heat liberated by this dung, the Indian housewife's main cooking fuel, is the thermal equivalent of 27 million tons of kerosene, 35 million tons of coal, or 68 million tons of wood. Since India has only small reserves of oil and coal and is already the victim of extensive deforestation, none of these fuels can be considered practical substitutes for cow dung. The thought of dung in the kitchen may not appeal to the average American, but Indian women regard it as a superior cooking fuel because it is finely adjusted to their domestic routines. Most Indian dishes are prepared with clarified butter known as *ghee,* for which cow dung is the preferred source of heat since it burns with a clean, slow, long-lasting flame that doesn't scorch the food. This enables the Indian housewife to start cooking her meals and to leave them unattended for several hours while she takes care of the children, helps out in the fields, or performs other chores. American housewives achieve a similar effect through a complex set of electronic controls that come as expensive options on late-model stoves.

Cow dung has at least one other major function. Mixed with water and made into a paste, it is used as a household flooring material. Smeared over a dirt floor and left to harden into a smooth surface, it keeps the dust down and can be swept clean with a broom.

Because cattle droppings have so many useful properties, every bit of dung is carefully collected. Village small fry are given the task of following the family cow around and of bringing home its daily petrochemical output. In the cities, sweeper castes enjoy a monopoly on the dung deposited by strays and earn their living by selling it to housewives. . . .

During droughts and famines, farmers are severely tempted to kill or sell their livestock. Those who succumb to this temptation seal their doom, even if they survive the drought, for when the rains come, they will be unable to plow their fields. I want to be even more emphatic: Massive slaughter of cattle under the duress of famine constitutes a much greater threat to aggregate welfare than any likely miscalculation by particular farmers concerning the usefulness of their animals during normal times. It seems probable that the sense of unutterable profanity elicited by cow slaughter has its roots in the excruciating contradiction between immediate needs and long-term conditions of survival. Cow love with its sacred symbols and holy doctrines protects the farmer against calculations that are "rational" only in the short term. To Western experts it looks as if "the Indian farmer would rather starve to death than eat his cow.". . . They don't realize that the farmer would rather eat his cow than starve, but that he will starve if he does eat it. . . .

Do I mean to say that cow love has no effect whatsoever on . . . the agricultural system? No. What I am saying is that cow love is an active element in a complex, finely articulated material and cultural order. Cow love mobilizes the latent capacity of human beings to persevere in a low-energy ecosystem in which there is little room for waste or indolence. Cow love contributes to the adaptive resilience of the human population by preserving temporarily dry or barren but still useful animals; by discouraging the growth of an energy-expensive beef industry; by protecting cattle that fatten in the public domain or at landlord's expense; and by preserving the recovery potential of the cattle population during droughts and famines. . . .

Wastefulness is more a characteristic of modern agribusiness than of traditional peasant economies. . . .

Automobiles and airplanes are faster than oxcarts, but they do not use energy more efficiently. In fact, more calories go up in useless heat and smoke during a single day of traffic jams in the United States than is wasted by all the cows of India during an entire year. The comparison is even less favorable when we consider the fact that the stalled vehicles are burning up irreplaceable reserves of petroleum that it took the earth tens of millions of years to accumulate. If you want to see a real sacred cow, go out and look at the family car.

CRITICAL-THINKING QUESTIONS

1. What evidence does Harris offer to support his argument that defining the cow as sacred is a necessary strategy for human survival in India?
2. If survival strategies make sense when we take a close look at them, why do they become so "encased" in elaborate cultural explanations?
3. Does India's recognition of the sacred cow help or hurt that nation's natural environment?
4. Following Harris's logic, can you think of reasons that people in some parts of the world (the Middle East, for instance) do not eat pork?

12

Manifesto of the Communist Party

Karl Marx and Friedrich Engels

Karl Marx, collaborating with Friedrich Engels, produced the "Manifesto" in 1848. This document is a well-known statement about the origin of social conflict in the process of material production. The ideas of Marx and Engels have been instrumental in shaping the political lives of more than one-fifth of the world's population, and of course, they have been instrumental in the development of the social-conflict paradigm in sociology.

BOURGEOIS AND PROLETARIANS[1]

The history of all hitherto existing society[2] is the history of class struggles.

Freeman and slave, patrician and plebeian, lord and serf, guild-master[3] and journeyman, in a word, oppressor and oppressed, stood in constant opposition to one another, carried on an uninterrupted, now hidden, now open fight, a fight that each time ended, either in a revolutionary reconstitution of society at large, or in the common ruin of the contending classes.

SOURCE: *Manifesto of the Communist Party,* Part I, by Karl Marx and Friedrich Engels.

In the earlier epochs of history, we find almost everywhere a complicated arrangement of society into various orders, a manifold gradation of social rank. In ancient Rome we have patricians, knights, plebeians, slaves; in the Middle Ages, feudal lords, vassals, guild-masters, journeymen, apprentices, serfs; in almost all of these classes, again, subordinate gradations.

The modern bourgeois society that has sprouted from the ruins of feudal society, has not done away with class antagonisms. It has but established new classes, new conditions of oppression, new forms of struggle in place of the old ones.

Our epoch, the epoch of the bourgeoisie, possesses, however, this distinctive feature; it has simplified the class antagonisms. Society as a whole is more and more splitting up into two great hostile camps, into two great classes directly facing each other: Bourgeoisie and Proletariat.

From the serfs of the Middle Ages sprang the chartered burghers of the earliest towns. From these burgesses the first elements of the bourgeoisie were developed.

The discovery of America, the rounding of the Cape, opened up fresh ground for the rising bourgeoisie. The East Indian and Chinese markets, the [colonization] of America, trade with the colonies, the increase in the means of exchange and in commodities generally, gave to commerce, to navigation, to industry, an impulse never before known, and thereby, to the revolutionary element in the tottering feudal society, a rapid development.

The feudal system of industry, under which industrial production was monopolized by close guilds, now no longer sufficed for the growing wants of the new markets. The manufacturing system took its place. The guild-masters were pushed on one side by the manufacturing middle class; division of labor between the different corporate guilds vanished in the face of division of labor in each single workshop.

Meantime the markets kept ever growing, the demand, ever rising. Even manufacture no longer sufficed. Thereupon, steam and machinery revolutionized industrial production. The place of manufacture was taken by the giant, Modern Industry, the place of the industrial middle class, by industrial millionaires, the leaders of whole industrial armies, the modern bourgeois.

Modern industry has established the world-market, for which the discovery of America paved the way. This market has given an immense development to commerce, to navigation, to communication by land. This development has, in its turn, reacted on the extension of industry; and in proportion as industry, commerce, navigation, railways extended, in the same proportion the bourgeoisie developed, increased its capital, and pushed into the background every class handed down from the Middle Ages.

We see, therefore, how the modern bourgeoisie is itself the product of a long course of development, of a series of revolutions in the modes of production and of exchange.

Each step in the development of the bourgeoisie was accompanied by a corresponding political advance of that class. An oppressed class under the sway of the feudal nobility, an armed and self-governing association in the mediaeval commune,[4] here independent urban republic (as in Italy and Germany), there taxable "third estate" of the monarchy (as in France), afterwards, in the period of manufacture proper, serving either the semi-feudal or the absolute monarchy as a counterpoise against the nobility, and, in fact, cornerstone of the great monarchies in general, the bourgeoisie has at last, since the establishment of Modern Industry and of the world-market, conquered for itself, in the modern representative State, exclusive political sway. The executive of the modern State is but a committee for managing the common affairs of the whole bourgeoisie.

The bourgeoisie, historically, has played a most revolutionary part.

The bourgeoisie, wherever it has got the upper hand, has put an end to all feudal, patriarchal, idyllic relations. It has pitilessly torn asunder the motley feudal ties that bound man to his "natural superiors," and has left remaining no other nexus between man and man than naked self-interest, than callous "cash payment." It has drowned the most heavenly ecstasies of religious fervour, of chivalrous enthusiasm, of philistine sentimentalism, in the icy water of egotistical calculation. It has resolved personal worth into exchange value, and in place of the numberless indefeasible chartered freedoms, has set up that single, unconscionable freedom—Free Trade. In one word, for exploitation, veiled by religious and political illusions, it has substituted naked, shameless, direct, brutal exploitation.

The bourgeoisie has stripped of its halo every occupation hitherto honoured and looked up to with reverent awe. It has converted the physician, the lawyer, the priest, the poet, the man of science, into its paid [wage-laborers].

The bourgeoisie has torn away from the family

its sentimental veil, and has reduced the family relation to a mere money relation.

The bourgeoisie has disclosed how it came to pass that the brutal display of vigour in the Middle Ages, which Reactionists so much admire, found its fitting complement in the most slothful indolence. It has been the first to show what man's activity can bring about. It has accomplished wonders far surpassing Egyptian pyramids, Roman aqueducts, and Gothic cathedrals; it has conducted expeditions that put in the shade all former Exoduses of nations and crusades.

The bourgeoisie cannot exist without constantly revolutionizing the instruments of production, and thereby the relations of production, and with them the whole relations of society. Conservation of the old modes of production in unaltered form, was, on the contrary, the first condition of existence for all earlier industrial classes. Constant revolutionizing of production, uninterrupted disturbance of all social conditions, everlasting uncertainty and agitation distinguish the bourgeois epoch from all earlier ones. All fixed, fast-frozen relations, with their train of ancient and venerable prejudices and opinions, are swept away, all new-formed ones become antiquated before they can ossify. All that is solid melts into air, all that is holy is profaned, and man is at last compelled to face with sober senses, his real conditions of life, and his relations with his kind.

The need of a constantly expanding market for its products chases the bourgeoisie over the whole surface of the globe. It must nestle everywhere, settle everywhere, establish [connections] everywhere.

The bourgeoisie has through its exploitation of the world-market given a cosmopolitan character to production and consumption in every country. To the great chagrin of Reactionists, it has drawn from under the feet of industry the national ground on which it stood. All old-established national industries have been destroyed or are daily being destroyed. They are dislodged by new industries, whose introduction becomes a life and death question for all civilised nations, by industries that no longer work up indigenous raw material, but raw material drawn from the remotest zones; industries whose products are consumed, not only at home, but in every quarter of the globe. In place of the old wants, satisfied by the productions of the country, we find new wants, requiring for their satisfaction the products of distant lands and climes. In place of the old local and national seclusion and self-sufficiency, we have intercourse in every direction, universal interdependence of nations. And as in material, so also in intellectual production. The intellectual creations of individual nations become common property. National one-sidedness and narrow-mindedness become more and more impossible, and from the numerous national and local literatures there arises a world-literature.

The bourgeoisie, by the rapid improvement of all instruments of production, by the immensely facilitated means of communication, draws all, even the most barbarian, nations into civilization. The cheap prices of its commodities are the heavy artillery with which it batters down all Chinese walls, with which it forces the barbarians' intensely obstinate hatred of foreigners to capitulate. It compels all nations, on pain of extinction, to adopt the bourgeois mode of production; it compels them to introduce what it calls civilization into their midst, i.e., to become bourgeois themselves. In a word, it creates a world after its own image.

The bourgeoisie has subjected the country to the rule of the towns. It has created enormous cities, has greatly increased the urban population as compared with the rural, and has thus rescued a considerable part of the population from the idiocy of rural life. Just as it has made the country dependent on the towns, so it has made barbarian and semi-barbarian countries dependent on the civilised ones, nations of peasants on nations of bourgeois, the East on the West.

The bourgeoisie keeps more and more doing away with the scattered state of the population, of the means of production, and of property. It has agglomerated population, centralized means of production, and has concentrated property in a few hands. The necessary consequence of this was political centralization. Independent, or but loosely connected provinces, with separate interests, laws, governments and systems of taxation, became lumped together in one nation, with one government, one code of laws, one national class-interest, one frontier and one customs-tariff.

The bourgeoisie, during its rule of scarce one hundred years, has created more massive and more colossal productive forces than have all preceding generations together. Subjection of Nature's forces to man, machinery, application of chemistry to industry and agriculture, steam-navigation, railways, electric telegraphs, clearing of whole continents for cultivation, canalization of rivers, whole populations conjured out of the ground—what earlier century had even a presentiment that such productive forces slumbered in the lap of social labor?

We see then: The means of production and of exchange on whose foundation the bourgeoisie built itself up, were generated in feudal society. At a certain stage in the development of these means of production and of exchange, the conditions under which feudal society produced and exchanged, the feudal organization of agriculture and manufacturing industry, in one word, the feudal relations of property became no longer compatible with the already developed productive forces; they became so many fetters. They had to burst asunder; they were burst asunder.

Into their places stepped free competition, accompanied by a social and political constitution adapted to it, and by the economical and political sway of the bourgeois class.

A similar movement is going on before our own eyes. Modern bourgeois society with its relations of production, of exchange and of property, a society that has conjured up such gigantic means of production and of exchange, is like the sorcerer, who is no longer able to control the powers of the nether world whom he has called up by his spells. For many a decade past the history of industry and commerce is but the history of the revolt of modern productive forces against modern conditions of production, against the property relations that are the conditions for the existence of the bourgeoisie and of its rule. It is enough to mention the commercial crises that by their periodical return put on its trial, each time more threateningly, the existence of the entire bourgeois society. In these crises a great part not only of the existing products, but also of the previously created productive forces, are periodically destroyed. In these crises there breaks out an epidemic that, in all earlier epochs, would have seemed an absurdity—the epidemic of overproduction. Society suddenly finds itself put back into a state of momentary barbarism; it appears as if a famine, a universal war of devastation had cut off the supply of every means of subsistence; industry and commerce seem to be destroyed; and why? Because there is too much civilization, too much means of subsistence, too much industry, too much commerce. The productive forces at the disposal of society no longer tend to further the development of the conditions of bourgeois property; on the contrary, they have become too powerful for these conditions, by which they are fettered, and so soon as they overcome these fetters, they bring disorder into the whole of bourgeois society, endanger the existence of bourgeois property. The conditions of bourgeois society are too narrow to comprise the wealth created by them. And how does the bourgeoisie get over these crises? On the one hand by enforced destruction of a mass of productive forces; on the other, by the conquest of new markets, and by the more thorough exploitation of the old ones. That is to say, by paving the way for more extensive and more destructive crises, and by diminishing the means whereby crises are prevented.

The weapons with which the bourgeoisie felled feudalism to the ground are now turned against the bourgeoisie itself.

But not only has the bourgeoisie forged the weapons that bring death to itself; it has also called into existence the men who are to wield those weapons—the modern working class—the proletarians.

In proportion as the bourgeoisie, i.e., capital, is developed, in the same proportion is the proletariat, the modern working class, developed, a class of laborers, who live only so long as they find work, and who find work only so long as their labor increases capital. These laborers, who must sell themselves piecemeal, are a commodity, like every other article of commerce, and are consequently exposed to all the vicissitudes of competition, to all the fluctuations of the market.

Owing to the extensive use of machinery and to division of labor, the work of the proletarians has lost all individual character, and, consequently, all charm for the workman. He becomes an appendage of the machine, and it is only the most simple, most monotonous, and most easily acquired knack that is required of him. Hence, the cost of production of a workman is restricted, almost entirely, to the means of subsistence that he requires for his maintenance, and for the propagation of his race. But the price of a commodity, and also of labor, is equal to its cost of production. In proportion, therefore, as the repulsiveness of the work increases, the wage decreases. Nay more, in proportion as the use of machinery and division of labor increases, in the same proportion the burden of toil also increases, whether by prolongation of the working hours, by increase of the work enacted in a given time, or by increased speed of the machinery, etc.

Modern industry has converted the little workshop of the patriarchal master into the great factory of the industrial capitalist. Masses of laborers, crowded into the factory, are organized like soldiers. As privates of the industrial army they are placed under the command of a perfect hierarchy of officers and sergeants. Not only are they the slaves of the bourgeois class, and of the bourgeois State, they are daily and hourly enslaved by the machine, by the over-looker, and, above all, by the individual bourgeois manufacturer himself. The more openly this despotism proclaims gain to be its end and aim, the more petty, the more hateful and the more embittering it is.

The less the skill and exertion or strength implied in manual labor, in other words, the more modern industry becomes developed, the more is the labor of men superseded by that of women. Differences of age and sex have no longer any distinctive social validity for the working class. All are instruments of labor, more or less expensive to use, according to their age and sex.

No sooner is the exploitation of the laborer by the manufacturer, so far, at an end, that he receives his wages in cash, than he is set upon by the other portions of the bourgeoisie, the landlord, the shopkeeper, the pawnbroker, etc.

The lower strata of the middle class—the small tradespeople, shopkeepers, and retired tradesmen generally, the handicraftsmen and peasants—all these sink gradually into the proletariat, partly because their diminutive capital does not suffice for the scale on which Modern Industry is carried on, and is swamped in the competition with the large capitalists, partly because their specialised skill is rendered worthless by new methods of production. Thus the proletariat is recruited from all classes of the population.

The proletariat goes through various stages of development. With its birth begins its struggle with the bourgeoisie. At first the contest is carried on by individual laborers, then by the workpeople of a factory, then by the operatives of one trade, in one locality, against the individual bourgeois who directly exploits them. They direct their attacks not against the bourgeois conditions of production, but against the instruments of production themselves; they destroy imported wares that compete with their labor, they smash to pieces machinery, they set factories ablaze, they seek to restore by force the vanished status of the workman of the Middle Ages.

At this stage the laborers still form an incoherent mass scattered over the whole country, and broken up by their mutual competition. If anywhere they unite to form more compact bodies, this is not yet the consequence of their own active union, but of the union of the bourgeoisie, which class, in order to attain its own political ends, is compelled to set the whole proletariat in motion, and is moreover yet, for a time, able to do so. At this stage, therefore, the proletarians do not fight their enemies, but the enemies of their enemies, the remnants of absolute monarchy, the landowners, the non-industrial bourgeois, the petty bourgeoisie. Thus the whole historical movement is concentrated in the hands of the bourgeoisie; every victory so obtained is a victory for the bourgeoisie.

But with the development of industry the proletariat not only increases in number, it becomes concentrated in greater masses, its strength grows, and it feels that strength more. The various interests and conditions of life within the ranks of the proletariat are more and more equalized, in proportion as machinery obliterates all distinctions of labor, and nearly everywhere reduces wages to the same low level. The growing competition among the bourgeois, and the resulting commercial crises, make the wages of the workers ever more fluctuating. The unceasing improvement of machinery, ever more rapidly developing, makes their livelihood more and more precarious; the collisions between individual workmen and individual bourgeois take more and more the character of collisions between two classes. Thereupon the workers begin to form combinations (Trades' Unions) against the bourgeois; they club together in order to keep up the rate of wages; they found permanent associations in order to make provision beforehand for these occasional revolts. Here and there the contest breaks out into riots.

Now and then the workers are victorious, but only for a time. The real fruit of their battles lies, not in the immediate result, but in the ever expanding union of the workers. This union is helped on by the improved means of communication that are created by modern industry, and that place the workers of different localities in contact with one another. It was just this contact that was needed to centralise the numerous local struggles, all of the same character, into one national struggle between classes. But every class struggle is a political struggle. And that union, to attain which the burghers of the Middle Ages, with their miserable highways, required centuries, the modern proletarians, thanks to railways, achieve in a few years.

This organization of the proletarians into a class, and consequently into a political party, is continually being upset again by the competition between the workers themselves. But it ever rises up again, stronger, firmer, mightier. It compels legislative recognition of particular interests of the workers, by taking advantage of the divisions among the bourgeoisie itself. Thus the ten-hours'-bill in England was carried.

Altogether collisions between the classes of the old society further, in many ways, the course of development of the proletariat. The bourgeoisie finds itself involved in a constant battle. At first with the aristocracy; later on, with those portions of the bourgeoisie itself, whose interests have become antagonistic to the progress of industry; at all times, with the bourgeoisie of foreign countries. In all these battles it sees itself compelled to appeal to the proletariat, to ask for its help, and thus, to drag it into the political arena. The bourgeoisie itself, therefore, supplies the proletariat with its own elements of political and general education, in other words, it furnishes the proletariat with weapons for fighting the bourgeoisie.

Further, as we have already seen, entire sections of the ruling classes are, by the advance of industry, precipitated into the proletariat, or are at least threatened in their conditions of existence. These also supply the proletariat with fresh elements of enlightenment and progress.

Finally, in times when the class-struggle nears the decisive hour, the process of dissolution going on within the ruling class, in fact within the whole range of old society, assumes such a violent, glaring character, that a small section of the ruling class cuts itself adrift, and joins the revolutionary class, the class that holds the future in its hands. Just as, therefore, at an earlier period, a section of the nobility went over to the bourgeoisie, so now a portion of the bourgeoisie goes over to the proletariat, and in particular, a portion of the bourgeois ideologists, who have raised themselves to the level of comprehending theoretically the historical movements as a whole.

Of all the classes that stand face to face with the bourgeoisie today, the proletariat alone is a really revolutionary class. The other classes decay and finally disappear in the face of modern industry; the proletariat is its special and essential product.

The lower-middle class, the small manufacturer, the shopkeeper, the artisan, the peasant, all these fight against the bourgeoisie, to save from extinction their existence as fractions of the middle class. They are therefore not revolutionary, but conservative. Nay more, they are reactionary, for they try to roll back the wheel of history. If by chance they are revolutionary, they are so, only in view of their impending transfer into the proletariat, they thus defend not their present, but their future interests, they desert their own standpoint to place themselves at that of the proletariat.

The "dangerous class," the social scum, that passively rotting mass thrown off by the lowest layers of old society, may, here and there, be swept into the movement by a proletarian revolution; its conditions of life, however, prepare it far more for the part of a bribed tool of reactionary intrigue.

In the conditions of the proletariat, those of old society at large are already virtually swamped. The proletarian is without property; his relation to his wife and children has no longer anything in common with the bourgeois family-relations; modern industrial labor, modern subjection to capital, the same in England as in France, in America as in Germany, has stripped him of every trace of national character. Law, morality, religion, are to him so many bourgeois prejudices, behind which lurk in ambush just as many bourgeois interests.

All the preceding classes that got the upper hand, sought to fortify their already acquired status by subjecting society at large to their conditions of appropriation. The proletarians cannot become masters of the productive forces of society, except by abolishing their own previous mode of appropriation, and thereby also every other previous mode of appropriation. They have nothing of their own to secure and to fortify; their mission is to destroy all previous securities for, and insurances of, individual property.

All previous historical movements were movements of minorities, or in the interest of minorities. The proletarian movement is the self-conscious, independent movement of the immense majority, in the interest of the immense majority. The proletariat, the lowest stratum of our present society, cannot stir, cannot raise itself up, without the whole superincumbent strata of official society being sprung into the air.

Though not in substance, yet in form, the struggle of the proletariat with the bourgeoisie is at first a national struggle. The proletariat of each country must, of course, first of all settle matters with its own bourgeoisie.

In depicting the most general phases of the development of the proletariat, we traced the more or less veiled civil war, raging within existing society, up to the point where that war breaks out into open revolution, and where the violent overthrow of the bourgeoisie, lays the foundation for the sway of the proletariat.

Hitherto, every form of society has been based, as we have already seen, on the antagonism of oppressing and oppressed classes. But in order to oppress a class, certain conditions must be assured to it under which it can, at least, continue its slavish existence. The serf, in the period of serfdom, raised himself to membership in the commune, just as the petty bourgeois, under the yoke of feudal absolutism, managed to develop into a bourgeois. The modern laborer, on the contrary, instead of rising with the progress of industry, sinks deeper and deeper below the conditions of existence of his own class. He becomes a pauper, and pauperism develops more rapidly than population and wealth. And here it becomes evident, that the bourgeoisie is unfit any longer to be the ruling class in society, and to impose its conditions of existence upon society as an overriding law. It is unfit to rule, because it is incompetent to assure an existence to its slave within his slavery, because it cannot help letting him sink into such a state, that it has to feed him, instead of being fed by him. Society can no longer live under this bourgeoisie, in other words, its existence is no longer compatible with society.

The essential condition for the existence, and for the sway of the bourgeois class, is the formation and augmentation of capital; the condition for capital is wage-labor. Wage-labor rests exclusively on competition between the laborers. The advance of industry, whose involuntary promoter is the bourgeoisie, replaces the isolation of the laborers, due to competition, by their involuntary combination, due to association. The development of Modern Industry, therefore, cuts from under its feet the very foundation on which the bourgeoisie produces and appropriates products. What the bourgeoisie therefore produces, above all, are its own grave-diggers. Its fall and the victory of the prole-tariat are equally inevitable.

CRITICAL-THINKING QUESTIONS

1. What are the distinguishing factors of "class conflict"? How does this differ from other kinds of conflict, as between individuals or nations?
2. Why do Marx and Engels argue that understanding society in the present requires investigating the society of the past?
3. On what grounds did Marx and Engels praise *industrial capitalism? On what grounds did they* condemn *the system?*

NOTES

1. By *bourgeoisie* is meant the class of modern capitalists, owners of the means of social production and employers of wage-labor. By proletariat, the class of modern wage-laborers who, having no means of production of their own, are reduced to selling their labor-power in order to live.

2. That is, all written history. In 1847, the prehistory of society, the social organization existing previous to recorded history, was all but unknown. Since then, Haxthausen discovered common ownership of land in Russia. Maurer proved it to be the social foundation from which all Teutonic races started in history, and by and bye village communities were found to be, or to have been, the primitive form of society everywhere from India to Ireland. The inner organization of this primitive Communistic society was laid bare, in its typical form, by Morgan's crowning discovery of the true nature of the gens and its relation to the tribe. With the dissolution of these primaeval communities society begins to be differentiated into separate and finally antagonistic classes. I have attempted to retrace this process of dissolution in: "Der Ursprung der Familie des, Privatelgenthums und des Staats," 2d ed., Stuttgart 1886.

3. Guild-master, that is a full member of a guild, a master within, not a head of, a guild.

4. "Commune" was the name taken, in France, by the nascent towns even before they had conquered from their feudal lords and masters, local self-government and political rights as "the Third Estate." Generally speaking, for the economical development of the bourgeoisie, England is here taken as the typical country, for its political development, France.

13

Gemeinschaft and Gesellschaft

Ferdinand Toennies

The German sociologist Ferdinand Toennies (1855–1936) described patterns of change by contrasting two types of social living: Gemeinschaft and Gesellschaft. In simple terms, Gemeinschaft is rooted in the rural, kinship-based life of the past; Gesellschaft, by contrast, finds its clearest expression in the commercial world of today's large, anonymous cities.

[A] relationship . . . and also the resulting association is conceived of either as real and organic life—this is the essential characteristic of the Gemeinschaft (community); or as imaginary and mechanical structure—this is the concept of Gesellschaft (society). . . .

All intimate, private, and exclusive living together, so we discover, is understood as life in Gemeinschaft (community). Gesellschaft (society) is public life—it is the world itself. In Gemeinschaft with one's family, one lives from birth on, bound to it in weal and woe. One goes into

Gesellschaft as one goes into a strange country. A young man is warned against bad Gesellschaft, but the expression bad Gemeinschaft violates the meaning of the word. Lawyers may speak of domestic (*häusliche*) Gesellschaft, thinking only of the legalistic concept of social association; but the domestic Gemeinschaft, or home life with its immeasurable influence upon the human soul, has been felt by everyone who ever shared it. Likewise, a bride or groom knows that he or she goes into marriage as a complete Gemeinschaft of life (*communio totius vitae*). A Gesellschaft of life would be a contradiction in and of itself. One keeps or enjoys another's Gesellschaft, but not his Gemeinschaft in this sense. One becomes a part of a religious Gemeinschaft; religious Gesellschaften (associations or societies), like any other groups formed for given purposes, exist only in so far as they, viewed from without, take their places among the institutions of a political body or as they represent conceptual elements of a theory; they do not touch upon the religious Gemeinschaft as such. There exists a Gemeinschaft of language, of folkways or mores, or of beliefs; but, by way of contrast, Gesellschaft exists in the realm of business, travel, or sciences. So of special importance are the commercial Gesellschaften; whereas, even though a certain familiarity and Gemeinschaft may exist among business partners, one could indeed hardly speak of commercial Gemeinschaft. To make the word combination "joint-stock Gemeinschaft" would be abominable. On the other hand, there exists a Gemeinschaft of ownership in fields, forest, and pasture. The Gemeinschaft of property between man and wife cannot be called Gesellschaft of property. Thus many differences become apparent.

Gemeinschaft is old; Gesellschaft is new as a name as well as a phenomenon. . . . [S]ays Bluntschli (*Staatswörterbuch IV*), "Wherever urban culture blossoms and bears fruits, Gesellschaft appears as its indispensable organ. The rural people know little of it." On the other hand, all praise of rural life has pointed out that the Gemeinschaft among people is stronger there and more alive; it is the lasting and genuine form of living together. In contrast to Gemeinschaft, Gesellschaft is transitory and superficial. Accordingly, Gemeinschaft should be understood as a living organism, Gesellschaft as a mechanical aggregate and artifact. . . .

The Gemeinschaft by blood, denoting unity of being, is developed and differentiated into Gemeinschaft of locality, which is based on a common habitat. A further differentiation leads to the Gemeinschaft of mind, which implies only cooperation and co-ordinated action for a common goal. Gemeinschaft of locality may be conceived as a community of physical life, just as Gemeinschaft of mind expresses the community of mental life. In conjunction with the others, this last type of Gemeinschaft represents the truly human and

supreme form of community. Kinship Gemeinschaft signifies a common relation to, and share in, human beings themselves, while in Gemeinschaft of locality such a common relation is established through collective ownership of land; and, in Gemeinschaft of mind, the common bond is represented by sacred places and worshiped deities. All three types of Gemeinschaft are closely interrelated in space as well as in time. They are, therefore, also related in all such single phenomena and in their development, as well as in general human culture and its history. Wherever human beings are related through their wills in an organic manner and affirm each other, we find one or another of the three types of Gemeinschaft. Either the earlier type involves the later one, or the later type has developed to relative independence from some earlier one. It is, therefore, possible to deal with (1) kinship, (2) neighborhood, and (3) friendship as definite and meaningful derivations of these original categories. . . .

The theory of the Gesellschaft deals with the artificial construction of an aggregate of human beings which superficially resembles the Gemeinschaft in so far as the individuals live and dwell together peacefully. However, in the Gemeinschaft they remain essentially united in spite of all separating factors, whereas in the Gesellschaft they are essentially separated in spite of all uniting factors. In the Gesellschaft, as contrasted with the Gemeinschaft, we find no actions that can be derived from an a priori and necessarily existing unity; no actions, therefore, which manifest the will and the spirit of the unity even if performed by the individual; no actions which, in so far as they are performed by the individual, take place on behalf of those united with him. In the Gesellschaft such actions do not exist. On the contrary, here everybody is by himself and isolated, and there exists a condition of tension against all others. Their spheres of activity and power are sharply separated, so that everybody refuses to everyone else contact with and admittance to his sphere; i.e., intrusions are regarded as hostile acts. Such a negative attitude toward one another becomes the normal and always underlying relation of these power-endowed individuals, and it characterizes the Gesellschaft in the condition of rest; nobody wants to grant and produce anything for another individual, nor will he be inclined to give ungrudgingly to another individual, if it be not in exchange for a gift or labor equivalent that he considers at least equal to what he has given. . . .

. . . In Gesellschaft every person strives for that which is to his own advantage and he affirms the actions of others only in so far as and as long as they can further his interest. Before and outside of convention and also before and outside of each special contract, the relation of all to all may therefore be conceived as potential hostility or latent war. Against this condition, all agreements of the will stand out as so many treaties and peace pacts. This conception is the only one which does justice to all facts of business and trade where all rights and duties can be reduced to mere value and definitions of ability to deliver. Every theory of pure private law or law of nature understood as pertaining to the Gesellschaft has to be considered as being based upon this conception.

CRITICAL-THINKING QUESTIONS

1. Describe the essential features of Gemeinschaft and Gesellschaft in order to clearly distinguish the two organizational types.

2. Why does Toennies link Gemeinschaft to kinship, neighborhood, and friendship? How is Gesellschaft linked to commerce?

3. Based on reading this selection, do you think Toennies found one type of social organization preferable to the other? If so, which one? Why?

SOCIETY

Contemporary

14

The Decline of U.S. Society

William J. Bennett

History reveals the rise and fall of many once-great nations. William J. Bennett, Secretary of Education from 1985 to 1988, uses eight "cultural indicators" to assess the moral, social, and behavioral climate in the United States. He concludes that our society is experiencing a cultural decline evident in weakening families, rising crime, and our government's inability to bring most social problems under control.

Is our culture declining? I have tried to quantify the answer to this question with the creation of the Index of Leading Cultural Indicators.

In the early 1960s, the Census Bureau began publishing the Index of Leading Economic Indicators. These eleven measurements, taken together, represent the best means we now have of interpreting current business developments and predicting future economic trends.

The Index of Leading Cultural Indicators, a compilation of the Heritage Foundation and Em-

power America, attempts to bring a similar kind of data-based analysis to cultural issues. It is a statistical portrait (from 1960 to the present) of the moral, social and behavioral conditions of modern American society—matters that, in our time, often travel under the banner of "values."

Perhaps no one will be surprised to learn that, according to the index, America's cultural condition is far from healthy. What is shocking is just how precipitously American life has declined in the past thirty years, despite the enormous governmental effort to improve it.

Since 1960, the U.S. population has increased 41 percent; the gross domestic product has nearly tripled; and total social spending by all levels of

SOURCE: "Quantifying America's Decline," by William J. Bennett, *The Wall Street Journal,* March 15, 1993. Reprinted with permission.

government (measured in constant 1990 dollars) has risen from $143.73 billion to $787 billion—more than a fivefold increase. Inflation-adjusted spending on welfare has increased by 630 percent, spending on education by 225 percent.

But during the same thirty-year period there has been a 560 percent increase in violent crime; a 419 percent increase in illegitimate births; a quadrupling in divorce rates; a tripling of the percentage of children living in single-parent homes; more than a 200 percent increase in the teenage suicide rate; and a drop of almost 80 points in SAT scores.

Clearly many modern-day social pathologies have gotten worse. More important, they seem impervious to government's attempts to cure them. Although the Great Society and its many social programs have had some good effects, there is a vast body of evidence suggesting that these "remedies" have reached the limits of their success.

Perhaps more than anything else, America's cultural decline is evidence of a shift in the public's attitudes and beliefs. Social scientist James Q. Wilson writes that "the powers exercised by the institutions of social control have been constrained and people, especially young people, have embraced an ethos that values self-expression over self-control." The findings of pollster Daniel Yankelovich seem to confirm this diagnosis. Our society now places less value than before on what we owe to others as a matter of moral obligation; less value on sacrifice as a moral good; less value on social conformity and respectability; and less value on correctness and restraint in matters of physical pleasure and sexuality.

Some writers have spoken eloquently on these matters. When the late Walker Percy was asked what concerned him most about America's future, he answered: "Probably the fear of seeing America, with all its great strength and beauty and freedom . . . gradually subside into decay through default and be defeated, not by the Communist movement, demonstrably a bankrupt system, but from within by weariness, boredom, cynicism, greed and in the end helplessness before its great problems." Alexander Solzhenitsyn, in a speech earlier this year, put it this way: "The West . . . has

been undergoing an erosion and obscuring of high moral and ethical ideals. The spiritual axis of life has grown dim." John Updike has written: "The fact that, compared to the inhabitants of Africa and Russia, we still live well cannot ease the pain of feeling we no longer live nobly."

Treatises have been written on why this decline has happened. The hard truth is that in a free society the ultimate responsibility rests with the people themselves. The good news is that what has been self-inflicted can be self-corrected.

There are a number of things we can do to encourage cultural renewal. First, government should heed the old injunction, "Do no harm." Over the years it has often done unintended harm to many of the people it was trying to help. The destructive incentives of the welfare system are perhaps the most glaring example of this.

Second, political leaders can help shape social attitudes through public discourse and through morally defensible social legislation. A thoughtful social agenda today would perhaps include: a more tough-minded criminal justice system, including more prisons; a radical reform of education through national standards and school choice; a system of child-support collection, whereby fathers would be made to take responsibility for their children; a rescinding of no-fault divorce laws for parents with children; and radical reform of the welfare system.

But even if these and other worthwhile efforts are made, we should temper our expectations of what government can do. A greater hope lies elsewhere.

Our social and civic institutions—families, churches, schools, neighborhoods and civic associations—have traditionally taken on the responsibility of providing our children with love, order and discipline—of teaching self-control, comparison, tolerance, civility, honesty, and respect for authority. Government, even at its best, can never be more than an auxiliary in the development of character.

The social regression of the past thirty years is due in large part to the enfeebled state of our social institutions and their failure to carry out their

Eight Cultural Indicators

Average Daily TV Viewing		SAT Scores	
1960	5:06 hours	1960	975
1965	5:29 hours	1965	969
1970	5:56 hours	1970	948
1975	6:07 hours	1975	910
1980	6:36 hours	1980	890
1985	7:07 hours	1985	906
1990	6:55 hours	1990	900
1992	7:04 hours	1992	899

Source: Nielsen Media Research   Source: The College Board

Violent Crime Rate (per 100,000)		Median Prison Sentence*	
1960	16.1	1954	22.5 days
1965	20.0	1964	12.1 days
1970	36.4	1974	5.5 days
1975	48.8	1984	7.7 days
1980	59.7	1988	8.5 days
1985	53.3	1990	8.0 days
1990	73.2		
1991	75.8		

Source: F.B.I.

*'Serious Crime': murder, rape, robbery, aggravated assault, burglary, larceny/theft and motor vehicle theft.

Source: National Center for Policy Analysis

Children on Welfare		Teen Suicide Rate	
1960	3.5%	1960	3.6%
1965	4.5%	1965	4.0%
1970	8.5%	1970	5.9%
1975	11.8%	1975	7.6%
1980	11.5%	1980	8.5%
1985	11.2%	1985	10.0%
1990	11.9%	1990	11.3%

Source: Bureau of the Census;   Source: National Center for
U.S. House of Representatives   Health Statistics

% of Illegitimate Births		Children with Single Mothers	
1960	5.3%	1960	8%
1970	10.7%	1970	11%
1980	18.4%	1980	18%
1990	26.2%	1990	22%

Source: National Center for Health Statistics

Sources: Bureau of the Census; Donald Hernandez, The American Child: Resources from Family, Government and the Economy

critical and time-honored tasks. We desperately need to recover a sense of the fundamental purpose of education, which is to engage in the architecture of souls. When a self-governing society ignores this responsibility, it does so at its peril.

CRITICAL-THINKING QUESTIONS

1. What cultural indicators does Bennett use to measure the decline of values in the United States? What other measures might be included?
2. Why, according to Bennett, is our culture declining? That is, who (or what) is to blame?
3. What remedies does Bennett propose? Do you agree or disagree with these solutions?

15

The Amish: A Small Society

John A. Hostetler

Some 100,000 Old Order Amish live in the rolling farmland of Pennsylvania, Ohio, Indiana, and southern Ontario. These descendants of sixteenth-century Germans, who fled persecution for their religious beliefs, constitute a distinctive "small society" that keeps the larger world at arm's length. This description of the Amish suggests the extent of cultural diversity within North America and raises questions about why some people would reject the "advantages" that many others take for granted.

Small communities, with their distinctive character—where life is stable and intensely human—are disappearing. Some have vanished from the face of the earth, others are dying slowly, but all have undergone changes as they have come into contact with an expanding machine civilization. The merging of diverse peoples into a common mass has produced tension among members of the minorities and the majority alike.

SOURCE: *Amish Society,* 3d ed., by John A. Hostetler (Baltimore: The Johns Hopkins University Press, 1980), pp. 3–12. Reprinted with permission.

The Old Order Amish, who arrived on American shores in colonial times, have survived in the modern world in distinctive, viable, small communities. They have resisted the homogenization process more successfully than others. In planting and harvest time one can see their bearded men working the fields with horses and their women hanging out the laundry in neat rows to dry. Many American people have seen Amish families, with the men wearing broad-brimmed black hats and the women in bonnets and long dresses, in railway depots or bus terminals. Although the Amish have lived with industrialized America for over two and a half centuries, they have moderated its influence on their personal lives, their families, communities, and their values.

The Amish are often perceived by other Americans to be relics of the past who live an austere, inflexible life dedicated to inconvenient and archaic customs. They are seen as renouncing both modern conveniences and the American dream of success and progress. But most people have no quarrel with the Amish for doing things the old-fashioned way. Their conscientious objection was tolerated in wartime, for after all, they are meticulous farmers who practice the virtues of work and thrift.

. . . The Amish are a church, a community, a spiritual union, a conservative branch of Christianity, a religion, a community whose members practice simple and austere living, a familistic entrepreneuring system, and an adaptive human community. . . .

The Amish are in some ways a little commonwealth, for their members claim to be ruled by the law of love and redemption. The bonds that unite them are many. Their beliefs, however, do not permit them solely to occupy and defend a particular territory. They are highly sensitive in caring for their own. They will move to other lands when circumstances force them to do so.

Commonwealth implies a place, a province, which means any part of a national domain that geographically and socially is sufficiently unified to have a true consciousness of its unity. Its inhabitants feel comfortable with their own ideas and customs, and the "place" possesses a sense of distinction from other parts of the country. Members of a commonwealth are not foot-loose. They have a sense of productivity and accountability in a province where "the general welfare" is accepted as a day-to-day reality. Commonwealth has come to have an archaic meaning in today's world, because when groups and institutions become too large, the sense of commonwealth or the common good is lost. Thus it is little wonder that the most recent dictionaries of the American English language render the meaning of commonwealth as

"obsolescent." In reality, the Amish are in part a commonwealth. There is, however, no provision for outcasts.

It may be argued that the Amish have retained elements of wholesome provincialism, a saving power to which the world in the future will need more and more to appeal. Provincialism need not turn to ancient narrowness and ignorance, confines from which many have sought to escape. A sense of province or commonwealth, with its cherished love of people and self-conscious dignity, is a necessary basis for relating to the wider world community. Respect for locality, place, custom, and local idealism can go a long way toward checking the monstrous growth of consolidation in the nation and thus help to save human freedom and individual dignity.

. . . Anthropologists, who have compared societies all over the world, have tended to call semi-isolated peoples "folk societies," "primitives," or merely "simple societies." These societies constitute an altogether different type in contrast to the industrialized, or so-called civilized, societies.

The "folk society," as conceptualized by Robert Redfield,[1] is a small, isolated, traditional, simple, homogeneous society in which oral communication and conventionalized ways are important factors in integrating the whole life. In such an ideal-type society, shared practical knowledge is more important than science, custom is valued more than critical knowledge, and associations are personal and emotional rather than abstract and categoric.

Folk societies are uncomfortable with the idea of change. Young people do what the old people did when they were young. Members communicate intimately with one another, not only by word of mouth but also through custom and symbols that reflect a strong sense of belonging to one another. A folk society is *Gemeinschaft*-like; there is a strong sense of "we-ness." Leadership is personal rather than institutionalized. There are no gross economic inequalities. Mutual aid is characteristic of the society's members. The goals of life are never stated as matters of doctrine, but neither are they questioned. They are implied by the acts that constitute living in a small society. Custom tends to become sacred. Behavior is strongly patterned, and acts as well as cultural objects are given symbolic meaning that is often pervasively religious. Religion is diffuse and all-pervasive. In the typical folk society, planting and harvesting are as sacred in their own ways as singing and praying.

The folk model lends itself well to understanding the tradition-directed character of Amish society. The heavy weight of tradition can scarcely be explained in any other way. The Amish, for example, have retained many of the customs and small-scale technologies that were common in rural society in the nineteenth century. Through a process of syncretism, Amish religious values have been fused with an earlier period of simple country living when everyone farmed with horses and on a scale where family members could work together. The Amish exist as a folk or "little" community in a rural subculture within the modern state. . . . The outsider who drives through an Amish settlement cannot help but recognize them by their clothing, farm homes, furnishings, fields, and other material traits of culture. Although they speak perfect English with outsiders, they speak a dialect of German among themselves.

Amish life is distinctive in that religion and custom blend into a way of life. The two are inseparable. The core values of the community are religious beliefs. Not only do the members worship a deity they understand through the revelation of Jesus Christ and the Bible, but their patterned behavior has a religious dimension. A distinctive way of life permeates daily life, agriculture, and the application of energy to economic ends. Their beliefs determine their conceptions of the self, the universe, and man's place in it. The Amish world view recognizes a certain spiritual worth and dignity in the universe in its natural form. Religious considerations determine hours of work and the daily, weekly, seasonal, and yearly rituals associated with life experience. Occupation, the means

and destinations of travel, and choice of friends and mate are determined by religious considerations. Religious and work attitudes are not far distant from each other. The universe includes the divine, and Amish society itself is considered divine insofar as the Amish recognize themselves as "a chosen people of God." The Amish do not seek to master nature or to work against the elements, but try to work with them. The affinity between Amish society and nature in the form of land, terrain, and vegetation is expressed in various degrees of intensity.

Religion is highly patterned, so one may properly speak of the Amish as a tradition-directed group. Though allusions to the Bible play an important role in determining their outlook on the world, and on life after death, these beliefs have been fused with several centuries of struggling to survive in community. Out of intense religious experience, societal conflict, and intimate agrarian experience, a mentality has developed that prefers the old rather than the new. While the principle seems to apply especially to religion, it has also become a charter for social behavior. "The old is the best, and the new is of the devil" has become a prevalent mode of thought. By living in closed communities where custom and a strong sense of togetherness prevail, the Amish have formed an integrated way of life and a folklike culture. Continuity of conformity and custom is assured and the needs of the individual from birth to death are met within an integrated and shared system of meanings. Oral tradition, custom, and conventionality play an important part in maintaining the group as a functioning whole. To the participant, religion and custom are inseparable. Commitment and culture are combined to produce a stable human existence.

. . . A century ago, hardly anyone knew the Amish existed. A half-century ago they were viewed as an obscure sect living by ridiculous customs, as stubborn people who resisted education and exploited the labor of their children. Today the Amish are the unwilling objects of a thriving tourist industry on the eastern seaboard. They are revered as hard-working, thrifty people with enormous agrarian stamina, and by some, as islands of sanity in a culture gripped by commercialism and technology run wild.

CRITICAL-THINKING QUESTIONS

1. Does this description of the Amish way of life make you think about your own way of life in different terms? How?

2. Why would the Amish reject technological advances, which most members of our society hold to be invaluable?

3. What might the majority of the U.S. population learn from the Amish?

NOTE

1. Robert Redfield, "The Folk Society," *Amer. J. of Soc.,* 52 (Jan. 1947), 293–308. See also his book *The Little Community* (Chicago: University of Chicago Press, 1955).

SOCIALIZATION

16

The Self

George Herbert Mead

The self is not the body but arises in social experience. Explaining this insight is perhaps the greatest contribution of George Herbert Mead. Mead argues that the basic shape of our personalities is derived from the social groupings in which we live. Note, too, that even the qualities that distinguish each of us from others emerge only within a social community.

In our statement of the development of intelligence we have already suggested that the language process is essential for the development of the self. The self has a character which is different from that of the physiological organism proper. The self is something which has a development; it is not initially there, at birth, but arises in the process of social experience and activity, that is, develops in the given individual as a result of his relations to that

SOURCE: *Mind, Self and Society: From the Standpoint of a Social Behaviorist* by George Herbert Mead (Chicago: University of Chicago Press, 1934), pp. 135–42, 144, 149–56, 158, 162–64. Copyright © 1934 by The University of Chicago. All rights reserved. Reprinted with permission.

process as a whole and to other individuals within that process. . . .

We can distinguish very definitely between the self and the body. The body can be there and can operate in a very intelligent fashion without there being a self involved in the experience. The self has the characteristic that it is an object to itself, and that characteristic distinguishes it from other objects and from the body. It is perfectly true that the eye can see the foot, but it does not see the body as a whole. We cannot see our backs; we can feel certain portions of them, if we are agile, but we cannot get an experience of our whole body. There are, of course, experiences which are somewhat vague and difficult of location, but the bodily experiences are for us organized about a self. The foot and hand belong to the self. We can see our feet, especially if we look at them from the wrong end of an opera glass, as strange things which we have difficulty in recognizing as our own. The parts of the body are quite distinguishable from the self. We can lose parts of the body without any serious invasion of the self. The mere ability to experience different parts of the body is not different from the experience of a table. The table presents a different feel from what the hand does when one hand feels another, but it is an experience of something with which we come definitely into contact. The body does not experience itself as a whole, in the sense in which the self in some way enters into the experience of the self.

It is the characteristic of the self as an object to itself that I want to bring out. This characteristic is represented in the word "self," which is a reflexive, and indicates that which can be both subject and object. This type of object is essentially different from other objects, and in the past it has been distinguished as conscious, a term which indicates an experience with, an experience of, one's self. It was assumed that consciousness in some way carried this capacity of being an object to itself. In giving a behavioristic statement of consciousness we have to look for some sort of experience in which the physical organism can become an object to itself.[1]

When one is running to get away from someone who is chasing him, he is entirely occupied in this action, and his experience may be swallowed up in the objects about him, so that he has, at the time being, no consciousness of self at all. We must be, of course, very completely occupied to have that take place, but we can, I think, recognize that sort of a possible experience in which the self does not enter. We can, perhaps, get some light on that situation through those experiences in which in very intense action there appear in the experience of the individual, back of this intense action, memories and anticipations. Tolstoi as an officer in the war gives an account of having pictures of his past experience in the midst of his most intense action. There are also the pictures that flash into a person's

mind when he is drowning. In such instances there is a contrast between an experience that is absolutely wound up in outside activity in which the self as an object does not enter, and an activity of memory and imagination in which the self is the principal object. The self is then entirely distinguishable from an organism that is surrounded by things and acts with reference to things, including parts of its own body. These latter may be objects like other objects, but they are just objects out there in the field, and they do not involve a self that is an object to the organism. This is, I think, frequently overlooked. It is that fact which makes our anthropomorphic reconstructions of animal life so fallacious. How can an individual get outside himself (experientially) in such a way as to become an object to himself? This is the essential psychological problem of selfhood or of self-consciousness; and its solution is to be found by referring to the process of social conduct or activity in which the given person or individual is implicated. The apparatus of reason would not be complete unless it swept itself into its own analysis of the field of experience; or unless the individual brought himself into the same experiential field as that of the other individual selves in relation to whom he acts in any given social situation. Reason cannot become impersonal unless it takes an objective, nonaffective attitude toward itself; otherwise we have just consciousness, not *self*-consciousness. And it is necessary to rational conduct that the individual should thus take an objective, impersonal attitude toward himself, that he should become an object to himself. For the individual organism is obviously an essential and important fact or constituent element of the empirical situation in which it acts; and without taking objective account of itself as such, it cannot act intelligently, or rationally.

The individual experiences himself as such, not directly, but only indirectly, from the particular standpoints of other individual members of the same social group, or from the generalized standpoint of the social group as a whole to which he belongs. For he enters his own experience as a self or individual, not directly or immediately, not by becoming a subject to himself, but only insofar as he first becomes an object to himself just as other individuals are objects to him or in his experience; and he becomes an object to himself only by taking the attitudes of other individuals toward himself within a social environment or context of experience and behavior in which both he and they are involved.

The importance of what we term "communication" lies in the fact that it provides a form of behavior in which the organism or the individual may become an object to himself. It is that sort of communication which we have been discussing—not communication in the sense of the cluck of the hen to the chickens, or the bark of a wolf to the pack, or the lowing of a cow, but communication in the sense of significant symbols, communication which is directed not only to others but also to the individual himself. So far as that type of communication is a part of behavior it at least introduces a self. Of course, one may hear without listening; one may see things that he does not realize; do things that he is not really aware of. But it is where one does respond to that which he addresses to another and where that response of his own becomes a part of his conduct, where he not only hears himself but responds to himself, talks and replies to himself as truly as the other person replies to him, that we have behavior in which the individuals become objects to themselves. . . .

The self, as that which can be an object to itself, is essentially a social structure, and it arises in social experience. After a self has arisen, it in a certain sense provides for itself its social experiences, and so we can conceive of an absolutely solitary self. But it is impossible to conceive of a self arising outside of social experience. When it has arisen we can think of a person in solitary confinement for the rest of his life, but who still has himself as a companion, and is able to think and to converse with himself as he had communicated with others. That process to which I have just referred, of responding to one's self as another responds to it, taking part in one's own conversation with others, being aware of what one is saying and using that awareness of what one is saying to determine what one is going to say thereafter—that is a process

with which we are all familiar. We are continually following up our own address to other persons by an understanding of what we are saying, and using that understanding in the direction of our continued speech. We are finding out what we are going to say, what we are going to do, by saying and doing, and in the process we are continually controlling the process itself. In the conversation of gestures what we say calls out a certain response in another and that in turn changes our own action, so that we shift from what we started to do because of the reply the other makes. The conversation of gestures is the beginning of communication. The individual comes to carry on a conversation of gestures with himself. He says something, and that calls out a certain reply in himself which makes him change what he was going to say. One starts to say something, we will presume an unpleasant something, but when he starts to say it he realizes it is cruel. The effect on himself of what he is saying checks him; there is here a conversation of gestures between the individual and himself. We mean by significant speech that the action is one that affects the individual himself, and that the effect upon the individual himself is part of the intelligent carrying-out of the conversation with others. Now we, so to speak, amputate that social phase and dispense with it for the time being, so that one is talking to one's self as one would talk to another person.[2]

This process of abstraction cannot be carried on indefinitely. One inevitably seeks an audience, has to pour himself out to somebody. In reflective intelligence one thinks to act, and to act solely so that this action remains a part of a social process. Thinking becomes preparatory to social action. The very process of thinking is, of course, simply an inner conversation that goes on, but it is a conversation of gestures which in its completion implies the expression of that which one thinks to an audience. One separates the significance of what he is saying to others from the actual speech and gets it ready before saying it. He thinks it out, and perhaps writes it in the form of a book; but it is still a part of social intercourse in which one is addressing other persons and at the same time addressing one's self, and in which one controls the address to other persons by the response made to one's own gesture. That the person should be responding to himself is necessary to the self, and it is this sort of social conduct which provides behavior within which that self appears. I know of no other form of behavior than the linguistic in which the individual is an object to himself, and, so far as I can see, the individual is not a self in the reflexive sense unless he is an object to himself. It is this fact that gives a critical importance to communication, since this is a type of behavior in which the individual does so respond to himself.

We realize in everyday conduct and experience that an individual does not mean a great deal of what he is doing and saying. We frequently say that such an individual is not himself. We come away from an interview with a realization that we have left out important things, that there are parts of the self that did not get into what was said. What determines the amount of the self that gets into communication is the social experience itself. Of course, a good deal of the self does not need to get expression. We carry on a whole series of different relationships to different people. We are one thing to one man and another thing to another. There are parts of the self which exist only for the self in relationship to itself. We divide ourselves up in all sorts of different selves with reference to our acquaintances. We discuss politics with one and religion with another. There are all sorts of different selves answering to all sorts of different social reactions. It is the social process itself that is responsible for the appearance of the self; it is not there as a self apart from this type of experience.

A multiple personality is in a certain sense normal, as I have just pointed out. . . .

The unity and structure of the complete self reflects the unity and structure of the social process as a whole; and each of the elementary selves of which it is composed reflects the unity and structure of one of the various aspects of that process in which the individual is implicated. In other words, the various elementary selves which constitute, or are organized into, a complete self are the various aspects of the structure of that complete self an-

swering to the various aspects of the structure of the social process as a whole; the structure of the complete self is thus a reflection of the complete social process. The organization and unification of a social group is identical with the organization and unification of any one of the selves arising within the social process in which that group is engaged, or which it is carrying on.[3]

. . . Another set of background factors in the genesis of the self is represented in the activities of play and the game. . . . We find in children . . . imaginary companions which a good many children produce in their own experience. They organize in this way the responses which they call out in other persons and call out also in themselves. Of course, this playing with an imaginary companion is only a peculiarly interesting phase of ordinary play. Play in this sense, especially the stage which precedes the organized games, is a play at something. A child plays at being a mother, at being a teacher, at being a policeman; that is, it is taking different roles, as we say. We have something that suggests this in what we call the play of animals: A cat will play with her kittens, and dogs play with each other. Two dogs playing with each other will attack and defend, in a process which if carried through would amount to an actual fight. There is a combination of responses which checks the depth of the bite. But we do not have in such a situation the dogs taking a definite role in the sense that a child deliberately takes the role of another. This tendency on the part of children is what we are working with in the kindergarten where the roles which the children assume are made the basis for training. When a child does assume a role he has in himself the stimuli which call out that particular response or group of responses. He may, of course, run away when he is chased, as the dog does, or he may turn around and strike back just as the dog does in his play. But that is not the same as playing at something. Children get together to "play Indian." This means that the child has a certain set of stimuli that call out in itself the responses that they would call out in others, and which answer to an Indian. In the play period the child utilizes his own responses to these stimuli which he makes use of in building a self. The response which he has a tendency to make to these stimuli organizes them. He plays that he is, for instance, offering himself something, and he buys it; he gives a letter to himself and takes it away; he addresses himself as a parent, as a teacher; he arrests himself as a policeman. He has a set of stimuli which call out in himself the sort of responses they call out in others. He takes this group of responses and organizes them into a certain whole. Such is the simplest form of being another to one's self. It involves a temporal situation. The child says something in one character and responds in another character, and then his responding in another character is a stimulus to himself in the first character, and so the conversation goes on. A certain organized structure arises in him and in his other which replies to it, and these carry on the conversation of gestures between themselves.

If we contrast play with the situation in an organized game, we note the essential difference that the child who plays in a game must be ready to take the attitude of everyone else involved in that game, and that these different roles must have a definite relationship to each other. Taking a very simple game such as hide-and-seek, everyone with the exception of the one who is hiding is a person who is hunting. A child does not require more than the person who is hunted and the one who is hunting. If a child is playing in the first sense he just goes on playing, but there is no basic organization gained. In that early stage he passes from one to another just as a whim takes him. But in a game where a number of individuals are involved, then the child taking one role must be ready to take the role of everyone else. If he gets in a ball nine he must have the responses of each position involved in his own position. He must know what everyone else is going to do in order to carry out his own play. He has to take all of these roles. They do not all have to be present in consciousness at the same time, but at some moments he has to have three or four individuals present in his own attitude, such as the one who is going to throw the ball, the one who is going to catch it, and so on. These responses must be, in some degree, present in his own make-up. In the game, then, there is a set of responses of such others so organized that the attitude of one calls out the appropriate attitudes of the other.

This organization is put in the form of the rules of the game. Children take a great interest in rules. They make rules on the spot in order to help themselves out of difficulties. Part of the enjoyment of the game is to get these rules. Now, the rules are the set of responses which a particular attitude calls out. You can demand a certain response in others if you take a certain attitude. These responses are all in yourself as well. There you get an organized set of such responses as that to which I have referred, which is something more elaborate than the roles found in play. Here there is just a set of responses that follow on each other indefinitely. At such a stage we speak of a child as not yet having a fully developed self. The child responds in a fairly intelligent fashion to the immediate stimuli that come to him, but they are not organized. He does not organize his life as we would like to have him do, namely, as a whole. There is just a set of responses of the type of play. The child reacts to a certain stimulus, and the reaction is in himself that is called out in others, but he is not a whole self. In his game he has to have an organization of these roles; otherwise he cannot play the game. The game represents the passage in the life of the child from taking the role of others in play to the organized part that is essential to self-consciousness in the full sense of the term.

. . . The fundamental difference between the game and play is that in the former the child must have the attitude of all the others involved in that game. The attitudes of the other players which the participant assumes organize into a sort of unit, and it is that organization which controls the response of the individual. The illustration used was of a person playing baseball. Each one of his own acts is determined by his assumption of the action of the others who are playing the game. What he does is controlled by his being everyone else on that team, at least insofar as those attitudes affect his own particular response. We get then an "other" which is an organization of the attitudes of those involved in the same process.

The organized community or social group which gives to the individual his unity of self may be called "the generalized other." The attitude of the generalized other is the attitude of the whole community.[4] Thus, for example, in the case of such a social group as a ball team, the team is the generalized other insofar as it enters—as an organized process or social activity—into the experience of any one of the individual members of it.

If the given human individual is to develop a self in the fullest sense, it is not sufficient for him merely to take the attitudes of other human individuals toward himself and toward one another within the human social process, and to bring that social process as a whole into his individual experience merely in these terms: He must also, in the same way that he takes the attitudes of other individuals toward himself and toward one another, take their attitudes toward the various phases or aspects of the common social activity or set of social undertakings in which, as members of an organized society or social group, they are all engaged; and he must then, by generalizing these individual attitudes of that organized society or social group itself, as a whole, act toward different social projects which at any given time it is carrying out, or toward the various larger phases of the general social process which constitutes its life and of which these projects are specific manifestations. This getting of the broad activities of any given social whole or organized society as such within the experiential field of any one of the individuals involved or included in that whole is, in other words, the essential basis and prerequisite of the fullest development of that individual's self: Only insofar as he takes the attitudes of the organized social group to which he belongs toward the organized, cooperative social activity or set of such activities in which that group as such is engaged, does he develop a complete self or possess the sort of complete self he has developed. And on the other hand, the complex cooperative processes and activities and institutional functionings of organized human society are also possible only insofar as every individual involved in them or belonging to that society can take the general attitudes of all other such individuals with reference to these processes and activities and institutional functionings, and to the organized social whole of experiential relations and interactions thereby constituted—and can direct his own behavior accordingly.

It is in the form of the generalized other that the social process influences the behavior of the individuals involved in it and carrying it on, i.e., that the community exercises control over the conduct of its individual members; for it is in this form that the social process or community enters as a determining factor into the individual's thinking. In abstract thought the individual takes the attitude of the generalized other[5] toward himself, without reference to its expression in any particular other individuals; and in concrete thought he takes that attitude insofar as it is expressed in the attitudes toward his behavior of those other individuals with whom he is involved in the given social situation or act. But only by taking the attitude of the generalized other toward himself, in one or another of these ways, can he think at all; for only thus can thinking—or the internalized conversation of gestures which constitutes thinking—occur. And only through the taking by individuals of the attitude or attitudes of the generalized other toward themselves is the existence of a universe of discourse, as that system of common or social meanings which thinking presupposes at its context, rendered possible.

. . . I have pointed out, then, that there are two general stages in the full development of the self. At the first of these stages, the individual's self is considered simply by an organization of the particular attitudes of other individuals toward himself and toward one another in the specific social acts in which he participates with them. But at the second stage in the full development of the individual's self that self is constituted not only by an organization of these particular individual attitudes, but also by an organization of the social attitudes of the generalized other or the social group as a whole to which he belongs. . . . So the self reaches its full development by organizing these individual attitudes of others into the organized social or group attitudes, and by thus becoming an individual reflection of the general systematic pattern of social or group behavior in which it and the others are all involved—a pattern which enters as a whole into the individual's experience in terms of these organized group attitudes which, through the mechanism of his central nervous system, he takes toward himself, just as he takes the individual attitudes of others.

. . . A person is a personality because he belongs to a community, because he takes over the institutions of that community into his own conduct. He takes its language as a medium by which he gets his personality, and then through a process of taking the different roles that all the others furnish he comes to get the attitude of the members of the community. Such, in a certain sense, is the structure of a man's personality. There are certain common responses which each individual has toward certain common things, and insofar as those common responses are awakened in the individual when he is affecting other persons he arouses his own self. The structure, then, on which the self is built is this response which is common to all, for one has to be a member of a community to be a self. Such responses are abstract attitudes, but they constitute just what we term a man's character. They give him what we term his principles, the acknowledged attitudes of all members of the community toward what are the values of that community. He is putting himself in the place of the generalized other, which represents the organized responses of all the members of the group. It is that which guides conduct controlled by principles, and a person who has such an organized group of responses is a man whom we say has character, in the moral sense.

. . . I have so far emphasized what I have called the structures upon which the self is constructed, the framework of the self, as it were. Of course we are not only what is common to all: Each one of the selves is different from everyone else; but there has to be such a common structure as I have sketched in order that we may be members of a community at all. We cannot be ourselves unless we are also members in whom there is a community of attitudes which control the attitudes of all.

We cannot have rights unless we have common attitudes. That which we have acquired as self-conscious persons makes us such members of society and gives us selves. Selves can only exist in definite relationships to other selves. No hard-and-fast line can be drawn between our own selves and the selves of others, since our own selves exist and enter as such into our experience only insofar as the selves of others exist and enter as such into our experience also. The individual possesses a self only in relation to the selves of the other members of his social group; and the structure of his self expresses or reflects the general behavior pattern of this social group to which he belongs, just as does the structure of the self of every other individual belonging to this social group.

CRITICAL-THINKING QUESTIONS

1. How does Mead distinguish between body and the self? What makes this a radically social *view of the self?*

2. How is the self both a subject and an object to itself? How is the ability to assume "the role of the other" vital to our humanity?

3. The idea that socialization produces conformity is easy to understand; but how does Mead argue that individual distinctiveness is also a result of social experience?

NOTES

1. Man's behavior is such in his social group that he is able to become an object to himself, a fact which constitutes him a more advanced product of evolutionary development than are the lower animals. Fundamentally it is this social fact—and not his alleged possession of a soul or mind with which he, as an individual, has been mysteriously and supernaturally endowed, and with which the lower animals have not been endowed—that differentiates him from them.

2. It is generally recognized that the specifically social expressions of intelligence, or the exercise of what is often called "social intelligence," depend upon the given individual's ability to take the roles of, or "put himself in the place of," the other individuals implicated with him in given social situations; and upon his consequent sensitivity to their attitudes toward himself and toward one another. These specifically social expressions of intelligence, of course, acquire unique significance in

terms of our view that the whole nature of intelligence is social to the very core—that this putting of one's self in the places of others, this taking by one's self of their roles or attitudes, is not merely one of the various aspects or expressions of intelligence or intelligent behavior, but is the very essence of its character. Spearman's "X factor" in intelligence—the unknown factor which, according to him, intelligence contains—is simply (if our social theory of intelligence is correct) this ability of the intelligent individual to take the attitude of the other, or the attitudes of others, thus realizing the significations or grasping the meanings of the symbols or gestures in terms of which thinking proceeds; and thus being able to carry on with himself the internal conversation with these symbols or gestures which thinking involves.

3. The unity of the mind is not identical with the unity of the self. The unity of the self is constituted by the unity of the entire relational pattern of social behavior and experience in which the individual is implicated, and which is reflected in the structure of the self; but many of the aspects or features of this entire pattern do not enter into consciousness, so that the unity of the mind is in a sense an abstraction from the more inclusive unity of the self.

4. It is possible for inanimate objects, no less than for other human organisms, to form parts of the generalized and organized—the completely socialized—other for any given human individual, insofar as he responds to such objects socially or in a social fashion (by means of the mechanism of thought, the internalized conversation of gestures). Any thing—any object or set of objects, whether animate or inanimate, human or animal, or merely physical—toward which he acts, or to which he responds, socially, is an element in what for him is the generalized other; by taking the attitudes of which toward himself he becomes conscious of himself as an object or individual, and thus develops a self or personality. Thus, for example, the cult, in its primitive form, is merely the social embodiment of the relation between the given social group or community and its physical environment—an organized social means, adopted by the individual members of that group or community, of entering into social relations with that environment, or (in a sense) of carrying on conversations with it; and in this way that environment becomes part of the total generalized other for each of the individual members of the given social group or community.

5. We have said that the internal conversation of the individual with himself in terms of words or significant gestures—the conversation which constitutes the process or activity of thinking—is carried on by the individual from the standpoint of the "generalized other." And the more abstract that conversation is, the more abstract thinking happens to be, the further removed is the generalized other from any connection with particular individuals. It is especially in abstract thinking, that is to say, that the conversation involved is carried on by the individual with the generalized other, rather than with any particular individuals. Thus it is, for example, that abstract concepts are concepts stated in terms of the attitudes of the entire social group or community; they are stated on the basis of the individual's consciousness of the attitudes of the generalized other toward them, as a result of his taking these attitudes of the generalized other and then responding to them. And thus it is also that abstract propositions are stated in a form which anyone—any other intelligent individual—will accept.

Contemporary

17

Cognitive Development: Children's Understandings of Homelessness

Mary E. Walsh

Homeless people must confront society's perceptions of their worth as people. Since a significant share of the homeless are families, thousands of children experience radical shifts in their identity. In this excerpt, Mary E. Walsh shows that children struggle with the questions of who they are, why they have lost their homes, and what the future will bring. Children's explanations of their plight become more complex, painful, and angry as their level of cognitive development increases.

IAN

Ian, who is fifteen, and his family have a history of unstable living situations. He and his mother have been in shelters on five previous occasions. Before coming to the current shelter, they were living in a hotel. Ian has also spent time in a residential school for troubled youths. During this shelter stay, he and his mother are joined by his

SOURCE: *"Moving to Nowhere": Children's Stories of Homelessness* by Mary E. Walsh (Auburn House, an imprint of Greenwood Publishing Group Inc., Westport, CT, 1992), pp. 33–36, and 38–46 *passim*. Copyright © 1992 by Mary E. Walsh. Abridged and reprinted with permission of Greenwood Publishing Group, Inc. All rights reserved.

one-year-old brother, David. Ian's father abandoned his mother prior to his birth. The mother was recently separated from his stepfather of many years.

We came here about December, the end of December. Now it's the end of June. We didn't have anywhere to live. We lived at my grandfather's, but my grandparents don't get along with my mother, so they kicked her out. So we came here. We were living with them about two or three years. My grandparents are rich. Wicked rich. They're low. They're wicked low. We're living in a shelter and my mother's mother and father are so rich. I hate them. I didn't like them even when we were there.

Not really. They're not normal. They're crazy. They treat my mother like crap all the time. There was five of them, mother's two brothers live there, and they're like twenty-four and twenty-eight and like if they make a mess my mother has to clean it up. Even if my uncle makes a mess, and he doesn't clean it up, my mother gets screamed at for it. Because when they were little my mother took care of the whole family because my grandmother and my grandfather were out making money. So, my mother quit school in ninth grade. She was the oldest one. She quit to take care of the kids. But now my grandmother doesn't understand that they're all adults and they all can take care of themselves. My mom can't do everything for everybody all the time. My mother wants respect and she told them and they got mad and so we had to get out. They get mad at my mother for not having her own place.

My grandmother wouldn't come to the shelter for my birthday. I don't know why. My friends won't visit me here either. They think it's a bum shelter. Bums! I wouldn't live with bums. I wouldn't let my mother or my brother live with bums either. I'd rob somebody before I'd live with bums. Some of my friends think it's pretty bad, but not all of them. Most of them understand. But some, they're not really my friends but I see them sometimes, they don't understand. I don't want anybody to know that I live here. They know because I told my other friends that live in the projects, my kind of friends, but I don't hang around with those other kids. Like one day I was skating with my friends and those other friends are with my friends and they found out where I live. They didn't say nothing though. One time, one of my friends talked, like joking around, and I didn't like it. He said, "Oh, I'm going to go take a shower in the shelter." And I almost beat the crap out of him. I took a fit and started screaming and pushing. He told me to come on and I hit him in the head. And then he goes "I was just joking." Because he was in a school like I used to be in, so I made fun of that too, so he says, "you made fun of that school." So that's why he said about the shelter and stuff. . . .

I don't know why we ended up here and not in another apartment. Somehow my mother went on welfare and she can't get her certificate for an apartment. So she's waiting. She wouldn't have enough money to do it on her own. And my step-father can't do it because he's paying all the car payments. My grandfather won't lend my mother any money either. He lends everybody else a lot of money to get nice houses and stuff, but he can't lend my mother the money to get a three-bedroom apartment. My grandmother treats my mother bad. I don't know, I think she used to abuse my mother or something. I think. I'm not sure. I think so though. Because my Uncle Joe told me when they were little that it happened. When my mother was pregnant with me, my grandfather punched her because my grandmother didn't want her to be pregnant because she wasn't married. They're wicked Catholic. I don't believe in God because it's so dumb. Sitting there praying to a wall. He doesn't do nothing back. It's just dumb. I don't like God. I just don't like him. I hate going to church. It's boring. You have to sit and listen to a priest say stuff you don't even know about. It doesn't make sense. You don't learn nothing. I don't learn nothing from going to church. I haven't been to church in three years. I don't like God. There is no God. He's not even there.

Living here is not that bad. My mother met a good friend, she made a good friend here. They're best friends right now. She's best friends with her. Her friend does a lot for us and we do a lot for her. Like chores and stuff. . . .

There's nothing good about living here, I just have to. We'll probably be here about five more months. We can't get out sooner because welfare stinks. And for housing you can't get the certificate. We're just waiting. There's three-bedroom apartments that we need. They're in the projects right now, but don't ask me why we can't have it. I don't understand it. I don't understand how they work. I know about the three-bedroom apartments because of my friends live in the projects and there's nobody living in those apartments. Two apartments have three bedrooms. And they're painted and cleaned out and everything. They're nice. I don't really want to go to the projects. One project is okay, but definitely not the other one. It has gang fights, knife fights, all different gangs. It's like, if you're not Black or Puerto Rican you'll get killed. . . .

Before we came to live here, my mother told me we were coming to a shelter. I was mad. I had no idea what I was going to get into. I was mad because a shelter is bad. It's pretty poor, pretty low living in a shelter. I hate it. It's pretty low because it's like you can't afford to live anywhere else. We could afford it but we just can't find a place and stuff.

The rest of the people are here because they're poor. They're poor just like anybody else. Or their houses burned down or something. I don't really talk to them that much. I talk to some of them. I ignore everybody when they talk on the phone. I don't talk to them about living here. Before I came, I thought it was going to be like a house where we just had our own room, except my mother and my brother would share one room and I had my own room. It was like different apartments in a house, like a hotel. I thought it was going to be like that. And I found out we got only one room, and I got pretty mad again. I was mad because of one room. It's better having your own room. Privacy's better. You can't just share a room with your mother and brother. I was real mad. I didn't know what to do. I didn't want to get mad, but you get mad about certain things, like when someone takes something away from you. You know how to get mad about that. I didn't know how to get mad about this because this has never happened before. I don't know. I was mad at my mom and stuff for not working and not putting David into daycare. She said she won't. She said that's why I took fits, because she wasn't around me enough. She's messed up. I don't know. I think she's messed up, but just like any other mom. She was twenty-one when I was born. I'm fifteen now. . . .

The worst part of living in a shelter is just not having an apartment, not having your own house to live in. Having to live in a shelter, that's the worst part. . . .

COMMENTARY

In [his] attempts to make meaning out of the experience of becoming homeless, . . . Ian . . . struggle[s] with the question of why [he] ha[s] lost [his] home. [A younger child's] explanation is concrete and simple: His mother didn't have enough money to pay the bills. Ian, [an older child], offers a more complex explanation. He presents multiple, interrelated reasons for why his family eventually became homeless. He is aware that homelessness ultimately reflects larger problems and issues: family dysfunction, substance abuse, social welfare services, and housing policies. Ian continually reflect[s], as all children do, on the reasons for [his] homelessness.

A major part of children's stories of homelessness is the explanation they give to themselves and to others about how they lost their home. What are the reasons that homelessness happened to their family, in particular, and to other families more generally? How do the children make meaning out of what has happened to them? What is the story children tell themselves, not only about what is happening, but most critically, about why it is happening? Children have many stories about the causes of their homelessness. While all children are generally aware that they are living in a shelter because they lost their home, children differ from one another in terms of how they explain why that has happened to their family. Their understanding of why they came to be homeless or had to live in a shelter is quite clearly related to their level of cognitive development.

Preschoolers' Explanations

Preschool-aged children, whose thinking processes are not yet logical, are unable to reason in terms of cause and effect. While they may report a cause for particular events in their lives, they are unable to explain how the cause produced the event. They explain the connection between events in terms of associations. Instead of being able to describe how a specific event produced their homelessness, they present only a disjointed account of some events that are associated with, but not necessarily the primary cause of, their homelessness. Consequently, they present a fairly confused and disconnected account of why they had to move out of their home. They have bits and pieces of a story that do not form a cohesive explanation. In accounting for why they lost their home, some young children may describe an incident as causing their becoming homeless, although from an adult's perspective, the incident only happened to coincide with, but did not cause, the event.

For example, a six-year-old boy, whose family had lived in many shelters, described the first time they lost their home, when he was four years old, and moved into the Salvation Army shelter. He attributed the loss of the home to the appearance of new tenants on the doorstep:

Once we were living in our place and some people came up the front stairs with all their stuff like brooms and suitcases and stuff. And when they got up the stairs they was moving in. So we had to get out by the back door. They was moving in the front door. They needed a place to live. They came to where we was living and we had no place to go. So we went to the Sally. (Bobby)

Another child, who was five years old, attributed her coming to the shelter to the stove in their old house. Explained Doreen:

We lived in Chicago. Why I came to here is because we had another one and then we moved out of there. And then we moved out of the other one and then we moved here. We moved out of the other one because in the other one, the stove, my mother was burning the whole house maybe. It was the stove. We had to move here.

Rather than a specific incident, a feeling associated with the move, such as a like or dislike, may be viewed by some young children as the event that caused the loss of home. Many young children, for example, attribute their moving from their old home to the preference of the parent rather than the necessity of circumstances. Referring to his old house, Daniel, a four-year-old, insisted they had moved "because I didn't like it and Mommy and Daddy didn't like it either." Arthur, a five-year-old who had moved with his mother and three younger sisters from the South to the North, attributed their leaving their home to the mother's preference for living in a pretty place. "Momma say to come here because she want us to come here. Because she liked it here. Because it's pretty." Arthur's mother, on the other hand, reported that she moved away from an abusive husband and came north for better job opportunities.

While some young children propose only a single cause, others list multiple causes. They simply list these causes as separate events and do not explain any connections between these causes. A seven-year-old girl, for example, provided several reasons for the move, each of which were associated with the family's moving out of the apartment. However, the reasons are not linked together in a logical manner and are disjointed and confusing:

We're not living in our house now because when we used to live there the owner went away for twenty days and after twenty days he came back and he told us to get out. I got lead poison there. It's like when I was a baby I drank paint and I got sick. . . . So I got lead poisoning there so the guy that owned the house came back. And a girl said "Get out." My mom and my dad said, "You can't do that. We lived here, then you moved out, so you can't come back in here. Too bad." Me and my mom owned that house. Me and my dad and my mom and my two brothers. Me and my brothers put some of our money in. We had two hundred bucks and put some of our money in and my mom and my dad put some of their money in. Everybody in our family, but me and my sister, they put some money in. (Gertie)

Because children at this age cannot reason in a logical fashion—that is, they do not understand that causes produce necessary effects—they do not see the world as a predictable place. Things happen randomly and chaotically. The positive aspect of this way of thinking is that it provides children with the ability to view the world in a hopeful way. Anything can happen "by magic." For example, they can believe that they will "have a house next week" without thinking about how that is going to happen. On the other hand, children's perception of events as random and magical occurrences does not foster a sense of control over the events around them. If events unfold spontaneously with no cause or necessary effect, then children are powerless to regulate any of the happenings in their lives. They are simply victims of whatever the environment does to them. It is this sense of lack of control that pervades young children's stories of how they became homeless.

While young children have varied explanations for the causes of their homelessness, surprisingly few, if any, attribute the homelessness to something that they did or failed to do. By contrast, in other traumatic situations, for example being placed in foster care or losing a parent to death, young children are very likely to report that they are personally responsible. The egocentric thinking characteristic of this stage of cognitive development leads them to believe that their actions have more effect than is actually possible. Consequently, they are inclined to believe that they are the cause of bad events. For example, an eight-year-old who had been placed in foster care when she was five clung to her early beliefs and explained that "we went into foster care because my brother and me didn't keep our room neat, it was a mess. The social work lady went all over our house and took us. The social workers are the bad people. They're off us now so we can keep our room how we want" (Jamie).

By contrast, young children who lose their homes do not seem to blame themselves as individuals for becoming homeless. It seems that children perceive their role in family separations quite differently from their role in the loss of their home. At the core of family separations are interpersonal relationships, in which children are active participants. Children learn from an early age that in these relationships they have certain power. For example, a child learns the connection "I smile, they smile." Thus, if these relationships go bad, children find it easy to believe that they played a significant role. Becoming homeless appears to be viewed as an issue of household management, an aspect of life in which children play no role. Getting money, paying bills, finding an apartment, and the like are "the stuff mommies and daddies do." These household management tasks are taken care of externally, and they are foreign to children. Thus, young children may perceive themselves as powerless to control these events. It may be that in this way children are spared from attributing the loss of their home to themselves.

School-aged Children's Explanations

In contrast to younger children, school-aged children between the ages of approximately seven and twelve do provide logically coherent explanations for their becoming homeless. Their explanations are likely to involve one or a few concrete events that they perceive as directly resulting in their homelessness, such as "the ceiling fell in," "we ran out of money," "boys hung around our house," or "Mom said to move." Unlike the case with younger children, these events are not merely associated with homelessness. Children at this age can provide some explanation for how each of these events led to homelessness. Some children focus on a single reason for their becoming homeless, such as "the owner kicked us out," while others offer multiple reasons for the family's becoming homeless.

Often children at this age offer a list of reasons. For example, after describing how her family had made many moves into "better apartments" within the city in order to get away from "bad apartments" in drug-infested areas, ten-year-old Isabella explained:

The last apartment was perfect, at first. But then the rain came in the spring and the ceiling got wet and fell down. And that's how we found out it had lead in the paint. That's bad. There was roaches too. I would kill them every time I see them. So my mother came here to the shelter to see if we could get in.

Isabella further explained that their homelessness also resulted from an inability to pay for another apartment, the presence of drugs in their previous neighborhoods, small apartments being inadequate for her family's size, and a landlord who was "very bad," having "lied to us about the lead paint." Isabella clearly attributed her homelessness to multiple causes.

While children in this stage can explain how each separate event or condition in and of itself led to homelessness, they are not usually able to explain how all these events are interconnected. Isabella could provide a string of causes and the specific effect of each, yet she was unable to articulate how these multiple causes were interrelated, for example, that lack of money made it difficult to get a good-sized, clean apartment in a safe neighborhood.

At this stage, the causes children offer are still concrete, but they are less individualistic and somewhat more general than those of younger children. For example, while a five-year-old might suggest that they are homeless "because my aunt Lisa kicked us out," school-aged children explain that "you can't stay with relatives because the landlord says there's too many people in the apartment." Children at this stage are also able to distinguish between different types of reasons, for example, momentary and more enduring causes. Tucker reported:

We came to the shelter because we moved up to our other grandmother's and they kicked us out! Well, our other grandmother didn't kind of kick us out, she just said "You gotta learn how to stay on your own. Your mother has to learn how to stay on her own, stand on her own feet, because soon I'm going to die and I'm not going to be there to help her." So that's why we came to the shelter.

Tucker realized that, while the immediate cause was his grandmother's order to get out, the more enduring cause was his mother's inability to manage on her own.

As a further extension of the ability to think in more general and less egocentric terms, children at this age are likely to recognize fundamental causes of homelessness rather than a series of discrete or distinct causes. For example, while school-aged children give many and diverse reasons for becoming homeless, nearly all include lack of money as one of those reasons. These children are quite aware that homelessness is a condition that affects not only their family, but many families, and that one cause for almost every family's homelessness is not having enough money to pay for a house.

Another, more general cause recognized by children this age is a "bad neighborhood," where there are a lot of problems, for example, drugs, violence, or substandard housing. They are beginning to recognize that there are better and worse places to live, and that they were living in the latter. While they cannot articulate the precise connection, they are aware that problems in finding a safe and adequate place to live are somehow related to their being homeless. A ten-year-old recalled:

First we lived on Westwood and then Main and then Central. We moved from Westwood because there was a lot of bad things in Westwood—a lot of drugs and bad things. And my mother then moved to Main and she had to move from Main because it was too stretchy, it was too little, the apartment, all our furniture wouldn't fit and from Main she moved to Central and Central was perfect, but one day the ceiling fell off on my house. (Isabella)

In a similar manner, children at this age also begin to recognize that the rules of the larger system play some role in their becoming homeless and in their ability to get another house. While they cannot explain all the pieces in a cohesive manner, some do understand that being homeless will actually help them to get better and more affordable housing. Some children in this age group talk about getting Section 8, the government subsidy program, and explain that this is why people come to the shelter. They do not completely understand the concept of Section 8, but they possess essential pieces of information about it, such as it makes an apartment cost less.

Adolescents' Explanations

Adolescents report the reasons for their becoming homeless in a much more complex manner. Like the seven- to twelve-year-olds, they are very aware of the concrete indicators, for example, roaches, broken glass, dirt, and violence in their neighborhoods. They are also able to articulate classes of causes, such as drugs or lack of money. However, they are also able to see the interconnections between these causes and to conceptualize the whole picture. While their story may leave some loose ends, it is evident that they do have some sense that a "leaky roof," "too many roaches," "drugs all over our neighborhood," "a landlord who wouldn't do anything," and "not enough money" are causes that are somehow linked to one another. A twelve-year-old whose family had moved from another country described the complex interplay of reasons:

We had to move because the owner kicked us out . . . because my mother didn't have a lot of money to pay the house. There was four of us living in the apartment. She run out of money because she had to stop working because she was going to have a baby. And the money she had to pay for rent became higher, became 700 dollars. It used to be four or five or something like that. The place we were living was small because when we came here we didn't have a lot of money to get a big place. There was only three rooms. It had one bedroom and one side there was the kitchen and the other side there was the living room. It was pretty crowded. Well, one day, the owner came to our house and said that we had to move because we didn't pay and that he'll meet us at court. We went to court but the owner chickened out. He wasn't there. And then these two people, workers, helped us and said that we were going to move to a shelter so that we could get a cheaper, bigger apartment later on. The shelter would help us to get a paper to get a new apartment. (Raymond)

Beginning to see that the causes of homelessness are somehow interconnected, that causes are feeding into one another in a circular fashion, also begins to sharpen children's sense of awareness of the trap they are in. The interdependence of causes is often described in stories in which children see no way out. While children at this age do not specifically articulate the concept of being trapped, their stories may describe situations for which they perceive no solutions. The story of a twelve-year-old boy explaining how he and his mother repeatedly became homeless described the trap the child felt:

We were in a shelter because we didn't have enough money. The place I was at was in—a school for bad kids—was having my mom give up all her money that she had and she got, so she quit her job. Then we moved to the shelter, and then she got another job, and then we moved to the trailer park. That was the best place we ever lived because it was our own house. But then we couldn't stay living in there because we couldn't make any more payments. And we were far away from my mom's job, because she was working at the same job. The place she worked was far away. When I heard we had to move from there I didn't say anything. I never say anything. (Ryan)

Children at this stage are not only aware of the complexity of reasons by which they became homeless but also are aware of the complexity and subtleties of the bureaucratic system. They come to know that the system's rules operate in an awkward and often inflexible manner, and that they must bend to the demands of the system in order to get what they need. For example, Dana and Haydn, who have been living in a suburb with their father, both realize that their mother, who was just released from jail, cannot get subsidized housing, which she desperately needs, unless her children are living with her in the shelter. While they are angry at the way the system works, they are realistic about doing what they must to help their mother.

At this stage, children also may attribute some of the reasons for their homelessness to their parents. They believe that if their parents had acted in a different manner, they would not have to be homeless. In addition, they may offer an understanding of psychological contributors to their parents' situation. Amidst Ian's list of multiple and interacting reasons for homelessness (a welfare system that "stinks," uncaring grandparents, mother's divorce from stepfather), he included his impression that his mother "wasn't around me enough." He then concluded, "I think she's messed up, but just like any other mom."

CRITICAL-THINKING QUESTIONS

1. What kinds of problems has Ian encountered? How does he explain his homelessness?

2. How do preschoolers, school-aged children,

and adolescents differ in their understandings of homelessness?

3. How does homelessness affect children's socialization in general? And their cognitive development in particular?

SOCIALIZATION

Cross-Cultural

18

Growing Up on the Streets

Elijah Anderson

How does persistent poverty, coupled to problems of crime and drug abuse, affect the social-ization process? In this selection, Elijah Anderson shows that even in poor communities there are competing versions of the right ways to live. Note, in his account of socialization in an African-American neighborhood in Philadelphia, the clash of values between the "old heads," who work to preserve traditional work and family beliefs, and the "new old heads," who en-gage in illegal behavior.

OF "OLD HEADS" AND YOUNG BOYS

The relationship between "old heads" and young boys represents an important institution of the tra-ditional black community. It has always been a central aspect of the social organization of North-ton, assisting the transition of young men from boyhood to manhood, from idle youth to stable

SOURCE: *Streetwise: Race, Class, and Change in an Ur-ban Community* by Elijah Anderson (Chicago: University of Chicago Press, 1990), pp. 102–11. Copyright © 1990 by The University of Chicago. All rights reserved. Reprinted with per-mission.

employment and participation in the regular man-ufacturing economy. The old head's acknowl-edged role was to teach, support, encourage, and in effect socialize young men to meet their re-sponsibilities with regard to the work ethic, fam-ily life, the law, and decency. But as meaningful employment has become increasingly scarce, drugs more accessible, and crime a way of life for many young black men, this institution has under-gone stress and significant change.

An old head was a man of stable means who was strongly committed to family life, to church, and, most important, to passing on his philosophy, developed through his own rewarding experience with work, to young boys he found worthy. He personified the work ethic and equated it with value and high standards of morality; in his eyes a workingman was a good, decent individual. . . .

The old head was a kind of guidance counselor and moral cheerleader who preached anticrime and antitrouble messages to his charges. Encouraging boys to work and make something of themselves, he would try to set a good example by living, as best he could, a stable, decent, worry-free life. His constant refrain was "Get yourself a trade, son," or "Do something with your life," or "Make something out of yourself." Displaying initiative, diligence, and pride, as a prime role model of the community, he lived "to have something," usually something material, though an intact nuclear family counted for much in the picture he painted. On the corners and in the alleys of Northton, he would point to others as examples of how hard work and decency could pay off. He might advise young boys to "pattern yourself after him." In these conversations and lectures, he would express great pride in his own outstanding work record, punctuality, good credit rating, and anything else reflecting his commitment to honesty, independence, hard work, and family values.

The old head could be a minister, a deacon in the church, a local policeman, a favorite teacher, an athletic coach, or a street corner man. He could be the uncle or even the father of a member of the local group of young boys. Very often the old head acted as surrogate father for those he considered in need of such attention. A youth in trouble would sometimes discuss his problem with an old head before going to his own father, if he had one, and the old head would be ready with a helping hand, sometimes a loan for a worthy purpose. . . .

In the old days young boys would gather around an old head on a street corner or after Sunday school to listen to the witty conversation and moral tales on hard work and decency. They truly felt they were learning something worthwhile from someone they could look up to and respect. One of the primary messages of the old head was about good manners and the value of hard work: how to dress for a job interview and deal with a prospec-

tive employer, how to work, and how to keep the job. Through stories, jokes, and conversation, the old head would convey his conception of the "tricks of the trade.". . .

Within the traditional black community, the old head [who, of course, can be a woman as well as a man] served as an important link to the more privileged classes. Often he could be seen pointing out the big shots and speaking about them in glowing terms. Through his example, he offered support to both the local and the wider systems of social stratification and inspired his boys to negotiate them through legitimate means. . . .

In the traditional black community, old heads had such legitimacy on the ghetto streets that they could chastise unknown boys and girls and expect the parents' support. . . . But today, given the high degree of mobility, segmentation, and anonymity within the local black community, which has been exacerbated by persistent poverty and crime combined with an elaborate drug culture, the young people are viewed as unpredictable and threatening. All of this encourages a very cautious approach to strange young people in Northton, if not total avoidance. As one middle-aged old head told me:

I have to watch what I do today, because you just don't know what you gettin' into when you speak to these youngsters. You could get cussed out or cut up. You just don't know, and many of the old heads are not sayin' anything.

The greatest complaint of female old heads is that young girls "don't listen" or that "they've changed so." So many young girls, they say, fail to ask advice or to heed it when it is offered gratuitously by "square old ladies." When rebuffed, they are inclined to call the younger women "fast" or "children who think they're grown." Such derisive comments seem warranted when they see girls on the streets with children in tow or answering a young man's call of "Hey, baby!" from across the street. Indeed, the female old heads know all about such young women, and they affirm their own identities as they discredit others. Likewise many of these young people, in self-defense, work to discredit older people at every turn. They tend to be socially disconnected; they may lack a father in the home or simply have an ineffectual family unit. Thus they have little sense of the values the old heads so badly want them to learn and adopt.

So female olds heads have also become more reticent. They keep out of the business of others. And where there is such disengagement by people who could be important role models, there is an even greater tendency for young women to lose their constraint against seriously deviant behavior, from having babies out of wedlock to experimenting with drugs.

THE NEW "OLD HEADS"

With the influx of the drug culture, new role models are being created. Engaged in fierce competition with the traditional old head—the standard-bearer of yesterday who worked hard in the factories and mills, and in the homes of the well-to-do, coming to value that way of life—the emerging old head is younger and may be the product of a street gang, making money fast and scorning the law and traditional values. If he works, he does so grudgingly. He makes ends meet through the underground economy, dabbling in the drug trade or participating full time. As far as family life goes, he shuns the traditional father's role. His is a "get over" mentality, and as the traditional old heads comment, he is out to beat the next fellow.

The new model for girls is often involved in the "high life" and hangs with her daytime group of friends, occasionally "getting high." She spends her meager income mainly on herself, buying fancy clothes, drugs, and alcohol. Like other members of her peer group, she may have one or two young children, whom she may dress up expensively as they compete over whose baby is the cutest. The babies' fathers may not be immediately involved in their lives, or they may be around part time. The woman may work at a local hospital or fast-food restaurant or she may be on welfare, but she generally has her hands full with child care, social activities, and men.

These emerging figures are in many respects the antithesis of the traditional old heads. The man derides family values and takes little responsibility for the family's financial welfare. He feels hardly any obligation to his string of women and the children he has fathered. In fact he considers it a measure of success if he can get away without being held legally accountable for his out-of-wedlock children. To his hustling mentality, generosity is a weakness. Given his unstable financial situation, he feels used when confronted with the prospect of taking care of someone else.

For him women are so many conquests, whose favors are obtained by "running a game," feigning to love and care for them to get what he wants, only to discard them at the slightest adversity. Self-aggrandizement consumes his whole being and is expressed in his penchant for a glamorous lifestyle, fine clothes, and fancy cars. On the corner he attempts to influence others by displaying the trappings of success. Eagerly awaiting his message are the young unemployed black men, demoralized by a hopeless financial situation but inclined to look up to this figure and, if they can, to emulate him. But for them broken lives and even early death may be in store. As one traditional old head commented:

See, when these young kids, especially these thirteen- and fourteen-year-olds, see, we got to get to them to let them know that that drug dealer you see riding down the street today in the Mercedes-Benz, next week you might read about him going to the cemetery, or in prison. We got to get to them and let them know this. Because what is happening is, we find these drug dealers, these kids on the corner, ten, twelve, they come from poverty-stricken families, things are going bad, they don't know half the time whether they gon' eat, what not gon' happen. So they see Joe Doe come by, maybe five or six years older than them. Joe Doe driving a new car. You know, he coming around, a group of guys coming around, and they look at 'em, and they say, "Wow, there go so and so there." He's down [hip], he got all the gold chains, and he got a big role of paper [money] on him, so they thinking, hey, I can do some of this too. And they go into it.

Now, I know, in a particular neighborhood, the young boys got a drug house in the area. So what the young boys doin', the young boys not selling dope, right? His father don't know this, but a lot of people had to get together and tell his father what was happenin'. The drug house got him watchin' and directin' company [customers]. He standin' on the corner, they payin' him like $50 a day, and that's big money to a kid like twelve or thirteen years old. Stand on the corner and tell somebody to come down to this house down here, that we dealing here. Stand on the corner and tell us when the police is coming. Now, this the kind of stuff that is happening.

For females the high life, welfare, prostitution, single parenthood, and crack addiction await. The high life holds out thrills for young girls, many of whom also seek independence from households with their mothers and sisters and brothers. Involved in sexually active peer groups, many settle for babies and participate in status games for which a "prize"—a cute baby—is the price of admission. They often act like adults too soon, coveting the grown-up life but unable to handle so much of it.

Awaiting them are the young male hipsters, who are there to trick them into "adulthood," into having "my baby," and leaving home and "be on your own." But this notion of success is little more than a dream that is seldom realized; it gets worked out in the local tenements among young children, meager resources, sometimes drugs, and a further need for "a good time." As such role models proliferate on the streets and in the homes of the community, they blur the line between themselves and the traditional old heads. Many of the young people fail to draw a distinction, having never known any attractive old heads other than those they now see, who provide a limited outlook. Consequently those who are looking for direction to achieve a more conventional life have little direct personal support.

AN OLD HEAD'S REACTION

But within the Northton community Tyrone Pitts, a traditional old head who has lived there for more than twenty years, is determined to make a difference. He lives on the boundary of the Village and has been much involved in local community life. Like other traditional old heads, he is concerned about his neighborhood; but Mr. Pitts has become so concerned that he has begun to engage in direct action against drugs in the local community. The following account is based on my interview with Mr. Pitts, edited and condensed into a narrative:

I had five teams, see. My football team. I was losing my players. Quarterback on crack, and I didn't know it. He didn't know what he was doing. See, I'm standing there one Saturday, telling him to do a running play, and he passing. I thought it was me. So I call it again, same thing happen. I call him over and ask if he's out of his mind. And one of the guys on the team says, "You know, Mr. Pitts, he's on that crack. He don't know what you talking about." That was in the winter. Then in the summer my baseball team, we getting' ready to have a championship baseball game. And one of my best players, he came but he was bombed out. My baseball pitcher got hooked on it. He was one of my best pitchers. This was my fourteen- to sixteen-year-old group. And this was what made me really start looking around. And then it start dawning on me, you know, what kind of problem I had.

So I went and started after-school drug and alcohol awareness [programs] and an after-school AIDS awareness, and after-school tutoring. I began to feel these things going on. So I began to start these things in the high school.

Then I looked around, and three or four of my nieces and nephews got hooked. And they got to robbing the family, you know. Yeah, I started to become very aware that it was just such a terrible problem all over. It was just frightening, all through the family, all over. It really got to me. And I didn't see no other leadership. No nothing. Nothing else happening. You know, I had decided I'd do something about this. I couldn't just let it happen like that. So, I'm gon' turn this energy to doing something, instead of just talking about it. Business to be done now. Ballplayers, nephews, nieces. Every time I look up I say, "Hey, wait a minute. This was one of my favorite kids here." I just had to just admit to myself that if you don't do nothing about it, then you gon' have to take the consequences.

I said, "Where's the leadership?" No one was around. Seem like the youth have taken on false opinions, like gold, funny TV shows, and dancing with any kind of myths. No concerns about education or survival of race. No recollection of history at all. Then on top of it all, drugs. To me this is more frightening than anything I've seen, you know. I mean like what's been dealt to us [blacks]. Lynchings, you know, we could deal with. That inspired us to fight more. That got us together. We weren't taking it. We could handle open affronts to us. But this thing [drugs] has everyone doing things that are really opposite to all we've ever been about.

Northton against Drugs is total reaction. It is a reaction out of frustration at seeing that nobody is in charge, and that somebody has to take charge again. We waiting on young people to say, "We not gon' involve ourselves [with drugs]." We looked up and seen they were being very passive about all this. From an older adult point of view, we had to take over the fight. Old heads had to reappear again. They had normal old heads in the sense of being ten to fifteen years older than the kids. Well these [Northton against Drugs] activists are almost thirty years older. See, the new [traditional old heads] batch didn't appear. There is a gap. A whole group did not appear. They didn't take the baton; that group [cohort] would now be about thirty years old. But they are the problem, see. The new old heads are these hoodlums. There is a gap in the leadership. The new old heads are not doing their parts. They are not doing anything. So the old old heads in fact have to do a double stint.

This was about two and a half years ago. First we were just trying to get them [drug dealers] off the corner of Spaulding Street. We had to get the neighbors to see there was no need to fear them, to get rid of the myth that we [the community] are afraid of them. You have to show them how tough we are. The little frightened fifth-grade dropout kids [grown up to be drug dealers]. They are using people's [neighbors'] fear as one of their weapons. We had to stop that.

The second thing is that you have to get everyone who has any gumption left in them to get out and fight. We have to get them [drug dealers] off the corner. You must force the police to do their job. See, the police who know that taxpayers are there [on the corner watching] have to behave differently. See, they were under the impression that didn't nobody black care. I've heard them [police] say that. They say, "What the heck? Don't seem like they care. Their own race don't care." But now we got the senators, the governor. See, all them people have come in. See some black people care. They really have started to react to our tactics. So we've been able to get really enthusiastic. The district attorney, U.S. senator, the governor was out. We've shook them all up.

There are old heads, and then there are bald-head old heads. We have to do the same battle we fought before. Before, we were doing it with anger and enthusiasm [1960s], with hope for the future. Now we are doing it because we ain't got no choice. We are the last line of defense. After this there's pure death [of our community]. That's why we don't mind stepping into the teeth of it. If we don't do that, then there is no hope for anything else. In our group, they come from all walks of life. Every one of them has a job; they know how to keep a job. Eight hours on the job and then seven more in the street, at night [vigils]. They range from semiprofessional to some who

are grandmothers [female old heads] who have to work and take care of grandchildren too [because daughters are on crack]. Bus drivers, parking-lot attendants, engineers, teachers, barbers, ministers, and restaurant owners, Village people, and we got Catholic sisters, priests. All kinds of people. The [drug] problem brought all kinds of people together. Black, white, Spanish, and Chinese together. It's a total rainbow coalition. We got a few yuppies in it too. We got some [white] factory workers from Arrington [Irish working-class neighborhood], some police officers, vets. You name a profession, and it's probably represented. Because we got over a thousand people [citywide]. See, this is what we do. We have about forty-five people. We have policemen. We [Northton against Drugs] pick a drug area that's really heavily infested. We go from our list and find a typical crack house. [We] block the corners, block the streets. Citizens and neighbors. We stand out there and shout. We have on our white hats [hard hats], our flashlights and bullhorns. We really dressed like a army. We [with the police] lock up the people coming by in cars buying [drugs]. We let some [our] people buy in the car. Then we have walkie-talkies and we call down the street and give the next person the license number. They stop the car. Take the car and the driver. That's been a big tactic. We just did one last night. We had nine cars last night. We lock up dealers that are selling. We stand in front of crack houses and shout 'em down. Tell 'em to come out. We gon' stay there until they stop selling poison to our children. We stay all night. Inside the crack house we find filth, dirt, no kind of living order. Piss in a bucket. Shit in the bucket. No running water. They steal the lights [electricity] from next door; it's usually an abandoned house. Matches all around.

In some cases we find small children, from one year to eight or nine. The mother brings them because she's on crack. The kids are out there. Hungry. It's just one of the worse sights you ever seen. Sometimes we catch them in the act, laying out, engaging in sex. It's unbelievable.

Then after we raid it [the crack house], we board it up. Soon as the police take them away, we start nailing it up. We put two-by-fours up and plywood boards, and we cement it. We seal it up right away, that night. And when they [drug dealers and customers] get back, they can't get back in there. Police arrest people on the spot. We bricked up twelve crack houses in Northton so far. When we finish with one, we look for the next one. We have a list. Now we teaching other neighborhoods to do the same thing. People think we supposed to stand by and just let them [drug dealers] do it, you know. I won't say it [drugs] won't win, but it won't win with me doing nothing [to fight back]. Its gon' have to catch me. We bust corner guys, alleys, houses. We search them out. We put heat on them. And they never seen no one come after them. They used to cops backing up from them. They teenagers up to thirty years old. This the group that was raised and never had to worry about discipline— you know what I mean. They didn't have any old heads telling them what to do. See, we had old heads [in the old days]. They took an interest in us. All that's gone now. The [young boys] try to go for bad, thinking teachers are afraid of them. They think everybody's afraid of them.

The old heads used to make us play ball, go to school, and tell us about athletes that made it, about jobs, and then take us to their jobs. But that left. They made us take responsibility for the community and one another. They showed wisdom when they talked to us. And I'm just doing what they showed me. I'm doing what they taught me to do. But see, after me, didn't none come around. We missed the other batch. I'm just doing the old head job, making as many as I can. I'm one of the dinosaurs, out of step with everybody.

Tyrone Pitts and others like him may manage to curb some of the drug activity within Northton and other areas of Eastern City. Northton against Drugs has even attracted the elements of the Village community, people who might find themselves at odds with Mr. Pitts on certain issues; but they agree profoundly on the issue of drugs. These are positive relationships. Together, through their direct actions, they put drug dealers and users under increasing pressure, driving the drug dealing from one area to the next. As they organize the heretofore passive old head contingent, including numerous frustrated and tired grandmothers who are pushed into service to raise a new generation, certain segments of the community become energized. They hold night vigils, and public officials begin to show interest in their activities, at times perhaps simply looking for publicity photos, at times delivering substantial resources to help such organizations help themselves.

In response to such campaigns, great numbers of local youths pause and think twice about trying drugs or other self-defeating behavior. But drug dealers also become more creative, responding to an important need of the local underclass—employment. The drug dealers promise money and the material "good life" where for many there is little hope. Hence there seems to be an endless supply of youths who are attracted by an often deadly game

of "follow the leader." As one goes out of commission, another is more than ready to take his place.

But, with the aid of the Tyrone Pittses of the world, traditional old heads, many of whom have taken their leave over the years, become emboldened. They come out of the woodwork to encourage once again a value system that emphasizes hard work, family life, and church. And this turn of events is positive indeed.

But regardless of their own values, many disadvantaged young blacks living in the ghetto of Northton find themselves surrounded by a complex world that seems arbitrary and unforgiving. Major changes in the regular economy, including cybernetics and the automation of industry, the decline of high-paying industrial jobs, and the rise of a service industry whose lowest levels pay only subsistence wages—combined with the massive influx of drugs into the local community—have exacerbated social breakdown. As inner-city manufacturing jobs have declined, the poorest segments of the community have yet to make an effective adjustment to this reality, and the underground economy competes effectively with the regular job market. All of this has undermined traditional social networks that once brought youths into the world of legitimate work and family life.

A good job is important to anyone, but particularly to someone trying to establish a family and become a productive citizen. What constitutes a "good job"? Thirty years ago, a black migrant from the South could find a job in a factory and take home about $100 a week, amounting to some $5,000 a year. This is equal to approximately $22,000 in today's dollars. In those days a man of the working class could look forward to raising a family with little financial strain. Today unskilled jobs with salaries even approaching this figure are scarce. Good jobs do exist in offices, hospitals, factories, and other large institutions that provide not only good pay but also increasingly important health care and other benefits. But since these jobs require training and are increasingly located in the suburbs—far from Northton and other inner-city areas—many young black men instead work at fast-food restaurants and make $5,000 to $8,500 a year, an amount that would not encourage any responsible person to try to establish a family.

When no good jobs are available the work ethic loses its force, for there is a basic incompatibility between theory and reality. However, some leaders in Northton continue to believe in the infinite availability of work in the traditional sense—high-paying jobs that require little training and skill. These are the words of the minister of a local congregation, who is a part-time taxi driver:

There are jobs out there for people who want to work. It may not be just what they want, but there is work to be done if you want it bad enough. Honest and honorable work. Something has happened to our community. Now you see a lot more violence than ever before. The drugs are everywhere, taking over our neighborhoods. A lot of our young people don't respect themselves today. Many of them don't know the value of work. Why, when I was growing up, the grown-ups taught us the value of work. I have a deep respect for it. Any man should want to work hard, for dignity comes with a job that enables a man to provide for his family.

But because of the lack of jobs and the seductive pull of the underground economy, the youngsters the minister preaches to do not believe him. His message falls on deaf ears, and his example is not trusted. Unemployed young men say, "You have to know someone." The common story is that you put in your application, but "you don't hear anything." But even when he knows "someone," the employment problems of a black youth are complicated by prejudice and by distrust about whether he will be a good worker who can be effectively managed. If the worker proves unmanageable, erratic, or unreliable, then the sponsor, who is likely to fit the traditional old head model, "looks bad" and worries about being "messed up" by his own helping efforts. Sponsors thus husband their reputations and limit their recommendations of those who seem the least bit marginal. Hence, increasing numbers of hard-core unemployed black youth have little use for the traditional old

head, and the old heads have even less respect for them.

To be sure, there are varying conceptions of work in Northton, and whether a person holds one or another of these conceptions may very well relate to his own place in the world of employment, particularly whether or not he holds a good job. Many of the employed consider the jobless to be personally at fault, their conditions the result of their own character flaws—a comfortable perspective. Those without jobs, on the other hand, are inclined to talk about how tough it is for young black men and women. These varying conceptions are voiced in charges and countercharges at local barbershops, taverns, and street corners, pitting one segment of the community against the other. Northton suffers from a host of strains, one being the profound incomparability between the newly emerging service economy and its potential workers. One strongly related and devastating effect is the perceptible breakdown of the family structure of poor people in Northton. Nowhere are the human consequences of persistent ghetto poverty better illustrated than in the social dynamics of teenage sexual behavior and pregnancy.

CRITICAL-THINKING QUESTIONS

1. How does the "new old head" differ from the traditional "old head" in terms of values, work, and attitudes about women and the family?
2. How have "old heads" tried to curb the influence of "new old heads" in the community?
3. How often, during the last few months, have you read articles, watched news reports, or heard discussions about urban communities—in predominantly minority neighborhoods—that reflect the traditional "old head" values of socialization? If such coverage has been rare, why do you think this is the case?

SOCIAL INTERACTION IN EVERYDAY LIFE

Classic

19

The Dyad and the Triad

Georg Simmel

Sometimes called the "Freud of sociology," Georg Simmel explored many of the intricate details of everyday life with a keen perceptiveness. In this selection, Simmel describes the distinctive qualities of human relationships with two members (the dyad) and three members (the triad).

THE DYAD

Everyday experiences show the specific character that a relationship attains by the fact that only two elements participate in it. A common fate or enterprise, an agreement or secret between two persons, ties each of them in a very different manner than if even only three have a part in it. This is perhaps most characteristic of the secret. General experience seems to indicate that this minimum of two, with which the secret ceases to be the property of the one individual, is at the same time the maximum at which its preservation is relatively secure. . . .

The social structure here rests immediately on the one and on the other of the two, and the secession of either would destroy the whole. The dyad, therefore, does not attain that super-personal life which the individual feels to be independent of himself. As soon, however, as there is a sociation of three, a group continues to exist even in case one of the members drops out.

. . . Neither of the two members can hide what he has done behind the group, nor hold the group responsible for what he has failed to do. Here the

SOURCE: *The Sociology of Georg Simmel,* trans. and ed. by Kurt H. Wolff. Copyright © 1950, renewed 1978 by The Free Press. Reprinted with permission of The Free Press, a Member of Paramount Publishing.

forces with which the group surpasses the individual—indefinitely and partially, to be sure, but yet quite perceptibly—cannot compensate for individual inadequacies, as they can in larger groups. There are many respects in which two united individuals accomplish more than two isolated individuals. Nevertheless, the decisive characteristic of the dyad is that each of the two must actually accomplish something, and that in case of failure only the other remains—not a super-individual force, as prevails in a group even of three.

. . . Precisely the fact that each of the two knows that he can depend only upon the other and on nobody else, gives the dyad a special consecration—as is seen in marriage and friendship, but also in more external associations, including political ones, that consist of two groups. In respect to its sociological destiny and in regard to any other destiny that depends on it, the dyadic element is much more frequently confronted with All or Nothing than is the member of the larger group.

THE TRIAD VS. THE DYAD

This peculiar closeness between two is most clearly revealed if the dyad is contrasted with the triad. For among three elements, each one operates as an intermediary between the other two, exhibiting the twofold function of such an organ, which is to unite and to separate. Where three elements, A, B, C, constitute a group, there is, in addition to the direct relationship between A and B, for instance, their indirect one, which is derived from their common relation to C. . . . Discords between two parties which they themselves cannot remedy, are accommodated by the third or by absorption in a comprehensive whole.

Yet the indirect relation does not only strengthen the direct one. It may also disturb it. No matter how close a triad may be, there is always the occasion on which two of the three members regard the third

as an intruder. The reason may be the mere fact that he shares in certain moods which can unfold in all their intensity and tenderness only when two can meet without distraction: The sensitive union of two is always irritated by the spectator. It may also be noted how extraordinarily difficult and rare it is for three people to attain a really uniform mood—when visiting a museum, for instance, or looking at a landscape—and how much more easily such a mood emerges between two. . . .

The sociological structure of the dyad is characterized by two phenomena that are absent from it. One is the intensification of relation by a third element, or by a social framework that transcends both members of the dyad. The other is any disturbance and distraction of pure and immediate reciprocity. In some cases it is precisely this absence which makes the dyadic relationship more intensive and strong. For, many otherwise undeveloped, unifying forces that derive from more remote psychical reservoirs come to life in the feeling of exclusive dependence upon one another and of hopelessness that cohesion might come from anywhere but immediate interaction. Likewise, they carefully avoid many disturbances and dangers into which confidence in a third party and in the triad itself might lead the two. This intimacy, which is the tendency of relations between two persons, is the reason why the dyad constitutes the chief seat of jealousy.

CRITICAL-THINKING QUESTIONS

1. Why do most people find their greatest experience of intimacy in a dyad?

2. What features of the dyad make this form of interaction unstable?

3. What are the characteristic strengths of the triad? What about weaknesses?

4. How might Simmel explain the common observation that "Two's company; three's a crowd"?

20

The Presentation of Self

Erving Goffman

Face-to-face interaction is a complex process by which people both convey and receive information about each other. In this selection, Erving Goffman presents basic observations about how everyone tries to influence how others perceive them. In addition, he suggests ways in which people can evaluate how honestly others present themselves.

When an individual enters the presence of others, they commonly seek to acquire information about him or to bring into play information about him already possessed. They will be interested in his general socioeconomic status, his conception of self, his attitude toward them, his competence, his trustworthiness, etc. Although some of this information seems to be sought almost as an end in itself, there are usually quite practical reasons for acquiring it. Information about the individual helps to define the situation, enabling others to know in advance what he will expect of them and what they may expect of him. Informed in these ways, the others will know how best to act in order to call forth a desired response from him.

For those present, many sources of information become accessible and many carriers (or "sign-vehicles") become available for conveying this information. If unacquainted with the individual, observers can glean clues from his conduct and appearance which allow them to apply their previous experience with individuals roughly similar to the one before them or, more important, to apply untested stereotypes to him. They can also assume from past experience that only individuals of a particular kind are likely to be found in a given social setting. They can rely on what the individual says about himself or on documentary evidence he provides as to who and what he is. If they know, or know of, the individual by virtue of experience prior to the interaction, they can rely on assumptions as to the persistence and generality of psychological traits as a means of predicting his present and future behavior.

However, during the period in which the individual is in the immediate presence of the others, few events may occur which directly provide the others with the conclusive information they will need if they are to direct wisely their own activity. Many crucial facts lie beyond the time and place of interaction or lie concealed within it. For example, the "true" or "real" attitudes, beliefs, and emotions of the individual can be ascertained only indirectly, through his avowals or through what appears to be involuntary expressive behavior. Similarly, if the individual offers the others a product or service, they will often find that during the interaction there will be no time and place immediately available for eating the pudding that the proof can be found in. They will be forced to accept some events as conventional or natural signs of something not directly available to the senses. In Ichheiser's terms,[1] the individual will have to act so that he intentionally or unintentionally *expresses* himself, and the others will in turn have to be *impressed* in some way by him.

The expressiveness of the individual (and therefore his capacity to give impressions) appears to involve two radically different kinds of sign activity: the expression that he *gives,* and the expression that he *gives off.* The first involves verbal symbols or their substitutes which he uses admittedly and solely to convey the information that he and the others are known to attach to these symbols. This is communication in the traditional and narrow sense. The second involves a wide range of action that others can treat as symptomatic of the actor, the expectation being that the action was performed for reasons other than the information conveyed in this way. As we shall have to see, this distinction has an only initial validity. The individual does of course intentionally convey misin-

formation by means of both of these types of communication, the first involving deceit, the second feigning.

. . . Let us now turn from the others to the point of view of the individual who presents himself before them. He may wish them to think highly of him, or to think that he thinks highly of them, or to perceive how in fact he feels toward them, or to obtain no clear-cut impression; he may wish to ensure sufficient harmony so that the interaction can be sustained, or to defraud, get rid of, confuse, mislead, antagonize, or insult them. Regardless of the particular objective which the individual has in mind and of his motive for having this objective, it will be in his interests to control the conduct of the others, especially their responsive treatment of him. This control is achieved largely by influencing the definition of the situation which the others come to formulate, and he can influence this definition by expressing himself in such a way as to give them the kind of impression that will lead them to act voluntarily in accordance with his own plan. Thus, when an individual appears in the presence of others, there will usually be some reason for him to mobilize his activity so that it will convey an impression to others which it is in his interests to convey. Since a girl's dormitory mates will glean evidence of her popularity from the calls she receives on the phone, we can suspect that some girls will arrange for calls to be made, and Willard Waller's finding can be anticipated:

It has been reported by many observers that a girl who is called to the telephone in the dormitories will often allow herself to be called several times, in order to give all the other girls ample opportunity to hear her paged.[2]

Of the two kinds of communication—expressions given and expressions given off—this report will be primarily concerned with the latter, with the more theatrical and contextual kind, the nonverbal, presumably unintentional kind, whether this communication be purposely engineered or not. As an example of what we must try to examine, I would like to cite at length a novelistic incident in which Preedy, a vacationing Englishman, makes his first appearance on the beach of his summer hotel in Spain:

But in any case he took care to avoid catching anyone's eye. First of all, he had to make it clear to those potential companions of his holiday that they were of no concern to him whatsoever. He stared through them, round them, over them—eyes lost in space. The beach might have been empty. If by chance a ball was thrown his way, he looked surprised; then let a smile of amusement lighten his face (Kindly Preedy), looked round dazed to see that there *were* people on the beach, tossed it back with a smile to himself and not a smile *at* the people, and then resumed carelessly his nonchalant survey of space.

But it was time to institute a little parade, the parade of the Ideal Preedy. By devious handlings he gave any who wanted to look a chance to see the title of his book—a Spanish translation of Homer, classic thus, but not daring, cosmopolitan too—and then gathered together his beach-wrap and bag into a neat sand-resistant pile (Methodical and Sensible Preedy), rose slowly to stretch at ease his huge frame (Big-Cat Preedy), and tossed aside his sandals (Carefree Preedy, after all).

The marriage of Preedy and the sea! There were alternative rituals. The first involved the stroll that turns into a run and a dive straight into the water, thereafter smoothing into a strong splashless crawl towards the horizon. But of course not really to the horizon. Quite suddenly he would turn on to his back and thrash great white splashes with his legs, somehow thus showing that he could have swum further had he wanted to, and then would stand up a quarter out of water for all to see who it was.

The alternative course was simpler, it avoided the cold-water shock and it avoided the risk of appearing too high-spirited. The point was to appear to be so used to the sea, the Mediterranean, and this particular beach, that one might as well be in the sea as out of it. It involved a slow stroll down and into the edge of the water—not even noticing his toes were wet, land and water all the same to *him!*—with his eyes up at the sky gravely surveying portents, invisible to others, of the weather (Local Fisherman Preedy).[3]

The novelist means us to see that Preedy is improperly concerned with the extensive impressions he feels his sheer bodily action is giving off to those around him. We can malign Preedy further by assuming that he has acted merely in order to give a particular impression, that this is a false impression, and that the others present receive either no impression at all, or, worse still, the impression that Preedy is affectedly trying to cause them to receive this particular impression. But the important point for us here is that the kind of impression Preedy thinks he is making is in fact the kind of impression that others correctly and incorrectly glean from someone in their midst. . . .

There is one aspect of the others' response that bears special comment here. Knowing that the individual is likely to present himself in a light that is favorable to him, the others may divide what they witness into two parts; a part that is relatively easy for the individual to manipulate at will, being chiefly his verbal assertions, and a part in regard to which he seems to have little concern or control, being chiefly derived from the expressions he gives off. The others may then use what are considered to be the ungovernable aspects of his expressive behavior as a check upon the validity of what is conveyed by the governable aspects. In this a fundamental asymmetry is demonstrated in the communication process, the individual presumably being aware of only one stream of his communication, the witnesses of this stream and one other. For example, in Shetland Isle one crofter's wife, in serving native dishes to a visitor from the mainland of Britain, would listen with a polite smile to his polite claims of liking what he was eating; at the same time she would take note of the rapidity with which the visitor lifted his fork or spoon to his mouth, the eagerness with which he passed food into his mouth, and the gusto expressed in chewing the food, using these signs as a check on the stated feelings of the eater. The same woman, in order to discover what one acquaintance (A) "actually" thought of another acquaintance (B), would wait until B was in the presence of A but engaged in conversation with still another person (C). She would then covertly examine the facial expressions of A as he regarded B in conversation with C. Not being in conversation with B, and not being directly observed by him, A would sometimes relax usual constraints and tactful deceptions, and freely express what he was "actually" feeling about B. This Shetlander, in short, would observe the unobserved observer.

Now given the fact that others are likely to check up on the more controllable aspects of behavior by means of the less controllable, one can expect that sometimes the individual will try to exploit this very possibility, guiding the impression he makes through behavior felt to be reliably informing.[4] For example, in gaining admission to a tight social circle, the participant observer may not only wear an accepting look while listening to an informant, but may also be careful to wear the same look when observing the informant talking to others; observers of the observer will then not as easily discover where he actually stands. A specific illustration may be cited from Shetland Isle. When a neighbor dropped in to have a cup of tea, he would ordinarily wear at least a hint of an expectant warm smile as he passed through the door into the cottage. Since lack of physical obstructions outside the cottage and lack of light within it usually made it possible to observe the visitor unobserved as he approached the house, islanders sometimes took pleasure in watching the visitor drop whatever expression he was manifesting and replace it with a sociable one just before reaching the door. However, some visitors, in appreciating that this examination was occurring, would blindly adopt a social face a long distance from the house, thus ensuring the projection of a constant image.

This kind of control upon the part of the individual reinstates the symmetry of the communication process, and sets the stage for a kind of information game—a potentially infinite cycle of concealment, discovery, false revelation, and rediscovery. It should be added that since the others are likely to be relatively unsuspicious of the presumably unguided aspects of the individual's conduct, he can gain much by controlling it. The others of course may sense that the individual is manipulating the presumably spontaneous aspects of his behavior, and seek in this very act of manipulation some shading of conduct that the individual has not managed to control. This again provides a check upon the individual's behavior, this time his presumably uncalculated behavior, thus re-establishing the asymmetry of the communication process. Here I would like only to add the suggestion that the arts of piercing an individual's effort at calculated unintentionality seem better developed than our capacity to manipulate our own behavior, so that regardless of how many steps have occurred in the information game, the witness is likely to have the advantage over the actor, and the initial asymmetry of the communication process is likely to be retained. . . .

In everyday life, of course, there is a clear understanding that first impressions are important. Thus, the work adjustment of those in service occupations will often hinge upon a capacity to seize and hold the initiative in the service relation, a capacity that will require subtle aggressiveness on the part of the server when he is of lower socioeconomic status than his client. W. F. Whyte suggests the waitress as an example:

The first point that stands out is that the waitress who bears up under pressure does not simply respond to her customers. She acts with some skill to control their behavior. The first question to ask when we look at the customer relationship is, "Does the waitress get the jump on the customer, or does the customer get the jump on the waitress?" The skilled waitress realizes the crucial nature of this question. . . .

The skilled waitress tackles the customer with confidence and without hesitation. For example, she may find that a new customer has seated himself before she could clear off the dirty dishes and change the cloth. He is now leaning on the table studying the menu. She greets him, says, "May I change the cover, please?" and, without waiting for an answer, takes his menu away from him so that he moves back from the table, and she goes about her work. The relationship is handled politely but firmly, and there is never any question as to who is in charge.[5]

When the interaction that is initiated by "first impressions" is itself merely the initial interaction in an extended series of interactions involving the same participants, we speak of "getting off on the right foot" and feel that it is crucial that we do so. Thus, one learns that some teachers take the following view:

You can't ever let them get the upper hand on you or you're through. So I start out tough. The first day I get a new class in, I let them know who's boss. . . . You've got to start off tough, then you can ease up as you go along. If you start out easy-going, when you try to get tough, they'll just look at you and laugh.[6]

. . . In stressing the fact that the initial definition of the situation projected by an individual tends to provide a plan for the cooperative activity that follows—in stressing this action point of view—we must not overlook the crucial fact that any projected definition of the situation also has a distinctive moral character. It is this moral character of projections that will chiefly concern us in this report. Society is organized on the principle that any individual who possesses certain social characteristics has a moral right to expect that others will value and treat him in an appropriate way. Connected with this principle is a second, namely that an individual who implicitly or explicitly signifies that he has certain social characteristics ought in fact to be what he claims he is. In consequence, when an individual projects a definition of the situation and thereby makes an implicit or explicit claim to be a person of a particular kind, he automatically exerts a moral demand upon the others, obliging them to value and treat him in the manner that persons of his kind have a right to expect. He also implicitly foregoes all claims to be things he does not appear to be[7] and hence foregoes the treatment that would be appropriate for such individuals. The others find, then, that the individual has informed them as to what is and as to what they *ought* to see as the "is."

One cannot judge the importance of definitional disruptions by the frequency with which they occur, for apparently they would occur more frequently were not constant precautions taken. We find that preventive practices are constantly employed to avoid these embarrassments and that corrective practices are constantly employed to compensate for discrediting occurrences that have not been successfully avoided. When the individual employs these strategies and tactics to protect his own projections, we may refer to them as "defensive practices"; when a participant employs them to save the definition of the situation projected by another, we speak of "protective prac-

tices" or "tact." Together, defensive and protective practices comprise the techniques employed to safeguard the impression fostered by an individual during his presence before others. It should be added that while we may be ready to see that no fostered impression would survive if defensive practices were not employed, we are less ready perhaps to see that few impressions could survive if those who received the impression did not exert tact in their reception of it.

In addition to the fact that precautions are taken to prevent disruption of projected definitions, we may also note that an intense interest in these disruptions comes to play a significant role in the social life of the group. Practical jokes and social games are played in which embarrassments which are to be taken unseriously are purposely engineered.[8] Fantasies are created in which devastating exposures occur. Anecdotes from the past—real, embroidered, or fictitious—are told and retold, detailing disruptions which occurred, almost occurred, or occurred and were admirably resolved. There seems to be no grouping which does not have a ready supply of these games, reveries, and cautionary tales, to be used as a source of humor, a catharsis for anxieties, and a sanction for inducing individuals to be modest in their claims and reasonable in their projected expectations. The individual may tell himself through dreams of getting into impossible positions. Families tell of the time a guest got his dates mixed and arrived when neither the house nor anyone in it was ready for him. Journalists tell of times when an all-too-meaningful misprint occurred, and the paper's assumption of objectivity or decorum was humorously discredited. Public servants tell of times a client ridiculously misunderstood form instructions, giving answers which implied an unanticipated and bizarre definition of the situation.[9] Seamen, whose home away from home is rigorously he-man, tell stories of coming back home and inadvertently asking mother to "pass the fucking butter."[10] Diplomats tell of the time a near-sighted queen asked a republican ambassador about the health of his king.[11]

To summarize, then, I assume that when an individual appears before others he will have many motives for trying to control the impression they receive of the situation.

CRITICAL-THINKING QUESTIONS

1. How does the "presentation of self" contribute to a definition of a situation in the minds of participants? How does this definition change over time?

2. Apply Goffman's approach to the classroom. What are the typical elements of the instructor's presentation of self? A student's presentation of self?

3. Can we evaluate the validity of people's presentations? How?

NOTES

1. Gustav Ichheiser, "Misunderstandings in Human Relations," supplement to *The American Journal of Sociology*, 55 (Sept. 1949), 6–7.

2. Willard Waller, "The Rating and Dating Complex," *American Sociological Review*, 2, 730.

3. William Sansom, *A Contest of Ladies* (London: Hogarth, 1956), pp. 230–32.

4. The widely read and rather sound writings of Stephen Potter are concerned in part with signs that can be engineered to give a shrewd observer the apparently incidental cues he needs to discover concealed virtues the gamesman does not in fact possess.

5. W. F. Whyte, "When Workers and Customers Meet," chap. 7, *Industry and Society*, ed. W. F. Whyte (New York: McGraw-Hill, 1946), pp. 132–33.

6. Teacher interview quoted by Howard S. Becker, "Social Class Variations in the Teacher-Pupil Relationship," *Journal of Educational Sociology*, 25, 459.

7. This role of the witness in limiting what it is the individual can be has been stressed by Existentialists, who see it as a basic threat to individual freedom. See Jean-Paul Sartre, *Being and Nothingness*, trans. Hazel E. Barnes (New York: Philosophical Library, 1956), pp. 365ff.

8. Goffman, op. cit., pp. 319–27.

9. Peter Blau, "Dynamics of Bureaucracy" (Ph.D. dissertation, Department of Sociology, Columbia University, forthcoming, University of Chicago Press), pp. 127–29.

10. Walter M. Beattie, Jr., "The Merchant Seaman" (unpublished M.A. Report, Department of Sociology, University of Chicago, 1950), p. 35.

11. Sir Frederick Ponsonby, *Recollections of Three Reigns* (New York: Dutton, 1952), p. 46.

21

You Just Don't Understand: Women and Men in Conversation

Deborah Tannen

Many men and women complain with frustration that they communicate on different "wave lengths." Deborah Tannen, a sociolinguist, explains why men and women often talk past each other in a host of everyday situations.

I was sitting in a suburban living room, speaking to a women's group that had invited men to join them for the occasion of my talk about communication between women and men. During the discussion, one man was particularly talkative, full of lengthy comments and explanations. When I made the observation that women often complain that their husbands don't talk to them enough, this man volunteered that he heartily agreed. He gestured toward his wife, who had sat silently beside him on the couch throughout

the evening, and said, "She's the talker in our family."

Everyone in the room burst into laughter. The man looked puzzled and hurt. "It's true," he explained. "When I come home from work, I usually have nothing to say, but she never runs out. If it weren't for her, we'd spend the whole evening in silence." Another woman expressed a similar paradox about her husband: "When we go out, he's the life of the party. If I happen to be in another room, I can always hear his voice above the others. But when we're home, he doesn't have that much to say. I do most of the talking."

Who talks more, women or men? According to

the stereotype, women talk too much. Linguist Jennifer Coates notes some proverbs:

A woman's tongue wags like a lamb's tail.
Foxes are all tail and women are all tongue.
The North Sea will sooner be found wanting in water than a woman be at a loss for a word.

Throughout history, women have been punished for talking too much or in the wrong way. Linguist Connie Eble lists a variety of physical punishments used in Colonial America: Women were strapped to ducking stools and held underwater until they nearly drowned, put into the stocks with signs pinned to them, gagged, and silenced by a cleft stick applied to their tongues.

Though such institutionalized corporal punishments have given way to informal, often psychological ones, modern stereotypes are not much different from those expressed in the old proverbs. Women are believed to talk too much. Yet study after study finds that it is men who talk more at meetings, in mixed-group discussions, and in classrooms where girls or young women sit next to boys or young men. For example, communications researchers Barbara and Gene Eakins tape-recorded and studied seven university faculty meetings. They found that, with one exception, men spoke more often and, without exception, spoke for a longer time. The men's turns ranged from 10.66 to 17.07 seconds, while the women's turns ranged from 3 to 10 seconds. In other words, the women's longest turns were still shorter than the men's shortest turns.

When a public lecture is followed by questions from the floor, or a talk show host opens the phones, the first voice to be heard asking a question is almost always a man's. And when they ask questions or offer comments from the audience, men tend to talk longer. Linguist Marjorie Swacker recorded question-and-answer sessions at academic conferences. Women were highly visible as speakers at the conferences studied; they presented 40.7 percent of the papers at the conferences studied and made up 42 percent of the audiences. But when it came to volunteering and being called on to ask questions, women contributed only 27.4 percent. Furthermore, the women's questions, on the average, took less than half as much time as the men's. (The mean was 23.1 seconds for women, 52.7 for men.) This happened, Swacker shows, because men (but not women) tended to preface their questions with statements, ask more than one question, and follow up the speaker's answer with another question or comment.

I have observed this pattern at my own lectures, which concern issues of direct relevance to women. Regardless of the proportion of women and men in the audience, men almost invariably ask the first question, more questions, and longer questions. In these situations, women often feel that men are talking too much. I recall one discussion period following a lecture I gave to a group assembled in a bookstore. The group was composed mostly of women, but most of the discussion was being conducted by men in the audience. At one point, a man sitting in the middle was talking at such great length that several women in the front rows began shifting in their seats and rolling their eyes at me. Ironically, what he was going on about was how frustrated he feels when he has to listen to women going on and on about topics he finds boring and unimportant.

RAPPORT-TALK AND REPORT-TALK

Who talks more, then, women or men? The seemingly contradictory evidence is reconciled by the difference between what I call *public* and *private* speaking. More men feel comfortable doing "public speaking," while more women feel comfortable doing "private" speaking. Another way of capturing these differences is by using the terms *report-talk* and *rapport-talk.*

For most women, the language of conversation is primarily a language of rapport: a way of establishing connections and negotiating relationships. Emphasis is placed on displaying similarities and matching experiences. From childhood, girls criticize peers who try to stand out or appear better than others. People feel their closest connections at home, or in settings where they *feel* at home—with one or a few people they feel close to and comfortable with—in other words, during private speaking. But even the most public situations can be approached like private speaking.

For most men, talk is primarily a means to preserve independence and negotiate and maintain status in a hierarchical social order. This is done by exhibiting knowledge and skill, and by holding center stage through verbal performance such as storytelling, joking, or imparting information. From childhood, men learn to use talking as a way to get and keep attention. So they are more comfortable speaking in larger groups made up of people they know less well—in the broadest sense, "public speaking." But even the most private situations can be approached like public speaking, more like giving a report than establishing rapport.

PRIVATE SPEAKING: THE WORDY WOMAN AND THE MUTE MAN

What is the source of the stereotype that women talk a lot? Dale Spender suggests that most people feel instinctively (if not consciously) that women, like children, should be seen and not heard, so any amount of talk from them seems like too much. Studies have shown that if women and men talk equally in a group, people think the women talked more. So there is truth to Spender's view. But another explanation is that men think women talk a lot because they hear women talking in situations where men would not: on the telephone; or in social situations with friends, when they are not discussing topics that men find inherently interesting; or, like the couple at the women's group, at home alone—in other words, in private speaking.

Home is the setting for an American icon that features the silent man and the talkative woman. And this icon, which grows out of the different goals and habits I have been describing, explains why the complaint most often voiced by women about the men with whom they are intimate is "He

doesn't talk to me"—and the second most frequent is "He doesn't listen to me."

A woman who wrote to Ann Landers is typical:

My husband never speaks to me when he comes home from work. When I ask, "How did everything go today?" he says, "Rough . . ." or "It's a jungle out there." (We live in Jersey and he works in New York City.)

It's a different story when we have guests or go visiting. Paul is the gabbiest guy in the crowd—a real spellbinder. He comes up with the most interesting stories. People hang on every word. I think to myself, "Why doesn't he ever tell *me* these things?"

This has been going on for thirty-eight years. Paul started to go quiet on me after ten years of marriage. I could never figure out why. Can you solve the mystery?
—The Invisible Woman

Ann Landers suggests that the husband may not want to talk because he is tired when he comes home from work. Yet women who work come home tired too, and they are nonetheless eager to tell their partners or friends everything that happened to them during the day and what these fleeting, daily dramas made them think and feel.

Sources as lofty as studies conducted by psychologists, as down to earth as letters written to advice columnists, and as sophisticated as movies and plays come up with the same insight: Men's silence at home is a disappointment to women. Again and again, women complain, "He seems to have everything to say to everyone else, and nothing to say to me."

The film *Divorce American Style* opens with a conversation in which Debbie Reynolds is claiming that she and Dick Van Dyke don't communicate, and he is protesting that he tells her everything that's on his mind. The doorbell interrupts their quarrel, and husband and wife compose themselves before opening the door to greet their guests with cheerful smiles.

Behind closed doors, many couples are having conversations like this. Like the character played by Debbie Reynolds, women feel men don't communicate. Like the husband played by Dick Van Dyke, men feel wrongly accused. How can she be convinced that he doesn't tell her anything, while he is equally convinced he tells her everything that's on his mind? How can women and men have such different ideas about the same conversations?

When something goes wrong, people look around for a source to blame: either the person they are trying to communicate with ("You're demanding, stubborn, self-centered") or the group that the other person belongs to ("All women are demanding"; "All men are self-centered"). Some generous-minded people blame the relationship ("We just can't communicate"). But underneath, or overlaid on these types of blame cast outward, most people believe that something is wrong with them.

If individual people or particular relationships were to blame, there wouldn't be so many different people having the same problems. The real problem is conversational style. Women and men have different ways of talking. Even with the best intentions, trying to settle the problem through talk can only make things worse if it is ways of talking that are causing trouble in the first place. . . .

"TALK TO ME!"

Women's dissatisfaction with men's silence at home is captured in the stock cartoon setting of a breakfast table at which a husband and wife are sitting: He's reading a newspaper; she's glaring at the back of the newspaper. In a Dagwood strip, Blondie complains, "Every morning all he sees is the newspaper! I'll bet you don't even know I'm here!" Dagwood reassures her, "Of course I know you're here. You're my wonderful wife and I love you very much." With this, he unseeingly pats the paw of the family dog, which the wife has put in her place before leaving the room. The cartoon strip shows that Blondie is justified in feeling like the woman who wrote to Ann Landers: invisible.

Another cartoon shows a husband opening a newspaper and asking his wife, "Is there anything you would like to say to me before I begin reading the newspaper?" The reader knows that there isn't—but that as soon as he begins reading the paper, she will think of something. The cartoon highlights the difference in what women and men think

talk is for: To him, talk is for information. So when his wife interrupts his reading, it must be to inform him of something that he needs to know. This being the case, she might as well tell him what she thinks he needs to know before he starts reading. But to her, talk is for interaction. Telling things is a way to show involvement, and listening is a way to show interest and caring. It is not an odd coincidence that she always thinks of things to tell him when he is reading. She feels the need for verbal interaction most keenly when he is (unaccountably, from her point of view) buried in the newspaper instead of talking to her.

Yet another cartoon shows a wedding cake that has, on top, in place of the plastic statues of bride and groom in tuxedo and gown, a breakfast scene in which an unshaven husband reads a newspaper across the table from his disgruntled wife. The cartoon reflects the enormous gulf between the romantic expectations of marriage represented by the plastic couple in traditional wedding costume, and the often disappointing reality represented by the two sides of the newspaper at the breakfast table—the front, which he is reading, and the back, at which she is glaring.

These cartoons, and many others on the same theme, are funny because people recognize their own experience in them. What's not funny is that many women are deeply hurt when men don't talk to them at home, and many men are deeply frustrated by feeling they have disappointed their partners, without understanding how they failed or how else they could have behaved.

Some men are further frustrated because, as one put it, "When in the world am I supposed to read the morning paper?" If many women are incredulous that many men do not exchange personal information with their friends, this man is incredulous that many women do not bother to read the morning paper. To him, reading the paper is an essential part of his morning ritual, and his whole day is awry if he doesn't get to read it. In his words, reading the newspaper in the morning is as important to him as putting on makeup in the morning is to many women he knows. Yet many women, he observed, either don't subscribe to a paper or don't read it until they get home in the evening. "I find this very puzzling," he said. "I can't tell you how often I have picked up a woman's morning newspaper from her front door in the evening and handed it to her when she opened the door for me."

To this man (and I am sure many others), a woman who objects to his reading the morning paper is trying to keep him from doing something essential and harmless. It's a violation of his independence—his freedom of action. But when a woman who expects her partner to talk to her is disappointed that he doesn't, she perceives his behavior as a failure of intimacy: He's keeping things from her; he's lost interest in her; he's pulling away. A woman I will call Rebecca, who is generally quite happily married, told me that this is the one source of serious dissatisfaction with her husband, Stuart. Her term for his taciturnity is *stinginess of spirit*. She tells him what she is thinking, and he listens silently. She asks him what he is thinking, and he takes a long time to answer, "I don't know." In frustration she challenges, "Is there nothing on your mind?"

For Rebecca, who is accustomed to expressing her fleeting thoughts and opinions as they come to her, *saying* nothing means *thinking* nothing. But Stuart does not assume that his passing thoughts are worthy of utterance. He is not in the habit of uttering his fleeting ruminations, so just as Rebecca "naturally" speaks her thoughts, he "naturally" dismisses his as soon as they occur to him. Speaking them would give them more weight and significance than he feels they merit. All her life she has had practice in verbalizing her thoughts and feelings in private conversations with people she is close to; all his life he has had practice in dismissing his and keeping them to himself. . . .

PUBLIC SPEAKING: THE TALKATIVE MAN AND THE SILENT WOMAN

So far I have been discussing the private scenes in which many men are silent and many women are talkative. But there are other scenes in which the

roles are reversed. Returning to Rebecca and Stuart, we saw that when they are home alone, Rebecca's thoughts find their way into words effortlessly, whereas Stuart finds he can't come up with anything to say. The reverse happens when they are in other situations. For example, at a meeting of the neighborhood council or the parents' association at their children's school, it is Stuart who stands up and speaks. In that situation, it is Rebecca who is silent, her tongue tied by an acute awareness of all the negative reactions people could have to what she might say, all the mistakes she might make in trying to express her ideas. If she musters her courage and prepares to say something, she needs time to formulate it and then waits to be recognized by the chair. She cannot just jump up and start talking the way Stuart and some other men can.

Eleanor Smeal, president of the Fund for the Feminist Majority, was a guest on a call-in radio talk show, discussing abortion. No subject could be of more direct concern to women, yet during the hour-long show, all the callers except two were men. Diane Rehm, host of a radio talk show, expresses puzzlement that although the audience for her show is evenly split between women and men, 90 percent of the callers to the show are men. I am convinced that the reason is not that women are uninterested in the subjects discussed on the show. I would wager that women listeners are bringing up the subjects they heard on *The Diane Rehm Show* to their friends and family over lunch, tea, and dinner. But fewer of them call in because to do so would be putting themselves on display, claiming public attention for what they have to say, catapulting themselves onto center stage.

I myself have been the guest on innumerable radio and television talk shows. Perhaps I am unusual in being completely at ease in this mode of display. But perhaps I am not unusual at all, because, although I am comfortable in the role of invited expert, I have never called in to a talk show I was listening to, although I have often had ideas to contribute. When I am the guest, my position of authority is granted before I begin to speak. Were I to call in, I would be claiming that right on my own. I would have to establish my credibility by explaining who I am, which might seem self-aggrandizing, or not explain who I am and risk having my comments ignored or not valued. For similar reasons, though I am comfortable lecturing to groups numbering in the thousands, I rarely ask questions following another lecturer's talk, unless I know both the subject and the group very well.

My own experience and that of talk show hosts seems to hold a clue to the difference in women's and men's attitudes toward talk: Many men are more comfortable than most women in using talk to claim attention. And this difference lies at the heart of the distinction between report-talk and rapport-talk.

CRITICAL-THINKING QUESTIONS

1. In general, who talks more, men or women? Who talks longer?

2. What is the difference between "report-talk" and "rapport-talk"? Between "private speaking" and "public speaking"?

3. In your opinion, is it possible to avoid some of the conflicts between report-talk and rapport-talk by developing a shared *conversational style between men and women? Or is this unlikely?*

SOCIAL INTERACTION IN EVERYDAY LIFE

Cross-Cultural

22

The Death of the Frito Bandito

Marty Westerman

By the end of this decade, one of three residents of the United States will be a member of a racial or ethnic minority. Even today, minorities represent a staggering commercial market—in excess of $500 billion annually. Corporations cannot afford insensitivity to the racial and cultural diversity of the U.S. This "bottom line" is bringing changes to advertising practices.

When minority groups speak these days, business listens. That's why Li'l Black Sambo and the Frito Bandito are dead. They were killed by the very ethnic groups they portrayed.

As minorities gain political and economic clout, they demand that advertisers stop portraying them in negative stereotypes and start portraying them in positive stereotypes. "Positive realism" is what the Burrell agency of Chicago calls the new type of ethnic ad, which it creates for

Coca-Cola and McDonald's. "We put blacks in authentic, optimistic settings, and we show them that the products are intended for them, not just the general market," says Burrell Public Relations president Jim Hill.

Blacks are a $218 billion market, according to the 1988 estimate of Johnson Publishing of Chicago, which produces *Ebony* and other magazines for the black market. Inc. Research in New York City estimates that Hispanics this year are worth $134 billion. The Los Angeles media firm of Muse, Cordero & Chen values the Asian market at about $35 billion.

The market size is impressive. Together, these

SOURCE: "Death of the Frito Bandito," by Marty Westerman, in *American Demographics,* vol. 11, no. 3, March 1989, pp. 28–32. Copyright © 1989. Reprinted with permission.

three groups now constitute 20 percent of the U.S. population. And their high rates of immigration and births mean that minorities might be close to 30 percent of the population by 2000.

Minority consumers typically have strong brand loyalties, and they are willing to pay extra for name brands. Marketing to them "is like 1950s consumerism all over again," says Gary Berman, president of Market Segment Research in Coral Gables, Florida.

Up to 70 percent of Asians and 50 percent of Hispanics are immigrants, and the majority are under the age of twenty-five. Their buying preferences are strongly influenced by their peers. They are ravenous for information about their new country, much of which they get from television. Companies that sell to these newcomers now can count on long-term loyalty to their products. Ethnic groups want positive media images that promise an upscale lifestyle in their future.

US AND THEM

In the nineteenth century, ethnic stereotypes "reflected the social fact of massive immigration to the United States from Europe and Asia," says M. Mark Stolarik, director of the Philadelphia-based Balch Institute for Ethnic Studies. "They were usually crude and condescending, and appealed to largely Anglo-American audiences who found it difficult to reconcile their visions of beauty, order, and behavior with those of non-Anglo-Americans."

In those days, there was the "real American" buying audience of white Anglo-Saxon Protestants. Then there were the advertising stereotypes: lively Latins, thrifty Scots, clean Dutch, Italian fruit peddlers, Mexican bandits, and pigtailed Chinese. Blacks were always subservient, like Uncle Ben, the Cream of Wheat chef Rastus, and a plantation mammy named Aunt Jemima.

Things began to change for two reasons. First, the civil-rights movement of the late 1950s and the 1960s signaled the rise of minority groups as voting blocks. Second, the dawn of segmented marketing in the 1970s led to increasing recognition of minorities as a market. This hastened the demise of negative ethnic stereotypes in advertising.

Frito-Lay dropped the Frito Bandito in 1971 after hearing from Hispanic groups who found the character demeaning. Today, Frito-Lay donates money to build playgrounds in Hispanic neighborhoods.

Ron Krieger, who in 1957 named his Lincoln City, Oregon, diner after the children's-book character Li'l Black Sambo, dropped "Black" from the name in the early 1970s. Then a California-based group created a nationwide Sambo's restaurant chain and tried to sidestep the racial issue by creating a new Sambo—a turbaned, tiger-riding Indian boy. The chain went out of business in 1982.

Quaker Foods, under pressure from black groups, transformed Aunt Jemima. She was once a servant mammy; now she's a black Betty Crocker. "We sell the product, not the logo," says Quaker spokesman Ron Batrell. But the logo has been in use since 1889, and Quaker has no intention of jeopardizing the brand's leading position by abandoning its image.

Uncle Ben and the black Cream of Wheat chef Rastus have evolved from full portraits to simple faces on the box. "It's an advantage to keep these characters as two-dimensional drawings," says Burrell's Jim Hill. "Bringing them to life in advertisements could only be a lose-lose proposition."

The challenge for advertisers now is to bring images to life that will motivate ethnic consumers without offending them.

"We're turning stereotypes into relevant cultural images," explains John Parlato, associate creative director for W. B. Doner Advertising in Baltimore. Doner has the Colt 45 Malt Liquor account for G. Heileman Brewing Company, and it recently completed work on two new Colt 45 television spots featuring actor Billy Dee Williams.

The original campaign portrayed Williams as a man on the make who used malt liquor to attract women. It drew heavy protest from feminist and black organizations. The new spots put Williams in attractive scenes with topflight dancers, status symbols such as cars and horses, independent women, and, of course, Colt 45.

The essence of advertising is reducing product attributes to concepts that can be conveyed at a glance. Often, doing this means relying on stereotypes. Ironically, products whose characters *can* be summarized in 30 seconds have a shot at immortality. Consumers remember Aunt Jemima. They remember the Frito Bandito. As Frito-Lay spokeswoman Beverly Holmes notes about the bandito character, "Audience recall was high, even among Hispanics."

"The shorthand images are a fact of life," says Parlato. "It is a question of what images to choose."

In consumer focus groups, blacks report that they want to see themselves portrayed as healthy people in integrated settings. They want to be accepted by their peers of all colors, to live good family lives in good neighborhoods, and to pursue the American Dream. That is the report from Tom Pirko, a consultant with BevMark Management of Los Angeles who analyzes product trends for the food and beverage industry.

"Blacks resent 'malt-liquor macho,'" says Pirko. "They don't want to see black women portrayed as sex symbols or homebound frumps, or black men as footloose, irresponsible studs. They don't want to see broken-home families in low-rent districts."

"Every marketer is looking for the magic formula to sell the black community," comments Richard Evans, editor of the trade journal *Beverage Beacon* in Los Angeles. "There's no secret. Like every other ethnic group, blacks want the best of what this country has to offer."

COKE RAISES THE DEAD

The American Dream is what motivates people to emigrate here from other countries, says David Chen, vice president for Asian marketing at Los Angeles–based Muse, Cordero & Chen. He asserts that blacks, Hispanics, and Asians share the same values. These include strong preferences for established, mainline American products, even if those brands are higher priced; strong family ties; a wish to preserve their native language and culture; and emphasis on education, achievement, and bringing honor to their families.

If minorities want to see themselves enjoying the American Dream, the media solution should be easy. Just shoot one commercial and substitute actors of different races and ethnic groups to appeal to whites, blacks, Hispanics, and Asians. But that doesn't work.

"These aren't just dark-skinned white people," Pirko points out. "Ethnic groups are complex markets with sophisticated social and cultural behaviors. Most advertisers look for homogeneous interests they can target to sell their products. They wouldn't think of doing that in the general market."

Most advertisers' first attempts to target ethnic markets involved translating their slogans directly. The results were often disastrous. The Coors beer slogan "get loose with Coors" in Spanish came out as "get the runs with Coors." Coca-Cola's "Coke adds life" in Japanese came out as "Coke brings your ancestors back from the dead." And Kentucky Fried Chicken learned that the Chinese do not judge the quality of their meals by whether they can lick their fingers afterward.

Even advertisers who did their translating homework were sometimes tripped up by dialects. When Hormel ran Spanish-language radio ads for its meats, Hispanic listeners had difficulty buying the product in neighborhood grocery stores. Hispanics pronounce the letter *j* as *h*, and they couldn't find meats labeled "Jormel" on the shelves. Hormel came back with advertising on TV and in posters.

Borden advertised ice cream to the Hispanic market by using the Mexican slang term *nieve,* which literally means "snow." The campaign worked in markets from Los Angeles to Texas. But in the East, Cubans, Central Americans, and Puerto Ricans thought Borden *was* selling snow.

BLACK SANTA CLAUS

The early successes in ethnic advertising confronted prejudice head-on. As early as 1967, Henry S. Levy & Sons in New York City had Chinese, blacks, and Native Americans telling the world in its ads, "You don't have to be Jewish to love Levy's real Jewish Rye." In 1972, Kodak and the J. Walter Thompson agency advertised Kodak's pocket Instamatic camera in *Ebony* magazine with a black Santa Claus.

The Levy's ad "sells a perception of openness and mutual respect for differences," says Carol Nathanson-Moog, whose firm, Creative Focus, in Bala Cynwyd, Pennsylvania, specializes in the psychological assessment of advertising. And Kodak's Instamatic ad directly addressed ethnic alienation from a white Santa Claus.

To avoid mistakes, consumer-product companies have hired black, Hispanic, and Asian specialists. Frito-Lay, a company that got its start by selling a Mexican corn-chip recipe invented by a San Antonio Hispanic, didn't do any active Hispanic marketing until 1984. It took the company that long because the bulk of its customers are white, says spokeswoman Beverly Holmes. RJR/Nabisco markets Ortega Mexican and Chun King Chinese food products the same way. "They aren't intended for the Hispanic or Asian markets," says RJR marketer Jim Chang, "just as Chef Boyar-dee products aren't intended for Italians."

"Using ethnic specialists, surveys, and focus groups is the best way for companies to avoid mistakes," says Kimberlee Reinmann of Berry, Brown in Dallas, which handles the advertising for Gatorade and other Quaker Foods products. These tools showed Quaker that a product's convenience is not an important attribute to Hispanic homemakers. "We discovered that Hispanic women cook Instant Quaker Oats on the stove, then refrigerate it to serve later as a pudding," she says.

Advertising approaches must be tailored to each product and target group. The macho approach, although repugnant to many men and women, does work for blue-collar drinkers of Colt 45 and other malt liquors.

Some celebrities—like Bill Cosby—have universal appeal. The "Cosby Show" is "a color-blind representation of American family life," says Tom Pirko. Other celebrities appeal only to certain groups. Michael Jackson doesn't sell Pepsi to twenty-five- to forty-year-old blacks. They think his plastic surgery and other eccentricities indicate that he is trying to cut his black ties. But PepsiCo research shows that Jackson excites twelve- to twenty-year-olds, the elderly, and Japanese Pepsi drinkers.

GET 'EM WHERE THEY LIVE

The most sophisticated ethnic marketers make buying their products a benefit to the ethnic community. That means buying ads in ethnic newspapers and on ethnic radio stations and using eight-sheet billboards in ethnic neighborhoods. It means marketing at the neighborhood level, emphasizing point-of-sale materials, and making sure products are available in local stores. It also means sponsoring local festivals and holidays.

The National Association for the Advancement of Colored People reports that some forty companies nationwide have now signed "Fair Share Agreements." While not legally binding, these agreements commit companies to expanding opportunities for blacks in employment, purchasing, procurement, media, and other areas. Coors and other national brewers have made their own separate covenants with black and Hispanic organizations. They run special ethnic-marketing programs, sponsor events, and actively solicit black suppliers.

Soft-drink, grocery, and fast-food companies have all signed covenants with Jesse Jackson's organization People United to Save Humanity (PUSH). The covenants are promises to fund sports teams, school programs, scholarships, and black cultural events. PepsiCo's latest effort is the Lionel Ritchie "Stay in School" tour. Coca-Cola is countering with a traveling exhibit about Jackie

Robinson. But not all forms of benevolence work with every group. Scholarships are more important to blacks and Hispanics than to Asians, according to Chen.

The ideal ethnic campaign will augment a company's image, inspire or entertain ethnic customers, and promote their integration into the mainstream of society. Today, the smart money is doing well by doing good.

CRITICAL-THINKING QUESTIONS

1. Why have businesses become more concerned with negative stereotypes in advertising?

2. Based on this analysis, do you think advertisers are well advised to devise a single commercial, shooting it many times and substituting various racial and ethnic actors? Why or why not?

3. Do you think more fair portrayal of minorities in advertising will improve minority-majority relations in general?

GROUPS AND ORGANIZATIONS

Classic

23

Primary Groups

Charles Horton Cooley

Charles Horton Cooley argues that human nature is a social *nature and is clearly expressed in group life. Cooley describes primary groups as "spheres of intimate association and cooperation" that are vital to the process of socialization.*

By primary groups I mean those characterized by intimate face-to-face association and cooperation. They are primary in several senses, but chiefly in that they are fundamental in forming the social nature and ideals of the individual. The result of intimate association, psychologically, is a certain fusion of individualities in a common whole, so that one's very self, for many purposes at least, is the common life and purpose of the group. Perhaps the simplest way of describing this wholeness is by saying that it is a "we"; it involves the sort of

SOURCE: *Social Organization: A Study of the Larger Mind* by Charles Horton Cooley (New York: Schocken Books, a subsidiary of Pantheon Books, 1962; orig. 1909), pp. 23–31. Reprinted with permission.

sympathy and mutual identification for which "we" is the natural expression. One lives in the feeling of the whole and finds the chief aims of his will in that feeling.

It is not to be supposed that the unity of the primary group is one of mere harmony and love. It is always a differentiated and usually a competitive unity, admitting of self-assertion and various appropriative passions; but these passions are socialized by sympathy, and come, or tend to come, under the discipline of a common spirit. The individual will be ambitious, but the chief object of his ambition will be some desired place in the thought of the others, and he will feel allegiance to common standards of service and fair play. So the boy will dispute with his fellows a place on the team, but above such disputes will place the common glory of his class and school.

The most important spheres of this intimate association and cooperation—though by no means the only ones—are the family, the play-group of children, and the neighborhood or community group of elders. These are practically universal, belonging to all times and all stages of development; and are accordingly a chief basis of what is universal in human nature and human ideals. The best comparative studies of the family, such as those of Westermarck[1] or Howard,[2] show it to us as not only a universal institution, but as more alike the world over than the exaggeration of exceptional customs by an earlier school had led us to suppose. Nor can anyone doubt the general prevalence of play-groups among children or of informal assemblies of various kinds among their elders. Such association is clearly the nursery of human nature in the world about us, and there is no apparent reason to suppose that the case has anywhere or at any time been essentially different.

As regards play, I might, were it not a matter of common observation, multiply illustrations of the universality and spontaneity of the group discussion and cooperation to which it gives rise. The general fact is that children, especially boys after about their twelfth year, live in fellowships in which their sympathy, ambition, and honor are engaged even more often than they are in the family. Most of us can recall examples of the endurance by boys of injustice and even cruelty, rather than appeal from their fellows to parents or teachers—as, for instance, in the hazing so prevalent at schools, and so difficult, for this very reason, to suppress. And how elaborate the discussion, how cogent the public opinion, how hot the ambitions in these fellowships.

Nor is this facility of juvenile association, as is sometimes supposed, a trait peculiar to English and American boys; since experience among our immigrant population seems to show that the offspring of the more restrictive civilizations of the continent of Europe form self-governing play-groups with almost equal readiness. Thus Miss

Jane Addams, after pointing out that the "gang" is almost universal, speaks of the interminable discussion which every detail of the gang's activity receives, remarking that "in these social folk-motes, so to speak, the young citizen learns to act upon his own determination."[3]

Of the neighborhood group it may be said, in general, that from the time men formed permanent settlements upon the land, down, at least, to the rise of modern industrial cities, it has played a main part of the primary, heart-to-heart life of the people. Among our Teutonic forefathers the village community was apparently the chief sphere of sympathy and mutual aid for the commons all through the "Dark" and Middle Ages, and for many purposes it remains so in rural districts at the present day. In some countries we still find it with all its ancient vitality, notably in Russia, where the *mir,* or self-governing village group, is the main theatre of life, along with the family, for perhaps 50 million peasants.

In our own life the intimacy of the neighborhood has been broken up by the growth of an intricate mesh of wider contacts which leaves us strangers to people who live in the same house. And even in the country the same principle is at work, though less obviously, diminishing our economic and spiritual community with our neighbors. How far this change is a healthy development, and how far a disease, is perhaps still uncertain.

Besides these almost universal kinds of primary association, there are many others whose form depends upon the particular state of civilization; the only essential thing, as I have said, being a certain intimacy and fusion of personalities. In our own society, being little bound by place, people easily form clubs, fraternal societies and the like, based on congeniality, which may give rise to real intimacy. Many such relations are formed at school and college, and among men and women brought together in the first instance by their occupations—as workmen in the same trade, or the like. Where there is a little common interest and activity, kindness grows like weeds by the roadside.

But the fact that the family and neighborhood groups are ascendant in the open and plastic time of childhood makes them even now incomparably more influential than all the rest.

Primary groups are primary in the sense that they give the individual his earliest and completest experience of social unity, and also in the sense that they do not change in the same degree as more elaborate relations, but form a comparatively permanent source out of which the latter are ever springing. Of course they are not independent of the larger society, but to some extent reflect its spirit; as the German family and the German school bear somewhat distinctly the print of German militarism. But this, after all, is like the tide setting back into creeks, and does not commonly go very far. Among the German, and still more among the Russian, peasantry are found habits of free cooperation and discussion almost uninfluenced by the character of the state; and it is a familiar and well-supported view that the village commune, self-governing as regards local affairs and habituated to discussion, is a very widespread institution in settled communities, and the continuator of a similar autonomy previously existing in the clan. "It is man who makes monarchies and establishes republics, but the commune seems to come directly from the hand of God."[4]

In our own cities the crowded tenements and the general economic and social confusion have sorely wounded the family and the neighborhood, but it is remarkable, in view of these conditions, what vitality they show; and there is nothing upon which the conscience of the time is more determined than upon restoring them to health.

These groups, then, are springs of life, not only for the individual but for social institutions. They are only in part moulded by special traditions, and, in larger degree, express a universal nature. The religion or government of other civilizations may seem alien to us, but the children or the family group wear the common life, and with them we can always make ourselves at home.

By human nature, I suppose, we may understand those sentiments and impulses that are human in being superior to those of lower animals, and also in the sense that they belong to mankind at large, and not to any particular race or time. It means, particularly, sympathy and the innumerable sentiments into which sympathy enters, such as love, resentment, ambition, vanity, hero-worship, and the feeling of social right and wrong.

Human nature in this sense is justly regarded as a comparatively permanent element in society. Always and everywhere men seek honor and dread ridicule, defer to public opinion, cherish their goods and their children, and admire courage, generosity, and success. It is always safe to assume that people are and have been human. . . .

To return to primary groups: The view here maintained is that human nature is not something existing separately in the individual, but a *group-nature or primary phase of society,* a relatively simple and general condition of the social mind. It is something more, on the one hand, than the mere instinct that is born in us—though that enters into it—and something else, on the other, than the more elaborate development of ideas and sentiments that makes up institutions. It is the nature which is developed and expressed in those simple, face-to-face groups that are somewhat alike in all societies; groups of the family, the playground, and the neighborhood. In the essential similarity of these is to be found the basis, in experience, for similar ideas and sentiments in the human mind. In these, everywhere, human nature comes into existence. Man does not have it at birth; he cannot acquire it except through fellowship, and it decays in isolation.

If this view does not recommend itself to common sense I do not know that elaboration will be of much avail. It simply means the application at this point of the idea that society and individuals are inseparable phases of a common whole, so that wherever we find an individual fact we may look for a social fact to go with it. If there is a universal nature in persons there must be something universal in association to correspond to it.

What else can human nature be than a trait of primary groups? Surely not an attribute of the separate individual—supposing there were any such thing—since its typical characteristics, such as affection, ambition, vanity, and resentment, are inconceivable apart from society. If it belongs, then, to man in association, what kind or degree of association is required to develop it? Evidently nothing elaborate, because elaborate phases of society are transient and diverse, while human nature is comparatively stable and universal. In short the family and neighborhood life is essential to its genesis and nothing more is.

Here as everywhere in the study of society we must learn to see mankind in psychical wholes, rather than in artificial separation. We must see and feel the communal life of family and local groups as immediate facts, not as combinations of something else. And perhaps we shall do this best by recalling our own experience and extending it through sympathetic observation. What, in our life, is the family and the fellowship; what do we know of the we-feeling? Thought of this kind may help us to get a concrete perception of that primary group-nature of which everything social is the outgrowth.

CRITICAL-THINKING QUESTIONS

1. Are primary groups necessarily devoid of conflict? How does Cooley address this issue?

2. For what reasons does Cooley employ the term primary *in his analysis? What are the characteristics of the implied opposite of primary groups: "secondary groups"?*

3. What is Cooley's view of human nature? Why does he think that society cannot be reduced to the behavior of many distinct individuals?

NOTES

1. *The History of Human Marriage.*
2. *A History of Matrimonial Institutions.*
3. *Newer Ideals of Peace,* 177.
4. De Tocqueville, *Democracy in America,* vol. 1, chap 5.

24

The Characteristics of Bureaucracy

Max Weber

According to Max Weber, human societies have historically been oriented by tradition of one kind or another. Modernity, in contrast, is marked by a different form of human consciousness: a rational world view. For Weber, there is no clearer expression of modern rationality than bureaucracy. In this selection, Weber identifies the characteristics of this organizational form.

Modern officialdom functions in the following specific manner:

I. There is the principle of fixed and official jurisdictional areas, which are generally ordered by rules, that is, by laws or administrative regulations. (1) The regular activities required for the purposes of the bureaucratically governed structure are distributed in a fixed way as official duties. (2) The authority to give the commands required for the discharge of these duties is distributed in a stable way and is strictly delimited by rules concerning

the coercive means, physical, sacerdotal, or otherwise, which may be placed at the disposal of officials. (3) Methodical provision is made for the regular and continuous fulfillment of these duties and for the execution of the corresponding rights; only persons who have the generally regulated qualifications to serve are employed.

In public and lawful government these three elements constitute "bureaucratic authority." In private economic domination, they constitute bureaucratic "management." Bureaucracy, thus understood, is fully developed in political and ecclesiastical communities only in the modern state, and, in the private economy, only in the most advanced institutions of capitalism. Permanent and public office authority, with fixed jurisdiction,

---

SOURCE: *From Max Weber: Essays in Sociology,* ed. and trans. H. H. Gerth and C. Wright Mills. Copyright © 1946 by Oxford University Press, Inc., pp. 196, 199–203. Renewed 1973 by Hans H. Gerth. Reprinted by permission of the publisher.

is not the historical rule but rather the exception. This is so even in large political structures such as those of the ancient Orient, the Germanic, and Mongolian empires of conquest, or of many feudal structures of state. In all these cases, the ruler executes the most important measures through personal trustees, table-companions, or court-servants. Their commissions and authority are not precisely delimited and are temporarily called into being for each case.

II. The principles of office hierarchy and of levels of graded authority mean a firmly ordered system of super- and subordination in which there is a supervision of the lower offices by the higher ones. Such a system offers the governed the possibility of appealing the decision of a lower office to its higher authority, in a definitely regulated manner. With the full development of the bureaucratic type, the office hierarchy is monocratically organized. The principle of hierarchical office authority is found in all bureaucratic structures: in state and ecclesiastical structures as well as in large party organizations and private enterprises. It does not matter for the character of bureaucracy whether its authority is called "private" or "public."

When the principle of jurisdictional "competency" is fully carried through, hierarchical subordination—at least in public office—does not mean that the "higher" authority is simply authorized to take over the business of the "lower." Indeed, the opposite is the rule. Once established and having fulfilled its task, an office tends to continue in existence and be held by another incumbent.

III. The management of the modern office is based upon written documents ("the files"), which are preserved in their original or draft form. There is, therefore, a staff of subaltern officials and scribes of all sorts. The body of officials actively engaged in a "public" office, along with the respective apparatus of material implements and the files, make up a "bureau." In private enterprise, "the bureau" is often called "the office."

In principle, the modern organization of the civil service separates the bureau from the private domicile of the official, and, in general, bureaucracy segregates official activity as something dis-

tinct from the sphere of private life. Public monies and equipment are divorced from the private property of the official. . . . In principle, the executive office is separated from the household, business from private correspondence, and business assets from private fortunes. The more consistently the modern type of business management has been carried through the more are these separations the case. The beginnings of this process are to be found as early as the Middle Ages.

It is the peculiarity of the modern entrepreneur that he conducts himself as the "first official" of his enterprise, in the very same way in which the ruler of a specifically modern bureaucratic state spoke of himself as "the first servant" of the state. The idea that the bureau activities of the state are intrinsically different in character from the management of private economic offices is a continental European notion and, by the way of contrast, is totally foreign to the American way.

IV. Office management, at least all specialized office management—and such management is distinctly modern—usually presupposes a thorough and expert training. This increasingly holds for the modern executive and employee of private enterprises, in the same manner as it holds for the state official.

V. When the office is fully developed, official activity demands the full working capacity of the official, irrespective of the fact that his obligatory time in the bureau may be firmly delimited. In the normal case, this is only the product of a long development, in the public as well as in the private office. Formerly, in all cases, the normal state of affairs was reversed: Official business was discharged as a secondary activity.

VI. The management of the office follows general rules, which are more or less stable, more or less exhaustive, and which can be learned. Knowledge of these rules represents a special technical learning which the officials possess. It involves jurisprudence, or administrative or business management.

The reduction of modern office management to rules is deeply embedded in its very nature. The theory of modern public administration, for instance, assumes that the authority to order certain matters by decree—which has been legally granted to public authorities—does not entitle the bureau to regulate the matter by commands given for each case, but only to regulate the matter abstractly. This stands in extreme contrast to the regulation of all relationships through individual privileges and bestowals of favor, which is absolutely dominant in patrimonialism, at least insofar as such relationships are not fixed by sacred tradition.

All this results in the following for the internal and external position of the official.

I. Office holding is a "vocation." This is shown, first, in the requirement of a firmly prescribed course of training, which demands the entire capacity for work for a long period of time, and in the generally prescribed and special examinations which are prerequisites of employment. Furthermore, the position of the official is in the nature of a duty. This determines the internal structure of his relations, in the following manner: Legally and actually, office holding is not considered a source to be exploited for rents or emoluments, as was normally the case during the Middle Ages and frequently up to the threshold of recent times. . . . Entrances into an office, including one in the private economy, is considered an acceptance of a specific obligation of faithful management in return for a secure existence. It is decisive for the specific nature of modern loyalty to an office that, in the pure type, it does not establish a relationship to a *person,* like the vassal's or disciple's faith in feudal or in patrimonial relations and authority. Modern loyalty is devoted to impersonal and functional purposes. . . .

II. The personal position of the official is patterned in the following way: (1) Whether he is in a private office or a public bureau, the modern official always strives and usually enjoys a distinct *social esteem* as compared with the governed. His social position is guaranteed by the prescriptive rules of rank order and, for the political official, by special definitions of the criminal code against "insults of officials" and "contempt" of state and church authorities.

The actual social position of the official is normally highest where, as in old civilized countries, the following conditions prevail: a strong demand for administration by trained experts; a strong and stable social differentiation, where the official predominantly derives from socially and economically privileged strata because of the social distribution of power; or where the costliness of the required training and status conventions are binding upon him. The possession of educational certificates—to be discussed elsewhere— are usually linked with qualification for office. Naturally, such certificates or patents enhance the "status element" in the social position of the official. . . .

Usually the social esteem of the officials as such is especially low where the demand for expert administration and the dominance of status conventions are weak. This is especially the case in the United States; it is often the case in new settlements by virtue of their wide fields for profit-taking and the great instability of their social stratification.

(2) The pure type of bureaucratic official is *appointed* by a superior authority. An official elected by the governed is not a purely bureaucratic figure. Of course, the formal existence of an election does not by itself mean that no appointment hides behind the election—in the state, especially, appointment by party chiefs. Whether or not this is the case does not depend upon legal statutes but upon the way in which the party mechanism functions. Once firmly organized, the parties can turn a formally free election into the mere acclamation of a candidate designated by the party chief. As a rule, however, a formally free election is turned into a fight, conducted according to definite rules, for votes in favor of one of two designated candidates. . . .

(3) Normally, the position of the official is held for life, at least in public bureaucracies; and this is increasingly the case for all similar structures. As a factual rule, *tenure for life* is presupposed, even where the giving of notice or periodic reappointment occurs. In contrast to the worker in a private enterprise, the official normally holds tenure. Legal or actual life-tenure, however, is not recog-

nized as the official's right to the possession of office, as was the case with many structures of authority in the past. Where legal guarantees against arbitrary dismissal of transfer are developed, they merely serve to guarantee a strictly objective discharge of specific office duties free from all personal considerations. . . .

(4) The official receives the regular *pecuniary* compensation of a normally fixed *salary* and the old age security provided by a pension. The salary is not measured like a wage in terms of work done, but according to "status," that is, according to the kind of function (the "rank") and, in addition, possibly, according to the length of service. The relatively great security of the official's income, as well as the rewards of social esteem, make the office a sought-after position. . . .

(5) The official is set for a *"career"* within the hierarchical order of the public service. He moves from the lower, less important, and lower paid to the higher positions. The average official naturally desires a mechanical fixing of the conditions of promotion: if not of the offices, at least of the salary levels. He wants these conditions fixed in terms of "seniority," or possibly according to grades achieved in a developed system of expert examinations. . . .

CRITICAL-THINKING QUESTIONS

1. In what respects is bureaucracy impersonal? What are some of the advantages and disadvantages of this impersonality?

2. Through most of human history, kinship has been the foundation of social organization. Why is kinship missing from Weber's analysis of bureaucracy? On what other basis are people selected for bureaucratic positions?

3. Why does bureaucracy take a hierarchical form? Do you think formal organization must be hierarchical?

25

The Female Advantage

Sally Helgesen

As the number of women managers increases, the workplace and the economy are being transformed. Sally Helgesen argues that "feminine principles of leading" include caring, making intuitive decisions, and being responsible to the world in using profits. In this selection, she describes how women's leadership styles differ from those of the archetypal "organization man."

[*In 1968, Henry Mintzberg published a Ph.D. dissertation based on keeping a minute-by-minute record of the activities of five executives. In 1973, these "diary studies" formed the foundation of several influential books on management. Sally Helgesen's research is based on observations of four women—two executives and two entrepreneurs.*]

The following are among the patterns of similarity and dissimilarity I found between the women I studied and Mintzberg's men.

1. The women worked at a steady pace, but with small breaks scheduled in throughout the day. Between 40 and 60 percent of their time was spent in formal, scheduled meetings; those in large corporations spent the most time this way. Unscheduled tasks quickly filled what remained of every day: calls to be returned, client follow-ups, brief informal conferences with subordinates and colleagues. The pace was steady and fast, but geared to cause a minimum of frantic stress, partly because the women worked at trying to schedule in very small breaks during the course of the day.

Frances Hesselbein, chief executive of the Girl Scouts, often closed her office door during lunch and read as she relaxed on the sofa; when traveling, she made an effort to arrive the night before her appointments, in order to "have some time to myself." Nancy Badore, director of Ford Motor Company's Executive Development Center, had her secretary leave fifteen-minute breaks between back-to-back meetings when possible, so that she "wouldn't have that desperate feeling of being squeezed." Dorothy Brunson, owner of several radio and television stations, was constantly "snatching at" little pieces of time "so I can just sit and catch my breath." Such deliberate pacing tactics derived from what Barbara Grogan, president of an industrial contracting company in Denver, described as "a recognition that I'm only human and I need my peace of mind."

2. *The women did not view unscheduled tasks and encounters as interruptions.* All four made a deliberate effort to be accessible, particularly to immediate subordinates. Barbara Grogan used head-high room dividers instead of walls for her office, "so that people will feel comfortable popping in." Dorothy Brunson's office wall was made of glass, "so that everyone can see I'm part of what's going on." Nancy Badore, as one of the highest ranking women at Ford, for years maintained an open-door policy for other women; on the day I was with her, she let her secretary make a lunch appointment for her with someone she did not quite remember "because I think she's some executive's daughter who wants advice." And Frances Hesselbein asks every Girl Scout employee—"from mailroom to management"—to write her with suggestions. "It doesn't matter if it's just a toaster oven for the seventh floor. They need to know that somebody cares."

Caring. Being involved. Helping. Being responsible. These were reasons the women in the diary studies gave for spending time with people who were not scheduled into their day, and whose concerns may only tangentially have affected their immediate business. Such encounters were not regarded as "usurpations" that impeded the flow of scheduled events, but rather as part of the flow itself. The difference in the women's view of interruptions from that of Mintzberg's men seemed to stem from the women's emphasis on keeping relationships in the organization in good repair, a concern that was reflected in the words they used. This female focus on relationships was noted in *The Managerial Woman,* though it was perceived by the authors as largely negative. They wrote that women in the workplace tend to "assume without thinking that the quality of relationships is [their] most important priority." This was contrasted in the book with men's supposedly more realistic focus on personal career objectives. But the diary studies reveal that women's concern with relationships gives them many advantages as managers—as will be seen in the following pages.

A final point in regard to interruptions. Because the women accepted them as a normal part of the flow, they did not expect their secretaries to provide them with "proper protection" from the world, as was the case with Mintzberg's men. Rather, they saw their secretaries as conduits who facilitated access to and communication with that world. As Frances Hesselbein remarked, "I'm fortunate to have three secretaries. It means I can keep in contact with more people."

3. *The women made time for activities not directly related to their work.* Although the open-ended nature of their jobs certainly demanded long hours, none permitted this to mean the sacrifice of important family time, or time to broaden their understanding of the world. Frances Hesselbein, a widow with a grown son, did say that her work consumed her life, but she characterized this as a conscious choice and said she had not permitted the same degree of absorption when her family was still living with her. Nancy Badore, the mother of a two-year-old, was strict about her hours; she came into the office at 8:30 (late by Ford's standards), and tried to make sure she was out by 6:00, so that she and her husband could enjoy evenings with their child. Barbara Grogan, divorced and with two school-aged children, never went into the office on weekends, and discouraged her employees from doing so because "they have families too." She summed up the prevailing view when she declared that her family life did not suffer because it was her *priority;* given a conflict, "I always put my children first." She was willing to put off work-related tasks that did not demand immediate attention in order to prevent business responsibilities from infringing on family time.

In addition, none of the women appeared to suffer from the intellectual isolation that Mintzberg noted among the men. In no case did a woman restrict her reading to material that related only to her work. Frances Hesselbein and Dorothy Brunson (whose two sons are in college) both characterized themselves as voracious readers, consuming books on history, management, and current events, as well as occasional novels or mystery stories. Nancy Badore reads "every magazine from *Vanity Fair* to the *National Enquirer,*" in order to keep current; both she and Dorothy Brunson study and collect art. Barbara Grogan devours "psychology and spiritual books" at night when she goes to bed, in order to keep herself on a "positive track." As Frances Hesselbein explained, "Everything I read relates in some way to managing the Girl Scouts. If it just broadens my understanding of the world, that helps."

4. The women preferred live action encounters, but scheduled time to attend to mail. They were similar to Mintzberg's men in their preference for dealing with people by telephone, or in brief, unscheduled meetings, but different in that none appeared to view her mail as a "burden." Nancy Badore reserved an hour every other day to go through it with her secretary; she dictated responses while the secretary took shorthand. Frances Hesselbein used a dictating machine to compose a constant stream of letters between meetings; she prided herself on answering every letter she received within three days, and asked everyone in her organization to do the same. Barbara Grogan wrote personal notes on yellow pads

by hand, then gave them to her secretary to type. "I have to scratch around, or it doesn't sound like me," she explained. The women's greater patience with the mail seemed to stem from their view of it as providing a way of keeping relationships in good repair by being polite, thoughtful, and personal.

5. They maintained a complex network of relationships with people outside their organizations. In this, they were no different than Mintzberg's men. They considered representing their companies a major aspect of their jobs, and spent between 20 and 40 percent of their time with clients, peers, and colleagues.

6. They focused on the ecology of leadership. Mintzberg noted that his men tended to become overly absorbed in the day-to-day tasks of management, and so rarely had time to contemplate the long range. This was not true of the women, who kept the long term in constant focus. For example, Dorothy Brunson monitored radio stations for at least two hours a day in whatever city she found herself: "I'm always looking at what people are doing, at what's going on. Every single trend that happens in this country has an effect on broadcasting."

However, as Frances Hesselbein points out, both male and female managers tend to be more big-picture oriented today than in Mintzberg's era, as a result of the advent of a global economy. What distinguishes the women's view of the big picture, however, is that it encompasses a vision of society—they relate decisions to their larger effect upon the role of the family, the American educational system, the environment, even world peace. This broad focus derives from their consciousness of themselves as participants in a revolution in expectations of and opportunities for women. This social dimension gives resonance to their view of the world and the importance of their place in it; they feel they must make a difference, not just to their companies, but to the world. This evidence of the women's big-picture thinking contradicts conventional wisdom about differences in how men and women manage. But much of what has been written on the subject has been based on comparisons between male CEOs and women in supervisory positions far down the ladder, rather than women in comparable leadership roles.

7. They saw their own identities as complex and multi-faceted. Unlike Mintzberg's men, who identified themselves with their positions, the women viewed their jobs as just one element of who they were. Other aspects of their lives simply took up too much time to permit total identification with their careers. "Raising two kids alone, how could I forget that I'm a mom *and* a manager?" asked Barbara Grogan. Being less identified with their careers permitted the women a measure of detachment. Nancy Badore: "Having a baby gives you a sense of what's really important. You still work like hell, but it's all in perspective."

Mintzberg noted that their *lack* of detachment made it difficult for the men he studied to consciously adopt various roles. They had a hard time playing whatever part was called for—figurehead, liaison, negotiator—because they identified too strongly with the position as a whole. The women were clearly more able to do this. "Sometimes, it's like I'm in a play," said Barbara Grogan. "I have different roles with different scripts, but *I'm* the same person. It's the same actress in those parts." Dorothy Brunson went so far as to keep two side-by-side offices in order to strengthen her sense of playing different roles. "In this little office, I wear my general manager's hat," she explained, standing behind one of her two desks. "I'm less important when I'm in here. In my big office, I can be more corporate." Brunson also took joyous relish in playing different parts with clients, bankers, and employees—whatever was called for at the moment. With some, she was the strict but concerned mother; with others, the savvy deal maker; with yet others, the wise and experienced leader. The process was very conscious. "It's not as if I'm different people. I'm just playing up different parts of who I am."

8. The women scheduled in time for sharing information. Whereas Mintzberg's men tended to hoard information, the women structured their days to include as much sharing as possible; it was a deliberate process, a major goal of every day. Frances Hesselbein invited employees to sit in her office and watch while she performed various tasks, such as giving telephone interviews. Dorothy Brunson met with a group of very young disc jockeys in order to get their input and share her thinking when she was confronted with a major format change at one of her stations. In her memorable phrase: "I see myself as a transmitter—picking up signals from everywhere, then beeping them out to where they need to go."

Again, this impulse to share information seemed to derive from the women's concern with relationships. Lots of give-and-take kept the network in good repair. Sharing was also facilitated by their view of themselves as being in the center of things rather than at the top; it's more natural to reach *out* than to reach *down*. They tended to structure their companies as networks or grids instead of hierarchies, which meant that information flowed along many circuits, rather than up and down in prescribed channels. . . . And since Mintzberg found that hoarding information added significantly to his executives' workloads, the women's willingness to share enabled them to keep their jobs from gobbling precious family and private time.

The characteristics of the women in the diary studies strongly interrelate with and reinforce one another. Their willingness to share information derived from a complex sense of their own identity, which enabled them to keep their careers in perspective. This broad sense of identity in turn encouraged a big-picture focus—on the *world* rather than just the organization—which was strengthened by the women's participation in activities that had nothing to do with their jobs. The scheduling of breaks into the day helped relieve the kind of pacing that can make unscheduled events seem like crises or interruptions. Being attentive to the mail was a way of sharing information.

The interrelation of these attitudes and qualities is reflected in the words the women use: *flow, in-*

teraction, access, conduit, involvement, network, reach. These are words that above all emphasize relationships with people; they are also *process* words that reveal a focus on the doing of various tasks rather than on the completion. A picture emerges from the diary studies of women who do not take an instrumental view of either work or people—that is, neither is simply the means to achieving the end of a certain position; both are rather ends in themselves.

REASONS FOR THE DIFFERENCES

Mintzberg's men, judged by their own ends-over-means standards, were highly successful. They held power, controlled information, made decisions, represented their companies, allocated resources, had authority and status; they had achieved their strategic objectives by reaching the very top of their respective fields. Yet in comparison with the women I studied—in the ways I have outlined—they often come off as less reflective and deliberate, narrower. Is it possible that I am stacking the deck in the women's favor? Judging them on their strengths and the men on their weaknesses?

I don't think so. There are specific reasons why the women in the diary studies have certain advantages in their ability to communicate, to prioritize, to see the broad picture. As mentioned before, the different eras in which the studies were conducted have everything to do with the way the women and men are perceived.

Mintzberg's men were managing their companies in the days when, in Betty Harragan's phrase, corporations were still "strictly male cloning productions." The organizations the men headed were hierarchically structured along the old military chain-of-command principle; having worked their way up through rigidly defined channels, the men naturally reflected their company's values. In those days, managers tended to stay with the company they started with, and this focus on security and loyalty made the "organization man" the archetypal figure of his era. Value was placed on nar-

row expertise (the sixties were the great age of the expert); on the mastery of prescribed skills; and on conformity to the corporate norm.

Today's organizations are very different. The hierarchical structure has given way in innovative companies to the lattice or the grid—less formal structures that deemphasize chain of command and seek to identify managerial talent in less rigid ways. The whole economy is more diverse; new ventures start up quickly; many talented men and women change companies every few years. The focus is on innovation and fast-paced informational exchange; cumbersome channels are looked on as counterproductive. Value is placed on breadth of vision, on what Jeffrey Sonnenfeld called a "diverse portfolio of skills," and on the ability to think creatively. The underlying mentality of our time is *ecological,* stressing the interrelatedness of all things. These are increasingly the values of today's reinvented corporation, and the women in the diary studies, as our contemporaries, share them.

Yet even accounting for this, the women may still be better managers than Mintzberg's men. Since a far smaller percentage of women than men make it to the top, it makes sense that the women who do would more likely be of a higher quality. According to studies done from a wide database at the Center for Values Research (CVR) in Dallas, top women managers are more likely to be what the center characterizes as "existential" leaders—that is, leaders who are able to reconcile a concern for bottom-line results with a concern for people; who focus on both ends and means; who are good at both planning and communication; and who are "reality-based," able to comprehend all the important aspects of *existence*—thus the term "existential." CVR estimates that this is so because a fiercer weeding-out process takes place among women managers; those who do survive must be the very best. Also, CVR has found that coworkers tend to be more hostile and negative toward women managers who lack human relations skills, which prevents women not strong in these skills from reaching positions of authority and influence.

Other reasons that the women in the diary studies appear to be better managers include the experiences and expectations they bring to the workplace. The experiences include their active involvement in the domestic sphere. Increasingly, motherhood is being recognized as an excellent school for managers, demanding many of the same skills: organization, pacing, the balancing of conflicting claims, teaching, guiding, leading, monitoring, handling disturbances, imparting information. The women in the diary studies agreed that their experience as mothers had been valuable. As Barbara Grogan put it, "If you can figure out which one gets the gumdrop, the four-year-old or the six-year-old, you can negotiate any contract in the world."

The women saw themselves as having no choice but to be actively involved in the domestic sphere; motherhood was not a responsibility that could be ducked. Unlike the men in Mintzberg's studies, they had no wives who could shield them from family problems; three of the four had no husbands living at home, which does not make them unrepresentative of the general situation. As a result, the women had every incentive to learn to balance conflicting demands. They achieved this in part by placing firm limits on time spent at work, and in part by integrating the public and private aspects of their lives. Over and over, the women in the diary studies talked about how their lives were "all of a piece," how "everything—home and work—just flows together." As Nancy Badore explained, "I compartmentalize nothing! I'm the same person at work as I am at home. What you see is exactly what you get. That feeling of wholeness unlocks my reserves, gives me a lot of energy. I don't think people who box their lives off in little pieces can *do* as much." Frances Hesselbein agreed. "What exhausts a person is not hard work, but the strain of feeling compartmentalized, limited, cut off, boxed in."

The integration of home and work was reflected in the diary studies by the women's mental involvement with their families during the workday. They called home, talked to children, housekeepers, and caretakers, occasionally they even noted chores relating to family on their office calendars.

By contrast, none of Mintzberg's men appeared to spend *a single moment* dealing with family issues. The men seemed to exist solely as managers when they were on the job; it was as if their fatherhood and husbandhood existed in a vacuum. Their identities had been tightly compartmentalized.

The need to integrate workplace and private sphere responsibilities made the women's lives more complex, but also gave them a certain advantage. Those in the diary studies simply had no choice but to become well-integrated individuals with strong psychological and spiritual resources in order to wrest what they sought from life. Mintzberg's men, deprived of this demanding imperative, developed into less rounded individuals, more subject to the human and intellectual alienation that makes the workplace, and life itself, sterile.

This alienation leads to the "quiet desperation" that Jan Halper found characterized many successful men. Although the majority saw their sacrifice of family and personal time as the inevitable cost of success, and claimed they would not do things differently if given a chance, they nevertheless confessed to deep feelings of emptiness, pointlessness, and resentment, a dissatisfaction that, though vague and inarticulated, was also profound. Having done what was expected of them, and given up everything else, they had not paid attention to their particular goals or dreams, and so were *unaware* of what they really wanted. The women in the diary studies, of course, had *not* done what was expected, so the paths they carved out for themselves were more truly theirs. They were more likely, in Joseph Campbell's memorable phrase, to be "following their bliss"—living their lives out of their own authentic center. Doing so would enhance the feeling of personal wholeness to which the women attributed the unlocking of their energies.

Women's expectations also played a role in preparing them to be outstanding managers. As already noted, the women in the diary studies did not consider their pace to be unbearably hectic; nor did they tend to view unscheduled encounters and calls as interruptions. As Barbara Grogan explained, "I don't think in terms of interruption.

When something unexpected needs my attention, it just goes to the top of my list. Maybe that comes from being a mom. If a kid suddenly has to go to the doctor, that isn't an interruption—that's a priority! As a mother, you find there's always something new to be fitted in. You learn not to expect to ever completely control your schedule."

The old adage may be at work here. Men are raised expecting their work to last from "sun to sun," while women know their kind of work will never be done. As Diana Meehan, head of The Institute for the Study of Men and Women at the University of Southern California, observes, "All over the world, women's work is essentially cyclical and unending; the tasks are not the kind that lend themselves to closure. And it's not just child-raising. The difference goes back to the organization of hunter-gatherer societies. The men get together and go out for the occasional big kill, a specific event that has a climax, and then it's over. But the women, who plant and gather, work at continuous tasks that need to be done again and again. This leads them to have more of a *process* orientation; and when you focus on process rather than on achievement or closure, you get more satisfaction from the work itself. You get pleasure from the actual *doing* of it, rather than from the abstract notion of getting it done."

CRITICAL-THINKING QUESTIONS

1. How do women's and men's managerial styles differ? In what sense is one better than the other?
2. Do you think that "feminine principles of leading" have a different impact on business versus nonprofit organizations? Small businesses versus large corporations? Female-dominated versus male-dominated workplaces?
3. Is Helgesen reinforcing sexist attitudes about women or blazing a trail for nonsexism in the workplace? (Evaluate this selection in terms of Reinharz's article on feminist research methods, Reading 6.)

GROUPS AND ORGANIZATIONS

26

Japanese Etiquette and Ethics in Business

Boye De Mente

Businesses in different cultures vary in managerial style and organizational philosophy. Members of our society have a growing interest in the organizational practices of Japan, a nation that has had remarkable economic success in recent decades. Because the economies of Japan and the United States are increasingly linked, there are practical benefits to understanding the cultural patterns of this economic superpower.

SHU-SHIN KOYO
(It's for Life)

Probably the most talked about and notorious facet of Japan's family-patterned company system is *shu-shin koyo* (shuu-sheen koe-yoe), or "lifetime employment," which applies, however, to only an elite minority of the nation's workers. Although a direct descendant of feudal Japan, when peasants and craftsmen were attached to a particular clan by birth, the lifetime employment system did not become characteristic of large-scale modern Japanese industry until the 1950s. In the immediate postwar period, losing one's job was tantamount to being sentenced to starvation. To prevent employees from being fired or arbitrarily laid off, national federation union leaders took advantage of their new freedom and the still weak position of industry to force adoption of the lifetime employment system by the country's major enterprises.

Under the lifetime employment system, all *permanent* employees of larger companies and government bureaus are, in practice, hired for life. These organizations generally hire only once a year, directly from schools. Well before the end of

SOURCE: *Japanese Etiquette and Ethics in Business,* 5th ed., by Boye De Mente (Lincolnwood, IL: NTC Business Books, 1987), pp. 71–81, 84–89, 91–97. Copyright © 1987. Reprinted with permission.

the school year, each company and government ministry or agency decides on how many new people it wants to bring in. The company or government bureau then invites students who are to graduate that year (in some cases only from certain universities) to take written and oral examinations for employment.

One company, for example, may plan on taking two hundred university graduates as administrative trainees, and five hundred junior and senior high school graduates for placement in blue-collar work. Since "permanent" employment is "for life," companies are careful to select candidates who have well-rounded personalities and are judged most likely to adjust to that particular company or agency's philosophy and "style."

This method of employee selection is known as *Shikaku Seido* or "Personal Qualifications System." This means that new employees are selected on the basis of their education, character, personality, and family backgrounds; as opposed to work experience or technological backgrounds.

A larger Japanese company hiring new employees, as well as firms entering into new business tie-ups, are sometimes compared to *miai kekkon* or "arranged marriages." The analogy is a good one. Both employment and joint-venture affiliations are, in principle, for life. Therefore, both parties want to be sure not only of the short-term intentions of the potential partner but also of the character and personality—even if there are any "black sheep" in the family. Thus both prospective employee and potential business partner must undergo close scrutiny. When the Japanese commit themselves, the commitment is expected to be total.

Choosing employees on the basis of personal qualifications is especially important to Japanese supervisors and managers, because they personally cannot hire, fire, or hold back promotions. They must acquire and keep the trust, goodwill, and cooperation of their subordinates, and manage by example and tact.

Besides exercising control over employee candidates by allowing only students from certain universities to take their entrance examinations, many companies in Japan also depend upon well-known professors in specific universities to recommend choice candidates to them each year. The reputations of some professors, especially in the physical sciences, are often such that they can actually "parcel out" the best students from their graduating classes to top firms in their field.

NENKO JORETSU
(The "Merit of Years")

Once hired by a larger company, the permanent Japanese employee who is a university graduate is on the first rung of a pay/promotion escalator system that over the years will gradually and automatically take him to or near the upper management level. This is the famous (or infamous) *nenko joretsu* (nane-koe joe-ray-t'sue), "long-service rank" or seniority system, under which pay and promotions are primarily based on longevity.

Not surprisingly, the employee, at least in administrative areas, is considered more important than the job in the Japanese company system. As a result, job classifications on the administrative level may be clear enough, but specific duties of individuals tend to be ill-defined or not defined at all. Work is more or less assigned on a collective basis, and each employee tends to work according to his or her ability and inclinations. Those who are capable, diligent, and ambitious naturally do most of the work. Those who turn out to be lazy or incompetent are given tasks befitting their abilities and interests.

Young management trainees are switched from one job to another every two or three years, and in larger companies they are often transferred to other offices or plants. The reason for this is to expose them to a wide range of experiences so they will be more valuable to the company as they go up the promotion ladder. Individuals are "monitored" and informally rated, and eventually the more capable are promoted faster than the other members of their age group. The ones promoted the fastest usually become managing directors; and one of their number generally becomes president.

During the first twelve to fifteen years of employment, the most capable junior managers accrue status instead of more pay raises and faster promotions. If they prove to be equally capable in their personal relations with others, they are the ones who are eventually singled out to reach the upper levels of the managerial hierarchy.

The seniority system in Japanese companies takes ordinary, even incapable, people who have toed the company line and made no blunders, to the head of departments, and occasionally to the head of companies. But their limitations are recognized, and the department or company is run by competent people below them, with little or no damage to the egos of the less capable executives or to the overall harmony within the firm.

Each work-section of a Japanese company is three-layered, consisting of young, on-the-job trainees (a status that often lasts for several years); mature, experienced workers who carry most of the burden; and older employees whose productivity has fallen off due to their age.

Direct, specific orders do not set well with the members of these work-sections. Such orders leave them with the impression they are not trusted and that management has no respect for them. Even the lowest clerk or delivery boy in a company is very sensitive about being treated with respect. The Japanese say they prefer general "ambiguous" instructions. All that work-groups want from management "are goals and direction."

Because human relations are given precedence in the Japanese management system, great importance is attached to the "unity of employees" within each of these groups. The primary responsibility of the senior manager in a group is not to direct the people in their work but to make "adjustments" among them in order to maintain harmonious relations within the group.

"What is required of the ideal manager," say the Japanese, "is that he know how to adjust human relations rather than be knowledgeable about the operation of his department or the overall function of the company. In fact, the man who is competent and works hard is not likely to be popular with

other members of his group and as a result does not make a good manager," they add.

Besides "appearing somewhat incompetent" as far as work is concerned while being skilled at preventing interemployee friction, the ideal Japanese manager has one other important trait. He is willing to shoulder all the responsibility for any mistakes or failings of his subordinates—hoping, of course, there will be no loss of face.

The efficient operation of this group system is naturally based on personal obligations and trust between the manager and his staff. The manager must make his staff obligated to him in order to keep their cooperation and in order to ensure that none of them will deliberately do anything or leave anything undone that would cause him embarrassment. Whatever knowledge and experience are required for the group to be productive is found among the manager's subordinates if he is weak in this area.

SEISHIN134
(*Training in Spirit*)

The Japanese associate productivity with employees having *seishin* (say-e-sheen), or "spirit," and being imbued with "Japanese morality." Company training, therefore, covers not only technical areas but also moral, philosophical, aesthetic, and political factors. Each of the larger companies has its own particular company philosophy and image, which are incorporated into its training and indoctrination programs. This is one of the prime reasons . . . major Japanese companies prefer not to hire older, experienced "outsiders"; it is assumed that they could not wholly accept or fit into the company mold.

ONJO SHUGI
(*"Mothering" Employees*)

The amount of loyalty, devotion, and hard work displayed by most Japanese employees is in direct proportion to the paternalism, *onjo shugi* (own-joe shuu-ghee), of the company management system. The more paternalistic (maternalistic would seem to be a better word) the company, the harder working and the more devoted and loyal employees tend to be. Japanese-style paternalism includes the concept that the employer is totally responsible for the livelihood and well-being of all employees and must be willing to go all the way for an employee when the need arises.

The degree of paternalism in Japanese companies varies tremendously, with some of them literally practicing cradle-to-grave responsibility for employees and their families. Many managers thus spend a great deal of time participating in social events involving their staff members—births, weddings, funerals, and so on.

Fringe benefits make up a very important part of the income of most Japanese workers, and they include such things as housing or housing subsidies, transportation allowances, family allowances, child allowances, health services, free recreational facilities, educational opportunities, retirement funds, etc.

The wide range of fringe benefits received by Japanese employees is an outgrowth of spiraling inflation and an increasingly heavy income tax system during the years between 1945 and 1955. Companies first began serving employees free lunches. Then larger companies built dormitories, apartments, and houses. Eventually, recreational, educational, and medical facilities were added to employee benefits.

Japan's famous twice-a-year bonuses, *shoyo* (show-yoe), were originally regarded as a fringe benefit by employees and management, but workers and unions have long since considered them an integral part of wages. Unions prefer to call the bonuses *kimatsu teate* (kee-mot-sue tay-ah-tay), or "seasonal allowances." The bonuses, usually the equivalent of two to six or eight months of base wages, are paid in midsummer just before *Obon* (Oh-bone), a major Buddhist festival honoring the dead, and just before the end of the calendar year in December.

RINJI SAIYO
(*The Outsiders*)

Not all employees of Japanese companies, including the larger ones, are hired for life or come under the *nenko joretsu* system of pay and promotion. There are two distinct categories of employees in most Japanese companies: those who are hired as permanent employees under the *shu-shin koyo* and *nenko joretsu* systems, and those hired under the *rinji saiyo* or "temporary appointment" system. The latter may be hired by the day or by the year, but they cannot be hired on contract for more than one year at a time. They are paid at a lower scale than permanent employees and may be laid off or fired at any time.

The *rinji saiyo* system of temporary employees is, of course, a direct outgrowth of the disadvantages of a permanent employment system, which at most is viable only in a booming, continuously growing economy.

The rapid internationalization of Japan's leading corporations is also having a profound effect on their policies regarding young Japanese who have graduated from foreign universities. Until the mid-1980s most Japanese companies simply would not consider hiring someone who had been partly or wholly educated abroad. Their rationale was that such people were no longer 100 percent Japanese and, therefore, would not fit into the training programs or the environment of Japanese companies.

Now a growing number of Japanese corporations with large international operations are looking for young people who have been educated abroad, speak a foreign language, and already have experience in living overseas. Ricoh, for example, now has a regular policy of hiring some of its annual crop of new employees from the group of Japanese students attending American universities.

Several Japanese employment agencies are now active among Japanese students in the U.S., providing them with information about job opportunities with Japanese companies overseas.

JIMUSHO NO HANA
(*"Office Flowers"*)

Women, mostly young, make up a highly visible percentage of Japan's labor force, particularly in offices (where they are often referred to as *jimusho no hana* or "office flowers") and in light manufacturing industries requiring precision handwork. Most of these young women are expected to leave the work force when they get married, but increasing numbers of them are staying on after marriage, at least until they begin having children, and are returning to the labor force after their children are raised.

Equally significant is that, little by little, women are beginning to cross the barrier between staff and management, and participate in the heady world of planning and decision-making.

While female managers are still generally confined to such industries as public relations, advertising, publishing, and retailing, economic and social pressures are gradually forcing other industries as well to begin thinking about desegregating their male-only management systems.

Another highly conspicuous phenomenon in Japan today is the growing number of women who head up their own successful companies in such areas as real estate, cosmetics, apparel, and the food business.

The world of Japanese business is still very much a male preserve, however, with many of the relationships and rituals that make up a vital part of daily business activity still closed to women. There are virtually no women in the numerous power groups, factions, clubs, and associations that characterize big business in Japan.

Foreign women who choose to do business in or with Japan face most of the same barriers that handicap Japanese women. They are unable to participate in the ritualistic after-work drinking and partying that are a major part of developing and maintaining effective business relations within the Japanese system. They cannot transcend their sex and be accepted as business persons first and foremost. They are unable to deal with other women on a managerial level in other companies simply because there generally are none.

They must also face the fact that most Japanese executives have had no experience in dealing with female managers, have no protocol for doing so, and are inclined to believe that women are not meant to be business managers in the first place.

This does not mean that foreign women cannot successfully engage in business in Japan, but they must understand the barriers, be able to accept them for what they are, and work around them. If they come on strong, as women or as managers, to Japanese businessmen who are traditionally oriented, they will most likely fail. They must walk a much finer line than men.

At the same time, a foreign woman who is both attractive and really clever in knowing how to use her femininity to manipulate men can succeed in Japan where others fail. This approach can be especially effective if the woman concerned is taken under the wing of an older, powerful Japanese businessman who likes her and takes a personal interest in her success.

Perhaps the most important lesson the foreign businesswoman in Japan must learn is that the Japanese regard business as a personal matter, and believe that the personal element must be satisfied before any actual business transpires. This means she must go through the process of establishing emotional rapport with her male Japanese counterparts, and convince them that she is a knowledgeable, experienced, trustworthy, and dependable business person.

It is often difficult for foreign men to develop this kind of relationship with Japanese businessmen, particularly when language is a problem, so the challenge to foreign women who want to do business in Japan (unless they go just as buyers or artists, etc.) is formidable.

The type of foreign woman who is most likely to do well in the Japanese environment is one who has a genuine affinity for the language and the culture, and appreciates both the opportunities and challenges offered by the situation. She must also have an outstanding sense of humor, be patient, and be willing to suppress some of her rational, liberal feelings.

RINGI SEIDO
(Putting It in Writing)

In addition to the cooperative-work approach based on each employee contributing according to his or her ability and desire, many large Japanese companies divide and diversify management responsibility by a system known as *ringi seido* (reen-ghee say-ee-doe), which means, more or less, "written proposal system." This is a process by which management decisions are based on proposals made by lower level managers, and it is responsible for the "bottom-up" management associated with many Japanese companies.

Briefly, the *ringi* system consists of proposals written by the initiating section or department that are circulated horizontally and vertically to all layers of management for approval. Managers and executives who approve of the proposal stamp the document with their *hanko* (hahn-koe) name seals in the prescribed place. Anyone who disapproves either passes the document on without stamping it or puts his seal on it sideways or upside down to indicate conditional approval.

When approval is not unanimous, higher executives may send the document back with recommendations that more staff work be done on it or that the opinions of those who disapprove be taken into consideration. Managers may attach comments to the proposal if they wish.

In practice, the man who originates a *ringi-sho* (written proposal document) informally consults with other managers before submitting it for official scrutiny. He may work for weeks or months in his efforts to get the idea approved unofficially. If he runs into resistance, he will invariably seek help from colleagues who owe him favors. They in turn will approach others who are obligated to them.

The efficiency and effectiveness of the *ringi seido* varies with the company. In some it is little more than a formality, and there is pressure from the top to eliminate the system altogether. In other companies the system reigns supreme, and there is strong opposition to any talk of eliminating it. The system is so deeply entrenched in both the traditional management philosophy of the Japanese and the aspirations and ambitions of younger managers that it will no doubt be around for a long time.

The foreign businessman negotiating with a Japanese company should be aware that his proposals may be the subject of one or more *ringi-sho* which not only takes up a great deal of time (they must be circulated in the proper chain-of-status order), it also exposes them to the scrutiny of as many as a dozen or more individuals whose interests and attitudes may differ.

Whether or not a *ringi* proposal is approved by the president is primarily determined by who has approved it by the time it gets to him. If all or most of the more important managers concerned have stamped the *ringi-sho*, chances are the president will also approve it.

While this system is cumbersome and slow, generally speaking it helps build and maintain a cooperative spirit within companies. In addition, it assures that when a policy change or new program is initiated, it will have the support of the majority of managers.

As can be seen from the still widespread use of the *ringi seido*, top managers in many Japanese companies are not always planners and decision-makers. Their main function is to see that the company operates smoothly and efficiently as a team, to see that new managers are nurtured within the system, and to "pass judgment" on proposals made by junior managers.

NEMAWASHI
(Behind the Scenes)

Just as the originator of a *ringi* proposal will generally not submit it until he is fairly sure it will be received favorably, Japanese managers in general do not, unlike their foreign counterparts, hold formal meetings to discuss subjects and make decisions. They meet to agree formally on what has already been decided in informal discussions behind the scenes.

These informal discussions are called *nemawashi* (nay-mah-wah-she) or "binding up the roots"—to make sure a plant's roots are protected when it is transplanted.

Nemawashi protocol does not require that all managers who might be concerned be consulted. But agreement must always be obtained from the "right" person—meaning the individual in the department, division, or upper echelon of the company management—who really exercises power. . . .

MIBUN
(*The Rights Have It*)

Everybody in Japan has his or her *mibun* (me-boon), "personal rights" or "station in life," and every *bun* has its special rights and responsibilities. There are special rights and special restrictions applying to managers only, to students only, to teachers only, to workers only, etc. The restrictions of a particular category are usually clear-cut and are intended to control the behavior of the people within these categories at all times—for example, the office employee even when he is not working or the student when he isn't in school.

The traditional purpose of the feudalistic *mibun* concept was to maintain harmony within and between different categories of people. A second purpose was to prevent anyone from bringing discredit or shame upon his category or his superiors.

A good example of the *mibun* system at work was once told by Konosuke Matsushita, founder of the huge Matsushita Electric Company (Panasonic, National, etc.). At the age of ten, Matsushita was apprenticed to a bicycle shop, which meant that he was practically a slave, forced to work from five in the morning until bedtime.

In addition to his regular duties, Matsushita had to run to a tobacco store several times a day for customers who came into the bicycle shop. Before he could go, however, he had to wash. After several months of this, he hit upon the idea of buying

several packs of cigarettes at one time, with his own meager savings, so that when a customer asked for tobacco, he not only could hand it to him immediately but also profit a few *sen* on each pack, since he received a discount by buying twenty packs at a time.

This pleased not only the bicycle shop customers but also Matsushita's master, who complimented him highly on his ingenuity. A few days later, however, the master of the shop told him that all the other workers were complaining about his enterprise and that he would have to stop it and return to the old system.

It was not within the *bun* of a mere flunky to demonstrate such ability.

The aims of foreign businessmen are often thwarted because they attempt to get things done by Japanese whose *bun* does not allow them to do whatever is necessary to accomplish the desired task. Instead of telling the businessmen they cannot do it or passing the matter on to someone who can, there is a tendency for the individual to wait a certain period, or until they are approached again by the businessmen, then announce that it is impossible.

In any dealings with a Japanese company, it is especially important to know the *bun* of the people representing the firm. The Japanese businessman who does have individual authority is often buttressed behind subordinates whose *bun* are strictly limited. If the outsider isn't careful, a great deal of time can be wasted on the wrong person.

It is the special freedoms or "rights" of the *bun* system that cause the most trouble. As is natural everywhere, the Japanese minimize the responsibilities of their *bun* and emphasize the rights, with the result that there are detailed and well-known rules outlining the rights of each category, but few rules covering the responsibilities.

As one disillusioned bureaucrat-turned-critic put it, "The rights of government and company bureaucrats tend to be limitless, while responsibilities are ignored or passed on to underlings. The underlings in turn say they are powerless to act without orders from above—or that it isn't their responsibility." The same critic also said that the only ability necessary to become a bureaucrat was that of escaping responsibility without being criticized.

A story related by a former editor of one of Japan's better known intellectual magazines illustrates how the *mibun* system penetrates into private life. While still an editor with the magazine, Mr. S went out one night for a few drinks with a very close writer-friend. While they were drinking, another writer, the noted Mr. D, came into the bar and joined them.

Mr. S continues: "I was not 'in charge' of Mr. D in my publishing house and didn't know him very well, but according to Japanese etiquette I should have bowed to him, paid him all kinds of high compliments, and told him how much I was obligated to him. But it was long after my working hours and I was enjoying a drink with a friend who was also a writer, so I just bowed and paid little attention to him.

"At this, Mr. D became angry and commanded me in a loud voice to go home. I refused to move, and he began shouting curses at me. I shouted back at him that I was drinking with a friend and it was none of his business, but he continued to abuse me loudly until my friend finally managed to quiet him down. Of course, I would have been fired the next day except that my friend was able to keep Mr. D from telling the directors of my company."

In doing business with a Japanese firm, it is important to find out the rank of each individual you deal with so you can determine the extent of his *bun*. It is also vital that you know the status of his particular section or department, which has its own ranking within the company.

There are other management characteristics that make it especially difficult for the uninitiated foreigner to deal with Japanese companies, including barriers to fast, efficient communication between levels of management within the companies. Everything must go through the proper chain of command, in a carefully prescribed, ritualistic way. If any link in this vertical chain is missing— away on business or sick—routine communication usually stops there. The ranking system does not allow Japanese management to delegate authority

or responsibility to any important extent. Generally, one person cannot speak for another.

In fact, some Japanese observers have begun criticizing the consensus system of business and political management, saying its absolute power represents a major threat to Japan in that it prevents rapid decision-making and often makes it impossible for the Japanese to react swiftly enough to either problems or opportunities.

HISHOKAN

(Where Are All the Secretaries?)

As most Western businessmen would readily admit, they simply could not get along without their secretaries. In many ways, secretaries are as important, if not more so, than the executives themselves. In Japan only the rare businessman has a secretary whose role approximates the function of the Western secretary.

The reason for the scarcity of secretaries in Japan is many-fold. The style of Japanese management—the collective work-groups, decision-making by consensus, face-to-face communication, and the role of the manager as harmony-keeper instead of director—practically precludes the secretarial function. Another factor is the language itself, and the different language levels demanded by the subordinate-superior system. Japanese does not lend itself to clear, precise instructions because of the requirements of etiquette. It cannot be transcribed easily or quickly, either in shorthand or by typewriter—although the appearance of Japanese-language computers in the early 1980s [began] to change that.

As a result, the Japanese are not prepared psychologically or practically for doing business through or with secretaries. The closest the typical Japanese company comes to having secretaries in the American sense are receptionists—usually pretty, young girls who are stationed at desks in building lobbies and in central floor and hall areas. They announce visitors who arrive with appointments and try to direct people who come in on business without specific appointments to the right section or department. When a caller who has never had any business with the company, and has no appointment, appears at one of the reception desks, the girl usually tries to line him up with someone in the General Affairs (*Somu Bu*) Department.

Small Japanese companies and many departments in larger companies do not have receptionists. In such cases, no specific individual is responsible for greeting and taking care of callers. The desks nearest the door are usually occupied by the lowest ranking members in the department, and it is usually up to the caller to get the attention of one of them and make his business known.

SHIGOTO
(*It's Not the Slot*)

The importance of face-to-face meetings in the conduct of business in Japan has already been mentioned. Regular, personal contact is also essential in maintaining "established relations" (the ability to *amaeru*) with business contacts. The longer two people have known each other and the more often they personally meet, the firmer this relationship.

This points up a particular handicap many foreign companies operating in Japan inadvertently impose on themselves by switching their personnel every two, three, or four years. In the normal course of business in Japan, it takes at least two years and sometimes as many as five years before the Japanese begin to feel like they really know their foreign employer, supplier, client, or colleague.

It also generally takes the foreign businessman transferred to Japan anywhere from one to three years or so to learn enough to really become effective in his job. Shortly afterward, he is transferred, recalled to the head office, is fired, or quits, and is replaced by someone else.

American businessmen in particular tend to pay too little attention to the disruption caused by personnel turnover, apparently because they think more in terms of the "position" or "slot" being

filled by a "body" that has whatever qualifications the job calls for. Generally speaking, they play down the personality and character of the person filling the position and often do not adequately concern themselves with the role of human relations in business.

This, of course, is just the opposite of the Japanese way of doing things, and it accounts for a great deal of the friction that develops between Japanese and Westerners in business matters. . . .

SEKININ SHA
(*Finding Where the Buck Stops*)

In Western countries there is almost always one person who has final authority and responsibility, and it is easy to identify this person. All you have to do is ask, "Who is in charge?" In Japanese companies, however, no one individual is in charge. Both authority and responsibility are dispersed among the managers as a group. The larger the company, the more people are involved. When there are mistakes or failures, Japanese management does not try to single out any individual to blame. They try to focus on the cause of the failing in an effort to find out why it happened. In this way, the employee who made the mistake (if one individual was involved) does not lose face, and all concerned have an opportunity to learn a lesson.

Ranking Japanese businessmen advise that it is difficult to determine who has real authority and who makes final decisions in a Japanese company. Said a Sony director: "Even a top executive must consult his colleagues before he 'makes' a decision because he has become a high executive more by his seniority than his leadership ability. To keep harmony in his company he must act as a member of a family." Sony's co-founder Akio Morita adds that because of this factor, the traditional concept of promotion by seniority may not have much of a future in Japan. He agrees, however, that it is not something that can be changed in a short period of time.

In approaching a Japanese company about a business matter, it is therefore almost always necessary to meet and talk with the heads of several sections and departments on different occasions. After having gone through this procedure, you may still not get a clear-cut response from anyone, particularly if the various managers you approached have not come to a favorable consensus among themselves. It is often left up to you to synthesize the individual responses you receive and draw your own conclusions.

It is always important and often absolutely essential that the outsider (foreign or Japanese) starting a new business relationship with a Japanese company establish good rapport with each level of management in the company. Only by doing so can the outsider be sure his side of the story, his needs and expectations, will get across to all the necessary management levels.

Earle Okumura, a Los Angeles-based consultant, and one of the few Americans who is bilingual and bicultural and has had extensive business experience in Japan, suggests the following approach to establishing "lines of communication" with a Japanese company when the project concerns the introductions of new technology to be used by the Japanese firm:

Step I. Ask a director or the head of the Research & Development Department to introduce you to the *kacho* (section chief) who is going to be directly in charge of your project within his department. Take the time to develop a personal relationship with the *kacho* (eating and drinking with him, etc.) then ask him to tell you exactly what you should do, and how you should go about trying to achieve and maintain the best possible working relationship with the company.

Step II. Ask the R&D *kacho,* with whom you now have at least the beginning of an *amae* relationship, to introduce you to his counterparts in the Production Department, Quality Control, and Sales Departments, etc., and go through the same get-acquainted process with each of them, telling them about yourself, your company, and your responsibilities. In all of these contacts, care must be taken not to pose any kind of threat or embarrassment to the different section managers.

Step III. After you have established a good, working relationship with the various *kacho* concerned, thoroughly explained your side of the project, and gained an understanding of their thinking, responsibilities, and capabilities, the third step is to get an appointment with the managing director or president of the company for a relaxed, casual conversation about policies, how much you appreciate being able to work with his company, and the advantages that should accrue to both parties as a result of the joint venture.

Do not, Okumura cautions, get involved in trying to pursue details of the project with the managing director or president. He will most likely not be familiar with them and, in any event, will be more concerned about your reliability, sincerity, and ability to deal with the company.

Before an American businessman commits himself to doing business with another company, he checks out the company's assets, technology, financial stability, etc. The Japanese businessman is first interested in the character and quality of the people in the other company and secondarily interested in its facilities and finances. The Japanese put more stock in goodwill and the quality of interpersonal relationships in their business dealings.

MIZU SHOBAI
(The "Water Business")

Mizu shobai (Mee-zoo show-bye), literally "water business," is a euphemism for the so-called entertainment trade—which is another euphemism for the hundreds of thousands of bars, cabarets, night clubs, "soap houses" (formerly known as Turkish baths), hotspring spas, and geisha inns that flourish in Japan. The term *mizu* is applied to this area of Japanese life because, like pleasure, water sparkles and soothes, then goes down the drain or evaporates into the air (and the business of catering to fleshly pleasures was traditionally associated with hot baths). *Shobai* or "business" is a very appropriate word, because the *mizu shobai* is one of the biggest businesses in Japan, employing some 5 million men and women.[1]

Drinking and enjoying the companionship of attractive young women in *mizu shobai* establishments is an important part of the lives of Japanese businessmen. There are basically two reasons for their regular drinking. First, ritualistic drinking developed into an integral part of religious life in ancient times, and from there it was carried over into social and business life.

Thus, for centuries, no formal function or business dealing of any kind has been complete without a drinking party (*uchiage*) (uu-chee-ah-gay) to mark the occasion. At such times, drinking is more of a duty than anything else. Only a person who cannot drink because of some physical condition or illness is normally excused.

The second reason for the volume of customary drinking that goes on in Japan is related to the distinctive subordinate-superior relationships between people and to the minutely prescribed etiquette that prevents the Japanese from being completely informal and frank with each other *except when drinking.*

Because the Japanese must be so circumspect in their behavior at all "normal" times, they believe it is impossible to really get to know a person without drinking with him. The sober person, they say, will always hold back and not reveal his true character. They feel ill at ease with anyone who refuses to drink with them at a party or outing. They feel that refusing to drink indicates a person is arrogant, excessively proud, and unfriendly. The ultimate expression of goodwill, trust, and humility is to drink to drunkenness with your coworkers and with close or important business associates in general. Those who choose for any reason not to go all the way must simulate drunkenness in order to fulfill the requirements of the custom.

Enjoying the companionship of pretty, young women has long been a universal prerogative of successful men everywhere. In Japan it often goes further than that. It has traditionally been used as an inducement to engage in business as well as to seal bargains, probably because it is regarded as the most intimate activity men can share.

When the Japanese businessman offers his Western guest or client intimate access to the charms of attractive and willing young women—something that still happens regularly—he is not "pandering" or engaging in any other "nasty" practice. He is merely offering the Western businessman a form of hospitality that has been popular in Japan since ancient times. In short, Japanese businessmen do openly and without guilt feelings, what many Western businessmen do furtively.

The foreign businessman who "passes" when offered the opportunity to indulge in this honorable Japanese custom, either before or after a bargain is struck, may be regarded as foolish or prudish for letting the opportunity go by, but he is no longer likely to be accused of insincerity.

Many Westerners find it difficult to join in wholeheartedly at the round of parties typically held for them by their Japanese hosts, especially if it is nothing more than a drinking party at a bar or cabaret. Westerners have been conditioned to intersperse their drinking with jokes, boasting, and long-winded opinions—supposedly rational—on religion, politics, business, or what-have-you.

Japanese businessmen, on the other hand, do not go to bars or clubs at night to have serious discussions. They go there to relax emotionally and physically—to let it all hang out. They joke, laugh, sing, dance, and make short, rapid-fire comments about work, their superiors, personal problems, and so on; but they do not have long, deep discussions.

When the otherwise reserved and carefully controlled Japanese businessman does relax in a bar, cabaret, or at a drinking party, he often acts—from a Western viewpoint—like a high school kid in his "cups" for the first time.

At a reception given by a group of American dignitaries at one of Tokyo's leading hotels, my table partner was the chief of the research division of the Japanese company being honored. The normally sober and distinguished scientist had had a few too many by the time the speeches began, and he was soon acting in the characteristic manner of the Japanese drunk. All during the speeches he giggled, sang, burped, and whooped it up, much to the embarrassment of both sides.

Most Japanese businessmen, particularly those

in lower and middle management, drink regularly and have developed an extraordinary capacity to drink heavily night after night and keep up their day-to-day work. Since they drink to loosen up and enjoy themselves, to be hospitable and to get to know their drinking partners, they are suspicious of anyone who drinks and remains formal and sober. They call this "killing the *sake*," with the added connotation that it also kills the pleasure.

During a boisterous drinking bout in which they sing and dance and trade risqué banter with hostesses or geisha, Japanese businessmen often sober up just long enough to have an important business exchange with a guest or colleague and then go back to the fun and games.

Foreign businessmen should be very cautious about trying to keep up with their Japanese hosts at such drinking rituals. It is all too common to see visiting businessmen being returned to their hotels well after midnight, sodden drunk. The key to this important ceremony is to drink moderately and simulate drunkenness.

In recent years, inflation has dimmed some of the nightly glow from geisha houses, the great cabarets, the bars, and the "in" restaurants in Japan's major cities. The feeling is also growing that the several billion dollars spent each year in the *mizu shobai* is incompatible with Japan's present-day needs. But like so many other aspects of Japanese life, the *mizu shobai* is deeply embedded in the overall socioeconomic system, as well as in the national psyche. It is not about to disappear in the foreseeable future.

Most of the money spent in the *mizu shobai* comes from the so-called *Sha-Yo Zoku* (Shah-Yoe Zoe-kuu), "Expense-Account Tribe"—the large number of salesmen, managers, and executives who are authorized to entertain clients, prospects, and guests at company expense. Japanese companies are permitted a substantial tax write-off for entertainment expenses to begin with, and most go way beyond the legal limit (based on their capital), according to both official and unofficial sources.

CRITICAL-THINKING QUESTIONS

1. Akio Morita, a founder of Sony Corporation, once commented that Japanese companies look more like social organizations than business enterprises (De Mente, 1987: 61). What evidence in this selection can be used to assess this observation?

2. How do Japanese business organizations differ from the ideal model of Western bureaucracy described by Max Weber (in Reading 24)?

3. What elements of Japanese business organizations explain the relatively slow entry of women into the work force, and especially into management positions?

NOTE

1. For more about the subject of *mizu shobai*, see *Bachelor's Japan* by Boye De Mente.

DEVIANCE

27

The Functions of Crime

Emile Durkheim

Common sense leads us to view crime, and all kinds of deviance, as pathological—*that is, as harmful to social life. Despite the obvious social costs of crime, however, Durkheim argues that crime is* normal *because it is part of all societies. Furthermore, he claims that crime makes important contributions to the operation of a social system.*

. . . Crime is present not only in the majority of societies of one particular species but in all societies of all types. There is no society that is not confronted with the problem of criminality. Its form changes; the acts thus characterized are not the same everywhere; but, everywhere and always, there have been men who have behaved in such a way as to draw upon themselves penal repression. . . . There is, then, no phenomenon that pre-

sents more indisputably all the symptoms of normality, since it appears closely connected with the conditions of all collective life. To make of crime a form of social morbidity would be to admit that morbidity is not something accidental, but, on the contrary, that in certain cases it grows out of the fundamental constitution of the living organism; it would result in wiping out all distinction between the physiological and the pathological. No doubt it is possible that crime itself will have abnormal forms, as, for example, when its rate is unusually high. This excess is, indeed, undoubtedly morbid in nature. What is normal, simply, is the existence of criminality. . . .

Here we are, then, in the presence of a conclusion in appearance quite paradoxical. Let us make

SOURCE: *The Rules of Sociological Method* by Emile Durkheim, trans. Sarah A. Solovay and John A. Mueller, ed. George E. G. Catlin. Copyright © 1938 by George E. G. Catlin, renewed 1966 by Sarah A. Solovay, John H. Mueller, and George E. G. Catlin. Reprinted with permission of The Free Press, Macmillan Publishing Company, a Member of Paramount Publishing.

no mistake. To classify crime among the phenomena of normal sociology is not to say merely that it is an inevitable, although regrettable, phenomenon, due to the incorrigible wickedness of men; it is to affirm that it is a factor in public health, an integral part of all healthy societies. This result is, at first glance, surprising enough to have puzzled even ourselves for a long time. Once this first surprise has been overcome, however, it is not difficult to find reasons explaining this normality and at the same time confirming it.

In the first place crime is normal because a society exempt from it is utterly impossible. Crime, we have shown elsewhere, consists of an act that offends certain very strong collective sentiments. In a society in which criminal acts are no longer committed, the sentiments they offend would have to be found without exception in all individual consciousnesses, and they must be found to exist with the same degree as sentiments contrary to them. Assuming that this condition could actually be realized, crime would not thereby disappear; it would only change its form, for the very cause which would thus dry up the sources of criminality would immediately open up new ones.

Indeed, for the collective sentiments which are protected by the penal law of a people at a specified moment of its history to take possession of the public conscience or for them to acquire a stronger hold where they have an insufficient grip, they must acquire an intensity greater than that which they had hitherto had. The community as a whole must experience them more vividly, for it can acquire from no other source the greater force necessary to control these individuals who formerly were the most refractory. For murderers to disappear, the horror of bloodshed must become greater in those social strata from which murderers are recruited; but, first it must become greater throughout the entire society. Moreover, the very absence of crime would directly contribute to produce this horror; because any sentiment seems much more respectable when it is always and uniformly respected.

One easily overlooks the consideration that these strong states of the common consciousness cannot be thus reinforced without reinforcing at the same time the more feeble states, whose violation previously gave birth to mere infraction of convention—since the weaker ones are only the prolongation, the attenuated form, of the stronger. Thus robbery and simple bad taste injure the same single altruistic sentiment, the respect for that which is another's. However, this same sentiment is less grievously offended by bad taste than by robbery; and since, in addition, the average consciousness has not sufficient intensity to react keenly to the bad taste, it is treated with greater tolerance. That is why the person guilty of bad taste is merely blamed, whereas the thief is punished. But, if this sentiment grows stronger, to the point of silencing in all consciousnesses the inclination which disposes man to steal, he will become more sensitive to the offenses which, until then, touched him but lightly. He will react against them, then, with more energy; they will be the object of greater opprobrium, which will transform certain of them from the simple moral faults that they were and give them the quality of crimes. For example, improper contracts, or contracts improperly executed, which only incur public blame or civil damages, will become offenses in law.

Imagine a society of saints, a perfect cloister of exemplary individuals. Crimes, properly so called, will there be unknown; but faults which appear venial to the layman will create there the same scandal that the ordinary offense does in ordinary consciousnesses. If, then, this society has the power to judge and punish, it will define these acts as criminal and will treat them as such. For the same reason, the perfect and upright man judges his smallest failings with a severity that the majority reserve for acts more truly in the nature of an offense. Formerly, acts of violence against persons were more frequent than they are today, because respect for individual dignity was less strong. As this has increased, these crimes have become more rare; and also, many acts violating this sentiment have been introduced into the penal law which were not included there in primitive times.[1] . . .

Crime is, then, necessary; it is bound up with

the fundamental conditions of all social life, and by that very fact it is useful, because these conditions of which it is a part are themselves indispensable to the normal evolution of morality and law.

Indeed, it is no longer possible today to dispute the fact that law and morality vary from one social type to the next, nor that they change within the same type if the conditions of life are modified. But, in order that these transformations may be possible, the collective sentiments at the basis of morality must not be hostile to change, and consequently must have but moderate energy. If they were too strong, they would no longer be plastic. Every pattern is an obstacle to new patterns, to the extent that the first pattern is inflexible. The better a structure is articulated, the more it offers a healthy resistance to all modification; and this is equally true of functional, as of anatomical, organization. If there were no crimes, this condition could not have been fulfilled; for such a hypothesis presupposes that collective sentiments have arrived at a degree of intensity unexampled in history. Nothing is good indefinitely and to an unlimited extent. The authority which the moral conscience enjoys must not be excessive; otherwise no one would dare criticize it, and it would too easily congeal into an immutable form. To make progress, individual originality must be able to express itself. In order that the originality of the idealist whose dreams transcend his century may find expression, it is necessary that the originality of the criminal, who is below the level of his time, shall also be possible. One does not occur without the other.

Nor is this all. Aside from this indirect utility, it happens that crime itself plays a useful role in this evolution. Crime implies not only that the way remains open to necessary changes but that in certain cases it directly prepares these changes. Where crime exists, collective sentiments are sufficiently flexible to take on a new form, and crime sometimes helps to determine the form they will take. How many times, indeed, it is only an anticipation of future morality—a step toward what will be! According to Athenian law, Socrates was a criminal, and his condemnation was no more than just. However, his crime, namely, the independence of his thought, rendered a service not only to humanity but to his country. . . .

From this point of view the fundamental facts of criminality present themselves to us in an entirely new light. Contrary to current ideas, the criminal no longer seems a totally unsociable being, a sort of parasitic element, a strange and unassimilable body, introduced into the midst of society. On the contrary, he plays a definite role in social life.

CRITICAL-THINKING QUESTIONS

1. On what grounds does Durkheim argue that crime should be considered a "normal" element of society?
2. Why is a society devoid of crime an impossibility?
3. What are the functional consequences of crime and deviance?

NOTE

1. Calumny, insults, slander, fraud, etc.

28

On Being Sane in Insane Places

David L. Rosenhan*

How do we know precisely what constitutes "normality" or mental illness? Conventional wisdom suggests that specially trained professionals have the ability to make reasonably accurate diagnoses. In this research, however, David Rosenhan provides evidence to challenge this assumption. What is—or is not—"normal" may have much to do with the labels that are applied to people in particular settings.

If sanity and insanity exist, how shall we know them?

The question is neither capricious nor itself insane. However much we may be personally convinced that we can tell the normal from the abnormal, the evidence is simply not compelling. It is commonplace, for example, to read about murder trials wherein eminent psychiatrists for the

defense are contradicted by equally eminent psychiatrists for the prosecution on the matter of the defendant's sanity. More generally, there are a great deal of conflicting data on the reliability, utility, and meaning of such terms as "sanity," "insanity," "mental illness," and "schizophrenia." Finally, as early as 1934, [Ruth] Benedict suggested that normality and abnormality are not universal.[1] What is viewed as normal in one culture may be seen as quite aberrant in another. Thus, notions of normality and abnormality may not be quite as accurate as people believe they are.

To raise questions regarding normality and abnormality is in no way to question the fact that some behaviors are deviant or odd. Murder is de-

* I thank W. Mischel, E. Orne, and M. S. Rosenhan for comments on an earlier draft of this manuscript.

SOURCE: "On Being Sane in Insane Places," by David L. Rosenhan, in *Science,* vol. 179 (January 1973), pp. 250–58. Copyright © 1973 by the American Association for the Advancement of Science. Reprinted with permission.

viant. So, too, are hallucinations. Nor does raising such questions deny the existence of the personal anguish that is often associated with "mental illness." Anxiety and depression exist. Psychological suffering exists. But normality and abnormality, sanity and insanity, and the diagnoses that flow from them may be less substantive than many believe them to be.

At its heart, the question of whether the sane can be distinguished from the insane (and whether degrees of insanity can be distinguished from each other) is a simple matter: Do the salient characteristics that lead to diagnoses reside in the patients themselves or in the environments and contexts in which observers find them? From Bleuler, through Kretchmer, through the formulators of the recently revised *Diagnostic and Statistical Manual* of the American Psychiatric Association, the belief has been strong that patients present symptoms, that those symptoms can be categorized, and, implicitly, that the sane are distinguishable from the insane. More recently, however, this belief has been questioned. Based in part on theoretical and anthropological considerations, but also on philosophical, legal, and therapeutic ones, the view has grown that psychological categorization of mental illness is useless at best and downright harmful, misleading, and pejorative at worst. Psychiatric diagnoses, in this view, are in the minds of the observers and are not valid summaries of characteristics displayed by the observed.

Gains can be made in deciding which of these is more nearly accurate by getting normal people (that is, people who do not have, and have never suffered, symptoms of serious psychiatric disorders) admitted to psychiatric hospitals and then determining whether they were discovered to be sane and, if so, how. If the sanity of such pseudopatients were always detected, there would be prima facie evidence that a sane individual can be distinguished from the insane context in which he is found. Normality (and presumably abnormality) is distinct enough that it can be recognized wherever it occurs, for it is carried within the person. If, on the other hand, the sanity of the pseudopatients were never discovered, serious difficulties would arise for those who support traditional modes of psychiatric diagnosis. Given that the hospital staff was not incompetent, that the pseudopatient had been behaving as sanely as he had been outside of the hospital, and that it had never been previously suggested that he belonged in a psychiatric hospital, such an unlikely outcome would support the view that psychiatric diagnosis betrays little about the patient but much about the environment in which an observer finds him.

This article describes such an experiment. Eight sane people gained secret admission to twelve different hospitals. Their diagnostic experiences constitute the data of the first part of this article; the remainder is devoted to a description of their experiences in psychiatric institutions. Too few psychiatrists and psychologists, even those who have worked in such hospitals, know what the experience is like. They rarely talk about it with former patients, perhaps because they distrust information coming from the previously insane. Those who have worked in psychiatric hospitals are likely to have adapted so thoroughly to the settings that they are insensitive to the impact of that experience. And while there have been occasional reports of researchers who submitted themselves to psychiatric hospitalization, these researchers have commonly remained in the hospitals for short periods of time, often with the knowledge of the hospital staff. It is difficult to know the extent to which they were treated like patients or like research colleagues. Nevertheless, their reports about the inside of the psychiatric hospital have been valuable. This article extends those efforts.

PSEUDOPATIENTS AND THEIR SETTINGS

The eight pseudopatients were a varied group. One was a psychology graduate student in his twenties. The remaining seven were older and "established." Among them were three psychologists, a pediatrician, a psychiatrist, a painter, and a housewife. Three pseudopatients were women, five were men. All of them employed pseudonyms, lest their alleged diagnoses embarrass them later. Those who were in mental health professions alleged another occupation in order to avoid the special attentions that might be accorded by staff, as a matter of courtesy or caution, to ailing colleagues.[2] With the exception of myself (I was the first pseudopatient and my presence was known to the hospital administrator and chief psychologist and, so far as I can tell, to them alone), the presence of pseudopatients and the nature of the research program was not known to the hospital staffs.[3]

The settings were similarly varied. In order to generalize the findings, admission into a variety of hospitals was sought. The twelve hospitals in the sample were located in five different states on the East and West coasts. Some were old and shabby, some were quite new. Some were research-oriented, others not. Some had good staff-patient ratios, others were quite understaffed. Only one was a strictly private hospital. All of the others were supported by state or federal funds or, in one instance, by university funds.

After calling the hospital for an appointment, the pseudopatient arrived at the admissions office complaining that he had been hearing voices. Asked what the voices said, he replied that they were often unclear, but as far as he could tell they said "empty," "hollow," and "thud." The voices were unfamiliar and were of the same sex as the pseudopatient. The choice of these symptoms was occasioned by their apparent similarity to existential symptoms. Such symptoms are alleged to arise from painful concerns about the perceived meaninglessness of one's life. It is as if the hallucinating person were saying, "My life is empty and hollow." The choice of these symptoms was also determined by the *absence* of a single report of existential psychoses in the literature.

Beyond alleging the symptoms and falsifying name, vocation, and employment, no further alterations of person, history, or circumstances were made. The significant events of the pseudopatient's life history were presented as they had actually occurred. Relationships with parents and siblings, with spouse and children, with people at work and in school, consistent with the aforementioned exceptions, were described as they were or had been. Frustrations and upsets were described along with joys and satisfactions. These facts are important to remember. If anything, they strongly biased the subsequent results in favor of detecting sanity, since none of their histories or current behaviors were seriously pathological in any way.

Immediately upon admission to the psychiatric ward, the pseudopatient ceased simulating *any* symptoms of abnormality. In some cases, there was a brief period of mild nervousness and anxiety, since none of the pseudopatients really believed that they would be admitted so easily. Indeed, their shared fear was that they would be immediately exposed as frauds and greatly embarrassed. Moreover, many of them had never visited a psychiatric ward; even those who had, nevertheless had some genuine fears about what might happen to them. Their nervousness, then, was quite appropriate to the novelty of the hospital setting, and it abated rapidly.

Apart from that short-lived nervousness, the pseudopatient behaved on the ward as he "normally" behaved. The pseudopatient spoke to patients and staff as he might ordinarily. Because there is uncommonly little to do on a psychiatric ward, he attempted to engage others in conversation. When asked by staff how he was feeling, he indicated that he was fine, that he no longer experienced symptoms. He responded to instructions from attendants, to calls for medication (which was not swallowed), and to dining-hall instructions. Beyond such activities as were available to him on the admissions ward, he spent his time writing down his observations about the ward, its patients, and the staff. Initially these notes were written "secretly," but as it soon became clear that no one much cared, they were subsequently written on standard tablets of paper in such public places as the dayroom. No secret was made of these activities.

The pseudopatient, very much as a true psychiatric patient, entered a hospital with no foreknowledge of when he would be discharged. Each was told that he would have to get out by his own devices, essentially by convincing the staff that he was sane. The psychological stresses associated with hospitalization were considerable, and all but one of the pseudopatients desired to be discharged almost immediately after being admitted. They were, therefore, motivated not only to behave sanely, but to be paragons of cooperation. That their behavior was in no way disruptive is confirmed by nursing reports, which have been obtained on most of the patients. These reports uniformly indicate that the patients were "friendly," "co-operative," and "exhibited no abnormal indications."

THE NORMAL ARE NOT DETECTABLY SANE

Despite their public "show" of sanity, the pseudopatients were never detected. Admitted, except in one case, with a diagnosis of schizophrenia,[4] each was discharged with a diagnosis of schizophrenia "in remission." The label "in remission" should in no way be dismissed as a formality, for at no time during any hospitalization had any question been raised about any pseudopatient's simulation. Nor are there any indications in the hospital records that the pseudopatient's status was suspect. Rather, the evidence is strong that, once labeled schizophrenic, the pseudopatient was stuck with that label. If the pseudopatient was to be discharged, he must naturally be "in remission"; but he was not sane, nor, in the institution's view, had he ever been sane.

The uniform failure to recognize sanity cannot be attributed to the quality of the hospitals, for, although there were considerable variations among them, several are considered excellent. Nor can it be alleged that there was simply not enough time to observe the pseudopatients. Length of hospitalization ranged from seven to fifty-two days, with an average of nineteen days. The pseudopatients were not, in fact, carefully observed, but this failure clearly speaks more to traditions within psychiatric hospitals than to lack of opportunity.

Finally, it cannot be said that the failure to recognize the pseudopatients' sanity was due to the fact that they were not behaving sanely. While there was clearly some tension present in all of them, their daily visitors could detect no serious behavioral consequences—nor, indeed, could other patients. It was quite common for the patients to "detect" the pseudopatients' sanity. During the first three hospitalizations, when accurate counts were kept, 35 of a total of 118 patients on the admissions ward voiced their suspicions, some vigorously. "You're not crazy. You're a journalist, or a professor [referring to the continual note-taking]. You're checking up on the hospital." While most of the patients were reassured by the pseudopatient's insistence that he had been sick before he came in but was fine now, some continued to believe that the pseudopatient was sane throughout his hospitalization. The fact that the patients often recognized normality when staff did not raises important questions.

Failure to detect sanity during the course of hospitalization may be due to the fact that physicians operate with a strong bias toward what statisticians call the type 2 error. This is to say that physicians are more inclined to call a healthy person sick (a false positive, type 2) than a sick person healthy (a false negative, type 1). The reasons for this are not hard to find: It is clearly more dangerous to misdiagnose illness than health. Better to err on the side of caution, to suspect illness even among the healthy.

But what holds for medicine does not hold equally well for psychiatry. Medical illnesses, while unfortunate, are not commonly pejorative. Psychiatric diagnoses, on the contrary, carry with them personal, legal, and social stigmas. It was therefore important to see whether the tendency toward diagnosing the sane insane could be reversed. The following experiment was arranged at a research and teaching hospital whose staff had heard these findings but doubted that such an error could occur in their hospital. The staff was informed that at some time during the following three months, one or more pseudopatients would attempt to be admitted into the psychiatric hospital. Each staff member was asked to rate each patient who presented himself at admissions or on the ward according to the likelihood that the patient was a pseudopatient. A 10-point scale was used, with a 1 and 2 reflecting high confidence that the patient was a pseudopatient.

Judgments were obtained on 193 patients who were admitted for psychiatric treatment. All staff who had had sustained contact with or primary responsibility for the patient—attendants, nurses, psychiatrists, physicians, and psychologists—were asked to make judgments. Forty-one patients were alleged, with high confidence, to be pseudopatients by at least one member of the staff. Twenty-three were considered suspect by at least one psychiatrist. Nineteen were suspected by one psychiatrist *and* one other staff member. Actually, no genuine pseudopatient (at least from my group) presented himself during this period.

The experiment is instructive. It indicates that the tendency to designate sane people as insane can be reversed when the stakes (in this case, prestige and diagnostic acumen) are high. But what can be said of the nineteen people who were suspected of being "sane" by one psychiatrist and another staff member? Were these people truly "sane," or was it rather the case that in the course of avoiding the type 2 error the staff tended to make more errors of the first sort—calling the crazy "sane"? There is no way of knowing. But one thing is certain: Any diagnostic process that lends itself so readily to massive errors of this sort cannot be a very reliable one.

THE STICKINESS OF PSYCHODIAGNOSTIC LABELS

Beyond the tendency to call the healthy sick—a tendency that accounts better for diagnostic behavior on admission than it does for such behavior after a lengthy period of exposure—the data speak to the massive role of labeling in psychiatric assessment. Having once been labeled schizophrenic, there is nothing the pseudopatient can do to overcome the tag. The tag profoundly colors others' perceptions of him and his behavior.

From one viewpoint, these data are hardly surprising, for it has long been known that elements are given meaning by the context in which they occur. Gestalt psychology made this point vigorously, and Asch[5] demonstrated that there are "central" personality traits (such as "warm" versus "cold") which are so powerful that they markedly color the meaning of other information in forming an impression of a given personality. "Insane," "schizophrenic," "manic-depressive," and "crazy" are probably among the most powerful of such central traits. Once a person is designated abnormal, all of his other behaviors and characteristics are colored by that label. Indeed, that label is so powerful that many of the pseudopatients' normal behaviors were overlooked entirely or profoundly misinterpreted. Some examples may clarify this issue.

Earlier I indicated that there were no changes in the pseudopatient's personal history and current status beyond those of name, employment, and, where necessary, vocation. Otherwise, a veridical description of personal history and circumstances was offered. Those circumstances were not psychotic. How were they made consonant with the diagnosis of psychosis? Or were those diagnoses modified in such a way as to bring them into accord with the circumstances of the pseudopatient's life, as described by him?

As far as I can determine, diagnoses were in no way affected by the relative health of the circumstances of a pseudopatient's life. Rather, the reverse occurred: The perception of his circumstances was shaped entirely by the diagnosis. A clear example of such translation is found in the case of a pseudopatient who had had a close relationship with his mother but was rather remote from his father during his early childhood. During adolescence and beyond, however, his father became a close friend, while his relationship with his mother cooled. His present relationship with his wife was characteristically close and warm. Apart from occasional angry exchanges, friction was minimal. The children had rarely been spanked. Surely there is nothing especially pathological about such a history. Indeed, many readers may see a similar pattern in their own experiences, with no markedly deleterious consequences. Observe, however, how such a history was translated in the psychopathological context, this from the case summary prepared after the patient was discharged.

This white thirty-nine-year-old male . . . manifests a long history of considerable ambivalence in close relationships, which begins in early childhood. A warm relationship with his mother cools during his adolescence. A distant relationship to his father is described as becoming very intense. Affective stability is absent. His attempts to control emotionality with his wife and children are punctuated by angry outbursts and, in the case of the children, spankings. And while he says that he has several good friends, one senses considerable ambivalence embedded in those relationships also. . . .

The facts of the case were unintentionally distorted by the staff to achieve consistency with a popular theory of the dynamics of a schizophrenic reaction. Nothing of an ambivalent nature had been described in relations with parents, spouse, or friends. To the extent that ambivalence could be inferred, it was probably not greater than is found in all human relationships. It is true the pseudopatient's relationships with his parents changed over time, but in the ordinary context that would hardly be remarkable—indeed, it might very well be expected. Clearly, the meaning ascribed to his verbalizations (that is, ambivalence, affective instability) was determined by the diagnosis: schizophrenia. An entirely different meaning would have been ascribed if it were known that the man was "normal."

All pseudopatients took extensive notes publicly. Under ordinary circumstances, such behavior would have raised questions in the minds of observers, as, in fact, it did among patients. Indeed, it seemed so certain that the notes would elicit suspicion that elaborate precautions were taken to remove them from the ward each day. But the precautions proved needless. The closest any staff member came to questioning these notes occurred when one pseudopatient asked his physician what kind of medication he was receiving and began to write down the response. "You needn't write it," he was told gently. "If you have trouble remembering, just ask me again."

If no questions were asked of the pseudopatients, how was their writing interpreted? Nursing records for three patients indicate that the writing was seen as an aspect of their pathological behavior. "Patient engages in writing behavior" was the daily nursing comment on one of the pseudopatients who was never questioned about his writing. Given that the patient is in the hospital, he must be psychologically disturbed. And given that he is disturbed, continuous writing must be a behavioral manifestation of that disturbance, perhaps a subset of the compulsive behaviors that are sometimes correlated with schizophrenia.

One tacit characteristic of psychiatric diagnosis is that it locates the sources of aberration within the individual and only rarely within the complex of stimuli that surrounds him. Consequently, behaviors that are stimulated by the environment are commonly misattributed to the patient's disorder. For example, one kindly nurse found a pseudopatient pacing the long hospital corridors. "Nervous, Mr. X?" she asked. "No, bored," he said.

The notes kept by pseudopatients are full of patient behaviors that were misinterpreted by well-intentioned staff. Often enough, a patient would go "berserk" because he had, wittingly or unwittingly, been mistreated by, say, an attendant. A nurse coming upon the scene would rarely inquire even cursorily into the environmental stimuli of the patient's behavior. Rather, she assumed that his upset derived from his pathology, not from his present interactions with other staff members. Occasionally, the staff might assume that the patient's family (especially when they had recently visited) or other patients had stimulated the outburst. But never were the staff found to assume that one of themselves or the structure of the hospital had anything to do with a patient's behavior. One psychiatrist pointed to a group of patients who were sitting outside the cafeteria entrance half an hour before lunchtime. To a group of young residents he indicated that such behavior was characteristic of the oral-acquisitive nature of the syndrome. It seemed not to occur to him that there were very few things to anticipate in a psychiatric hospital besides eating.

A psychiatric label has a life and an influence of its own. Once the impression has been formed that the patient is schizophrenic, the expectation is that he will continue to be schizophrenic. When a sufficient amount of time has passed, during which the patient has done nothing bizarre, he is considered to be in remission and available for discharge. But the label endures beyond discharge, with the unconfirmed expectation that he will behave as a schizophrenic again. Such labels, conferred by mental health professionals, are as influential on the patient as they are on his relatives and friends, and it should not surprise anyone that the diagnosis acts on all of them as a self-fulfilling prophecy. Eventually, the patient himself accepts the diagnosis, with all of its surplus meanings and expectations, and behaves accordingly.

The inferences to be made from these matters are quite simple. Much as Zigler and Phillips have demonstrated that there is enormous overlap in the symptoms presented by patients who have been variously diagnosed,[6] so there is enormous overlap in the behaviors of the sane and the insane. The sane are not "sane" all of the time. We lose our tempers "for no good reason." We are occasionally depressed or anxious, again for no good reason. And we may find it difficult to get along with one or another person—again for no reason that we can specify. Similarly, the insane are not always insane. Indeed, it was the impression of the pseudopatients while living with them that they were sane for long periods of time—that the bizarre behaviors upon which their diagnoses were allegedly predicated constituted only a small fraction of their total behavior. If it makes no sense to label ourselves permanently depressed on the basis of an occasional depression, then it takes better evidence than is presently available to label all patients insane or schizophrenic on the basis of bizarre behaviors or cognitions. It seems more useful, as Mischel[7] has pointed out, to limit our discussions to *behaviors,* the stimuli that provoke them, and their correlates.

It is not known why powerful impressions of personality traits, such as "crazy" or "insane," arise. Conceivably, when the origins of and stimuli that give rise to a behavior are remote or unknown, or when the behavior strikes us as immutable, trait labels regarding the *behaver* arise. When, on the other hand, the origins and stimuli are known and available, discourse is limited to the behavior itself. Thus, I may hallucinate because I am sleeping, or I may hallucinate because I have ingested a peculiar drug. These are termed sleep-induced hallucinations, or dreams, and drug-induced hallucinations, respectively. But when the stimuli to my hallucinations are unknown, that is called craziness, or schizophrenia—as if that inference were somehow as illuminating as the others.

THE EXPERIENCE OF PSYCHIATRIC HOSPITALIZATION

The term "mental illness" is of recent origin. It was coined by people who were humane in their inclinations and who wanted very much to raise the station of (and the public's sympathies toward) the psychologically disturbed from that of witches and "crazies" to one that was akin to the physically ill. And they were at least partially successful, for the treatment of the mentally ill *has* improved considerably over the years. But while treatment has improved, it is doubtful that people really regard the mentally ill in the same way that they view the physically ill. A broken leg is something one recovers from, but mental illness allegedly endures forever. A broken leg does not threaten the observer, but a crazy schizophrenic? There is by now a host of evidence that attitudes toward the mentally ill are characterized by fear, hostility, aloofness, suspicion, and dread. The mentally ill are society's lepers.

That such attitudes infect the general population is perhaps not surprising, only upsetting. But that they affect the professionals—attendants, nurses, physicians, psychologists, and social workers—who treat and deal with the mentally ill is more disconcerting, both because such attitudes are self-evidently pernicious and because they are unwitting. Most mental health professionals would insist that they are sympathetic toward the mentally ill, that they are neither avoidant nor hostile. But it is more likely that an exquisite ambivalence characterizes their relations with psychiatric patients, such that their avowed impulses are only part of their entire attitude. Negative attitudes are there too and can easily be detected. Such attitudes should not surprise us. They are the natural offspring of the labels patients wear and the places in which they are found.

Consider the structure of the typical psychiatric hospital. Staff and patients are strictly segregated. Staff have their own living space, including their dining facilities, bathrooms, and assembly places. The glassed quarters that contain the professional staff, which the pseudopatients came to call "the cage," sit out on every dayroom. The staff emerge primarily for caretaking purposes—to give medication, to conduct a therapy or group meeting, to instruct or reprimand a patient. Otherwise, staff keep to themselves, almost as if the disorder that afflicts their charges is somehow catching.

So much is patient-staff segregation the rule that, for four public hospitals in which an attempt was made to measure the degree to which staff and patients mingle, it was necessary to use "time out of the staff cage" as the operational measure. While it was not the case that all time spent out of the cage was spent mingling with patients (attendants, for example, would occasionally emerge to watch television in the dayroom), it was the only way in which one could gather reliable data on time for measuring.

The average amount of time spent by attendants outside of the cage was 11.3 percent (range, 3 to 52 percent). This figure does not represent only time spent mingling with patients, but also includes time spent on such chores as folding laundry, supervising patients while they shave, directing ward cleanup, and sending patients to off-ward activities. It was the relatively rare attendant who spent time talking with patients or playing games with them. It proved impossible to obtain a "percent mingling time" for nurses, since the amount of time they spent out of the cage was

too brief. Rather, we counted instances of emergence from the cage. On the average, daytime nurses emerged from the cage 11.5 times per shift, including instances when they left the ward entirely (range, 4 to 39 times). Late afternoon and night nurses were even less available, emerging on the average 9.4 times per shift (range, 4 to 41 times). Data on early morning nurses, who arrived usually after midnight and departed at 8 A.M., are not available because patients were asleep during most of this period.

Physicians, especially psychiatrists, were even less available. They were rarely seen on the wards. Quite commonly, they would be seen only when they arrived and departed, with the remaining time being spent in their offices or in the cage. On the average, physicians emerged on the ward 6.7 times per day (range, 1 to 17 times). It proved difficult to make an accurate estimate in this regard, since physicians often maintained hours that allowed them to come and go at different times.

The hierarchical organization of the psychiatric hospital has been commented on before, but the latent meaning of that kind of organization is worth noting again. Those with the most power have least to do with patients, and those with the least power are most involved with them. Recall, however, that the acquisition of role-appropriate behaviors occurs mainly through the observation of others, with the most powerful having the most influence. Consequently, it is understandable that attendants not only spend more time with patients than do any other members of the staff—that is required by their station in the hierarchy—but also, insofar as they learn from their superiors' behavior, spend as little time with patients as they can. Attendants are seen mainly in the cage, which is where the models, the action, and the power are.

I turn now to a different set of studies, these dealing with staff response to patient-initiated contact. It has long been known that the amount of time a person spends with you can be an index of your significance to him. If he initiates and maintains eye contact, there is reason to believe that he is considering your requests and needs. If he pauses to chat or actually stops and talks, there is added reason to infer that he is individuating you. In four hospitals, the pseudopatient approached the staff member with a request which took the following form: "Pardon me, Mr. [or Dr. or Mrs.] X, could you tell me when I will be eligible for grounds privileges?" (or ". . . when I will be presented at the staff meeting?" or ". . . when I am likely to be discharged?"). While the content of the question varied according to the appropriateness of the target and the pseudopatient's (apparent) current needs the form was always a courteous and relevant request for information. Care was taken never to approach a particular member of the staff more than once a day, lest the staff member become suspicious or irritated. . . . [R]emember that the behavior of the pseudopatients was neither bizarre nor disruptive. One could indeed engage in good conversation with them.

. . . Minor differences between these four institutions were overwhelmed by the degree to which staff avoided continuing contacts that patients had initiated. By far, their most common response consisted of either a brief response to the question, offered while they were "on the move" and with head averted, or no response at all.

The encounter frequently took the following bizarre form: (pseudopatient) "Pardon me, Dr. X. Could you tell me when I am eligible for grounds privileges?" (physician) "Good morning, Dave. How are you today?" (Moves off without waiting for a response.). . .

POWERLESSNESS AND DEPERSONALIZATION

Eye contact and verbal contact reflect concern and individuation; their absence, avoidance and depersonalization. The data I have presented do not do justice to the rich daily encounters that grew up around matters of depersonalization and avoidance. I have records of patients who were beaten by staff for the sin of having initiated verbal contact. During my own experience, for example, one patient was beaten in the presence of other patients for having approached an attendant and [telling]

him, "I like you." Occasionally, punishment meted out to patients for misdemeanors seemed so excessive that it could not be justified by the most radical interpretations of psychiatric canon. Nevertheless, they appeared to go unquestioned. Tempers were often short. A patient who had not heard a call for medication would be roundly excoriated, and the morning attendants would often wake patients with, "Come on, you m—f—s, out of bed!"

Neither anecdotal nor "hard" data can convey the overwhelming sense of powerlessness which invades the individual as he is continually exposed to the depersonalization of the psychiatric hospital. It hardly matters *which* psychiatric hospital— the excellent public ones and the very plush private hospital were better than the rural and shabby ones in this regard, but again, the features that psychiatric hospitals had in common overwhelmed by far their apparent differences.

Powerlessness was evident everywhere. The patient is deprived of many of his legal rights by dint of his psychiatric commitment. He is shorn of credibility by virtue of his psychiatric label. His freedom of movement is restricted. He cannot initiate contact with the staff, but may only respond to such overtures as they make. Personal privacy is minimal. Patient quarters can be entered and possessions examined by any staff member, for whatever reason. His personal history and anguish is available to any staff member (often including the "grey lady" and "candy striper" volunteer) who chooses to read his folder, regardless of their therapeutic relationship to him. His personal hygiene and waste evacuation are often monitored. The water closets may have no doors.

At times, depersonalization reached such proportions that pseudopatients had the sense that they were invisible, or at least unworthy of account. Upon being admitted, I and other pseudopatients took the initial physical examinations in a semipublic room, where staff members went about their own business as if we were not there.

On the ward, attendants delivered verbal and occasionally serious physical abuse to patients in the presence of other observing patients, some of whom (the pseudopatients) were writing it all down. Abusive behavior, on the other hand, terminated quite abruptly when other staff members were known to be coming. Staff are credible witnesses. Patients are not.

A nurse unbuttoned her uniform to adjust her brassiere in the presence of an entire ward of viewing men. One did not have the sense that she was being seductive. Rather, she didn't notice us. A group of staff persons might point to a patient in the dayroom and discuss him animatedly, as if he were not there.

One illuminating instance of depersonalization and invisibility occurred with regard to medications. All told, the pseudopatients were administered nearly 2100 pills, including Elavil, Stelazine, Compazine, and Thorazine, to name but a few. (That such a variety of medications should have been administered to patients presenting identical symptoms is itself worthy of note.) Only two were swallowed. The rest were either pocketed or deposited in the toilet. The pseudopatients were not alone in this. Although I have no precise records on how many patients rejected their medications, the pseudopatients frequently found the medications of other patients in the toilet before they deposited their own. As long as they were cooperative, their behavior and the pseudopatients' own in this matter, as in other important matters, went unnoticed throughout.

Reactions to such depersonalization among pseudopatients were intense. Although they had come to the hospital as participant observers and were fully aware that they did not "belong," they nevertheless found themselves caught up in and fighting the process of depersonalization. Some examples: A graduate student in psychology asked his wife to bring his textbooks to the hospital so he could "catch up on his homework"—this despite the elaborate precautions taken to conceal his professional association. The same student, who had trained for quite some time to get into the hospital, and who had looked forward to the experience, "remembered" some drag races that he had wanted to see on the weekend and insisted that he be discharged by that time. Another pseudopatient attempted a romance with a nurse. Subsequently, he

informed the staff that he was applying for admission to graduate school in psychology and was very likely to be admitted, since a graduate professor was one of his regular hospital visitors. The same person began to engage in psychotherapy with other patients—all of this as a way of becoming a person in an impersonal environment.

THE SOURCES OF DEPERSONALIZATION

What are the origins of depersonalization? I have already mentioned two. First are attitudes held by all of us toward the mentally ill—including those who treat them—attitudes characterized by fear, distrust, and horrible expectations on the one hand, and benevolent intentions on the other. Our ambivalence leads, in this instance as in others, to avoidance.

Second, and not entirely separate, the hierarchical structure of the psychiatric hospital facilitates depersonalization. Those who are at the top have least to do with patients, and their behavior inspires the rest of the staff. Average daily contact with psychiatrists, psychologists, residents, and physicians combined ranged from 3.9 to 25.1 minutes, with an overall mean of 6.8 (six pseudopatients over a total of 129 days of hospitalization). Included in this average are time spent in the admissions interview, ward meetings in the presence of a senior staff member, group and individual psychotherapy contacts, case presentation conferences, and discharge meetings. Clearly, patients do not spend much time in interpersonal contact with doctoral staff. And doctoral staff serve as models for nurses and attendants.

There are probably other sources. Psychiatric installations are presently in serious financial straits. Staff shortages are pervasive, staff time at a premium. Something has to give, and that something is patient contact. Yet, while financial stresses are realities, too much can be made of them. I have the impression that the psychological forces that result in depersonalization are much stronger than the fiscal ones and that the addition of more staff would not correspondingly improve patient care in this regard. The incidence of staff meetings and the enormous amount of record-keeping on patients, for example, have not been as substantially reduced as has patient contact. Priorities exist, even during hard times. Patient contact is not a significant priority in the traditional psychiatric hospital, and fiscal pressures do not account for this. Avoidance and depersonalization may.

Heavy reliance upon psychotropic medication tacitly contributes to depersonalization by convincing staff that treatment is indeed being conducted and that further patient contact may not be necessary. Even here, however, caution needs to be exercised in understanding the role of psychotropic drugs. If patients were powerful rather than powerless, if they were viewed as interesting individuals rather than diagnostic entities, if they were socially significant rather than social lepers, if their anguish truly and wholly compelled our sympathies and concerns, would we not *seek* contact with them, despite the availability of medications? Perhaps for the pleasure of it all?

THE CONSEQUENCES OF LABELING AND DEPERSONALIZATION

Whenever the ratio of what is known to what needs to be known approaches zero, we tend to invent "knowledge" and assume that we understand more than we actually do. We seem unable to acknowledge that we simply don't know. The needs for diagnosis and remediation of behavioral and emotional problems are enormous. But rather than acknowledge that we are just embarking on understanding, we continue to label patients "schizophrenic," "manic-depressive," and "insane," as if in those words we had captured the essence of understanding. The facts of the matter are that we have known for a long time that diagnoses are often not useful or reliable, but we have nevertheless continued to use them. We now know that we cannot distinguish insanity from sanity. It is depressing to consider how that information will be used.

Not merely depressing, but frightening. How many people, one wonders, are sane but not recognized as such in our psychiatric institutions? How many have been needlessly stripped of their privileges of citizenship, from the right to vote and drive to that of handling their own accounts? How many have feigned insanity in order to avoid the criminal consequences of their behavior, and, conversely, how many would rather stand trial than live interminably in a psychiatric hospital—but are wrongly thought to be mentally ill? How many have been stigmatized by well-intentioned, but nevertheless erroneous, diagnoses? On the last point, recall again that a "type 2 error" in psychiatric diagnosis does not have the same consequences it does in medical diagnosis. A diagnosis of cancer that has been found to be in error is cause for celebration. But psychiatric diagnoses are rarely found to be in error. The label sticks, a mark of inadequacy forever.

Finally, how many patients might be "sane" outside the psychiatric hospital but seem insane in it—not because craziness resides in them, as it were, but because they are responding to a bizarre setting, one that may be unique to institutions which harbor nether people? Goffman[8] calls the process of socialization to such institutions "mortification"—an apt metaphor that includes the processes of depersonalization that have been described here. And while it is impossible to know whether the pseudopatients' responses to these processes are characteristic of all inmates—they were, after all, not real patients—it is difficult to believe that these processes of socialization to a psychiatric hospital provide useful attitudes or habits of response for living in the "real world."

SUMMARY AND CONCLUSIONS

It is clear that we cannot distinguish the sane from the insane in psychiatric hospitals. The hospital itself imposes a special environment in which the meanings of behavior can easily be misunderstood. The consequences to patients hospitalized in such an environment—the powerlessness, depersonalization, segregation, mortification, and self-labeling—seem undoubtedly counter-therapeutic.

I do not, even now, understand this problem well enough to perceive solutions. But two matters seem to have some promise. The first concerns the proliferation of community mental health facilities, of crisis intervention centers, of the human potential movement, and of behavior therapies that, for all of their own problems, tend to avoid psychiatric labels, to focus on specific problems and behaviors, and to retain the individual in a relatively nonpejorative environment. Clearly, to the extent that we refrain from sending the distressed to insane places, our impressions of them are less likely to be distorted. (The risk of distorted perceptions, it seems to me, is always present, since we are much more sensitive to an individual's behaviors and verbalizations than we are to the subtle contextual stimuli that often promote them. At issue here is a matter of magnitude. And, as I have shown, the magnitude of distortion is exceedingly high in the extreme context that is a psychiatric hospital.)

The second matter that might prove promising speaks to the need to increase the sensitivity of mental health workers and researchers to the Catch-22 position of psychiatric patients. Simply reading materials in this area will be of help to some such workers and researchers. For others, directly experiencing the impact of psychiatric hospitalization will be of enormous use. Clearly, further research into the social psychology of such total institutions will both facilitate treatment and deepen understanding.

I and the other pseudopatients in the psychiatric setting had distinctly negative reactions. We do not pretend to describe the subjective experiences of true patients. Theirs may be different from ours, particularly with the passage of time and the necessary process of adaptation to one's environment. But we can and do speak to the relatively more objective indices of treatment within the hospital. It could be a mistake, and a very unfortunate one, to consider that what happened to us derived from malice or stupidity on the part of the staff. Quite the contrary, our overwhelming impression of them was of people who really cared, who were committed and who were uncommonly intelligent. Where they failed, as they sometimes did painfully, it would be more accurate to attribute those failures to the environment in which they, too, found themselves than to personal callousness. Their perceptions and behavior were controlled by the situation, rather than being motivated by a malicious disposition. In a more benign environment, one that was less attached to global diagnosis, their behaviors and judgments might have been more benign and effective.

CRITICAL-THINKING QUESTIONS

1. How does this research illustrate the basic ideas of labeling theory in sociology?
2. Once the "patients" were admitted to the hospitals, how was their subsequent behavior understood in terms of the label of "mentally ill"? Did the label of mental illness disappear at the point at which the "patients" were discharged from the hospitals?
3. What, if any, ethical issues are raised by the way in which this research was conducted?

NOTES

1. R. Benedict, *J. Gen. Psychol.,* 10 (1934), 59.

2. Beyond the personal difficulties that the pseudopatient is likely to experience in the hospital, there are legal and social ones that, combined, require considerable attention before entry. For example, once admitted to a psychiatric institution, it is difficult, if not impossible, to be discharged on short notice, state law to the contrary notwithstanding. I was not sensitive to these difficulties at the outset of the project, nor to the personal and situational emergencies that can arise, but later a writ of habeas corpus was prepared for each of the entering pseudopatients and an attorney was kept "on call" during every hospitalization. I am grateful to John Kaplan and Robert Bartels for legal advice and assistance in these matters.

3. However distasteful such concealment is, it was a necessary first step to examining these questions. Without concealment, there would have been no way to know how valid these experiences were; nor was there any way of knowing whether whatever detections occurred were a tribute to the diagnostic acumen of the staff or to the hospital's rumor network. Obviously, since my concerns are general ones that cut across

individual hospitals and staffs, I have respected their anonymity and have eliminated clues that might lead to their identification.

4. Interestingly, of the twelve admissions, eleven were diagnosed as schizophrenic and one, with the identical symptomatology, as manic-depressive psychosis. This diagnosis has a more favorable prognosis, and it was given by the only private hospital in our sample. On the relations between social class and psychiatric diagnosis, see A. deB. Hollingshead and F. C. Redlich, *Social Class and Mental Illness: A Community Study* (New York: John Wiley, 1958).

5. S. E. Asch, *J. Abnorm. Soc. Psychol.,* 41(1946); *Social Psychology* (Englewood Cliffs, NJ: Prentice-Hall, 1952).

6. E. Zigler and L. Phillips, *J. Abnorm. Soc. Psychol.,* 63 (1961), 69. See also R. K. Freudenberg and J. P. Robertson, *A.M.A. Arch. Neurol. Psychiatr.,* 76 (1956),14.

7. W. Mischel, *Personality and Assessment* (New York: John Wiley, 1968).

8. E. Goffman, *Asylums* (Garden City, NY: Doubleday, 1961).

29

Crime in World Perspective

Elliott Currie

The problem of crime is far worse in the United States than it is in most other industrial societies. In this selection, Elliott Currie suggests that the reasons for this are deep in our society itself—and include the sharp contrast between rich and poor, the high unemployment, and the general lack of strong family and community ties. The strong emphasis on individualism in U.S. culture not only promotes crime but also directs us rather simplistically to blame crime on criminals, so that the war on crime is largely a matter of stiffer sentences and more prisons.

. . . No one living in a major American city needs much convincing that despite more than a decade of ever-"tougher" policies against crime, the United States remains wracked by violence and fear. Criminal violence is woven deeply into our social fabric—a brutal and appalling affront to any reasonable conception of civilized social life.

In recent months, these incidents took place in

the United States: In Illinois, armed marauders attacked travelers on an interstate highway, robbing the occupants of two cars and killing a twelve-year-old boy. In Florida, a passing motorist's intervention barely saved a young woman from attack by a crowd of nearly a hundred men. In New York, gangs of youths robbed and beat participants in a charity walkathon in Central Park. In Fort Lauderdale, Florida, a bandit held up an entire church congregation during an evening service. Not far away, near Pompano Beach, two intrepid men broke *into* a prison and robbed two inmates. A United States senator and his companion, on their way to dinner with the mayor of New York, were mugged by two men just down the street from the mayor's mansion. In Los Angeles, eleven people died in a single weekend in episodes of youth-gang violence, while the home of the chief of the Los Angeles Police Department was burglarized—twice.

The public response to criminal violence has become correspondingly bitter and even desperate. Three-fifths of the American public expressed their support for a self-styled vigilante who shot down four young black men after they asked him for five dollars in a New York subway; respected commentators urge people living in cities to "adopt the tough attitudes of an embattled population."

To live in the urban United States in the 1980s is to feel that the elementary bonds of society are badly frayed. The sense of social disintegration is so pervasive that it is easy to forget that things are not the same elsewhere. Violence on the American level comes to seem like a fact of life, an inevitable feature of modern society. It is not. Most of us are aware that we are worse off, in this respect, than other advanced industrial countries. How *much* worse, however, is truly startling.

Criminal statistics are notoriously tricky, and comparisons of one country's statistics with another's even more so. But the differences in national crime rates—at least for serious crimes of violence, which we rightly fear the most—are large enough to transcend the limitations of the data. In recent years, Americans have faced roughly seven to ten times the risk of death by homicide as the residents of most European countries and Japan. Our closest European competitor in homicide rates is Finland, and we murder one another at more than three times the rate the Finns do.

These differences are sometimes explained as the result of America's "frontier" ethos or its abundance of firearms. Both of these are important, but neither even begins to explain the dimensions of these international differences. With similar frontier traditions, Australia and Canada have murder rates that are, respectively, less than a fourth and less than a third of ours. Though their numbers are roughly the same, Californians are murdered almost six times as often as Canadians. Nor does this simply reflect the relative ease with which Americans can obtain handguns: More Californians are killed with knives alone than Canadians are by *all* means put together. And Canada ranks fairly high, internationally, in homicide rates.

What holds for homicide also holds for other serious crimes of violence. Here the comparisons are more chancy, because of greater problems of definition and measurement. But careful research reveals that Americans are more than three times as likely to be raped than West Germans, and six times as likely to be robbed. These rates were derived from police statistics, which are known to be subject to strong biases. But similar results come from "victimization" studies, which calculate crime rates by asking people whether, and how often, they have been the victims of crime.

In the first English study of this kind, the British Home Office (using a sample of eleven thousand respondents) estimated that the British robbery rate in 1981 was about twenty for every ten thousand people over age sixteen in 1981. In the same year, a comparable American survey by the Bureau of Justice Statistics estimated a robbery rate nearly four times higher. The British study turned up not one rape and only a single attempted rape: The American survey estimated an overall rape rate of about ten per ten thousand (three completed, seven attempted). And Britain is by no means one of the most tranquil of European countries: Rates of serious criminal violence in Denmark, Norway, Switzerland, and the Netherlands are lower still.

In the severity of its crime rates, the United States more closely resembles some of the most volatile countries of the Third World than other developed Western societies; and we won't begin to understand the problem of criminal violence in the United States without taking that stark difference as our point of departure. Its consequences are enormous. If we were blessed with the moderately low homicide rate of Sweden, we would suffer well under three thousand homicide deaths a year, thereby saving close to sixteen thousand American lives—nearly three times as many as were lost in battle annually, on average, during the height of the Vietnam War.

The magnitude of the contrast between the United States and most other developed societies is often ignored as we scrutinize the fluctuations in our own crime rates from year to year. We watch the state of the public safety, like that of the economy, with a kind of desperate hopefulness. Just as the economy has "recovered" several times in recent years, so we have periodically "turned the corner on crime." And indeed, by the mid-1980s, the level of violent crime had fallen off from the disastrous peak it had reached at the start of the decade. That respite was certainly welcome; but it should not obscure the more troubling general upward trend since the sixties. From 1969 through 1983, the rate of violent crime—as measured by police reports—rose nationwide by 61 percent. Rape went up 82 percent, robbery 44 percent, and homicide 14 percent (the first two figures are almost certainly inflated because of changes in reporting, the third probably not). Measured this way, the more recent declines have only returned us to the already horrendous levels of the late 1970s, just before we suffered one of the sharpest *increases* in criminal violence in American history. Still more disturbingly, reported rapes and aggravated assaults *rose* again in 1984—at the fastest pace since 1980. Criminal victimization surveys offer a somewhat different but scarcely more encouraging picture, indicating virtually no change in crimes of violence for the past decade, with a slight decline in many violent crimes in 1983—but a slight *rise* in others in 1984.

The recent dip in crime, moreover, has been ominously uneven. Between 1982 and 1983, the murder rate in the economically depressed states of Illinois and Michigan rose by 10 percent; reported rapes shot up by 20 percent in Michigan and 27 percent in Wisconsin. Detroit's murder rate jumped 17 percent from 1981 to 1983; that of East St. Louis, Illinois, by an astonishing 96 percent. Drug-related gang wars helped boost the homicide rate in Oakland, California, by 17 percent between 1983 and 1984. The national crime rate, in short, may have improved—but the situation in some of America's inner cities was worsening.

What makes all this so troubling is that our high crime rates have resisted the most extraordinary efforts to reduce them. Since 1973, we have more than doubled the national incarceration rate—the proportion of the population locked up in state and federal prisons and in local jails. In 1983, the prison inmates alone would have filled a city the size of Atlanta, Georgia; including the inmates of local jails (a number that jumped by more than a *third* between 1978 and 1982 alone) would have swollen the "city" to the size of Washington, DC. And this number doesn't include those confined in juvenile detention facilities, military prisons, and psychiatric facilities for the criminally insane. . . .

How did we arrive at this impasse?

As with many other issues of social policy in the eighties, there is a pervasive sense that older ways of thinking about crime have lost their usefulness and credibility; but no convincing alternatives have come forward to take their place. It is painfully apparent that the decade-long conservative experiment in crime control has failed to live up to its promises. That experiment, launched with high hopes and much self-righteous certainty, was based on the alluringly simple premise that crime was pervasive in the United States because we were too lenient with criminals; in the economic jargon fashionable during the seventies, the "costs" of crime had fallen too low. The reverse side of the argument was that other ways of dealing with crime—through "rehabilitating" offenders or improving social conditions—at best didn't work and at worst had made the streets more dangerous. But the policies that resulted from these premises have left us with both the world's highest rate of incarceration for "street" crimes *and* the highest levels of criminal violence outside of some developing countries. We have created an overstuffed and volatile penal system of overwhelming barbarity, yet we endure levels of violence significantly higher than in the more "permissive" sixties.

To be sure, it is likely that some part of the recent dip in the crime rate is a result of the huge increases in incarceration in the past several years; after all, it would be remarkable if they had had *no* effect on crime. But the hard fact is that violent crime is worse in America today than before the "prison boom" of the seventies and eighties began, and indeed was highest just when our rate of incarceration was increasing the fastest. At best, very little has been accomplished, at great social cost. To borrow a medical analogy, it's plausible to argue that a series of drastic and unpleasant treatments has relieved some of the symptoms of the disease; it is not plausible to argue that the patient is well, or even demonstrably recovering. And as we shall see, there is little ground for hope that the same strategies can accomplish much more in the future, short of draconian measures on a scale that would transform our criminal justice system—and American society as a whole—beyond recognition.

It could, of course, be argued that this strategy *would* have worked, if it had only gone far enough—but that it was undermined by the leniency and obstinacy of officials and the public, especially the unwillingness of legislators to vote for more prisons. If the streets are still unsafe despite the swelling of the prisons, blame it on the failure to build enough new prison cells and the consequent vacillation of judges hesitant to pack still more criminals into the time-bombs that our prisons have mainly become. In 1984, for example, the Federation of New York Judges declared that the streets had become "lawless marches of robbers, rapists, and felons of every kind," and called for more prisons, on the ground that "swift and severe punishment is the only defense against predators." Appellate Justice Murphy even went so far as to argue that without a greater investment in punishment "we will live in the sickly twilight of a soulless people too weak to drive predators out of their own house." Justice Murphy and his colleagues were apparently unfazed by the fact that criminals had "taken the city" despite the doubling of New York's incarceration rate during the previous decade.

So proponents of this "get-even-tougher" approach are confronted with a formidable job of persuasion. It is difficult to think of any social experiment in recent years whose central ideas have been so thoroughly and consistently carried out. The number of people we have put behind bars, for ever-longer terms, is unprecedented in American history. And unlike most such experiments, which are usually undertaken with minimal funding and on a limited scale, this one has been both massively financed and carried out on a grand scale in nearly every state of the union. If it has failed to work in the way its promoters expected, they have fewer excuses than most applied social theorists.

We have become a country in which it is possible to be sentenced to a year behind bars for stealing six dollars' worth of meat from a supermarket, but we are still by far the most dangerous society in the developed world. That paradox has deeply undercut the credibility of the conservative strategy of crime control in the eighties. No one today seriously disagrees that we need a strong and effective criminal justice system; that is no longer a matter for real debate. But that is a far cry from believing that we can rely on the prisons to solve the crime problem. Clearly, we need more creative approaches to crime—and we need them urgently.

But I do not think that the earlier perspective, which for want of a more precise term I will call "liberal criminology," can, by itself, offer a sufficiently compelling alternative. It is risky to generalize about that perspective, because it included several diverse—and not always compatible—lines of thought and practice. But there were common themes. Most liberal criminology linked crime to the pressures of social and economic inequality and deprivation, and assumed that a combination of rehabilitation for offenders, better opportunities for the disadvantaged, and a more humane, less intrusive criminal-justice system would reduce crime, if not end it. By the end of the sixties, that vision was a shambles, undermined by the apparent "paradox" of rising crime rates in the face of the Great Society's social programs, the general improvement in the American standard of living, and the reduction of unemployment. Conservatives made much of the fact that American society seemed to be becoming more dangerous just when it was also becoming both more affluent and more committed to action against poverty, inequality, and racial subordination.

That "paradox" . . . was highly exaggerated.

And indeed, the vision of the liberal criminology of the sixties has been unfairly maligned and often misunderstood. Much of what it had to say about the roots of crime and about the potentials of the criminal-justice system remains both remarkably fresh and, more important, correct. It rested on several crucial perceptions that have stood up well under the test of time and experience. One was that crime could not be dealt with through the criminal-justice system alone, and that the system is likely to crack if we load it with that burden. Another was that if we wanted to deal with crime in America in other than marginal ways, we would have to move beyond the level of merely patching up, punishing, or quarantining individuals who had gone wrong to confront a range of deep and long-standing social and economic problems. Both of these principles fell out of fashion during the seventies, but both were right—and both must be a part of any credible analysis of crime in the future.

But the liberalism of the sixties had important limitations as well. At times, it seemed to say that crime wasn't really as much of a problem as the public naïvely thought it was—a position that won few friends outside the relatively tranquil preserves of the academic world. Most other Americans were afraid of crime, or enraged by it, and they had good reason to be. It didn't help to imply, as some liberal and radical criminologists did, that worrying overmuch about being mugged or raped was a sign of incipient racism or an authoritarian character. Likewise, it didn't help when liberals, pressed for answers to the problem of violent street crime, responded by insisting that the crimes of white-collar people and corporate executives were *also* costly and vicious. That was certainly true, but it simply sidestepped the question at hand. . . .

If we are to build a society that is less dangerous, less fearful, and less torn by violence, we will have to move beyond *both* perspectives—liberal and conservative. Can we do so? I think we can. . . . Doing so, however, will require hard choices and a serious commitment of social and economic resources. In a society traditionally drawn to the quick fix, many people, at all points

on the political spectrum, want to know what will stop crime next month, and are impatient with the idea that we are in for a long haul. But the hard truth is that there are no magic buttons to push, no program waiting just around the corner to reform the courts or strengthen the police or organize the neighborhood that will make criminal violence disappear tomorrow. There are, however, steps we can take now that can begin to make a difference in the safety of our streets and homes—and to reverse the tragic waste of lives that criminal violence involves.

Many of those steps are based on evidence that has been available for years. It was often said during the seventies that we knew very little about the causes of crime. That was not true then, and it is even less true now, after several more years of research and experience. We do not know as much as we would like, but we are not groping in the dark, either. To agree that more research needs to be done is not the same as saying that we don't know enough to start. . . .

But there is another, still more important reason for our failure to come to grips with criminal violence. It is not lack of knowledge or technical prowess that keeps us from launching an honest and serious fight against crime; the obstacles are much more often ideological and political. What seem on the surface to be technical arguments about what we can and cannot do about crime often turn out, on closer inspection, to be moral or political arguments about what we should or should not do; and these in turn are rooted in larger disagreements about what sort of society we want for ourselves and our children. If we are serious about rethinking the problem of crime, we need to engage the issues on that higher level of moral and political values. It is always easier, as R. H. Tawney once observed, to "set up a new department, and appoint new officials, and invent a new name to express their resolution" to do things differently. "But unless they will take the pains," Tawney cautioned, "not only to act, but to reflect, they end by effecting nothing.". . .

A hard look at the comparative evidence allows us to dispose of several myths that have hindered our coming to grips with violent crime in America. It is not, for example, unusual leniency with criminals that distinguishes us from less violent nations. On the contrary, as we've seen, we are far more punitive in our response to crime (if often less efficient—two outcomes that are complementary, not contradictory): We rely far more on the formal apparatus of punishment and use it more severely than most other advanced societies. Likewise, the comparative evidence quickly dispenses with the myths that the growth of the welfare state or laxity in the punishment of children are to blame for our crime rate, since the welfare state is distinctly underdeveloped in the United States as compared with other industrial societies and our support for punitive discipline far greater.

On the other hand, we've seen that the United States differs from other industrial societies in several dimensions of social and economic life that are crucial in accounting for our high levels of criminal violence. These include a wider spread of inequality, greater extremes of poverty and insecurity, the relative absence of effective policies to deal with unemployment and subemployment, greater disruption of community and family ties through job destruction and migration, and fewer supports for families and individuals in the face of economic and technological change and material deprivation.

Some of the roots of these differences—particularly our heritage of racial subordination—reach deep into our history in ways that would create profound difficulties for even the most generous and active social policy. Others, however, represent more or less conscious and current choices, for which we pay a steep price in social disintegration and violence. The result has been an unusual degree of erosion of the institutions that bear much of the responsibility for achieving socialization and social cohesion. Like all serious tasks, these require sufficient and appropriate resources—in particular a supportive and nurturing human "ecology" that, among other things, provides for the attentive and undisturbed care of the young and ensures that individuals can contribute to the larger community and in turn be rewarded by it with esteem and respect. Such a supportive ecology does not simply flow automatically from the operation of the economic market. On the contrary, the natural tendency of the marketplace is to put considerable strain on the institutions of family, work, and community that are its chief components. The growth of urban-industrial consumer society has increased those strains throughout the world. In most developed nations, this process has been ameliorated to some extent by countervailing mechanisms of social obligation and support. In the United States, by contrast, this growth has been marked by the relatively unbuffered play of market forces and has been exceptionally disruptive of the institutions essential for the healthy development of character and community. In these differences we may begin to understand why we suffer the worst violent-crime rate among industrial societies—and why we are forced to resort to levels of punishment that sharply distinguish us from all but the most notoriously repressive among them.

The general nature of the remedy is implicit in the diagnosis. If we are serious about attacking the roots of this American affliction, we must build a society that is less unequal, less depriving, less insecure, less disruptive of family and community ties, less corrosive of cooperative values. In short, we must begin to take on the enormous task of creating the conditions of community life in which individuals can live together in compassionate and cooperative ways.

CRITICAL-THINKING QUESTIONS

1. How does the rate of serious street crimes in the United States compare with that of other industrial societies?

2. Why does Currie argue that reducing crime is hindered by ideological and political constraints?

3. In what ways does he suggest crime might be reduced? Do you think most members of our society would agree with his analysis?

30

Some Principles of Stratification

Kingsley Davis and Wilbert Moore
with a response by Melvin Tumin

Why is some degree of social stratification found everywhere? This selection outlines what has become known as the "Davis and Moore thesis": Social stratification is a consequence of the fact that some social positions are more important to the operation of a social system than others. The selection is followed by a critical response by Melvin Tumin, who suggests a number of ways in which social stratification is dysfunctional *for society.*

Starting from the proposition that no society is "classless," or unstratified, an effort is made to explain, in functional terms, the universal necessity which calls forth stratification in any social system. Next, an attempt is made to explain the roughly uniform distribution of prestige as between the major types of positions in every society. Since, however, there occur between one

SOURCES: "Some Principles of Stratification," by Kingsley Davis and Wilbert E. Moore, in *American Sociological Review,* vol. 10, no. 2 (April 1945), pp. 242–44.

"Some Principles of Stratification: A Critical Analysis," by Melvin Tumin, in *American Sociological Review,* vol. 18, no. 4 (Aug. 1953), pp. 387–93. Reprinted with permission.

society and another great differences in the degree and kind of stratification, some attention is also given to the varieties of social inequality and the variable factors that give rise to them. . . .

Throughout, it will be necessary to keep in mind one thing—namely, that the discussion relates to the system of positions, not to the individuals occupying those positions. It is one thing to ask why different positions carry different degrees of prestige, and quite another to ask how certain individuals get into those positions. Although, as the argument will try to show, both questions are related, it is essential to keep them separate in our thinking. Most of the literature on stratification has tried to answer the second question (particularly with regard to the ease or difficulty of mobility between strata) without tackling the first. The first question, however, is logically prior and, in the case of any particular individual or group, factually prior.

THE FUNCTIONAL NECESSITY OF STRATIFICATION

Curiously, however, the main functional necessity explaining the universal presence of stratification is precisely the requirement faced by any society of placing and motivating individuals in the social structure. As a functioning mechanism a society must somehow distribute its members in social positions and induce them to perform the duties of these positions. It must thus concern itself with motivation at two different levels: to instill in the proper individuals the desire to fill certain positions, and, once in these positions, the desire to perform the duties attached to them. Even though the social order may be relatively static in form, there is a continuous process of metabolism as new individuals are born into it, shift with age, and die off. Their absorption into the positional system must somehow be arranged and motivated. This is true whether the system is competitive or noncompetitive. A competitive system gives greater importance to the motivation to achieve positions, whereas a noncompetitive system gives perhaps greater importance to the motivation to perform the duties of the positions; but in any system both types of motivation are required.

If the duties associated with the various positions were all equally pleasant to the human organism, all equally important to societal survival, and all equally in need of the same ability or talent, it would make no difference who got into which positions, and the problem of social placement would be greatly reduced. But actually it does make a great deal of difference who gets into which positions, not only because some positions are inherently more agreeable than others, but also because some require special talents or training and some are functionally more important than others. Also, it is essential that the duties of the positions be performed with the diligence that their importance requires. Inevitably, then, a society must have, first, some kind of rewards that it can use as inducements, and, second, some way of distributing these rewards differentially according to positions. The rewards and their distribution become a part of the social order, and thus give rise to stratification.

One may ask what kind of rewards a society has at its disposal in distributing its personnel and securing essential services. It has, first of all, the things that contribute to sustenance and comfort. It has, second, the things that contribute to humor and diversion. And it has, finally, the things that contribute to self-respect and ego expansion. The last, because of the peculiarly social character of the self, is largely a function of the opinion of others, but it nonetheless ranks in importance with the first two. In any social system all three kinds of rewards must be dispensed differentially according to positions.

In a sense the rewards are "built into" the position. They consist in the "rights" associated with the position, plus what may be called its accompaniments or perquisites. Often the rights, and sometimes the accompaniments, are functionally related to the duties of the position. (Rights as viewed by the incumbent are usually duties as viewed by other members of the community.) However, there may be a host of subsidiary rights and perquisites that are not essential to the function of the position and have only an indirect and symbolic connection with its duties, but which still may be of considerable importance in inducing people to seek the positions and fulfill the essential duties.

If the rights and perquisites of different positions in a society must be unequal, then the society must be stratified, because that is precisely what stratification means. Social inequality is thus an unconsciously evolved device by which societies insure that the most important positions are conscientiously filled by the most qualified persons. Hence every society, no matter how simple or complex, must differentiate persons in terms of both prestige and esteem, and must therefore possess a certain amount of institutionalized inequality.

It does not follow that the amount or type of inequality need be the same in all societies. This is largely a function of factors that will be discussed presently.

THE TWO DETERMINANTS OF POSITIONAL RANK

Granting the general function that inequality subserves, one can specify the two factors that determine the relative rank of different positions. In general those positions convey the best reward, and hence have the highest rank, which (a) have the greatest importance for the society and (b) require the greatest training or talent. The first factor concerns function and is a matter of relative significance; the second concerns means and is a matter of scarcity.

Differential Functional Importance. Actually a society does not need to reward positions in proportion to their functional importance. It merely needs to give sufficient reward to them to insure that they will be filled competently. In other words, it must see that less essential positions do not compete successfully with more essential ones. If a position is easily filled, it need not be heavily rewarded, even though important. On the other hand, if it is important but hard to fill, the reward must be high enough to get it filled anyway. Functional importance is therefore a necessary but not a sufficient cause of high rank being assigned to a position.[1]

Differential Scarcity of Personnel. Practically all positions, no matter how acquired, require some form of skill or capacity for performance. This is implicit in the very notion of position, which implies that the incumbent must, by virtue of his incumbency, accomplish certain things.

There are, ultimately, only two ways in which a person's qualifications come about: through in-

herent capacity or through training. Obviously, in concrete activities both are always necessary, but from a practical standpoint the scarcity may lie primarily in one or the other, as well as in both. Some positions require innate talents of such high degree that the persons who fill them are bound to be rare. In many cases, however, talent is fairly abundant in the population but the training process is so long, costly, and elaborate that relatively few can qualify. Modern medicine, for example, is within the mental capacity of most individuals, but a medical education is so burdensome and expensive that virtually none would undertake it if the position of the M.D. did not carry a reward commensurate with the sacrifice.

If the talents required for a position are abundant and the training easy, the method of acquiring the position may have little to do with its duties. There may be, in fact, a virtually accidental relationship. But if the skills required are scarce by reason of the rarity of talent or the costliness of training, the position, if functionally important, must have an attractive power that will draw the necessary skills in competition with other positions. This means, in effect, that the position must be high in the social scale—must command great prestige, high salary, ample leisure, and the like.

How Variations Are to Be Understood. Insofar as there is a difference between one system of stratification and another, it is attributable to whatever factors affect the two determinants of differential reward—namely, functional importance and scarcity of personnel. Positions important in one society may not be important in another, because the conditions faced by the societies, or their degree of internal development, may be different. The same conditions, in turn, may affect the question of scarcity; for in some societies the stage of development, or the external situation, may wholly obviate the necessity of certain kinds of skill or talent. Any particular system of stratification, then, can be understood as a product of the special conditions affecting the two aforementioned grounds of differential reward.

CRITICAL RESPONSE
BY MELVIN TUMIN

The fact of social inequality in human society is marked by its ubiquity and its antiquity. Every known society, past and present, distributes its scarce and demanded goods and services unequally. And there are attached to the positions which command unequal amounts of such goods and services certain highly morally-toned evaluations of their importance for the society.

The ubiquity and the antiquity of such inequality has given rise to the assumption that there must be something both inevitable and positively functional about such social arrangements. . . . Clearly, the truth or falsity of such an assumption is a strategic question for any general theory of social organization. It is therefore most curious that the basic premises and implications of the assumption have only been most casually explored by American sociologists. . . .

Let us take [the Davis and Moore] propositions and examine them *seriatim.*

(1) *Certain positions in any society are more functionally important than others and require special skills for their performance.*

The key term here is "functionally important." The functionalist theory of social organization is by no means clear and explicit about this term. The minimum common referent is to something known as the "survival value" of a social structure. This concept immediately involves a number of perplexing questions. Among these are: (a) the issue of minimum vs. maximum survival, and the possible empirical referents which can be given to those terms; (b) whether such a proposition is a useless tautology since any *status quo* at any given moment is nothing more and nothing less than everything present in the *status quo.* In these terms, all acts and structures must be judged positively functional in that they constitute essential portions of the *status quo*; (c) what kind of calculus of functionality exists which will enable us, at this point in our development, to add and subtract long and short range consequences, with their mixed qualities, and arrive at some summative judgment regarding the rating an act or structure should receive on a scale of greater or lesser functionality? At best, we tend to make primarily intuitive judgments. Often enough, these judgments involve the use of value-laden criteria, or, at least, criteria which are chosen in preference to others not for any sociologically systematic reasons but by reason of certain implicit value preferences. . . .

A generalized theory of social stratification must recognize that the prevailing system of inducements and rewards is only one of many variants in the whole range of possible systems of motivation which, at least theoretically, are capable of working in human society. It is quite conceivable, of course, that a system of norms could be institutionalized in which the idea of threatened withdrawal of services, except under the most extreme circumstances, would be considered as absolute moral anathema. In such a case, the whole notion of relative functionality, as advanced by Davis and Moore, would have to be radically revised.

(2) *Only a limited number of individuals in any society have the talents which can be trained into the skills appropriate to these positions (i.e., the more functionally important positions).*

The truth of this proposition depends at least in part on the truth of proposition 1 above. It is, therefore, subject to all the limitations indicated above. But for the moment, let us assume the validity of the first proposition and concentrate on the question of the rarity of appropriate talent.

If all that is meant is that in every society there is a *range* of talent, and that some members of any society are by nature more talented than others, no sensible contradiction can be offered, but a question must be raised here regarding the amount of sound knowledge present in any society concerning the presence of talent in the population.

For, in every society there is some demonstrable ignorance regarding the amount of talent present in the population. *And the more rigidly stratified a society is, the less chance does that society have of discovering any new facts about the talents of its members.* Smoothly working and stable systems of stratification, wherever found, tend to build-in obstacles to the further exploration of the range of available talent. This is especially true in those societies where the opportunity to discover talent in any one generation varies with the differential resources of the parent generation. Where, for instance, access to education depends upon the wealth of one's parents, and where wealth is differentially distributed, large segments of the population are likely to be deprived of the chance even to *discover* what are their talents.

Whether or not differential rewards and opportunities are functional in any one generation, it is clear that if those differentials are allowed to be socially inherited by the next generation, then the stratification system is specifically dysfunctional for the discovery of talents in the next generation. In this fashion, systems of social stratification tend to limit the chances available to maximize the efficiency of discovery, recruitment and training of "functionally important talent."

. . . In this context, it may be asserted that there is some noticeable tendency for elites to restrict further access to their privileged positions, once they have sufficient power to enforce such restrictions. This is especially true in a culture where it is possible for an elite to contrive a high demand and a proportionately higher reward for its work by restricting the numbers of the elite available to do the work. The recruitment and training of doctors in modern United States is at least partly a case in point. . . .

(3) *The conversion of talents into skills involves a training period during which sacrifices of one kind or another are made by those undergoing the training.*

Davis and Moore introduce here a concept, "sacrifice," which comes closer than any of the rest of their vocabulary of analysis to being a direct reflection of the rationalizations, offered by the more fortunate members of a society, of the rightness of their occupancy of privileged positions. It is the least critically thought-out concept in the repertoire, and can also be shown to be least supported by the actual facts.

In our present society, for example, what are the sacrifices which talented persons undergo in the training period? The possibly serious losses involve the surrender of earning power and the cost of the training. The latter is generally borne by the parents of the talented youth undergoing training, and not by the trainees themselves. But this cost tends to be paid out of income which the parents were able to earn generally by virtue of *their* privileged positions in the hierarchy of stratification. That is to say, the parents' ability to pay for the training of their children is part of the differential *reward* they, the parents, received for their privileged positions in the society. And to charge this sum up against sacrifices made by the youth is falsely to perpetrate a bill or a debt already paid by the society to the parents. . . .

What tends to be completely overlooked, in addition, are the psychic and spiritual rewards which are available to the elite trainees by comparison with their age peers in the labor force. There is, first, the much higher prestige enjoyed by the college student and the professional-school student as compared with persons in shops and offices. There is, second, the extremely highly valued privilege of having greater opportunity for self-development. There is, third, all the psychic gain involved in being allowed to delay the assumption of adult responsibilities such as earning a living and supporting a family. There is, fourth, the access to leisure and freedom of a kind not likely to be experienced by the persons already at work.

If these are never taken into account as rewards of the training period it is not because they are not concretely present, but because the emphasis in American concepts of reward is almost exclusively placed on the material returns of positions. The emphases on enjoyment, entertainment, ego enhancement, prestige and esteem are introduced only when the differentials in these which accrue to the skilled positions need to be justified. If these other rewards were taken into account, it would be much more difficult to demonstrate that the training period, as presently operative, is really sacrificial. Indeed, it might turn out to be the case that even at this point in their careers, the elite trainees were being differentially rewarded relative to their age peers in the labor force. . . .

(4) *In order to induce the talented persons to undergo these sacrifices and acquire the training, their future positions must carry an inducement value in the form of differential, i.e., privileged and disproportionate access to the scarce and desired rewards which the society has to offer.*

Let us assume, for the purposes of the discussion, that the training period is sacrificial and the talent is rare in every conceivable human society. There is still the basic problem as to whether the allocation of differential rewards in scarce and desired goods and services is the only or the most efficient way of recruiting the appropriate talent to these positions.

For there are a number of alternative motivational schemes whose efficiency and adequacy ought at least to be considered in this context. What can be said, for instance, on behalf of the motivation which De Man called "joy in work," Veblen termed "instinct for workmanship" and which we latterly have come to identify as "intrinsic work satisfaction"? Or, to what extent could the motivation of "social duty" be institutionalized in such a fashion that self-interest and social interest come closely to coincide? Or, how much prospective confidence can be placed in the possibilities of institutionalizing "social service" as a widespread motivation for seeking one's appropriate position and fulfilling it conscientiously?

Are not these types of motivations, we may ask, likely to prove most appropriate for precisely the "most functionally important positions"? Especially in a mass industrial society, where the vast majority of positions become standardized and routinized, it is the skilled jobs which are likely to retain most of the quality of "intrinsic job satisfaction" and be most readily identifiable as socially serviceable. Is it indeed impossible then to build these motivations into the socialization pattern to which we expose our talented youth? . . .

(5) *These scarce and desired goods consist of rights and perquisites attached to, or built into, the positions and can be classified into those things which contribute to (a) sustenance and comfort; (b) humor and diversion; (c) self-respect and ego expansion.*

(6) *This differential access to the basic rewards of the society has as a consequence the differentiation of the prestige and esteem which various strata acquire. This may be said, along with the rights and perquisites, to constitute institutionalized social inequality, i.e., stratification.*

With the classification of the rewards offered by Davis and Moore there need be little argument. Some question must be raised, however, as to whether any reward system, built into a general stratification system, must allocate equal amounts of all three types of reward in order to function effectively, or whether one type of reward may be emphasized to the virtual neglect of others. This raises the further question regarding which type of emphasis is likely to prove most effective as a differential inducer. Nothing in the known facts about human motivation impels us to favor one type of reward over the other, or to insist that all three types of reward must be built into the positions in comparable amounts if the position is to have an inducement value.

It is well known, of course, that societies differ considerably in the kinds of rewards they emphasize in their efforts to maintain a reasonable balance between responsibility and reward. There are, for instance, numerous societies in which the conspicuous display of differential economic advantage is considered extremely bad taste. In short, our present knowledge commends to us the possibility of considerable plasticity in the way in which different types of rewards can be structured into a functioning society. This is to say, it cannot yet be demonstrated that it is *unavoidable* that differential prestige and esteem shall accrue to positions which command differential rewards in power and property.

What does seem to be unavoidable is that differential prestige shall be given to those in any society who conform to the normative order as against those who deviate from that order in a way judged immoral and detrimental. On the assumption that the continuity of a society depends on the continuity and stability of its normative order, some such distinction between conformists and deviants seems inescapable.

It also seems to be unavoidable that in any society, no matter how literate its tradition, the older, wiser and more experienced individuals who are charged with the enculturation and socialization of the young must have more power than the young, on the assumption that the task of effective socialization demands such differential power.

But this differentiation in prestige between the conformist and the deviant is by no means the same distinction as that between strata of individuals each of which operates *within* the normative order, and is composed of adults. . . .

(7) *Therefore, social inequality among different strata in the amounts of scarce and desired goods, and the amounts of prestige and esteem which they receive, is both positively functional and inevitable in any society.*

If the objections which have heretofore been raised are taken as reasonable, then it may be stated that the only items which any society *must* distribute unequally are the power and property necessary for the performance of different tasks. If such differential power and property are viewed by all as commensurate with the differential responsibilities, and if they are culturally defined as *resources* and not as rewards, then no differentials in prestige and esteem need follow.

Historically, the evidence seems to be that every time power and property are distributed unequally, no matter what the cultural definition, prestige and esteem differentiations have tended to result as well. Historically, however, no systematic effort has ever been made, under propitious circumstances, to develop the tradition that each man is as socially worthy as all other men so long as he performs his appropriate tasks conscientiously. While such a tradition seems utterly utopian, no known facts in psychological or social science have yet demonstrated its impossibility or its dysfunctionality for the continuity of a society. The achievement of a full institutionalization of such a tradition seems far too remote to contemplate. Some successive approximations at such a tradition, however, are not out of the range of prospective social innovation.

What, then, of the "positive functionality" of social stratification? Are there other, negative, functions of institutionalized social inequality which can be identified, if only tentatively? Some such dysfunctions of stratification have already been suggested in the body of this paper. Along with others they may now be stated, in the form of provisional assertions, as follows:

1. Social stratification systems function to limit the possibility of discovery of the full range of talent available in a society. This results from the fact of unequal access to appropriate motivation, channels of recruitment and centers of training.

2. In foreshortening the range of available talent, social stratification systems function to set limits upon the possibility of expanding the productive resources of the society, at least relative to what might be the case under conditions of greater equality of opportunity.

3. Social stratification systems function to provide the elite with the political power necessary to procure acceptance and dominance of an ideology which rationalizes the *status quo*, whatever it may be, as "logical," "natural" and "morally right." In this manner, social stratification systems function as essentially conservative influences in the societies in which they are found.

4. Social stratification systems function to distribute favorable self-images unequally throughout a population. To the extent that such favorable self-images are requisite to the development of the creative potential inherent in men, to that extent stratification systems function to limit the development of this creative potential.

5. To the extent that inequalities in social rewards cannot be made fully acceptable to the less privileged in a society, social stratification systems function to encourage hostility, suspicion and distrust among the various segments of a society and thus to limit the possibilities of extensive social integration.

6. To the extent that the sense of significant membership in a society depends on one's place on the prestige ladder of the society, social stratification systems function to distribute unequally the sense of significant membership in the population.

7. To the extent that loyalty to a society depends on a sense of significant membership in the society, social stratification systems function to distribute loyalty unequally in the population.

8. To the extent that participation and apathy depend upon the sense of significant membership in the society, social stratification systems function to distribute the motivation to participate unequally in a population.

Each of the eight foregoing propositions contains implicit hypotheses regarding the consequences of unequal distribution of rewards in a society in accordance with some notion of the functional importance of various positions. These are empirical hypotheses, subject to test. They are offered here only as exemplary of the kinds of consequences of social stratification which are not often taken into account in dealing with the problem. They should also serve to reinforce the doubt that social inequality is a device which is uniformly functional for the role of guaranteeing that the most important tasks in a society will be performed conscientiously by the most competent persons.

The obviously mixed character of the functions of social inequality should come as no surprise to anyone. If sociology is sophisticated in any sense, it is certainly with regard to its awareness of the mixed nature of any social arrangement, when the observer takes into account long- as well as short-range consequences and latent as well as manifest dimensions.

CRITICAL-THINKING QUESTIONS

1. Why do Davis and Moore argue that all societies attach greater rewards to some positions than to others?

2. Does the "Davis and Moore thesis" justify social stratification as it presently exists in the United States (or anywhere else)?

3. In what ways does Tumin argue that social stratification is dysfunctional *for a social system?*

NOTE

1. Unfortunately, functional importance is difficult to establish. To use the position's prestige to establish it, as is often unconsciously done, constitutes circular reasoning from our point of view. There are, however, two independent clues: (a) the degree to which a position is functionally unique, there being no other positions that can perform the same function satisfactorily; and (b) the degree to which other positions are dependent on the one in question. Both clues are best exemplified in organized systems of positions built around one major function. Thus in most complex societies the religious, political, economic and educational functions are handled by distinct structures not easily interchangeable. In addition each structure possesses many different positions, some clearly dependent on, if not subordinate to, others. In sum, when an institutional nucleus becomes differentiated around one main function, and at the same time organizes a large portion of the population into its relationships, *key* positions in it are of the highest functional importance. The absence of such specialization does not prove functional unimportance, for the whole society may be relatively unspecialized; but it is safe to assume that the more important functions receive the first and clearest structural differentiation.

SOCIAL STRATIFICATION

Contemporary

31

The Global Economy: Consequences for U.S. Inequality

Robert B. Reich

The U.S. economy is increasingly linked to the rest of the world. But what effect does the emerging global economy have for U.S. social stratification? Robert Reich argues that one consequence is a growing disparity in income. Some employees—especially those in upper management positions—are benefiting from the global economy; others—primarily rank and file workers—are losing ground.

Between 1978 and 1987, the poorest fifth of American families became 8 percent poorer, and the richest fifth became 13 percent richer. That leaves the poorest fifth with less than 5 percent of the nation's income, and the richest fifth with more than 40 percent. This widening gap can't be blamed on the growth in single-parent lower-income families, which in fact slowed markedly after the late 1970s. Nor is it due mainly to the stingy social policy of the Reagan years. Granted, Food Stamp benefits have dropped in real terms by about 13

percent since 1981, and many states have failed to raise benefits for the poor and unemployed to keep up with inflation. But this doesn't come close to accounting for the growing inequality. Rather, the trend is connected to a profound change in the American economy as it merges with the global economy. And because the merging is far from complete, this trend will not stop of its own accord anytime soon.

It is significant that the growth of inequality shows up most strikingly among Americans who have jobs. Through most of the postwar era, the wages of Americans at different income levels rose at about the same pace. Although different workers occupied different steps on the escalator, every-

SOURCE: "As the World Turns," by Robert B. Reich, in *The New Republic,* vol. 200, no. 18, May 1, 1989, pp. 23, 26–28. Reprinted by permission.

one moved up together. In those days poverty was the condition of *jobless* Americans, and the major economic challenge was to create enough jobs for everyone. Once people were safely on the work force escalator, their problems were assumed to be over. Thus "full employment" became a liberal rallying cry, while conservatives fretted over the inflationary tendencies of a full-employment economy.

In recent years working Americans have been traveling on two escalators—one going up, the other going down. In 1987 the average hourly earnings of non-supervisory workers, adjusted for inflation, were lower than in any year since 1966. Middle-level managers fared much better, although their median real earnings were only slightly above the levels of the 1970s. Executives, however, did spectacularly well. In 1988 alone, CEOs of the hundred largest publicly held industrial corporations received raises averaging almost 12 percent. The remunerations of lesser executives rose almost as much, and executives of smaller companies followed close behind.

Between 1978 and 1987, as the real earnings of unskilled workers were declining, the real incomes of workers in the securities industry (investment bankers, arbitrageurs, and brokers) rose 21 percent. Few investment bankers pocket anything near the $50 million lavished yearly upon the partners of Kohlberg, Kravis, Roberts & Company, or the $550 million commandeered last year by Michael Milken, but it is not unusual for a run-of-the-mill investment banker to bring home comfortably over a million dollars. Partners in America's largest corporate law firms are comparatively deprived, enjoying average yearly earnings of only $400,000 to $1.2 million.

Meanwhile, the number of impoverished *working* Americans climbed by nearly two million, or 23 percent, between 1978 and 1987. The number who worked full time and year round but were poor climbed faster, by 43 percent. Nearly 60 percent of the 20 million people who now fall below the Census Bureau's poverty line are from families with at least one member in full-time or part-time work.

The American economy, in short, is creating a wider range of earnings than at any other time in the postwar era. The most basic reason, put simply, is that America itself is ceasing to exist as a system of production and exchange separate from the rest of the world. One can no more meaningfully speak of an "American economy" than of a "Delaware economy." We are becoming but a region—albeit still a relatively wealthy region—of a global economy, whose technologies, savings, and investments move effortlessly across borders, making it harder for individual nations to control their economic destinies.

By now Washington officials well understand that the nation's fiscal and monetary policies cannot be set without taking account of the savings that will slosh in or slosh out of the nation in consequence. Less understood is the speed and ease with which new technologies now spread across the globe, from computers in, say, San Jose, to satellite, and then back down to computers in Taiwan. (America's efforts to stop the Japanese from copying our commercial designs and the Soviets from copying our military designs are about equally doomed.) And we have yet to come to terms with the rise of the global corporation, whose managers, shareholders, and employees span the world. Our debates over the future of American jobs still focus on topics like the competitiveness of the American automobile industry or the future of American manufacturing. But these categories are increasingly irrelevant. They assume the existence of a separate American economy in which all the jobs associated with a particular industry, or even more generally with a particular sector, are bound together, facing a common fate.

New technologies of worldwide communication and transportation have redrawn the playing field. American industries no longer compete against Japanese or European industries. Rather, a company with headquarters in the United States, production facilities in Taiwan, and a marketing force spread across many nations competes with another, similarly ecumenical company. So when General Motors, say, is doing well, that probably is good news for a lot of executives in Detroit, and for GM shareholders across the globe, but it isn't necessarily good news for a lot of assembly-line workers in Detroit, because there may, in fact, be very few GM assembly-line workers in Detroit, or anywhere else in America. The welfare of assembly-line workers in Detroit may depend, instead, on the health of corporations based in Japan or Canada.

More to the point, even if those Canadian and Japanese corporations are doing well, these workers may be in trouble. For they are increasingly part of an international labor market, encompassing Asia, Africa, Western Europe—and perhaps, before long, Eastern Europe. Corporations can with relative ease relocate their production centers, and alter their international lines of communication and transportation accordingly, to take advantage of low wages. So American workers find themselves settling for low wages in order to hold on to their jobs. More and more, your "competitiveness" as a worker depends not on the fortunes of any American corporation, or of any American industry, but on what function you serve within the global economy. GM executives are becoming more "competitive" even as GM production workers become less so, because the functions that GM executives perform are more highly valued in the world market than the functions that GM production workers perform.

In order to see in greater detail what is happening to American jobs, it helps to view the work Americans do in terms of functional categories that reflect the real competitive positions of workers in the global economy. Essentially, three broad categories are emerging. Call them symbolic-analytic services, routine production services, and routine personal services.

(1) *Symbolic-analytic services* are based on the manipulation of information: data, words, and oral and visual symbols. Symbolic analysis comprises some (but by no means all) of the work undertaken by people who call themselves lawyers, investment bankers, commercial bankers, management consultants, research scientists, academics, public-relations executives, real estate developers, and even a few creative accountants. Also: advertising and marketing specialists, art directors, design engineers, architects, writers and editors, musicians, and television and film producers. Some of the manipulations performed by symbolic analysts reveal ways of more efficiently deploying resources or shifting financial assets, or of otherwise saving time and energy. Other manipulations grab money from people who are too slow or naive to protect themselves by manipulation in response. Still others serve to entertain the recipients.

Most symbolic analysts work alone or in small teams. If they work with others, they often have partners rather than bosses or supervisors, and their yearly income is variable, depending on how much value they add to the business. Their work environments tend to be quiet and tastefully decorated, often within tall steel-and-glass buildings. They rarely come in direct contact with the ultimate beneficiaries of their work. When they are not analyzing, designing, or strategizing, they are in meetings or on the telephone—giving advice or making deals. Many of them spend inordinate time in jet planes and hotels. They are articulate and well groomed. The vast majority are white males.

Symbolic analysis now accounts for more than 40 percent of America's gross national product, and almost 20 percent of our jobs. Within what we still term our "manufacturing sector," symbolic-analytic jobs have been increasing at a rate almost three times that of total manufacturing employment in the United States, as routine manufacturing jobs have drifted overseas or been mastered by machines.

The services performed by America's symbolic analysts are in high demand around the world, regardless of whether the symbolic analysts provide them in person or transmit them via satellite and fiber-optic cable. The Japanese are buying up the insights and inventions of America's scientists and engineers (who are only too happy to sell them at a fat profit). The Europeans, meanwhile, are hiring our management consultants, business strategists, and investment bankers. Developing nations are hiring our civil and design engineers; and almost everyone is buying the output of our pop musicians, television stars, and film producers.

It is the same with the global corporation. The central offices of these sprawling entities, headquartered in America, are filled with symbolic analysts who manipulate information and then export their insights via the corporation's far-flung enterprise. IBM doesn't export machines from the United States; it makes machines all over the globe, and services them on the spot. IBM world headquarters, in Armonk, New York, just exports strategic planning and related management services.

Thus has the standard of living of America's symbolic analysts risen. They increasingly find themselves part of a global labor market, not a national one. And because the United States has a highly developed economy, and an excellent university system, they find that the services they have to offer are quite scarce in the context of the whole world. So elementary laws of supply and demand ensure that their salaries are quite high.

These salaries are likely to go even higher in the years ahead, as the world market for symbolic analysis continues to grow. Foreigners are trying to learn these skills and techniques, to be sure, but they still have a long way to go. No other country does a better job of preparing its most fortunate citizens for symbolic analysis than does the United States. None has surpassed America in providing experience and training, often with entire regions specializing in one or another kind of symbolic analysis (New York and Chicago for finance, Los Angeles for music and film, the San Francisco Bay area and greater Boston for science and engineering). In this we can take pride. But for the second major category of American workers—the providers of routine production services—the laws of supply and demand don't bode well.

(2) *Routine production services* involve tasks that are repeated over and over, as one step in a sequence of steps for producing a finished product. Although we tend to associate these jobs with manufacturing, they are becoming common in the storage and retrieval of information. Banking, insurance, wholesaling, retailing, health care—all employ hordes of people who spend their days processing data, often putting information into computers or taking it out.

Most providers of routine production services work with many other people who do similar work within large, centralized facilities. They are overseen by supervisors, who in turn are monitored by more senior supervisors. They are usually paid an hourly wage. Their jobs are monotonous. Most of these people do not have a college education; they need only be able to take directions and, occasionally, undertake simple computations. Those who deal with metal are mostly white males; those who deal with fabrics or information tend to be female and/or minorities.

Decades ago, jobs like these were relatively well paid. Henry Ford gave his early production workers five dollars a day, a remarkable sum for the time, in the (correct) belief that they and their neighbors would be among the major buyers of Fords. But in recent years America's providers of routine production services have found themselves in direct competition with millions of foreign workers, most of whom are eager to work for a fraction of the pay of American workers. Through the miracle of satellite transmission, even routine data-processing can now be undertaken in relatively poor nations, thousands of miles away from the skyscrapers where the data are finally used. This fact has given management-level symbolic analysts ever greater bargaining leverage. If routine producers living in America don't agree to reduce their wages, then the work will go abroad.

And it has. In 1950 routine production services constituted about 30 percent of our national product and well over half of American jobs. Today such services represent about 20 percent of national product and one-fourth of jobs. And the scattering of foreign-owned factories placed here to circumvent American protectionism isn't going to reverse the trend. So the standard of living of America's routine production workers will likely keep declining. The dynamics behind the wage concessions, plant closings, and union-busting that have become commonplace are not likely to change.

(3) *Routine personal services* also entail sim-

ple, repetitive work, but, unlike routine production services, they are provided in person. Their immediate objects are specific customers rather than streams of metal, fabric, or data. Included in this employment category are restaurant and hotel workers, barbers and beauticians, retail sales personnel, cabdrivers, household cleaners, day-care workers, hospital attendants and orderlies, truck drivers, and—among the fastest-growing of all—custodians and security guards.

Like production workers, providers of personal services are usually paid by the hour, are carefully supervised, and rarely have more than a high school education. But unlike people in the other two categories of work, these people are in direct contact with the ultimate beneficiaries of what they do. And the companies they work for are often small. In fact, some routine personal-service workers turn entrepreneurial. (Most new businesses and new jobs in America come from this sector—now constituting about 20 percent of GNP and 30 percent of jobs.) Women and minorities make up the bulk of routine personal-service workers.

Apart from the small number who strike out on their own, these workers are paid poorly. They are sheltered from the direct effects of global competition, but not the indirect effects. They often compete with illegal aliens willing to work for low wages, or with former or would-be production workers who can't find well-paying production jobs, or with labor-saving machinery (automated tellers, self-service gas pumps, computerized cashiers) dreamed up by symbolic analysts in America and manufactured in Asia. And because they tend to be unskilled and dispersed among small businesses, personal-service workers rarely hire a union or a powerful lobby group to stand up for their interests. When the economy turns sour, they are among the first to feel the effects. These workers will continue to have jobs in the years ahead and may experience some small increase in real wages. They will have demographics on their side, as the American work force shrinks. But for all the foregoing reasons, the gap between their earnings and those of the symbolic analysts will continue to grow.

These three functional categories—symbolic analysis, routine production, and routine personal service—cover at least three out of four American jobs. The rest of the nation's work force consists mainly of government employees (including public school teachers), employees in regulated industries (like utility workers), and government-financed workers (engineers working on defense weapons systems), many of whom are sheltered from global competition. One further clarification: Some traditional job categories overlap with several functional categories. People called "secretaries," for example, include those who actually spend their time doing symbolic-analytic work closely allied to what their bosses do; those who do routine data entry or retrieval of a sort that will eventually be automated or done overseas; and those who provide routine personal services.

The important point is that workers in these three functional categories are coming to have a different competitive position in the world economy. Symbolic analysts hold a commanding position in an increasingly global labor market. Routine production workers hold a relatively weak position in an increasingly global labor market. Personal-service workers still find themselves in a national labor market, but for various reasons they suffer the indirect effects of competition from workers abroad.

How should we respond to these trends? One response is to accept them as inevitable consequences of change, but try to offset their polarizing effects through a truly progressive income tax, coupled with more generous income assistance—including health insurance—for poor working Americans. (For a start, we might reverse the extraordinarily regressive Social Security amendments of 1983, through which poor working Americans are now financing the federal budget deficit, often paying more in payroll taxes than in income taxes.)

A more ambitious response would be to guard against class rigidities by ensuring that any talented American kid can become a symbolic analyst—regardless of family income or race. Here we see the upside of a globalized economy. Unlike America's old vertically integrated economy, whose white-collar jobs were necessarily limited in proportion to the number of blue-collar jobs beneath them, the global economy imposes no particular limit upon the number of Americans who can sell symbolic-analytic services. In principle, all of America's routine production workers could become symbolic analysts and let their old jobs drift overseas. In practice, of course, we can't even inch toward such a state anytime soon. Not even America's gifted but poor children can aspire to such jobs until the government spends substantially more than it does now to ensure excellent public schools in every city and region to which talented children can go, and ample financial help when they are ready to attend college.

Of course, it isn't clear that even under those circumstances there would be radical growth in the number of Americans who became research scientists, design engineers, musicians, management consultants, or (even if the world needed them) investment bankers and lawyers. So other responses are also needed. Perhaps the most ambitious would be to increase the numbers of Americans who could apply symbolic analysis to production and to personal services.

There is ample evidence, for example, that access to computerized information can enrich production jobs by enabling workers to alter the flow of materials and components in ways that generate new efficiencies. (Shoshana Zuboff's recent book *In the Age of the Smart Machine* carefully documents these possibilities.) Production workers who thus have broader responsibilities and more control over how production is organized cease to be "routine" workers—becoming, in effect, symbolic analysts at a level very close to the production process. The same transformation can occur in personal-service jobs. Consider, for example, the checkout clerk whose computer enables her to control inventory and decide when to reorder items from the factory.

The number of such technologically empowered jobs, of course, is limited by the ability of workers to learn on the job. That means a far greater number of Americans will need good health care (including prenatal and postnatal) and also a good grounding in mathematics, basic science, and reading and communicating. So once again, comfortably integrating the American work force into the new world economy turns out to rest heavily on education.

Education and health care for poor children are apt to be costly. Since poorer working Americans, already under a heavy tax load, can't afford it, the cost would have to be borne by wealthier Americans—who also would have to bear the cost of any income redistribution plans designed to neutralize the polarizing domestic effects of a globalized economy. Thus a central question is the willingness of the more fortunate American citizens—especially symbolic analysts, who constitute the most fortunate fifth, with 40 percent of the nation's income—to bear the burden. But here lies a Catch-22. For as our economic fates diverge, the top fifth may be losing the sense of connectedness with the bottom fifth, or even the bottom half, that would elicit such generosity.

The conservative tide that has swept the land during the last decade surely has many causes, but these economic fundamentals should not be discounted. It is now possible for the most fortunate fifth to sell their expertise directly in the global market, and thus maintain and enhance their standard of living and that of their children, even as that of other Americans declines. There is less and less basis for a strong sense of interclass interdependence. Meanwhile, the fortunate fifth have also been able to insulate themselves from the less fortunate, by living in suburban enclaves far removed from the effects of poverty. Neither patriotism nor altruism may be sufficient to overcome these realities. Yet without the active support of the fortunate fifth, it will be difficult to muster the political will necessary for change.

George Bush speaks eloquently of "a thousand points of light" and of the importance of generosity. But so far his administration has set a poor example. A minuscule sum has been budgeted for education, training, and health care for the poor. The president says we can't afford any more. Meanwhile, he pushes a reduction in the capital gains rate—another boon to the fortunate fifth.

On withdrawing from the presidential race of 1988, Paul Simon of Illinois said, "Americans instinctively know that we are one nation, one family, and when anyone in that family hurts, all of us hurt." Sadly, that is coming to be less and less the case.

CRITICAL-THINKING QUESTIONS

1. In the past, Reich argues, poverty was the plight of the jobless; today, the ranks of the working poor are swelling. Why?

2. What evidence suggests that the United States is more and more bound up with a global economy? What effect does this have on U.S. workers at various occupational levels?

3. What does Reich suggest that the federal government should do in response to growing economic inequality in the United States?

Cross-Cultural

32

Women's Poverty in Africa

Daphne Topouzis

The concept "feminization of poverty" refers to the increasing share of poor people who are women. Poverty is growing faster in Africa than in any other part of the world. In this article, Daphne Topouzis discusses why the poorest of the poor in African countries are women and their dependent families. Note the interplay among economic, social, political, and environmental factors that create a "vicious circle of poverty" that will be difficult for even the most well-intentioned policies to break.

An alarming trend with potentially devastating economic, social, and environmental consequences is developing across Africa, with evidence showing that nearly two-thirds of Africa's fast-growing, poverty-stricken population consists of women. The picture becomes bleaker considering that between 1970 and 1985, the number of Africans living in abject poverty rose by 75 per-

cent to about 270 million, or half the population of the continent, according to the International Labor Organization.

Poor shelter, malnutrition, disease, illiteracy, overwork, a short life expectancy, and high maternal and infant mortality rates mark the lives of the poorest of poor women and their dependent families. Poverty is growing faster in Africa than in any other part of the world. Even more alarming, perhaps, is the fact that the feminization of poverty is becoming increasingly structural, advancing well beyond the reach of policy-makers and development projects. As a result, it is becoming virtually

SOURCE: "The Feminization of Poverty," by Daphne Topouzis, *Africa Report,* July/August 1990, pp. 60–63. Copyright © 1990 by the African-American Institute. Reprinted by permission of *Africa Report.*

impossible for women to escape the cycle of crushing poverty in which they are entrenched.

If this trend is not reversed, however, about 400 million Africans will be living in absolute poverty by 1995, argues the newly released UNDP *1990 Human Development Report,* and up to 260 million could be women.

The feminization of poverty is only beginning to be recognized as a pressing problem in Africa and elsewhere in the world, and there are as yet no statistical indicators or figures available to help identify the magnitude of the crisis. At best, studies on poverty refer to it in passing, but more often, they fail to appreciate the ramifications of this shift in the pattern of poverty on overall economic development.

The reasons behind the increasing concentration of poverty among women in Africa are as varied as they are complex. A combination of prolonged drought and the debt crisis have triggered large-scale male migrations to the cities, leaving one-third of all rural households headed by women. In some regions of sub-Saharan Africa, up to 43 percent of all households are headed by women, according to the UN *1989 World Survey on Women in Development.*

This phenomenon is transforming the family structure and socioeconomic fabric of African societies across the continent, placing additional financial burdens on already poor and overworked women. Women heads of households tend to have more dependents, fewer breadwinning family members, and restricted access to productive resources. "Female members of a poor household are often worse off than male members because of gender-based differences in the distribution of food and other entitlements within the family," adds the *1990 Human Development Report.*

The poverty crisis has been further aggravated by ill-fated agricultural policies or a neglect of agriculture by national governments, rapid population growth, and pressure on land available for cultivation—all of which have contributed to declining productivity and food consumption in many African countries. Between 1980 and 1985, per capita income in Africa declined by 30 percent,

taking into account the negative terms of trade. The first victims of food shortages and famine tend to be women with young children, which is not surprising, considering that just under half of all African women and 63 percent of pregnant women suffer from anemia.

The adverse effects of the economic recession and remedial structural adjustment programs should be added to the list of factors that have contributed to the impoverishment of women. Structural adjustment has in many cases increased unemployment in the cities, and women are again the first to be laid off in the formal sector. Austerity measures have also decreased women's purchasing power and removed subsidies on basic foodstuffs. Thus, already overworked women have no choice but to work even longer hours to keep their families afloat, often at the expense of caring for their children and their own health. According to the UN Fund for Population Activity's *State of the World Population 1990,* rural African women tend to have more children in order to lighten their load with food production.

And last but not least, armed conflicts in Sudan, Ethiopia, Angola, Mozambique, and civil unrest in several other countries have left thousands of women widowed, displaced, or abandoned to a life of permanent emergency as refugees: An estimated two-thirds of the 5 million adult refugee population on the continent are women. "When armies march, there is no harvest," reads one African saying. As a result, women refugees often become almost totally dependent on relief from international organizations whose resources for them are currently on the decline.

THE PLIGHT OF RURAL WOMEN

From near food self-sufficiency in 1970, Africa over the past two decades has witnessed a marked decline in food production and consumption per person, while real per capita access to resources has decreased accordingly. African women, who produce, process, and market over 75 percent of the food, suffer greater deprivations than men and continue to be ignored by national policy-makers and international aid organizations.

Thus, even though the past two years have seen bumper crops in many Sahelian countries, women farmers have not benefitted from this, and the poorest among them are still unable to grow enough food to sustain their families. One of the reasons is that, as a whole, they remain excluded from access to improved technology, credit, extension services, and land. Landless, unskilled, and illiterate rural women often live precarious lives on the edge of impoverishment, regardless of how hard they work.

Women in developing countries work twice as many hours as men for one-tenth of the income. In East Africa, women spend up to sixteen hours every day growing, processing, and preparing food, gathering fuel and water, and performing other household chores, in addition to caring for their children and the extended family. In Malawi, women put in twice as many hours as men cultivating maize, the main cash crop, and the same number of hours in cotton, in addition to doing all the housework.

In South Africa's homelands, women walk from three to five miles every other day to collect fuelwood weighing up to sixty-five pounds, according to *Apartheid's Environmental Toll,* a report released by Worldwatch Institute in Washington, D.C. Environmental degradation affects women directly, as they have to walk longer distances to fetch fuelwood and water. In turn, impoverished women—most of whom live in ecologically fragile areas—have little alternative but to continue degrading their environment in order to survive. Poverty, overpopulation, and environmental degradation are not only inextricably linked, but they continually reinforce one another.

URBAN WOMEN IN "PINK COLLAR JOBS"

Women are still a minority in the public sector in Africa: In Benin and Togo, 21 percent of public sector employees are women, while in Tanzania,

their share in formal employment was 15.6 percent in 1983. Poor urban women have little professional training. As a result, they are reduced to low-wage, low-status, or "pink collar" jobs, which include clerical, teaching, and social services. In Kenya, 78.9 percent of the female work force in the service sector is employed in pink collar jobs, while only 6.1 percent is employed in high-paying jobs. The economic crisis has had a profound effect on these women, with unemployment rising by 10 percent annually in the period 1980–1985. In Botswana and Nigeria, the rate of unemployment among young women under 20 was 44 percent and 42 percent respectively in 1987, as opposed to males of the same age group, at 23.5 and 22.2 percent. For those who retained their jobs, wages were often slashed by one-third.

The vast majority of urban women work in the informal sector where earnings are meager, and there is no legal protection or job security: In Ghana, 85 percent of all employment in trade in 1970 was accounted for by women; in Nigeria, 94 percent of the street food vendors are women. These women earn substantially less than their male counterparts and often live on the edge of poverty, so that a slight deterioration in economic conditions, such as price rises of essential foodstuffs, can directly threaten their survival, as well as that of their families. In Dar es Salaam, argues the *1990 Human Development Report,* poor women had to cut back from three meals a day to two. In extreme cases, poor urban women have resorted to begging, prostitution, and other illicit activities in order to survive.

STRUCTURAL ADJUSTMENT

Structural adjustment programs prescribed by international financial institutions have largely failed to integrate women into economic development and have imposed drastic cuts in education and health services, thereby exacerbating existing inequalities and marginalizing women further. A recent study conducted by a group of experts set up by the Commonwealth Ministers Responsible for Women, entitled *Engendering Adjustment for the 1990s,* argues that women in developing countries "have been at the epicenter of the crisis and have borne the brunt of the adjustment efforts."

Particularly alarming is the fact that for the first time in many years, maternal and infant mortality rates are beginning to rise and girls' school enrollments are starting to fall. "If you educate a man, you simply educate an individual, but if you educate a woman, you educate a family," said J. E. Aggrey, a Ghanaian educator. Few, however, have taken this message seriously: Illiteracy in Africa is four times as high among women as among men, and the higher the level of education, the lower the percentage of girls. In Côte d'Ivoire, 82 women among 707 students completed university studies in 1983. In thirteen out of eighteen African countries for which figures are available, expenditure per pupil in primary school decreased dramatically, up to 40 percent, between 1980 and 1984/5.

Women's health has also suffered severe setbacks as a result of structural adjustment programs. In Nigeria, where health fees and social service subsidies were slashed, health care and food costs have spiraled by 400 to 600 percent, according to a recent report in *West Africa.* About 75,000 women die each year from causes related to pregnancy or childbirth in Nigeria alone—that is, one woman every seven minutes, according to the same source. In Benin, Cameroon, Nigeria, Malawi, Mali, and Mozambique, one out of five fifteen-year-old women dies before she reaches forty-five years of age for reasons related to pregnancy and childbirth.

WOMEN IN DEVELOPMENT

Between 1965 and 1986, women were neglected by development planners largely due to misconceptions and misdirected efforts and as a result, hardly benefitted from development aid, argued a 1988 World Bank report. Thus, it was taken for granted that all households are male-headed, that women do not work, and that by increasing the income of a household, everyone will benefit. Rural development projects geared toward women tended to emphasize training and health, hygiene, nutrition, and child care, neglecting to help women improve their capabilities as farmers. Women were barred from access to credit and improved technology because it was the men who were addressed as the real producers.

A case in point is the Sedhiou Project in Senegal, which provided credit to cooperatives but refused female membership. In a British-funded cotton growing project in Bura, Kenya, women have no access to plots where they can grow food, and malnutrition has increased among their children; at an integrated rural development project in Zambia, women have little time to grow food and care for their families because they have to work long hours on their husbands' cash crop, to mention but a few examples.

The devastating drought, famines, and the economic crisis of the 1980s pressured African governments and development organizations into recognizing the vital role women play in economic development. Most African governments now have a ministry, bureau, or department dealing with women's affairs and some legislative adjustments have been made to improve the socioeconomic status of women. These initiatives, however, have not reached the most vulnerable and impoverished of women, not least because their needs are multisectoral and are unlikely to be met by a single government department, while being ignored or given token recognition by other ministries.

In essence, women's economic contributions remain largely overlooked and equitable development strategies have yet to be translated into effective plans of action. In many countries, African women still cannot own the land they cultivate or get access to credit. In Lesotho, women lack the most basic legal and social rights: They cannot sign contracts, borrow money, or slaughter cattle without their husbands' consent.

Sustainable development has to become synonymous with equitable development, and economic recovery will only come about if the feminization of poverty is tackled as an economic and social problem rather than as a purely developmental or exclusively a women's problem. There are some encouraging initiatives in Ghana, Tanzania, and Nigeria, where farmers' cooperatives are obtaining loans for poor women from local banks.

However, a formidable task awaits national governments and development workers: Access to productive resources such as land, capital, and technology, fair wages, training, and education and basic health care are essential conditions if African women are to break out of the vicious circle of poverty and underdevelopment. Equally pressing, however, are policy-making and legislative reforms to combat discrimination against women and change male attitudes regarding women's contributions to social and economic life.

CRITICAL-THINKING QUESTIONS

1. What are the reasons for the "feminization of poverty" in many African countries?
2. In 1970, most Africans were self-sufficient in food production and consumption. Why has this self-sufficiency decreased dramatically in the last two decades?
3. How have attitudes about *women shaped economic and educational policies* toward *women?*

RACE AND ETHNICITY

Classic

33

The Souls of Black Folks

W. E. Burghart Du Bois

W. E. B. Du Bois, a pioneering U.S. sociologist and the first African American to receive a doctorate from Harvard University, describes how a color-conscious society casts black people as "strangers in their own homes." One result, Du Bois explains, is that African Americans develop a "double consciousness," seeing themselves as Americans but always, gazing back at themselves through the eyes of the white majority, as people set below and apart by color.

Between me and the other world there is ever an unasked question: unasked by some through feelings of delicacy; by others through the difficulty of rightly framing it. All, nevertheless, flutter round it. They approach me in a half-hesitant sort of way, eye me curiously or compassionately, and then, instead of saying directly, How does it feel to be a problem? they say, I know an excellent colored man in my town; or, I fought at Mechan-

SOURCE: *The Souls of Black Folks* by W. E. Burghart Du Bois (New York: Penguin, 1982; orig. 1903), pp. 43–53. Reprinted with permission.

icsville; or, Do not these Southern outrages make your blood boil? At these I smile, or am interested, or reduce the boiling to a simmer, as the occasion may require. To the real question, How does it feel to be a problem? I answer seldom a word.

And yet, being a problem is a strange experience,—peculiar even for one who has never been anything else, save perhaps in babyhood and in Europe. It is in the early days of rollicking boyhood that the revelation first bursts upon one, all in a day, as it were. I remember well when the shadow swept across me. I was a little thing, away up in the hills of New England, where the dark Housatonic winds between Hoosac and Taghkanic to the sea. In a wee wooden schoolhouse, something put it into the boys' and girls' heads to buy gorgeous visiting-cards—ten cents a package—and exchange. The exchange was merry, till one girl, a tall newcomer, refused my card,—refused it peremptorily, with a glance. Then it dawned upon me with a certain suddenness that I was different from the others; or like, mayhap, in heart and life and longing, but shut out from their world by a vast veil. I had thereafter no desire to tear down that veil, to creep through; I held all beyond it in common contempt, and lived above it in a region of blue sky and great wandering shadows. That sky was bluest when I could beat my mates at examination-time, or beat them at a foot-race, or even beat their stringy heads. Alas, with the years all this fine contempt began to fade; for the words I longed for, and all their dazzling opportunities, were theirs, not mine. But they should not keep these prizes, I said; some, all, I would wrest from them. Just how I would do it I could never decide: by reading law, by healing the sick, by telling the wonderful tales that swam in my head,—some way. With other black boys the strife was not so fiercely sunny: Their youth shrunk into tasteless sycophancy, or into silent hatred of the pale world about them and mocking distrust of everything white; or wasted itself in a bitter cry, Why did God make me an outcast and a stranger in mine own house? The shades of the prison-house closed round about us all: walls strait and stubborn to the whitest, but relentlessly narrow, tall, and unscalable to sons of night who must plod darkly on in resignation, or beat unavailing palms against the stone, or steadily, half hopelessly, watch the streak of blue above.

After the Egyptian and Indian, the Greek and Roman, the Teuton and Mongolian, the Negro is a sort of seventh son, born with a veil, and gifted with second-sight in this American world,—a world which yields him no true self-consciousness, but only lets him see himself through the revelation of the other world. It is a peculiar sensation, this double-consciousness, this sense of always looking at one's self through the eyes of others, of measuring one's soul by the tape of a world that looks on in amused contempt and pity. One ever feels his twoness,—an American, a Negro; two souls, two thoughts, two unreconciled strivings; two warring ideals in one dark body, whose dogged strength alone keeps it from being torn asunder.

The history of the American Negro is the history of this strife,—this longing to attain self-conscious manhood, to merge his double self into a better and truer self. In this merging he wishes neither of the older selves to be lost. He would not Africanize America, for America has too much to teach the world and Africa. He would not bleach his Negro soul in a flood of white Americanism, for he knows that Negro blood has a message for the world. He simply wishes to make it possible for a man to be both a Negro and an American, without being cursed and spit upon by his fellows, without having the doors of Opportunity closed roughly in his face.

This, then, is the end of his striving: to be a coworker in the kingdom of culture, to escape both death and isolation, to husband and use his best powers and his latent genius. These powers of body and mind have in the past been strangely wasted, dispersed, or forgotten. The shadow of a mighty Negro past flits through the tale of Ethiopia the Shadowy and of Egypt the Sphinx. Through history, the powers of single black men flash here and there like falling stars, and die sometimes before the world has rightly gauged their brightness. Here in America, in the few days since Emancipation, the black man's turning hither and thither in hesitant and doubtful striving has often made his very strength to lose effectiveness, to seem like absence of power, like weakness. And yet it is not weakness,—it is the contradiction of double aims. The double-aimed struggle of the black artisan on the one hand to escape white contempt for a nation of mere hewers of wood and drawers of water, and on the other hand to plough and nail and dig for a poverty-stricken horde—could only result in making him a poor craftsman, for he had but half a heart in either cause. By the poverty and ignorance of his people, the Negro minister or doctor was tempted toward quackery and demagogy; and by the criticism of the other world, toward ideals that made him ashamed of his lowly tasks. The would-be black *savant* was confronted by the paradox that the knowledge his people needed was a twice-told tale to his white neighbors, while the knowledge which would teach the white world was Greek to his own flesh and blood. The innate love of harmony and beauty that set the ruder souls of his people a-dancing and a-singing raised but confusion and doubt in the soul of the black artist; for the beauty revealed to him was the soul-beauty of a race which his larger audience despised, and he could not articulate the message of another people. This waste of double aims, this seeking to satisfy two unreconciled ideals, has wrought sad havoc with the courage and faith and deeds of ten thousand thousand people,—has sent them often wooing false gods and invoking false means of salvation, and at times has even seemed about to make them ashamed of themselves.

Away back in the days of bondage they thought to see in one divine event the end of all doubt and disappointment; few men ever worshipped Freedom with half such unquestioning faith as did the American Negro for two centuries. To him, so far as he thought and dreamed, slavery was indeed the sum of all villainies, the cause of all sorrow, the root of all prejudice; Emancipation was the key to a promised land of sweeter beauty than ever stretched before the eyes of wearied Israelites. In song and exhortation swelled one refrain—Liberty; in his tears and curses the God he implored had Freedom in his right hand. At last it came,—suddenly, fearfully, like a dream. With one wild carnival of blood and passion came the message in his own plaintive cadences:—

> Shout, O children!
> Shout, you're free!
> For God has bought your liberty!

Years have passed away since then,—ten, twenty, forty; forty years of national life, forty years of renewal and development, and yet the swarthy spectre sits in its accustomed seat at the Nation's feast. In vain do we cry to this our vastest social problem:—

> Take any shape but that, and my firm nerves
> Shall never tremble!

The Nation has not yet found peace from its sins; the freedman has not yet found in freedom his promised land. Whatever of good may have come in these years of change, the shadow of a deep disappointment rests upon the Negro people,—a disappointment all the more bitter because the unattained ideal was unbounded save by the simple ignorance of a lowly people.

The first decade was merely a prolongation of the vain search for freedom, the boon that seemed ever barely to elude their grasp,—like a tantalizing will-o'-the-wisp, maddening and misleading the headless host. The holocaust of war, the terrors of the Ku-Klux Klan, the lies of carpet-baggers, the disorganization of industry, and the contradictory advice of friends and foes, left the bewildered serf with no new watchword beyond the old cry for freedom. As the time flew, however, he began to grasp a new idea. The ideal of liberty demanded for its attainment powerful means, and these the Fifteenth Amendment gave him. The ballot, which before he had looked upon as a visible sign of freedom, he now regarded as the chief means of gaining and perfecting the liberty with which war had partially endowed him. And why not? Had not votes made war and emancipated millions? Had not votes enfranchised the freedmen? Was anything impossible to a power that had done all this? A million black men started with renewed zeal to vote themselves into the kingdom. So the decade flew away, the revolution of 1876 came, and left the half-free serf weary, wondering, but still inspired. Slowly but steadily, in the following years, a new vision began gradually to replace the dream of political power,—a powerful movement, the rise of another ideal to guide the unguided, another pillar of fire by night after a clouded day. It was the ideal of "book-learning"; the curiosity, born of compulsory ignorance, to know and test the power of the cabalistic letters of the white man, the longing to know. Here at last seemed to have been discovered the mountain path to Canaan; longer than the highway of Emancipation and law, steep and rugged, but straight, leading to heights high enough to overlook life.

Up the new path the advance guard toiled, slowly, heavily, doggedly; only those who have watched and guided the faltering feet, the misty minds, the dull understandings, of the dark pupils of these schools know how faithfully, how piteously, this people strove to learn. It was weary work. The cold statistician wrote down the inches of progress here and there, noted also where here and there a foot had slipped or some one had fallen. To the tired climbers, the horizon was ever dark, the mists were often cold, the Canaan was always dim and far away. If, however, the vistas disclosed as yet no goal, no resting-place, little but flattery and criticism, the journey at least gave leisure for reflection and self-examination; it changed the child of Emancipation to the youth with dawning self-consciousness, self-realization, self-respect. In those sombre forests of his striving his own soul rose before him, and he saw himself,—darkly as through a veil; and yet he saw in himself some faint revelation of his power, of his mission. He began to have a dim feeling that, to attain his place in the world, he must be himself, and not another. For the first time he sought to analyze the burden he bore upon his back, that dead-weight of social degradation partially masked behind a half-named Negro problem. He felt his poverty; without a cent, without a home, without land, tools, or savings, he had entered into competition with rich, landed, skilled neighbors. To be a poor man is hard, but to be a poor race in a land of dollars is the very bottom of hardships. He felt the weight of his ignorance,—not simply of letters, but of life, of business, of the humanities; the accumulated sloth and shirking and awkwardness of decades and centuries shackled his hands and feet. Nor was his burden all poverty and ignorance. The red stain of bastardy, which two centuries of systematic legal defilement of Negro women had stamped upon his race, meant not only the loss of ancient African chastity, but also the hereditary weight of a mass

of corruption from white adulterers, threatening almost the obliteration of the Negro home.

A people thus handicapped ought not to be asked to race with the world, but rather allowed to give all its time and thought to its own social problems. But alas! while sociologists gleefully count his bastards and his prostitutes, the very soul of the toiling, sweating black man is darkened by the shadow of a vast despair. Men call the shadow prejudice, and learnedly explain it as the natural defence of culture against barbarism, learning against ignorance, purity against crime, the "higher" against the "lower" races. To which the Negro cries Amen! and swears that to so much of this strange prejudice as is founded on just homage to civilization, culture, righteousness, and progress, he humbly bows and meekly does obeisance. But before that nameless prejudice that leaps beyond all this he stands helpless, dismayed, and well-nigh speechless; before that personal disrespect and mockery, the ridicule and systematic humiliation, the distortion of fact and wanton license of fancy, the cynical ignoring of the better and the boisterous welcoming of the worse, the all-pervading desire to inculcate disdain for everything black, from Toussaint to the devil,—before this there rises a sickening despair that would disarm and discourage any nation save that black host to whom "discouragement" is an unwritten word.

But the facing of so vast a prejudice could not but bring the inevitable self-questioning, self-disparagement, and lowering of ideals which ever accompany repression and breed in an atmosphere of contempt and hate. Whisperings and portents came borne upon the four winds: Lo! we are diseased and dying, cried the dark hosts; we cannot write, our voting is vain; what need of education, since we must always cook and serve? And the Nation echoed and enforced this self-criticism saying: Be content to be servants, and nothing more; what need of higher culture for half-men? Away with the black man's ballot, by force or fraud,—and behold the suicide of a race! Nevertheless, out of the evil came something of good,—the more careful adjustment of education to real life, the clearer perception of the Negroes' social responsibilities, and the sobering realization of the meaning of progress.

So dawned the time of *Sturm und Drang:* Storm and stress to-day rocks our little boat on the mad waters of the world-sea; there is within and without the sound of conflict, the burning of body and rending of soul; inspiration strives with doubt, and faith with vain questionings. The bright ideals of the past,— physical freedom, political power, the training of brains and the training of hands,—all these in turn have waxed and waned, until even the last grows dim and overcast. Are they all wrong,— all false? No, not that, but each alone was oversimple and incomplete,—the dreams of a credulous race-childhood, or the fond imaginings of the other world which does not know and does not want to know our power. To be really true, all these ideals must be melted and welded into one. The training of the schools we need to-day more than ever,—the training of deft hands, quick eyes and ears, and above all the broader, deeper, higher culture of gifted minds and pure hearts. The power of the ballot we need in sheer self-defence,—else what shall save us from a second slavery? Freedom, too, the long-sought, we still seek,—the freedom of life and limb, the freedom to work and think, the freedom to love and aspire. Work, culture, liberty,—all these we need, not singly but together, not successively but together, each growing and aiding each, and all striving toward that vaster ideal that swims before the Negro people, the ideal of human brotherhood, gained through the unifying ideal of Race; the ideal of fostering and developing the traits and talents of the Negro, not in opposition to or contempt for other races, but rather in large conformity to the greater ideals of the American Republic, in order that some day on American soil two world-races may give each to each those characteristics both so sadly lack. We the darker ones come even now not altogether empty-handed: There are to-day no truer exponents of the pure human spirit of the Declaration of Independence than the American Negroes; there is no true American music but the wild sweet melodies of the Negro slave, the American fairy tales and folklore are Indian and African; and, all in all, we black men seem the sole oasis of simple faith and reverence in a dusty desert of dollars and smartness. Will America be poorer if she replace her brutal dyspeptic blundering with lighthearted but determined Negro humility? or her coarse and cruel wit with loving jovial good-humor? or her vulgar music with the soul of the Sorrow Songs?

Merely a concrete test of the underlying principles of the great republic is the Negro Problem, and the spiritual striving of the freedmen's sons is the travail of souls whose burden is almost beyond the measure of their strength, but who bear it in the name of an historic race, in the name of this the land of their fathers' fathers, and in the name of human opportunity.

CRITICAL-THINKING QUESTIONS

1. What does Du Bois mean by the "double consciousness" of African Americans?
2. Du Bois writes that people of color aspire to realizing a "better and truer self." What do you think he imagines such a self to be?
3. What are some of the reasons, according to Du Bois, that Emancipation (from slavery in 1863) brought disappointment to former slaves, at least in the short run?
4. Does this essay seem optimistic or pessimistic about the future of U.S. race relations? Why?

RACE AND ETHNICITY

Contemporary

34

The Black Ghetto Underclass

William Julius Wilson

The term underclass *refers to chronically poor people living in our country's central cities. The underclass is disproportionately black, leading many members of our society to assume that racial discrimination is the central cause of urban ghettos. William Julius Wilson claims that discrimination is, indeed, important. But he argues that the plight of poor, urban blacks is more complex, involving the interaction of many social and economic forces, both past and present.*

Why have the social conditions of the ghetto underclass deteriorated so rapidly in recent years? Racial discrimination is the most frequently invoked explanation, and it is undeniable that discrimination continues to aggravate the social and economic problems of poor blacks. But is discrimination really greater today than it was in 1948, when black unemployment was less than half of what it is now, and when the gap between black and white jobless rates was narrower?

SOURCE: *The Truly Disadvantaged: The Inner City, the Underclass, and Public Policy* by William Julius Wilson (Chicago: University of Chicago Press, 1987), pp. 140–46. Copyright © 1987 by The University of Chicago. All rights reserved. Reprinted with permission.

As for the poor black family, it apparently began to fall apart not before but after the mid-twentieth century. Until publication in 1976 of Herbert Gutman's *The Black Family in Slavery and Freedom,* most scholars had believed otherwise. Stimulated by the acrimonious debate over the Moynihan report, Gutman produced data demonstrating that the black family was not significantly disrupted during slavery or even during the early years of the first migration to the urban North, beginning after the turn of the century. The problems of the modern black family, he implied, were associated with modern forces.

Those who cite discrimination as the root cause of poverty often fail to make a distinction between the effects of *historic* discrimination (i.e., discrimination prior to the mid-twentieth century) and the effects of *contemporary* discrimination. Thus they find it hard to explain why the economic position of the black underclass started to worsen soon after Congress enacted, and the White House began to enforce, the most sweeping civil rights legislation since Reconstruction.

The point to be emphasized is that historic discrimination is more important than contemporary discrimination in understanding the plight of the ghetto underclass—that in any event there is more to the story than discrimination (of whichever kind). Historic discrimination certainly helped create an impoverished urban black community in the first place. In his recent *A Piece of the Pie: Black and White Immigrants since 1880,* Stanley Lieberson shows how, in many areas of life, including the labor market, black newcomers from the rural South were far more severely discriminated against in northern cities than were the new white immigrants from southern, central, and eastern Europe. Skin color was part of the problem but it was not all of it.

The disadvantage of skin color—the fact that the dominant whites preferred whites over nonwhites—is one that blacks shared with the Japanese, Chinese, and others. Yet the experience of the Asians, who also experienced harsh discriminatory treatment in the communities where they were concentrated, but who went on to prosper in their adopted land, suggests that skin color per se was not an insuperable obstacle. Indeed Lieberson argues that the greater success enjoyed by Asians may well be explained largely by the different context of their contact with whites. Because changes in immigration policy cut off Asian migration to America in the late nineteenth century, the Japanese and Chinese population did not reach large numbers and therefore did not pose as great a threat as did blacks.

Furthermore, the discontinuation of large-scale immigration from Japan and China enabled those Chinese and Japanese already in the United States to solidify networks of ethnic contacts and to occupy particular occupational niches in small, relatively stable communities. For blacks, the situation was different. The 1970 census recorded 22,580,000 blacks in the United States but only 435,000 Chinese and 591,000 Japanese.

If different population sizes accounted for a good deal of the difference in the economic success of blacks and Asians, they also helped determine the dissimilar rates of progress of urban blacks and the new European arrivals. European immigration was curtailed during the 1920s, but black migration to the urban North continued through the 1960s. With each passing decade there were many more blacks who were recent migrants to the North, whereas the immigrant component of the new Europeans dropped off over time. Eventually, other whites muffled their dislike of the Poles and Italians and Jews and directed their antagonism against blacks.

In addition to the problem of historic discrimination, the black migration to New York, Philadelphia, Chicago, and other northern cities—the continued replenishment of black populations there by poor newcomers—predictably skewed the age profile of the urban black community and kept it relatively young. The number of central-city black youths aged sixteen to nineteen increased by almost 75 percent from 1960 to 1969. Young black adults (aged twenty to twenty-four) increased in number by two-thirds during the same period, three times the increase for young white adults. In the nation's inner cities in 1977, the median age for whites was 30.3, for blacks 23.9. The importance of this jump in the number of young minorities in the ghetto, many of them lacking one or more parents, cannot be overemphasized.

Age correlates with many things. For example, the higher the median age of a group, the higher its income; the lower the median age, the higher the unemployment rate and the higher the crime rate (more than half of those arrested in 1980 for violent and property crimes in American cities were under twenty-one). The younger a woman is, the more likely she is to bear a child out of wedlock, head up a new household, and depend on welfare.

In short, part of what had gone awry in the ghetto was due to the sheer increase in the number of black youth.

The population explosion among minority youth occurred at a time when changes in the economy were beginning to pose serious problems for unskilled workers. Urban minorities have been particularly vulnerable to the structural economic changes of the past two decades: the shift from goods-producing to service-producing industries, the increasing polarization of the labor market into low-wage and high-wage sectors, innovations in technology, and the relocation of manufacturing industries out of the central cities.

Most unemployed blacks in the United States reside within the central cities. Their situation, already more difficult than that of any other major ethnic group in the country, continues to worsen. Not only are there more blacks without jobs every year; men, especially young males, are dropping out of the labor force in record proportions. Also, more and more black youth, including many who are no longer in school, are obtaining no job experience at all.

However, the growing problem of joblessness in the inner city both exacerbates and is in turn partly created by the changing social composition of inner-city neighborhoods. These areas have undergone a profound social transformation in the last several years, as reflected not only in their increasing rates of social dislocation but also in the changing class structure of ghetto neighborhoods. In the 1940s, 1950s, and even the 1960s, lower-class, working-class, and middle-class black urban families all resided more or less in the same ghetto areas, albeit on different streets. Although black middle-class professionals today tend to be employed in mainstream occupations outside the black community and neither live nor frequently interact with ghetto residents, the black middle-class professionals of the 1940s and 1950s (doctors, lawyers, teachers, social workers, etc.) resided in the higher-income areas of the inner city and serviced the ghetto community. The exodus of black middle-class professionals from the inner city has been increasingly accompanied by a movement of stable working-class blacks to higher-income neighborhoods in other parts of the city and to the suburbs. Confined by restrictive covenants to communities also inhabited by the urban black lower classes, the black working and middle classes in earlier years provided stability to inner-city neighborhoods and perpetuated and reinforced societal norms and values. In short, their very presence enhanced the social organization of ghetto communities. If strong norms and sanctions against aberrant behavior, a sense of community, and positive neighborhood identification are the essential features of social organization in urban areas, inner-city neighborhoods today suffer from a severe lack of social organization.

Unlike in previous years, today's ghetto residents represent almost exclusively the most disadvantaged segments of the urban black community—including those families that have experienced long-term spells of poverty and/or welfare dependency, individuals who lack training and skills and have either experienced periods of persistent unemployment or have dropped out of the labor force altogether, and individuals who are frequently involved in street criminal activity. The term *ghetto underclass* refers to this heterogeneous group of families and individuals who inhabit the cores of the nation's central cities. The term suggests that a fundamental social transformation has taken place in ghetto neighborhoods, and the groups represented by this term are collectively different from and much more socially isolated than those that lived in these communities in earlier years.

The significance of changes embodied in the social transformation of the inner city is perhaps best captured by the concepts *concentration effects* and *social buffer.* The former refers to the constraints and opportunities associated with living in a neighborhood in which the population is overwhelmingly socially disadvantaged—constraints and opportunities that include the kinds of ecological niches that the residents of these communities occupy in terms of access to jobs, availability of marriageable partners, and exposure to conventional role models. The latter refers to the presence of a sufficient number of working- and middle-class professional families to absorb the shock or cushion the effect of uneven economic growth and periodic recessions on inner-city neighborhoods. The basic thesis is not that ghetto culture went unchecked following the removal of higher-income families in the inner city, but that the removal of these families made it more difficult to sustain the basic institutions in the inner city (including churches, stores, schools, recreational facilities, etc.) in the face of prolonged joblessness. And as the basic institutions declined, the social organization of inner-city neighborhoods (defined here to include a sense of community, positive neighborhood identification, and explicit norms and sanctions against aberrant behavior) likewise declined. Indeed, the social organization of any neighborhood depends in large measure on the viability of social institutions in that neighborhood. It is true that the presence of stable working- and middle-class families in the ghetto provides mainstream role models that reinforce mainstream values pertaining to employment, education, and family structure. But, in the final analysis, a far more important effect is the institutional stability that these families are able to provide in their neighborhoods because of their greater economic and educational resources, especially during periods of an economic downturn—periods in which joblessness in poor urban areas tends to substantially increase.

In underlining joblessness as an important aspect of inner-city social transformations, we are reminded that in the 1960s scholars readily attributed poor black family deterioration to problems of employment. Nonetheless, in the last several years, in the face of the overwhelming attention given to welfare as the major source of black family breakup, concerns about the importance of joblessness have diminished, despite the existence of evidence strongly suggesting the need for renewed scholarly and public policy attention to the relationship between the disintegration of

poor black families and black male labor-market experiences.

Although changing social and cultural trends have often been said to explain some of the dynamic shifts in the structure of the family, they appear to have more relevance for changes in family structure among whites. And contrary to popular opinion, there is little evidence to support the argument that welfare is the primary cause of family out-of-wedlock births, breakups, and female-headed households. Welfare does seem to have a modest effect on separation and divorce, particularly for white women, but recent evidence indicates that its total effect on the proportion of all female householders is small.

By contrast, the evidence for the influence of joblessness on family structure is much more conclusive. Research has demonstrated, for example, a connection between an encouraging economic situation and the early marriage of young people. In this connection, black women are more likely to delay marriage and less likely to remarry. Although black and white teenagers expect to become parents at about the same ages, black teenagers expect to marry at later ages. The black delay in marriage and the lower rate of remarriage, each associated with high percentages of out-of-wedlock births and female-headed households, can be directly tied to the employment status of black males. Indeed, black women, especially young black women, are confronting a shrinking pool of "marriageable" (that is economically stable) men.

White women are not experiencing this problem. Our "male marriageable pool index" shows that the number of employed white men per one hundred white women in different age categories has either remained roughly the same or has only slightly increased in the last two decades. There is little reason, therefore, to assume a connection between the recent growth of female-headed white families and patterns of white male employment. That the pool of "marriageable" white men has not decreased over the years is perhaps reflected in the earlier age of first marriage and the higher rate of remarriage among white women. It is therefore reasonable to hypothesize that the rise in rates of separation and divorce among whites is due mainly to the increased economic independence of white women and related social and cultural factors embodied in the feminist movement.

The argument that the decline in the incidence of intact marriages among blacks is associated with the declining economic status of black men is further supported by an analysis of regional data on female headship and the "male marriageable pool." Whereas changes in the ratios of employed men to women among whites have been minimal for all regions of the country regardless of age from 1960 to 1980, the ratios among blacks have declined significantly in all regions except the West, with the greatest declines in the northeastern and north-central regions of the country. On the basis of these trends, it would be expected that the growth in numbers of black female-headed households would occur most rapidly in the northern regions, followed by the South and the West. Regional data on the "male marriageable pool index" support this conclusion, except for the larger-than-expected increase in black female-headed families in the West—a function of patterns of selective black migration to the West.

The sharp decline in the black "male marriageable pool" in the northeastern and north-central regions is related to recent changes in the basic economic organization in American society. In the two northern regions, the shift in economic activity from goods production to services has been as-sociated with changes in the location of production, including an interregional movement of industry from the North to the South and West and, more important, a movement of certain industries out of the older central cities where blacks are concentrated. Moreover, the shrinkage of the male marriageable pool for ages sixteen to twenty-four in the South from 1960 to 1980 is related to the mechanization of agriculture, which lowered substantially the demand for low-skilled agricultural labor, especially during the 1960s. For all these reasons, it is often necessary to go beyond the specific issue of current racial discrimination to understand factors that contribute directly to poor black joblessness and indirectly to related social problems such as family instability in the inner city. But this point has not been readily grasped by policymakers and civil rights leaders.

CRITICAL-THINKING QUESTIONS

1. In what respects, according to Wilson, has the historical experience of blacks in the United States differed from that of Asians and other categories of minorities?

2. What elements of social disorganization characterize much of the nation's poor, black neighborhoods? What are the consequences for those living there?

3. How has economic insecurity affected family patterns within poor, black communities?

35

The Rise of Hispanic Affluence

William O'Hare

Social scientists have documented the disadvantages endured by various U.S. minorities. Yet no minority is internally homogeneous. Although, taken as a whole, Hispanics receive only two-thirds of the average U.S. income, the number of affluent Hispanic households grew sharply during the 1980s.

The mainstream media usually portray America's Hispanics as a group of impoverished, newly arrived immigrants from Mexico or Central America. The truth is more complex. A significant share of the Hispanic community has moved into affluence since 1970, and upscale Hispanic households are one of the nation's fastest-growing market segments.

Affluence means different things to different people, but most analyses put households with annual incomes of $50,000 or more in the affluent category. The number of Hispanic* households with an income of $50,000 or more (in 1988 dol- lars) grew from 191,000 in 1972 to 638,000 in 1988, a 234 percent increase.

Most of this increase occurred during the 1980s. The number of affluent Hispanic house- holds grew by only 129,000 between 1972 and 1980, then gained 318,000 between 1980 and 1988. More than 2.6 million Hispanics live in these 638,000 affluent households.

In 1972, 7.2 percent of Hispanic households were affluent. That share grew to 8.2 percent by 1980 and 10.8 percent in 1988. It is a higher pro- portion than the share of black households that are affluent (9.8 percent) but much lower than the fig-

SOURCE: "The Rise of Hispanic Affluence," by William O'Hare, in *American Demographics,* vol. 12, no. 8, August 1990, pp. 40–43. Reprinted with permission.

* In this article, the terms black and white refer to non-His- panic blacks and non-Hispanic whites.

ure for whites (23.2 percent). And only 1.3 percent of Hispanic households are in the super-affluent category, with annual incomes of more than $100,000.

A DIFFERENT MARKET

Among all Hispanic households, average income is low because the average incomes of recent immigrants are so low. However, the averages obscure the rapid growth of affluent Hispanics.

TABLE 35-1 Affluent Americans: A Comparison of Wealthy Hispanics and Whites

Demographic	Affluent Hispanics (%)	Affluent Whites (%)
Age		
15–24	10	7
25–44	54	40
45–64	25	25
65 and older	11	28
Marital Status		
Married	78	82
Widowed	3	3
Divorced/separated	11	7
Never married	8	8
Education		
Less than high school	19	6
High school graduate	28	27
1–3 years college	25	19
College graduate	29	48
Household Size		
1 person	3	6
2 people	19	33
3 or more people	78	61
Tenure		
Owner	74	86
Renter	26	14
Region		
Northeast	18	26
Midwest	9	24
South	30	30
West	42	20
Metropolitan Status		
Central city	36	24
Suburbs	61	60
Rural	4	15

NOTE: Distribution of affluent Hispanics and affluent non-Hispanic whites by selected characteristics of householder, 1988.
SOURCE: Current Population Survey, March 1989, Bureau of the Census.

Upscale Hispanics represent a growing but often underserved consumer market.

Affluent Hispanics are similar to other affluent groups in some respects, but their differences are important. Like most affluent households, Hispanics achieve affluence by having multiple paychecks. Of the 11.9 million Hispanic workers reported by the Census Bureau in 1988, only 211,000, or 1.8 percent, individually made more than $50,000. Of these, 84 percent were men. Of the 638,000 Hispanic households that were affluent in 1988, 504,000 of them were married couples.

Hispanic households tend to be larger than white households, and affluent Hispanics are no exception. Seventy-eight percent of affluent Hispanic households include three or more people, compared with only 61 percent of white households. One-third of white households contain just two people, and 6 percent are people who live alone, compared with only 19 percent and 3 percent of affluent Hispanic households.

Affluent Hispanics are more likely than affluent whites to be young adults, and they are less likely to be aged sixty-five or older. Fifty-four percent of affluent Hispanics are aged twenty-five to forty-four, for example, compared with only 40 percent of affluent whites. Twenty-eight percent of affluent whites are aged sixty-five or older, compared with 11 percent of affluent Hispanics. This reflects the younger age structure of the Hispanic population in general.

Education is a powerful influence on the affluence of Hispanic households, but the average educational level of affluent Hispanics is still less than that of affluent whites. Almost half (48 percent) of affluent white householders have at least a four-year college degree, compared with only 29 percent of affluent Hispanic householders. Fully 19 percent of affluent Hispanic householders are high school dropouts, versus just 6 percent of whites.

WHERE THEY LIVE

Location is one of the major differences between affluent Hispanics and other affluent groups.

Forty-two percent of all affluent Hispanic households are in the West, compared with only 20 percent of affluent white households. Only 9 percent of affluent Hispanics live in the Midwest, compared with one-quarter of affluent whites.

Affluent Hispanics are also twice as likely as affluent whites to live in a large metropolitan area. One-third of affluent Hispanics live in metropolitan areas of 1 million or more, partly because so many live in Los Angeles. While 15 percent of affluent whites live in nonmetropolitan areas, only 4 percent of affluent Hispanics live outside of metros.

Within metropolitan areas, affluent Hispanics are much more likely than affluent whites to live in the central city. About 60 percent of both Hispanic and white affluent households are in the suburbs of large cities. But 36 percent of affluent Hispanics live in the central cities, compared with 24 percent of whites. This may explain why only about three-quarters of affluent Hispanics are homeowners, compared with 86 percent of affluent whites.

The latest reliable data on affluent Hispanics within specific metropolitan areas are from the 1980 census. To locate pockets of affluence in the nation's metropolitan areas, I examined the share of Hispanic households with incomes of $35,000 or more in 1979, which is roughly equivalent to an income of $50,000 or more in 1988. This analysis revealed that the metropolitan areas where Hispanic households are most likely to be affluent are not the areas with the largest Hispanic populations. In fact, the share of Hispanic households with 1979 incomes of $35,000 or more was lower in metropolitan areas where Hispanics made up a large share of the total population.

At the top of the list is Honolulu where more than one-quarter of all Hispanic households had incomes of more than $35,000 in 1980. Honolulu is followed by Washington, DC, Detroit, and Nassau-Suffolk, New York. Despite Miami's relatively affluent Cuban community, that metropolitan area ended up ninth in this ranking. And almost all of the metros at the bottom of the list are heavily His-

TABLE 32-2 Concentrations of Affluent Hispanics

Metropolitan Area	Percent Affluent	Metropolitan Area	Percent Affluent
1. Honolulu, HI	25.3	22. Tucson, AZ	7.5
2. Washington, DC-MD-VA	24.6	23. Phoenix, AZ	7.2
3. Detroit, MI	18.7	24. Albuquerque, NM	7.1
4. Nassau-Suffolk, NY	15.8	25. Philadelphia, PA-NJ	7.1
5. San Francisco-Oakland, CA	15.1	26. Austin, TX	6.5
6. San Jose, CA	14.8	27. Boston-Lowell-Brockton-Lawrence-Haverhill, MA	6.5
7. Anaheim-Santa Ana-Garden Grove, CA	14.2	28. Salinas-Seaside-Monterey, CA	6.3
8. New Orleans, LA	13.2	29. Stockton, CA	6.3
9. Miami, FL	11.5	30. Corpus Christi, TX	6.1
10. Houston, TX	11.3	31. Laredo, TX	5.7
11. Chicago, IL	10.9	32. Jersey City, NJ	5.5
12. Oxnard-Simi Valley-Ventura, CA	10.2	33. Bakersfield, CA	5.5
13. Newark, NJ	9.8	34. Bergen-Passaic, NJ	5.1
14. Tampa-St. Petersburg, FL	9.8	35. San Antonio, TX	4.8
15. Denver-Boulder, CO	9.3	36. New York, NY-NJ	4.7
16. Sacramento, CA	9.1	37. Fresno, CA	4.7
17. Los Angeles-Long Beach, CA	8.7	38. El Paso, TX	4.6
18. Santa Barbara-Santa Maria-Lompoc, CA	8.6	39. Las Cruces, NM	4.2
19. Riverside-San Bernardino-Oakland, CA	8.3	40. McAllen-Pharr-Edinburg, TX	3.6
20. San Diego, CA	8.2	41. Brownsville-Harlingen-San Benito, TX	3.5
21. Dallas -Fort Worth, TX	8.1	42. Visalia-Tulare-Porterville, CA	3.3

NOTES: Percent of Hispanic households with incomes of $50,000 or more in 1989 dollars, in selected metropolitan areas, 1979 ($50,000 in 1989 dollars is roughly equivalent to $35,000 in 1979). Ranking is based on unrounded percentages.

SOURCE: 1980 census.

panic and located in the Southwest. In Brownsville-McAllen, Texas, and Visalia, California, fewer than 4 percent of Hispanic households had 1979 incomes of $35,000 or more.

The number of affluent Hispanics is growing because Hispanics are becoming a larger share of our population, and also because an ever-growing share of Hispanics are moving up in U.S. society. Like other groups, most affluent Hispanic households are married couples where both husband and wife work. But affluent Hispanics are heavily concentrated in the West, in large (1 million plus) metropolitan areas, and in central cities. The remarkable economic strides Hispanics have made in the 1980s should show up when the 1990 census results are released beginning next year. . . .

CRITICAL-THINKING QUESTIONS

1. How affluent are Hispanics compared with whites? Compared to African Americans?

2. In what respects do affluent Hispanics differ from affluent whites?

3. What evidence supports the conclusion that Hispanics have improved their social position in recent decades? What evidence leads to the conclusion that they have not?

36

The Transculturation
of Native American College Students

Terry Huffman

Anyone can experience discomfort in an unfamiliar cultural setting; many Native Americans have a difficult time adjusting to the college campus. According to the author, traditional Native Americans embrace cultural systems that do not mesh well with the individualistic, competitive, and white-European world typical of U.S. colleges. This fact goes a long way toward explaining low educational achievement among Native Americans. But, he continues, the concept of transculturation suggests an alternative by which new learning may be compatible with a traditional way of life.

I have advised my people this way—when you find something good in the white man's road, pick it up. When you find something that is bad or turns out bad, drop it, leave it alone. We shall master his machinery, and his inventions, his skills, his medicine, his planning, but we will retain our beauty and still be Indians.

—Sitting Bull

SOURCE: "The Transculturation of Native American College Students," by Terry Huffman, in *American Mosaic: Selected Readings on America's Multicultural Heritage,* ed. Young I. Song and Eugene C. Kim. Englewood Cliffs, NJ: Prentice Hall, 1993. Reprinted with permission.

Native Americans have one of the lowest levels of higher educational achievement among American racial and ethnic groups. It has been estimated that a mere 6 percent of Native American students complete their college education (Astin 1982).

A variety of factors have been identified to account for this dismal record of educational achievement. The lack of success has been attributed to low achievement motivation, poor academic preparation, inadequate financial support, and lack of parental and community support (Guyette and Heth 1983; Falk and Aitken 1984; Lin 1985; McIntosch 1987; Scott 1986; and West 1988). There is little doubt that these factors, individually and cumulatively, pose barriers for Native Americans. However, perhaps none of these factors are more problematic for those students and mysterious to researchers than the potential for cultural conflict that often seems to be inherent in the college setting.

College is an institution of values, norms, and attitudes. Moreover, it embodies a cultural milieu which reflects middle-class America. Many Native Americans find this cultural milieu foreign, even alien. These are individuals oriented toward cultural expectations different than those found institutionalized in the college setting.

For those who face cultural conflicts the options are seemingly few: Withdraw from the institution in an attempt to preserve one's "Indianness," or adopt non-Indian ways and pursue assimilation. However, there is another alternative. There are students who have been successful at retaining their cultural heritage while negotiating the complexities of the non-Indian institution. These rather unique individuals bridge the cultures and while they have largely been ignored by researchers, they are worth investigating. This bridging and the progression of values, attitudes, behaviors, and feelings associated with it, are referred to as transculturation.

METHODS

The results of this paper are part of an ongoing research project involving Native Americans who are attending or have attended South Dakota colleges. The subjects consist of Native American students attending predominately non-Indian institutions and students who have attended reservation community colleges and non-Indian institutions.

The research design utilizes a "double-barreled" approach utilizing both quantitative and qualitative methodologies. The quantitative approach involves a questionnaire designed, among other things, to obtain information on cultural, social, academic, and financial problems encountered by Native Americans. The qualitative approach involves in-depth interviews in order to gain greater insight into Native Americans' subjective thoughts and views regarding their college experience.

At the time of this writing, thirty subjects have participated in the project.

The Phenomenon of Native-American Transculturation

Not all Native American students face cultural conflicts in college. Many are not appreciatively different from their fellow non-Indian classmates. That is, there are those students who have spent little or none of their lives on reservations and have relatively little contact with "traditional" Indian culture. As they generally identify with and are assimilated into the American cultural mainstream, these individuals feel no great sense of cultural conflict (Huffman and Rosonke 1989).

On the other hand, there are those students who have a strong identification with traditional Indian culture. Typically they have lived a great deal, if not all, of their lives on reservations. These students find assimilation repulsive and thus reject the notion. For these individuals the potential for cultural conflict looms large (Huffman and Rosonke 1989).

A large proportion of the students who encounter cultural conflict simply leave college (Chadwick 1972; Falk and Aitken 1984). Scott (1986), who describes the attachment to traditional Indian culture as the "difficult situation," reported:

The data confirm that being a "cultural Indian" reduces the likelihood of academic success . . . those committed to Indian ways are less likely to become integrated into the university community, and consequently less likely to succeed. (p. 381)

Certainly many "cultural Indians" desire to leave once they encounter the cultural dilemmas of college life (Huffman and Rosonke 1989). The students who succumb to this temptation stand out in the literature as examples of Native Americans who have failed to make the necessary adjustments to the gesellschaft world of academia.

What then separates those who persist from those who become another Native American attrition statistic? It cannot be merely assumed that academically successful traditional Native Americans have experienced a radical form of assimilation. There is a growing body of evidence to refute the assimilationist model of Native American education (Huffman, Sill, and Brokenleg 1986; Kerbo 1981; McFee 1972). Rather, it is the very retention of traditional culture that has enhanced the performance of many "cultural Indians." That is, these more culturally traditional Native American students undergo a process of transculturation that is fundamental to their academic success.

The Concept of Transculturation

Transculturation is the process by which an individual of one culture can enter and interact in the milieu of another culture without loss of the person's native cultural identity and ways. Hallowell (1972) has defined transculturation as:

It is a phenomenon that involves the fate of persons rather than changes in sociocultural systems. . . . It is the process whereby individuals under a variety of circumstances temporarily or permanently detached from one group . . . enter the web of social relations that constitute another society, and come under the influence of its customs, ideas, and values to a greater or lesser degree. (p. 206)

Transculturation has some important distinctions from the more commonly used concept of biculturalism. Quite often biculturalism is treated as rather one-dimensional. That is, biculturalism typically is associated with bilingualism (Medicine 1986; Pizzillo 1976; Vasquez 1979).

The synonymous use of biculturalism and bilingualism has come under attack as naive (Fishman 1980; Matute-Bianchi 1980). Yet, the detractors will admit the usefulness of equating the two terms

in finding support for a particular "crosscultural" program (Bartlett 1979). A fact that could explain why biculturalism has endured with relatively little refinement. For instance, Pratte (1979) has commented:

Even though interrelated and interdependent, biculturalism and bilingualism are not identical terms. Bilingualism, in its most ordinary employment, means fluency in at least two languages, including oral communication, the encoding and decoding of written symbols, and the correct inflection and pitch, commonly called the superimposed structure of a language. . . . Biculturalism, on the other hand, refers to the cultural elements that may include language but go beyond language, insofar as it is a functional awareness and participation in two contrasting sociocultures (statuses, roles, values, etc.). Thus for the purpose of clarifying the conceptual difficulty here, if it is only the fluency that is assessed as bilingual, it is obvious that bilingualism is not biculturalism. . . . There is a sense in which it would be hard to find a better example of the danger of naively defining a term in educational discourse in order to win acceptance of the program offered. (pp. 183–85)

Also the idea of biculturalism typically implies a kind of acculturated end product. The idea generally is that biculturalism follows a linear pattern with the individual, like a mathematical equation, adding elements from the host culture while relinquishing elements from the native culture (McFee 1972). Ultimately the result is a sort of "hybrid" with the necessary repertoire of cultural skills (i.e., language) to relate to two cultures. In this sense, biculturalism has simply been a variation on the idea of acculturation.

Furthermore, how an individual receives a blended cultural repertoire is largely ignored. The point of emphasis is that the bicultural individual is a product rather than a process. Only a few attempts have been made to formulate a bicultural process. For instance, Szapocznik and his colleagues have formulated a three-dimensional bicultural process consisting of: (1) the acculturation of cultural elements from the host culture, (2) the retention and relinquishing of native cultural elements, (3) the syncretization of the two cultures resulting in a bicultural individual (Szapocznik and Kurtines 1979; Szapocznik, Kurtines, and Fernandez 1980; Szapocznik, Santisteban, Kurtines, Perez-Vidal, and Hervis 1984; Szapocznik and Hernandez 1988). However, even in this attempt the implication is nevertheless of an end product.

Transculturation, on the other hand, implies a continual ongoing process of cultural encounters and resultant realignments (Sill 1967). The individual in a cross-cultural situation never achieves the "end product" of biculturalism. This is more analogous to a person on an international journey experiencing many differing cultural encounters, some of which he/she can relate to, many others in which he/she cannot. At first, the traveler is disoriented and finds little with which to relate. This is the time of first awareness. Each cultural element needs to be tested and evaluated. In time the traveler learns to relate to the new culture on its own terms. This does not mean, however, that the individual has surrendered the native cultural heritage. On the contrary, the individual has simply put it aside long enough to make way in the new cultural setting.

When the individual returns to his/her native cultural milieu, former ways have not been lost. Experience and skills are certainly broadened but not at the expense of native ways and skills (as implied in biculturalism) (Ortiz 1947; Polgar 1960). An international sojourner typically returns with a widened cultural perspective and worldview. The individual, nevertheless, is still the cultural product of his/her society.

When the cross-cultural experience involves members of subcultures within a larger society, the same process applies. Here too journeys into the mainstream result in an enriched and broadened worldview. The important point is that the cultural heritage still remains intact; however, new options exist.

Transculturation is a process of exploring evermore deeply into a cultural context, testing out another culture, realigning with what is learned, and leading to more discovery. Therefore, it is also a journey into one's own culture. Each new discovery about a new culture leads to a revelation about the complexities of one's own cultural world. Thus, an individual never arrives as a "product," but rather is learning how to learn a new and old culture.

The difference in the use of the transculturation and biculturalism is more than a mere matter of semantics. It is a matter of theoretical and practical implication. The use of transculturation reduces the subtlety of assimilation that resides somewhat below the surface of biculturalism and attempts to give recognition to the resilience, integrity, and undergirding strength of minority cultures in a pluralistic society (Ortiz 1947).

The Process of Transculturation

The challenge for traditional Native American students is to interact on two cultural levels simultaneously (Davis and Pyatskowit 1976). That is, successful performance in college requires dual operation at a Native American cultural level and a college mainstream level.

Transculturated students have the unique ability to interact within and between cultures as demanded by the situation (Qoyawayma 1964). However, the process leading through this cultural-social-psychological maze is not easy. Through interviews with students, four stages of the Native American transculturational process have been identified: initial alienation, self-discovery, realignment, and participation [Figure 36-1].

Stage 1: Initial Alienation. Because traditional Native American students first experience the mainstream college as cultural "outsiders," their initial feeling is one of alienation. At first there are very few things about college life with which they can relate. The institution itself (i.e., administration policies and procedures, even to an extent classroom etiquette, etc.) seems rigid, overly formalized, and altogether strange.

A young man who had spent his entire life on the Cheyenne River (South Dakota) reservation, who was active in Native American religion, and reported a great deal of cultural difficulties while

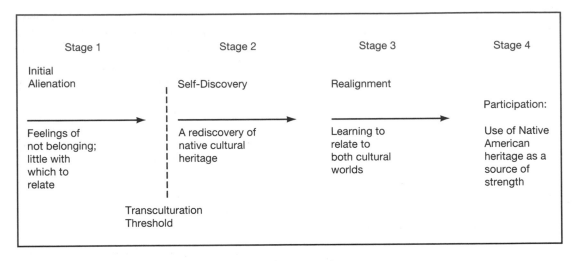

FIGURE 36-1   Stages of Native American Transculturation

in college (he was, in fact, nearing the end of his first semester when the interview took place) is typical of the impression and reaction of many culturally traditional Native American students:

I felt like I'm where I didn't belong. . . . I set a lot of goals, I wanted to come to school. But when I got here I found that it was really hard. I had a lot of problems with wanting to leave. . . . My first impression was to get back into my car and just go home.

Another young man from the Pine Ridge (South Dakota) reservation succinctly summarized his college experience in a similar manner by simply stating: "I feel like I don't belong."

Many students are overwhelmed by the lack of familiar cultural connections. Little contact is made with non-Indian students and the institution itself begins to be regarded with suspicion (due to a growing perception that it is simply another agent of assimilation). Often traditional Native American students even feel alienated from their fellow Native American classmates, particularly those who are more assimilated, viewing them with some contempt as "urban Indians." The same Cheyenne River student stated:

I just try to keep to myself. . . . It's like they (other Native American students) more or less have accepted the values of non-Indians over Indian ones.

At this stage, traditional Native Americans are extremely vulnerable. An experience in which the perceived threat of assimilation looms large compounded by feelings of isolation from other Native Americans leaves many students disillusioned and thus they reject the college experience. In this sense, Scott's idea of the "difficult situation" is to a point correct. That is, Native American cultural traditionalism and the rigors of academic life do not at first make a blissful marriage.

A student who had lived all his life on the Turtle Mountain (North Dakota) reservation contemplated on the difficulties that he and many other students experience:

I really think they (Indian students) become disenchanted really quick. I think they perceive it (college) as this huge, monstrous institution rather than a person walking daily. Because it's foreign, I know for a fact, that they do suffer some sort of "culture shock" because the surroundings are new and the way of life is new. The objectives of your time, how you spend your time, what you do, is all new. The emphasis is placed on self and trying to fend for yourself and I think that there are a lot of handicaps like that . . . ! think that because the cultures are so opposed that it would be a hard transaction; that they won't see the benefits of it right away and might become disenchanted.

Because of their disenfranchisement from college life, it is at this early stage of college life that traditional Native Americans have the greatest potential for unsuccessful academic careers. Many students leave college because of the alienation they feel. Unfortunately, it is these students who often stand out in the literature and serve as stereotypical models of Native Americans who could not release the "old Indian ways" and make the necessary adjustments to the mainstream.

Yet, despite these difficulties, many muddle through. Every day of the first few months (in some cases even years) is a test to their commitment and endurance. A Standing Rock (North Dakota) student, who was nearing the end of his academic career, reflected:

I felt like this was the last place on earth I wanted to be because there was nothing that I could relate to. It was all just really different. . . . I had a bunch of walls around me. It was hard for me to be here. I look at it as being afraid, being out of place, feeling like I was different and a lot of people treated me different. . . . I just had to take it one step at a time.

Stage 2: Self-Discovery. If traditional Native American students can endure the pangs of the initial alienation, they reach a transculturation threshold. At this point they begin to realize that they have not been snared in a web of assimilation, that they can compete academically, and that they can interact with Indians and non-Indians alike, all without a loss to their cultural self. In short, they come to realize that they have not lost their "Indianness" and yet they have survived academically.

Thus, they begin an introspection and make a most curious discovery. They have succeeded because they are Indian and have not attempted to be anything else. It is striking to this writer just how profound this stage is in the experience of the transculturated Native Americans interviewed. Virtually all the transculturated students could relate a

specific time in their academic career when they had to take stock of their cultural selves.

At that transculturation threshold a conscious and deliberate decision is made to attempt to relate to both cultural worlds when necessary while using traditional Native American values and heritage as a personal anchor. The Turtle Mountain reservation student referred to above recalled reaching his threshold:

I really had to do some searching and really some finding out; am I going to accept the way I am or am I going to try to conform or am I just going to leave it alone? Finally I had to accept what I was and that there are some things that are more to being an Indian than just the "Indian." There was [sic] feelings and family and culture, there was [sic] ways of doing things. When I learned to separate the two and learned that this is the way you do it at work, this is the way you do it at home, and you conduct your family affairs this way, then that's good. I think the turning point came when I decided to separate the two. . . . Then I resolved my "Indianness" and the way the system works.

A Standing Rock reservation student who was president of his college's honor program and the president of the campus Native American student organization put it this way:

The first thing I found out when I came to college is how much Indian I was . . . I'd say my strongest identification with my own "Indianness" has been since I've been here. . . . It's a real source of strength because I guess it sort of gives me a reason for being here.

Stage 3: Realignment. With the strength and confidence they find in their cultural identity, Native American students begin a realignment process. At this stage, students make the necessary practical adjustments in their personal, social, and academic worlds. That is, they begin to learn to relate at both cultural levels as demanded by the situation. The Standing Rock student cited above referred to this stage as "learning to play the game."

Students reassess themselves and their situation. They evaluate their repertoire of values, attitudes, and goals and measure them against those institutionalized in the fabric of higher education. They can then begin to align themselves with the nature of academia and use the appropriate norms and behaviors as needed. In short, they learn to cross cultural boundaries when necessary. At this stage, they are well into the process of transculturation.

A middle-aged woman from Pine Ridge, by any standards a traditional Indian person (whose late father was a well known Lakota spiritual leader), described the realignment process this way:

When we go to school we live a non-Indian way but we still keep our values. . . . I could put my values aside just long enough to learn what it is I want to learn but that doesn't mean I'm going to forget them. I think that is how strong they are with me.

Stage 4: Participation. At this stage students begin to settle in. They have largely overcome the alienation of their early college experience and discovered that it is possible to be an "Indian" in the heart of the non-Indian world. They learn that they can interact with both Indians and non-Indians alike. Also, typically their goals and desires are crystallized.

Much like other students, at this stage Native American students begin to concentrate on their studies. Interestingly they also make maximum use of their Native American heritage as a source of strength, confidence, and identity. The Pine Ridge student cited above observed:

I think that the time we spend away from our people, we appreciate our ways and our people even more. People that have left the reservation to go away to school, I have never seen them participate in things like pow-wows or sweats or sun dances. I've never seen them do that. Yet they go away for four or five years and then they come back and they are really strong into spirituality; they're really different. And I was thinking that they appreciate things more when they are away like that. They must think about it or something happens while they are away.

Support from others is important to sustain the participation of this stage. Native American students look to others for the moral support necessary to continue the educational process that still proves to be difficult. The same Pine Ridge student stated:

I had a lot of elderly people talk to me and tell me that I wasn't here for them (prejudiced whites), that I was here to learn and that someday I was going home to help them out and not to pay attention to them. "Put those feelings aside. Remember what you're doing but also why you are doing." So that's where my support comes from. From the elderly people from home. When I go home, I get handshakes, I get hugs. I come back all renewed again. I can handle anything that comes my way.

DISCUSSION

Transculturated students are the least researched and understood among Native American college students. The reasons for this lack of recognition are several fold. First is a conceptualization difficulty related to the very ability these students have to operate at two cultural levels. That is, the ability to operate in the college mainstream has led some to assume that these students are simply assimilated (Boutwell, Low, Williams, and Proffit 1973; Carroll 1978). Working from such an assumption there is a failure to recognize the retention of Native American cultural traditions implied by transculturation (Medicine 1986).

Second is a methodological difficulty. Most studies have been quantitative attempts to measure the degree of assimilation (Huffman et al. 1986; Roy 1962; Scott 1986). Typically these instruments have not been sensitive to the transculturational phenomena. Unfortunately few attempts have been qualitative research designs dealing with the perceptions of Native Americans on their academic experience. Such research strategies are better suited to the articulation of transculturation process.

Third, and underlying the first two reasons, is the problem of ethnocentrism. In the past it has been explicitly advanced that assimilation is and should be the key to educational success of all minorities, especially for Native Americans. Therefore, examples of Native American educational achievement that contradicted the assimilation model were either dismissed as an aberration or simply ignored (Medicine 1986). In essence, assimilation theory tends to assume a "melting pot" or appropriate mainstream American culture, whereas transculturation theory is appropriate to a pluralistic view of American society.

CONCLUSION

There is an important implication that arises from this work on transculturation. Success in college for traditional Native Americans does not impinge on greater assimilation at all. Rather, contrary to much of the thinking of the past, for many students the retention of traditional cultural identity and heritage is crucial for greater academic achievement and success. Indeed, it is apparent that traditionalism is the instrumental factor in facilitating a strong sense of personal self-identity and confidence in Native American students.

Cultural traditionalism becomes a "blessing" rather than a "burden," however, when one is able to cross the transculturation threshold between alienation and self-discovery. When Native Americans discover or appropriate the strength that comes from being Indian, they have in place the social psychological mechanism to participate and achieve in the mainstream.

Unfortunately, many traditional Native American college students fail to cross that threshold, resulting in academic failure which further perpetuates the notion that traditionalism poses a "difficult situation." In reality it is not the traditionalism that is the difficult situation, but rather overcoming the alienation that comes along with being a culturally traditional Native American in the non-Indian academic world.

CRITICAL-THINKING QUESTIONS

1. Define the concept of transculturation. In this process, what changes and what stays the same?
2. What are the four stages of transculturation? Why do some students not complete the stages of development?
3. Do you think the theory of transculturation has a useful application to the experiences of African Americans on a predominantly white campus? Of Latinos on a mostly Anglo campus?

REFERENCES

ASTIN, A. W. 1982. Minorities in American higher education: Final report of the Commission on the Higher Education of Minorities. San Francisco, CA: Jossey-Bass.

BARTLETT, G. 1979. Two approaches to acculturation: Bilingual education and ESL. *Journal of American Indian Education,* 18: 15–19.

BOUTWELL, R. C., W. C. LOW, K. WILLIAMS, and T. PROFFIT. 1973. Red apples. *Journal of American Indian Education,* 12: 111–14.

CARROLL, R. E. 1978. Academic performance and cultural marginality. *Journal of American Indian Education,* 18: 11–16.

CHADWICK, B. A. 1972. The inedible feast. In *Native Americans today: Sociological perspectives,* ed. H. M. Bahr, B. A. Chadwick, and R. C. Day. New York: Harper & Row.

DAVIS, T., and A. PYATSKOWIT. 1976. Bicognitive education: A new future for the Indian child. *Journal of American Education,* 15: 14–21.

FALK, D. R., and L. P. AITKEN. 1984. Promoting retention among American Indian college students. *Journal of American Indian Education,* 23: 24–31.

FISHMAN, J. A. 1980. Bilingualism and biculturation as individual and as societal phenomenon. *Journal of Multilingual and Multicultural Development,* 1: 2–15.

GUYETTE, S., and C. HETH. 1983. *American Indian higher education: Needs and projections.* Paper presented at the meeting of the American Educational Research Association, Montreal, Quebec, April.

HALLOWELL, I. A. 1972. American Indians, white, and black: The phenomenon of transculturation. In *Native Americans today: Sociological perspectives,* ed. H. M. Bahr, B. A. Chadwick, and R. C. Day. New York: Harper & Row.

HUFFMAN, T. E., and J. R. ROSONKE. 1989. *Four profiles of Native American college students.* Paper presented at the meeting of the Midwest Sociological Society, St. Louis, MO, April.

HUFFMAN, T. E., M. L. SILL, and M. BROKENLEG. 1986. College achievement among Sioux and white South Dakota students. *Journal of American Indian Education,* 25: 32–38.

KERBO, H. R. 1981. College achievement among Native Americans: A research note. *Social Forces,* 59: 1275–80.

LIN, R. L. 1985. The promise and problems of the Native American student. *Journal of American Indian Education,* 25: 6–16.

MATUTE-BIANCHI, M. C. 1980. What is bicultural about bilingual-bicultural education? *Urban Review,* 12: 91–108.

MEDICINE, B. 1986. Contemporary cultural revisitation: Bilingual and bicultural education. *Wicazo Sa Review,* 2: 31–35.

MCFEE, M. 1972. The 150 percent man, a product of Blackfeet acculturation. In *Native Americans today: Sociological perspectives,* ed. H. M. Bahr, B. A. Chadwick, and R. C. Day. New York: Harper & Row.

MCINTOSCH, B. J. 1987. *Special needs of American Indian college students.* Office of Research and Development, Mesa Community College, AZ.

ORTIZ, F. 1947. *Cuban counterpoint: Tobacco and sugar.* New York: Knopf.

PIZZILLO, J. J. 1976. Bilingualism in the United States and its relationship to pluralism. *Current Issues in Education,* 1.

POLGAR, S. 1960. Biculturation of Mesquakie teenage boys. *American Anthropologist,* 62: 217–35.

PRATTE, R. 1979. *Pluralism in education: Conflict, clarity and commitment.* Springfield, IL: Charles C. Thomas.

QOYAWAYMA, P. 1964. *No turning back: A Hopi Indian woman's struggle to live in two worlds.* Albuquerque: University of New Mexico Press.

ROY, P. 1962. The measurement of assimilation: The Spokane Indians. *American Journal of Sociology,* 67: 541–51.

SILL, M. L. 1967. Transculturation in four not-so-easy stages. In *The Peace Corps experience,* ed. Roy Hopes. New York: Clarkson N. Potter.

SCOTT, W. F. 1986. Attachment to Indian culture and the "difficult situation": A study of American Indian college students. *Youth and Society,* 17: 381–95.

SZAPOCZNIK, J., and R. HERNANDEZ. 1988. The Cuban-American family. In *Ethnic families in America: Patterns and variations,* ed. C. H. Mindel. New York: Elsevier.

SZAPOCZNIK, J., and W. KURTINES. 1979. Acculturation, biculturalism and adjustment among Cuban Americans. In *Psychological dimensions on the acculturation process: Theory, models, and some new findings,* ed. A. Padilla. Boulder, CO: Westview.

SZAPOCZNIK, J., W. KURTINES, and T. FERNANDEZ. 1980. Bicultural involvement and adjustment in Hispanic American youths. *International Journal of Intercultural Relations,* 4: 353–66.

SZAPOCZNIK, J., D. SANTISTEBAN, W. KURTINES, A. PEREZ-VIDAL, and O. HERVIS. 1984. Bicultural effectiveness training: A treatment intervention for enhancing intercultural adjustment. *Hispanic Journal of Behavioral Sciences,* 6: 317–44.

VASQUEZ, J. 1979. Bilingual education's needed third dimension. *Educational Leadership,* 37: 166–68.

WEST, D. K. 1988. Comparisons of career maturity and its relationship with academic performance. *Journal of American Indian Education,* 27: 1–7.

SEX AND GENDER

Classic

37

Sex and Temperament in Three Primitive Societies

Margaret Mead

The work of anthropologist Margaret Mead laid the foundation for much of our contemporary sociological research and debate on gender. Are "masculine" and "feminine" traits innate or learned? Do men and women differ because of nature (heredity) or nurture (socialization)? Based on her studies of three "primitive peoples" in New Guinea, Margaret Mead argues that cultural conditioning is more important than biology in shaping women's and men's behavior.

We have now considered in detail the approved personalities of each sex among three primitive peoples. We found the Arapesh—both men and women—displaying a personality that, out of our historically limited preoccupations, we would call maternal in its parental aspects, and feminine in its sexual aspects. We found men, as well as women, trained to be co-operative, unaggressive, responsive to the needs and demands of others. We found no idea that sex was a powerful driving force either for men or for women. In marked contrast to

SOURCE: *Sex and Temperament in Three Primitive Societies* by Margaret Mead (New York: Morrow, 1963; orig. 1935), pp. 279–88. Copyright© 1935, 1950, 1963 by Margaret Mead. Reprinted with permission of William Morrow & Co., Inc.

these attitudes, we found among the Mundugumor that both men and women developed as ruthless, aggressive, positively sexed individuals, with the maternal cherishing aspects of personality at a minimum. Both men and women approximated to a personality type that we in our culture would find only in an undisciplined and very violent male. Neither the Arapesh nor the Mundugumor profit by a contrast between the sexes; the Arapesh ideal is the mild, responsive man married to the mild, responsive woman; the Mundugumor ideal is the violent aggressive man married to the violent aggressive woman. In the third tribe, the Tchambuli, we found a genuine reversal of the sex attitudes of our own culture, with the woman the dominant, impersonal, managing partner, the man the less responsible and the emotionally dependent person. These three situations suggest, then, a very definite conclusion. If those temperamental attitudes which we have traditionally regarded as feminine—such as passivity, responsiveness, and a willingness to cherish children—can so easily be set up as the masculine pattern in one tribe, and in another be outlawed for the majority of women as well as for the majority of men, we no longer have any basis for regarding such aspects of behaviour as sex-linked. And this conclusion becomes even stronger when we consider the actual reversal in Tchambuli of the position of dominance of the two sexes, in spite of the existence of formal patrilineal institutions.

The material suggests that we may say that many, if not all, of the personality traits which we have called masculine or feminine are as lightly linked to sex as are the clothing, the manners, and the form of head-dress that a society at a given period assigns to either sex. When we consider the behaviour of the typical Arapesh man or woman as contrasted with the behaviour of the typical Mundugumor man or woman, the evidence is overwhelmingly in favour of the strength of social conditioning. In no other way can we account for the almost complete uniformity with which Arapesh children develop into contented, passive, secure persons, while Mundugumor children develop as characteristically into violent, aggressive, insecure persons. Only to the impact of the whole of the integrated culture upon the growing child can we lay the formation of the contrasting types. There is no other explanation of race, or diet, or selection that can be adduced to explain them. We are forced to conclude that human nature is almost unbelievably malleable, responding accurately and contrastingly to contrasting cultural conditions. The differences between individuals who are members of different cultures, like the differences between individuals within a culture, are almost entirely to be laid to differences in conditioning, especially during early childhood, and the form of this conditioning is culturally determined. Standardized personality differences between the sexes

are of this order, cultural creations to which each generation, male and female, is trained to conform. There remains, however, the problem of the origin of these socially standardized differences.

While the basic importance of social conditioning is still imperfectly recognized—not only in lay thought, but even by the scientist specifically concerned with such matters—to go beyond it and consider the possible influence of variations in hereditary equipment is a hazardous matter. The following pages will read very differently to one who has made a part of his thinking a recognition of the whole amazing mechanism of cultural conditioning—who has really accepted the fact that the same infant could be developed into a full participant in any one of these three cultures—than they will read to one who still believes that the minutiae of cultural behaviour are carried in the individual germ-plasm. If it is said, therefore, that when we have grasped the full significance of the malleability of the human organism and the preponderant importance of cultural conditioning, there are still further problems to solve, it must be remembered that these problems come *after* such a comprehension of the force of conditioning; they cannot precede it. The forces that make children born among the Arapesh grow up into typical Arapesh personalities are entirely social, and any discussion of the variations which do occur must be looked at against this social background.

With this warning firmly in mind, we can ask a further question. Granting the malleability of human nature, whence arise the differences between the standardized personalities that different cultures decree for all of their members, or which one culture decrees for the members of one sex as contrasted with the members of the opposite sex? If such differences are culturally created, as this material would most strongly suggest that they are, if the new-born child can be shaped with equal ease into an unaggressive Arapesh or an aggressive Mundugumor, why do these striking contrasts occur at all? If the clues to the different personalities decreed for men and women in Tchambuli do not lie in the physical constitution of the two sexes—an assumption that we must reject both for the

Tchambuli and for our own society—where can we find the clues upon which the Tchambuli, the Arapesh, the Mundugumor, have built? Cultures are man-made, they are built of human materials; they are diverse but comparable structures within which human beings can attain full human stature. Upon what have they built their diversities?

We recognize that a homogeneous culture committed in all of its gravest institutions and slightest usages to a co-operative, unaggressive course can bend every child to that emphasis, some to a perfect accord with it, the majority to an easy acceptance, while only a few deviants fail to receive the cultural imprint. To consider such traits as aggressiveness or passivity to be sex-linked is not possible in the light of the facts. Have such traits, then, as aggressiveness or passivity, pride or humility, objectivity or a preoccupation with personal relationships, an easy response to the needs of the young and the weak or a hostility to the young and the weak, a tendency to initiate sex-relations or merely to respond to the dictates of a situation or another person's advances—have these traits any basis in temperament at all? Are they potentialities of all human temperaments that can be developed by different kinds of social conditioning and which will not appear if the necessary conditioning is absent?

When we ask this question we shift our emphasis. If we ask why an Arapesh man or an Arapesh woman shows the kind of personality that we have considered in the first section of this book, the answer is: Because of the Arapesh culture, because of the intricate, elaborate, and unfailing fashion in which a culture is able to shape each new-born child to the cultural image. And if we ask the same question about a Mundugumor man or woman, or about a Tchambuli man as compared with a Tchambuli woman, the answer is of the same kind. They display the personalities that are peculiar to the cultures in which they were born and educated. Our attention has been on the differences between Arapesh men and women as a group and Mundugumor men and women as a group. It is as if we had represented the Arapesh personality by a soft yellow, the Mundugumor by

a deep red, while the Tchambuli female personality was deep orange, and that of the Tchambuli male, pale green. But if we now ask whence came the original direction in each culture, so that one now shows yellow, another red, the third orange and green by sex, then we must peer more closely. And leaning closer to the picture, it is as if behind the bright consistent yellow of the Arapesh, and the deep equally consistent red of the Mundugumor, behind the orange and green that are Tchambuli, we found in each case the delicate, just discernible outlines of the whole spectrum, differently overlaid in each case by the monotone which covers it. This spectrum is the range of individual differences which lie back of the so much more conspicuous cultural emphases, and it is to this that we must turn to find the explanation of cultural inspiration, of the source from which each culture has drawn.

There appears to be about the same range of basic temperamental variation among the Arapesh and among the Mundugumor, although the violent man is a misfit in the first society and a leader in the second. If human nature were completely homogeneous raw material, lacking specific drives and characterized by no important constitutional differences between individuals, then individuals who display personality traits so antithetical to the social pressure should not reappear in societies of such differing emphases. If the variations between individuals were to be set down to accidents in the genetic process, the same accidents should not be repeated with similar frequency in strikingly different cultures, with strongly contrasting methods of education.

But because this same relative distribution of individual differences does appear in culture after culture, in spite of the divergence between the cultures, it seems pertinent to offer a hypothesis to explain upon what basis the personalities of men and women have been differently standardized so often in the history of the human race. This hypothesis is an extension of that advanced by Ruth Benedict in her *Patterns of Culture*. Let us assume that there are definite temperamental differences between human beings which if not entirely hereditary at least are established on a hereditary base very soon after birth. (Further than this we cannot at present narrow the matter.) These differences finally embodied in the character structure of adults, then, are the clues from which culture works, selecting one temperament, or a combination of related and congruent types, as desirable, and embodying this choice in every thread of the social fabric—in the care of the young child, the games the children play, the songs the people sing, the structure of political organization, the religious observance, the art and the philosophy.

Some primitive societies have had the time and the robustness to revamp all of their institutions to fit one extreme type, and to develop educational techniques which will ensure that the majority of each generation will show a personality congruent with this extreme emphasis. Other societies have pursued a less definitive course, selecting their models not from the most extreme, most highly differentiated individuals, but from the less marked types. In such societies the approved personality is less pronounced, and the culture often contains the types of inconsistencies that many human beings display also; one institution may be adjusted to the uses of pride, another to a casual humility that is congruent neither with pride nor with inverted pride. Such societies, which have taken the more usual and less sharply defined types as models, often show also a less definitely patterned social structure. The culture of such societies may be likened to a house the decoration of which has been informed by no definite and precise taste, no exclusive emphasis upon dignity or comfort or pretentiousness or beauty, but in which a little of each effect has been included.

Alternatively, a culture may take its clues not from one temperament, but from several temperaments. But instead of mixing together into an inconsistent hotchpotch the choices and emphases of different temperaments, or blending them together into a smooth but not particularly distinguished whole, it may isolate each type by making it the basis for the approved social personality for an age-group, a sex-group, a caste-group, or an occupational group. In this way society becomes not a monotone with a few discrepant patches of an intrusive colour, but a mosaic, with different groups displaying different personality traits. Such specializations as these may be based upon any facet of human endowment—different intellectual abilities, different artistic abilities, different emotional traits. So the Samoans decree that all young people must show the personality trait of unaggressiveness and punish with opprobrium the aggressive child who displays traits regarded as appropriate only in titled middle-aged men. In societies based upon elaborate ideas of rank, members of the aristocracy will be permitted, even compelled, to display a pride, a sensitivity to insult, that would be deprecated as inappropriate in members of the plebeian class. So also in professional groups or in religious sects some temperamental traits are selected and institutionalized, and taught to each new member who enters the profession or sect. Thus the physician learns the bedside manner, which is the natural behaviour of some temperaments and the standard behaviour of the general practitioner in the medical profession; the Quaker learns at least the outward behaviour and the rudiments of meditation, the capacity for which is not necessarily an innate characteristic of many of the members of the Society of Friends.

So it is with the social personalities of the two sexes. The traits that occur in some members of each sex are specially assigned to one sex, and disallowed in the other. The history of the social definition of sex-differences is filled with such arbitrary arrangements in the intellectual and artistic field, but because of the assumed congruence between physiological sex and emotional endowment we have been less able to recognize that a similar arbitrary selection is being made among emotional traits also. We have assumed that because it is convenient for a mother to wish to care for her child, this is a trait with which women have been more generously endowed by a carefully teleological process of evolution. We have assumed that because men have hunted, an activity requiring enterprise, bravery, and initiative, they have been endowed with these useful attitudes as part of their sex-temperament.

Societies have made these assumptions both overtly and implicitly. If a society insists that warfare is the major occupation for the male sex, it is therefore insisting that all male children display bravery and pugnacity. Even if the insistence upon the differential bravery of men and women is not made articulate, the difference in occupation makes this point implicitly. When, however, a society goes further and defines men as brave and women as timorous, when men are forbidden to show fear and women are indulged in the most flagrant display of fear, a more explicit element enters in. Bravery, hatred of any weakness, of flinching before pain or danger—this attitude which is so strong a component of *some human* temperaments has been selected as the key to masculine behaviour. The easy unashamed display of fear or suffering that is congenial to a different temperament has been made the key to feminine behaviour.

Originally two variations of human temperament, a hatred of fear or willingness to display fear, they have been socially translated into inalienable aspects of the personalities of the two sexes. And to that defined sex-personality every child will be educated, if a boy, to suppress fear, if a girl, to show it. If there has been no social selection in regard to this trait, the proud temperament that is repelled by any betrayal of feeling will display itself, regardless of sex, by keeping a stiff upper lip. Without an express prohibition of such behaviour the expressive unashamed man or woman will weep, or comment upon fear or suffering. Such attitudes, strongly marked in certain temperaments, may by social selection be standardized for everyone, or outlawed for everyone, or ignored by society, or made the exclusive and approved behaviour of one sex only.

Neither the Arapesh nor the Mundugumor have made any attitude specific for one sex. All of the energies of the culture have gone towards the creation of a single human type, regardless of class, age, or sex. There is no division into age-classes for which different motives or different moral attitudes are regarded as suitable. There is no class of seers or mediums who stand apart drawing inspiration from psychological sources not available to the majority of the people. The Mundugumor have, it is true, made one arbitrary selection, in that they recognize artistic ability only among individuals born with the cord about their necks, and firmly deny the happy exercise of artistic ability to those less unusually born. The Arapesh boy with a tinea infection has been socially selected to be a disgruntled, antisocial individual, and the society forces upon sunny co-operative children cursed with this affliction a final approximation to the behaviour appropriate to a pariah. With these two exceptions no emotional role is forced upon an individual because of birth or accident. As there is no idea of rank which declares that some are of high estate and some of low, so there is no idea of sex-difference which declares that one sex must feel differently from the other. One possible imaginative social construct, the attribution of different personalities to different members of the community classified into sex-, age-, or caste-groups, is lacking.

When we turn however to the Tchambuli, we find a situation that while bizarre in one respect, seems nevertheless more intelligible in another. The Tchambuli have at least made the point of sex-difference; they have used the obvious fact of sex as an organizing point for the formation of social personality, even though they seem to us to have reversed the normal picture. While there is reason to believe that not every Tchambuli woman is born with a dominating, organizing, administrative temperament, actively sexed and willing to initiate sex-relations, possessive, definite, robust, practical and impersonal in outlook, still most Tchambuli girls grow up to display these traits. And while there is definite evidence to show that all Tchambuli men are not, by native endowment, the delicate responsive actors of a play staged for the women's benefit, still most Tchambuli boys manifest this coquettish play-acting personality most of the time. Because the Tchambuli formulation of sex-attitudes contradicts our usual premises, we can see clearly that Tchambuli culture has arbitrarily permitted certain human traits to women, and allotted others, equally arbitrarily, to men.

CRITICAL-THINKING QUESTIONS

*1. How do female and male personality traits dif-
fer among the Arapesh, the Mundugumor, and the
Tchambuli?*

*2. How does Mead explain these differences?
What does she mean, for example, when she states
that "human nature is unbelievably malleable to
cultural conditions"?*

*3. Most people in the United States still describe
men as aggressive, strong, confident, and ambitious while characterizing women as emotional,
talkative, romantic, and nurturing. Does this mean
that biology is more important than environment
in shaping our personality and behavior?*

38

The Beauty Myth

Naomi Wolf

Despite women's recent strides toward social equality—or, perhaps, because of them—the concept of beauty has emerged as a barrier to feminist goals. What Wolf calls the "beauty myth" influences women to measure their worth against unrealistic standards of physical attractiveness, and also encourages men to want to possess beautiful women. To understand why women in our society spend some $50 billion annually on dieting and cosmetics, Wolf explains, we need to examine the political construction of the concept of beauty itself.

At last, after a long silence, women took to the streets. In the two decades of radical action that followed the rebirth of feminism in the early 1970s, Western women gained legal and reproductive rights, pursued higher education, entered the trades and the professions, and overturned ancient and revered beliefs about their social role. A generation on, do women feel free?

The affluent, educated, liberated women of the First World, who can enjoy freedoms unavailable

SOURCE: *The Beauty Myth: How Images of Beauty Are Used Against Women* by Naomi Wolf (New York: Morrow, 1990), pp. 9–19. Copyright © 1991 by Naomi Wolf. Reprinted with permission of William Morrow & Company, Inc. and Random House of Canada Limited.

to any women ever before, do not feel as free as they want to. And they can no longer restrict to the subconscious their sense that this lack of freedom has something to do with—with apparently frivolous issues, things that really should not matter. Many are ashamed to admit that such trivial concerns—to do with physical appearance, bodies, faces, hair, clothes—matter so much. But in spite of shame, guilt, and denial, more and more women are wondering if it isn't that they are entirely neurotic and alone but rather that something important is indeed at stake that has to do with the relationship between female liberation and female beauty.

The more legal and material hindrances

women have broken through, the more strictly and heavily and cruelly images of female beauty have come to weigh upon us. Many women sense that women's collective progress has stalled; compared with the heady momentum of earlier days, there is a dispiriting climate of confusion, division, cynicism, and above all, exhaustion. After years of much struggle and little recognition, many older women feel burned out; after years of taking its light for granted, many younger women show little interest in touching new fire to the torch.

During the past decade, women breached the power structure; meanwhile, eating disorders rose exponentially and cosmetic surgery became the fastest-growing medical specialty. During the past five years, consumer spending doubled, pornography became the main media category, ahead of legitimate films and records combined, and thirty-three thousand American women told researchers that they would rather lose ten to fifteen pounds than achieve any other goal. More women have more money and power and scope and legal recognition than we have ever had before; but in terms of how we feel about ourselves *physically,* we may actually be worse off than our unliberated grandmothers. Recent research consistently shows that inside the majority of the West's controlled, attractive, successful working women, there is a secret "underlife" poisoning our freedom; infused with notions of beauty, it is a dark vein of self-hatred, physical obsessions, terror of aging, and dread of lost control.

It is no accident that so many potentially powerful women feel this way. We are in the midst of a violent backlash against feminism that uses images of female beauty as a political weapon against women's advancement: the beauty myth. It is the modern version of a social reflex that has been in force since the Industrial Revolution. As women released themselves from the feminine mystique of domesticity, the beauty myth took over its lost ground, expanding as it waned to carry on its work of social control.

The contemporary backlash is so violent because the ideology of beauty is the last one remaining of the old feminine ideologies that still has the power to control those women whom second wave feminism would have otherwise made relatively uncontrollable: It has grown stronger to take over the work of social coercion that myths about motherhood, domesticity, chastity, and passivity, no longer can manage. It is seeking right now to undo psychologically and covertly all the good things that feminism did for women materially and overtly.

This counterforce is operating to checkmate the inheritance of feminism on every level in the lives of Western women. Feminism gave us laws against job discrimination based on gender; immediately case law evolved in Britain and the United States that institutionalized job discrimination based on women's appearances. Patriarchal religion declined; new religious dogma, using some of the mind-altering techniques of older cults and sects, arose around age and weight to functionally supplant traditional ritual. Feminists, inspired by Friedan, broke the stranglehold on the women's popular press of advertisers for household products, who were promoting the feminine mystique; at once, the diet and skin care industries became the new cultural censors of women's intellectual space, and because of their pressure, the gaunt, youthful model supplanted the happy housewife as the arbiter of successful womanhood. The sexual revolution promoted the discovery of female sexuality; "beauty pornography"—which for the first time in women's history artificially links a commodified "beauty" directly and explicitly to sexuality—invaded the mainstream to undermine women's new and vulnerable sense of sexual self-worth. Reproductive rights gave Western women control over our own bodies; the weight of fashion models plummeted to 23 percent below that of ordinary women, eating disorders rose exponentially, and a mass neurosis was promoted that used food and weight to strip women of that sense of control. Women insisted on politicizing health; new technologies of invasive, potentially deadly "cosmetic" surgeries developed apace to re-exert old forms of medical control of women.

Every generation since about 1830 has had to fight its version of the beauty myth. "It is very little to me," said the suffragist Lucy Stone in 1855, "to have the right to vote, to own property, etcetera, if I may not keep my body, and its uses, in my absolute right." Eighty years later, after women had won the vote, and the first wave of the organized women's movement had subsided, Virginia Woolf wrote that it would still be decades before women could tell the truth about their bodies. In 1962, Betty Friedan quoted a young woman trapped in the Feminine Mystique: "Lately, I look in the mirror, and I'm so afraid I'm going to look like my mother." Eight years after that, heralding the cataclysmic second wave of feminism, Germaine Greer described "the Stereotype": "To her belongs all that is beautiful, even the very word beauty itself . . . she is a doll . . . I'm sick of the masquerade." In spite of the great revolution of the second wave, we are not exempt. Now we can look out over ruined barricades: A revolution has come upon us and changed everything in its path, enough time has passed since then for babies to have grown into women, but there still remains a final right not fully claimed.

The beauty myth tells a story: The quality called "beauty" objectively and universally exists. Women must want to embody it and men must want to possess women who embody it. This embodiment is an imperative for women and not for men, which situation is necessary and natural because it is biological, sexual, and evolutionary: Strong men battle for beautiful women, and beautiful women are more reproductively successful. Women's beauty must correlate to their fertility, and since this system is based on sexual selection, it is inevitable and changeless.

None of this is true. "Beauty" is a currency system like the gold standard. Like any economy, it is determined by politics, and in the modern age in the West it is the last, best belief system that keeps male dominance intact. In assigning value to women in a vertical hierarchy according to a culturally imposed physical standard, it is an expression of power relations in which women must unnaturally compete for resources that men have appropriated for themselves.

"Beauty" is not universal or changeless, though the West pretends that all ideals of female beauty stem from one Platonic Ideal Woman; the Maori admire a fat vulva, and the Padung, droopy breasts. Nor is "beauty" a function of evolution: Its ideals change at a pace far more rapid than that of the evolution of species, and Charles Darwin was himself unconvinced by his own explanation that "beauty" resulted from a "sexual selection" that deviated from the rule of natural selection; for women to compete with women through "beauty" is a reversal of the way in which natural selection affects all other mammals. Anthropology has overturned the notion that females must be "beautiful" to be selected to mate: Evelyn Reed, Elaine Morgan, and others have dismissed sociobiological assertions of innate male polygamy and female monogamy. Female higher primates are the sexual initiators; not only do they seek out and enjoy sex with many partners, but "every nonpregnant female takes her turn at being the most desirable of all her troop. And that cycle keeps turning as long as she lives." The inflamed pink sexual organs of primates are often cited by male sociobiologists as analogous to human arrangements relating to female "beauty," when in fact that is a universal, nonhierarchical female primate characteristic.

Nor has the beauty myth always been this way. Though the pairing of the older rich men with young, "beautiful" women is taken to be somehow inevitable, in the matriarchal Goddess religions that dominated the Mediterranean from about 25,000 B.C.E. to about 700 B.C.E., the situation was reversed: "In every culture, the Goddess has many lovers. . . . The clear pattern is of an older woman with a beautiful but expendable youth—Ishtar and Tammuz, Venus and Adonis, Cybele and Attis, Isis and Osiris . . . their only function the service of the divine 'womb.' " Nor is it something only women do and only men watch: Among the Nigerian Wodaabes, the women hold economic power and the tribe is obsessed with male beauty; Wodaabe men spend hours together in elaborate makeup sessions, and compete—provocatively painted and dressed, with swaying hips and seductive expressions—in beauty contests judged by women. There is no legitimate historical or biological justification for the beauty myth; what it is doing to women today is a result of nothing more exalted than the need of today's power structure, economy, and culture to mount a counteroffensive against women.

If the beauty myth is not based on evolution, sex, gender, aesthetics, or God, on what is it based? It claims to be about intimacy and sex and life, a celebration of women. It is actually composed of emotional distance, politics, finance, and sexual repression. The beauty myth is not about women at all. It is about men's institutions and institutional power.

The qualities that a given period calls beautiful in women are merely symbols of the female behavior that that period considers desirable: *The beauty myth is always actually prescribing behavior and not appearance.* Competition between women has been made part of the myth so that women will be divided from one another. Youth and (until recently) virginity have been "beautiful" in women since they stand for experiential and sexual ignorance. Aging in women is "unbeautiful" since women grow more powerful with time, and since the links between generations of women must always be newly broken: Older women fear young ones, young women fear old, and the beauty myth truncates for all the female life span. Most urgently, women's identity must be premised upon our "beauty" so that we will remain vulnerable to outside approval, carrying the vital sensitive organ of self-esteem exposed to the air.

Though there has, of course, been a beauty myth in some form for as long as there has been patriarchy, the beauty myth in its modern form is a fairly recent invention. The myth flourishes when material constraints on women are dangerously loosened. Before the Industrial Revolution, the average woman could not have had the same feelings about "beauty" that modern women do who experience the myth as continual comparison to a mass-disseminated physical ideal. Before the

development of technologies of mass production—daguerrotypes, photographs, etc.—an ordinary woman was exposed to few such images outside the Church. Since the family was a productive unit and women's work complemented men's, the value of women who were not aristocrats or prostitutes lay in their work skills, economic shrewdness, physical strength, and fertility. Physical attraction, obviously, played its part; but "beauty" as we understand it was not, for ordinary women, a serious issue in the marriage marketplace. The beauty myth in its modern form gained ground after the upheavals of industrialization, as the work unit of the family was destroyed, and urbanization and the emerging factory system demanded what social engineers of the time termed the "separate sphere" of domesticity, which supported the new labor category of the "breadwinner" who left home for the workplace during the day. The middle class expanded, the standards of living and of literacy rose, the size of families shrank; a new class of literate, idle women developed, on whose submission to enforced domesticity the evolving system of industrial capitalism depended. Most of our assumptions about the way women have always thought about "beauty" date from no earlier than the 1830s, when the cult of domesticity was first consolidated and the beauty index invented.

For the first time new technologies could reproduce—in fashion plates, daguerreotypes, tintypes, and rotogravures—images of how women should look. In the 1840s the first nude photographs of prostitutes were taken; advertisements using images of "beautiful" women first appeared in mid-century. Copies of classical artworks, postcards of society beauties and royal mistresses, Currier and Ives prints, and porcelain figurines flooded the separate sphere to which middle-class women were confined.

Since the Industrial Revolution, middle-class Western women have been controlled by ideals and stereotypes as much as by material constraints. This situation, unique to this group, means that analyses that trace "cultural conspiracies" are uniquely plausible in relation to them. The rise of the beauty myth was just one of several emerging social fictions that masqueraded as natural components of the feminine sphere, the better to enclose those women inside it. Other such fictions arose contemporaneously: a version of childhood that required continual maternal supervision; a concept of female biology that required middle-class women to act out the roles of hysterics and hypochondriacs; a conviction that respectable women were sexually anesthetic; and a definition of women's work that occupied them with repetitive, time-consuming, and painstaking tasks such as needlepoint and lacemaking. All such Victorian inventions as these served a double function—that is, though they were encouraged as a means to expend female energy and intelligence in harmless ways, women often used them to express genuine creativity and passion.

But in spite of middle-class women's creativity with fashion and embroidery and child rearing, and, a century later, with the role of the suburban housewife that devolved from these social fictions, the fictions' main purpose was served: During a century and a half of unprecedented feminist agitation, they effectively counteracted middle-class women's dangerous new leisure, literacy, and relative freedom from material constraints.

Though these time- and mind-consuming fictions about women's natural role adapted themselves to resurface in the postwar Feminine Mystique, when the second wave of the women's movement took apart what women's magazines had portrayed as the "romance," "science," and "adventure" of homemaking and suburban family life, they temporarily failed. The cloying domestic fiction of "togetherness" lost its meaning and middle-class women walked out of their front doors in masses.

So the fictions simply transformed themselves once more: Since the women's movement had successfully taken apart most other necessary fictions of femininity, all the work of social control once spread out over the whole network of these fictions had to be reassigned to the only strand left intact, which action consequently strengthened it a hundredfold. This reimposed onto liberated women's faces and bodies all the limitations, taboos, and punishments of the repressive laws, religious injunctions and reproductive enslavement that no longer carried sufficient force. Inexhaustible but ephemeral beauty work took over from inexhaustible but ephemeral housework. As the economy, law, religion, sexual mores, education, and culture were forcibly opened up to include women more fairly, a private reality colonized female consciousness. By using ideas about "beauty," it reconstructed an alternative female world with its own laws, economy, religion, sexuality, education, and culture, each element as repressive as any that had gone before.

Since middle-class Western women can best be weakened psychologically now that we are stronger materially, the beauty myth, as it has resurfaced in the last generation, has had to draw on more technological sophistication and reactionary fervor than ever before. The modern arsenal of the myth is a dissemination of millions of images of the current ideal; although this barrage is generally seen as a collective sexual fantasy, there is in fact little that is sexual about it. It is summoned out of political fear on the part of male-dominated institutions threatened by women's freedom, and it exploits female guilt and apprehension about our own liberation—latent fears that we might be going too far. This frantic aggregation of imagery is a collective reactionary hallucination willed into being by both men and women stunned and disoriented by the rapidity with which gender relations have been transformed: a bulwark of reassurance against the flood of change. The mass depiction of the modern woman as a "beauty" is a contradiction: Where modern women are growing, moving, and expressing their individuality, as the myth has it, "beauty" is by definition inert, timeless, and generic. That this hallucination is necessary and deliberate is evident in the way "beauty" so directly contradicts women's real situation.

And the unconscious hallucination grows ever more influential and pervasive because of what is now conscious market manipulation: powerful industries—the $33-billion-a-year diet industry, the $20-billion cosmetics industry, the $300-million cosmetic surgery industry, and the $7-billion pornography industry—have arisen from the capital made out of unconscious anxieties, and are in turn able, through their influence on mass culture, to use, stimulate, and reinforce the hallucination in a rising economic spiral.

This is not a conspiracy theory; it doesn't have to be. Societies tell themselves necessary fictions in the same way that individuals and families do. Henrik Ibsen called them "vital lies," and psychologist Daniel Goleman describes them working the same way on the social level that they do within families: "The collusion is maintained by directing attention away from the fearsome fact, or by repackaging its meaning in an acceptable format." The costs of these social blind spots, he writes, are destructive communal illusions. Possibilities for women have become so open-ended that they threaten to destabilize the institutions on which a male-dominated culture has depended, and a collective panic reaction on the part of both sexes has forced a demand for counterimages.

The resulting hallucination materializes, for women, as something all too real. No longer just an idea, it becomes three-dimensional, incorporating within itself how women live and how they do not live: It becomes the Iron Maiden. The original Iron Maiden was a medieval German instrument of torture, a body-shaped casket painted with the limbs and features of a lovely, smiling young woman. The unlucky victim was slowly enclosed inside her; the lid fell shut to immobilize the victim, who died either of starvation or, less cruelly, of the metal spikes embedded in her interior. The modern hallucination in which women are trapped or trap themselves is similarly rigid, cruel, and euphemistically painted. Contemporary culture directs attention to imagery of the Iron Maiden, while censoring real women's faces and bodies.

Why does the social order feel the need to defend itself by evading the fact of real women, our faces and voices and bodies, and reducing the meaning of women to these formulaic and endlessly reproduced "beautiful" images? Though unconscious personal anxieties can be a powerful force in the creation of a vital lie, economic necessity practically guarantees it. An economy that depends on slavery needs to promote images of slaves that "justify" the institution of slavery. Western economies are absolutely dependent now on the continued underpayment of women. An ideology that makes women feel "worth less" was urgently needed to counteract the way feminism had begun to make us feel worth more. This does not require a conspiracy; merely an atmosphere. The contemporary economy depends right now on the representation of women within the beauty myth. Economist John Kenneth Galbraith offers an economic explanation for "the persistence of the view of homemaking as a 'higher calling' ": The concept of women as naturally trapped within the Feminine Mystique, he feels, "has been forced on us by popular sociology, by magazines, and by fiction to disguise the fact that woman in her role of consumer has been essential to the development of our industrial society. . . . Behavior that is essential for economic reasons is transformed into a social virtue." As soon as a woman's primary social value could no longer be defined as the attainment of virtuous domesticity, the beauty myth redefined it as the attainment of virtuous beauty. It did so to substitute both a new consumer imperative and a new justification for economic unfairness in the workplace where the old ones had lost their hold over newly liberated women.

Another hallucination arose to accompany that of the Iron Maiden: The caricature of the Ugly Feminist was resurrected to dog the steps of the women's movement. The caricature is unoriginal; it was coined to ridicule the feminists of the nineteenth century. Lucy Stone herself, whom supporters saw as "a prototype of womanly grace . . . fresh and fair as the morning," was derided by detractors with "the usual report" about Victorian feminists: "a big masculine woman, wearing boots, smoking a cigar, swearing like a trooper." As Betty Friedan put it presciently in 1960, even before the savage revamping of that old caricature: "The unpleasant image of feminists today resembles less the feminists themselves than the image fostered by the interests who so bitterly opposed the vote for women in state after state." Thirty years on, her conclusion is more true than ever: That resurrected caricature, which sought to punish women for their public acts by going after their private sense of self, became the paradigm for new limits placed on aspiring women everywhere. After the success of the women's movement's second wave, the beauty myth was perfected to checkmate power at every level in individual women's lives. The modern neuroses of life in the female body spread to woman after woman at epidemic rates. The myth is undermining—slowly, imperceptibly, without our being aware of the real forces of erosion—the ground women have gained through long, hard, honorable struggle.

The beauty myth of the present is more insidious than any mystique of femininity yet: A century ago, Nora slammed the door of the doll's house; a generation ago, women turned their backs on the consumer heaven of the isolated multiapplianced home; but where women are trapped today, there is no door to slam. The contemporary ravages of the beauty backlash are destroying women physically and depleting us psychologically. If we are to free ourselves from the dead weight that has once again been made out of femaleness, it is not ballots or lobbyists or placards that women will need first; it is a new way to see.

CRITICAL-THINKING QUESTIONS

1. Why, according to conventional understandings, is beauty more central to the lives of women than to men? Do you see a connection between our ideas about beauty and eating disorders (which, to various degrees, affect almost half of college-age women)?

2. Why has a heightened concern with physical beauty developed historically at a time of women's progress toward social equality?

3. According to Wolf, is there such a thing as "beauty"? How and why does a society come to define people in such terms?

39

*Why Many Women
Don't Report Sexual Harassment*

Stephanie Riger

Although sexual harassment has always existed, it had a generally low profile until the 1991 Senate confirmation hearings of Clarence Thomas, now a member of the U.S. Supreme Court. Then the issue of sexual harassment received national attention when Anita Hill, a law professor at the University of Oklahoma, testified that Thomas had sexually harassed her in the early 1980s while he was her boss and director of the Equal Employment Opportunity Commission. Why didn't Anita Hill report the harassment when it occurred? In this article, Stephanie Riger offers some answers.

Sexual harassment—unwanted sexually oriented behavior in a work context—is the most recent form of victimization of women to be redefined as a social rather than a personal problem, following rape and wife abuse. A sizeable proportion of women surveyed in a wide variety of work settings reported being subject to unwanted sexual attention, sexual comments or jokes, offensive touching, or attempts to coerce compliance with or punish rejection of sexual advances. In 1980 the U.S. Merit Systems Protection Board (1981) conducted the first comprehensive national survey of sexual harassment among federal employees: About 4 out of 10 of the 10,648 women surveyed reported having been the target of sexual harassment during the previous twenty-four months. A recent update of this survey found that the frequency of harassment in 1988 was identical to that reported earlier: 42 percent of all

SOURCE: "Gender Dilemmas in Sexual Harassment Policies and Procedures," by Stephanie Riger, *American Psychologist,* vol. 46, no. 5, May 1991. Copyright 1991 by the American Psychological Association. Reprinted by permission.

women surveyed in 1988 reported that they had experienced some form of unwanted and uninvited sexual attention compared to exactly the same percentage of women in 1980 (U.S. Merit Systems Protection Board 1988). . . .

Despite the high rates found in surveys of sexual harassment of women, few complaints are pursued through official grievance procedures. Dzeich and Weiner (1984) concluded, after reviewing survey findings, that 20 percent to 30 percent of female college students experience sexual harassment. Yet academic institutions averaged only 4.3 complaints each during the 1982–1983 academic year (Robertson, Dyer, and Campbell 1988), a period roughly consecutive with the surveys cited by Dzeich and Weiner. In another study conducted at a university in 1984, of thirty-eight women who reported harassment, only one reported the behavior to the offender's supervisor and two reported the behavior to an adviser, another professor, or employer (Reilly, Lott, and Gallogly 1986). Similar findings have been reported on other college campuses. . . .

It is the contention of this article that the low rate of utilization of grievance procedures is due to gender bias in sexual harassment policies that discourages their use by women. Policies are written in gender-neutral language and are intended to apply equally to men and women. However, these policies are experienced differently by women than men because of gender differences in perceptions of harassment and orientation toward conflict. Although victims of all forms of discrimination are reluctant to pursue grievances, women, who are most likely to be the victims of sexual harassment, are especially disinclined to pursue sexual harassment grievances for at least two reasons. First, the interpretation in policies of what constitutes harassment may not reflect women's viewpoints, and their complaints may not be seen as valid. Second, the procedures in some policies that are designed to resolve disputes may be inimical to women because they are not compatible with the way that many women view conflict resolution. Gender bias in policies, rather than an absence of harassment or lack of as-

sertiveness on the part of victims, produces low numbers of complaints.

GENDER BIAS IN THE DEFINITION OF SEXUAL HARASSMENT

The first way that gender bias affects sexual harassment policies stems from differences between men and women in the interpretation of the definition of harassment. Those writing sexual harassment policies for organizations typically look to the courts for the distinction between illegal sexual harassment and permissible (although perhaps unwanted) social interaction. The definition of harassment in policies typically is that provided by the U.S. Equal Employment Opportunity Commission (1980) guidelines:

Unwelcome sexual advances, requests for sexual favors, and other verbal or physical conduct of a sexual nature constitute sexual harassment when (1) submission to such conduct is made either explicitly or implicitly a term or condition of an individual's employment, (2) submission to or rejection of such conduct by an individual is used as the basis for employment decisions affecting such individual, or (3) such conduct has the purpose or effect of unreasonably interfering with an individual's work performance or creating an intimidating, hostile, or offensive working environment. (p. 74677)

The first two parts of the definition refer to a quid pro quo relationship involving people in positions of unequal status, as superior status is usually necessary to have control over another's employment. In such cases bribes, threats, or punishments are used. Incidents of this type need happen only once to fall under the definition of sexual harassment. However, courts have required that incidents falling into the third category, "an intimidating, hostile, or offensive working environment," must be repeated in order to establish that such an environment exists; these incidents must be both pervasive and so severe that they affect the victim's psychological well-being. Harassment of this type can come from peers or even subordinates as well as superiors.

In all three of these categories, harassment is judged on the basis of conduct and its effects on the recipient, not the intentions of the harasser. Thus, two typical defenses given by accused harassers—"I was just being friendly," or "I touch everyone, I'm that kind of person"—do not hold up in court. Yet behavior may have an intimidating or offensive effect on some people but be inoffensive or even welcome to others. In deciding whose standards should be used, the courts employ what is called the *reasonable person rule,* asking whether a reasonable person would be offended by the conduct in question. The dilemma in applying this to sexual harassment is that a reasonable woman and a reasonable man are likely to differ in their judgments of what is offensive.

Definitions of sexual harassment are socially constructed, varying not only with characteristics of the perceiver but also those of the situational context and actors involved. Behavior is more likely to be labeled harassment when it [is] done by someone with greater power than the victim; when it involves physical advances accompanied by threats of punishment for noncompliance; when the response to it is negative; when the behavior reflects persistent negative intentions toward a woman; the more inappropriate it is for the actor's social role; and the more flagrant and frequent the harasser's actions. Among women, professionals are more likely than those in secretarial–clerical positions to report the more subtle behaviors as harassment.

The variable that most consistently predicts variation in people's definition of sexual harassment is the sex of the rater. Men label fewer behaviors at work as sexual harassment (Kenig and Ryan 1986; Konrad and Gutek 1986; Lester et al. 1986; Powell 1986). Men tend to find sexual overtures from women at work to be flattering, whereas women find similar approaches from men to be insulting (Gutek 1985). Both men and women agree that certain blatant behaviors, such as sexual assault or sexual bribery, constitute harassment, but women are more likely to see as ha-

rassment more subtle behavior such as sexual teasing or looks or gestures (Kenig and Ryan 1986; U.S. Merit Systems Protection Board 1981). Even when they do identify behavior as harassment, men are more likely to think that women will be flattered by it (Kirk 1988). Men are also more likely than women to blame women for being sexually harassed (Kenig and Ryan 1986; Jensen and Gutek 1982). . . .

GENDER BIAS IN GRIEVANCE PROCEDURES

Typically, procedures for resolving disputes about sexual harassment are written in gender-neutral terms so that they may apply to both women and men. However, men and women may react quite differently to the same procedures. . . .

Comparison of Informal and Formal Grievance Procedures

Informal attempts to resolve disputes differ from formal procedures in important ways (for a general discussion of dispute resolution systems, see Brett, Goldberg, and Ury 1990). First, their goal is to solve a problem, rather than to judge the harasser's guilt or innocence. The assumptions underlying these processes are that both parties in a dispute perceive a problem (although they may define that problem differently); that both share a common interest in solving that problem; and that together they can negotiate an agreement that will be satisfactory to everyone involved. Typically, the goal of informal processes is to end the harassment of the complainant rather than judge (and punish, if appropriate) the offender. The focus is on what will happen in the future between the disputing parties, rather than on what has happened in the past. Often policies do not specify the format of informal problem solving, but accept a wide variety of strategies of reconciliation. For example, a complainant might write a letter to the offender, or someone might talk to the offender on the complainant's behalf. The offender and victim might participate in mediation, in which a third party helps them negotiate an agreement. Many policies accept a wide array of strategies as good-faith attempts to solve the problem informally.

In contrast, formal procedures generally require a written complaint and have a specified procedure for handling cases, usually by bringing the complaint to a group officially designated to hear the case, such as a hearing board. The informal process typically ends when the complainant is satisfied (or decides to drop the complaint); the formal procedure ends when the hearing board decides on the guilt or innocence of the alleged harasser. Thus, control over the outcome usually rests with the complainant in the case of informal mechanisms, and with the official governance body in the case of a hearing. Compliance with a decision is usually voluntary in informal procedures, whereas the decision in a formal procedure is binding unless appealed to a higher authority. Formal procedures are adversarial in nature, with the complainant and defendant competing to see whose position will prevail.

A typical case might proceed as follows: A student with a complaint writes a letter to the harasser (an informal procedure). If not satisfied with the response, she submits a written complaint to the sexual harassment hearing board, which then hears both sides of the case, reviews available evidence, and decides on the guilt or innocence of the accused (a formal procedure). If the accused is found guilty, the appropriate officer of the institution decides on punishment.

Gender Differences in Orientation to Conflict

Women and men may differ in their reactions to dispute resolution procedures for at least two reasons. First, women typically have less power than men in organizations (Kanter 1977). Using a grievance procedure, such as appearing before a hearing board, may be inimical because of the possibility of retaliation for a complaint. Miller (1976) suggested that differences in status and power affect the way that people handle conflict:

As soon as a group attains dominance it tends inevitably to produce a situation of conflict and . . . it also, simultaneously, seeks to suppress conflict. Moreover, subordinates who accept the dominant's conception of them as passive and malleable do not openly engage in conflict. Conflict . . . is forced underground. (p. 127)

This may explain why some women do not report complaints at all. When they do complain, however, their relative lack of power or their values may predispose women to prefer informal rather than formal procedures. Beliefs about the appropriate way to handle disputes vary among social groups. Gilligan's (1982) distinction between an orientation toward rights and justice compared with an emphasis on responsibilities to others and caring is likely to be reflected in people's preferences for ways of handling disputes (Kolb and Coolidge 1988). Neither of these orientations is exclusive to one sex, but according to Gilligan, women are more likely to emphasize caring. Women's orientation to caring may be due to their subordinate status. Empirical support for Gilligan's theories is inconclusive (see, e.g., Mednick 1989, for a summary of criticisms). Yet the fact that most victims of sexual harassment state that they simply want an end to the offending behavior rather than punishment of the offender suggests a "caring" rather than "justice" perspective (or possibly, a fear of reprisals).

In the context of dispute resolution, an emphasis on responsibilities and caring is compatible with the goals of informal procedures to restore harmony or at least peaceful coexistence among the parties involved, whereas that of justice is compatible with formal procedures that attempt to judge guilt or innocence of the offender. Thus women may prefer to use informal procedures to resolve conflicts, and indeed most cases in educational institutions are handled through informal mechanisms (Robertson et al. 1988). Policies that do not include an informal dispute resolution option are likely to discourage many women from bringing complaints. . . .

OTHER OBSTACLES TO REPORTING COMPLAINTS

Belief That Sexual Harassment of Women Is Normative

Because of differences in perception of behavior, men and women involved in a sexual harassment case are likely to have sharply divergent interpretations of that case, particularly when a hostile environment claim is involved. To women, the behavior in question is offensive, and they are likely to see themselves as victims of male actions. The requirement that an attempt be made to mediate the dispute or solve it through informal processes may violate their perception of the situation and of themselves as victims of a crime. By comparison, a victim of a mugging is not required to solve the problem with the mugger through mediation (B. Sandler, personal communication, 1988). To many men, the behavior is not offensive, but normative. In their eyes, no crime has been committed, and there is no problem to be solved.

Some women may also consider sexual harassment to be normative. Women may believe that these sorts of behaviors are simply routine, a commonplace part of everyday life, and thus not something that can be challenged. Younger women—who are more likely to be victims—are more tolerant of harassment than are older women (Lott et al. 1982; Reilly et al. 1986). Indeed, Lott et al. concluded that "younger women in particular have accepted the idea that prowling men are a 'fact of life' " (p. 318). This attitude might prevent women from labelling a negative experience as harassment. Surveys that ask women about sexual harassment and about the frequency of experiencing specific sexually harassing behaviors find discrepancies in responses to these questions (Fitzgerald et al. 1988). Women report higher rates when asked if they have been the target of specific harassing behaviors than when asked a general question about whether they have been harassed. Women are also more willing to report negative reactions to offensive behaviors than they are to label those behaviors as sexual harassment (Brewer 1982).

Normative beliefs may deter some male victims of harassment from reporting complaints also, because men are expected to welcome sexual advances if those advances are from women.

Negative Outcomes for Victims Who Bring Complaints

The outcome of grievance procedures does not appear to provide much satisfaction to victims who bring complaints. In academic settings, despite considerable publicity given to a few isolated cases in which tenured faculty have been fired, punishments are rarely inflicted on harassers, and the punishments that are given are mild, such as verbal warnings (Robertson et al. 1988). Among federal workers, 33 percent of those who used formal grievance procedures to protest sexual harassment found that it "made things worse" (Livingston 1982). More than 65 percent of the cases of formal charges of sexual harassment filed with the Illinois Department of Human Rights involved job discharge of the complaint (Terpstra and Cook 1985). Less than one-third of those cases resulted in a favorable settlement for the complainant, and those who received financial compensation got an average settlement of $3,234 (Terpstra and Baker 1988). Similar findings in California were reported by Coles (1986), with the average cash settlement there of $973, representing approximately one month's pay. Although a few legal cases have resulted in large settlements, these studies suggest that typical settlements are low. Formal actions may take years to complete, and in legal suits the victim usually must hire legal counsel at considerable expense (Livingston 1982). These small settlements seem unlikely to compensate victims for the emotional stress, notoriety, and financial costs involved in filing a public complaint. Given the consistency with which victimization falls more often to women than men, it is ironic that one of the largest settlements awarded to an individual in a sexual harassment case ($196,500 in damages) was made to a man who brought suit against his female supervisor (Brewer and Berk 1982), perhaps because sexual aggression by a woman is seen as especially egregious.

Emotional Consequences of Harassment

In academic settings, harassment can adversely affect students' learning, and therefore their academic standing. It can deprive them of educational and career opportunities because they wish to avoid threatening situations. Students who have been harassed report that they consequently avoid taking a class from or working with a particular faculty member, change their major, or leave a threatening situation. Lowered self-esteem follows the conclusion that rewards, such as a high grade, may have been based on sexual attraction rather than one's abilities (McCormack 1985). Decreased feelings of competence and confidence and increased feelings of anger, frustration, depression, and anxiety all can result from harassment. The psychological stress produced by harassment is compounded when women are fired or quit their jobs in fear or frustration.

Meek and Lynch (1983) proposed that victims of harassment typically go through several stages of reaction, at first questioning the offender's true intentions and then blaming themselves for the offender's behavior. Women with traditional sex-role beliefs are more likely to blame themselves for being harassed (Jensen and Gutek 1982). Victims then worry about being believed by others and about possible retaliation if they take formal steps to protest the behavior. A victim may be too frightened or confused to assert herself or punish the offender. Psychologists who work with victims of harassment would do well to recognize that not only victims' emotional reactions but also the nature of the grievance process as discussed in this article may discourage women from bringing formal complaints.

CRITICAL-THINKING QUESTIONS

1. How does gender bias affect sexual harassment policies? Why do men and women react differently to the same sexual harassment grievance procedures?

2. Riger describes several obstacles to reporting sexual harassment complaints. Do these obstacles explain why you (or someone you know) have never reported sexual harassment incidents?

3. As this article explains, sexual harassment is a widespread problem with serious economic and emotional consequences. How can sexual harassment be prevented on campuses or in workplaces? Has your campus or workplace eliminated the obstacles to reporting sexual harassment complaints that Riger describes?

REFERENCES

BRETT, J. M., S. B. GOLDBERG, and W. L. URY. 1990. Designing systems for resolving disputes in organizations. *American Psychologist,* 45:162–70.

BREWER, M. 1982. Further beyond nine to five: An integration and future directions. *Journal of Social Issues,* 38:149–57.

BREWER, M. B., and R. A. BERK. 1982. Beyond nine to five: Introduction. *Journal of Social Issues,* 38: 1–4.

COLES, F. S. 1986. Forced to quit: Sexual harassment complaints and agency response. *Sex Roles,* 14:81–95.

DZIECH, B., and L. WEINER. 1984. *The lecherous professor.* Boston: Beacon Press.

FITZGERALD, L. F., S. L. SCHULLMAN, N. BAILEY, M. RICHARDS, J. SWECKER, Y. GOLD, M. ORMEROD, and L. WEITZMAN. 1988. The incidence and dimensions of sexual harassment in academia and the workplace. *Journal of Vocational Behavior,* 32:152–75.

GILLIGAN, C. 1982. *In a different voice: Psychological theory and women's development.* Cambridge: Harvard University Press.

GUTEK, B. A. 1985. *Sex and the workplace.* San Francisco: Jossey-Bass.

JENSEN, I. W., and B. A. GUTEK. 1982. Attributions and assignment of responsibility in sexual harassment. *Journal of Social Issues,* 38:121–36.

KANTER, R. M. 1977. *Men and women of the corporation.* New York: Basic Books.

KENIG, S., and J. RYAN. 1986. Sex differences in levels of tolerance and attribution of blame for sexual harassment on a university campus. *Sex Roles,* 15: 535–49.

KIRK, D. 1988. *Gender differences in the perception of sexual harassment.* Paper presented at the Academy of Management National Meeting, Anaheim, CA, August.

KOLB, D. M., and G. G. COOLIDGE. 1988. *Her place at the table: A consideration of gender issues in negotiation* (Working paper series 88-5). Harvard Law School, Program on Negotiation.

KONRAD, A. M., and B. A. GUTEK. 1986. Impact of work experiences on attitudes toward sexual harassment. *Administrative Science Quarterly,* 31:422–38.

LESTER, D., B. BANTA, J. BARTON, N. ELIAN, L. MAC-KIEWICZ, and J. WINKELRIED. 1986. Judgments about sexual harassment: Effects of the power of the harasser. *Perceptual and Motor Skills,* 63:990.

LIVINGSTON, J. A. 1982. Responses to sexual harassment on the job: Legal, organizational, and individual actions. *Journal of Social Issues,* 38(4):5–22.

LOTT, B., M. E. REILLY, and D. R. HOWARD. 1982. Sexual assault and harassment: A campus community case study. *Signs: Journal of Women in Culture and Society,* 8:296–319.

McCORMACK, A. 1985. The sexual harassment of students by teachers: The case of students in science. *Sex Roles,* 13:21–32.

MEDNICK, M. T. 1989. On the politics of psychological constructs: Stop the bandwagon, I want to get off. *American Psychologist,* 44:1118–23.

MEEK, P. M., and A. Q. LYNCH. 1983. Establishing an informal grievance procedure for cases of sexual harassment of students. *Journal of the National Association for Women Deans, Administrators, and Counselors,* 46:30–33.

MILLER, I. B. 1976. *Toward a new psychology of women.* Boston: Beacon Press.

POWELL, G. N. 1986. Effects of sex role identity and sex on definitions of sexual harassment. *Sex Roles,* 14: 9–19.

REILLY, M. E., B. LOTT, and S. GALLOGLY. 1986. Sexual harassment of university students. *Sex Roles,* 15:333–58.

ROBERTSON, C., C. E. DYER, and D. CAMPBELL. 1988. Campus harassment: Sexual harassment policies and procedures at institutions of higher learning. *Signs: Journal of Women in Culture and Society,* 13:792–812.

TERPSTRA, D. E., and D. D. BAKER. 1988. Outcomes of sexual harassment charges. *Academy of Management Journal,* 31:185–94.

TERPSTRA, D. E., and S. E. COOK. 1985. Complainant characteristics and reported behaviors and consequences associated with formal sexual harassment charges. *Personnel Psychology,* 38:559–74.

U.S. EQUAL EMPLOYMENT OPPORTUNITY COMMISSION. 1980, November 10. Final amendment to guidelines on discrimination because of sex under Title VII of the Civil Rights Act of 1964, as amended. 29 CFR Part 1604. *Federal Register,* 45:74675–77.

U.S. MERIT SYSTEMS PROTECTION BOARD. 1981. *Sexual harassment in the federal workplace: Is it a problem?* Washington, DC: U.S. Government Printing Office.

U.S. MERIT SYSTEMS PROTECTION BOARD. 1988. *Sexual harassment in the federal government: An update.* Washington, DC: U.S. Government Printing Office.

Cross-Cultural

40

Homosexual Behavior
in Cross-Cultural Perspective

J. M. Carrier*

Although sexuality is a biological process, the meaning of sexuality is culturally variable. Carrier shows that attitudes toward homosexuality are far from uniform around the world. Some societies are quite accommodating about sexual practices that other societies punish harshly.

The available cross-cultural data clearly show that the ways in which individuals organize their sexual behavior vary considerably between societies (Westermarck 1908; Ford and Beach 1951; Broude and Greene 1976). Although biological and psychological factors help explain variations of sexual behavior between individuals within a given society, intercultural variations in patterns of human sexual behavior are mainly related to social and cultural differences occurring between societies around the world. The purpose of this chapter is to consider what kinds of variations in homosexual behavior occur between societies, and to determine which sociocultural factors appear to account for the variance of the behavior cross-culturally.[1]

THE CROSS-CULTURAL DATA

Data available on homosexual behavior in most of the world's societies, past or present, are meager. Much is known about the dominant middle-

* The author is particularly indebted to Evelyn Hooker for her invaluable comments and criticisms; and to the Gender Identity Research Group at UCLA for an early critique of the ideas presented in this paper.

class white populations of the United States, England, and northern European countries where most scientific research on human sexual behavior has been done, but very little is known about homosexual behavior in the rest of the world. The lack of knowledge stems from the irrational fear and prejudice surrounding the study of human sexual behavior, and from the difficulties associated with the collection of information on a topic that is so personal and highly regulated in most societies.

Most of the cross-cultural information on sexual behavior has been gathered by Western anthropologists. The quality of the information collected and published, however, varies considerably. Based on a survey of the literature, Marshall and Suggs (1971) report that: "Sexual behavior is occasionally touched upon in anthropological publications but is seldom the topic of either articles or monographs by anthropologists." Broude and Greene (1976), after coding the sexual attitudes and practices in 186 societies using the Human Relations Area Files, note:[2]

... information of any sort on sexual habits and beliefs is hard to come by.... when data do exist concerning sexual attitudes and practices, they are often sketchy and vague; what is more, such information is usually suspect in terms of its reliability, either because of distortions on the part of the subjects or because of biases introduced by the ethnographer. ...

Cross-cultural data on homosexual behavior is further complicated by the prejudice of many observers who consider the behavior unnatural, dysfunctional, or associated with mental illness, and by the fact that in many of the societies studied the behavior is stigmatized and thus not usually carried out openly. Under these circumstances, the behavior is not easily talked about. At the turn of the twentieth century such adjectives as disgusting, vile, and detestable were still being used to describe homosexual behavior; and even in the mid-1930s some anthropologists continued to view the behavior as unnatural. In discussing sodomy with some of his New Guinea informants, Williams (1936), for example, asked them if they "had ever been subjected to an unnatural practice." With the acceptance of the view in the mid-1930s that homosexual behavior should be classified as a mental illness (or at best dysfunctional), many anthropologists replaced "unnatural" with the medical model. This model still finds adherents among researchers at present, especially those in the branch of anthropology referred to as psychological anthropology.

Because of the prejudice with which many researchers and observers approached the subject, statements about the reported absence of homosexual behavior, or the limited extent of the behavior where reported, should be viewed with some skepticism. Mead (1961) suggests that statements of this kind "can only be accepted with the greatest caution and with very careful analysis of the personality and training of the investigator." She further notes that: "Denials of a practice cannot be regarded as meaningful if that practice is verbally recognized among a given people, even though a strong taboo exists against it."

This chapter will mainly utilize the published research findings of empirical studies which have considered homosexual behavior in some detail. It will examine homosexual behavior in preliterate, peasant, and complex modern societies in all the major geographical regions of the world.[3] Where necessary, these findings will be supplemented with information found in accounts given by travelers, missionaries, and novelists.

SOCIOCULTURAL FACTORS

A number of sociocultural factors help explain variations of homosexual behavior between societies. Two of the most important are: cultural attitudes and proscriptions related to cross-gender behavior, and availability of sexual partners.[4] The latter is in turn related to such variables as segregation of sexes prior to marriage, expectations with respect to virginity, age at marriage, and available economic resources and/or distribution of income.

Cross-Gender and Homosexual Behavior

Different expectations for male persons as opposed to female persons are culturally elaborated from birth onward in every known society. Although behavioral boundaries between the sexes may vary culturally, male persons are clearly differentiated from female persons; and progeny is assured by normative societal rules which correlate male and female gender roles with sexual behavior, marriage, and the family. There is a general expectation in every society that a majority of adult men and women will cohabit and produce the next generation. Social pressure is thus applied in the direction of marriage. The general rule is that one should not remain single.

The cross-cultural data on human sexual behavior suggest that a significant relationship exists between much of the homosexual behavior reported cross culturally and the continuing need of societies to deal with cross-gender behavior. Feminine male behavior, and the set of anxieties associated with its occurrence in the male part of the population, appears to have brought about more elaborate cultural responses temporally and spatially than has masculine female behavior. There are no doubt many reasons why this is so, but it appears to be related in general to the higher status accorded men than women in most societies; and, in particular, to the defense role that men have historically played in protecting women and children from outsiders.

Societies in which homosexual behavior can be linked to cultural responses to cross-gender behavior may be categorized according to the type of response made. Three major cultural types have been identified: those societies which make a basic accommodation to cross-gender behavior, those societies which outlaw the behavior as scandalous and/or criminal, and those societies which neither make an accommodation to such behavior nor outlaw it but instead have a cultural formulation which tries to ensure that cross-gender behavior does not occur.

Accommodating Societies

Societies making an accommodation to cross-gender behavior in one form or another have been reported in many different parts of the world. Munroe et al. (1969), for example, put together a list of societies having what they call "institutionalized male transvestism . . . the permanent adoption by males of aspects of female dress and/or behavior in accordance with customary expectations within a given society." Their list includes Indian societies in North and South America, island societies in Polynesia and Southeast Asia, and preliterate and peasant societies in mainland Asia and Africa. Although reported for both sexes male cross-gender behavior appears in the literature more often than female.

A folk belief exists in some of these societies that in every generation a certain number of individuals will play the gender role of the opposite sex, usually beginning at or prior to puberty and often identified at a very early age. The Mohave Indians of the American Southwest, for example, used to hold the following belief—typical of many Indian societies in North America—about cross-gender behavior of both sexes:

> Ever since the world began at the magic mountain . . . it was said that there would be transvestites. In the beginning, if they were to become transvestites, the process started during their intrauterine life. When they grew up they were given toys according to their sex. They did not like these toys however. (Devereux 1937)

In southern Mexico one group of Zapotec Indians believes that "effeminate males" are born not made: "Typical comments include: But what can we do; he was born that way; he is like God made him. A related belief also exists that . . . it is a thing of the blood" (Royce 1973). In Tahiti, the belief exists that there is at least one cross-gender behaving male, called a *māhū*, in all villages: "When one dies then another substitutes . . . God arranges it like this. It isn't allowed (that there should be) two *māhū* in one place" (Levy 1973).

Cross-gender behavior is accepted in other societies because it is believed that some supernatural event makes people that way prior to birth, or that the behavior is acquired through some mystical force or dream after birth. In India, for example, the following belief exists about the *Hijadā*, cross-gender behaving males thought to be impotent at birth who later have their genitals removed:

When we ask a Hijadā or an ordinary man in Gujarat "Why does a man become a Hijadā?" the usual reply is "One does not become a Hijadā by one's own will; it is only by the command of the mātā that one becomes a Hijadā." The same idea is found in a myth about the origin of the Hijadās. It is said that one receives the mātā's command either in dreams or when one sits in meditation before her image. (Shah 1961)

Among the Chukchee of northeastern Asia, a role reversal was accepted because of an unusual dream or vision:

Transformation takes place by the command of the *ka'let* (spirits) usually at the critical age of early youth when shamanistic inspiration first manifests itself. (Bogores 1904)

Among the Lango in Africa:

A number of Lango men dress as women, simulate menstruation, and become one of the wives of other males. They are believed to be impotent and to have been afflicted by some supernatural agency. (Ford and Beach 1951)

Although not necessarily accepted gladly, the various folk beliefs make the behavior acceptable, and a certain number of cross-gender behaving individuals are to be expected in every generation. Expectations about the extent to which the opposite gender role is to be played, however, appear to have changed over time with acculturation. Affected individuals in the past often were required to make a public ritualized change of gender and cross-dress and behave in accordance with their new identity. Among the Mohave, for example,

there was an initiation ceremony and it was important for the initiate "to duplicate the behavior pattern of his adopted sex and make 'normal' individuals of his anatomic sex feel toward him as though he truly belonged to his adopted sex" (Devereux 1937). The *māhū* in Tahiti were described in the latter part of the eighteenth century as follows:

These men are in some respects like the Eunichs [*sic*] in India but are not castrated. They never cohabit with women but live as they do. They pick their beard out and dress as women, dance and sing with them and are as effeminate in their voice. (Morrison 1935)

Affected individuals in most societies at present are allowed a choice as to the extent they want to play the role; e.g., how far they want to identify with the opposite sex, whether they want to cross-dress or not, etc. Levy (1973) notes, for example, that in Tahiti: "Being a *māhū* does not now usually entail actually dressing as a woman." The North American Indian societies who used to have initiation ceremonies discontinued them long ago; and, although expectations about cross-gender behaving individuals persist, only remnants of the original belief system are remembered currently. They continue, however, to be tolerant and "there apparently is no body of role behavior aimed at humiliating boys who are feminine or men who prefer men sexually" (Stoller 1976).

The link between cross-gender behavior and homosexual behavior is the belief that there should be concordance between gender role and sexual object choice. When a male behaves like a female, he should be expected therefore to want a male sexual partner and to play the female sex role—that is, to play the insertee role in anal intercourse or fellatio. The same concordance should be expected when a female behaves like a male. As a result of beliefs about concordance, it is important to note that a society may not conceptualize the sexual behavior or its participants as "homosexual."

There is some evidence in support of this linking of gender role and homosexual behavior in societies making an accommodation and providing a social role for cross-gender behaving individuals. Kroeber (1940), for example, concluded from his investigations that: "In most of primitive northern Asia and North America, men of homosexual trends adopted women's dress, work, and status, and were accepted as nonphysiological but institutionalized women." Devereux's Mohave informants said that the males who changed their gender role to female had male husbands and that both anal intercourse and fellatio were practiced, with the participants playing the appropriate gender sex role. The informants noted the same concordance for females who behaved like males.

Unfortunately, the anthropological data do not always make clear whether cultural expectations in a given society were for concordance between gender role and erotic object; or, in terms of actual behavior, how many cross-gender behaving individuals chose same sex, opposite sex, or both sexes as erotic objects. In the paper I just quoted, Kroeber also concluded: "How far invert erotic practices accompanied the status is not always clear from the data, and it probably varied. At any rate, the North American attitude toward the berdache stresses not his erotic life but his social status; born a male, he became accepted as a woman socially."

Many anthropologists and other observers confounded their findings by assuming an equivalence between "transvestite" and "homosexual."[5] Thus, when an informant described cross-gender behavior, they may have concluded without foundation that a same-sex erotic object choice was part of the behavior being described, and that they were eliciting information on "homosexuals." Angelino and Shedd (1955) provide supporting evidence. They reviewed the literature on an often used anthropological concept, berdache, and concluded that the "term has been used in an exceedingly ambiguous way, being used as a synonym for homosexualism, hermaphroditism, transvestism, and effeminism." They also note that the meaning of berdache changed over time; going from kept boy/male prostitute, to individuals who played a passive role in sodomy, to males who played a passive sex role and cross-dressed.

In spite of the confusion between "transvestite" and "homosexual," the available data suggest that in many of the societies providing a social role for cross-gender behavior, the selection of sexual partners was based on the adopted gender role; and, though they might be subjected to ridicule, neither partner in the sexual relationship was penalized for the role played.

The *māhū* role in Tahiti provides a contemporary look at how one Polynesian society continues to provide a social role for cross-gender behavior. According to Levy (1973), villagers in his area of study do not agree on the sexual behavior of the *māhū*—some "believe that *māhū* do not generally engage in homosexual intercourse." Information from both *māhū* and *non-māhū* informants, however, leads to the conclusion that probably a majority of the *māhūs* prefer adolescent males with whom they perform "ote moa" (literally, "penis sucking"). The following are some aspects of the role and the community response to it:

It is said to be exclusive. Its essential defining characteristic is "doing woman's work," that is, a role reversal which is *publicly demonstrated*—either through clothes or through other public aspects of women's role playing. Most villagers approve of, and are pleased by, the role reversal. But homosexual behavior is a covert part of the role, and it is disapproved by many villagers. Men who have sexual relations with the *māhū*. . . do not consider themselves abnormal. Villagers who know of such activities may disapprove, but they do not label the partners as unmanly. The *māhū* is considered as a substitute woman for the partner. A new word, *raerae*, which reportedly originated in Papeete, is used by some to designate nontraditional types of homosexual behavior. (Levy 1973)

It should also be noted that in Levy's village of study *māhūs* were the only adult men reported to be engaging in homosexual intercourse.

Another contemporary example of a social role for cross-gender behavior is the *Hijadā* role provided cross-gender behaving males in northwestern India. Given slightly different names by different observers (*Hijarās, Hinjrās,* and *Hijirās*), these males appear to be playing the same role. There is general agreement on the fact that they cross-dress, beg alms, and collect dues at special ceremonies where they dance and sing as women. There is a considerable difference of opinion, however, as to whether they engage in homosexual intercourse or in any sexual activity for that matter. From the available data, it appears that they live mostly in towns in communes, with each commune having a definite jurisdiction of villages and towns "where its members can beg alms and collect dues" (Shah 1961). They are also reported to live separately by themselves. From the findings of Carstairs (1956) and Shah (1961), one can at least conclude that the *Hijadās* living alone are sexually active:

Carstairs is wrong in considering all the Hijadās as homosexual, but there seems to be some truth in his information about the homosexuality of the Deoli Hijadā. (Note: Deoli is the village of Carstairs' study.) Faridi and Mehta also note that some Hijadās practice "sodomy." This, however, is not institutionalized homosexuality. (Shah 1961)

The finding by Opler (1960) that "they cannot carry on sexual activities and do not marry" may apply to the majority of *Hijadās* living in communes. The question of what kind of sexual behavior the *Hijadās* practice, if any, cannot be answered definitively with the data available. That they are still a viable group in India is confirmed by a recent Associated Press release:

About 2000 eunuchs dressed in brightly colored saris and other female garb were converging on this northern town from all over India this weekend for a private convention of song, dance and prayer.

Local reaction to the gathering was mixed. "They're perverts," commented a local peanut vendor. "We should have nothing to do with them. They should be run out of town."

A New Delhi social worker . . . said they sometimes supplement their income as paid lovers of homosexuals. (Excerpts from AP, February 6, 1979)

Disapproving Societies

Societies in which cross-gender behavior produces strong emotional negative reactions in large segments of the population tend to have the following commonalities: (1) negative reactions produced by the behavior are essentially limited to the male part of the population and relate mainly to effeminate males; (2) cross-gender behavior is controlled by laws which prohibit cross-dressing, and by laws and public opinion which consider other attributes associated with the behavior as scandalous; (3) gender roles are sharply dichotomized; and (4) a general belief exists that anyone demonstrating cross-gender behavior is homosexual.

A number of complex modern and peasant societies in the Middle East, North Africa, southern Europe, and Central and South America have the commonalities listed. The author's research in Mexico (Carrier 1976 and 1977) illustrates how homosexual behavior in these societies appears to be linked to social responses to cross-gender behavior. The comments that follow are limited to male homosexual behavior. Female homosexuality is known to exist in these societies, but too little is known about the behavior to be included in the discussion.

Mexican Homosexual Behavior. The Mexican mestizo culture places a high value on manliness. One of the salient features of the society is thus a sharp delimitation between the roles played by males and females. Role expectations in general are for the male to be dominant and independent and for the female to be submissive and dependent. The continued sharp boundary between male and female roles in Mexico appears to be due in part to a culturally defined hypermasculine ideal model of manliness, referred to under the label *machismo*. The ideal female role is generally believed to be the reciprocal of the macho (male) role.[6]

As a consequence of the high status given manliness, Mexican males from birth onward are expected to behave in as manly a way as possible. Peñalosa (1968) sums it up as follows: "Any signs of feminization are severely repressed in the boy." McGinn (1966) concludes: "The young Mexican boy may be severely scolded for engaging in feminine activities, such as playing with dolls or jacks. Parents verbally and physically punish 'feminine' traits in their male children." The importance of manly behavior continues throughout the life span of Mexican males.

One result of the sharp dichotomization of male and female gender roles is the widely held belief that effeminate males basically prefer to play the female role rather than the male. The link between male effeminacy and homosexuality is the additional belief that as a result of this role preference effeminate males are sexually interested only in masculine males with whom they play the passive sex role. Although the motivations of males participating in homosexual encounters are without question diverse and complex, the fact remains that in Mexico cultural pressure is brought to bear on effeminate males to play the passive insertee role in sexual intercourse, and a kind of de facto cultural approval is given (that is, no particular stigma is attached to) masculine males who want to play the active insertor role in homosexual intercourse.

The beliefs linking effeminate males with homosexuality are culturally transmitted by a vocabulary which provides the appropriate labels, by homosexually oriented jokes and word games (*albures*), and by the mass media. The links are established at a very early age. From early childhood on, Mexican males are made aware of the labels used to denote male homosexuals and the connection is always clearly made that these homosexual males are guilty of unmanly effeminate behavior.

The author's data also support the notion that prior to puberty effeminate males in Mexico are targeted as sexual objects for adolescent and adult males, and are expected to play the passive insertee sex role in anal intercourse. Following the onset of puberty, they continue to be sexual targets for other males because of their effeminacy. The consensus of my effeminate respondents in Mexico is that regardless of whether they are at school, in a movie theater, on the downtown streets, in a park, or in their own neighborhood, they are sought out and expected to play the anal passive sex role by more masculine males. As one

fourteen-year-old respondent put it, in response to the question of where he had looked for sexual contacts during the year prior to the interview: "I didn't have to search for them . . . they looked for me."

The other side of the coin is represented by masculine male participants in homosexual encounters. Given the fact that effeminate males in Mexico are assumed homosexual and thus considered available as sexual outlets, how do the cultural factors contribute to the willingness of masculine males to play the active insertor sex role? The available data suggest that, insofar as the social variables are concerned, their willingness to participate in homosexual encounters is due to the relatively high level of sexual awareness that exists among males in the society, to the lack of stigmatization of the insertor sex role, and to the restraints that may be placed on alternative sexual outlets by available income and/or by marital status. The only cultural proscriptions are that "masculine" males should not play the passive sex role and should not be exclusively involved with homosexual intercourse.

The passive sex role is by inference—through the cultural equivalence of effeminacy with homosexuality—prescribed for "effeminate" males. It becomes a self-fulfilling prophecy of the society that effeminate males (a majority?) are eventually, if not from the beginning, pushed toward exclusively homosexual behavior. Some do engage in heterosexual intercourse, and some marry and set up households; but these probably are a minority of the identifiably effeminate males among the mestizos of the Mexican population.

Brazilian Homosexual Behavior. Both Young (1973) and Fry (1974) note the relationship between cross-gender behavior and homosexuality in Brazil:

Brazilians are still pretty hung-up about sexual roles. Many Brazilians believe in the *bicha/bofe* (femme/ butch) dichotomy and try to live by it. In Brazil, the average person doesn't even recognize the existence of the masculine homosexual. For example, among working-class men, it is considered all right to fuck a *bicha*, an accomplishment of sorts, just like fucking a woman. (Young 1973)

In the simplest of terms, a male is a man until he is assumed or proved to have "given" in which case he becomes a *bicha*. With very few exceptions, males who "eat" *bichas* are not classified as anything other than "real men." Under this classificatory scheme they differ in no way from males who restrict themselves to "eating" females. (Note: the male who gives is an insertee, the one who eats is an insertor.) (Fry 1974)

Southern European Homosexual Behavior. Contemporary patterns of male homosexual behavior in Greece appear similar to those observed by the author in Mexico. An American anthropologist who collected data on homosexual behavior in Greece while working there on an archaeological project (Bialor 1975) found, for example, that preferences for playing one sex role or the other (anal insertor or anal insertee) appear to be highly developed among Greek males. Little or no stigma is attached to the masculine male who plays the active insertor role. The social setting in modern Greece also appears to be strikingly similar to that in modern Mexico. Karlen (1971) describes it as follows:

The father spends his spare time with other men in cafes; society is a male club, and there all true companionship lies. Women live separate, sequestered lives. Girls' virginity is carefully protected, and the majority of homicides are committed over the "honor" of daughters and sisters. In some Greek villages a woman does not leave her home unaccompanied by a relative between puberty and old age. Women walk the street, even in Athens, with their eyes down; a woman who looks up when a man speaks to her is, quite simply, a whore. The young male goes to prostitutes and may carry on homosexual connections; it is not unusual for him to marry at thirty having had no sexual experience save with prostitutes and male friends. (p. 16)

In an evaluation of the strategy of Turkish boys' verbal dueling rhymes, Dundes, Leach, and Ozkok (1972) make the following observations about homosexual behavior in Turkey:

It is extremely important to note that the insult refers to *passive* homosexuality, not to homosexuality in general. In this context there is nothing insulting about being the active homosexual. In a homosexual relationship, the active phallic aggressor gains status; the passive victim of such aggression loses status. It is important to play the active role in a homosexual relationship; it is shameful and demeaning to be forced to take the passive role.

Moroccan Homosexual Behavior. The author does not know of any formal studies of homosexual behavior in Morocco. The available information suggests, however, that contemporary patterns of homosexual behavior in Morocco are similar to those in Mexico; that is, as long as Moroccan males play the active, insertor sex role in the relationship, there is never any question of their being considered homosexual. Based on his field work in Morocco shortly after the turn of the century, Westermarck (1908) believed that "a very large proportion of the men" in some parts of the country were involved in homosexual activity. He also noted that: "In Morocco active pederasty is regarded with almost complete indifference, whilst the passive sodomite, if a grown-up individual, is spoken of with scorn. Dr. Polak says the same of the Persians." Contemporary patterns of homosexual behavior in the Islamic Arab countries of North Africa are probably similar to those in Morocco. . . .

DISCUSSION

Heterosexual intercourse, marriage, and the creation of a family are culturally established as primary objectives for adults living in all of the societies discussed above. Ford and Beach (1951) concluded from their cross-cultural survey that "all known cultures are strongly biased in favor of copulation between males and females as contrasted with alternative avenues of sexual expression." They further note that this viewpoint is biologically adaptive in that it favors perpetuation of the species and social group, and that societies favoring other nonreproductive forms of sexual expression for adults would not be likely to survive for many generations.

Homosexual intercourse appears to be the most important alternative form of sexual expression utilized by people living around the world. All cultures have established rules and regulations that govern the selection of a sexual partner or partners. With respect to homosexual behavior, however, there appear to be greater variations of the rules and regulations. And male homosexual behavior generally appears to be more regulated by cultures than female homosexual behavior. This difference may be the result of females being less likely than males to engage in homosexual activity; but it may also just be the result of a lack of data on female as compared with male homosexual behavior cross-culturally.

Exclusive homosexuality, however, because of the cultural dictums concerning marriage and the family, appears to be generally excluded as a sexual option even in those societies where homosexual behavior is generally approved. For example, the two societies where all male individuals are free to participate in homosexual activity if they choose, Siwan and East Bay, do not sanction exclusive homosexuality.[7] Although nearly all male members of these two societies are reported to engage in extensive homosexual activities, they are not permitted to do so exclusively over their adult life span. Davenport (1965) reports "that East Bay is a society which permits men to be either heterosexual or bisexual in their behavior, but denies the possibility of the exclusively homosexual man." He notes that "they have no concept and therefore no word for the exclusive homosexual." There are not much data available on the Siwans, but it has been reported that whether single or married Siwan males "are expected to have both homosexual and heterosexual affairs" (Ford and Beach 1951).

In East Bay there are two categories of homosexual relationships. One category appears similar to that found in a number of Melanesian societies; an older man plays the active (insertor) sex role in anal intercourse with younger boys "from seven to perhaps eleven years of age." Davenport notes:

The man always plays the active role, and it is considered obligatory for him to give the boy presents in return for accommodating him. A man would not engage his own son in such a relationship, but fathers do not object when friends use their young sons in this way, provided the adult is kind and generous. (p. 200)

The other category is between young single men of the same age group who play both sex roles in anal intercourse. The young men, however, "are not regarded as homosexual lovers. They are simply friends or relatives, who, understanding each other's needs and desires, accommodate one another thus fulfilling some of the obligations of kinship and friendship." This category may be related to several social factors which limit heterosexual contacts of young single men. First, the population is highly masculine with a male/female ratio of 120:100 in the fifteen- to twenty-five-year-old age group. Second, females have historically been brought in as wives for those who could afford the bride price. Third, sexual relations between unmarried individuals and adultery are forbidden. Both relationships are classed as larcenies and "only murder carries a more severe punishment." At first marriage a bride is expected to be a virgin. Chastity is highly valued in that it indicates adultery is less likely to occur after marriage. And fourth, there is "an extensive system for separating the sexes by what amounts to a general social avoidance between men and women in all but a few situations." From early adolescence on, unmarried men and boys sleep and eat in the men's house; and married men spend much of their time there during the day. Davenport notes that both masturbation and anal copulation are socially approved and regarded as substitutes for heterosexual intercourse by members of the society. Female homosexual activity is not reported in East Bay.

Among Siwan males the accepted homosexual relationship is "between a man and a boy but not between adult men or between two young boys" (Bullough 1976). They are reported to practice anal intercourse with the adult man always playing the active (insertor) sex role. In this society, boys are more valued than girls. Allah (1917) reports that

bringing up of a boy costs very little whereas the girl needs ornaments, clothing, and stains. Moreover the boy is a very fruitful source of profit for the father, not for the work he does, but because he is hired by his father to another man to be used as a catamite. Sometimes two men exchange their sons. If they are asked about this, they are not ashamed to mention it.

Homosexual activity is not reported for Siwan females.

The way in which cross-gender behavior is linked to homosexual behavior, and the meaning ascribed to the "homosexual" behavior by participants and significant others, differ between the three categories of societies identified in this study. What is considered homosexuality in one culture may be considered appropriate behavior within prescribed gender roles in another, a homosexual act only on the part of one participant in another, or a ritual act involving growth and masculinity in still another. Care must therefore be taken when judging sexual behavior cross-culturally with such culture-bound labels as "homosexual" and "homosexuality."

From a cultural point of view, deviations from sexual mores in a given society appear most likely to occur as a result of the lack of appropriate sexual partners and/or a result of conditioning in approved sexual behavior which is limited by age or ritual (for example, where homosexual intercourse is only appropriate for a certain age group and/or ritual time period and inappropriate thereafter). Homosexual activity initiated by sociocultural variables may over time through interaction with personality variables, produce an outcome not in accordance with the sexual mores of the society.

The findings presented in this chapter illustrate the profound influence of culture on the structuring of individual patterns of sexual behavior. Whether from biological or psychological causation, cross-gender behaving individuals in many societies must cope with a cultural formulation which equates their behavior with homosexual ac-

tivity and thus makes it a self-fulfilling prophecy that they become homosexually involved. There are also individuals in many societies who might *prefer* to be exclusively homosexual but are prevented from doing so by cultural edicts. From whatever causes that homosexual impulses originate, whether they be biological or psychological, culture provides an additional dimension that cannot be ignored.

CRITICAL-THINKING QUESTIONS

1. What type of society tends to be accepting of homosexuality? What kind of society is disapproving of this sexual orientation? Why?
2. What insights can be drawn from this article that help to explain violence and discrimination directed toward gay people in U.S. society?
3. Are data about sexuality easily available to researchers? Why not?

NOTES

1. Homosexual behavior or activity will be used here to describe sexual behavior between individuals of the same sex; and it may have nothing to do with sexual object choice or sexual orientation of the individuals involved. Additionally, the terms "sex role" and "gender role" will be used to describe different behavioral phenomena. As Hooker (1965) points out, they "are often used interchangeably, and with resulting confusion." Following her suggestion, the term "sex role," when homosexual practices are described, will refer to typical sexual performance only. "The gender connotations (M-F) of these performances need not then be implicitly assumed." The term gender role will refer to the expected attitudes and behavior that distinguish males from females.

2. The Human Relations Area Files (HRAF) contain information on the habits, practices, customs, and behavior of populations in hundreds of societies around the world. These files utilize accounts given not only by anthropologists but also by travelers, writers, missionaries, and explorers. Most cross-cultural surveys of sexual behavior, like those of Ford and Beach and Broude and Greene, have been based on HRAF information. A major criticism of the HRAF information on sexual behavior relates to the difficulty of assessing the reliability of the data collected in different time periods by different people with varying amounts of scientific training as observers.

3. "Preliterate" refers to essentially tribal societies that do not have a written language; "peasant" refers to essentially

agrarian literate societies; and "complex modern" refers to highly industrialized societies.

4. In one of the first scholarly surveys of homosexual behavior done by an anthropologist, Westermarck (1908) concluded that: "A very important cause of homosexual practices is absence of the other sex."

5. The confounding of transvestism with homosexuality still occurs. For example, Minturn, Grosse, and Haider (1969) coded male homosexuality with transvestism in a recent study of the patterning of sexual beliefs and behavior, "because it is often difficult to distinguish between the two practices, and because they are assumed to be manifestations of the same psychological processes and to have similar causes."

6. The roles described represent the normative cultural ideals of the mestizoized national culture. Mestizos are Mexican nationals of mixed Indian and Spanish ancestry. They make up a large majority of the population, and their culture is the dominant one.

7. Both societies are small, each totaling less than one thousand inhabitants. The Siwans live in an oasis in the Libyan desert. The people of East Bay (a pseudonym) live in a number of small coastal villages in an island in Melanesia.

REFERENCES

ALLAH, M. 1917. Siwan customs. *Harvard African Studies,* 1:7.

ANGELINO, A., and C. SHEDD. 1955. A note on berdache. *American Anthropologist,* 57:121–25.

ASSOCIATED PRESS. 1979. Eunuchs gather for convention in India. Panipat, February 6, 1979.

BIALOR, P. 1975. Personal communication.

BOGORES, W. 1904. The Chukchee. *Memoirs of American Museum of Natural History,* 2: 449–51.

BROUDE, G., and S. GREENE. 1976. Cross-cultural codes on twenty sexual attitudes and practices. *Ethnology,* 15(4):410–11.

BULLOUGH, V. 1976. *Sexual variance in society and history* (pp. 22–49). New York: John Wiley.

CARRIER, J. 1976. Cultural factors affecting urban Mexican male homosexual behavior. *Archives of Sexual Behavior,* 5(2):103–24.

———. 1977. Sex-role preference as an explanatory variable in homosexual behavior. *Archives of Sexual Behavior,* 6(1):53–65.

CARSTAIRS, G. 1956. Hinjra and Jiryan: Two derivatives of Hindu attitudes to sexuality. *British Journal of Medical Psychology,* 2:129–32.

DAVENPORT, W. 1965. Sexual patterns and their regulation in a society of the southwest Pacific. In *Sex and behavior* (pp. 164–207). New York: John Wiley.

DEVEREUX, G. 1937. Institutionalized homosexuality of the Mohave Indians. In *The problem of homosexuality in modern society* (pp. 183–226). New York: E. P. Dutton.

DUNDES, A., J. LEACH, and B. OZKOK. 1972. The strategy of Turkish boys' verbal dueling. In *Directions in sociolinguistics: The ethnography of communication.* New York: Holt.

FORD, C .S., and F. A. BEACH. 1951. *Patterns of sexual behavior.* New York: Harper & Row.

FRY, P. 1974. Male homosexuality and Afro-Brazilian possession cults. Unpublished paper presented to Symposium on Homosexuality in Crosscultural Perspective, 73rd Annual Meeting of the American Anthropological Association, Mexico City.

HOOKER, E. 1965. An empirical study of some relations between sexual patterns and gender identity in male homosexuals. In *Sex research: New developments* (pp. 24–25). New York: Holt.

KARLEN, A. 1971. *Sexuality and homosexuality: A new view.* New York: W. W. Norton & Co., Inc.

KROEBER, A. 1940. Psychosis or social sanction. *Character and Personality,* 8:204–15. Reprinted in *The nature of culture* (Chicago: University of Chicago Press, 1952), p. 313.

LEVY, R. 1973. *Tahitians.* Chicago: University of Chicago Press.

MARSHALL, D., and R. SUGGS. 1971. *Human sexual behavior* (pp. 220–21). New York: Basic Books.

McGINN, N. 1966. Marriage and family in middle-class Mexico. *Journal of Marriage and Family Counseling,* 28:305–13.

MEAD, M. 1961. Cultural determinants of sexual behavior. In *Sex and internal secretions* (pp. 1433–79). Baltimore: Williams & Wilkins.

MINTURN, L., M. GROSSE, and S. HAIDER. 1969. Cultural patterning of sexual beliefs and behavior. *Ethnology,* 8(3):3.

MORRISON, J. 1935. *The journal of James Morrison.* London: Golden Cockeral Press.

MUNROE, R., J. WHITING, and D. HALLY. 1969. Institutionalized male transvestism and sex distinctions. *American Anthropologist,* 71:87–91.

OPLER, M. 1960. The Hijarā (hermaphrodites) of India and Indian national character: A rejoinder. *American Anthropologist,* 62(3):505–11.

PEÑALOSA, F. 1968. Mexican family roles. *Journal of Marriage and Family Counseling,* 30:680–89.

SHAH, A. 1961. A note on the Hijadās of Gujarat. *American Anthropologist,* 63(6):1325–30.

STOLLER, R. 1976. Two feminized male American Indians. *Archives of Sexual Behavior,* 5(6):536.

WESTERMARCK, E. 1908. On homosexual love. In *The origin and development of the moral ideas.* London: Macmillan.

WILLIAMS, F. 1936. *Papuans of the trans-fly.* London: Oxford University Press.

YOUNG, A. 1973. Gay gringo in Brazil. In *The gay liberation book* (pp. 60–67), ed. L. Richmond and G. Noguera. San Francisco: Ramparts Press.

41

The Tragedy of Old Age in America

Robert N. Butler

The United States has often been described as a "youth culture," in which youth is a measure of personal worth. In this selection, Robert Butler explores the U.S. view of the elderly, which he finds to be fraught with myths and prejudices. He argues that these not only hurt elderly people but also disadvantage everyone.

What is it like to be old in the United States? What will our own lives be like when we are old? Americans find it difficult to think about old age until they are propelled into the midst of it by their own aging and that of relatives and friends. Aging is the neglected stepchild of the human life cycle. Though we have begun to examine the socially taboo subjects of dying and death, we have leaped over that long period of time preceding death known as old age. In truth, it is easier to manage the problem of death than the problem of living as

an old person. Death is a dramatic, one-time crisis while old age is a day-by-day and year-by-year confrontation with powerful external and internal forces, a bittersweet coming to terms with one's own personality and one's life.

Those of us who are not old barricade ourselves from discussions of old age by declaring the subject morbid, boring, or in poor taste. Optimism and euphemism are other common devices. People will speak of looking forward to their "retirement years." The elderly are described respectfully as "senior citizens," "golden agers," "our elders," and one hears of old people who are considered inspirations and examples of how to "age well" or "gracefully." There is the popularly accepted opinion that Social Security and pensions provide a

SOURCE: *Why Survive? Being Old in America* by Robert N. Butler, M.D., pp. 1–2, 6–12, 15–16. Copyright © 1975 by Robert N. Butler, M.D. Reprinted with permission of Harper-Collins Publishers, Inc.

comfortable and reliable flow of funds so the elderly have few financial worries. Medicare has lulled the population into reassuring itself that the once terrible financial burdens of late-life illnesses are now eradicated. Advertisements and travel folders show relaxed, happy, well-dressed older people enjoying recreation, travel, and their grandchildren. If they are no longer living in the old family home, they are pictured as delighted residents of retirement communities with names like Leisure World and Sun City, with lots of grass, clean air, and fun. This is the American ideal of the "golden years" toward which millions of citizens are expectantly toiling through their workdays.

But this is not the full story. A second theme runs through the popular view of old age. Our colloquialisms reveal a great deal: Once you are old you are "fading fast," "over the hill," "out to pasture," "down the drain," "finished," "out of date," an "old crock," "fogy," "geezer," or "biddy." One hears children saying they are afraid to get old, middle-aged people declaring they want to die after they have passed their prime, and numbers of old people wishing they were dead.

What can we possibly conclude from these discrepant points of view? Our popular attitudes could be summed up as a combination of wishful thinking and stark terror. We base our feelings on primitive fears, prejudice, and stereotypes rather than on knowledge and insight. In reality, the way one experiences old age is contingent upon physical health, personality, earlier-life experiences, the actual circumstances of late-life events (in what order they occur, how they occur, when they occur), and the social supports one receives: adequate finances, shelter, medical care, social roles, religious support, recreation. All of these are crucial and interconnected elements which together determine the quality of late life. . . .

MYTHS AND STEREOTYPES ABOUT THE OLD

In addition to dealing with the difficulties of physical and economic survival, older people are af-

fected by the multitude of myths and stereotypes surrounding old age:

An older person thinks and moves slowly. He does not think as he used to or as creatively. He is bound to himself and to his past and can no longer change or grow. He can learn neither well nor swiftly and, even if he could, he would not wish to. Tied to his personal traditions and growing conservatism, he dislikes innovations and is not disposed to new ideas. Not only can he not move forward, he often moves backward. He enters a second childhood, caught up in increasing egocentricity and demanding more from his environment than he is willing to give to it. Sometimes he becomes an intensification of himself, a caricature of a lifelong personality. He becomes irritable and cantankerous, yet shallow and enfeebled. He lives in his past; he is behind the times. He is aimless and wandering of mind, reminiscing and garrulous. Indeed, he is a study in decline, the picture of mental and physical failure. He has lost and cannot replace friends, spouse, job, status, power, influence, income. He is often stricken by diseases which, in turn, restrict his movement, his enjoyment of food, the pleasures of well-being. He has lost his desire and capacity for sex. His body shrinks, and so too does the flow of blood to his brain. His mind does not utilize oxygen and sugar at the same rate as formerly. Feeble, uninteresting, he awaits his death, a burden to society, to his family and to himself.

In its essentials, this view I have sketched approximates the picture of old age held by many Americans. As in all clichés, stereotypes, and myths there are bits of truth. But many of the current views of old age represent confusions, misunderstandings, or simply a lack of knowledge about old age. Others may be completely inaccurate or biased, reflecting prejudice or outright hostility. Certain prevalent myths need closer examination.

The Myth of "Aging"

The idea of chronological aging (measuring one's age by the number of years one has lived) is a kind of myth. It is clear that there are great differences in the rates of physiological, chronological, psychological, and social aging within the person and from person to person. In fact, physiological indicators show a greater range from the mean in old age than in any other age group, and this is true of personality as well. Older people actually become more diverse rather than more similar with advancing years. There are extraordinarily "young" eighty-year-olds as well as "old" eighty-year-olds. Chronological age, therefore, is a convenient but imprecise indicator of physical, mental, and emotional status. For the purposes of this book old age may be considered to commence at the conventionally accepted point of sixty-five.

We do know that organic brain damage can create such extensive intellectual impairment that people of all types and personalities may become dull-eyed, blank-faced, and unresponsive. Massive destruction of the brain and body has a "leveling" effect which can produce increasing homogeneity among the elderly. But most older people do not suffer impairment of this magnitude during the greater part of their later life.

The Myth of Unproductivity

Many believe the old to be unproductive. But in the absence of diseases and social adversities, old people tend to remain productive and actively involved in life. There are dazzling examples like octogenarians Georgia O'Keeffe continuing to paint and Pope John XXIII revitalizing his church, and septuagenarians Duke Ellington composing and working his hectic concert schedule and Golda Meir acting as her country's vigorous Prime Minister. Substantial numbers of people become unusually creative for the first time in old age, when exceptional and inborn talents may be discovered and expressed. What is most pertinent to our discussion here, however, is the fact that many old people continue to contribute usefully to their families and community in a variety of ways, including active employment. The 1971 Bureau of Labor Statistics figures show 1,780,000 people over sixty-five working full time and 1,257,000 part time. Since society and business practice do not encourage the continued employment of the elderly, it is obvious that many more would work if jobs were available.

When productive incapacity develops, it can be traced more directly to a variety of losses, diseases,

or circumstances than to that mysterious process called aging. Even then, in spite of the presence of severe handicaps, activity and involvement are often maintained.

The Myth of Disengagement

This is related to the previous myth and holds that older people prefer to disengage from life, to withdraw into themselves, choosing to live alone or perhaps only with their peers. Ironically, some gerontologists themselves hold these views. One study, *Growing Old: The Process of Disengagement,* presents the theory that mutual separation of the aged person from his society is a natural part of the aging experience. There is no evidence to support this generalization. Disengagement is only one of many patterns of reaction to old age.

The Myth of Inflexibility

The ability to change and adapt has little to do with one's age and more to do with one's lifelong character. But even this statement has to be qualified. One is not necessarily destined to maintain one's character in earlier life permanently. True, the endurance, the strength, and the stability in human character structure are remarkable and protective. But most, if not all, people change and remain open to change throughout the course of life, right up to its termination. The old notion, whether ascribed to Pope Alexander VI or Sigmund Freud, that character is laid down in final form by the fifth year of life can be confidently refuted. Change is the hallmark of living. The notion that older people become less responsive to innovation and change because of age is not supported by scientific studies of healthy older people living in the community or by everyday observations and clinical psychiatric experience.

A related cliché is that political conservatism increases with age. If one's options are constricted by job discrimination, reduced or fixed income, and runaway inflation, as older people's are, one may become conservative out of economic necessity rather than out of qualities innate in the psy-

nipulation by older people is best recognized for what it is—a valuable clue that there is energy available which should be redirected toward greater benefit for themselves and others.

It must also be remembered that the old can have many prejudices against the young. These may be a result of their attractiveness, vigor, and sexual prowess. Older people may be troubled by the extraordinary changes that they see in the world around them and blame the younger generation. They may be angry at the brevity of life and begrudge someone the fresh chance of living out a life span which they have already completed.

Angry and ambivalent feelings flow, too, between the old and the middle-aged, who are caught up in the problems unique to their age and position within the life cycle. The middle-aged bear the heaviest personal and social responsibilities since they are called upon to help support—individually and collectively—both ends of the life cycle: the nurture and education of their young and the financial, emotional, and physical care of the old. Many have not been prepared for their heavy responsibilities and are surprised and overwhelmed by them. Frequently these responsibilities trap them in their careers or life styles until the children grow up or their parents die. A common reaction is anger at both the young and the old. The effects of financial pressures are seen primarily in the middle and lower economic classes. But the middle-aged of all classes are inclined to be ambivalent toward the young and old since both age groups remind them of their own waning youth. In addition—with reason—they fear technological or professional obsolescence as they see what has happened to their elders and feel the pressure of youth pushing its way toward their position in society. Furthermore, their responsibilities are likely to increase in the future as more and more of their parents and grandparents live longer life spans.

CRITICAL-THINKING QUESTIONS

1. Butler presents several "themes" that shape popular views of old age in the United States. What evidence of these do you find in the mass media? What about in your own attitudes and behavior toward elderly people?

2. Why do you think our society has developed views of aging that are not realistic?

3. How do the elderly themselves sometimes reinforce ageism?

NOTES

1. Human beings react in varying ways to brain disease just as they do to other serious threats to their persons. They may become anxious, rigid, depressed, and hypochondriacal. (Hypochondriasis comprises bodily symptoms or fear of diseases that are not due to physical changes but to emotional concerns. They are no less real simply because they do not have a physical origin.) These reactions can be ameliorated by sensitive, humane concern, talk, and understanding even though the underlying physical process cannot be reversed. Therefore, even the irreversible brain syndromes require proper diagnosis and treatment of their emotional consequences.

2. No less a thinker than Aristotle failed to distinguish between the intrinsic features of aging and the reaction of the elderly to their lives. He considered cowardice, resentment, vindictiveness, and what he called "senile avarice" to be intrinsic to late life. Cicero took a warmer and more positive view of old age. He understood, for example, "If old men are morose, troubled, fretful, and hard to please . . . these are faults of character and not of age." So he explained in his essay *"De Senectute."*

42

My Quest for the Fountain of Age

Betty Friedan

Betty Friedan, whose book The Feminine Mystique *was an important source of the feminist movement that emerged in the 1960s, argues here that the elderly are trapped by many of the stereotypes that have blocked the road to greater opportunities for women. Thus, we must reconsider the truth in the widespread "aging mystique"—the notion that growing old amounts to little more than losing youthful beauty and earlier vitality.*

At the start of my quest, I sat at my desk trying to make sense of some strange discrepancies between image and reality in the pile of clippings and studies I had been accumulating about age. On the one hand, despite continued reports of advances in our life expectancy, there was a curious absence—in effect, a blackout—of images of people over sixty-five, especially women, doing, or even selling, anything at all in the mass media. On the other hand, there was an increasing obsession with the "problem" of age and how to avoid it personally, through diet, exercise, chemical formulas, plastic surgery, moisturizing creams, psychological defenses and outright denial—as early and as long as possible. And there seemed to be a growing impatience for some final solution to that problem—before the multiplying numbers of invisible, unproductive, dependent older people, unfortunately living beyond sixty-five, placed an "intolerable burden" on their families and society with their senility, chronic illnesses, Medicare, Meals on Wheels and nursing homes.

SOURCE: "My Quest for the Fountain of Age," by Betty Friedan from *The Fountain of Age* (New York: Simon & Schuster, 1993). Copyright © 1993 by Betty Friedan. Reprinted with permission.

Consider the following, a random selection from my pile:

- In a study of characters appearing in prime-time network television drama monitored for one week in a major city, of 464 role portrayals, only seven (or 1.5 percent) appeared to be over sixty-four years of age. Another study found that only two out of a hundred television commercials contained older characters.
- In an analysis of 265 articles on aging in a large Midwestern newspaper, none depicted older people still active in their communities. All dealt with the "problem" of age, like nursing homes, or had retirees reminiscing about the "good old days."
- In a nationwide survey of American adults conducted for the National Council on Aging to determine popular images of aging, Louis Harris found the great majority of Americans agreed that "most people over sixty-five" were not very "sexually active," not very "open-minded and adaptable," not very "useful members of their communities."

I went through all the major mass-market magazines for August 1986—fashion, general, women's, men's, news—studying every ad or illustration showing identifiable faces. The nonexistence of images that were not "young" was dismaying: the seeming disappearance of people who could be over sixty-five, except for those extremely rich or famous—and they were shown as "young."

Even articles that dealt with people known to be in their sixties were, for the most part, illustrated with pictures of those same people in their youth. The main illustration in a *Vanity Fair* article on Imelda Marcos showed her at forty-five. A *Vogue* article on Jean Harris did not show her white-haired, as she was in prison, or in the dramatic years of her mid-life murder trial, but a brown-haired, younger picture "taken six years before Hy's death." Four out of six illustrations for the article on Rock Hudson's death from AIDS were of the "young" Rock Hudson.

THE MYSTIQUE OF AGE

Staring at these images—and thinking about what they left out—I became aware that I had been on this road before. I remembered when some thirty years ago I had suddenly sensed there was something missing in the image of woman in the women's magazines I was then reading and writing for. That image defined a woman only in sexual relation to a man—as wife, mother, sex object, server of physical needs of husband, children, home. But I had heard women groping to articulate a "problem that had no name," because it didn't have to do with husband, children, home or even sex. And I became aware that the image of women we all accepted left out woman as a person, defining herself by her own actions in society.

I asked myself, then, what it meant, this discrepancy between the reality of our being as women and the image by which we were trying to live our lives. I began to call that image the "Feminine Mystique" and to figure out how it had come about and what it was doing to us. I began to see the "woman problem," as it was called then, in new terms, and to see how that Feminine Mystique masked, even created, the real problems.

So now I asked why there was no image of age with which I could identify the person I am today. What did the image of the "plight" or "problem" of age leave out? What explained the absence of any image of older people leading active and productive lives? The image of age as inevitable decline and deterioration, I realized, was also a mystique of sorts, but one emanating not an aura of desirability but a miasma of dread. I asked myself how this dread of age fitted or distorted reality, making age so terrifying that we have to deny its very existence. And I wondered if that dread, and the denial it breeds, was actually helping to *create* the "problem" of age.

I could already see, from the panic that kept dogging my own search, that the Mystique of Age was much more deadly than the Feminine Mystique, more terrifying to confront, harder to break through. Even as age came closer and closer to me personally, I kept asking myself if denial isn't better, healthier. Did I really want to open this sinister Pandora's box? For there was truly nothing to look forward to—nothing to identify with, nothing I wanted to claim as "us"—in the image of age as decay and deterioration. Was the terrifying Mystique of Age—and the real "plight" of the elderly—somehow created by our obsession with and idealization of youth and the refusal even to look at the reality of age on its own terms?

All forms of denial of age, it seems to me, ultimately spring that dread trap we try to avoid. How long and how well can we really live by trying to pass as young, as all those articles and books seem to advise? By the fourth face-lift (or third?) we begin to look grotesque, no longer human. Obsessed with stopping age, passing as young, we do not seek new functions in the years of life now open to us beyond the sexual, child-rearing, power-seeking female and male roles of our youth.

Seeing age only as decline from youth, we make age itself the problem—and never face the real problems that keep us from evolving and leading continually useful, vital and productive lives.

THE FOUNTAIN OF AGE

Why have gerontologists not looked seriously at abilities and qualities that develop in the later years of life? Why are the political programs for age confined to those proliferating care services that work toward increased dependence and segregation of the elderly, as opposed to the integration of people over sixty-five into roles in society in which they can continue to function as independent persons and make their own choices?

Why the increased emphasis by professional age experts and the media on the nursing home as the locus of age when, in fact, more than 95 percent of those over sixty-five continue to live in the community? Why the preoccupation with senility, Alzheimer's disease, when less than 5 percent of people over sixty-five will suffer it? Why the persistent image of the aged as "sick" and "helpless," as a burden on our hospitals and health-care system, when, in fact, people over sixty-five are less likely than those who are younger to suffer from the acute illnesses that require hospitalization? Why the persistent image of those over sixty-five as sexless when research shows people capable of

sex until ninety, if they are healthy and not shamed out of seeking or otherwise deprived of sex partners? Why don't most people know that current research shows some *positive* changes in certain mental abilities, as well as muscular, sexual and immune processes, that can compensate for age-related declines?

What are we doing to ourselves—and to our society—by denying age? (Peter Pan and Dorian Gray found it hell staying "forever young.") Is there some serious foreclosure of human fulfillment, forfeiture of values, in that definition of age as "problem"? In fact, the more we seek the perpetual fountain of youth and go on denying age, defining age itself as "problem," that "problem" will only get worse. For we will never know what we could be, and we will not organize in our maturity to break through the barriers that keep us from using our evolving gifts in society, or demand the structures we need to nourish them.

I think it is time we start searching for the Fountain of Age, time that we stop denying our growing older and look at the actuality of our experience and that of other women and men who have gone beyond denial to a new place in their sixties, seventies and eighties. It is time to look at age on its own terms and put names on its values and strengths, breaking through the definition of age solely as deterioration or decline from youth.

Only then will we see that the problem is not age itself, to be denied or warded off as long as possible; that the problem is not those increasing numbers of people living beyond sixty-five, to be segregated from the useful, pleasurable activities of society so that the rest of us can keep our illusion of staying forever young. Nor is the basic political problem the burden on society of those forced into deterioration, second childhood, even senility. The problem is, first of all, how to break through the cocoon of our illusory youth and risk a new stage in life, where there are no prescribed roles, no models, no guideposts, no rigid rules or visible rewards—how to step out into the true existential unknown of these years of life now open to us and to find our own terms for living them.

GENERATIVITY

In their "late style," artists and scientists tend to move beyond tumult and discord, distracting details and seemingly irreconcilable differences, and move on to unifying principles that give fresh meaning to what has gone before and presage the agenda for the next generation. Erik Erikson, finding a dearth of meaning in age in our time, conceptualized "generativity" as the promise beyond stagnation. The very lack of rigidly proscribed roles, or forced retirement from those rigidly separate sex roles of our youth and the parenting years, can make possible another kind of wholeness in the third age. But that often is achieved only painfully or can find no expression because the age mystique denies us new possibilities. At this point, it takes real strength and a compelling drive to generativity to break through that mystique and find ways to express such wholeness in society. Some people retreat in bitterness or find what meaning they can in the routines of daily survival and the trivial pursuits prescribed for "senior citizens." But others, in their work or love, express a generativity that, as much as any truly revolutionary artistic creation or scientific discovery, may preview for a future generation new values and directions.

Some examples of this generativity in action:

- Since its inception in 1967, the Senior Concert Orchestra of New York has played almost ninety free concerts to more than 100,000 citizens in high schools and colleges, as well as a free concert in Carnegie Hall attended by many who may never have been to a concert before. Begun by the Senior Musicians Association under the auspices of Local 802, American Federation of Musicians, the orchestra includes retirees of the New York Philharmonic, the Metropolitan Opera, and the NBC Symphony Orchestra under Toscanini; it seeks the funding it needs to do its work as "a viable symbol for benign aging and productivity."
- The Seasoned Citizens Theater Company plays at senior centers, nursing homes and hospitals. Helen Mayer, the founder-director, has to seek voluntary contributions, since senior centers and hospitals can't afford to pay more than $150 for performances that cost $500 to mount. The motto at the bottom of the company's letterhead says, "We do not stop playing

because we grow old . . . We grow old because we stop playing."
- At St. Mark's Episcopal Church on Capitol Hill, my old college friend Mary Jackson Craighill, in her early seventies, leads the Senior Dance Company, a group of dancers who have been working together for many years, in "religious dance alongside secular dance." They perform in Washington and Virginia public schools, hold workshops for teachers and students, and in recent years have held dance series, followed by conversations with the audience, at veterans' hospitals, soldiers' and airmen's homes, and many nursing and retirement homes.
- In New York, the Retired Faculty Community Linkage Project was conceived in the mid-1980s to match the expertise of retired Columbia University faculty members with the needs of institutions and organizations in the community. Linkage projects ranged from Nobel laureate physicist Isidor Rabi's lectures before New York City public school students to a community festival of photography, film and discussion, called "Creativity in the '80s," organized at Columbia for the surrounding Harlem community by a retired architect, composer and professor of religion. The concept, pioneered by the Brookdale Institute on Aging and Adult Human Development, is being adopted at other universities.

Generativity is expressed in more mundane terms whenever older people's talents are truly used as a community resource, or where they are allowed or encouraged to use their wisdom in work with younger people. In Fort Ord, California, "foster grandparents" went into Army homes where there were problems of child abuse, as the mainstay of the Army Community Service child-abuse program. They were valued by the Army agency because they went in as "respected, nonthreatening presences and helped the mothers learn to care for their children without violence."

At seventy-four, George Kreidler, a former linebacker for the Green Bay Packers who retired at sixty-five after thirty-one years supervising the construction of oil refineries and nuclear power plants for Bechtel Corp., was overseeing house construction for Habitat for Humanity. Retiring to Asheville, North Carolina, he was described as part of "a new breed of active, independent retirees, for whom a need to help society at large is as important as personal enrichment." Through the North

Carolina Center for Creative Retirement, he also served as the mentor to a young college athlete, not to win more games but for his "academic performance and future direction." Others tutored grade and high school students. Asked his qualifications for tutoring grade school students, a retired locomotive engineer wrote, "I have my act together."

THE PERSONAL IS AGAIN POLITICAL

In the early years of the women's movement, after we broke through the Feminine Mystique and began to take ourselves seriously, we recognized possibilities in ourselves that we hadn't dared put a name to until we heard about them from each other. The personal is political, we said, as we began moving to break through the barriers that had kept us isolated from society. We had no real role models then, because our mothers and the women who went before us hadn't faced the new road now open to us. We had to be role models for each other.

The same holds true now, I believe, for women and men facing this unprecedented and uncharted territory of age. We have to tell each other the way it really is, growing older, and help each other name the possibilities we hardly recognize or dare put a name to when we sense them in ourselves. I think we need new kinds of consciousness raising, to make that evolutionary leap into new age, to help each other move on uncharted paths.

How do we help each other finally affirm the integrity of full personhood at last—that radiant inner self that seems to carry the mystery and meaning of our life—and break through the barriers that keep us from really using what we dimly recognize as our own unique late style? How do we find ways to use the wisdom we have derived from the painful, joyful experience of our lives as we have lived them in society, so that we may live out our generativity?

Part of the answer to these questions has to be uniquely personal; and yet it may be very hard to find, in isolation, against the total blankness of the uncharted age, that expectation only of decline, and the age ostracism—the graylash.

No one has seen the generativity of age for what I believe it is or could be: a stage of evolution in our own lives, one that could be key to the evolution and survival of our aging society. And since the personal is political, I think part of the answer has to be a political movement that will effect the changes necessary for society to use productively the wisdom and generativity of age.

Acceptance, however, must first come from ourselves. How do we create new roles for older people in society? That will take a lot of us saying no to the age mystique and demanding a continuation of our human birthright—to move in the new years of life as full persons in society, using our unique human capabilities as they have evolved through years of work and love and our capacities for wisdom, helping society transcend decline and move in new life-affirming directions. That, in turn, given the way our society is, will require new social structures and political policies.

One thing is certain. We cannot even begin to help create the new patterns that are needed if we are barred in age from participating in the institutions that carry society forward. It is only now, as women are reaching critical mass in every field and institution, that we can even glimpse the possibilities of style and structure, policy and practice, that were hidden when the very rubrics were defined solely in terms of male experience. The "different voice" of women is only now beginning to be heard in new political and economic, psychological and theological terms, transforming the male model in medicine and law, university and business, and every church and academic discipline. And it is only now that the empowerment of women can be seen in its evolutionary significance—as solution, not just problem, in the crises of family and church, economy and government, threatening the very fabric of our society.

THE EMPOWERMENT OF AGE

For these same reasons, we must seek the empowerment of age, new roles for people over sixty, seventy, eighty that use their wisdom to help solve the problems of our aging society. But I do not think we can seek the empowerment of age on the same terms as the women's movement, or the black civil rights movement, or the labor movement. There is a danger in seeing age as a special-interest group, even though it has already become clear how much power it might mobilize.

I have been enormously impressed by the possibilities of the American Association of Retired Persons on the issues it does address, and its power to market to and inform that huge population of older Americans, to help bring about the paradigm shift necessary to break through the age mystique. But I am not sure that any model for age as a special-interest group comprises the needed political shift: a new movement that will use the wisdom and resources of older women and men, who by the year 2000 will be the dominant population group of our aging society, not so much for protection of their own Social Security and health care but to set new priorities and measures of success in business and the national budget, new integration of all members of all families to grow and to care for each other.

The movement that flows from the Fountain of Age cannot be a special-interest group. It would be a violation of our own wisdom and generativity to empower ourselves in age only for our own security and care. It would be a denial of the true power of age. Even now, many supposed retirement enclaves are evolving into subversive pools of new activism, combining play and learning with work, to face each other's and the whole community's needs for care. And companies on the cutting edge are meeting their own new problems by calling us back to work out of retirement or giving us new options that will use our abilities beyond retirement in tandem with the young.

The flexibility, autonomy and meaning that we now demand of work, the responsibility that we insist on sharing, are what industry and professions now urgently need for their own survival. Such flexibility and shared responsibility and shorter working hours are also urgently needed now by the new families—two paycheck or single parent or three generational.

A REAL CONTRIBUTION

This new conception of human age has to have some function in the survival of the whole community, stretching into the future. In evolutionary terms, the function of age must go beyond reproduction to contribute in some other way to the survival of our species. Our legacy has to be more than those memories of meaning we write down for our grandchildren. It is only by continuing to work on the various problems confronting our society right now with whatever wisdom and generativity we have attained over our own lifetime that we leave a legacy to our grandchildren, helping enrich and shape that future, expressing and conserving the generativity of the whole human community.

And through our actions, we will create a new image of age—free and joyous, living with pain, saying what we really think and feel at last—knowing who we are, realizing that we know more than we ever knew we knew, not afraid of what anyone thinks of us anymore, moving with wonder into that unknown future we have helped shape for the generations coming after us. There will not have to be such dread and denial for them in living their age if we use our own age in new adventures, breaking the old rules and inhibitions, changing the patterns and possibilities of love and work, learning and play, worship and creation, discovery and political responsibility, and resolving the seeming irreconcilable conflicts between us.

I began this quest with my own denial and fear of age. It ends with acceptance, affirmation and celebration. Somewhere along the way, I recognized, with relief and excitement, my liberation from the power politics of the women's movement. I recognized my own compelling need to transcend the war between the sexes, the no-win battles of women as a whole sex, oppressed victims, against men as a whole sex, the oppressors. I recognized that my need to reconcile feminism and families comes from my own generativity, my personal truth as mother to my children, and my commitment to the future through the women's movement.

The unexpectedness of this new quest has been

my adventure into age. I realized that all the experiences I have had—as daughter, student, youthful radical, reporter, battler for women's rights, wife, mother, grandmother, teacher, leader, friend and lover, confronting real or phantom enemies and dangers, the terrors of divorce and my own denial of age, and even a kind of ostracism from some of the organizations I helped start—all of it, mistakes, triumphs, battles lost and won, and moments of despair and exaltation, are part of me now: I am myself at this age. It took me all these years to put the missing pieces together, to confront my own age

in terms of integrity and generativity, moving into the unknown future with a comfort now, instead of being stuck in the past. I have never felt so free.

CRITICAL-THINKING QUESTIONS

1. What does Friedan argue is missing in our society's images of the elderly?

2. How does our image of growing old actually create the "problem" of old age?

3. What are the alternatives to seeing aging simply as the decline of youth?

43

The Aged As Teachers

Donald O. Cowgill

In contrast to Western countries, there are many societies in which the aged are revered as historians and educators. This is true primarily of preindustrial societies, in which traditions are strong and social change is slow. Thus wisdom accumulated over a lifetime sets old people apart as elders—*people worthy of the highest honor and respect.*

Almost forty years ago, Simmons (1945: 40) asserted: "Few generalizations concerning the aged in primitive societies can be made with greater confidence than that they have almost universally been regarded as the custodians of knowledge *par excellence* and the chief instructors of the people." Maxwell and Silverman (1970) hypothesized that control of useful knowledge is a primary basis of the high esteem in which older people are held in such societies. Later, Watson and Maxwell (1977) confirmed this hypothesis after correlating an information control scale with a scale for esteem of elderly in twenty-six societies. This implies that control of useful information partially explains the high esteem of the elderly in primitive societies, but, conversely, the loss of such control in modern societies helps explain the decline in the status of the elderly in these societies.

Among the Aleuts in the late nineteenth century, every village reportedly had one or two men whose special function was to educate the children (Elliot 1886). In many societies this becomes the particular prerogative of grandparents. Thus it

SOURCE: *Aging Around the World* by Donald O. Cowgill (Belmont, CA: Wadsworth, 1986), pp. 168–74. Copyright © 1986 by Wadsworth, Inc. Reprinted with permission.

is the grandparents, not the parents, who represent the chief transgenerational conveyors of a society's culture (Tomashevich 1981: 21). So it is among the !Kung Bushmen, where the grandparents care for small children while their mothers are away on their gathering forays (Biesele and Howell 1981: 89). The elder generation spends much of its time in teaching the grandchildren the skills, traditions, and values of the society. In fact the Baganda define a good grandparent as "one who teaches, loves and cares for his or her grandchildren" (Nahemow 1983: 112). Though grandparents of both sexes are included in this definition, it seems to apply with special force to the grandmother. This is true also in Dahomean society, where older people spend much of their time educating their grandchildren, using storytelling as the chief medium (Tomashevich 1981: 28). But this is neither a matter of convenience nor of blood relationship; it is very much a matter of age and experience. Age and wisdom are so closely identified that it is not unusual for an African, regardless of blood relationship, to refer to a person noted for his or her wisdom as "grandfather" or "grandmother" (Fuller 1972: 58).

It is natural that such wise persons should be advisors as well as teachers. Among the Igbo of Nigeria, the elders not only transmit information, they are also recognized as the moral agents of youth (Boyd 1973: 37). Elders are revered as advisors among the Kogi of Colombia (Reichal-Dolmatoff 1951) and the Haida of British Columbia (Tomashevich 1981: 29). Older women admonish the young, and the male elders serve as advisors and interpreters of tradition to all ages among the Hutterites (Boyd 1973: 39). Older men are often sought out for advice by younger Thai villagers (Blanchard 1957: 405).

The content of the elders' teaching is as wide as the term *culture*. Certainly it includes the history, mythology, and folklore of the society itself. Among the Incas, certain elders were assigned the task of remembering the important events of their history and recording by means of knots and threads all of the laws, the succession of kings, and the time

in which each ruled (Simmons 1945: 136). As an aid to memory, songs were composed in which historical events were recounted. These then could be memorized and handed down from generation to generation. Otherwise, among a nonliterate people, the history is bounded, as Bleck said of the Bushmen, by the memory of the oldest person (Simmons 1945: 139). When their hair turns gray, Kapauku Papuans stop working in the fields and spend much of their time educating their grandchildren in the history and folklore of their society (Pospisil 1963). The elders are considered repositories of tradition in Swaziland and among the Semai of Malaya (Boyd 1973: 39). Pritchard gave an account of elderly Samoans assembling in an evening to rehearse the deeds of their ancestors or relate the legends of their gods (Simmons 1945: 137).

Creation stories are usually among the legends. Such a story was related by the elderly teachers, along with historical events and tales about the old style of life, in a Mexican village (Adams 1972: 111). Another feature of lore that is preserved and transmitted by the elderly is the genealogy of the lineage. This has been noted among the Gwambe (Fuller 1972: 59), the Tiwi (Boyd 1973: 39), the Toda (Simmons 1945: 137), the Samoans (Holmes 1972: 81), and certainly it is a prevalent preoccupation of the elderly among the Chinese.

Another area in which the knowledge of older people is extensive and relevant is the physical environment within which the people live. Fuller notes (1972: 59) that among the Zulu, information supplied by him about the natural environment was distrusted because he "was not old enough to know." The only credible information came from their own elderly. The elderly of the Maori are a veritable storehouse of nature lore. The names of all living things are known (some 280 plant names, 100 birds, and 60 insects), and this represents only a fragment of the information stored in the memories of elderly Maori people (Simmons 1945: 138). The older men among the Aranda of Australia teach the young the tracks of various animals and the location of the best sources of food (Tomashevich 1981: 30). Most elderly Kirghiz men are steeped in local history and ecology, and some are noted for their veterinary skills (Shahrani 1981: 189).

Perhaps even more notable among the teaching skills of the elderly are those in the realm of arts and crafts. These range broadly through music, art, pottery, weaving, tanning, dance, flower arranging, and calligraphy. Among the Omaha Indians, only the older men knew the old songs perfectly and could teach them to the oncoming generations (Simmons 1945: 133). The Hopis are noted for their crafts, and the aged among them are the best technicians, the older women in pottery and basketry and the older men in weaving and tanning. In Japan the folk arts in which older people excel and which they in turn teach to the young include calligraphy, flower arranging, the tea ceremony, *bonsai* horticulture, and several stylized forms of poetry (Maeda 1978: 66–67). Among the Bantus of southern Africa, an elderly male or female usually initiated a dance, performing the first steps, and an elder began the first drumming (Fuller 1972: 63). The treasured knowledge of the elders of the Coast Salish included methods of construction and canoe making (Amoss 1981: 227). On the island of Truk, the art of traditional massage is a monopoly of the elderly, who only reluctantly pass it on to the younger generations (Borthwick 1977: 201). In instances where social change involves change of language, it is the elderly who retain the old language and, to the extent that it is taught at all, teach it to the young. In the old lacquer village of Ban Khern in northern Thailand in 1965, most of the older people still spoke Khern (from the Shan states of Burma), but less than 20 percent of the children understood the language. In modern China older people are the most frequent participants in the daily early morning meditation/exercise known as Tai Chi (Haber 1979: 7), and some of them proudly display their certificates as teachers of the art.

A favorite medium through which the elderly carry out their educator role is storytelling. Some develop this to a high art, and the education is at the same time amusement and entertainment. Such was the case with the old men of the Asmat tribe. Be-

ginning at about the age of eight, boys would gather at the fireplace of their grandfather to listen to the adventures of fictional characters, the Asmat equivalent of the American "Dick and Jane," or of animals such as a dog, or a bird such as a cockatoo. In the course of such stories, the children would learn much about their jungle environment and the natural resources of the area (Van Arsdale 1981: 116–17). The young defer to the elderly among the !Kung Bushmen, and the elderly take great delight in telling and retelling stories of their own exploits or those of mythical beings (Biesele and Howell 1981: 88–89). Oratory is a prized art form in Samoa, and the young orator chiefs often gather in the evening to listen to their elders as they discuss myths, legends, customs, family history, and genealogy. The aged are considered storehouses of information, and this is the customary method of imparting it (Holmes and Rhoads 1983: 123). Incidentally, the Samoans employ another interesting art form, the chanting of legends (Simmons 1945: 97). This is akin to the songs and song contests that will be discussed later. Turnbull (1965: 120) tells of the involvement of the aged Mbuti pygmies in storytelling, recitation of myths and legends, and even imitation of the behavior of various animals, all for the edification and entertainment of the children.

I observed an interesting variation in the use of older people for oral history in China in 1978. Here the elderly were encouraged to tell about their lives before the Revolution of 1949. The intent was the opposite of most oral history; instead of glorifying the past, the purpose was to portray the horrible conditions that obtained in China before the revolution and in the process to justify it and attest to the progress since then. Haber (1979: 7) observed the same phenomenon and was told that the elderly often visit schools to tell their "bitterness stories." In performing this role, the elderly are presented as heroes in Chinese society (Missine 1982: 7).

Borthwick (1977: 194) observed singing contests between villages on the island of Truk. These were not especially for older people, but some older people participated. Months of rehearsal preceded the actual contests. Rivalry was also involved in the posing of riddles by elders among the Bantu (Fuller 1972: 63). In addition, they vied with each other in telling myths and legends.

What do older people get in return for these activities? Often the returns are very tangible and very practical. In fact the simplest answer to the question is: They get a living. In some societies this is supplied in a quid pro quo exchange; that is, in return for a given bit of valued information, the elder may receive definite remuneration. Aged men among the Navaho charged high prices for information about cures, sacred names, legends, secrets, and songs (Simmons 1945: 135). They were paid in sheep, cattle, or horses. Elders in the secret societies of the Akamba actually held a monopoly over certain information and charged dearly for sharing it. When a person needed knowledge about a certain custom, he or she had to go to an elder for it and pay with a goat or, if he or she was rich, a bull (Simmons 1945: 139). Such a monopoly was planned and husbanded. The elders would resist sharing all of their treasured knowledge until very late in life. Aged Dieri systematically kept certain knowledge from the young in order to increase their power over them (Simmons 1945: 138).

In other instances the exchange was less explicit and less crassly economic. Marshall (1976) reports that among the !Kung Bushmen, a hunter is expected to share any kill with his parents and with his wife's parents. Such sharing is not conceived of as payment to those elders for their roles as educators, but in a general sense that is the nature of the bargain.

But apart from the economic rewards, which may be specific and explicit or quite general and implicit, there are other rewards. When the information imparted is valued, its possessors and teachers will also be valued, and this implies some other intangible dividends in the form of prestige, honor, respect, and a sense of importance to the community. The feeling of being a significant member of the society and having a secure and accepted role in it is certainly a part of the role of the aged in the preindustrial societies that have constituted the bulk of our examples in this chapter. It

is a role that tends to be eroded in the process of modernization.

We can see the beginnings of this erosion in many places around the world and its veritable completion in many modernized countries. The current fad of preservation and revival of traditional ethnic cultures is symptomatic of the process. There is a temporary nostalgic satisfaction in recalling the old days and the way things were, and the recording of these recollections supplies the occasion for a curtain call for some elderly people. They may enjoy a brief round of applause before the old theater finally closes. The former life of the Coast Salish can never return. Some of the current cohort of elderly may remember and tell us about it; we may even revive parts of it in pageantry, but it is all playacting. The reality is gone, and shortly those living memories will be replaced by books, films, and tapes stored away in our modern libraries. Even the oldest of the Oklahoma Indians can no longer recall earlier forms of ceremonial behavior, past lifestyles, or the movements and exploits of a hunting and gathering existence (Williams 1980:109). Indeed the current demand for revival produces some stress among their elderly because they are being pressed to recall and reproduce events they never actually experienced.

The fact of the matter is that rapid social change, such as the contemporary process of modernization, renders older people obsolete. Their classic role as conservators and transmitters of vital information is destroyed. Much that they know is no longer pertinent, and much that they don't know is essential. Watson and Maxwell (1977: 55) note that in Samoa the elderly are becoming less and less useful as sources of information, and Adams (1972: 119) notes the "increasing irrelevancy" of the knowledge of elderly Mexicans. In fully modernized societies the aged are reduced to "a roleless role." They have not only lost their economic function and some political influence, their roles as religious and educational leaders have also been eroded.

However, modernization not only renders useless much of the knowledge possessed by older people, the new forms of education and the values that accompany them also expose the deception that the elderly have sometimes used to bolster their privileged positions. Finley (1981) notes that in Guatemala modern education has undercut the traditional "cargo" system through which men worked themselves up to positions of power and status, resulting in extremely powerful roles in old age. Modernized people no longer share the mystical beliefs that supported such a system.

CRITICAL-THINKING QUESTIONS

1. Describe the roles and functions of the aged in preserving and transmitting culture.
2. How are the aged rewarded for their teaching activities?
3. How is social change (i.e., modernization) destroying the traditional role of the elderly?

REFERENCES

ADAMS, F. 1972. The role of old people in Santo Tomás Mazaltepec. In *Aging and modernization* (pp. 103–26), ed. D. O. Cowgill and L. D. Holmes. New York: Appleton-Century-Crofts.

AMOSS, P. T. 1981. Coast Salish elders. In *Other ways of growing old* (pp. 227–47), ed. P. T. Amoss and S. Harrell. Stanford, CA: Stanford University Press.

BIESELE, M., and N. HOWELL. 1981. The old people give you life: Aging among !Kung hunter gatherers. In *Other ways of growing old: Anthropological perspectives* (pp. 77–98), ed. P. T. Amoss and S. Harrell. Stanford, CA: Stanford University Press.

BLANCHARD, W. 1957. *Thailand: Its people, its society, its culture.* New Haven, CT: Human Relations Area Files.

BORTHWICK, M. 1977. *Traditional and bureaucratic forms of old age assistance in the Truk District, U.S. Trust Territory of the Pacific Islands.* Report to the U.S. Social Security Administration.

BOYD, R. R. 1973. Preliterate prologues to modern aging roles. In *Foundations of practical gerontology* (2d ed., rev., pp. 35–46), ed. R. R. Boyd and C. G. Oakes. Columbia: University of South Carolina Press.

ELLIOTT, H. W. 1886. *Our Arctic province: Alaska and the Seal Islands.* New York: Scribner's.

FINLEY, G. E. 1981. Aging in Latin America. *Spanish-lang. Psych.,* 1:223-48.

FULLER, C. E. 1972. Aging among Southern African Bantu. In *Aging and modernization* (pp. 51–72), ed. D. O. Cowgill and L. D. Holmes. New York: Appleton-Century-Crofts.

HABER, D. 1979, NOV.–DEC. Impressions of old age in China. *Aging,* nos. 301–2:7–9.

HOLMES, L. D. 1972. The role and status of the aged in changing Samoa. In *Aging and modernization* (pp. 73–89), ed. D. O. Cowgill and L. D. Holmes. New York: Appleton-Century-Crofts.

HOLMES, L. D., and E. C. RHOADS. 1983. Aging and change in modern Samoa. In *Growing old in different cultures* (pp. 119–29), ed. J. Sokolovsky, Belmont, CA: Wadsworth.

MAEDA, D. 1978. Ageing in Eastern society. In *The social challenge of ageing* (pp. 45–72), ed. D. Hobman. New York: St. Martin's Press.

MARSHALL, L. 1976. Sharing, talking and giving. In *Kalahari hunter gatherers: Studies of !Kung San and their neighbors* (pp. 349–71), ed. R. B. Lee and I. DeVore. Cambridge: Harvard University Press.

MAXWELL, R. J., and P. SILVERMAN. 1970. Information and esteem: Cultural considerations in the treatment of the elderly. *Aging and Human Dev.,* 1:361–92.

MISSINE, L. E. 1982, Nov.–Dec. Elders are educators. *Perspective on Aging,* 11(6):5–8.

NAHEMOW, N. 1983. Grandparenthood in Baganda: Role option in old age? In *Growing old in different societies: Cross-cultural perspectives* (pp. 104–15), ed. J. Sokolovsky. Belmont, CA: Wadsworth.

POSPISIL, L. 1963. *Kapauku Papuan economy.* New Haven, CT: Yale University Publications in Anthropology.

REICHAL-DOLMATOFF, G. 1951. *Los Kogi: Una tribu de la Sierra Nevada de Santa Marta, Colombia.* Bogota: Editorial Iquelma.

SHAHRANI, M. N. 1981. Growing in respect: Aging among the Kirghiz of Afghanistan. In *Other ways of growing old: Anthropological perspectives* (pp. 175–92), ed. P. Amoss and S. Harrell. Stanford, CA: Stanford University Press.

SIMMONS, L. 1945. *The role of the aged in primitive society.* London: Oxford University Press.

TOMASHEVICH, G. V. 1981. Aging and the aged in various cultures. In *Aging in America and other cultures* (pp. 17–41), ed. G. Falk, U. Falk, and G. V. Tomashevich. Saratoga, CA: Century Twenty One Publishing.

TURNBULL, C. M. 1965. *Wayward servants*. Garden City, NY: Natural History Press.

VAN ARSDALE, P. W. 1981. The elderly Asmat of New Guinea. In *Other ways of growing old: Anthropological perspectives* (pp. 111–23), ed. P. T. Amoss and S. Harrell. Stanford, CA: Stanford University Press.

WATSON, W. H., and R. J. MAXWELL, EDS. 1977. *Human aging and dying: A study in sociocultural gerontology*. New York: St. Martin's Press.

WILLIAMS, G. C. 1980. Warriors no more: A study of the American Indian elderly. In *Aging in culture and society* (pp. 101–11), ed. C. L. Fry. Brooklyn, NY: J. F. Bergin.

44

Alienated Labor

Karl Marx

The human species, argues Karl Marx, is social by nature and expresses that social nature in the act of production. But within the capitalist economic system, Marx claims, the process of production does not affirm human nature but denies it. The result is what he terms "alienated labor."

. . . [We] have shown that the worker sinks to the level of a commodity, and to a most miserable commodity; that the misery of the worker increases with the power and volume of his production; that the necessary result of competition is the accumulation of capital in a few hands, and thus a restoration of monopoly in a more terrible form; and finally that the distinction between capitalist and landlord, and between agricultural laborer and industrial worker, must disappear, and the whole of society divide into the two classes of property *owners* and *propertyless* workers. . . .

Thus we have now to grasp the real connexion between this whole system of alienation—private property, acquisitiveness, the separation of labor, capital and land, exchange and competition, value and the devaluation of man, monopoly and competition—and the system of *money*. . . .

We shall begin from a *contemporary* economic fact. The worker becomes poorer the more wealth he produces and the more his production increases in power and extent. The worker becomes an ever cheaper commodity the more goods he creates. The *devaluation* of the human world increases in direct relation with the *increase in value* of the

SOURCE: "Alienated Labor" by Karl Marx in *Karl Marx: Early Writings,* trans. and ed. T. B. Bottomore (New York: McGraw-Hill, 1963), pp. 120–27. Reprinted by permission of McGraw-Hill.

world of things. Labor does not only create goods; it also produces itself and the worker as a *commodity*, and indeed in the same proportion as it produces goods.

This fact simply implies that the object produced by labor, its product, now stands opposed to it as an *alien being,* as a *power independent* of the producer. The product of labor is labor which has been embodied in an object and turned into a physical thing; this product is an *objectification* of labor. The performance of work is at the same time its objectification. The performance of work appears in the sphere of political economy as a *vitiation*[1] of the worker, objectification as a *loss* and as *servitude to the object,* and appropriation as *alienation.*

So much does the performance of work appear as vitiation that the worker is vitiated to the point of starvation. So much does objectification appear as loss of the object that the worker is deprived of the most essential things not only of life but also of work. Labor itself becomes an object which he can acquire only by the greatest effort and with unpredictable interruptions. So much does the appropriation of the object appear as alienation that the more objects the worker produces the fewer he can possess and the more he falls under the domination of his product, of capital.

All these consequences follow from the fact that the worker is related to the *product of his labor* as to an *alien* object. For it is clear on this presupposition that the more the worker expends himself in work the more powerful becomes the world of objects which he creates in face of himself, the poorer he becomes in his inner life, and the less he belongs to himself. It is just the same as in religion. The more of himself man attributes to God the less he has left in himself. The worker puts his life into the object, and his life then belongs no longer to himself but to the object. The greater his activity, therefore, the less he possesses. What is embodied in the product of his labor is no longer his own. The greater this product is, therefore, the more he is diminished. The *alienation* of the worker in his product means not only that his labor becomes an object, assumes an *external* existence, but that it exists independently, *outside himself,* and alien to him, and that it stands opposed to him as an autonomous power. The life which he has given to the object sets itself against him as an alien and hostile force.

Let us now examine more closely the phenomenon of *objectification;* the worker's production and the *alienation* and *loss* of the object it produces, which is involved in it. The worker can create nothing without *nature,* without the *sensuous external world.* The latter is the material in which his labor is realized, in which it is active, out of which and through which it produces things.

But just as nature affords the *means of existence* of labor, in the sense that labor cannot *live* without objects upon which it can be exercised, so also it provides the *means of existence* in a narrower sense; namely the means of physical existence for the *worker* himself. Thus, the more the worker *appropriates* the external world of sensuous nature by his labor the more he deprives himself of *means of existence,* in two respects: First, that the sensuous external world becomes progressively less an object belonging to his labor or a means of existence of his labor, and secondly, that it becomes progressively less a means of existence in the direct sense, a means for the physical subsistence of the worker.

In both respects, therefore, the worker becomes a slave of the object; first, in that he receives an *object of work,* i.e. receives *work,* and secondly, in that he receives *means of subsistence.* Thus the object enables him to exist, first as a *worker* and secondly, as a *physical subject.* The culmination of this enslavement is that he can only maintain himself as a *physical subject* so far as he is a *worker,* and that it is only as a *physical subject* that he is a worker.

(The alienation of the worker in his object is expressed as follows in the laws of political economy: The more the worker produces the less he has to consume; the more value he creates the more worthless he becomes; the more refined his product the more crude and misshapen the worker; the more civilized the product the more barbarous the worker; the more powerful the work the more feeble the worker; the more the work manifests intelligence the more the worker declines in intelligence and becomes a slave of nature.)

Political economy conceals the alienation in the nature of labor insofar as it does not examine the direct relationship between the worker (work) and production. Labor certainly produces marvels for the rich but it produces privation for the worker. It produces palaces, but hovels for the worker. It produces beauty, but deformity for the worker. It replaces labor by machinery, but it casts some of the workers back into a barbarous kind of work and turns the others into machines. It produces intelligence, but also stupidity and cretinism for the workers.

The direct relationship of labor to its products is the relationship of the worker to the objects of his production. The relationship of property owners to the objects of production and to production itself is merely a *consequence* of this first relationship and confirms it. We shall consider this second aspect later.

Thus, when we ask what is the important relationship of labor, we are concerned with the relationship of the *worker* to production.

So far we have considered the alienation of the worker only from one aspect; namely, *his relationship with the products of his labor.* However, alienation appears not merely in the result but also in the *process of production,* within *productive activity* itself. How could the worker stand in an alien relationship to the product of his activity if he did not alienate himself in the act of production itself? The product is indeed only the *résumé* of activity, of production. Consequently, if the product of labor is alienation, production itself must be active alienation—the alienation of activity and the activity of alienation. The alienation of the object of labor merely summarizes the alienation in the work activity itself.

What constitutes the alienation of labor? First, that the work is *external* to the worker, that it is not part of his nature; and that, consequently, he does not fulfil himself in his work but denies himself, has a feeling of misery rather than well-being, does not develop freely his mental and physical energies but is physically exhausted and mentally debased. The worker, therefore, feels himself at home only during his leisure time, whereas at work he feels homeless. His work is not voluntary but imposed, *forced labor.* It is not the satisfaction of a need, but only a *means* for satisfying other needs. Its alien character is clearly shown by the fact that as soon as there is no physical or other compulsion it is avoided like the plague. External labor, labor in which man alienates himself, is a labor of self-sacrifice, of mortification. Finally, the external character of work for the worker is shown by the fact that it is not his own work but work for someone else, that in work he does not belong to himself but to another person. . . .

We arrive at the result that man (the worker) feels himself to be freely active only in his animal functions—eating, drinking and procreating, or at most also in his dwelling and in personal adornment—while in his human functions he is reduced to an animal. The animal becomes human and the human becomes animal.

Eating, drinking, and procreating are of course also genuine human functions. But abstractly considered, apart from the environment of human activities, and turned into final and sole ends, they are animal functions.

We have now considered the act of alienation of practical human activity, labor, from two aspects: (1) the relationship of the worker to the *product of labor* as an alien object which dominates him. This relationship is at the same time the relationship to the sensuous external world, to natural objects, as an alien and hostile world; (2) the relationship of labor to the *act of production* within *labor.* This is the relationship of the worker to his own activity as something alien and not belonging to him, activity as suffering (passivity), strength as powerlessness, creation as emasculation, the *personal* physical and mental energy of the worker, his personal life (for what is life but activity?), as an activity which is directed against himself, independent of him and not belonging to him. This is *self-alienation* as against the [afore]mentioned alienation of the *thing.*

We have now to infer a third characteristic of *alienated labor* from the two we have considered.

Man is a species-being not only in the sense that he makes the community (his own as well as those of other things) his object both practically and theoretically, but also (and this is simply another expression for the same thing) in the sense that he treats himself as the present, living species, as a *universal* and consequently free being.

Species-life, for man as for animals, has its physical basis in the fact that man (like animals) lives from inorganic nature, and since man is more universal than an animal so the range of inorganic nature from which he lives is more universal. Plants, animals, minerals, air, light, etc. constitute, from the theoretical aspect, a part of human consciousness as objects of natural science and art; they are man's spiritual inorganic nature, his intellectual means of life, which he must first prepare for enjoyment and perpetuation. So also, from the practical aspect, they form a part of human life and activity. In practice man lives only from these natural products, whether in the form of food, heating, clothing, housing, etc. The universality of man appears in practice in the universality which makes the whole of nature into his inorganic body: (1) as a direct means of life; and equally (2) as the material object and instrument of his life activity. Nature is the inorganic body of man; that is to say nature, excluding the human body itself. To say that man *lives* from nature means that nature is his *body* with which he must remain in a continuous interchange in order not to die. The statement that the physical and mental life of man, and nature, are interdependent means simply that nature is interdependent with itself, for man is a part of nature.

Since alienated labor (1) alienates nature from man; and (2) alienates man from himself, from his own active function, his life activity; so it alienates him from the species. It makes *species-life* into a means of individual life. In the first place it alienates species-life and individual life, and secondly, it turns the latter, as an abstraction, into the purpose of the former, also in its abstract and alienated form.

For labor, *life activity, productive life*, now appear to man only as *means* for the satisfaction of a need, the need to maintain his physical existence. Productive life is, however, species-life. It is life creating life. In the type of life activity resides the whole character of a species, its species-character; and free, conscious activity is the species-character of human beings. Life itself appears only as a *means of life*.

The animal is one with its life activity. It does not distinguish the activity from itself. It is *its activity*. But man makes his life activity itself an object of his will and consciousness. He has a conscious life activity. It is not a determination with which he is completely identified. Conscious life activity distinguishes man from the life activity of animals. Only for this reason is he a species-being. Or rather, he is only a self-conscious being, i.e., his own life is an object for him, because he is a species-being. Only for this reason is his activity free activity. Alienated labor reverses the relationship, in that man because he is a self-conscious being makes his life activity, his *being,* only a means for his *existence.*

CRITICAL-THINKING QUESTIONS

1. Does Marx argue that work is inevitably alienating? Why does work within a capitalist economy produce alienation?

2. In what different respects does labor within capitalism alienate the worker?

3. Based on this analysis, under what conditions do you think Marx would argue that labor is not alienating?

NOTE

1. Debasement.

THE ECONOMY AND WORK

Contemporary

45

The Corporate Closet

James D. Woods with Jay H. Lucas

In a predominantly heterosexual society, many gay men and lesbians have not "come out of the closet" because they fear social and economic reprisals. Using in-depth interviews with seventy men, James Woods describes strategies devised by professional gay men for managing their sexual identity at work. One such strategy is social withdrawal.

When a gay man is unwilling to remain in the closet but mindful of the dangers that lie outside its protective walls, he may try to find middle ground. Between the extremes of deception and disclosure, between counterfeiting and coming out, he seeks an alternative. He wants a way of protecting himself that doesn't require an elaborate, tiresome fiction. More than anything, he wants to avoid the issue altogether.

Unfortunately, avoidance tactics can rob a gay man of social contact. His dodges and evasions can

SOURCE: *The Corporate Closet: The Professional Lives of Gay Men in America* by James D. Woods (Jay Lucas, Research Associate). Copyright © 1993 by James D. Woods. Reprinted with permission of The Free Press, an imprint of Simon & Schuster.

leave him feeling isolated and detached, denied even the distorted social feedback that would be possible if he were willing to don a heterosexual mask. Men who counterfeit a sexual identity often complain that their social lives do not reflect their psychic realities, that they are treated as if they were "someone else." Avoidance tactics, on the other hand, can rob them of *all* contact.

When asked to describe the biggest disadvantage of refusing to talk about sexuality at work, gay men say that it severely limits their social involvement with peers. "I have to exclude certain people from my life," says Terry. "I might be more social. I would encourage people to have drinks with me, except that I don't want to get too close to them. You miss out on some things." Miguel voices a similar frustration. "There are so many people in the hospital who are really, really nice," he says. "And I'm sure if I didn't have this concern about being gay, I would have excellent relationships with them. So that's something that's getting lost."

In particular, these men are often deprived of the sense that others understand or appreciate their lives. Milton, a Washington attorney known for his pro bono efforts on behalf of African Americans and people with AIDS, finds that this is the most distressing aspect of his situation. "I would like to maintain some level of privacy," he says. "Still, there are times when I wish people would come to me and say, 'How are you doing?' and, 'How does it feel to lose so many friends to AIDS at such a young age?' 'How has all this affected you on a personal level?' And people never do. I wish they would ask me, sometimes, 'What is it like to be a successful gay black man? What are the challenges, what are the difficulties, what are the rewards?' I wish they would, but they don't." Like everyone else Milton wants to be noticed and cared about. His social withdrawal discourages such caring.

"It's a little numbing," says Derek, to forgo contact in this way. "It's no big deal because I've always had to do it," he explains. "I can't imagine what it would be like to be able to show affection, or to allow anybody to think that you're even *capable* of feeling affection as they do: a wife stopping by, and everybody wanting to meet her; a discussion about what your family did the night before; admitting that you had a fight and having people care or offer their token advice. Imagine the thrill of being able to show public affection the way other people do, to let somebody know that you're sitting next to somebody you happen to love, not somebody that you happened to watch the football game with that afternoon. It must be *bliss*; I can't comprehend it. To me it's only a concept."

Derek recalls a situation in which his own silence became almost unbearable. An employee in New York, a man named Charlie, told Derek that he had been diagnosed with AIDS. A few days later, during a meeting, Derek realized that Char-

lie's condition might put him in a compromising position. His response was to feign ignorance:

I'm so ashamed . . . that when Charlie called me, when I heard this, the first thing I thought about was not that this very charming, lovely, adorable, almost little brother-son to me, had this disease. The first thing I thought about was *me*. Not that I was ill, but that my career might suffer. And I was so ashamed . . . for an entire day I was calculating how I would deal with this. It's demeaning when I'm sitting in the room, and we talk about medical expenses going up, not the fact that we've got this kid with AIDS: "We've got to be more careful about the way we hire. . . . We've got to be sure that we're not going to be hiring any homosexuals in here."

In these meetings Derek felt muzzled and paralyzed, as if his voice had suddenly been stolen. He was unable to explain the situation or acknowledge his feelings about it, because to do so might impede his own efforts to avoid exposure. Derek recognizes that he has some tough choices to make in the coming months. "People will be asking, 'Wasn't this your friend, Derek?' It's going to be very tough."

In fact, personal problems or crises are often cited as experiences that gay men would most like to share with coworkers. "Heterosexuals who are having family problems or kid problems or money problems or *anything* can pretty much talk to someone about it," says Glen. "They can just say, 'I'm having a shitty day.' Just saying that much is enough." Chip explains, "I don't get to share my personal life in the same way that heterosexual workers do, all the little day-to-day things. You know, 'I went on a date with my girlfriend,' or 'I've been dating the same person for two years, and she's important to me,' or 'I've had a fight with Frank, and today's a bitchy day for me.' "

The invisibility of their lovers and friends is a source of particular frustration. Because these most meaningful relationships go unacknowledged at work, gay men are denied the support and affirmation of peers. In a survey by *Out/Look,* 29 percent of lesbians and gay men who had come out at work said that they did so in order to "improve relationships with a boss or coworker," while 25 percent said they wanted to "include a spouse" in social activities with people at work. Larry, the managing partner in a small Washington law firm, recalls the end of his relationship with a lover of ten years. "In the office I toughed it out," he says. "I don't think I ever said to anyone, 'My most important relationship has broken up, by the way.' So I did the usual thing I do in those kinds of situations: bifurcate it, split it up, get my support outside the office where I knew I was safe, and pretend that everything was fine at work. I look back now at how awful it was not to have the kind of support anyone else would have gotten in the workplace."

Chris suffered an equally painful "divorce" from his lover of many years. Both men worked for the same firm but had carefully concealed their relationship at work. "Here's one of the most traumatic things that can happen to you—the end of a relationship," says Chris. "I think if I had been straight I would have gone to my employer and said, 'My wife and I are getting a divorce, and it's a tough time for me.' But I didn't do that." Years later Chris looks back at that time with great sadness. "Divorces among straight people are so public," he says. "Gays don't have that."

Even when their personal lives are stable, gay professionals find that they miss out on the friendships that often develop in work situations. Tip still has regrets about a friendship that ultimately fell apart when he found himself unable, after months of indecision, to reveal that he is gay. He and Fred were both surgical residents and had become close over the years in school. "Fred was one of my best friends," Tip says. "Actually, I took him hunting with me a few times, and he met my family." The problems began when Fred and his wife tried to arrange a date for Tip:

He and his wife kept trying to set me up. The last time we spoke was about six months ago on the phone. Actually, we had a direct confrontation. He came out and said, "Tip, what's going on? I've been trying to set you up with this girl that works with my wife." I said, "No, Fred, I don't like being set up. If I don't like her, then it's going to hurt your wife's feelings." I had used that excuse before, and he wouldn't let it go this time. He said, "Tip, I'm doing you a favor. All you have to do is show up and drop your pants. That's all you've got to do." And I'm thinking that's exactly what I *don't* want

to do. And he says, "What is this, are you gay or something?" That's what he asked me. I said, "Fred, forget it. Look, the girl's already pissed. She's already asked your wife why I wouldn't want to go out with her, so it's already doomed and I haven't even met her."

After this confrontation Tip and Fred quickly drifted apart. Tip remained unwilling to come out, worried that he would be too vulnerable at work. Still, he acknowledges, "The way I'm doing this is costly. It's caused me to lose two friends because I didn't socialize with them. I didn't produce a date; I avoided the whole situation. It caused me to lose a friend, and Fred was a good friend."

Even so, Tip feels that these friendships must be sacrificed if he is to protect his job. "People aren't happy knowing you without knowing something about your social life. If I had it to do over again I probably wouldn't say a word. I'd rather not know a lot of the people that I know now, because it's like starting a friendship and only being able to carry it out halfway. It would have been better if I had just done my work and gone to the library or something."

Not all gay professionals mourn the loss of social opportunities at work, however. Some have little interest in spending more time with coworkers they consider dull or with whom they have little in common. Some consider themselves antisocial or private "by nature." Still others feel it is sufficient to build a small, intimate network of contacts, keeping the rest of the office at arm's length. There are certain advantages, they point out, to social withdrawal.

Mitch prefers to focus his attention on a small number of coworkers with whom he is especially close. "There's a core group of people with whom I feel I can discuss what's going on in my life," he says. "The people with whom I deal most frequently, including my secretary and the other people in my department—they know what my social situation is. So if something is going on in my life that's impacting the way I'm working, then it's fine." Consequently, while Mitch has told a select group of associates that he is gay, he avoids the issue with others. "If I felt there was nobody at work that I could walk into their office and talk to, that would be a problem. But that's not the case."

Some men feel that it is simply their nature to be reserved, and have little tolerance for what they perceive are intrusions from coworkers. "It doesn't bother me that people don't know that I'm gay," says Nick, who avoids after-hours socializing with coworkers. "There's no elaborate company event that I want to take my boyfriend to. I don't want to go to the football games myself." "As a human matter, I think you need just a certain amount of intimacy, a certain number of friends," says Roger. "I have to make a certain amount of contact in order to feel like I'm human, to feel that I'm connecting up with the rest of the race. But my experience is that most people have maybe five or six very close friends, no more. A lot of people *know* a lot of people, but there's only so much intimacy that you need or can develop in the world."

In most organizations, however, it is virtually impossible to distinguish work performance from participation in the social life of the office. Managerial jobs, in particular, require a man to operate a network of relationships—with clients, peers, bosses, suppliers, and support staff—and place a premium on his social competence. If he withdraws from others, he may be unable to do his job. Especially when the relevant tasks require teamwork, avoidance strategies sometimes leave a man little elbow room. Geoff describes his office as a small, "family-oriented" place, in which he has been reluctant to reveal very much about his personal life. "I think that's something that probably bothers the others. I'm not a warm, friendly, slap-each-other-on-the-back, go-out-for-a-couple-of-beers kind of guy. I ask a question, get an answer, and go on and do my job. Get in, get out. So I'm not real warm and friendly around them, which I think bothers them."

Some will eventually bump into a "glass ceiling" imposed by their social isolation. Greg feels that his social withdrawal helps explain his inability to "fit in" with the other men and women at his former employer. Although his coworkers were a tight-knit group, Greg was careful to reveal almost nothing about himself. "I think that's the problem when you withhold these kinds of personal feelings in your relationships with people. It's a great handicap, I think. People tend to think that you're uninteresting, that you don't have a personal life." Greg admits that he also found his coworkers somewhat dull, further discouraging him from taking part in the social life of the office. Still, he wonders if his aloofness, his reluctance to discuss even the most mundane aspects of his life outside the office, is one of the reasons he was recently fired. "I didn't associate with these people very much, except at the office," he says. "I was kind of a loner there."

Stuart received a similarly harsh lesson in the importance of being social at work. Five years out of law school he knew that he was considered something of an enigma at work. "I never held casual conversations with the other attorneys," he recalls. "I didn't stop by to chat with people unless I felt I absolutely had to. I kept the door to my office closed a lot of the time, especially when I took personal calls at work, because I didn't want my conversations to be monitored. Other people didn't do that. I also knew that I wasn't everyone's favorite luncheon companion. I would see other groups of people going to lunch, and there was an inner clique of people who ate together at least once a week. They would have lunch for two or three hours, drinking and socializing. I was only invited when I ran into them in the elevator or in the hallways, so that they were embarrassed and had to ask me along."

It wasn't that Stuart disliked the other attorneys or considered himself an especially shy or unfriendly person. "It's just that those sorts of encounters are painful for me," he says, "because they force me to play-act. The other attorneys talk about choosing a stroller, getting their kids into the right kindergarten, raising a family. I never feel that I fit in, since almost everyone else in the firm can be categorized as 'young and married.'" The same is true of company sporting events. "I never took part in the softball team, because the prospect of spending several hours with people from my office, playing sports—it guaranteed that I would feel like an outsider. But it was a big deal for them. Even the women in the department adopted masculine tastes in sports. There was a betting pool, and it was highly publicized. Every day during the summer I would get a memo about the games coming up, the current bets, and who had participated. It was a big self-promotional vehicle for the people who took part in it. But for me softball would have been a dangerous game. I wasn't scared of being hit by the ball; I was scared of being asked questions about my social life, questions that would just naturally come up in that context."

By this time Stuart's social isolation had also begun to affect his work. "Because I wasn't interacting with everyone socially, I wasn't getting work the way other people were. Projects are supposed to be doled out by an assigning partner on the basis of who is busy, who has experience in a particular area, and so forth. But in practice, whenever a project came up, whoever happened to be friendly with a particular partner at a particular time would get the job. Hanging out in someone else's office, talking about nothing, meant that you got work. I would always hear about projects for which I was ideally suited that had been assigned to somebody else. Sometimes it made me really angry. In order to make partner, I knew I had to work for as many people as possible, to demonstrate my skills to as many people as possible. And that simply wasn't happening. Most of the partners simply weren't thinking of me because I never talked to them."

At the end of his fifth year with the firm, Stuart was called in for his annual performance review. Two of the partners in the department discussed his work over the past year, emphasizing how pleased clients were. "During the first part of the review, they talked about how excellent my work was. One of them said that I wrote and thought clearly and professionally, skills that he said couldn't be taught. They praised me for the responsibility I had shown on several key projects. But then they said that there was a problem. They said that I didn't talk to them often enough. They said that while they didn't expect me to go out drinking with them—they could see I wasn't a back-slapper—they did expect me to spend more of my social time with them. Then they warned me, quite explicitly, that this was going to be a problem for me in making partner. They made it clear that there was no problem with my work, that they didn't expect me to socialize with them on a grand scale. But they did expect me to schmooze with them, to hang out and be casual with them." Hearing this, Stuart knew where the conversation was headed. "It was suggested," he recalls, "that I start planning a career elsewhere, somewhere that was a better fit for me."

CRITICAL-THINKING QUESTIONS

1. What are the advantages and disadvantages of social withdrawal in "managing" a gay identity in the workplace?

2. How does social isolation affect gay professional men's work? Do you think that lesbians encounter similar problems?

3. In the last few years, many corporations have embraced the idea of "cultural diversity." For example, they have sponsored workshops, provided training sessions, and incorporated cultural diversity into mission statements. Based on your experiences and observations as well as this article, does cultural diversity also include gay men and lesbians?

THE ECONOMY AND WORK

Cross-Cultural

46

Maid in the U.S.A.

Mary Romero

Domestic work—almost exclusively performed by women of color—is both underpaid and undervalued in our society. In this selection, Mary Romero describes some of the strategies Chicana domestics use to eliminate the demeaning aspects of their work, to define the relationships between themselves and employers in more equal terms, and to professionalize their jobs.

Although Chicanas consider flexibility, autonomy and independence the advantages of domestic service over other jobs, these characteristics are not inherent features. Domestics have to negotiate directly with employers to establish a flexible work schedule and autonomy on the job. An analysis of their work histories in domestic service reveals that Chicana domestics actively negotiate informal labor arrangements that include both strategies to eliminate the most oppressive aspects of the occupation and to develop instrumental employer-employee relationships aimed at professionalizing it.

SOURCE: *Maid in the U.S.A.* by Mary Romero (New York: Routledge, 1992), pp. 146–47, 149–56, 156–61. Copyright © 1992 by Routledge, Chapman and Hall, Inc. Reprinted with permission.

Unable to find employment offering job security, advancement, or benefits, Chicanas make calculated attempts to improve the occupation by minimizing employer control and personalism. . . .

NEGOTIATING SPECIFIC TASKS

In the informal labor arrangement, domestic and employer must verbally negotiate working conditions, including tasks, timing, technique, the length of the working day, and payment. When starting with a new employer, the domestic works one day, and if the employer is satisfied with her work, the two agree upon a work schedule and the specific tasks to be accomplished. Mrs. Rodriquez describes the ideal situation: "Once the person learns that you're going to do the job they just totally leave you to your own. It's like it's your own home." This ideal is similar to the informal arrangements Glenn reports.[1] However, half of the women I interviewed explain that the ideal situation is achieved after some supervision and negotiation. Such an experience is alluded to in Mrs. Portillo's explanation of why she left an employer: "I don't want somebody right behind me telling me what to do. I will not work like that and that's why I didn't stay any longer with this lady."

The priority of domestics in the informal labor arrangement is to negotiate a work structure that provides autonomy and independence. Autonomy on the job is created when the worker controls the planning and organization of the housework, as well as the work pace and method. Gaining autonomy also assures the worker that the parameters of the work are maintained. The ideal situation is to have the worker structuring the work, with the employer removed from direct supervision. Chicana domestics stated their desire for autonomy, using the common expression "being your own boss."

Fifteen of the Chicanas make a practice of carefully distinguishing specific tasks that are considered part of the agreement from other tasks that are undertaken only for additional pay. Although informal work arrangements frequently imply a set number of hours, the typical arrangement is referred to as "charging by the house." Mrs. Salazar explains the verbal contract:

When you say you're going to clean a house, after you find out how big it is, you tell them [the employer] "I'll clean it for say sixty dollars." You're not saying how long you're going to be there. To me, that was just a contract between you and the customer and after awhile when you've been there awhile, you know how fast you can work and I was doing it in less than eight hours.

Mrs. Lopez expresses her preference for "charging by the house": "I never liked to work by the hour because if I would work by the hour the lady would just go crazy loading me up with work, with more work and more work to do."

Charging a flat rate also eliminates employers'

attempts at speedup by adding more tasks and forcing the domestic to increase the work pace. Glenn also found that Japanese American domestics attempt to limit the amount of work by specifying tasks rather than time. Charging a flat rate is a significant change in the occupation, particularly in light of the broad range of physical and emotional labor domestics report. The list of tasks suggests that many employers purchase labor power rather than labor services; that is, workers are not hired simply to provide the labor service of cleaning the house but their labor is purchased for a certain amount of hours to do a variety of unspecified tasks. "Charging by the house" involves specifying the specific tasks and, thus, placing boundaries on the job description.

All but one of the women interviewed attempt to control the work load and establish a concrete verbal contract outlining the specific tasks. Mrs. Gallegos is the only woman I interviewed who voiced a different strategy for controlling the amount of tasks given by the employer.

When you work by the hour, they're [employers] not going to line up any work. And once you start using a system, you can do it . . . take your time, you know, I see a lot of ladies—they [employees] want too much when they [employers] do pay them so much but they [employees] ask too much. I won't go for that. I told them [employers] I work by the hour, I will not take a flat rate cause if it takes me five, six hours, I want to get paid and if it takes four hours that's my problem. I will not work flat rate.

Mrs. Gallegos argues that the hourly wage places a limit on the amount of work and assures the worker that she is paid for all of her labor.

Like the dialectic between employer and employee Glenn describes, there is an ongoing negotiation as the domestic attempts to maintain the agreement while the employer attempts to lengthen the work day or to add more tasks. For instance, Mrs. Tafoya recalls an incident in which an employer attempted to extract additional unpaid labor:

I guess the niece came home. I knew the record player was playing and she was kinda—but I thought she was just tapping like you would tap [indicates with her hand on the table], you know. She was dancing and I guess the wax wasn't dry. She made a mess. I said to Mrs. Johnson [employer], I says I'm not going to clean that again. You get your niece to clean that. I did it once and it was beautiful. And I did it because nobody was here and I know that it would dry right. So if you want it redone you have your niece do it. And she says but you're getting paid for it. I says yea, I got paid for it and I did it.

By refusing to wax the floor over again, Mrs. Tafoya maintained the original labor arrangement.

Mrs. Sanchez gave an account that illustrates her attempt to place limits on the amount of work done and her efforts to maintain the original verbal contract. Mrs. Sanchez described a current problem she was having with an employer who is attempting to add more work. Mimicking the high-pitched voice of her employer, she repeated the employer's question: "Would you mind doing this? Would you mind doing that?" Mrs. Sanchez confided that she wanted to respond by saying, "Yes I do mind and I won't do it" but instead she said "Well, I'll do it this time." She expressed the importance of pointing out to the employer that the task would be done this time but was not to be expected in the future.

Another strategy Chicanas use to limit the work and reduce employers' efforts to extract unpaid labor involves developing a routine for handling "extras." The women describe preparing a monthly or bimonthly schedule for rotating particular tasks, such as cleaning the stove or refrigerator, and thereby avoid many special requests. Another common practice is to establish an understanding with the employer that if one task is added, another is eliminated. If the employer does not identify the tasks to be eliminated, the employee simply selects one and later explains that there was not enough time for both. Mrs. Garcia recalls learning this strategy from her cousin:

My cousin said, "Do the same thing every time you come in, as far as changing the sheets, vacuum and dust, and window sills, pictures on the walls, and stuff like that unless they ask you to do something extra. Then, maybe don't clean the tile in the bathroom, or just do the windows that really need it, so you can have some time to do this other stuff that they wanted you to do extra."

And she said, "Never do more than what they ask you to do, because if you do then you're not really getting paid for it." . . .

Chicana domestics, not unlike African American and Japanese American domestics, did not necessarily find an affective relationship the ingredient for a satisfying working relationship. In fact, the opposite is the case, because affective relationships provide more opportunities for exploitation. Frequently, close friendships result in fictitious kinship references, such as a younger employer adopting the domestic as a surrogate mother. Redefining the work obligation as a "family" obligation places the domestic in a difficult position. As Mrs. Portillo explains, the personal nature of the relationship creates an atmosphere conducive to manipulation: "Some people use their generosity to pressure you." Maintaining the conditions of the contract also becomes difficult because extra requests are made as if from a friend rather than from an employer. When employers use personalism as a means to extract additional labor, many domestics are able to increase their pay by threatening to quit. However, when they no longer feel in control, many choose to quit and find another employer.

MINIMIZING CONTACT WITH EMPLOYERS

Domestics commonly report conflict over the work process. In order to structure the work as a meaningful and nondegrading activity, domestics struggle to remove employers from control of decisions. When employers control the work process, domestics are reduced to unskilled labor and housecleaning becomes mindless hourly work. Furthermore, domestics strive to eliminate the rituals of deference and the stigma of servitude. Minimizing the contact with employers was the most successful strategy for gaining control over the work process.

Employers are reluctant to turn over the control of the process to the domestic. Instead they attempt to structure the work to be supervised and monitored. Chicanas report that some employers give detailed instructions on how to clean their homes; they specified washing the floor on hands and knees, using newspaper instead of paper towels on the windows, or even in which direction to scrub the wall. Mrs. Portillo, a retired domestic with thirty years of experience, expresses the frustration of working for an employer who retained control of the work process:

I used to have one lady that used to work right along with me. I worked with her three years. I found it hard. I was taking orders. I'm not the type to want to take orders. I know what I'm going to do. I know what general housecleaning is.

Under supervised conditions, domestics find themselves simply taking orders, which reduces their work activity to quick, monotonous gestures.

Mrs. Sanchez voices the general consensus that the less interaction there is with employers, the better are the working conditions: "The conflicts have been mostly with people who stay at home and really just demand the impossible." Five domestics even commented that they selected employers on the basis of whether the employer worked outside the home.

Chicanas argue that working women are more appreciative of the housework done and are relieved to turn over the planning and execution of cleaning to the domestic. Unemployed women, on the other hand, are portrayed as "picky" and unwilling to relinquish control. Three domestics whom I interviewed suggested that unemployed women feel guilty because they are not doing the work themselves and thus retain control and responsibility for the housework. Mrs. Lucero's description represents the distinctions domestics make between working women and full-time homemakers:

I think women that weren't working were the ones that always had something to complain about. The ones that did work were always satisfied. I've never come across a lady that works that has not been satisfied. Those that are home and have the time to do it themselves, and don't want to do it, they are the ones that are always com-

plaining, you know, not satisfied, they always want more and more. You can't really satisfy them.

Working women tend to be ideal employers because they are rarely home and are unable to supervise.

The selection of employers is essential in maximizing the advantages of domestic service over other available jobs. For instance, Mrs. Gallegos explains that she selects jobs on the basis of the type of work that she wants to avoid: "Well, if I can help it, I don't like to do ovens. I hardly do that anymore. . . . I don't like to work for people who are very dirty either." Four characteristics that the women most frequently mention as qualities of a good employer are trust, respect, the understanding that family responsibilities come before work, and the ability to maintain a system for housecleaning. Only employers who trust their employees will allow the worker to structure the housework. Such respect indicates that employers are not trying to affirm and enhance their status by establishing the domestic's inferior status. Most of the women felt that family obligations, such as a sick child, superseded the work obligation. Therefore, they sought employers who were willing to accommodate occasional changes in the schedule and did not threaten to fire the worker. Domestics prefer to work for employers who maintain the house between cleanings and are not "dirty." Bad employers are characterized as "constantly looking over their shoulder," expecting the domestic to pick up after the children, leaving too many notes, and adding extra tasks. Domestics control their work environments to a large degree by replacing undesirable employers with more compatible ones.

A high turnover rate has always been characteristic of contemporary domestic service. Nevertheless, if a good working arrangement is established, domestics continue with an employer for some time. Over half of the women in this study worked for the same employer for at least two-thirds of their work histories as domestics. The women with the most extensive domestic experience have very impressive records. For instance,

Mrs. Portillo, a sixty-eight-year-old retired domestic, had the same employers for the entire thirty years of her employment. Another woman, Mrs. Rivas, a fifty-three-year-old domestic with thirty-two years of experience, had the same employer for twenty years. Two younger women, Mrs. Montoya, age thirty-three, and Mrs. Rivera, age thirty-two, both have twelve years of experience and have worked for the same employer for eleven years.

Half of the women stated that they consider the first couple of days with a new employer a time to decide whether to keep the employer. For instance, Mrs. Fernandez bases her decision to stay with a new employer on watching for signs of supervision and monitoring and unreasonable expectations.

You can tell if they're [employers] going to trust you or not. If they're not overlooking—see, you know—over you all the time. If they start looking or saying "I don't want this moved or I don't want this done or be careful with this"—well, you know, you can be so careful but there's accidents happen. So if they start being picky I won't stay.

Mrs. Lopez classifies the type of employer by the attitude they expose in the first few minutes of their first encounter:

I have had ladies that have said "I know you know what to do so I'll leave it to you" or they pull out their cleaning stuff and tell you "This is for this and this is for that" and I say "I know I've done this before." "Oh, ok. I'll let you do it."

Supervision and monitoring of workers not only function to control the work process but remind the worker of her subordinate position in society. Offering unsolicited advice about cleaning techniques—such as scrubbing floors on hands and knees rather than with a mop, or the safest way to bend while picking up the vacuum cleaner and moving heavy furniture—symbolizes a level of servitude. Asking a domestic to scrub floors on hands and knees—not a common practice of housewives today—is experienced as demeaning.

The inferior status of the domestic is also evident in the employer's instructions on how to bend without themselves offering assistance.

BECOMING AN EXPERT

Another strategy used by Chicanas in the struggle to transform domestic service is to define themselves as expert cleaners or housekeepers. It is a unique strategy not reported among the African Americans studied by Rollins, Coley, or Dill or the Japanese Americans in Glenn's study.[2] This strategy attempts to transform the employee-employer relationship, creating an ideal situation in which employers turn over responsibility for the housework to the domestic. Establishing themselves as expert housecleaners involved defining a routine set of housework tasks and eliminating personal services such as babysitting, laundry, or ironing. Older Chicanas recalled babysitting, ironing, cooking and doing laundry, but in recent years they rarely do such tasks. Even younger Chicanas in their thirties, some with twelve years' experience, do ironing or laundry only for employers they started with ten years ago.

The importance of redefining social relationships in domestic service is most apparent in the women's distinctions between the work they do and maid's work. Mrs. Fernandez, a thirty-five-year-old domestic, indicates the distinction in the following account:

They [the employer's children] started to introduce me to their friends as their maid. "This is our maid Angela." I would say "I'm not your maid. I've come to clean your house and a maid is someone who takes care of you and lives here or comes in every day and I come once a week and it is to take care of what you have messed up. I'm not your maid. I'm your housekeeper."

These Chicanas define their work as different from maid's work. Mrs. Montoya's statement illustrates the equation of personal services with maid's work:

I figure I'm not there to be their personal maid. I'm there to do their housecleaning—their upkeep of the house.

Most of the women I work for are professionals and so they feel it's not my job to run around behind them. Just to keep their house maintenance clean and that's all they ask.

Mrs. Rojas, a thirty-three-year-old domestic with twelve years of experience, equates deferential behavior with being a maid.

One or two [employers] that I work for now have children that are snotty, you know they thought that I was their maid or they would treat me like a maid you know instead of a cleaning lady.

These workers resisted attempts by employers and their families to structure the work around rituals of deference and avoided doing the emotional labor attached to personal services.

The Chicanas interviewed consider themselves experts. They are aware of the broad range of knowledge that they have acquired from cleaning a variety of homes. This includes the removal of stains on various surfaces, tips for reorganizing the home, and the pros and cons of certain brands of appliances. A source of pride among the women was the fact that they had introduced a labor-saving device or tactic into the employer's home. Mrs. Garcia's experience in removing stains illustrates the assistance domestics give employers:

They [employers] just wipe their stoves and then complain "this doesn't come off anymore." They never took a SOS pad or a scrub brush to scrub it off. They expect it just to come off because they wiped. . . . Their kitchen floors would have Kool-Aid stains or they would have it on the counters, so I would just pour Clorox on it and the Clorox would just bring it right up and they would say "But you'll ruin it!" "No it will be alright." "Are you sure?" I never ruined anything from helping them out. . . .

CREATING A BUSINESSLIKE ENVIRONMENT

As in other female-dominated occupations—such as nursing and teaching—private household workers lack authority and must therefore rely on the employers' cooperation to change the structure of the work and social relationships. Mrs. Rojas describes one woman she worked for who accepted her obligation as an employer and maintained the agreement to hire Mrs. Rojas every Wednesday.

I use to work for her on Wednesday and she would be going on a trip away with her husband and stuff because he did a lot of out-of-state work and she would go with him and being that I was going to be there on Wednesday and she wasn't she'd pay me anyway so I got paid from her whether I went [to work] or not as long as it was her who was going to be gone and not an excuse from me or something. She is about the only one that ever did that.

This employer is unique because most employers in domestic service expect the domestic to keep a work schedule to clean their houses on a regular basis but do not accept the responsibility of providing the work they promised.

In another account about an employer's daughter expecting her to be subordinate, Mrs. Rojas illustrates the role some employers play in eliminating servitude aspects of the occupation.

I told a young lady something about leaving her underclothes thrown around, and she asked me what was I there for? I went straight in, called her mother and told her the situation. Her mother came home from work and let the young lady have it. She [the mother] was thoroughly upset. I was not there to be her [the daughter's] personal maid and she was told that in no uncertain terms.

Analysis of the informal networks used by both employers and employees points to a key role in establishing a businesslike environment. The informal network between employers and employees socializes both to the value of modernizing trends in the occupation. Chicana work histories revealed that, particularly for younger workers, the introduction to domestic service involved an informal apprenticeship program. Like the domestics interviewed in Coley's study, the new recruit accompanied a relative to work for several days or weeks until the new recruit decided she was ready to work alone. Mrs. Rodriquez describes the introduction and "training" into domestic service she received from her sister:

She would go look it over and see if I missed anything or like in the bathroom you have to polish all the chrome and I didn't know that so I cleaned it and it was clean but she's the one that gave me all these tips on polishing up the chrome and stuff.

While assisting her sister, Mrs. Garcia pointed out the advantages of charging a "flat rate" rather than by the hour:

When I was working with my sister, I told her she shouldn't be cleaning by the hour because it's not worth it to be cleaning by the hour. You are there too many hours and you don't make much money that way.

Although the Chicanas identified these training sessions as providing experience in cleaning, learning about new products or appliances, and discovering the pros and cons of structuring the work in particular ways, the most important function may have been the socialization of new recruits to expect certain working conditions and wages and to learn ways to negotiate with employers. . . .

CONCLUSION

Faced with limited job opportunities, Chicanas turn to domestic service and restructure the occupation to resemble a businesslike arrangement. Similarly to the union members in Coley's study, the Chicana household workers I interviewed define themselves as professional cleaners hired to do general housework. They urge their employers to turn over the planning along with the execution of the work. They consider themselves skilled laborers who are well able to schedule tasks, determine cleaning techniques, select the appropriate work materials, and set the work pace. Verbal agreements specifying tasks minimize supervision and increase the degree of autonomy. Eliminating the employer from a supervisory role also removes the worker from a subordinate position. Like the household worker's collective that Salzinger studied in the Bay area, Chicanas are "redefining domestic work as skilled labor, and on that basis struggling for increased pay and security and for autonomy and control over their work," and "they are in fact engaged in what in other contexts has been called a 'professionalization project.' "[3] Domestics' ability to select and change employers is the critical locus of autonomy and control in what would otherwise be a powerless, subservient position. Working for a different employer—and in many cases two to three employers—places Chicanas in a strong negotiating position.

Like other full-time domestics, Chicanas employed as day workers in private households are moving away from "wage work" and from selling their "labor time" toward a "flat rate" in which a "job" is exchanged for a specified amount of money. In this situation, any efficiency realized by the worker saves her time and can sometimes be converted into profit that will accrue to her. Chicanas are attempting to transform domestic work in the direction of the petit-bourgeois relation of customer-vendor rather than the preindustrial relation of mistress-servant or even the wage worker-employer relation of capitalism. This arrangement is most successful with employed housewives who readily accept the skills of domestics. The strategy to transform domestic service by selling labor services rather than labor power is also useful in eliminating potentially exploitative aspects of the domestic-mistress relationship. Strategies described by Chicanas in the study are consistent with the emergence of cleaning agencies that advertise expert and skilled labor.

Although there is a long history of attempts to organize maid's unions,[4] most private household workers are isolated from each other and struggle for better working conditions on an individual basis. Nevertheless, the goals of individual struggle have similarities with issues of collective action: raising wages; providing benefits such as paid vacations, holidays, sick leave, and workers' unemployment compensation; changing attitudes toward the occupation; and creating public awareness about the value of the labor.

CRITICAL-THINKING QUESTIONS

1. Why do domestic workers try to redefine their work on the basis of a contract rather than hourly work?

2. How do domestic workers negotiate specific tasks? minimize their contact with employers? create a businesslike environment?

3. Some observers argue that domestic work should be eliminated and all of us should "pick up after ourselves" instead of expecting others to do our dirty work. Do you agree or disagree?

NOTES

1. Evelyn Nakano Glenn, "Occupational Ghettoization: Japanese American Women and Domestic Service, 1905–1970," *Ethnicity*, 7, no. 4 (1981), 352–86.

2. Soraya Moore Coley, " 'And Still I Rise': An Exploratory Study of Contemporary Black Private Household Workers" (Ph.D. diss., Bryn Mawr College, 1981); Bonnie Thornton Dill, "Making Your Job Good Yourself: Domestic Service and the Construction of Personal Dignity," in *Women and the Politics of Empowerment,* ed. Ann Bookman and Sandra Morgen (Philadelphia: Temple University Press, 1988), pp. 33–52; Judith Rollins, *Between Women: Domestics and Their Employers* (Philadelphia: Temple University Press, 1985).

3. Leslie Salzinger, "A Maid by Any Other Name: The Transformation of 'Dirty Work' by Central American Immigrants," in *Ethnography Unbound: Power and Resistance in the Modern Metropolis,* ed. Michael Buraway et al. (Berkeley and Los Angeles: University of California Press, 1991), pp. 139–60.

4. Phyllis Palmer, *Domesticity and Dirt: Housewives and Domestic Servants in the United States, 1920–1945* (Philadelphia: Temple University Press, 1989).

Classic

47

The Power Elite

C. Wright Mills

Conventional wisdom suggests that U.S. society operates as a democracy, guided by the "voice of the people." C. Wright Mills argues that above ordinary people—and even above many politicians—are "the higher circles," those who run the corporations, operate the military establishment, and manipulate the machinery of the state. It is this relative handful of people whom Mills calls "the power elite."

The powers of ordinary men are circumscribed by the everyday worlds in which they live, yet even in these rounds of job, family, and neighborhood they often seem driven by forces they can neither understand nor govern. "Great changes" are beyond their control, but affect their conduct and outlook nonetheless. The very framework of modern society confines them to projects not their own, but from every side, such changes now press upon the men and women of the mass society, who accord-

ingly feel that they are without purpose in an epoch in which they are without power.

But not all men are in this sense ordinary. As the means of information and of power are centralized, some men come to occupy positions in American society from which they can look down upon, so to speak, and by their decisions mightily affect, the everyday worlds of ordinary men and women. They are not made by their jobs; they set up and break down jobs for thousands of others; they are not confined by simple family responsibilities; they can escape. They may live in many hotels and houses, but they are bound by no one community. They need not merely "meet the demands of the day and hour"; in some part, they create these demands, and cause others to meet them. Whether or not they profess their power, their technical and political experience of it far transcends that of the underlying population. What Jacob Burckhardt said of "great men," most Americans might well say of their elite: "They are all that we are not."

The power elite is composed of men whose positions enable them to transcend the ordinary environments of ordinary men and women; they are in positions to make decisions having major consequences. Whether they do or do not make such decisions is less important than the fact that they do occupy such pivotal positions: Their failure to act, their failure to make decisions, is itself an act that is often of greater consequence than the decisions they do make. For they are in command of the major hierarchies and organizations of modern society. They rule the big corporations. They run the machinery of the state and claim its prerogatives. They direct the military establishment. They occupy the strategic command posts of the social structure, in which are now centered the effective means of the power and the wealth and the celebrity which they enjoy.

The power elite are not solitary rulers. Advisers and consultants, spokesmen and opinion-makers are often the captains of their higher thought and decision. Immediately below the elite are the professional politicians of the middle levels of power, in the Congress and in the pressure groups, as well as among the new and old upper classes of town and city and region. Mingling with them, in curious ways which we shall explore, are those professional celebrities who live by being continually displayed but are never, so long as they remain celebrities, displayed enough. If such celebrities are not at the head of any dominating hierarchy, they do often have the power to distract the attention of the public or afford sensations to the masses, or, more directly, to gain the ear of those who do occupy positions of direct power. More or less unattached, as critics of morality and technicians of power, as spokesmen of God and creators of mass sensibility, such celebrities and consultants are part of the immediate scene in which the drama of the elite is enacted. But that drama itself is centered in the command posts of the major institutional hierarchies.

The truth about the nature and the power of the elite is not some secret which men of affairs know but will not tell. Such men hold quite various theories about their own roles in the sequence of event and decision. Often they are uncertain about their roles, and even more often they allow their fears and their hopes to affect their assessment of their own power. No matter how great their actual power, they tend to be less acutely aware of it than of the resistances of others to its use. Moreover, most American men of affairs have learned well the rhetoric of public relations, in some cases even to the point of using it when they are alone, and thus coming to believe it. The personal awareness of the actors is only one of the several sources one must examine in order to understand the higher circles. Yet many who believe that there is no elite, or at any rate none of any consequence, rest their argument upon what men of affairs believe about themselves, or at least assert in public.

There is, however, another view: Those who feel, even if vaguely, that a compact and powerful elite of great importance does now prevail in America often base that feeling upon the historical trend of our time. They have felt, for example, the domination of the military event, and from this they infer that generals and admirals, as well as other men of decision influenced by them, must be enormously powerful. They hear that the Congress has again abdicated to a handful of men decisions clearly related to the issue of war or peace. They know that the bomb was dropped over Japan in the name of the United States of America, although they were at no time consulted about the matter. They feel that they live in a time of big decisions; they know that they are not making any. Accordingly, as they consider the present as history, they infer that at its center, making decisions or failing to make them, there must be an elite of power.

On the one hand, those who share this feeling about big historical events assume that there is an elite and that its power is great. On the other hand, those who listen carefully to the reports of men apparently involved in the great decisions often do not believe that there is an elite whose powers are of decisive consequence.

Both views must be taken into account, but neither is adequate. The way to understand the power of the American elite lies neither solely in recognizing the historic scale of events nor in accepting the personal awareness reported by men of apparent decision. Behind such men and behind the events of history, linking the two, are the major institutions of modern society. These hierarchies of state and corporation and army constitute the means of power; as such they are now of a consequence not before equaled in human history—and at their summits, there are now those command posts of modern society which offer us the sociological key to an understanding of the role of the higher circles in America.

Within American society, major national power now resides in the economic, the political, and the military domains. Other institutions seem off to the side of modern history, and, on occasion, duly subordinated to these. No family is as directly powerful in national affairs as any major corporation; no church is as directly powerful in the external biographies of young men in America today as the military establishment; no college is as powerful in the shaping of momentous events as the National Security Council. Religious, educational, and family institutions are not autonomous centers of national power; on the contrary, these decentralized areas are increasingly shaped by the big three, in which developments of decisive and immediate consequence now occur.

Families and churches and schools adapt to modern life; governments and armies and corporations shape it; and, as they do so, they turn these lesser institutions into means for their ends. Religious institutions provide chaplains to the armed forces where they are used as a means of increasing the effectiveness of its morale to kill. Schools select and train men for their jobs in corporations and their specialized tasks in the armed forces. The extended family has, of course, long been broken up by the industrial revolution, and now the son and the father are removed from the family, by

compulsion if need be, whenever the army of the state sends out the call. And the symbols of all these lesser institutions are used to legitimate the power and the decisions of the big three.

The life-fate of the modern individual depends not only upon the family into which he was born or which he enters by marriage, but increasingly upon the corporation in which he spends the most alert hours of his best years; not only upon the school where he is educated as a child and adolescent, but also upon the state which touches him throughout his life; not only upon the church in which on occasion he hears the word of God, but also upon the army in which he is disciplined.

If the centralized state could not rely upon the inculcation of nationalist loyalties in public and private schools, its leaders would promptly seek to modify the decentralized educational system. If the bankruptcy rate among the top 500 corporations were as high as the general divorce rate among the 37 million married couples, there would be economic catastrophe on an international scale. If members of armies gave to them no more of their lives than do believers to the churches to which they belong, there would be a military crisis.

Within each of the big three, the typical institutional unit has become enlarged, has become administrative, and, in the power of its decisions, has become centralized. Behind these developments there is a fabulous technology, for as institutions, they have incorporated this technology and guide it, even as it shapes and paces their developments.

The economy—once a great scatter of small productive units in autonomous balance—has become dominated by two or three hundred giant corporations, administratively and politically interrelated, which together hold the keys to economic decisions.

The political order, once a decentralized set of several dozen states with a weak spinal cord, has become a centralized, executive establishment which has taken up into itself many powers previously scattered, and now enters into each and every cranny of the social structure.

The military order, once a slim establishment in a context of distrust fed by state militia, has become the largest and most expensive feature of government, and, although well-versed in smiling public relations, now has all the grim and clumsy efficiency of a sprawling bureaucratic domain.

In each of these institutional areas, the means of power at the disposal of decision makers have increased enormously; their central executive powers have been enhanced; within each of them modern administrative routines have been elaborated and tightened up.

As each of these domains becomes enlarged and centralized, the consequences of its activities become greater, and its traffic with the others increases. The decisions of a handful of corporations bear upon military and political as well as upon economic developments around the world. The decisions of the military establishment rest upon and grievously affect political life as well as the very level of economic activity. The decisions made within the political domain determine economic activities and military programs. There is no longer, on the one hand, an economy, and, on the other hand, a political order containing a military establishment unimportant to politics and to money-making. There is a political economy linked, in a thousand ways, with military institutions and decisions. On each side of the world-split running through central Europe and around the Asiatic rimlands, there is an ever-increasing interlocking of economic, military, and political structures. If there is government intervention in the corporate economy, so is there corporate intervention in the governmental process. In the structural sense, this triangle of power is the source of the interlocking directorate that is most important for the historical structure of the present.

The fact of the interlocking is clearly revealed at each of the points of crisis of modern capitalist society—slump, war, and boom. In each, men of decision are led to an awareness of the interdependence of the major institutional orders. In the nineteenth century, when the scale of all institutions was smaller, their liberal integration was achieved in the automatic economy, by an autonomous play of market forces, and in the automatic political domain, by the bargain and the vote.

It was then assumed that out of the imbalance and friction that followed the limited decisions then possible a new equilibrium would in due course emerge. That can no longer be assumed, and it is not assumed by the men at the top of each of the three dominant hierarchies.

For given the scope of their consequences, decisions—and indecisions—in any one of these ramify into the others, and hence top decisions tend either to become coordinated or to lead to a commanding indecision. It has not always been like this. When numerous small entrepreneurs made up the economy, for example, many of them could fail and the consequences still remain local; political and military authorities did not intervene. But now, given political expectations and military commitments, can they afford to allow key units of the private corporate economy to break down in slump? Increasingly, they do intervene in economic affairs, and as they do so, the controlling decisions in each order are inspected by agents of the other two, and economic, military, and political structures are interlocked.

At the pinnacle of each of the three enlarged and centralized domains, there have arisen those higher circles which make up the economic, the political, and the military elites. At the top of the economy, among the corporate rich, there are the chief executives; at the top of the political order, the members of the political directorate; at the top of the military establishment, the elite of soldier-statesmen clustered in and around the Joint Chiefs of Staff and the upper echelon. As each of these domains has coincided with the others, as decisions tend to become total in their consequence, the leading men in each of the three domains of power—the warlords, the corporation chieftains, the political directorate—tend to come together, to form the power elite of America.

The higher circles in and around these command posts are often thought of in terms of what their members possess: They have a greater share than other people of the things and experiences that are most highly valued. From this point of view, the elite are simply those who have the most of what there is to have, which is generally held to include money, power, and prestige—as well as all the ways of life to which these lead. But the elite are not simply those who have the most, for they could not "have the most" were it not for their positions in the great institutions. For such institutions are the necessary bases of power, of wealth, and of prestige, and at the same time, the chief means of exercising power, of acquiring and retaining wealth, and of cashing in the higher claims for prestige.

By the powerful we mean, of course, those who are able to realize their will, even if others resist it. No one, accordingly, can be truly powerful unless he has access to the command of major institutions, for it is over these institutional means of power that the truly powerful are, in the first instance, powerful. Higher politicians and key officials of government command such institutional power; so do admirals and generals, and so do the major owners and executives of the larger corporations. Not all power, it is true, is anchored in and exercised by means of such institutions, but only within and through them can power be more or less continuous and important.

Wealth also is acquired and held in and through institutions. The pyramid of wealth cannot be understood merely in terms of the very rich; for the great inheriting families, as we shall see, are now supplemented by the corporate institutions of modern society: Every one of the very rich families has been and is closely connected—always legally and frequently managerially as well—with one of the multimillion-dollar corporations.

The modern corporation is the prime source of wealth, but, in latter-day capitalism, the political apparatus also opens and closes many avenues to wealth. The amount as well as the source of income, the power over consumer's goods as well as over productive capital, are determined by position within the political economy. If our interest in the very rich goes beyond their lavish or their miserly consumption, we must examine their relations to modern forms of corporate property as well as to the state; for such relations now determine the chances of men to secure big property and to receive high income.

Great prestige increasingly follows the major institutional units of the social structure. It is obvious that prestige depends, often quite decisively, upon access to the publicity machines that are now a central and normal feature of all the big institutions of modern America. Moreover, one feature of these hierarchies of corporation, state, and military establishment is that their top positions are increasingly interchangeable. One result of this is the accumulative nature of prestige. Claims for prestige, for example, may be initially based on military roles, then expressed in and augmented by an educational institution run by corporate executives, and cashed in, finally, in the political order, where, for General Eisenhower and those he represents, power and prestige finally meet at the very peak. Like wealth and power, prestige tends to be cumulative: The more of it you have, the more you can get. These values also tend to be translatable into one another: The wealthy find it easier than the poor to gain power; those with status find it easier than those without it to control opportunities for wealth.

If we took the one-hundred most powerful men in America, the one-hundred wealthiest, and the one-hundred most celebrated away from the institutional positions they now occupy, away from their resources of men and women and money, away from the media of mass communication that are now focused upon them—then they would be powerless and poor and uncelebrated. For power is not of a man. Wealth does not center in the person of the wealthy. Celebrity is not inherent in any personality. To be celebrated, to be wealthy, to have power requires access to major institutions, for the institutional positions men occupy determine in large part their chances to have and to hold these valued experiences.

The people of the higher circles may also be conceived as members of a top social stratum, as a set of groups whose members know one another, see one another socially and at business, and so, in making decisions, take one another into account. The elite, according to this conception, feel themselves to be, and are felt by others to be, the inner circle of "the upper social classes." They form a more or less compact social and psychological entity; they have become self-conscious members of a social class. People are either accepted into this class or they are not, and there is a qualitative split, rather than merely a numerical scale, separating them from those who are not elite. They are more or less aware of themselves as a social class and they behave toward one another differently from the way they do toward members of other classes. They accept one another, understand one another, marry one another, tend to work and to think if not together at least alike.

Now, we do not want by our definition to prejudge whether the elite of the command posts are conscious members of such a socially recognized class, or whether considerable proportions of the elite derive from such a clear and distinct class. These are matters to be investigated. Yet in order to be able to recognize what we intend to investigate, we must note something that all biographies and memoirs of the wealthy and the powerful and the eminent make clear: No matter what else they may be, the people of these higher circles are involved in a set of overlapping "crowds" and intricately connected "cliques." There is a kind of mutual attraction among those who "sit on the same terrace"—although this often becomes clear to them, as well as to others, only at the point at which they feel the need to draw the line; only when, in their common defense, they come to understand what they have in common, and so close their ranks against outsiders.

The idea of such ruling stratum implies that most of its members have similar social origins, that throughout their lives they maintain a network of informal connections, and that to some degree there is an interchangeability of position between the various hierarchies of money and power and celebrity. We must, of course, note at once that if such an elite stratum does exist, its social visibility and its form, for very solid historical reasons, are quite different from those of the noble cousinhoods that once ruled various European nations.

That American society has never passed through a feudal epoch is of decisive importance to the na-

ture of the American elite, as well as to American society as a historic whole. For it means that no nobility or aristocracy, established before the capitalist era, has stood in tense opposition to the higher bourgeoisie. It means that this bourgeoisie has monopolized not only wealth but prestige and power as well. It means that no set of noble families has commanded the top positions and monopolized the values that are generally held in high esteem; and certainly that no set has done so explicitly by inherited right. It means that no high church dignitaries or court nobilities, no entrenched landlords with honorific accouterments, no monopolists of high army posts have opposed the enriched bourgeoisie and in the name of birth and prerogative successfully resisted its self-making.

But this does *not* mean that there are no upper strata in the United States. That they emerged from a "middle class" that had no recognized aristocratic superiors does not mean they remained middle class when enormous increases in wealth made their own superiority possible. Their origins and their newness may have made the upper strata less visible in America than elsewhere. But in America today there are in fact tiers and ranges of wealth and power of which people in the middle and lower ranks know very little and may not even dream. There are families who, in their well-being, are quite insulated from the economic jolts and lurches felt by the merely prosperous and those farther down the scale. There are also men of power who in quite small groups make decisions of enormous consequence for the underlying population. . . .

CRITICAL-THINKING QUESTIONS

1. What institutions form the "interlocking triangle" in Mills's analysis? Why does he think these are the more powerful social institutions?
2. Explain how Mills argues that the existence of a power elite is not a consequence of people *per se but a result of the institutions of U.S. society.*
3. Does the lack of an aristocratic history mean that power is dispersed throughout U.S. society?

48

Pornography: Morality or Politics?

Catharine A. MacKinnon

In conventional usage, the term "politics" evokes thoughts of campaigns and elections for office. Critics of the status quo, however, typically argue that various dimensions of everyday life are political insofar as some category of humanity wields power over others. Thus feminists contend that pornography—widely thought of as obscenity—is more correctly understood as a type of sexual politics *expressing male power over women. To Catharine MacKinnon, a leading feminist and lawyer, pornography is not a moral issue but an important political matter.*

A critique of pornography[1] is to feminism what its defense is to male supremacy. Central to the institutionalization of male dominance, pornography cannot be reformed or suppressed or banned. It can only be changed. The legal doctrine of obscenity, the state's closest approximation to addressing the pornography question, has made the First Amend-

SOURCE: *Feminism Unmodified: Discourses on Life and Law* by Catharine A. MacKinnon (Cambridge: Harvard University Press, 1987), pp. 146–53, 162. Copyright © 1987 by the President and Fellows of Harvard College. Reprinted by permission of the publishers.

ment[2] into a barrier to this process. . . . Obscenity law is concerned with morality, specifically morals from the male point of view, meaning the stand point of male dominance. The feminist critique of pornography is about politics, specifically politics from women's point of view, meaning the standpoint of the subordination of women to men.[3] Morality here means good and evil; politics means power and powerlessness. Obscenity is a moral idea; pornography is a political practice. Obscenity is abstract; pornography is concrete. The two concepts represent two entirely different things. Nudity, explicitness, excess of candor, arousal or excitement, prurience, unnaturalness—these qualities bother obscenity law when sex is depicted or portrayed. Abortion, birth control information, and treatments for "restoring sexual virility" (whose, do you suppose?) have also been included.[4] Sex forced on real women so that it can be sold at a profit to be forced on other real women; women's bodies trussed and maimed and raped and made into things to be hurt and obtained and accessed, and this presented as the nature of women; the coercion that is visible and the coercion that has become invisible—this and more bothers feminists about pornography. Obscenity as such probably does little harm,[5] pornography causes attitudes and behaviors of violence and discrimination that define the treatment and status of half of the population.[6] To make the legal and philosophical consequences of this distinction clear, I will describe the feminist critique of pornography, criticize the law of obscenity in terms of it, then discuss the criticism that pornography "dehumanizes" women to distinguish the male morality of liberalism and obscenity law from a feminist political critique of pornography.[7] . . .

Pornography, in the feminist view, is a form of forced sex, a practice of sexual politics, an institution of gender inequality. In this perspective, pornography is not harmless fantasy or a corrupt and confused misrepresentation of an otherwise natural and healthy sexuality. Along with the rape and prostitution in which it participates, pornography institutionalizes the sexuality of male supremacy, which fuses the erotization of dominance and submission with the social construction of male and female.[8] Gender is sexual. Pornography constitutes the meaning of that sexuality. Men treat women as who they see women as being. Pornography constructs who that is. Men's power over women means that the way men see women defines who women can be. Pornography is that way.

In pornography, women desire dispossession and cruelty. Men, permitted to put words (and other things) in women's mouths, create scenes in which women desperately want to be bound, bat-

tered, tortured, humiliated, and killed. Or merely taken and used. This is erotic to the male point of view. Subjection itself, with self-determination ecstatically relinquished, is the content of women's sexual desire and desirability. Women are there to be violated and possessed, men to violate and possess them, either on screen or by camera or pen, on behalf of the viewer.

One can be for or against this pornography without getting beyond liberalism. The critical yet formally liberal view of Susan Griffin, for example, conceptualizes eroticism as natural and healthy but corrupted and confused by "the pornographic mind."[9] Pornography distorts Eros, which preexists and persists, despite male culture's pornographic "revenge" upon it. Eros is, unaccountably, *still there*. Pornography mistakes it, mis-images it, misrepresents it. There is no critique of *reality* here, only objections to how it is seen; no critique of that reality that pornography imposes on women's real lives, those lives that are so seamlessly *consistent* with the pornography that pornography can be credibly defended by saying it is only a mirror of reality.

Contrast this view with the feminist analysis of Andrea Dworkin, in which sexuality itself is a social construct, gendered to the ground. Male dominance here is not an artificial overlay upon an underlying inalterable substratum of uncorrupted essential sexual being. Sexuality free of male dominance will require *change*, not reconceptualization, transcendence, or excavation. Pornography is not imagery in some relation to a reality elsewhere constructed. It is not a distortion, reflection, projection, expression, fantasy, representation, or symbol either. It is sexual reality. Dworkin's *Pornography: Men Possessing Women*[10] presents a sexual theory of gender inequality of which pornography is a core constitutive practice. The way pornography produces its meaning constructs and defines men and women as such. Gender is what gender means.[11] It has no basis in anything other than the social reality its hegemony constructs. The process that gives sexuality its male supremacist meaning is therefore the process through which gender inequality becomes socially real.

In this analysis the liberal defense of pornography as human sexual liberation, as derepression—whether by feminists, lawyers, or neo-Freudians[12]—is a defense not only of force and sexual terrorism, but of the subordination of women. Sexual liberation in the liberal sense frees male sexual aggression in the feminist sense. What looks like love and romance in the liberal view looks a lot like hatred and torture in the feminist view. Pleasure and eroticism become violation. Desire appears as lust for dominance and submission. The vulnerability of women's projected sexual availability—that acting we are allowed: Asking to be acted upon—is victimization. Play conforms to scripted roles, fantasy expresses ideology—is not exempt from it—and admiration of natural physical beauty becomes objectification.

The experience of the (overwhelmingly) male audiences who consume pornography[13] is therefore not fantasy or simulation or catharsis[14] but sexual reality: the level of reality on which sex itself largely operates. To understand this, one does not have to notice that pornography models are real women to whom something real is being done,[15] nor does one have to inquire into the systematic infliction of pornographic sexuality upon women,[16] although it helps. The aesthetic of pornography itself, the *way* it provides what those who consume it want, is itself the evidence. When uncensored explicit—that is, the most pornographic—pornography tells all, all means what a distanced detached observer would report about who did what to whom. This is the turn-on. Why does observing sex objectively presented cause the male viewer to experience his own sexuality? Because his eroticism is, socially, a watched thing. . . . It is not that life and art imitate each other; in sexuality, they *are* each other.

The law of obscenity,[17] the state's primary approach[18] to its version of the pornography question, has literally nothing in common with this feminist critique. Their obscenity is not our pornography. One commentator has said, "Obscenity is not suppressed primarily for the protection of others. Much of it is suppressed for the

purity of the 'community.' Obscenity, at bottom, is not a crime. Obscenity is a sin."[19] This is, on one level, literally accurate. Men are turned on by obscenity, including its suppression, the same way they are by sin. Animated by morality from the male standpoint, in which violation—of women and rules—is eroticized, obscenity law can be seen to proceed according to the interest of male power, robed in gender-neutral good and evil.

Morality in its specifically liberal form (although, as with most dimensions of male dominance, the distinction between left and right is more formal than substantive) revolves around a set of parallel distinctions that can be consistently traced through obscenity law. Even though the approach this law takes to the problem it envisions has shifted over time, its fundamental norms remain consistent: Public is opposed to private, in parallel with ethics and morality, and factual is opposed to valued determinations. Under male supremacy, these distinctions are gender-based: Female is private, moral, valued, subjective; male is public, ethical, factual, objective.[20] If such gendered concepts are constructs of the male experience, imposed from the male standpoint on society as a whole, liberal morality expresses male supremacist politics. That is, discourse conducted in terms of good and evil that does not expose the gendered foundations of these concepts proceeds oblivious to—and serves to disguise—the position of power that underlies, and is furthered by, that discourse. . . .

Reexamining the law of obscenity in light of the feminist critique of pornography that has become possible, it becomes clear that male morality sees as good that which maintains its power and sees as evil that which undermines or qualifies it or questions its absoluteness. Differences in the law over time—such as the liberalization of obscenity doctrine—reflect either changes in the group of men in power or shifts in their perceptions of the best strategy for maintaining male supremacy—probably some of both. But it must be made to work. The outcome, descriptively analyzed, is that obscenity law prohibits what it sees as immoral, which from a feminist standpoint tends to be relatively harmless, while protecting what it sees as moral, which from a feminist standpoint is often that which is damaging to women. So it, too, is a politics, only covertly so. What male morality finds evil, meaning threatening to its power, feminist politics tends to find comparatively harmless. What feminist politics identifies as central in our subordination—the erotization of dominance and submission—male morality tends to find comparatively harmless or defends as affirmatively valuable, hence protected speech.

In 1973 obscenity under law came to mean that which " 'the average person applying contemporary community standards' would find that, . . . taken as a whole, appeals to the prurient interest . . . [which] depicts or describes, in a patently offensive way, sexual conduct specifically defined by the applicable state law; and [which], taken as a whole, lacks serious literary, artistic, political, or scientific value."[21] Feminism doubts whether the average person, gender neutral, exists; has more questions about the content and process of definition of community standards than about deviations from them; wonders why prurience counts but powerlessness doesn't; why sensibilities are better protected from offense than women are from exploitation; defines sexuality, hence its violation and expropriation, more broadly than does any state law and wonders why a body of law that can't in practice tell rape from intercourse should be entrusted with telling pornography from anything less. The law of obscenity says that intercourse on street corners is not legitimized by the fact that the persons are "simultaneously engaged in a valid political dialogue."[22] But, in a feminist light, one sees that the requirement that a work be considered "as a whole" legitimizes something very like that on the level of publications like *Playboy*.[23] Experimental evidence is beginning to support what victims have long known: Legitimate settings diminish the injury perceived as done to the women whose trivialization and objectification it contextualizes.[24] Besides, if a woman is subjected, why should it matter that the work has other value?[25] Perhaps what redeems a work's value among men *enhances* its injury to

women. Existing standards of literature, art, science, and politics are, in feminist light, remarkably consonant with pornography's mode, meaning, and message. Finally and foremost, a feminist approach reveals that although the content and dynamic of pornography are about women—about the sexuality of women, about women as sexuality—in the same way that the vast majority of "obscenities" refer specifically to women's bodies, our invisibility has been such that the law of obscenity has *never even considered pornography a women's issue.*[26]. . .

. . . [T]he law of obscenity has the same surface theme and the same underlying theme as pornography itself. Superficially both involve morality: rules made and transgressed for purposes of sexual arousal. Actually, both are about power, about the equation between the erotic and the control of women by men: *women* made and transgressed for purposes of sexual arousal. It seems essential to the kick of pornography that it be to some degree against the rules, but it is never truly unavailable or truly illegitimate. Thus obscenity law, like the law of rape, preserves the value of, without restricting the ability to get, that which it purports to both devalue and to prohibit. Obscenity law helps keep pornography sexy by putting state power—force, hierarchy—behind its purported prohibition on what men can have sexual access to. The law of obscenity is to pornography as pornography is to sex: a map that purports to be a mirror, a legitimization and authorization and set of directions and guiding controls that project themselves onto social reality while claiming merely to reflect the image of what is already there. Pornography presents itself as fantasy or illusion or idea, which can be good or bad as it is accurate or inaccurate, while it actually, *hence accurately,* distributes power. Liberal morality cannot deal with illusions that *constitute* reality because its theory of reality, lacking a substantive critique of the distribution of social power, cannot get behind the empirical world, truth by correspondence. On the surface, both pornography and the law of obscenity are about sex. In fact, it is the status of women that is at stake.

CRITICAL-THINKING QUESTIONS

1. According to MacKinnon, how does pornography involve constructing a definition of masculinity and femininity? What does it mean to suggest that reality is "gendered"?

2. What is the conventional understanding of pornography as a moral issue? Why does MacKinnon reject that as incorrect, as a "masculine" analysis, and as inconsistent with the political goals of feminism?

3. Based on a reading of MacKinnon's article, why do conservatives often criticize feminism for "politicizing" everyday life?

NOTES

Many of the ideas in this essay were developed and refined in close collaboration with Andrea Dworkin. It is difficult at times to distinguish the contribution of each of us to a body of work that—through shared teaching, writing, speaking, organizing, and political action on every level—has been created together. I have tried to credit specific contributions that I am aware are distinctly hers. This text is mine; she does not necessarily agree with everything in it.

1. This speech as a whole is intended to communicate what I mean by pornography. The key work on the subject is Andrea Dworkin, *Pornography: Men Possessing Women* (1981). No definition can convey the meaning of a word as well as its use in context can. However, what Andrea Dworkin and I mean by pornography is rather well captured in our legal definition: "Pornography is the graphic sexually explicit subordination of women, whether in pictures or in words, that also includes one or more of the following: (1) women are presented dehumanized as sexual objects, things, or commodities; or (2) women are presented as sexual objects who enjoy pain or humiliation; or (3) women are presented as sexual objects who experience sexual pleasure in being raped; or (4) women are presented as sexual objects tied up or cut up or mutilated or bruised or physically hurt; or (5) women are presented in postures of sexual submission, servility, or display; or (6) women's body parts—including but not limited to vaginas, breasts, and buttocks—are exhibited, such that women are reduced to those parts; or (7) women are presented as whores by nature; or (8) women are presented being penetrated by objects or animals; or (9) women are presented in scenarios of degradation, injury, torture, shown as filthy or inferior, bleeding, bruised, or hurt in a context that makes these conditions sexual." Pornography also includes "the use of men, children, or transsexuals in the place of women." Pornography, thus defined, is discrimination on the basis of sex and, as such, a civil rights violation. This definition is a slightly modified version of the one passed by the Minneapolis City Council on December 30, 1983. Minneapolis, Minn., Ordinance amending Tit. 7, chs. 139 and 141, Minneapolis Code of Ordinances Relating to Civil Rights (Dec. 30, 1983). The ordinance was vetoed by the mayor, reintroduced, passed again, and vetoed again in 1984.

2. "Congress shall make no law . . . abridging the freedom of speech, or of the press . . ." U.S. Const. amend. I.

3. The sense in which I mean women's perspective as different from men's is like that of Virginia Woolf's reference to "the difference of view, the difference of standard" in her "George Eliot," 1 *Collected Essays* 204 (1966). Neither of us uses the notion of a gender difference to refer to something biological or natural or transcendental or existential. Perspective parallels standards because the social experience of gender is confined by gender. *See* Catharine A. MacKinnon, *Sexual Harassment of Working Women,* 107–41 (1979). . . ; Virginia Woolf, *Three Guineas* (1938); *see also* Andrea Dworkin, "The Root Cause," in *Our Blood: Essays and Discourses on Sexual Politics,* 96 (1976). I do not refer to the gender difference here descriptively, leaving its roots and implications unspecified, so they could be biological, existential, transcendental, in any sense inherent, or social but necessary. I mean "point of view" as a view, hence a standard, that is imposed on women by force of sex inequality, which is a political condition. "Male," which is an adjective here, is a social and political concept, not a biological attribute; it is a status socially conferred upon a person because of a condition of birth. As I use "male," it has nothing whatever to do with inherency, preexistence, nature, inevitability, or body as such. Because it is in the interest of men to be male in the system we live under (male being powerful as well as human), they seldom question its rewards or even see it as a status at all.

4. Criminal Code, Can. Rev. Stat. chap. c-34, § 159(2)(c) and (d)(1970). People v. Sanger, 222 N.Y. 192, 118 N.E. 637 (1918).

5. *The Report of the Commission on Obscenity and Pornography* (1970) (majority report). The accuracy of the commission's findings is called into question by: (1) widespread criticism of the commission's methodology from a variety of perspectives, e.g., L. Sunderland, *Obscenity—The Court, the Congress and the President's Commission* (1975); Edward Donnerstein, "Pornography Commission Revisited: Aggression—Erotica and Violence against Women," 39 *Journal of Personality and Social Psychology,* 269 (1980); Ann Garry, "Pornography and Respect for Women," 4 *Social Theory and Practice* 395 (Summer 1978); Irene Diamond, "Pornography and Repression," 5 *Signs: A Journal of Women in Culture and Society* 686 (1980); Victor Cline, "Another View: Pornography Effects, the State of the Art," in *Where Do You Draw the Line?* (V. B. Cline, Ed. 1974); Pauline Bart and Margaret Jozsa, "Dirty Books, Dirty Films, and Dirty Data," in *Take Back the Night: Women on Pornography* 204 (Laura Lederer, Ed. 1982); (2) the commission's tendency to minimize the significance of its own findings, *e.g.,* those by Donald Mosher on the differential effects of exposure by gender; and (3) the design of the commission's research. The commission did not focus on questions about gender, did its best to eliminate "violence" from its materials (so as not to overlap with the Violence Commission), and propounded unscientific theories such as Puritan guilt to explain women's negative responses to the materials.

Further, scientific causality is unnecessary to legally validate an obscenity regulation: "But, it is argued, there is no scientific data which conclusively demonstrate that exposure to obscene materials adversely affects men and women or their society. It is [urged] that, absent such a demonstration, any kind of state regulation is 'impermissible.' *We reject this argument.* It is not for us to resolve empirical uncertainties underlying state legislation, save in the exceptional case where that legislation plainly impinges upon rights protected by the Constitution itself. . . . Although there is no conclusive proof of a connection between antisocial behavior and obscene material, the legislature of Georgia could quite reasonably determine that such a connection does or might exist." Paris Adult Theatre I v. Slaton, 413 U.S. 49, 60–61 (1973) (Burger, J., for the majority) (emphasis added); see also Roth v. U.S., 354 U.S. 476, 501 (1957).

6. Some of the harm of pornography to women, as defined in note 1 . . . , and as discussed in this talk, has been documented in empirical studies. Recent studies have found that exposure to pornography increases the willingness of normal men to aggress against women under laboratory conditions; makes both women and men substantially less able to perceive accounts of rape as accounts of rape; makes normal men more closely resemble convicted rapists psychologically; increases attitudinal measures that are known to correlate with rape, such as hostility toward women, propensity to rape, condoning rape, and predictions that one would rape or force sex on a woman if one knew one would not get caught; and produces other attitude changes in men, such as increasing the extent of their trivialization, dehumanization, and objectification of women. Diana E. H. Russell, "Pornography and Violence: What Does the New Research Say?" in Lederer, note [5] . . . , at 216; Neil M. Malamuth and Edward Donnerstein, Eds., *Pornography and Sexual Aggression* (1984); Dolph Zillman, *The Connection between Sex and Aggression* (1984); J. V. P. Check, N. Malamuth, and R. Stille, "Hostility to Women Scale" (1983) (unpublished manuscript); Edward Donnerstein, "Pornography: Its Effects on Violence against Women," in Malamuth and Donnerstein, Eds., *Pornography and Sexual Aggression* (1984); Neil M. Malamuth and J. V. P. Check, "The Effects of Mass Media Exposure on Acceptance of Violence against Women: A Field Experiment," 15 *Journal of Research in Personality* 436 (1981); Neil M. Malamuth, "Rape Proclivities among Males," 37 *Journal of Social Issues* 138 (1981); Neil M. Malamuth and Barry Spinner, "A Longitudinal Content Analysis of Sexual Violence in the Best-Selling Erotic Magazines," 16 *Journal of Sex Research* 226 (1980); Mosher, "Sex Callousness Towards Women," in 8 *Technical Report of the Commission on Obscenity and Pornography* 313 (1971); Dolph Zillman and J. Bryant, "Effects of Massive Exposure to Pornography," in Malamuth and Donnerstein, Eds., *Pornography and Sexual Aggression* (1984).

7. The following are illustrative, not exhaustive, of the body of work I term the "feminist critique of pornography." Andrea Dworkin, note 1 . . . ; Dorchen Leidholdt, "Where Pornography Meets Fascism," *Win,* Mar. 15, 1983, at 18; George Steiner, "Night Words," in *The Case Against Pornography,* 227 (D. Holbrook, Ed. 1973); Susan Brownmiller, *Against Our Will: Men, Women and Rape,* 394 (1975); Robin Morgan, "Pornography and Rape: Theory and Practice," in *Going Too Far,* 165 (Robin Morgan, Ed. 1977); Kathleen Barry, *Female Sexual Slavery* (1979); *Against Sado-Masochism: A Radical Feminist Analysis* (R. R. Linden, D. R. Pagano, D. E. H. Rus

sell, and S. L. Star, Eds. 1982), especially chapters by Ti-Grace Atkinson, Judy Butler, Andrea Dworkin, Alice Walker, John Stoltenberg, Audre Lorde, and Susan Leigh Star; Alice Walker, "Coming Apart," in Lederer, *Take Back the Night,* note [5] . . . , and other articles in that volume with the exception of the legal ones; Gore Vidal, "Women's Liberation Meets the Miller-Mailer-Manson Man," in *Homage to Daniel Shays: Collected Essays 1952–1972,* 389 (1972); Linda Lovelace and Michael McGrady, *Ordeal* (1980). Works basic to the perspective taken here are Kate Millett, *Sexual Politics* (1969) and Florence Rush, *The Best-Kept Secret: Sexual Abuse of Children* (1980). "Violent Pornography: Degradation of Women versus Right of Free Speech," 8 *New York University Review of Law and Social Change,* 181 (1978) contains both feminist and nonfeminist arguments.

8. [For more extensive discussions of this subject, *see* my prior work, especially "Feminism, Marxism, Method and the State: An Agenda for Theory," 7 *Signs: Journal of Women in Culture and Society,* 515 (1982)], [hereinafter cited as *Signs* I].

9. Susan Griffin, *Pornography and Silence: Culture's Revenge Against Nature,* 2–4, 251–65 (1981).

10. Dworkin, note 1.

11. *See also* Dworkin, note [3]. . . .

12. The position that pornography is sex—that [whenever] you think of sex you think of pornography—underlies nearly every treatment of the subject. In particular, nearly every nonfeminist treatment proceeds on the implicit or explicit assumption, argument, criticism, or suspicion that pornography is sexually liberating in some way, a position unifying an otherwise diverse literature. *See, e.g.,* D. H. Lawrence, "Pornography and Obscenity," in his *Sex, Literature and Censorship,* 64 (1959); Hugh Hefner, "The Playboy Philosophy," *Playboy,* Dec. 1962, at 73, and *Playboy,* Feb. 1963, at 43; Henry Miller, "Obscenity and the Law of Reflection," in his *Remember to Remember,* 274, 286 (1947); Deirdre English, "The Politics of Porn: Can Feminists Walk the Line?" *Mother Jones,* April 1980, at 20; Jean Bethke Elshtain, "The Victim Syndrome: A Troubling Turn in Feminism," *The Progressive,* June 1982, at 42. To choose an example at random: "In opposition to the Victorian view that narrowly defines proper sexual function in a rigid way that is analogous to ideas of excremental regularity and moderation, pornography builds a model of plastic variety and joyful excess in sexuality. In opposition to the sorrowing Catholic dismissal of sexuality as an unfortunate and spiritually superficial concomitant of propagation, pornography affords the alternative idea of the independent status of sexuality as a profound and shattering ecstasy." David Richards, "Free Speech and Obscenity Law: Toward a Moral Theory of the First Amendment," 123 *University of Pennsylvania Law Review,* 45, 81 (1974) (footnotes omitted). *See also* F. Schauer, "Response: Pornography and the First Amendment," 40 *University of Pittsburgh Law Review,* 605, 616 (1979).

13. Spending time around adult bookstores, attending pornographic movies, and talking with pornographers (who, like all smart pimps, do some form of market research), as well as analyzing the pornography itself in sex/gender terms, all confirm that pornography is for men. That women may attend or otherwise consume it does not make it any less for men, any more than the observation that mostly men consume pornog

raphy means that pornography does not harm women. *See* Martha Langelan, "The Political Economy of Pornography," *Aegis: Magazine on Ending Violence against Women,* Autumn 1981, at 5; J. Cook, "The X-Rated Economy," *Forbes,* Sept. 18, 1978, at 60. Personal observation reveals that most women tend to avoid pornography as much as possible—which is not very much, as it turns out.

14. The "fantasy" and "catharsis" hypotheses, together, assert that pornography cathects sexuality on the level of fantasy fulfillment. The work of Edward Donnerstein, particularly, shows that the opposite is true. The more pornography is viewed, the *more* pornography—and the more brutal pornography—is both wanted and required for sexual arousal. What occurs is not catharsis, but desensitization, requiring progressively more potent stimulation. See works cited note [6] . . . ; Murray Straus, "Leveling, Civility, and Violence in the Family," 36 *Journal of Marriage & The Family,* 13 (1974).

15. Lovelace and McGrady, note [7] . . . , provides an account by one coerced pornography model. *See also* Andrea Dworkin, "Pornography's 'Exquisite Volunteers,' " *Ms.,* March 1981, at 65.

16. However, for one such inquiry, see Russell, note [6] . . . , at 228: A random sample of 930 San Francisco households found that 10 percent of women had at least once "been upset by anyone trying to get you to do what they'd seen in pornographic pictures, movies or books." Obviously, this figure could only include those who knew that the pornography was the source of the sex, so this finding is conservative. *See also* Diana E. H. Russell, *Rape in Marriage,* 27–41 (1983) (discussing the data base). The hearings Andrea Dworkin and I held for the Minneapolis City Council on the ordinance cited in note 1 produced many accounts of the use of pornography to force sex on women and children. *Public Hearings on Ordinances to Add Pornography as Discrimination against Women,* Committee on Government Operations, City Council, Minneapolis, Minn., Dec. 12–13, 1983. (Hereinafter cited as *Hearings.*)

17. To body of law ably encompassed and footnoted by William Lockhart and Robert McClure, "Literature, the Law of Obscenity and the Constitution," 38 *Minnesota Law Review,* 295 (1954) and "Censorship of Obscenity," 45 *Minnesota Law Review,* 5 (1960), I add only the most important cases since then: Stanley v. Georgia, 394 U.S. 557 (1969); U.S. v. Reidel, 402 U.S. 351 (1970); Miller v. California, 413 U.S. 15 (1973); Paris Adult Theatre I v. Slaton, 413 U.S. 49 (1973); Hamling v. U.S., 418 U.S. 87 (1973); Jenkins v. Georgia, 418 U.S. 153 (1973); U.S. v. 12 200-Ft. Reels of Super 8mm Film, 413 U.S. 123 (1973); Erznoznik v. City of Jacksonville, 422 U.S. 205 (1975); Splawn v. California, 431 U.S. 595 (1976); Ward v. Illinois, 431 U.S. 767 (1976); Lovisi v. Slayton, 539 F.2d 349 (4th Cir. 1976). *See also* New York v. Ferber, 458 U.S. 747 (1982).

18. For a discussion of the role of the law of privacy in supporting the existence of pornography, see Ruth Colker, "Pornography and Privacy: Towards the Development of a Group Based Theory for Sex Based Intrusions of Privacy," 1 *Law and Inequality: A Journal of Theory and Practice,* 191 (1983).

19. Louis Henkin, "Morals and the Constitution: The Sin of Obscenity," 63 *Columbia Law Review,* 391, 395 (1963).

20. These parallels are discussed more fully in *Signs* II. It may seem odd to denominate "moral" as *female* here, since this article discusses male morality. Under male supremacy, men define things; I am describing that. Men define women *as* "moral." This is the male view of women. My analysis, a feminist critique of the male standpoint, terms "moral" the concept that pornography is about good and evil. This is *my* analysis of *them,* as contrasted with their attributions to women.

21. Miller v. California, 413 U.S. 15, 24 (1973).

22. Paris Adult Theatre I v. Slaton, 413 U.S. 49, 67 (1973). *See also* Miller v. California, 413 U.S. 15, 25 n.7 ("A quotation from Voltaire in the flyleaf of a book will not constitutionally redeem an otherwise obscene publication," quoting Kois v. Wisconsin, 408 U.S. 229, 231 [1972]).

23. Penthouse International v. McAuliffe, 610 F.2d 1353, 1362–73 (5th Cir. 1980). For a study in enforcement, *see* Coble v. City of Birmingham, 389 So.2d 527 (Ala. Ct. App. 1980).

24. Malamuth and Spinner, note [6] . . . (". . . the portrayal of sexual aggression within such 'legitimate' magazines as *Playboy* and *Penthouse* may have a greater impact than similar portrayals in hard-core pornography"); Neil M. Malamuth and Edward Donnerstein, "The Effects of Aggressive-Pornographic Mass Media Stimuli," 15 *Advances in Experimental Social Psychology,* 103, 130 (1982).

25. Some courts, under the obscenity rubric, seem to have understood that the quality of artistry does not undo the damage. People v. Mature Enterprises, 343 N.Y.S.2d 911, 925 n. 14(N.Y. Sup. 1973) ("This court will not adopt a rule of law which states that obscenity is suppressible but that well-written or technically well produced obscenity is not," quoting, in part, People v. Fritch, 13 N.Y.2d 119, 126, 243 N.Y.S.2d, 1, 7, 192 N.E.2d 713 [1963]). More to the point of my argument here is Justice O'Connor's observation that "[t]he compelling interests identified in today's opinion . . . suggest that the Constitution might in fact permit New York to ban knowing distribution of works depicting minors engaged in explicit sexual conduct, regardless of the social value of the depictions. For example, a twelve-year-old child photographed while masturbating surely suffers the same psychological harm whether the community labels the photograph 'edifying' or 'tasteless.' The audience's appreciation of the depiction is simply irrelevant to New York's asserted interest in protecting children from psychological, emotional, and mental harm." New York v. Ferber, 458 U.S. 747, 774–75 (1982) (concurring). Put another way, how does it make a harmed child *not harmed* that what was produced by harming him is great art?

26. Women typically get mentioned in obscenity law only in the phrase, "women and men," used as a synonym for "people." At the same time, exactly who the victim of pornography is, has long been a great mystery. The few references to "exploitation" in obscenity litigation do not evoke a woman victim. For example, one reference to "a system of commercial exploitation of people with sadomasochistic sexual aberrations" concerned the customers of women dominatrixes, all of whom were men. State v. Von Cleef, 102 N.J. Super. 104, 245 A.2d 495, 505 (1968). The children at issue in *Ferber* were boys. Similarly, Justice Frankfurter invoked the "sordid exploitation of man's nature and impulses" in discussing his conception of pornography in Kingsley Pictures Corp. v. Regents, 360 U.S. 684, 692 (1958).

POLITICS, GOVERNMENT, AND THE MILITARY

Cross-Cultural

49

Arms Control and the New World Order

Jack Mendelsohn

The collapse of the former Soviet Union and the Eastern Bloc provides a historic opportunity to pursue the goals of arms control and enhancing global security. But, in the shadow of superpower confrontation, we also see rising fears about inadvertent use of nuclear weapons as well as resurging local and regional conflicts. This article assesses the prospects for peace in the post–Cold War era.

The collapse of communism and the promise of a more cooperative East-West relationship have transformed the world of arms control. Goals that were once unthinkable—making enormous cuts in strategic forces or actually destroying nuclear warheads—are now at the top of the agenda. Developments that were always dangerous but of only secondary concern because of the primary East-West confrontation—the widespread deployment of short-range nuclear weapons or the spread of conventional weapons to the developing world—have now become urgent issues. And verification measures, originally born of deep distrust between East and West and intended to inform adversaries about each other's military programs, are now available to help monitor agreements, build trust, and reduce tensions.

NUCLEAR WEAPONS

Understandably, the most immediate concern of both the United States and Europe is the future of nuclear weapons in a disintegrating Soviet empire. For now, at least, the goals of the United States and

SOURCE: *The Brookings Review,* Spring 1992, pp. 34–39. Copyright © 1992 by the Brookings Institution. Reprinted by permission.

Russia seem to be congruent: to ensure the centralized command and control of the nuclear forces of the newly formed Commonwealth of Independent States (CIS), to encourage the safe and secure withdrawal of tactical (and, eventually, strategic) nuclear weapons from the outlying republics to Russia, and to prevent the spread of nuclear hardware and brainpower to third countries. Programs to address these problems are already under way or under consideration, although concern about their continued successful implementation will certainly persist.

In the longer term a different set of nuclear arms control issues will challenge policymakers. The end of the Cold War offers a unique opportunity to push the size of U.S. and Russian strategic nuclear forces down to considerably lower levels. As [former Soviet president Gorbachev and former U.S. president Bush agreed], the United States and Russia could readily cut in half the number of strategic weapons permitted under the Strategic Arms Reduction Treaty (START).

How low strategic forces can ultimately be taken will depend on the actual role assigned to nuclear weapons. Most analysts agree that the United States can maintain its present "warfighting" strategy with as few as 3,000–4,000 nuclear weapons. . . . If, on the other hand, the United States were prepared to abandon its current warfighting strategy, which targets thousands of military, political, and economic sites, in favor of a purely deterrent one involving a very limited set of military-industrial targets, it would facilitate even steeper reductions in strategic warheads. This is apparently the strategy that underlies Russian President Boris Yeltsin's recent offer to reduce strategic arsenals to 2,000–2,500 warheads.

An essentially deterrent strategy would be based on the premise that relatively few warheads are required to dissuade an adversary from launching a deliberate nuclear attack. According to former Secretary of Defense Robert McNamara, during the 1962 Cuban missile crisis, when the United States had approximately 5,000 strategic warheads to the Soviet Union's 300, "President Kennedy and I were deterred from even consider-

ing a nuclear attack on the USSR by the knowledge that, although such a strike would destroy the Soviet Union, *tens* of their weapons would survive to be launched against the United States" (emphasis added). Nothing in the past thirty years has invalidated that conclusion or diminished the deterrent of even a few nuclear weapons.

PREVENTING INADVERTENT CONFLICT

With the end of the adversarial relationship between the United States and Russia and the prospect of large-scale reductions in existing nuclear arsenals, longstanding fears of deliberate attack have yielded to a new concern about inadvertent conflict. To respond to this concern, the two nations will need to make it as difficult as possible to launch their nuclear weapons. They will have to ensure that all nuclear weapons are subject to both physical safeguards and chain-of-command arrangements that cannot be defeated or circumvented. To this end, all deployed and non-deployed nuclear weapons should have the latest technology electronic locks to prevent unauthorized use. Both arming and release codes for all nuclear weapons should be held by the national command authority (on-board commanders have access to the codes for U.S. ballistic missile submarines).

Another way to reduce the risk of inadvertent war is to increase the overall confidence of both sides in the survivability of their nuclear forces. This can be done by some relatively simple measures. For example, the president has proposed that land-based ballistic missile systems be limited by agreement to one warhead. That is one way to eliminate the concern that a small number of land-based multiple-warhead missiles on one side could be used early in a crisis and, in theory at least, destroy large numbers of similar systems on the other side. Alternatively, land-based systems could be made mobile or dispersed among multiple protective shelters. Finally, overall warhead reductions, on the scale discussed above, would by themselves decrease the number of multiple warhead systems and increase survivability by making it difficult, if not impossible, to undertake a disarming strike against the nuclear forces of the other side.

As one confidence-building measure, warheads could be removed from a portion of the land-based missile force and the systems taken off high state of alert. Ballistic missile submarines could patrol out of range of their targets, and aggressive anti-submarine warfare training activities could be strictly limited. Strategic bombers should remain off alert and their weapons stored away from operational bases. The sides could also limit the size and frequency of large-scale exercises and enhance confidence by exchanging data and giving advance notice of strategic force tests or practice alerts.

Finally, the United States, Russia, and the relevant CIS countries should agree to destroy the existing stockpile of retired and surplus nuclear weapons, perhaps 15,000 to 18,000 warheads on each side. As the two sides reduce their tactical and strategic arsenals, the number of warheads in storage will increase dramatically—as will concern over their possible theft, sale, misappropriation, or rapid redeployment. The destruction of redundant warheads should be coupled with a ban on the further production of fissile material for weapons purposes, a monitored limit on the production of new warheads to replace existing systems, and the storage, under international safeguards, of fissile material withdrawn from retired weapons.

STRATEGIC DEFENSES

Closely related to the question of nuclear force reductions and to the shift from preparing for deliberate war to preventing inadvertent war is the issue of preserving the Anti-Ballistic Missile (ABM) Treaty's strict limits on strategic defensive systems. Despite the boost given anti-missile systems by the Scud-Patriot encounters during the Gulf war, the United States will have to tread carefully in its approach to tactical and strategic ballistic missile defenses. Strategic defenses, by their nature, undercut confidence in the retaliatory capability of strategic offensive forces and could therefore lessen the willingness of one side or another to make big cuts in strategic offensive forces. In some cases, such as those involving the relatively small national deterrent forces of France and Britain, deploying even a low level of strategic defenses may actually stimulate an increase in arsenals in order to overcome these anti-missile systems.

Thus the Bush administration's interest in rewriting the ABM Treaty to permit large-scale deployment of its newest version of Star Wars, known as Global Protection against Limited Strikes (GPALS), runs contrary to a fundamental U.S. interest: to reduce nuclear arsenals in the CIS to as low a level as possible. Moreover, the goal cited by the administration in support of GPALS—to protect the United States against threats from third world "nondeterrables"—is questionable. CIA Director Robert Gates has predicted that it will be at least a decade before any country other than China or the CIS could strike the United States with long-range ballistic missiles. And most observers believe that long-range ballistic missiles would not be the delivery system of choice for any third world nation attempting to threaten the United States.

Although Yeltsin proposed a joint SDI program, it is unlikely, given the economic situation in the CIS, that in the long run Russia will really pursue such a costly defensive project. The same should be true for the United States. If the United States nonetheless persists in its efforts to deploy defenses, and if the Russians acquiesce to a similar program, then it will be critically important that any eventual strategic defensive deployments be limited to very few fixed land-based interceptors only. Anti-tactical ballistic missile systems, which are likely to be of interest to both sides and which are not prohibited by the ABM Treaty, should be designed so that neither their capability nor their widespread deployment will erode confidence in either side's strategic offensive retaliatory capabilities.

CONVENTIONAL WEAPONS

In the short term, U.S., European, and CIS arms control goals regarding conventional weapons are likely to be similar: to encourage the prompt adherence to, and implementation of, past and pending arms control obligations, especially the recently concluded Conventional Armed Forces in Europe (CFE) agreement, and to complete the Open Skies and CFE follow-on talks (the former to create an aerial inspection regime and the latter to establish politically binding limits on troop levels). A third goal, to ensure the orderly transfer of conventional military forces from Union control to the newly formed states, is certainly shared by the West and Russia. But tensions among the states of the new CIS may make it difficult, or even impossible, to distribute conventional forces quickly or smoothly. . . .

In the longer term, now that the fear of a massive land war in Europe has become, in the words of the CIA director, "virtually nonexistent," the conventional weapons arms control agenda is likely to be occupied with four principal issues. The first is greater openness, or transparency, in military programs and activities. After several decades of relying primarily on satellites and sensors to monitor military activities, and as the infatuation with on-site inspection fades, we are just now beginning to recognize and exploit the potential of relatively straightforward cooperative measures to provide intelligence. Through extensive and intensive multilateral exchange, nations can increase the information available on budgets, force size, production levels, research, development and modernization programs, deployment plans, arms transfers, and operational practices. As such openness improves our ability to predict the evolution of the overall security environment, it will enhance stability and reduce the risk of overreaction.

A second objective regarding conventional arms is to defuse the dangers of localized or ethnic strife in Europe. While the threat of a general war in Europe is minimal, numerous potential regional flash points, such as Croatia-Serbia or Armenia-Azerbaijan, still exist. Even if the CFE treaty enters into force, a concentrated effort will still have to be made to deal with these problem areas by subregional arms control. Subregional constraints might involve lowering force levels in geographically restricted areas (force allotments in Hungary and Romania, for example, could be 25 percent beneath CFE levels); establishing disengagement zones (Hungary and Romania could both agree not to deploy military forces within 50 kilometers of their common border); or instituting special monitoring measures such as intensive aerial overflights or third-party inspections.

A third issue, how to integrate large numbers of demobilized soldiers into civilian life and forestall a "black market" in conventional military hardware, will be one of the most challenging, albeit nontraditional, new arms control tasks. But it may also be the one most amenable to direct economic intervention. The United States has already offered the CIS $400 million to help dismantle its nuclear and chemical warheads. The United States and its European allies may wish to consider establishing a similar Conference on Security and Cooperation in Europe (CSCE) fund to help destroy, securely store, or ultimately buy up surplus war material from Eastern Europe and the CIS states to keep it from leaking into the black market (as apparently happened during the Croatian-Serbian conflict).

We may also wish to use an international fund to help train, house, employ, or provide severance pay to demobilized CIS soldiers to keep them from becoming a disruptive social or political force. Germany did as much to speed the evacuation of Soviet soldiers from its territory, and the current Russian military budget has designated all its capital investment for housing. We may also wish to institute programs to train soldiers who remain in uniform to work on disaster relief, environmental clean-up, and other civil support missions.

Finally, with or without U.S. participation, the European states will need to work toward creating European-based peacekeeping, peacemaking (that is, interventionary), and conflict-resolution institutions to deal with continent-wide security issues. The U.S. government does not now favor such institutions because it fears that they would undercut U.S. influence in European security issues. But, at some point, the tensions created by Yugoslavian-type crises, where the United States adopted a hands-off policy and Europe had very limited tools to manage the conflict, will force the empowerment of one or another of the Euro-based organizations (the Conference on Security and Cooperation in Europe, the Western European Union, or the North Atlantic Cooperation Council), the United Nations, or another specially created body to deal directly and forcefully with subregional challenges to European security. Once some international institution is designated as the executive forum, it will have to earmark multinational forces for the peacekeeping task, and the member states will have to devise a decisionmaking process that keeps the parties to the problem from blocking action.

STEMMING THE SPREAD OF WEAPONS

As the enormous changes in Europe have eased concerns about East-West conflict, the United States and other developed nations have turned their attention to the challenges to international security posed by the spread of weapons in the developing world. Ironically, the problem is largely the result of the developed world's own policies during the Cold War, when arming the enemy of one's enemy was considered to be the height of sophisticated geopolitics. Meeting the proliferation challenge will require of the developed world a full and rare measure of political will and self-restraint.

To be sure, regimes to control several types of proliferation already exist or are under negotiation. The nuclear Non-Proliferation Treaty, with some 140 members, has been a highly successful example of international cooperation and common perspective for a quarter of a century. Negotiations on a Chemical Weapons Convention are far advanced and likely to be concluded in the not-too-distant future. And major supplier groups (to control nuclear technology, chemical and biological weapons, missile technology, and conventional

arms transfers to the Middle East) have already been established and are expanding their scope.

Building on the existing nonproliferation structures, arms control can make several useful contributions. The first is to encourage stronger supplier restraint. Supplier states first must resist domestic political or economic pressures to sell arms, and then they will have to demonstrate a high level of political skill to balance the concerns of the developed world with objections from less advanced countries that nonproliferation regimes will spark. The nuclear supplier group clearly increased the time and cost of Iraq's nuclear weapons program. Nonetheless, the extent of Iraq's program surprised almost everyone, a fact that underscores the need to strengthen and expand nuclear export guidelines to include limits on "dual use" items—an effort already under way.

The United States and the other major arms exporters will also have to make more explicit efforts to limit sales of conventional weapons to areas of tension. For example, in conjunction with a supplier regime, "caps" might be placed on the value of arms exports approved by the supplier group to any one country in any one year. . . . That would require an international register of arms transfer and agreement among at least the "big five" exporters (the United States, the United Kingdom, France, the former Soviet Union, and China, which accounted for nearly 90 percent of the arms trade in 1990) to declare transfers and respect the cap. Pressure could also be applied to potential arms recipients by linking, directly or informally, U.S. aid, as well as aid from international lending institutions, to military spending levels.

As important as supplier restraint may be, regional arms control will undoubtedly remain the best long-term way to slow proliferation. Models already exist: The Treaty of Tlatelolco (establishing a nuclear-free zone in Latin America) and the Conventional Forces in Europe treaty are examples. Rallying the political will and muscle to apply these models to regions of the world where the underlying tension has not been directly eased by the new cooperative spirit in Europe will be a challenge. But easing these regional concerns is the key to taking the pressure off the "demand" side of proliferation: In fact, supplier restraint should only be a tool to buy time for regional efforts to work.

Regional arms control in areas such as the Middle East, South Asia, and Korea will have to involve major outside players. The United States, Russia, France, or Britain, depending on the region involved, will have to take an active interest and leading role in bringing about even a modest reconciliation. This reconciliation process would involve, first, political dialogue (as between the two Koreas and at the Middle East peace talks), then transparency (as in the Sinai and on the Golan Heights), supplier restraint, confidence-building measures, and, eventually, explicit arms control measures to limit forces and disengage (or separate) threatening forces.

Improved verification and monitoring would also strengthen nonproliferation efforts. Confidence in arms control regimes and regional security arrangements can, in general, be buttressed by increased transparency and predictability. In the proliferation arena, where one is dealing, almost by definition, with countries trying to acquire military capabilities by clandestine means, comprehensive intelligence, monitoring, and verification regimes are critical. First, as the Iraq experience has demonstrated, all agreements dealing with weapons of mass destruction must permit the right to challenge inspections of suspect sites. Second, nations with sophisticated intelligence capabilities, the United States in particular, will have to begin to share intelligence more widely. Making information more generally accessible will increase the stake of other participating states in the nonproliferation regime, enhance their confidence in its viability, and strengthen any eventual case against violators.

Finally, arms control by example is an important adjunct to specific nonproliferation treaties and cooperative measures. Although it cannot by itself stop states or leaders determined to violate an international agreement or tacit understanding, it can enhance the moral authority of the major powers. Evidence of serious intent to implement supplier restraint, to pursue deeper nuclear force reductions, to destroy conventional weapons and nuclear warheads, to stop fissionable materials production, and to cease nuclear testing would bolster the case for "demand" reduction in the proliferation arena. It would also strengthen the hand of the major powers in making the case for taking collective action—whether export controls, political and economic sanctions, or military measures—against any state that violates international agreements or standards.

CRITICAL-THINKING QUESTIONS

1. Why are the prospects for ensuring global peace historically great at present?

2. In light of the ending of the Cold War, what security concerns are taking on greater importance?

3. Why do some analysts see the growing military power of poor countries as a particular problem at this time?

FAMILY

Classic

50

"His" and "Her" Marriage

Jessie Bernard

Social scientists have found that men and women are not joined at the hip by a wedding ceremony. Rather, their subsequent lives differ in terms of gender roles, power, and ways of communicating. Bernard was among the first sociologists to point out that marriage has a different meaning for women and men. As this selection shows, spouses rarely define reality in the same way, even with regard to simple routines such as sweeping the floor or mowing the lawn.

. . . [T]here is by now a very considerable body of well-authenticated research to show that there really are two marriages in every marital union, and that they do not always coincide.

"HIS" AND "HER" MARRIAGES

. . . [T]he differences in the marriages of husbands and wives have come under the careful scrutiny of a score of researchers. They have found that when

they ask husbands and wives identical questions about the union, they often get quite different replies. There is usually agreement on the number of children they have and a few other such verifiable items, although not, for example, on length of premarital acquaintance and of engagement, on age at marriage, and interval between marriage and birth of first child. Indeed, with respect to even such basic components of the marriage as frequency of sexual relations, social interaction, household tasks, and decision making, they seem to be reporting on different marriages. As, I think, they are.

In the area of sexual relations, for example, Kinsey and his associates found different responses in from one- to two-thirds of the couples

SOURCE: *The Future of Marriage* by Jessie Bernard. Copyright © 1972 by Jessie Bernard. Reprinted with permission.

they studied. Kinsey interpreted these differences in terms of selective perception. In the generation he was studying, husbands wanted sexual relations oftener than the wives did, thus "the females may be overestimating the actual frequencies" and "the husbands . . . are probably underestimating the frequencies." The differences might also have been vestiges of the probable situation earlier in the marriage when the desired frequency of sexual relations was about six to seven times greater among husbands than among wives. This difference may have become so impressed on the spouses that it remained in their minds even after the difference itself had disappeared or even been reversed. In a sample of happily married, middle-class couples a generation later, Harold Feldman found that both spouses attributed to their mates more influence in the area of sex than they did to themselves.

Companionship, as reflected in talking together, he found, was another area where differences showed up. Replies differed on three-fourths of all the items studied, including the topics talked about, the amount of time spent talking with each other, and which partner initiated conversation. Both partners claimed that whereas they talked more about topics of interest to their mates, their mates initiated conversations about topics primarily of interest to themselves. Harold Feldman concluded that projection in terms of needs was distorting even simple, everyday events, and lack of communication was permitting the distortions to continue. It seemed to him that "if these sex differences can occur so often among these generally well-satisfied couples, it would not be surprising to find even less consensus and more distortion in other less satisfied couples."

Although, by and large, husbands and wives tend to become more alike with age, in this study of middle-class couples, differences increased with length of marriage rather than decreased, as one might logically have expected. More couples in the later than in the earlier years, for example, had differing pictures in their heads about how often they laughed together, discussed together, exchanged ideas, or worked together on projects, and about how well things were going between them.

The special nature of sex and the amorphousness of social interaction help to explain why differences in response might occur. But household tasks? They are fairly objective and clear-cut and not all that emotion-laden. Yet even here there are his-and-her versions. Since the division of labor in the household is becoming increasingly an issue in marriage, the uncovering of differing replies in this area is especially relevant. Hard as it is to believe, Granbois and Willett tell us that more than half of the partners in one sample disagreed on who kept track of money and bills. On the question, who mows the lawn? more than a fourth disagreed. Even family income was not universally agreed on.

These differences about sexual relations, companionship, and domestic duties tell us a great deal about the two marriages. But power or decision making can cover all aspects of a relationship. The question of who makes decisions or who exercises power has therefore attracted a great deal of research attention. If we were interested in who really had the power or who really made the decisions, the research would be hopeless. Would it be possible to draw any conclusion from a situation in which both partners agree that the husband ordered the wife to make all the decisions? Still, an enormous literature documents the quest of researchers for answers to the question of marital power. The major contribution it has made has been to reveal the existence of differences in replies between husbands and wives.

The presence of such inconsistent replies did not at first cause much concern. The researchers apologized for them but interpreted them as due to methodological inadequacies; if only they could find a better way to approach the problem, the differences would disappear. Alternatively, the use of only the wife's responses, which were more easily available, was justified on the grounds that differences in one direction between the partners in one marriage compensated for differences in another direction between the partners in another marriage and thus canceled them out. As, indeed, they did. For when Granbois and Willett, two market researchers, analyzed the replies of husbands and wives separately, the overall picture was in fact the same for both wives and husbands. Such cancel-ing out of differences in the total sample, however, concealed almost as much as it revealed about the individual couples who composed it. Granbois and Willett concluded, as Kinsey had earlier, that the "discrepancies . . . reflect differing perceptions on the part of responding partners." And this was the heart of the matter.

Differing reactions to common situations, it should be noted, are not at all uncommon. They are recognized in the folk wisdom embedded in the story of the blind men all giving different replies to questions on the nature of the elephant. One of the oldest experiments in juridical psychology demonstrates how different the statements of wit-nesses of the same act can be. Even in laboratory studies, it takes intensive training of raters to make it possible for them to arrive at agreement on the behavior they observe.

It has long been known that people with differ-ent backgrounds see things differently. We know, for example, that poor children perceive coins as larger than do children from more affluent homes. Boys and girls perceive differently. A good deal of the foundation for projective tests rests on the dif-ferent ways in which individuals see identical stim-uli. And this perception—or, as the sociologists put it, definition of the situation—is reality for them. In this sense, the realities of the husband's marriage are different from those of the wife's.

Finally, one of the most perceptive of the re-searchers, Constantina Safilios-Rothschild, asked the crucial question: Was what they were getting, even with the best research techniques, family so-ciology or wives' family sociology? She answered her own question: What the researchers who relied on wives' replies exclusively were reporting on was the wife's marriage. The husband's was not necessarily the same. There were, in fact, two mar-riages present:

One explanation of discrepancies between the responses of husbands and wives may be the possibility of two "re-alities," the husband's subjective reality and the wife's subjective reality—two perspectives which do not al-ways coincide. Each spouse perceives "facts" and situ-ations differently according to his own needs, values,

attitudes, and beliefs. An "objective" reality could pos-sibly exist only in the trained observer's evaluation, if it does exist at all.

Interpreting the different replies of husbands and wives in terms of selective perception, pro-jection of needs, values, attitudes, and beliefs, or different definitions of the situation, by no means renders them trivial or incidental or justifies dis-missing or ignoring them. They are, rather, funda-mental for an understanding of the two marriages, his and hers, and we ignore them at the peril of se-rious misunderstanding of marriage, present as well as future.

IS THERE AN OBJECTIVE REALITY IN MARRIAGE?

Whether or not husbands and wives perceive dif-ferently or define situations differently, still sexual relations are taking place, companionship is or is not occurring, tasks about the house are being per-formed, and decisions are being made every day by someone. In this sense, some sort of "reality" does exist. David Olson went to the laboratory to see if he could uncover it.

He first asked young couples expecting babies such questions as these: Which one of them would decide whether to buy insurance for the newborn child? Which one would decide the husband's part in diaper changing? Which one would decide whether the new mother would return to work or to school? When there were differences in the an-swers each gave individually on the questionnaire, he set up a situation in which together they had to arrive at a decision in his laboratory. He could then compare the results of the questionnaire with the results in the simulated situation. He found neither spouse's questionnaire response any more accu-rate than the other's; that is, neither conformed bet-ter to the behavioral "reality" of the laboratory than the other did.

The most interesting thing, however, was that husbands, as shown on their questionnaire re-sponse, perceived themselves as having more power than they actually did have in the laboratory "reality," and wives perceived that they had less. Thus, whereas three-fourths (73 percent) of the husbands overestimated their power in decision making, 70 percent of the wives underestimated theirs. Turk and Bell found similar results in Canada. Both spouses tend to attribute decision-making power to the one who has the "right" to make the decision. Their replies, that is, conform to the model of marriage that has characterized civilized mankind for millennia. It is this model rather than their own actual behavior that husbands and wives tend to perceive.

We are now zeroing in on the basic reality. We can remove the quotation marks. For there is, in fact, an objective reality in marriage. It is a reality that resides in the cultural—legal, moral, and conventional—prescriptions and proscriptions and, hence, expectations that constitute marriage. It is the reality that is reflected in the minds of the spouses themselves. The differences between the marriages of husbands and of wives are structural realities, and it is these structural differences that constitute the basis for the different psychological realities.

THE AUTHORITY STRUCTURE OF MARRIAGE

Authority is an institutional phenomenon; it is strongly bound up with faith. It must be believed in; it cannot be enforced unless it also has power. Authority resides not in the person on whom it is conferred by the group or society, but in the recognition and acceptance it elicits in others. Power, on the other hand, may dispense with the prop of authority. It may take the form of the ability to coerce or to veto; it is often personal, charismatic, not institutional. This kind of personal power is self-enforcing. It does not require shoring up by access to force. In fact, it may even operate subversively. A woman with this kind of power may or may not know that she possesses it. If she does know she has it, she will probably disguise her exercise of it.

In the West, the institutional structure of marriage has invested the husband with authority and backed it by the power of church and state. The marriages of wives have thus been officially dominated by the husband. Hebrew, Christian, and Islamic versions of deity were in complete accord on this matter. The laws, written or unwritten, religious or civil, which have defined the marital union have been based on male conceptions, and they have undergirded male authority.

Adam came first. Eve was created to supply him with companionship, not vice versa. And God himself had told her that Adam would rule over her; her wishes had to conform to his. The New Testament authors agreed. Women were created for men, not men for women; women were therefore commanded to be obedient. If they wanted to learn anything, let them ask their husbands in private, for it was shameful for them to talk in the church. They should submit themselves to their husbands, because husbands were superior to wives; and wives should be as subject to their husbands as the church was to Christ. Timothy wrapped it all up: "Let the woman learn in silence with all subjection. But I suffer not a woman to teach, nor to usurp authority over the man, but to be in silence." Male Jews continued for millennia to thank God three times a day that they were not women. And the Koran teaches women that men are naturally their superiors because God made them that way; naturally, their own status is one of subordination.

The state as well as the church had the same conception of marriage, assigning to the husband and father control over his dependents, including his wife. Sometimes this power was well-nigh absolute, as in the case of the Roman patria potestas—or the English common law, which flatly said, "The husband and wife are as one and that one is the husband." There are rules still lingering today with the same, though less extreme, slant. Diane B. Schulder has summarized the legal framework of the wife's marriage as laid down in the common law.

The legal responsibilities of a wife are to live in the home established by her husband; to perform the domestic chores (cleaning, cooking, washing, etc.) necessary to help maintain that home; to care for her husband and children. . . . A husband may force his wife to have sexual relations as long as his demands are reasonable and her health is not endangered. . . . The law allows a wife to take a job if she wishes. However, she must see that her domestic chores are completed, and, if there are children, that they receive proper care during her absence.

A wife is not entitled to payment for household work; and some jurisdictions in the United States expressly deny payment for it. In some states, the wife's earnings are under the control of her husband, and in four, special court approval and in some cases husband's consent are required if a wife wishes to start a business of her own.

The male counterpart to these obligations includes that of supporting his wife. He may not disinherit her. She has a third interest in property owned by him, even if it is held in his name only. Her name is required when he sells property.

Not only divine and civil law but also rules of etiquette have defined authority as a husband's prerogative. One of the first books published in England was a *Boke of Good Manners,* translated from the French of Jacques Le Grand in 1487, which included a chapter on "How Wymmen Ought to Be Gouerned." The thirty-third rule of Plutarch's *Rules for Husbands and Wives* was that women should obey their husbands; if they "try to rule over their husbands they make a worse mistake than the husbands do who let themselves be ruled." The husband's rule should not, of course, be brutal; he should not rule his wife "as a master does his chattel, but as the soul governs the body, by feeling with her and being linked to her by affection." Wives, according to Richard Baxter, a seventeenth-century English divine, had to obey even a wicked husband, the only exception being that a wife need not obey a husband if he ordered her to change her religion. But, again, like Plutarch, Baxter warned that the husband should love his wife; his authority should not be so coercive or so harsh as to destroy love. Among his twelve rules for carrying out the duties of conjugal love, however, was one to the effect that love must not be so imprudent as to destroy authority.

As late as the nineteenth century, Tocqueville noted that in the United States the ideals of democracy did not apply between husbands and wives:

Nor have the Americans ever supposed that one consequence of democratic principles is the subversion of marital power, or the confusion of the natural authorities in families. They hold that every association must have a head in order to accomplish its objective, and that the natural head of the conjugal association is man. They do not therefore deny him the right of directing his partner; and they maintain, that in the smaller association of husband and wife, as well as in the great social community, the object of democracy is to regulate and legalize the powers which are necessary, not to subvert all power.

This opinion is not peculiar to men and contested by women; I never observed that the women of America consider conjugal authority as an unfortunate usurpation [by men] of their rights, nor that they thought themselves degraded by submitting to it. It appears to me, on the contrary, that they attach a sort of pride to the voluntary surrender of their own will, and make it their boast to bend themselves to the yoke, not to shake it off.

The point here is not to document once more the specific ways (religious, legal, moral, traditional) in which male authority has been built into the marital union—that has been done a great many times—but merely to illustrate how different (structurally or "objectively" as well as perceptually or "subjectively") the wife's marriage has actually been from the husband's throughout history.

THE SUBVERSIVENESS OF NATURE

The rationale for male authority rested not only on biblical grounds but also on nature or natural law, on the generally accepted natural superiority of men. For nothing could be more self-evident than that the patriarchal conception of marriage, in which the husband was unequivocally the boss, was natural, resting as it did on the unchallenged superiority of males.

Actually, nature, if not deity, is subversive. Power, or the ability to coerce or to veto, is widely distributed in both sexes, among women as well as among men. And whatever the theoretical or conceptual picture may have been, the actual, day-by-day relationships between husbands and wives have been determined by the men and women themselves. All that the institutional machinery could do was to confer authority; it could not create personal power, for such power cannot be conferred, and women can generate it as well as men. . . . Thus, keeping women in their place has been a universal problem, in spite of the fact that almost without exception institutional patterns give men positions of superiority over them.

If the sexes were, in fact, categorically distinct, with no overlapping, so that no man was inferior to any woman or any woman superior to any man, or vice versa, marriage would have been a great deal simpler. But there is no such sharp cleavage between the sexes except with respect to the presence or absence of certain organs. With all the other characteristics of each sex, there is greater or less overlapping, some men being more "feminine" than the average woman and some women more "masculine" than the average man. The structure of families and societies reflects the positions assigned to men and women. The bottom stratum includes children, slaves, servants, and outcasts of all kinds, males as well as females. As one ascends the structural hierarchy, the proportion of males increases, so that at the apex there are only males.

When societies fall back on the lazy expedient—as all societies everywhere have done—of allocating the rewards and punishments of life on the basis of sex, they are bound to create a host of anomalies, square pegs in round holes, societal misfits. Roles have been allocated on the basis of sex which did not fit a sizable number of both sexes—women, for example, who chafed at subordinate status and men who could not master superordinate status. The history of the relations of the sexes is replete with examples of such misfits.

Unless a modus vivendi is arrived at, unhappy marriages are the result.

There is, though, a difference between the exercise of power by husbands and by wives. When women exert power, they are not rewarded; they may even be punished. They are "deviant." Turk and Bell note that "wives who . . . have the greater influence in decision making may experience guilt over this fact." They must therefore dissemble to maintain the illusion, even to themselves, that they are subservient. They tend to feel less powerful than they are because they *ought* to be.

When men exert power, on the other hand, they are rewarded; it is the natural expression of authority. They feel no guilt about it. The prestige of authority goes to the husband whether or not he is actually the one who exercises it. It is not often even noticed when the wife does so. She sees to it that it is not.

There are two marriages, then, in every marital union, his and hers. And his . . . is better than hers. The questions, therefore, are these: In what direction will they change in the future? Will one change more than the other? Will they tend to converge or to diverge? Will the future continue to favor the husband's marriage? And if the wife's marriage is improved, will it cost the husband's anything, or will his benefit along with hers?

CRITICAL-THINKING QUESTIONS

1. What evidence does Bernard offer to support her conclusion that there are "his" and "her" marriages rather than "our" marriage?
2. Does the traditional inequality of men and women support or undermine marital roles? How?
3. What are the consequences for marriage of the gradual process by which the two sexes are becoming more socially equal?

51

Are Families Really Important?

Norval D. Glenn

Sociologists distinguish attitudes (what people say) from behavior (what people do). As this selection shows, there is a big gap between what members of our society say about their families and what they actually do to support them. Norval Glenn argues that although a majority of people claim that family is the most important priority in their lives, most of us put our personal freedom, jobs, and even possessions before our family responsibilities.

If you believe what Americans say about their values, then families are doing fine. In survey after survey, traditional relationships among parents, children, and siblings are identified as the most important aspect of life. Families are seen as more important than work, recreation, friendships, or status. Researchers have been asking Americans about their families for over half a century, and Americans have always replied that the family takes priority over everything else in their lives.

But if you watch what Americans do, traditional family relationships are in trouble. If current divorce rates continue, about two out of three marriages that begin this year will not survive as long as both spouses live. The proportion of American adults who are married is decreasing, the share of out-of-wedlock births has soared, and most children under age eighteen will spend part of their childhood living with only one parent.

In other words, Americans continue to say they embrace traditional family values—but their family relations have changed dramatically. Why has this happened? What are the consequences? These are important questions, and business leaders must

---

SOURCE: "What Does Family Mean?" by Norval D. Glenn, in *American Demographics,* vol. 14, no. 6, June 1992. Copyright © June 1992, *American Demographics*, Ithaca, New York. Reprinted with permission.

address them if they are to deal effectively with employees and consumers.

WHAT AMERICANS SAY

Surveys taken in 1971 and 1989 show how little expressed attitudes toward the family have changed. In the earlier study, the Quality of Life Survey conducted by the Institute for Social Research at the University of Michigan, people were asked to rate twelve goals, including "an interesting job," "a large bank account," "having good friends," and "a happy marriage." Three-quarters of those responding rated "having a happy marriage" as extremely important, while 70 percent gave that rating to "being in good health," and 69 percent rated "having a good family life" the same. In contrast, only 38 percent said that "having an interesting job" was extremely important.

A more recent survey shows similar results. In the 1989 Massachusetts Mutual American Family Value Study, family-related variables such as "respecting one's parents," "respecting one's children," "being able to provide emotional support to your family," and "having a happy marriage" ranked far above more individually centered goals. For example, such goals as "being financially secure," "earning a good living," "having a rewarding job," "having nice things," and "being free from obligations so I can do whatever I want to" were reported to be relatively unimportant.

Among American high school seniors, family values were on top in both the 1970s and the 1980s. "Having a good marriage and family life" ranked first for all students from 1976 through 1986. Three-quarters of all seniors rated it extremely important in both years. Only "being able to find steady work," "having strong friendships," and "finding purpose and meaning in life" came close in importance.

Studies that interview the same people every few years show that family tends to become even more important in the years following high school graduation. The National Longitudinal Study of High School and Beyond found that high school

boys, on average, considered "being successful in work" and "having steady work" somewhat more important than "having a happy family life." But four years after graduation, the same respondents rated "having a happy family life" first.

Other surveys indicate that having a happy family life really is the key to overall happiness. Satisfaction with family life was highly correlated with overall life satisfaction in the 1971 Quality of Life Survey: After family, satisfaction with marriage and satisfaction with financial situation ranked high as predictors of overall life satisfaction. But a poor marriage may be worse than no marriage at all. Bad marriages wreak havoc on happiness; people who do not characterize their marriage as "very happy" report the lowest overall happiness of any category of people, according to the General Social Surveys conducted by the National Opinion Research Center.

The link between strong family ties and overall happiness indicates that family should be more important than anything else. But the truth is that many if not most Americans will sacrifice traditional family ties for activities they claim are less important. It is common for Americans to let the pursuit of more individualistic goals interfere with their family life, even when doing so is clearly contrary to their best interests.

WHAT THEY DO

What is responsible for the gap between professed family values and life choices? Some of it is probably due to economic, technological, and demographic trends that make it harder for families to stay together. But the surveys indicate that shifting ideas about the family are also driving the changes. In the 1990s, new values are colliding with notions of family stability.

Probably the most important recent change in attitudes about the family has been a decline in the ideal of marital permanence. You can see this decline in the Study of American Families, which interviewed the same sample of mothers at four different dates. In recent years, it found a sharp increase in the percentage of women who said parents who do not get along should split up rather than stay together for the sake of the children. This percentage went from 51 in 1962 to 82 in 1985.

Of course, an increased acceptance of divorce may not imply a weakening of family values. Some analysts argue that the decreased willingness to tolerate unsatisfactory marriages reflects the importance that people now place on marriage. Indeed, the change might be seen as the weakening of one family value and the strengthening of another to replace it.

Previous generations of Americans saw marriage as an institution to be joined and supported. But today, most people value marriage primarily for what they personally can gain from it, not for what it does for their children, extended family, or community. The goal of "having a happy marriage" currently ranks well above "being married to the same person for life" and even farther above simply "being married." Such a ranking indicates that Americans value marriage primarily as a means to individual happiness. Their tendency to value it for any other reason has seen a substantial decline in recent years.

Other surveys have shown an increase in expressed negative attitudes toward marriage. This is not surprising, in view of the fact that Americans' propensity to marry and remarry has declined in recent years. According to the Americans View Their Mental Health Surveys, the percentage of respondents who said that marriage changes a person's life in positive ways went from 43 in 1957 to 30 in 1976. Meanwhile, negative responses increased from 23 percent to 28 percent.

The importance people attach to marital happiness has almost certainly increased in recent years, but attaining marital happiness has become less likely. That gap may account for some of the growth of negative attitudes about marriage. The share of Americans who are still in their first marriages after ten years and who rated those marriages "very happy" has declined substantially. It was 46 percent among those who married in the mid-1960s, but 33 percent of those who married in the middle to late 1970s, according to the General

Social Surveys. The proportion of all married Americans who said their marriages were "very happy" also declined.

Negative attitudes toward parenthood have also increased since World War II, according to the Mental Health Surveys. In 1957 and 1976, parents were asked how having children affects a person's life. Positive responses decreased from 58 percent to 44 percent, while negative responses increased from 22 to 28 percent.

Values that emphasize materialistic gain and individual achievement have also increased, at least among young Americans. The share of high school seniors who said "having lots of money" was extremely important grew from 15 percent in 1976 to 28 percent in 1986, and those who ranked "being successful in my line of work" as extremely important grew from 53 percent to 61 percent, according to the University of Michigan's Monitoring the Future Surveys.

Likewise, the proportion of first-year college students who said that "to be very well-off financially" was a very important or essential life goal went from 40 percent in the early 1970s to 70 percent in 1985, according to surveys taken by the American Council on Education and UCLA.

Americans may be more materialistic and achievement-oriented than they are willing to admit. The same respondents who ranked "having nice things" and "being financially secure" near the bottom of a list of "most important" priorities were asked, in the 1989 Massachusetts Mutual Study, to imagine that they were thirty-eight years old and were offered a new job requiring more work hours and less time with their families. The hypothetical job would provide higher rewards, including greater prestige and more pay. Almost one-third said that their acceptance of such an offer would be "very likely," and an additional one-third said it would be "somewhat likely." Not a single one of the 1,200 respondents said it would be "very unlikely."

The evidence is clear. When personal and family goals conflict, many people who express strong support for family values do not live up to those values.

BRIDGING THE GAP

While most Americans express positive views of their own families, they do not hesitate to point out problems in the family next door. Only 6 percent of the respondents in the Massachusetts Mutual survey rated American family life in general "excellent," compared with 54 percent who rated it "only fair" or "poor." Sixty-two percent said family values in this country had gotten weaker, while only 14 percent said stronger. An overwhelming majority (85 percent) said Americans value material things more than family. And only 5 percent predicted that America's family life would be "excellent" in 1999; 59 percent said it would be "only fair" or "poor."

The same people who hold a dim view of America's family life express satisfaction with their own families. Although the Massachusetts Mutual survey respondents rated family life "only fair," 71 percent claimed they were "extremely satisfied" or "very satisfied" with their own family life.

The same gap shows up when you ask Americans about the state of marriage as an institution. Almost two-thirds of the married respondents to the recent General Social Surveys rate their own marriages "very happy," but most of the respondents to each of the several Virginia Slims Women's Opinion Polls said they thought the institution of marriage was weaker than it was ten years earlier. In 1986, one-third of the high school seniors included in the Monitoring the Future Survey agreed with the statement that "One sees so few good or happy marriages that one questions it as a way of life."

One reason for this skewed picture of American family life may be the media's emphasis on negative trends and events. Another is that people tend to deny the extent of problems in their own families. Indeed, other evidence on the prevalence of family problems suggests that the survey respondents' negative perception of other families may be more accurate than their reported positive feelings about their own family life.

The recent confusion surrounding the American family as an institution should be telling us something. While it may be the temporary outcome of major shifts in our social environment, the rift between word and deed is important. Trend-spotters who predict the resurgence of the traditional American family may be engaging in wishful thinking.

Many authorities on the American family still believe that family life is basically healthy and that family values are as strong as ever. But this positive view is largely based on a literal interpretation of people's responses to family-value questions on polls and surveys. A growing minority of family watchers are looking at family-related behavior and taking a less sanguine view. References to "the decline of the family," long common among political and religious leaders, are now frequent in academic literature.

Business decisions that address domestic needs must be based on a clear understanding of the complex relationship between values and family life. Americans need to resolve the inconsistency between their actions and their stated values. Businesses can help by designing new family services, revising employee benefit packages, and speaking out for the rights of children.

CRITICAL-THINKING QUESTIONS

1. Why, according to Glenn, are traditional family relationships in trouble?

2. What is the precise difference between what most of us say about the importance of the family and what we actually do to maintain strong families?

3. Glenn maintains that businesses can address family problems by "designing new family services, revising employee benefit packages, and speaking out for the rights of children." Why, in your opinion, have businesses not done so? Do you think that the business community will address family needs in the future?

FAMILY

Cross-Cultural

52

Love, Arranged Marriage, and the Indian Social Structure

Giri Raj Gupta

Although most people in the United States cannot imagine a wedding without love, romance plays little or no part in marriage in many traditional societies. In much of China, India, Africa, and South America, marriages are arranged by families. In this selection, Gupta explains how arranged marriages unify families, support religion, and solidify the class structure.

Marriage is an immemorial institution which, in some form, is found everywhere. Mating patterns are closely associated with marriage, more so with the social structure. It's not the institution of marriage itself, but the institutionalization of mating patterns which determine the nature of family relationships in a society. Primitive societies present a wide array of practices ranging from marriage by capture to mutual love and elopement. Yet, the people who marry through customary practice are those who are eligibles, who consciously followed the established norms, and who did the kind of things they were supposed to do. The main purpose of marriage is to establish a family, to produce children, and to further the family's economic and social position. Perhaps, there are some transcendental goals too. Generally, women hope for kind and vigorous providers and protectors and men for faithful mothers and good housekeepers; both undoubtedly hope for mutual devotion and affection too. Irrespective of the various ways of instituting marriage, most marriages seem to have these common goals.

There are few works commenting on mating patterns in India. Though some monographs on tribal and rural India have treated the subject, nev-

SOURCE: "Love, Arranged Marriage and the Indian Social Structure," by Giri Raj Gupta, in *Cross-Cultural Perspectives of Mate-Selection and Marriage,* ed. George Kurian. Copyright © 1979 by George Kurian. Reprinted with permission of Greenwood Publishing Group, Inc., Westport, CT.

ertheless, serious sociological attention has only infrequently been given. The present paper attempts to explain the variables as a part of the cultural system which help in promotion and sustenance of the arranged marriage, particularly in the Hindu society in India. In addition, the paper also critically analyzes the present-day mating patterns which relate to precautionary controls working against the potentially disintegrative forces of change; especially those endangering family unity, religious structure, and the stratification system.

ROMANTIC LOVE VERSUS CONJUGAL LOVE

One is intrigued by the cultural pattern in India where the family is characterized by arranged marriage. Infatuation as well as romantic love, though, is reported quite in abundance in the literature, sacred books, and scriptures, yet is not thought to be an element in prospective marital alliance (see Meyer 1953: 322–39).

Sanskrit or Hindi terms like *sneh* (affection) and *prem* or *muhbbat* carry two different meanings. *Sneh* is nonsensual love, while *prem* is a generic term connoting love with god, people, nation, family, [neighbor], and, of course, lover or beloved. In fact, there is a hierarchy of relationships. In Urdu literature, concepts like *ishque ruhani* (love with the spirit), *ishque majazi* (love with the supreme being), and *ishque haqiqi* (love with the lover or beloved) are commonly referred to love relationships. Interestingly, the humans supposedly reach the highest goal of being in love with god through the love they cherish among humans. Great love stories in mythology and history illustrate the emotion, as opposed to reason, which characterizes the thoughts and acts of persons in love. The quality of the emotions may be characterized best by the altruistic expressions of a person for the person in love. Most people in India do not go around singing of their love as one might imagine after watching Indian movies and dramatic performances. Even the proximity, intimacy,

freedom, and permissiveness characterized in such media are rarely commonplace in the reality of the day-to-day life. In general, to verbalize and manifest romantic expressions of love is looked upon as a product of poets' or novelists' fantasies. Yet, at least theoretically, to be in love with someone is a highly cherished ideal.

In one of the most ancient scriptures, Rgveda, it was wished that a person's life be of a hundred-year duration. The Hindu sages in their theory of *purusharthas* suggested four aims of life: *dharma,* righteousness, which provides a link between animal and god in man; *artha,* acquisitive instinct in man, enjoyment of wealth and its manifestations; *kama,* instinctive and emotional life of man and the satisfaction of sex drives and aesthetic urges; and *moksha,* the end of life and the realization of an inner spirituality in man (see Kapadia 1966: 25).

The Hindu scriptures written during 200 B.C. to 900 A.D. mention eight modes of acquiring a wife known as Brahma, Daiva, Arsha, Prajapatya, Asura, Gandharva, Rakshasa, and Paisacha. Only the first four are known as *dharmya,* that is, according to religion. An exchange of gifts between the subjects' families marks the wedding ceremony, but no dowry is paid. In the Asura form payment of the bride price is the main element, while Rakshasa and Paisacha, respectively, pertain to the abduction and seduction of a girl when she is unconscious. The Gandharva marriage refers to a marriage by mutual choice. The Hindu lawgivers differ in their opinions and interpretations of this kind of marriage; some called it the best mode of marriage, while others viewed it stigmatic on religious and moral grounds. However, there is no reliable data to support or justify the popularity of any one of these modes of marriage. The first four kinds pertain to arranged marriages in which the parental couple ritually gives away the daughter to a suitable person, and this ideal continues to be maintained in the Hindu society. Opposed to these are four others, three of which were objected to by the scriptwriters in the past and viewed as illegal today, though nevertheless, they happen. The Gandharva mode, though opposed to the accepted norm, is nearest to what may be variously termed as "free-choice," "romantic," or "love" marriage. Yet through the ages Hindu revivalism and other socioreligious and economic factors discredited the importance of Gandharva marriage.

Diversified sects of Muslims and Christians view marriage as a civil contract as opposed to a sacrament.[1] However, marriages are arranged most often with the consent of the subjects. The Muslims, at least theoretically, permit polygamy according to Islamic law; however, they prefer monogamy. As opposed to Hindu and Christian communities it is customary that the boy's party initiates a marriage proposal (see Kapadia 1966: 209–14; Kurian 1974: 357–58, 1975).

Most Indian marriages are arranged, although sometimes opinions of the partners are consulted, and in cases of adults, their opinions are seriously considered. Another aspect of this pattern is that individuals come to believe that their life mate is predestined, their fate is preordained, they are "right for each other," they are helpless as far as choice is concerned and therefore must succumb to the celestial forces of the universe. That the entire syndrome, typical for the society, represents a complex set of forces working around and upon the individual to get married to a person whom one is destined to love. It is also believed to be good and desirable that critical issues like the choosing of a life partner should be handled by responsible persons of family and kin group. However, it is generally possible that persons in love could marry if related prohibitions have been effectively observed.

Generally, love is considered a weak basis for marriage because its presence may overshadow suitable qualities in spouses. Therefore, arranged marriages result from more or less intense care given to the selection of suitable partners so that the family ideals, companionship, and co-parenthood can grow, leading to love. Ernest Van Den Haag writes about the United States:

A hundred years ago, there was every reason to marry young—though middle-class people seldom did. The unmarried state had heavy disadvantages for both sexes. Custom did not permit girls to be educated, to work, or to have social, let alone sexual, freedom. . . . And, though, less restricted than girls shackled to their fami-

lies, single men often led a grim and uncomfortable life. A wife was nearly indispensable, if only to darn socks, sew, cook, clean, take care of her man. (1973: 181)

Goode views romantic love paradoxically, and calls it the antithesis of "conjugal love," because marriage is not based upon it; actually a couple strives to seek it within the marital bond (1959: 40). The latter, presumably, protect the couple against the harmful effects of individualism, freedom, and untoward personality growth. It may be worthwhile here to analyze the structural conditions under which mating relationships occur and to see how they relate to various values and goals in Indian society.

A study conducted in 1968, on 240 families in Kerala, a state which has the highest literacy rate in India, reveals that practical consideration in the selection of mates rather than free-choice or romantic love becomes the basis of marriage. In order of importance, the study reports that the major qualities among the girls considered important are: good character, obedience, ability to manage home, good cook, should take active part in social and political affairs, educated, religious, depending entirely on husband for major decisions, fair complexion, good companion with similar intellectual interests, and beauty (Kurian 1974: 335). Among the boy's qualities, his appearance, charm, and romantic manifestation do not count much, while the social and economic status of his family, education, and earning potential overshadow his personal qualities (Kurian 1974: 355; see also Ross 1961: 259).

The Kerala study further illustrates some interesting trends, such as: that only 59 percent of the respondents thought that meeting the prospective wife before marriage contributes to marital happiness. The parental preferences about the nature of choice of spouse of their children showed that 5.8 percent wanted to arrange the marriage without consulting sons and daughters, while 75.6 percent wanted to arrange the marriage with the consent of sons and daughters, 17.3 percent were willing to allow free choice to their children with their approval, and only 1.3 percent will allow freedom of choice without parental interference (Kurian 1974: 358). In fact, what Srinivas observed over three decades ago in Mysore was that "romantic love as a basis of marriage is still not very deep or widely spread in the family mores of India today," has not yet changed much (see Srinivas 1942: 60).

The dilemma of a boy who had fallen in love with a girl from a lower caste is reported from a study of Bangalore, a city of about a million people:

My love affair has caused me great trouble, for my intense love of the girl and the devotion to my parents cannot be reconciled. My parents don't like our engagement, and I cannot displease them, but on the other hand I cannot give up my girl who has done so much for me. She is responsible for progress and the bright future which everyone says is ahead of me. The problem is my greatest headache at the present time. (Ross 1961: 269)

During my own fieldwork during 1963–67, in Awan, a community of about three thousand people in Rajasthan state, having extensive and frequent urban contacts, it took me no time to figure out that a question inquiring about "romantic" or "love" marriage would be futile, because people simply laughed it away. Parental opinion was reinforced by several other considerations. One man, a community elite, remarked:

Young people do not know what love is; they are, if at all, infatuated which is very transitory and does not entail considerations of good marital life. If my son marries, I wish to see that the girl is well-raised, obedient, preserves the family traditions, ready to bear the hardships with us, and to nurse us in our old age.

Love, a premarital manifestation, is thus thought to be a disruptive element in upsetting the firmly established close ties in the family, a transference of loyalty from the family of orientation to a person, and a loss of allegiance of a person, leaving the family and kin group in disdain for personal goals.

Continued loyalty of the individual to the family of orientation and kin group is the most cherished ideal in the Indian family system. To preserve this ideal, certainly the simplest recourse is child marriage or adolescent marriage. The child is betrothed, married, and most often placed in a job and generally provides the deference demanded by the elders. Though this pattern does not give much opportunity to the individual to act freely in matrimonial affairs, it maintains a close link of the couple with the father's household which requires much physical, social, and emotional care throughout the family cycle and particularly in old age. The relationships in the extended joint family are all-important.

The Hindu scriptural texts prescribe that a person should go through *grahstashrama* (a stage of householder's life) which includes procreation of children. The status system gives high prestige to the parents of large families. Kinship and religious values stress the need for a male heir. Large families provide security, both in economic and social terms, for the old and the destitute and the ill in a country where old-age pensions, disability, sickness benefits, and unemployment as well as medical insurance are either nonexistent or inadequate. When a family has several children, their marriages have to be spaced for economic as well as social reasons, which in turn necessitates early marriages.

Similar to other indigenous civilizations, a high value is placed upon chastity, especially female virginity in its ideal form. Love as play or premarital activity is not encouraged. Rather, elders consider it as their most important duty to supervise nubile girls. Marriage is an ideal, a duty, and a social responsibility usually preceded by highly ritualized ceremonial and festive events illustrating gradual involvement, especially of the female preparatory to the initiation of her marital role. Interestingly, all these ritual activities are role oriented (such as contributing to the long and prosperous life of the prospective husband) rather than person oriented (such as taking vows for the success of a person who is in love). This is one of those most pertinent factors which infuses longevity to the marital bond. The upper caste ideal that a girl could be ritually married only once in her lifetime and destined to marry the same person in lives to come continues to determine explicit and categorical aversion among girls to premarital interactions with strangers. Paradoxically, though, there is an implicit assumption that a person's marriage to a person of the opposite sex is governed by supreme celestial forces; in actual practice, mundane realities usually settle a marriage.

The early marriage of the person does not permit much personal independence and is further linked with another structural pattern in which the kinship rules define a class (caste, subcaste, regional group) of eligible future spouses. In other words, in the interest of homogamy and sanctity of the kin group, marriage should occur early. Thus, this would eliminate the chances of an unmarried adult to disregard a link with his or her kin group and caste. Problems arise at times when a person goes across the narrow limits of a group, often losing his chances of obtaining the usual support from the family, the kin group, and the caste. However, transgressions of basic family norms by an individual which may cause loss of identity, rejection, and an aggravated departure from the value system are rare. Often it is circumventing rather than contradicting the system which provides clues to change. Under such a pattern, elders negotiate and arrange marriages of their children and dependents with a likelihood of minimum generational conflict reinforcing greater chances of family unity. Adolescent physical and social segregation is marked by a greater emphasis on the learning of discrete sex roles idealizing, at least theoretically, parental roles.

As found in Western cultures, the youth culture frees the individual from family attachments thus permitting the individual to fall in love; and love becomes a substitute for the interlocking of kinship roles. The structural isolation of the Western family also frees the married partners' affective inclinations, that they are able to love one another (Parsons 1949: 187–89). Such a pattern is absent in the Indian family system.

Contrary to this, in India, marriage of a boy indirectly strengthens his bonds with the family of orientation. It is one of the major crises which marks his adulthood and defines his responsibilities towards his parents and the kin group. His faith and sentimental involvement in the family of orientation is an acknowledgment of the usual obligations incurred in his raising and training. A pervasive philosophy of individualism appears to be spreading and suggests a trend toward free mate choices, equality for women, equal divorce rights, and taking up of traditionally known ritually inferior but lucrative occupations; this militantly asserts the importance of the welfare of the person over any considerations of the continuity of the group. The trend toward conjugal family systems, widespread as it is, is generally confined to the urbanized regions (Gore 1958; Kapur 1970). Moreover, these changes where they appear on one hand, are viewed as social problems and as symptoms of the breakdown of time-honored ways; on the other, they are looked at as indicators of personal achievement, individual fulfillment, and family prestige.

SOCIALIZATION

The cultural pattern demands that a child in India cannot isolate himself from his parents, siblings, and other members of the extended family.

The maturation process is rarely fraught with problems or turmoil associated with parent and adolescent children as they all learn to play new roles and feel new feelings. A child's expanding world gradually gives a mature sense of responsibilities to share in most of the important decisions in his life cycle. Covert parent-child conflict is shadowed by affection and sentimental ties helping the adolescents to achieve desirable balance between rebellion and conformity, individual wishes and feelings of the parents. Occasionally, this causes some problems. Since parents make decisions about most significant aspects of the family, including the marriage of their children, passive, indifferent, and sometimes negative feelings develop in the children as they seek to be dependent on other members of the family.

The family in India is known for its cohesive function, especially providing for the emotional needs of its members. Most often, this function is effectively performed by the extended kin group which, in fact, is a segment of the caste or subcaste. Adults, as well as children, must have love and security in order to maintain emotional stability under the stresses of life and in order to meet the emotional demands made upon them by the crises. In addition to providing the positive emotional needs of its members by personal sacrifices done by the members on a regular basis throughout the life cycle of the family, it also provides a safe outlet for negative feelings. Conflicts arising from interpersonal relations are generally handled by the older members, and care is taken by them to ensure that roles and responsibilities are clearly defined. Conflicts are resolved and mitigated by a general concern in the group favoring the emotional satisfaction of the individual. A person throughout his adolescence is never isolated from the family. Thus, not only generations, but extended and local units of kin groups are forced into a more intensive relationship. The affectional ties are solidified by mutual care, help in crisis situations, and assistance provided. This often destroys negative feelings. Several rituals, rites, and ceremonial occasions reinforce the unity of the family (Dube 1955: 131–58; Gupta 1974: 104–16). In general, a person substantially invests his emotions and feelings in his family and kin group, denial of which may be hazardous to his psyche. Such a deep involvement of the individual causes his emotional dependence on the family and acceptance to its wishes in most of the crucial decisions and events in his life, including marriage.

PREMARITAL INTERACTION AND MATE SELECTION

India is perhaps the only subcontinent which provides a wide variety of mate selection processes from an open to a very closed system, from marriage by capture in the primitives to the arranged marriage among Hindus and Muslims. Moreover, rules prohibiting certain classes of persons from marrying one another also vary, such as three to four clan avoidance rules in central and northern parts to preferential cross-cousin or maternal uncle and niece marriages in the south. In other words, rules regarding the definition of incest or areas of potential mates vary substantially. Most people in the Northern states, for example, prohibit marriage between persons of similarly named clans and extend this rule to several other related clans, such as of mother's clan, mother's mother clan, and father's mother clan. The people bearing these clan names may be living several hundred miles away . . . but are usually thought to be related. From this point of view, then, the ideal mate for any person could also be a stranger, an outsider, but an individual related to him in distant terms. . . . A person living across a state belonging to one's caste has a greater chance of being an eligible for a prospective mate than a person belonging to some other caste living next door. Caste is thus an extended kin group and, at least theoretically, membership in which is related through various kinds of kinship ties. Marriage alliances within the *jati* (caste or subcaste) reinforce kinship and family ties and cause a sort of evolution of the class system. Class generally determines future marital alliances within the caste. The resources assessed by a family in seeking a marital alliance from another family play a crucial role in determining the decision about the alliance. The voices of the significant members of the family are crucial in making a marriage since newlywed couples are barely into adulthood and have neither the material nor psychological resources to start a household of their own. Later in their married life when they have resources, they may still consider the opinions of the significant members because the disadvantages of not adhering to such opinions are greater than the annoyances of living together.

A SOCIOLOGICAL PARADIGM OF ARRANGED MARRIAGES

Recent research on the changing aspects of the family in India (Collver 1963; Conklin 1974; Desai 1964; Gore 1965; Gould 1968; Gupta 1974; Hooja 1968; Kapur 1970; Kurian 1961, 1974;

Orenstein 1959, 1961, 1966; Ross 1961; Shah 1974; Singer 1968) suggests that there has been little change in the joint family system in India, which is a vanguard of the arranged marriage.

The above discussion gives us to understand that what is needed in our approach to arranged marriage is a frame of reference which is more fully on the sociological level. As a step toward this goal, a general theoretical approach to the arranged marriage or "conjugal love" relationship has been formulated which, it is believed, takes account of the historical, cultural, and psychological levels, and brings into central focus the sociological level. The following tentative theoretical formulation is proposed only as a first attempt to outline what sociological factors are generally responsible to the growth of "conjugal love" as opposed to "romantic love." By any conservative estimate, love marriages occur in only less than 1 percent of the population.

1. It is important to note that arranged marriages are closely associated with "closed systems" wherein the hierarchies are very intricate and more than one factor such as historical origins, ritual positions, occupational affiliations, and social distance determinants play significant roles in defining the in-group and the out-group, particularly in marital alliances. In such systems, group identity is marked by strong senses of esoteric values, and such values are preserved and reinforced by attributes which distinguish a group in rank and its interaction with others. That is, most proximate ties of the individuals ought to be within their own group.

2. Continuity and unity of the extended family is well-preserved since all the significant members of the family share the mate-selection decision make-up which involves several persons who are supposedly known to have experience and qualifications to find a better choice as against the free choice of the subject. Obviously, this leads to lower age at marriage and, in turn, strengthens the predominance of the family over the individual choice.

3. Any possible problems emerging from a couple's functioning in marital life become problems for the whole family. Advice and counseling from the members of the extended family to improve the couple's relationship, weathering life's storms, or even ing in-crises are reinforced by the shared responsibilities.

This is also partly responsible for denouncing the idea of divorce and forces working against it. This is not to say that this, in fact, resolves all the conflicts in marriage.

4. As long as the social system is unable to develop a value system to promote individualism, economic security outside the family system, and a value system which advances the ideals of nuclear family, the individuals in such a system continue to demand support from the family which, in turn, would lead to reemphasizing the importance of arranged marriage. Forces of modernization supporting the "romantic ideal" would continue to find partial support in such a system as long as the sources of moral and material support for the individual are based in the extended/joint family system.

5. It is difficult to assume that arranged marriage is related to the low status of a woman since man is also a party to it. If the concept of "free choice" is applicable to either sex, perhaps it will not support the ideal of arranged marriage. Apparently, an individual who opts for free choice or a "love marriage" is likely to dissociate from his/her family, kin group, caste, and possibly community, which he/she cannot afford unless he/she has been ensured tremendous support from sources other than these conventional institutions.

6. Arranged marriages, in general, irrespective of caste or class categories, help in maintaining closer ties with several generations. Families in such a system are an insurance for the old and the orthodox, a recluse for the devout and the defiant, a haven for the invalid and the insipid.

7. The demographic situation in India, as in most developing societies, is also a contributing factor, among others, to the early arranged marriages. After independence, India has made many advancements in science, technology, and medicine. . . . life expectancy, which was twenty-nine years in 1947, is now fifty-four years. However, the vicious circle of early child marriage, early pregnancy, high mortality rate, and replacement of the population are closely interwoven to ensure society from extinction. While the value system notoriously maintains this chainwork, the declining mortality rate further accentuates early marriages to shelve off the economic burden of the family by spacing weddings. The family protects and insulates from ruining itself by arranging marriages as early as possible and for using its resources for status aggrandizement.

Since the changes in Indian society often present a welter of traditional and modern, conventional as well as prestige and [glamor]-oriented marital role models with significant changes in the value system, it is quite probable that in the long run, "romantic ideal" will pervade the system. Whether such changes will be a part of a continuum, that is, revitalization of the mythological past or acceptance of the ideals of the modern West, preserving tenacity and positive elements of its own against the swaggering forces of change, has yet to be seen.

CRITICAL-THINKING QUESTIONS

1. How common is arranged marriage among India's Hindus, Muslims, and Christians? Are there other types of marriage?
2. Why is romantic love devalued in traditional societies?
3. Do you think arranged marriages and a lesser emphasis on romantic love would reduce the frequency of divorce in the United States?

NOTE

1. The observation that "diversified sects of Muslims and Christians view marriage as a civil contract as opposed to a sacrament" does not hold good universally. In India, at any rate, for all Christians, to whichever denomination they belong, marriage is a sacrament.

REFERENCES

CHEKKI, D. A. 1968. Mate selection, age at marriage and propinquity among the Lingayats of India. *Journal of Marriage and the Family,* 30 (Nov.):707–11.

COLLVER, A. 1963. The family cycle in India and the United States. *American Sociological Review,* 28: 86–96.

CONKLIN, G. H. 1974. The extended family as an independent factor in social change: A case from India. *Journal of Marriage and Family,* 36 (Nov.): 798–804.

CORMACK, M. 1953. *The Hindu woman.* New York: Bureau of Publications, Columbia University.

DESAI, I. P. 1964. *Some aspects of family in Mahuva.* Bombay: Asia Publishing House.

DUBE, S. C. 1955. *Indian village.* New York: Cornell University Press.

GOODE, W. J. 1959. The theoretical importance of love. *American Sociological Review,* 24:38–47.

———. 1963. *World revolution and family patterns.* New York: Free Press.

GORE, M. S. 1968. *Urbanization and family change.* Bombay: Popular Prakashan.

GUPTA, G. R. 1974. *Marriage, religion and society: Pattern of change in an Indian village.* New York: Halsted Press.

HATE, C. A. 1970. Raising the age at marriage. *The Indian Journal of Social Work,* 30:303–9.

HOOJA, S. 1968. Dowry system among the Hindus in North India: A case study. *The Indian Journal of Social Work,* 38:411–26.

KAPADIA, K. M. 1966. *Marriage and family in India.* 3d ed. London: Oxford University Press.

KAPUR, P. 1970. *Marriage and the working woman in India.* Delhi: Vikas Publications.

KARVE, I. 1965. *Kinship organization in India.* Bombay: Asia Publishing House.

KLASS, M. 1966. Marriage rules in Bengal. *American Anthropologist,* 68: 951–70.

KURIAN, G. 1961. *The Indian family in transition.* The Hague: Mouton.

———. 1974. Modern trends in mate selection and marriage with special reference to Kerala. In *The family in India—A regional view* (pp. 351–67), ed. G. Kurian. The Hague: Mouton.

———. 1975. Structural changes in the family in Kerala, India. In *Psychological Anthropology,* ed. T. R. Williams. The Hague: Mouton.

MADAN, T. N. 1965. *Family and kinship: A study of the Pandits of rural Kashmir.* New York: Asia Publishing House.

MANDELBAUM, D. G. 1970. *Society in India,* vols. 1 & 2. Berkeley: University of California Press.

MEYER, J. J. 1953. *Sexual life in ancient India.* New York: Barnes & Noble.

ORENSTEIN, H. 1959. The recent history of the extended family in India. *Social Problems,* 8:341–50.

———. 1961. The recent history of family in India. *Social Problems,* 8 (Spring):341–50.

——— 1966. The Hindu joint family: The norms and the numbers. *Pacific Affairs,* 39 (Fall–Winter): 314–25.

PARSONS, T. 1949. *Essays in sociological theory.* Glencoe, IL: Free Press.

Ross, A. D. 1961. *The Hindu family in its urban setting.* Toronto: University of Toronto Press.

Shah, A. M. 1974. *The household dimension of family in India.* Berkeley: University of California Press.

Singer, M. 1968. The Indian joint family in modern industry. In *Structure and change in Indian society,* ed. M. Singer & B. S. Cohn. Chicago: Aldine Publishing Co.

Srinivas, M. N. 1942. Marriage and family in Mysore. Bombay: New Book Co.

Van Den Haag, E. 1973. Love or marriage. In *Love, marriage and family: A developmental approach* (pp. 181–86), ed. M. E. Lasswell and T. E. Lasswell. Glenview, IL: Scott, Foresman and Co.

Vatuk, S. 1972. *Kinship and urbanization.* Berkeley: University of California Press.

Classic

53

The Protestant Ethic and the Spirit of Capitalism

Max Weber

In perhaps his most well known treatise, Max Weber argues that a major factor in the development of the capitalist economic system was the distinctive world view of early, ascetic Protestantism, especially Calvinism and Puritanism. In this excerpt from his classic analysis, Weber explains that religious ideas about work and materials initially fostered capitalism's growth; ultimately, he concludes, capitalism was able to stand on its own without religious supports.

A product of modern European civilization, studying any problem of universal history, is bound to ask himself to what combination of circumstances the fact should be attributed that in Western civilization, and in Western civilization only, cultural phenomena have appeared which (as we like to think) lie in a line of development having *universal* significance and value. . . . All over the world

SOURCE: *The Protestant Ethic and the Spirit of Capitalism* by Max Weber, trans. Talcott Parsons. Copyright © 1958 by Charles Scribner's Sons; copyright renewed 1986. Reprinted with permission of Macmillan College Publishing Company.

there have been merchants, wholesale and retail, local and engaged in foreign trade. . . .

But in modern times the Occident has developed, in addition to this, a very different form of capitalism which has appeared nowhere else: the rational capitalistic organization of (formally) free labour. Only suggestions of it are found elsewhere. Even the organization of unfree labour reached a considerable degree of rationality only on plantations and to a very limited extent in the *Ergasteria* of antiquity. In the manors, manorial workshops, and domestic industries on estates with serf labour it was probably somewhat less developed. Even real domestic industries with free labour have definitely been proved to have existed in only a few isolated cases outside the Occident. . . .

Rational industrial organization, attuned to a regular market, and neither to political nor irrationally speculative opportunities for profit, is not, however, the only peculiarity of Western capitalism. The modern rational organization of the capitalistic enterprise would not have been possible without two other important factors in its development: the separation of business from the household, which completely dominates modern economic life, and closely connected with it, rational book-keeping. . . .

Hence in a universal history of culture the central problem for us is not, in the last analysis, even from a purely economic view-point, the development of capitalistic activity as such, differing in different cultures only in form: the adventurer type, or capitalism in trade, war, politics, or administration as sources of gain. It is rather the origin of this sober bourgeois capitalism with its rational organization of free labour. Or in terms of cultural history, the problem is that of the origin of the Western bourgeois class and of its peculiarities, a problem which is certainly closely connected with that of the origin of the capitalistic organization of labour, but is not quite the same thing. For the bourgeois as a class existed prior to the development of the peculiar modern form of capitalism, though, it is true, only in the Western hemisphere.

Now the peculiar modern Western form of capitalism has been, at first sight, strongly influenced by the development of technical possibilities. Its rationality is to-day essentially dependent on the calculability of the most important technical factors. But this means fundamentally that it is dependent on the peculiarities of modern science, especially the natural sciences based on mathematics and exact and rational experiment. On the other hand, the development of these sciences and of the technique resting upon them now receives important stimulation from these capitalistic interests in its practical economic application. It is true that the origin of Western science cannot be attributed to such interests. Calculation, even with decimals, and algebra have been carried on in In-

dia, where the decimal system was invented. But it was only made use of by developing capitalism in the West, while in India it led to no modern arithmetic or book-keeping. Neither was the origin of mathematics and mechanics determined by capitalistic interests. But the *technical* utilization of scientific knowledge, so important for the living conditions of the mass of people, was certainly encouraged by economic considerations, which were extremely favourable to it in the Occident. But this encouragement was derived from the peculiarities of the social structure of the Occident. We must hence ask, from *what* parts of that structure was it derived, since not all of them have been of equal importance?

Among those of undoubted importance are the rational structures of law and of administration. For modern rational capitalism has need, not only of the technical means of production, but of a calculable legal system and of administration in terms of formal rules. Without it adventurous and speculative trading capitalism and all sorts of politically determined capitalisms are possible, but no rational enterprise under individual initiative, with fixed capital and certainty of calculations. Such a legal system and such administration have been available for economic activity in a comparative state of legal and formalistic perfection only in the Occident. We must hence inquire where that law came from. Among other circumstances, capitalistic interests have in turn undoubtedly also helped, but by no means alone nor even principally, to prepare the way for the predominance in law and administration of a class of jurists specially trained in rational law. But these interests did not themselves create that law. Quite different forces were at work in this development. And why did not the capitalistic interests do the same in China or India? Why did not the scientific, the artistic, the political, or the economic development there enter upon that path of rationalization which is peculiar to the Occident?

For in all the above cases it is a question of the specific and peculiar rationalism of Western culture. . . . It is hence our first concern to work out and to explain genetically the special peculiarity of Occidental rationalism, and within this field that of the modern Occidental form. Every such attempt at explanation must, recognizing the fundamental importance of the economic factor, above all take account of the economic conditions. But at the same time the opposite correlation must not be left out of consideration. For though the development of economic rationalism is partly dependent on rational technique and law, it is at the same time determined by the ability and disposition of men to adopt certain types of practical rational conduct. When these types have been obstructed by spiritual obstacles, the development of rational economic conduct has also met serious inner resistance. The magical and religious forces, and the ethical ideas of duty based upon them, have in the past always been among the most important formative influences on conduct. In the studies collected here we shall be concerned with these forces.

Two older essays have been placed at the beginning which attempt, at one important point, to approach the side of the problem which is generally most difficult to grasp: the influence of certain religious ideas on the development of an economic spirit, or the *ethos* of an economic system. In this case we are dealing with the connection of the spirit of modern economic life with the rational ethics of ascetic Protestantism. Thus we treat here only one side of the causal chain. . . .

. . . [T]hat side of English Puritanism which was derived from Calvinism gives the most consistent religious basis for the idea of the calling. . . . For the saints' everlasting rest is in the next world; on earth man must, to be certain of his state of grace, "do the works of him who sent him, as long as it is yet day." Not leisure and enjoyment, but only activity serves to increase the glory of God according to the definite manifestations of His will.

Waste of time is thus the first and in principle the deadliest of sins. The span of human life is infinitely short and precious to make sure of one's own election. Loss of time through sociability, idle talk, luxury, even more sleep than is necessary for health, six to at most eight hours, is worthy of absolute moral condemnation. It does not yet hold, with Franklin, that time is money, but the proposition is true in a certain spiritual sense. It is infinitely valuable because every hour lost is lost to labour for the glory of God. Thus inactive contemplation is also valueless, or even directly reprehensible if it is at the expense of one's daily work. . . .

[T]he same prescription is given for all sexual temptation as is used against religious doubts and a sense of moral unworthiness: "Work hard in your calling." But the most important thing was that even beyond that labour came to be considered in itself the end of life, ordained as such by God. St. Paul's "He who will not work shall not eat" holds unconditionally for everyone. Unwillingness to work is symptomatic of the lack of grace.

Here the difference from the mediæval viewpoint becomes quite evident. Thomas Aquinas also gave an interpretation of that statement of St. Paul. But for him labour is only necessary *naturali ratione* for the maintenance of individual and community. Where this end is achieved, the precept ceases to have any meaning. Moreover, it holds only for the race, not for every individual. It does not apply to anyone who can live without labour on his possessions, and of course contemplation, as a spiritual form of action in the Kingdom of God, takes precedence over the commandment in its literal sense. Moreover, for the popular theology of the time, the highest form of monastic productivity lay in the increase of the *Thesaurus ecclesiæ* through prayer and chant.

. . . For everyone without exception God's Providence has prepared a calling, which he should profess and in which he should labour. And this calling is not, as it was for the Lutheran, a fate to which he must submit and which he must make the best of, but God's commandment to the individual to work for the divine glory. This seemingly subtle difference had far-reaching psychological consequences, and became connected with a further development of the providential interpretation of the economic order which had begun in scholasticism.

It is true that the usefulness of a calling, and thus its favour in the sight of God, is measured primarily in moral terms, and thus in terms of the importance of the goods produced in it for the community. But a further, and, above all, in practice the most important, criterion is found in private profitableness. For if that God, whose hand the Puritan sees in all the occurrences of life, shows one of His elect a chance of profit, he must do it with a purpose. Hence the faithful Christian must follow the call by taking advantage of the opportunity. "If God show you a way in which you may lawfully get more than in another way (without wrong to your soul or to any other), if you refuse this, and choose the less gainful way, you cross one of the ends of your calling, and you refuse to be God's steward, and to accept His gifts and use them for Him when He requireth it: You may labour to be rich for God, though not for the flesh and sin.". . .

The superior indulgence of the *seigneur* and the parvenu ostentation of the *nouveau riche* are equally detestable to asceticism. But, on the other hand, it has the highest ethical appreciation of the sober, middle-class, self-made man. "God blesseth His trade" is a stock remark about those good men who had successfully followed the divine hints. The whole power of the God of the Old Testament, who rewards His people for their obedience in this life, necessarily exercised a similar influence on the Puritan who . . . compared his own state of grace with that of the heroes of the Bible. . . .

Although we cannot here enter upon a discussion of the influence of Puritanism in all . . . directions, we should call attention to the fact that the toleration of pleasure in cultural goods, which contributed to purely aesthetic or athletic enjoyment, certainly always ran up against one characteristic limitation: They must not cost anything. Man is only a trustee of the goods which have come to him through God's grace. He must, like the servant in the parable, give an account of every penny entrusted to him, and it is at least hazardous to spend any of it for a purpose which does not serve the glory of God but only one's own enjoyment. What person, who keeps his eyes open, has not met representatives of this view-point even in the present? The idea of a man's duty to his possessions, to which he subordinates himself as an obedient steward, or even as an acquisitive machine, bears with chilling weight on his life. The greater the possessions the heavier, if the ascetic attitude toward life stands the test, the feeling of responsibility for them, for holding them undiminished for the glory of God and increasing them by restless effort. The origin of this type of life also extends in certain roots, like so many aspects of the spirit of capitalism, back into the Middle Ages. But it was in the ethic of ascetic Protestantism that it first found a consistent ethical foundation. Its significance for the development of capitalism is obvious.

This worldly Protestant asceticism, as we may recapitulate up to this point, acted powerfully against the spontaneous enjoyment of possessions; it restricted consumption, especially of luxuries. On the other hand, it had the psychological effect of freeing the acquisition of goods from the inhibitions of traditionalistic ethics. It broke the bonds of the impulse of acquisition in that it not only legalized it, but (in the sense discussed) looked upon it as directly willed by God. . . .

As far as the influence of the Puritan outlook extended, under all circumstances—and this is, of course, much more important than the mere encouragement of capital accumulation—it favoured the development of a rational bourgeois economic life; it was the most important, and above all the only consistent influence in the development of that life. It stood at the cradle of the modern economic man.

To be sure, these Puritanical ideals tended to give way under excessive pressure from the temptations of wealth, as the Puritans themselves knew very well. With great regularity we find the most genuine adherents of Puritanism among the classes which were rising from a lowly status, the small bourgeois and farmers, while the *beati possidentes,* even among Quakers, are often found tending to repudiate the old ideals. It was the same fate which again and again befell the predecessor of this worldly asceticism, the monastic asceticism of the Middle Ages. In the latter case, when rational economic activity had worked out its full effects by strict regulation of conduct and limitation of consumption, the wealth accumulated either succumbed directly to the nobility, as in the time before the Reformation, or monastic discipline threatened to break down, and one of the numerous reformations became necessary.

In fact the whole history of monasticism is in a certain sense the history of a continual struggle with the problem of the secularizing influence of wealth. The same is true on a grand scale of the worldly asceticism of Puritanism. The great revival of Methodism, which preceded the expansion of English industry toward the end of the eighteenth century, may well be compared with such a monastic reform. We may hence quote here a passage from John Wesley himself which might well serve as a motto for everything which has been said above. For it shows that the leaders of these ascetic movements understood the seemingly paradoxical relationships which we have here analysed perfectly well, and in the same sense that we have given them. He wrote:

I fear, wherever riches have increased, the essence of religion has decreased in the same proportion. Therefore I do not see how it is possible, in the nature of things, for any revival of true religion to continue long. For religion must necessarily produce both industry and frugality, and these cannot but produce riches. But as riches increase, so will pride, anger, and love of the world in all its branches. How then is it possible that Methodism, that is, a religion of the heart, though it flourishes now as a green bay tree, should continue in this state? For the Methodists in every place grow diligent and frugal; consequently they increase in goods. Hence they proportionately increase in pride, in anger, in the desire of the flesh, the desire of the eyes, and the pride of life. So, although the form of religion remains, the spirit is swiftly vanishing away. Is there no way to prevent this—this continual decay of pure religion? We ought not to prevent people from being diligent and frugal; *we must exhort all Christians to gain all they can, and to save all they can; that is, in effect, to grow rich.*

As Wesley here says, the full economic effect of those great religious movements, whose significance for economic development lay above all in their ascetic educative influence, generally came only after the peak of the purely religious enthusiasm was past. Then the intensity of the search for

the Kingdom of God commenced gradually to pass over into sober economic virtue; the religious roots died out slowly, giving way to utilitarian worldliness. Then, as Dowden puts it, as in *Robinson Crusoe,* the isolated economic man who carries on missionary activities on the side takes the place of the lonely spiritual search for the Kingdom of Heaven of Bunyan's pilgrim, hurrying through the market-place of Vanity. . . .

A specifically bourgeois economic ethic had grown up. With the consciousness of standing in the fullness of God's grace and being visibly blessed by Him, the bourgeois business man, as long as he remained within the bounds of formal correctness, as long as his moral conduct was spotless and the use to which he put his wealth was not objectionable, could follow his pecuniary interests as he would and feel that he was fulfilling a duty in doing so. The power of religious asceticism provided him in addition with sober, conscientious, and unusually industrious workmen, who clung to their work as to a life purpose willed by God.

Finally, it gave him the comforting assurance that the unequal distribution of the goods of this world was a special dispensation of Divine Providence, which in these differences, as in particular grace, pursued secret ends unknown to men. . . .

One of the fundamental elements of the spirit of modern capitalism, and not only of that but of all modern culture: Rational conduct on the basis of the idea of the calling, was born—that is what this discussion has sought to demonstrate—from the spirit of Christian asceticism. One has only to re-read the passage from Franklin, quoted at the beginning of this essay, in order to see that the essential elements of the attitude which was there called the spirit of capitalism are the same as what we have just shown to be the content of the Puritan worldly asceticism, only without the religious basis, which by Franklin's time had died away. . . .

Since asceticism undertook to remodel the world and to work out its ideals in the world, material goods have gained an increasing and finally an inexorable power over the lives of men as at no previous period in history. To-day the spirit of religious asceticism—whether finally, who knows?—has escaped from the cage. But victorious capitalism, since it rests on mechanical foundations, needs its support no longer. The rosy blush of its laughing heir, the Enlightenment, seems also to be irretrievably fading, and the idea of duty in one's calling prowls about in our lives like the ghost of dead religious beliefs. Where the fulfillment of the calling cannot directly be related to the highest spiritual and cultural values, or when, on the other hand, it need not be felt simply as economic compulsion, the individual generally abandons the attempt to justify it at all. In the field of its highest development, in the United States, the pursuit of wealth, stripped of its religious and ethical meaning, tends to become associated with purely mundane passions, which often actually give it the character of sport.

No one knows who will live in this cage in the future, or whether at the end of this tremendous development entirely new prophets will arise, or there will be a great rebirth of old ideas and ideals, or, if neither, mechanized petrification, embellished with a sort of convulsive self-importance. For of the last stage of this cultural development, it might well be truly said: "Specialists without spirit, sensualists without heart; this nullity imagines that it has attained a level of civilization never before achieved."

But this brings us to the world of judgments of value and of faith, with which this purely historical discussion need not be burdened. . . .

Here we have only attempted to trace the fact and the direction of its influence to their motives in one, though a very important point. But it would also further be necessary to investigate how Protestant Asceticism was in turn influenced in its development and its character by the totality of social conditions, especially economic. The modern man is in general, even with the best will, unable to give religious ideas a significance for culture and national character which they deserve. But it is, of course, not my aim to substitute for a one-sided materialistic an equally one-sided spiritualistic causal interpretation of culture and of history. Each is equally possible, but each, if it does not serve as the preparation, but as the conclusion of an investigation, accomplishes equally little in the interest of historical truth.

CRITICAL-THINKING QUESTIONS

1. What are the distinctive characteristics of the religious orientation that Weber called the "Protestant ethic"? In what ways did they promote the development of the capitalist economic system?

2. In what respects do early Calvinists with a sense of "calling" differ from today's "workaholics"?

3. In what sense does Weber's analysis differ from the materialist orientation of Karl Marx (Reading 44), who suggested that productive forces shape the world of ideas?

54

Evangelicals in America

Kenneth A. Briggs

Much of the growth in Christianity in recent decades has been among so-called "evangelicals." Who are these Christians? The following article examines the past and present standing of evangelical Christianity and its effective use of the "electronic church."

No word has so dominated recent talk of American religion—or been pronounced in so many ways—as the term "evangelical." Its sudden prominence took place seemingly by accident. Jimmy Carter casually described himself as having been "born-again" to a group of surprised reporters during his 1976 presidential campaign. That incident unleashed a torrent of reporting on an aspect of America's religious tradition that had escaped widespread awareness for several decades.

In the decade between then and now, much fact and fiction has grown up around the evangelical

SOURCE: "Religion in America," by Kenneth A. Briggs, in *The Gallup Report,* no. 259, April 1987, pp. 3–5. Reprinted with permission.

movement. Much of the "fact" had to do with the long evangelical heritage that led to modern expressions of evangelical revivalism. Much of the "fiction" has been spun around the false notion that evangelicals comprised a religious subculture far from mainstream Christianity.

The treatment of evangelicals as a distinct movement was not, of course, without some basis in truth. Churches with evangelical labels had sprung up and other religious bodies, such as the Southern Baptists, became synonymous with the term almost solely by dint of reputation. But the tendency toward defining evangelicals as a separate religious entity ignored the longstanding evangelical character of nearly all American Christianity and, indeed, the church from earliest times. Perhaps it was only the American propensity toward breaking things down into "specialized" categories that forced evangelicals farther toward isolation than they deserved to be.

The "Dictionary of Christian Theology" describes "evangelical" as "that which is contained in, or relates to, the four Gospels" and "those beliefs that are in conformity with the Gospels." From a traditional standpoint, then, the word is generic to Christianity, applying validity to a broad spectrum of believers. The Protestant Reformation gave poignancy to this understanding by underscoring it as one of the two distinguishing marks of a truly renewed church: evangelical and reformed.

Despite this esteemed legacy, the term fell into some disrepute earlier this century by becoming linked with discredited fundamentalism. In the fifty years between the Scopes Monkey Trial and Jimmy Carter's presidential campaign, the term became associated more closely with a set of evangelistic methods and beliefs in Biblical inerrancy. As such, the group considered evangelical was relegated to the margins of religious establishments, often considered extremist and aberrant.

The sudden jump into visibility during the 1970s revealed how much the evangelical revival had changed while the country was paying so little attention to it. Evangelicals had entered the mainstream of economic and social life in considerable numbers. They were no longer seen as confined to certain exclusively evangelical churches. They were gaining political momentum. And many of their representatives were anchoring their own television ministries.

With the surge of interest in evangelicals—came a flurry of efforts to study the movement. Because the basic evangelical theme is so deeply embedded in all Christianity, it became difficult to distinguish the more self-conscious evangelicals who fit a uniquely American Protestant conservative mold from those of other, mainstream churches who share an evangelical spirit but do not identify themselves as heirs of American revivalism. The search for definitions goes on.

From the studies that have been conducted over the past decade, what can be said about the direction of the self-consciously evangelical movement? Has it, as many media accounts seem to imply, grown by leaps and bounds as a religious and political force, or do the indicators show a different pattern?

A comparison of surveys of "born-again" experience over the decade helps frame a response to the question. The most recent polls show that one-third of Americans identify themselves as "born-again" or evangelical. Women outnumber men by 36 to 29 percent, 36 percent are age fifty and older, and the preponderance, 50 percent, live in the South.

Results from a decade ago are remarkably similar. *Religion in America, 1977–78,* reported that the same proportion of Americans said they considered themselves "born-again."

Applying more exacting standards has reduced that one-third figure on several polls. If the true evangelical is assumed to be one who, in addition to having a "born-again" experience, must believe in the literal truth of the Bible and has engaged in efforts to convert others, the percentage drops to the 20 percent range.

Various surveys turn up some variation on the totals of "born-again" Christians, measured by that one criterion alone, but nothing has indicated a consistent pattern of significant growth in the numbers of Americans who are self-consciously evangelical. This suggests little, if any, actual growth. Much has been made of the decrease of membership among many mainline Protestant churches, usually contrasted with the presumed spurt among evangelical churches. Some explicitly evangelical churches have made steady gains, but the overall proportion of the public calling itself evangelical or "born-again" does not appear to have changed over the past decade.

Likewise, the spread of evangelicals across the denominational spectrum seems constant over the same period. In the 1977–78 report, for example, 61 percent of Baptists and 11 percent of Episcopalians described themselves as "born-again." The latest figures for these groups are virtually identical. A slight shift has taken place among Catholics. Ten years ago, 18 percent of Catholics said they were "born-again" compared to 11 percent on the latest polls. One explanation for the drop is that the Catholic charismatic renewal, which emphasizes personal, direct encounters with the Holy Spirit in the manner of the "born-again" style, was flourishing in the mid-1970s and has since ebbed.

If evangelical loyalties have not dramatically increased, the apparent ability of the movement to hold its own in the face of many challenges can be considered something of a feat. Liberal Christianity has been largely in decline. Secular ideologies have made inroads into all denominations, lowering the level of religious commitment among many church members, experts say. From the vantage point of some analysts, the middle ground between clear-cut, evangelical faith and unbelief, the churched and the unchurched, seems to be eroding. In the struggle for hearts and minds, the analysts say, nominal Christianity and cultural forms of civil religion become less viable options. Evangelicals pose the alternative by holding a set of beliefs firmly and unequivocally. Observers note that, while evangelicals draw criticism from those who regard their ways as too simplistic or rigid, the evangelical presence keeps alive the choice of taking faith seriously.

Whether evangelical strength can overcome the recent scandals involving television preachers is the latest test. Gallup Polls conducted soon after the demise of Jim and Tammy Bakker and the controversy over the fund-raising appeals of Oral Roberts show serious public distrust of television evangelists in general. Whether the disaffection with television evangelists reflects detrimentally on the wider evangelical movement remains to be seen.

An immediate concern for evangelical leaders is what impact the turmoil might have among evangelicals themselves. Evangelicals are far more likely to tune in TV evangelists than nonevangelicals and while their disillusion with the media preachers registers lower than that of nonevangelicals, it could spell trouble within the ranks.

Overall, the percentage of the public regarding TV evangelists as "untrustworthy" shot up from 36 percent in 1980 to 63 percent just after the recently publicized troubles. In 1980, 53 percent believed the preachers were honest. That figure dropped to 34 percent.

Among those who watch religious TV programs weekly, largely an evangelical audience, 47 percent said they saw TV evangelists as "untrustworthy." Fifty-three percent of these weekly viewers said they believe TV evangelists were honest, compared to 34 percent of the general public.

Survey results have shown that viewers of religious television do so in order to confirm their faith and gain added assurance. The TV evangelists, then, appear to have functioned as reinforcers of those who are already believers. Should confidence in these spokespersons for the faith suffer seriously, the evangelical movement could be quite adversely affected. But the capacity for recovery has been one of the movement's great assets and the outcome is far from clear. The latest surveys show the need for rebuilding support. Among evangelicals, 35 percent believe TV evangelists are dishonest, 33 percent think they are insincere, and 38 percent say that television preachers do not have a special relationship with God.

The acceptability of evangelicals as presidential candidates offers one indication of the movement's current standing on a wider public basis. In the aftermath of the conflicts among the TV evangelists, 29 percent of Americans said they were "less likely" to vote for a candidate "who considers himself a born-again evangelical Christian." The percentage is three times what it had been in 1980.

Demographic factors continue to shape the evangelical community. Those who describe themselves as "born-again" are disproportionately Protestant, black, poor, and Southern. Forty-four percent of blacks call themselves evangelical, as compared to 31 percent of whites. Nearly four of ten evangelicals belong to households whose income is $15,000 or less, compared to about two in ten whose income is $40,000 and above. Nearly four in ten have not completed high school.

Though many evangelicals have prospered in recent years by climbing the educational and job ladders, large numbers of evangelicals have not. The question is whether the movement can retain the allegiance of the majority of those who become upwardly mobile. Conversely, how does the relative lack of formal education and economic hardship relate to the fostering of an evangelical identity?

Differences in the economic well-being of members of various denominations are striking. Among all Baptists, the total household income is $15,000 or under for 44 percent and $40,000 or over for 11 percent; comparable figures for other church bodies are: all Methodists, 30 percent and 18 percent, respectively; all Lutherans, 27 percent and 20 percent; all Presbyterians, 30 percent and 30 percent; all Episcopalians, 20 percent and 31 percent. Clearly Presbyterians and Episcopalians continue to have the largest percentages of affluent members.

By nature, evangelical churches have seen the way forward as beset by obstacles and challenges. The propagation and development of faith has always been seen by its leaders as the most compelling and formidable of tasks. Surveys indicate tough sledding ahead just to maintain the level of relative stability that has marked the past ten years.

Some evangelicals believe the key to evangelism may lie in the ability of the movement to broaden its moral perspective. Personal morality has been the hallmark of modern evangelicalism, but, as many religious historians point out, their forebears in the nineteenth century were in the forefront of the struggle for the broader goals of societal justice.

Jimmy Carter himself has stood in that tradition, embracing both personal and social ethics. Billy Graham, the evangelist with the highest public standing, has placed concern for the arms race at the heart of his ministry.

In the tide of political and social conservatism during the Reagan presidency, the vision and aspirations of evangelicals have found a receptive climate in many centers of political power. The support has, in the view of most analysts, buoyed the movement. A change in climate in the years ahead could place the cause of evangelical Americans in a much different context; its moral and spiritual agenda could become more difficult to achieve.

But evangelicals have been building resources. They now have a more complex network of churches, schools, colleges, and media ministries than ever before. Those resources will be needed as never before in the effort by evangelicals to retain their toehold in American religious life.

CRITICAL-THINKING QUESTIONS

1. Has the "born-again" population changed during the last decade?
2. Have the recently publicized troubles of televangelists such as Jim and Tammy Bakker had any impact on the viewers?
3. What is the "demographic profile" of the televangelical community?

55

Women and Islam

Jane I. Smith

Many Westerners have a vague notion that women in Iran, Saudi Arabia, and other Islamic societies are subject to relentless control by men. Although there is some truth to this stereotype, a more realistic account of the relationship between Islam and gender must begin with a basic understanding of this unfamiliar religion. In this article, Jane Smith provides an overview of Islamic tenets, explores some of the variations that divide the vast Islamic world, and assesses the relative social standing of the sexes—as Muslims themselves understand it.

To attempt to talk about women in Islam is of course to venture into an area fraught with the perils of overgeneralization, oversimplification, and the almost unavoidable limitations of a Western bias. The first problem is simply one of raw numbers. There are perhaps close to half a billion Muslim women inhabiting all major areas of the world today. Is it possible to say anything that holds true for all of them, let alone for their sisters over the past fourteen centuries of Islam?

Then one must consider all the various elements that comprise the picture of Islamic womanhood. Many of these elements are directly related to the religion of Islam itself, such as past and present legal realities, roles permitted and enforced as a result of Muslim images of women, and the variety of Islamic and hetero-Islamic rites and practices in which Islamic women have traditionally participated. Other elements contributing to the full picture of women in Islam—such as education, political rights, professional employment oppor-

SOURCE: "Women and Islam," by Jane I. Smith, in *Women in World Religions,* ed. Arvind Sharma. Copyright © 1987 by SUNY Press. Reprinted by permission of the State University of New York Press.

tunities, and the like—have less to do with the religion per se but are still influenced by it.

The Holy Qur'ān (sometimes transliterated as "Koran") still forms the basis of prevailing family law in most areas of the Muslim world. It has always been and still is considered to be the last in a series of divine revelations from God given in the seventh century C.E. to humanity through the vehicle of his final prophet Muhammad. The Qur'ān is therefore the literal and unmitigated word of God, collected and ordered by the young Muslim community but untainted with the thoughts and interpretations of any persons, including Muhammad himself. It is obvious, then, why the regulations formulated by the Qur'ān in regard to women have been adhered to with strictness and why changes in Muslim family law are coming about only very slowly in the Islamic world.

The circumstances of women in pre-Islamic Arabia are subject to a variety of interpretations. On the one hand, certain women—soothsayers, priestesses, queens, and even singular individuals—did play powerful roles in society. On the other hand, whatever the earlier realities for women in terms of marriage, divorce, and inheritance of property, it is clear that the Qur'ān did introduce very significant changes that were advantageous for women. Contemporary Muslims are fond of pointing out, quite correctly, that Islam brought legal advantages for women quite unknown in corresponding areas of the Western Christian world. What, then, does the Qur'ān say about women?

The earliest messages of the Qur'ān, and the twin themes that run through all the chapters, are of the realities of the oneness of God and the inevitability of the day of judgment. All persons, men and women, are called upon to testify to those realities. . . . Religiously speaking, then, men and women are fully equal in the eyes of God according to the Qur'ān.

Before looking at the specifics of the legal injunctions for women, it is necessary to consider two verses that have caused a great deal of consternation to Westerners. One is 2:228, which says literally that men are a step above women, and the other is 4:34, clarifying that men are the protectors of women (or are in charge of women) because God has given preference to one over the other and because men provide support for women. Perhaps because these verses have been so troublesome for non-Muslims (especially feminists), they have been subject to an enormous amount of explanation and interpretation by contemporary Muslim apologists eager to present a defense of their religion. These writers, men and women, affirm that it is precisely because men are invested with the responsibility of taking care of women, financially and otherwise, that they are given authority over the females of their families. And that, affirm many Muslim women today, is exactly the way it should be. We will return to this perspective later, particularly in light of what a desire for liberation means—and does not mean—for many Muslim women. . . . .

According to the Qur'ān, a man may marry up to four wives, so long as he is able to provide for each equally. He may marry a Muslim woman or a member of the Jewish or Christian faith, or a slave woman. A Muslim woman, however, may marry only one husband, and he must be a Muslim. Contemporary Muslim apologists are quick to point out that these restrictions are for the benefit of women, ensuring that they will not be left unprotected. In Islam, marriage is not a sacrament but a legal contract, and according to the Qur'ān a woman has clearly defined legal rights in negotiating this contract. She can dictate the terms and can receive the dowry herself. This dowry (*mahr*) she is permitted to keep and maintain as a source of personal pride and comfort.

Polygamy (or more strictly polygyny, plurality of wives) is practiced by only a small percentage of the contemporary Muslim population, and a man with more than two wives is extremely rare. Many countries are now taking steps to modify the circumstances in which a husband may take more than one wife, although only in two countries, Turkey and Tunisia, are multiple marriages actually illegal. Other countries have made such moves as requiring the husband to have the permission of the court (as in Iraq and Syria) or to get the permission of the first wife (as in Egypt), or permitting the wife to write into her marriage contract that she will not allow a cowife (as in Morocco and Lebanon). It seems reasonable to expect that other countries will make changes and modifications. It is interesting to note that while for some finances have dictated monogamy—most husbands have simply not been able to afford more than one wife—changing economic realities may again dictate that a man contemplate the possibility of having several wives to work and supply income for the family.

Muslim women traditionally have been married at an extremely young age, sometimes even before puberty. This practice is related, of course, to the historical fact that fathers and other male relatives generally have chosen the grooms themselves, despite the guarantee of the Qur'ān that marriage is a contract into which male and female enter equally. While it is true that technically a girl cannot be forced into a marriage she does not want, pressures from family and the youth of the bride often have made this prerogative difficult to exercise. Today, the right of a male member of the family to contract an engagement for a girl against her wishes has been legally revoked in most places, although it is still a common practice, especially in rural areas. . . .

In the contemporary Islamic world, divorce rates vary considerably from one country to the next. Muslim apologists insist that divorce is not nearly as common in Islamic countries as it is, for example, in the United States. This statement is generally true, although in some countries, such as Morocco, the rate is high and continues to grow. Often what is really only the breaking of the engagement contract is included in divorce statistics, skewing the measure. Many countries are now considering serious changes in divorce procedures. The simultaneous triple repudiation generally has been declared illegal, and in many countries divorce initiated by either party, the man or the woman, must take place in the court of law. Other countries add special stipulations generally favorable to the woman. It remains true, however, that men can divorce for less cause than women,

and often divorces hung up in courts with male judges can prove enormously difficult for women to gain.

In accordance with Islamic law, custody of the children traditionally has gone to the father at some time between the age of seven and nine for boys and between seven and puberty for girls, depending on the legal school. This practice too is slowly changing, and in most areas women who have been divorced by their husbands are allowed to keep their sons until puberty and their daughters until they are of an age to be married.

It is considered one of the great innovations of the Qur'ān over earlier practices that women are permitted to inherit and own property. Non-Muslims have generally found great difficulty with the Qur'ānic stipulation that a woman is allowed to inherit property but that the inheritance should be only half that of a male. According to the Islamic understanding, however, the rationale is precisely that which applies to the verse saying that men are in charge of women. Because women are permitted to keep and maintain their own property without responsibility for taking care of their families financially, it is only reasonable that the male, who must spend his own earning and inheritance for the maintenance of women, should receive twice as much. . . .

According to the Qur'ān, women should not expose themselves to public view with lack of modesty. It does not say that they should be covered specifically from head to toe, nor that they should wear face veils or masks or other of the paraphernalia that has adorned many Islamic women through the ages. The Qur'ān also suggests that the wives of the Prophet Muhammad, when speaking to other men, should do so from behind a partition, again for purposes of propriety. It has been open to question whether this statement is meant to apply to all women. In the early Islamic community, these verses were exaggerated and their underlying ideas elaborated and defined in ways that led fairly quickly to a seclusion of women which seems quite at odds with what the Qur'ān intended or the Prophet wanted. When the community in Medina was established, women participated fully with men in all activities of worship and prayer. Soon they became segregated, however, to the point where an often-quoted hadīth (no doubt spurious) attributed to Muhammad has him saying that women pray better at home than in the mosque, and best of all in their own closets. Today a number of contemporary Muslim writers are urging a return to the practices of the young Muslim community, with women no longer segregated from the mosque or relegated to certain rear or side portions as they generally have been, but participating fully in worship with men. . . .

What is popularly known as "veiling" is part of the general phenomenon of the segregation of women and yet is also distinctly apart from it. The two are increasingly seen as separate by contemporary Islamic women seeking to affirm a new identity in relation to their religion. Veils traditionally have taken a number of forms: a veil covering the face from just below the eyes down; a *chador* or *burka* covering the entire body, including the face, often with a woven screen in front through which women can see but not be seen; and a full face mask with small slits through the eyes, still worn in some areas of the Arabian Gulf. These costumes, so seemingly oppressive to Western eyes, at least have allowed women to observe without being observed, thus affording their wearers a degree of anonymity that on some occasions has proven useful.

The general movement toward unveiling had its ostensible beginning in the mid-1920s, when the Egyptian feminist Huda Sha'rawi cast off her veil after arriving in Egypt from an international meeting of women. She was followed literally and symbolically by masses of women in the succeeding years, and Egyptian women as well as those in other Middle Eastern countries made great strides in adopting Western dress. At the present time in the history of Islam, however, one finds a quite different phenomenon. Partly in reaction against Western liberation and Western ideals in general, women in many parts of the Islamic world are self-consciously adopting forms of dress by which they can identify with Islam rather than with what they now see as the imperialist West. Islamic dress, gen-erally chosen by Muslim women themselves rather than forced upon them by males, signals for many an identification with a way of life that they are increasingly convinced represents a more viable alternative than that offered by the West. . . .

We see, then, that while legal circumstances for women have undergone some significant changes in the past half-century, the dictates of the Qur'ān continue to be enormously influential in the molding of new laws as well as in the personal choices of Muslim men and women. . . .

I have stressed here the insistence of the Qur'ān on the religious and spiritual equality of men and women. And aside from some unfortunate hadīths with very weak chains of authority suggesting that the majority of women will be in the Fire on the Day of Judgment because of their mental and physical inferiority, religious literature in general, when talking about human responsibility and concomitant judgment, makes women full partners with men under the divine command to live lives of integrity and righteousness. . . .

Of course, women do participate in many of the activities and duties considered incumbent on all good Muslims, but generally these practices have a somewhat different function for them than for men. Prayer for women, as we have said, is usually in the home rather than in the mosque, and does not necessarily follow the pattern of the regularized five times a day. Participation in the fast itself is normally the same as for the men (except when women are pregnant, nursing, or menstruating), but the particular joys of preparing the fast-breaking meals are for the women alone. While the husband determines the amount of money or goods to be distributed for almsgiving, another responsibility of all Muslims, it is often the wife who takes charge of the actual distribution.

The last duty incumbent on Muslims after the testimony to the oneness of God and prophethood of his apostle Muhammad, the prayer, the fast, and paying the almstax is the pilgrimage once in a lifetime to the holy city of Mecca. Women do participate in this journey, and as transportation becomes easier and the care provided for pilgrims in Saudi Arabia becomes more regularized with modernization, increasing numbers of females join the throngs which gather to circumambulate the Xaaba at Mecca each year. . . .

Saints in Islam are both male and female. One is normally recognized as a saint not by any process of canonization but because of some miraculous deed(s) performed or through a dream communication after death with a living person requesting that a shrine be erected over his or her tomb. Often a woman is favored with these dreams and after the construction of the shrine she becomes the carekeeper of the tomb, a position of some honor and responsibility. . . .

While women in the Islamic world have been segregated and secluded, and historically have been considered second-class citizens by the vast majority of males in the community, they have not been totally without power. They have been able to maintain a degree of control over their own lives and over the men with whom they live through many of the religious practices described above. The fact that they alone have the ability to bear children, the influence they continue to play in the lives of their sons, and the power they have over their son's wives are subtle indications that there are certain checks and balances on the obvious authority invested by the Qur'ān in men. From sexuality to control of the network of communications in the family to manipulation of such external agencies as spirits and supernatural beings, women have had at their control a variety of means to exert their will over the men in their families and over their own circumstances. The subtle means of control available to women throughout the world have of course been exploited: withholding sexual favors (a questionable but often-quoted hadīth says that if a woman refuses to sleep with her husband, the angels will curse her until the morning), doing small things to undermine a husband's honor such as embarrassing him in front of guests, indulging in various forms of gossip and social control, and the like. . . .

Until fairly recently, education for women in the Muslim world has been minimal. Girls were given the rudiments of an Islamic education, mainly a little instruction in the Qur'ān and the tra-

ditions so as to be able to recite their prayers properly. Beyond that their training was not academic but domestic. In the late nineteenth and early twentieth century, Islamic leaders awoke with a start to the reality that Muslims were significantly behind the West in a variety of ways, including technology and the education necessary to understand and develop it. Many of these leaders recognized that if Islamic nations were to compete successfully in the contemporary world, it had to be with the aid of a well-educated and responsible female sector. Thus, this century has seen a number of educational advances for women, and in some countries, such as Egypt, Iraq, and Kuwait, women constitute very significant numbers of the university population. Nonetheless, illiteracy in many Muslim nations continues to be high, and the gap between male and female literacy rates is even increasing in some areas. In Saudi Arabia, where at present the economic resources are certainly available, large numbers of Saudi girls are receiving a full education, though separated from boys, and are taught either by men through television transmission or by women.

In education as in most areas of life, the male understanding of women as encouraged by certain parts of the Islamic tradition continues to play an important role. The Qur'ān does state, along with the stipulation that women can inherit only half of what men inherit, that the witness (in the court of law) of one man is equal to that of two women. This unfortunately has been interpreted by some in the history of Islam to mean that women are intellectually inferior to men, unstable in their judgment, and too easily swayed by emotion. Such perspectives are certainly not shared by all but nonetheless have been influential (and in some places are increasingly so today) in making it difficult for a woman to have access to the same kinds of educational opportunities that are available to men. Certain subjects are deemed "appropriate" for a woman to study, particularly those geared to make her the best and most productive wife, mother, and female participant in the family structure.

The prevalent view, confirmed by the Qur'ān,

is that women should be modest and should neither expose themselves to men nor be too much in public places, where they will be subject to men's observation or forced to interact with males not in their immediate families. This view obviously has contributed to the difficulties of receiving a full education and of securing employment outside the home. More employment opportunities are open to women today than in the past, however, and in many countries women hold high-level positions in business, government, civil service, education, and other sectors. Statistics differ greatly across the Islamic world and are difficult to assess because they often fail to take into account the rural woman who may work full-time in the fields or other occupation outside the house but does not earn an independent salary. . . .

Saudi Arabia presents an interesting case study of the confrontation of Islamic ideas with contemporary reality. Women are greatly inhibited in the labor arena; because of conservative religious attitudes they must be veiled and covered, are not permitted to drive or even ride in a taxi with a strange man, and in general are unable to participate on the social and professional level with males. However, in a country in which production is both necessary and economically possible and which suffers from a lack of manpower, the use of women in the work force or increased importation of foreign labor seem the only two (both undesirable) alternatives. Thus more Saudi women are working, and because of their right to inherit, are accumulating very substantial amounts of money. It is interesting to note the rapid rate of construction of new banks exclusively for women in places like Jiddah and Riyadh.

The aforementioned Qur'ān verse about the witness of two women being equal to that of one man and the supporting literature attesting to female intellectual, physical (and in fact sometimes moral) inferiority have made it difficult for Muslim women to achieve equal political rights. In most Arab countries (except Saudi Arabia and certain of the Gulf States), as well as in most other parts of the Islamic world, women have now been given the vote. Centuries of passivity in the polit-

ical realm, however, have made it difficult for women to take advantage of the opportunities now available to them. In some countries, such as Egypt, women are playing major political roles, but generally women politicians find little support from men or even from other women for their aspirations. This is not to underestimate the strong current in Islamic thinking which encourages the full participation of women in politics, as well as in the educational and professional fields.

Like an intricate and complex geometric pattern on a Persian rug or a frieze decorating a mosque, the practices, roles, opportunities, prescriptions, hopes, and frustrations of Islamic women are woven together in a whole. The colors are sometimes bold and striking, at other times muted and subtle. Some contemporary Muslim women are progressive and aggressive, no longer content to fit the traditionally prescribed patterns. Others are passive and accepting, not yet able to discern what new possibilities may be open to them, let alone whether or not they might want to take advantage of such opportunities. Some are Westernized as their mothers and grandmothers were and have every intention of staying that way, while others are increasingly clear in their feelings that the West does not have the answers and that Islam, particularly the Islam of the Qur'ān and the community of the Prophet Muhammad, is God's chosen way for humankind. For the latter, their dress, their relationships with their husbands and families, and their verbal assent to Islamic priorities reflect this conviction that the time has come to cease a fruitless preoccupation with things Western and to reaffirm their identity as Muslim women.

It is difficult for Western feminists to grasp exactly what the Muslim woman may mean by "liberation." For many Islamic women, the fruits of liberation in the West are too many broken marriages, women left without the security of men who will provide for them, deteriorating relations between men and women, and sexual license that appears as rank immorality. They see the Islamic system as affirmed by the Qur'ān as one in which male authority over them ensures their care and protection and provides a structure in which the family is solid, children are inculcated with lasting values, and the balance of responsibility between man and woman is one in which absolute equality is less highly prized than cooperation and complementarity.

The new Islamic woman, then, is morally and religiously conservative and affirms the absolute value of the true Islamic system for human relationships. She is intolerant of the kind of Islam in which women are subjugated and relegated to roles insignificant to the full functioning of society, and she wants to take full advantage of educational and professional opportunities. She may agree, however, that certain fields of education are more appropriate for women than others, and that certain professions are more natural to males than to females. She participates as a contributor to and decisionmaker for the family, yet recognizes that in any complex relationship final authority must rest with one person. And she is content to delegate that authority to her husband, father, or other male relative in return for the solidarity of the family structure and the support and protection that it gives her and her children.

That not all, or even most, Muslim women subscribe to this point of view is clear. And yet, at the time of this writing, it seems equally clear that, if Western observers are to understand women in the contemporary Islamic world, they must appreciate a point of view that is more and more prevalent. The West is increasingly identified with imperialism, and solutions viable for women in the Islamic community are necessarily different from the kinds of solutions that many Western women seem to have chosen for themselves. For the Muslim the words of the Qur'ān are divine, and the prescriptions for the roles and rights of females, like the other messages of the holy book, are seen as part of God's divinely ordered plan for all humanity. Change will come slowly and whatever kinds of liberation ultimately prevail will be cloaked in a garb that is—in one or another of its various aspects—essentially Islamic.

CRITICAL-THINKING QUESTIONS

1. In what formal ways does Islam confer on men authority over women?

2. In what formal and informal ways does Islam give power to women to affect their own lives and those of men?

3. From a Muslim perspective, what are some of the problems with Western living and, particularly, Western feminism?

EDUCATION

56

Education and Inequality

Samuel Bowles and Herbert Gintis

Education has long been held to be a means to realizing U.S. ideals of equal opportunity. As Lester Ward notes at the beginning of this selection, the promise of education is to allow "natural" abilities to win out over the "artificial" inequalities of class, race, and sex. Samuel Bowles and Herbert Gintis claim that this has happened very little in the United States. Rather, they argue, schooling has more to do with maintaining *existing social hierarchy.*

Universal education is the power, which is destined to overthrow every species of hierarchy. It is destined to remove all artificial inequality and leave the natural inequalities to find their true level. With the artificial inequalities of caste, rank, title, blood, birth, race, color, sex, etc., will fall nearly all the oppression, abuse, prejudice, enmity, and injustice, that humanity is now subject to. (Lester Frank Ward, *Education* © 1872)

A review of educational history hardly supports the optimistic pronouncements of liberal educa-

tional theory. The politics of education are better understood in terms of the need for social control in an unequal and rapidly changing economic order. The founders of the modern U.S. school system understood that the capitalist economy produces great extremes of wealth and poverty, of social elevation and degradation. Horace Mann and other school reformers of the antebellum period knew well the seamy side of the burgeoning industrial and urban centers. "Here," wrote Henry Barnard, the first state superintendent of education in both Connecticut and Rhode Island, and later to become the first U.S. Commissioner of Education, "the wealth, enterprise and professional talent of the state are concentrated . . . but here also are

SOURCE: *Schooling in Capitalist America: Educational Reform and the Contradictions of Economic Life* by Samuel Bowles and Herbert Gintis. Copyright © 1976 by Basic Books, Inc. Reprinted with permission of Basic Books, a division of HarperCollins Publishers, Inc.

poverty, ignorance profligacy and irreligion, and a classification of society as broad and deep as ever divided the plebeian and patrician of ancient Rome."[1] They lived in a world in which, to use de Tocqueville's words, ". . . small aristocratic societies . . . are formed by some manufacturers in the midst of the immense democracy of our age [in which] . . . some men are opulent and a multitude . . . are wretchedly poor."[2] The rapid rise of the factory system, particularly in New England, was celebrated by the early school reformers; yet, the alarming transition from a relatively simple rural society to a highly stratified industrial economy could not be ignored. They shared the fears that de Tocqueville had expressed following his visit to the United States in 1831:

When a work man is unceasingly and exclusively engaged in the fabrication of one thing, he ultimately does his work with singular dexterity; but at the same time he loses the general faculty of applying his mind to the direction of the work. . . . [While] the science of manufacture lowers the class of workmen, it raises the class of masters. . . . [If] ever a permanent inequality of conditions . . . again penetrates into the world, it may be predicted that this is the gate by which they will enter.[3]

While deeply committed to the emerging industrial order, the farsighted school reformers of the mid-nineteenth century understood the explosive potential of the glaring inequalities of factory life. Deploring the widening of social divisions and fearing increasing unrest, Mann, Barnard, and others proposed educational expansion and reform. In his Fifth Report as Secretary of the Massachusetts Board of Education, Horace Mann wrote:

Education, then beyond all other devices of human origin, is the great equalizer of the conditions of men—the balance wheel of the social machinery. . . . It does better than to disarm the poor of their hostility toward the rich; it prevents being poor.[4]

Mann and his followers appeared to be at least as interested in disarming the poor as in preventing poverty. They saw in the spread of universal and free education a means of alleviating social distress without redistributing wealth and power or altering the broad outlines of the economic system. Education, it seems, had almost magical powers.

The main idea set forth in the creeds of some political reformers, or revolutionizers, is, that some people are poor because others are rich. This idea supposed a fixed amount of property in the community . . . and the problem presented for solution is, how to transfer a portion of this property from those who are supposed to have too much to those who feel and know that they have too little. At this point, both their theory and their expectation of reform stop. But the beneficent power of education would not be exhausted, even though it should peaceably abolish all the miseries that spring from the coexistence, side by side, of enormous wealth and squalid want. It has a higher function. Beyond the power of diffusing old wealth, it has the prerogative of creating new.[5]

The early educators viewed the poor as the foreign element that they were. Mill hands were recruited throughout New England, often disrupting the small towns in which textile and other rapidly growing industries had located. Following the Irish potato famine of the 1840s, thousands of Irish workers settled in the cities and towns of the northeastern United States. Schooling was seen as a means of integrating this "uncouth and dangerous" element into the social fabric of American life. The inferiority of the foreigner was taken for granted. The editors of the influential *Massachusetts Teacher,* a leader in the educational reform movement, writing in 1851, saw ". . . the increasing influx of foreigners . . ." as a moral and social problem:

Will it, like the muddy Missouri, as it pours its waters into the clear Mississippi and contaminates the whole united mass, spread ignorance and vice, crime and disease, through our native population?

If . . . we can by any means purify this foreign people, enlighten their ignorance and bring them up to our level, we shall perform a work of true and perfect charity, blessing the giver and receiver in equal measure. . . .

With the old not much can be done; but with their children, the great remedy is *education.* The rising generation must be taught as our own children are taught. We say *must be* because in many cases this can only be accomplished by coercion.[6]

Since the mid-nineteenth century the dual objectives of educational reformers—equality of opportunity and social control—have been intermingled, the merger of these two threads sometimes so nearly complete that it becomes impossible to distinguish between the two. Schooling has been at once something done for the poor and to the poor.

The basic assumptions which underlay this commingling help explain the educational reform movement's social legacy. First, educational reformers did not question the fundamental economic institutions of capitalism: Capitalist ownership and control of the means of production and dependent wage labor were taken for granted. In fact, education was to helps preserve and extend the capitalist order. The function of the school system was to accommodate workers to its most rapid possible development. Second, it was assumed that people (often classes of people or "races") are differentially equipped by nature or social origins to occupy the varied economic and social levels in the class structure. By providing equal opportunity, the school system was to elevate the masses, guiding them sensibly and fairly to the manifold political, social, and economic roles of adult life.

Jefferson's educational thought strikingly illustrates this perspective. In 1779, he proposed a two-track educational system which would prepare individuals for adulthood in one of the two classes of society: the "laboring and the learned."[7] Even children of the laboring class would qualify for leadership. Scholarships would allow ". . . those persons whom nature hath endowed with genius and virtue. . ." to ". . . be rendered by liberal education worthy to receive and able to guard the sacred deposit of the rights and liberties of their fellow citizens."[8] Such a system, Jefferson asserted, would succeed in ". . . raking a few geniuses from the rubbish."[9] Jefferson's two-tiered educational plan presents in stark relief the outlines and motivation for the stratified structure of U.S. education which has endured up to the present. At the top, there is the highly selective aristocratic tradition, the elite university training future leaders. At the base is mass education for all, dedicated to uplift and control. The two traditions have always coexisted although their meeting point has drifted upward over the years, as mass education has spread upward from elementary school through high school, and now up to the post-high-school level.

Though schooling was consciously molded to reflect the class structure, education was seen as a means of enhancing wealth and morality, which would work to the advantage of all. Horace Mann, in his 1842 report to the State Board of Education, reproduced this comment by a Massachusetts industrialist:

The great majority always have been and probably always will be comparatively poor, while a few will possess the greatest share of this world's goods. And it is a wise provision of Providence which connects so intimately, and as I think so indissolubly, the greatest good of the many with the highest interests in the few.[10]

Much of the content of education over the past century and a half can only be construed as an unvarnished attempt to persuade the "many" to make the best of the inevitable.

The unequal contest between social control and social justice is evident in the total functioning of U.S. education. The system as it stands today provides eloquent testimony to the ability of the well-to-do to perpetuate in the name of equality of opportunity an arrangement which consistently yields to themselves disproportional advantages, while thwarting the aspirations and needs of the working people of the United States. However grating this judgment may sound to the ears of the undaunted optimist, it is by no means excessive in light of the massive statistical data on inequality in the United States. Let us look at the contemporary evidence.

We may begin with the basic issue of inequalities in the years of schooling. As can be seen in [Figure 56-1], the number of years of schooling attained by an individual is strongly associated with parental socioeconomic status. This figure presents the estimated distribution of years of schooling attained by individuals of varying socioeconomic backgrounds. If we define socioeconomic background by a weighted sum of income, occupation, and educational level of the parents, a child from the ninetieth percentile may expect, on the average, five more years of schooling than a child in the tenth percentile.[11]

... We have chosen a sample of white males because the most complete statistics are available for this group. Moreover, if inequality for white males can be documented, the proposition is merely strengthened when sexual and racial differences are taken into account.

Additional census data dramatize one aspect of

FIGURE 56-1 Educational Attainments Are Strongly Dependent on Social Background Even for People of Similar Childhood IQs. Notes: For each socioeconomic group, the left-hand bar indicates the estimated average number of years of schooling attained by all men from that group. The right-hand bar indicates the estimated average number of years of schooling attained by men with IQ scores equal to the average for the entire sample. The sample refers to "non-Negro" men of "nonfarm" backgrounds, aged 35–44 years in 1962. Source: Samuel Bowles and Valerie Nelson, "The 'Inheritance of IQ' and the Intergenerational Transmission of Economic Inequality," *The Review of Economics and Statistics,* vol. LVI, no. 1 (Feb. 1974).

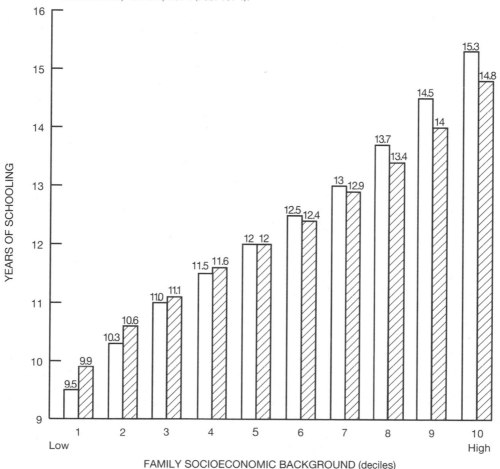

educational inequalities: the relationship between family income and college attendance. Even among those who had graduated from high school in the early 1960s, children of families earning less than $3,000 per year were over six times as likely *not* to attend college as were the children of families earning over $15,000.[12] Moreover, children from less well-off families are *both* less likely to have graduated from high school and more likely to attend inexpensive, two-year community colleges rather than a four-year B.A. program if they do make it to college.[13]

Not surprisingly, the results of schooling differ greatly for children of different social backgrounds. Most easily measured, but of limited importance, are differences in scholastic achievement. If we measure the output of schooling by scores on nationally standardized achievement tests, children whose parents were themselves highly educated outperform the children of parents with less education by a wide margin. Data collected for the U.S. Office of Education Survey of Educational Opportunity reveal, for example, that among white high-school seniors, those whose parents were in the top education decile were, on the average, well over three grade levels in measured scholastic achievement ahead of those whose parents were in the bottom decile.[14]

Given these differences in scholastic achievement, inequalities in years of schooling among individuals of different social backgrounds are to be expected. Thus one might be tempted to argue that the close dependence of years of schooling attained on background displayed in the left-hand bars of [Figure 56-1] is simply a reflection of unequal intellectual abilities, or that inequalities in college attendance are the consequences of differing levels of scholastic achievement in high school and do not reflect any additional social class inequalities peculiar to the process of college admission.

This view, so comforting to the admissions personnel in our elite universities, is unsupported by the data, some of which is presented in [the figure]. The right-hand bars of [the figure] indicate that even among children with identical IQ test scores at ages six and eight, those with rich, well-

educated, high-status parents could expect a much higher level of schooling than those with less-favored origins. Indeed, the closeness of the left-hand and right-hand bars in [the figure] shows that only a small portion of the observed social class differences in educational attainment is related to IQ differences across social classes.[15] The dependence of education attained on background is almost as strong for individuals with the same IQ as for all individuals. Thus, while [the figure] indicates that an individual in the ninetieth percentile in social class background is likely to receive five more years of education than an individual in the tenth percentile, it also indicated that he is likely to receive 4.25 more years schooling than an individual from the tenth percentile with the same IQ. Similar results are obtained when we look specifically at access to college education for students with the same measured IQ. Project Talent data indicates that for "high ability" students (top 25 percent as measured by a composite of tests of "general aptitude"), those of high socioeconomic background (top 25 percent as measured by a composite of family income, parents' education, and occupation) are nearly twice as likely to attend college than students of low socioeconomic background (bottom 25 percent). For "low ability" students (bottom 25 percent), those of high-social background are more than four times as likely to attend college as are their low-social background counterparts.[16]

Inequality in years of schooling is, of course, only symptomatic of broader inequalities in the educational system. Not only do less well-off children go to school for fewer years, they are treated with less attention (or more precisely, less benevolent attention) when they are there. These broader inequalities are not easily measured. Some show up in statistics on the different levels of expenditure for the education of children of different socioeconomic backgrounds. Taking account of the inequality in financial resources for each year in school and the inequality in years of schooling obtained, Jencks estimated that a child whose parents were in the top fifth of the income distribution receives roughly twice the educational resources in dollar terms as does a child whose parents are in the bottom fifth.[17]

The social class inequalities in our school system, then, are too evident to be denied. Defenders of the educational system are forced back on the assertion that things are getting better; the inequalities of the past were far worse. And, indeed, there can be no doubt that some of the inequalities of the past have been mitigated. Yet new inequalities have apparently developed to take their place, for the available historical evidence lends little support to the idea that our schools are on the road to equality of educational opportunity. For example, data from a recent U.S. Census survey reported in Spady indicate that graduation from college has become no less dependent on one's social background. This is true despite the fact that high-school graduation is becoming increasingly equal across social classes.[18] Additional data confirm this impression. The statistical association (coefficient of correlation) between parents' social status and years of education attained by individuals who completed their schooling three or four decades ago is virtually identical to the same correlation for individuals who terminated their schooling in recent years.[19] On balance, the available data suggest that the number of years of school attained by a child depends upon family background as much in the recent period as it did fifty years ago.

Thus, we have empirical reasons for doubting the egalitarian impact of schooling. . . . We conclude that U.S. education is highly unequal, the chances of attaining much or little schooling being substantially dependent on one's race and parents' economic level. Moreover, where there is a discernible trend toward a more equal educational system—as in the narrowing of the black education deficit, for example—the impact on the structure of economic opportunity is minimal at best.

CRITICAL-THINKING QUESTIONS

1. Describe how the educational system of the United States has historically had two objectives: *increasing opportunity on the one hand, and stabilizing an unequal society on the other. Which is emphasized in most public discussions of schooling?*
2. In what respects, according to Bowles and Gintis, has schooling supported the capitalist economic system? What character does this confer to the educational system?
3. What are Bowles and Gintis's conclusions about the relationship between schooling and natural ability? Between schooling and social background?

NOTES

1. H. Barnard, *Papers for the Teacher: 2nd Series* (New York: F. C. Brownell, 1866), pp. 293–310.

2. A. de Tocqueville, as quoted in Jeremy Brecher, *Strike!* (San Francisco: Straight Arrow Books, 1972), pp. xi, xii.

3. Ibid., p. 172.

4. Horace Mann as quoted in Michael Katz, ed., *School Reform Past and Present* (Boston: Little, Brown, 1971), p. 141.

5. Ibid., p. 145.

6. *The Massachusetts Teacher* (Oct. 1851), quoted in Katz, pp. 169–70.

7. D. Tyack, *Turning Points in American Educational History* (Waltham, MA: Blaisdell, 1967), p. 89.

8. Ibid., p. 109.

9. Ibid., p. 89.

10. Mann, quoted in Katz, p. 147.

11. This calculation is based on data reported in full in Samuel Bowles and Valerie Nelson, "The 'Inheritance of IQ' and the Intergenerational Transmission of Economic Inequality," *The Review of Economics and Statistics,* vol. 56, no. 1 (Feb. 1974). It refers to non-Negro males from nonfarm backgrounds, aged 35–44 years. The zero-order correlation coefficient between socioeconomic background and years of schooling was estimated at 0.646. The estimated standard deviation of years of schooling was 3.02. The results for other age groups are similar.

12. These figures refer to individuals who were high-school seniors in October 1965, and who subsequently graduated from high school. College attendance refers to both two- and four-year institutions. Family income is for the twelve months preceding October 1965. Data is drawn from U.S. Bureau of the Census, *Current Population Reports,* Series P-60, No. 183 (May 1969).

13. For further evidence, see ibid.; and Jerome Karabel, "Community Colleges and Social Stratification," *Harvard Educational Review,* vol. 424, no. 42 (Nov. 1972).

14. Calculation based on data in James S. Coleman et al., *Equality of Educational Opportunity* (Washington, DC: U.S. Government Printing Office, 1966), and the authors.

15. The data relating to IQ are from a 1966 survey of veterans by the National Opinion Research Center; and from N. Bayley and E. S. Schaefer, "Correlations of Maternal and Child Behaviors with the Development of Mental Ability: Data from the Berkeley Growth Study," *Monographs of Social Research in Child Development,* vol. 29, no. 6 (1964).

16. Based on a large sample of U.S. high-school students as reported in John C. Flannagan and William W. Cooley, *Project Talent, One Year Follow-up Study,* Cooperative Research Project, No. 2333 (Pittsburgh: University of Pittsburgh, School of Education, 1966).

17. C. Jencks et al., *Inequality: A Reassessment of the Effects of Family and Schooling in America* (New York: Basic Books, 1972), p. 48.

18. W. L. Spady, "Educational Mobility and Access: Growth and Paradoxes," in *American Journal of Sociology,* vol. 73, no. 3 (Nov. 1967); and Peter Blau and Otis D. Duncan, *The American Occupational Structure* (New York: John Wiley, 1967). More recent data support the evidence of no trend toward equality. See U.S. Bureau of Census, op. cit.

19. Blau and Duncan, ibid.

57

Why Don't College Students Participate?

David A. Karp and William C. Yoels

Perhaps surprisingly, the classroom—where many sociologists spend most of their time—has rarely been the focus of research. This study is based on the observation of ten university classes and questionnaires completed by students. Analyzing the results, David Karp and William Yoels offer insights concerning a widespread educational problem—the apparent apathy of most students in the classroom.

While there has been . . . a good deal written about higher education in general, there has been comparatively little research specifically on the *college classroom*. . . . Rarely have researchers attempted to consider the processes through which students and teachers formulate definitions of the classroom as a social setting. The problem of how students and teachers assign "meaning" to the classroom situation has been largely neglected. . . . Although writing about primary and secondary

SOURCE: "The College Classroom: Some Observations on the Meaning of Student Participation," by David A. Karp and William C. Yoels, in *Sociology and Social Research,* vol. 60, no. 4, July 1976, pp. 421–39. Reprinted with permission.

school classrooms, we would suggest that the following statement from Jackson's (1968: vii) *Life in Classrooms* holds true for college classrooms as well. He writes that:

Classroom life . . . is too complex an affair to be viewed or talked about from any single perspective. Accordingly, as we try to grasp the meaning of what school is like for students and teachers, we must not hesitate to use all the ways of knowing at our disposal. This means we must read and look and listen and count things, and talk to people, and even muse introspectively. . . .

The present study focuses on the meanings of student participation in the college classroom. Our examination of this problem will center on the way in which definitions of classrooms held by students and teachers relate to their actual behavior in the classroom.

METHODS OF STUDY

In an attempt to investigate the issues mentioned above we initiated an exploratory study of classroom behavior in several classes of a private university located in a large city in the northeastern United States. . . .

Ten classes were selected for observation. The observers were undergraduate and graduate sociology students who were doing the research as part of a Readings and Research arrangement. The classes were not randomly selected but were chosen in terms of the observers' time schedules and the possibility of their observing behavior in the classrooms on a regular basis throughout the semester. The observed classes were located in the following departments: sociology, philosophy, English, psychology, economics, theology. While the classes are certainly not a representative sample of all classes taught in this university, questionnaire responses from an additional sample of students in classes selected at random at the end of the semester indicate a remarkable similarity to the questionnaire responses of the students in the ten classes under observation.[1]

At the end of the semester a questionnaire was distributed in class to the students in the ten classes which had been under prior observation. A shortened version of this questionnaire was also given to the teachers of these classes. Questionnaire items centered on factors deemed important in influencing students' decisions on whether to talk or not in class.

FINDINGS

. . . Classes with [fewer] than forty students have a higher average number of interactions per session than those with more than forty students.

More important, however, is the fact that in both categories of class size the *average number* of students participating is almost identical. Moreover, a handful of students account for more than 50 percent of the total interactions in both under forty and over forty classes. In classes with [fewer] than forty students, between four and five students account for 75 percent of the total interactions per session; in classes of more than forty students between two and three students account for 51 percent of the total interactions per session. . . . [I]t would appear that class size has relatively little effect on the average number of students participating in class. Such a finding is particularly interesting in view of the fact . . . that more than 65 percent of both male and female students indicated that the large size of the class was an important factor in why students would choose not to talk in class.

Data also indicate that students have a conception of classroom participation as being concentrated in the hands of a few students. Ninety-three percent of the males and 94 percent of the females strongly agreed or agreed with the item "In most of my classes there are a small number of students who do most of the talking." Such a conception is in congruence with the observations of actual classroom behavior. . . .

The students' conception that a handful of students do most of the talking is also coupled with annoyance on the part of many students at those who "talk too much." Responses to a questionnaire item indicated that 62 percent of the males and 61 percent of the females strongly agreed or agreed with the item "I sometimes find myself getting annoyed with students who talk too much in class."

Students also believe it possible to make a decision very early in the semester as to whether professors really want class discussion. Ninety-four percent of the males and 96 percent of the females strongly agreed or agreed with the item "students can tell pretty quickly whether a professor really wants discussion in his/her class."

Students were also asked whether the teacher's sex is likely to influence their participation in class. The overwhelming response of both male and female students to this question is that the professor's sex makes *no difference* in their likelihood of participating in class. Over 93 percent of the males and 91 percent of the female students answered "No Difference" to this question. In effect, then, both male and female students tend to define the classroom as a situation in which the sexual component of the professor's identity is completely irrelevant.

. . . [But] the data indicate a very clear-cut relationship between the sex of the teacher and the likelihood of male or female participation in class. In male taught classes men account for 75.4 percent of the interactions, three times the percentage for women—24.6 percent. In female taught classes, men still account for more of the interactions than women—57.8 percent to 42.2 percent—but the percentage of female participation increases almost 75 percent from 24.7 percent in male taught classes to 42.2 percent in female taught classes. Female student participation is maximized under the influence of female professors.

. . . The participation of men and women may be a function of their proportion in class. . . . [But] in both male and female taught classes the percentage of male and female students is almost equal, therefore eliminating the possibility that the rate of male-female participation is a function of male student overrepresentation in these classes.

. . . [W]hat [were] students responding to when they participated in classroom interactions[?] There was very little student-to-student interaction occurring in the ten classes under observation. Ten percent of the total number of classroom interactions involved cases in which students responded to the questions or comments of other students, . . . [so] that the actions of the teacher are indeed most crucial in promoting classroom interaction. Questions posed by the teacher and teacher comments accounted for 88 percent of the classroom interactions. Especially significant is the fact that very few cases occur in which the teacher directly calls on a particular student to answer a question. . . . Indeed, it might be argued that the current norm in college classrooms is for both students and teach-

ers to avoid any type of direct *personal confrontation* with one another. It might be that "amicability" in the classroom is part of the larger process, described by Riesman (1950) in *The Lonely Crowd,* in which the desire to "get ahead" is subordinated to the desire to "get along." In the college classroom "getting along" means students and teachers avoiding any situation that might be potentially embarrassing to one or the other.

. . . [I]n male taught classes male students are more likely than female students to be directly questioned by the instructor (7.1 percent to 3.1 percent). In addition, men are twice as likely as female students (30.3 percent to 15.0 percent) to respond to a comment made by a male teacher. In female taught classes the percentages of male and female responses are almost identical in each category under observation. Of interest here is the fact that female teachers are equally likely to directly question male and female students (12.8 percent versus 12.5 percent).

Table 57-1 presents the student responses to a series of items concerning why students would choose not to talk in class. The items are ranked in terms of the percentage of students who indicated that the particular item was important in keeping them from talking. As the rankings indicate, male and female students are virtually identical in their conceptions of what factors inhibit or promote their classroom participation. The items accorded the most importance—not doing the assigned reading, ignorance of the subject matter, etc.—are in the highest ranks. The lowest ranking items are those dealing with students and teachers not respecting the student's point of view, the grade being negatively affected by classroom participation, etc.

In comparing the teachers' rankings of these same items with that of the students, it appears that, with one important exception, the rankings are very similar. About 42 percent of both male and female students ranked as important the item concerning the possibility that other students would find them unintelligent. Eighty percent of the teachers, on the other hand, indicated that this was likely an important factor in keeping students from talking.

TABLE 57-1 Percentage of Students Who Indicated That an Item Was an Important Factor in Why Students Would Choose Not to Talk in Class, by Sex of Student (in rank order)

	Male			Female	
Rank	Item	%	Rank	Item	%
1. I had not done the assigned reading		80.9	1. The feeling that I don't know enough about the subject matter		84.8
2. The feeling that I don't know enough about the subject matter		79.6	2. I had not done the assigned reading		76.3
3. The large size of the class		70.4	3. The feeling that my ideas are not well enough formulated		71.1
4. The feeling that my ideas are not well enough formulated		69.8	4. The large size of the class		68.9
5. The course simply isn't meaningful to me		67.3	5. The course simply isn't meaningful to me		65.1
6. The chance that I would appear unintelligent in the eyes of the teacher		43.2	6. The chance that I would appear unintelligent in the eyes of other students		45.4
7. The chance that I would appear unintelligent in the eyes of other students		42.9	7. The chance that I would appear unintelligent in the eyes of the teacher		41.4
8. The small size of the class		31.0	8. The small size of the class		33.6
9. The possibility that my comments might negatively affect my grade		29.6	9. The possibility that my comments might negatively affect my grade		24.3
10. The possibility that other students in the class would not respect my point of view		16.7	10. The possibility that the teacher would not respect my point of view		21.1
11. The possibility that the teacher would not respect my point of view		12.3	11. The possibility that other students in the class would not respect my point of view		12.5

DISCUSSION

Although we did not begin this study with any explicit hypotheses to be tested, we did begin with some general guiding questions. Most comprehensive among these, and of necessary importance from a symbolic interactionist perspective, was the question, "What is a college classroom?" We wanted to know how both students and teachers were defining the social setting, and how these definitions manifested themselves in the activity that goes on in the college classrooms. More specifically, we wanted to understand what it was about the definition of the situation held by students and teachers that led to, in most instances, rather little classroom interaction.

What knowledge, we might now ask, do students have of college classrooms that makes the decision not to talk a "realistic" decision? There would seem to be two factors of considerable importance as indicated by our data.

First, students believe that they can tell very early in the semester whether or not a professor really wants class discussion. Students are also well aware that there exists in college classrooms a rather distinctive "consolidation of responsibility." In any classroom there seems almost inevitably to be a small group of students who can be counted on to respond to questions asked by the professor or to generally have comments on virtually any issue raised in class. Our observational data . . . indicated that on the average a very small number of students are responsible for the majority of all talk that occurs in class on any given day. The fact that this "consolidation of responsibility" looms large in students' consciousness is indicated by the fact, reported earlier, that more than 90 percent of the students strongly agreed or agreed with the statement "In most of my classes there are a small number of students who do most of the talking."

Once the group of "talkers" gets established and identified in a college classroom the remaining students develop a strong expectation that these "talkers" can be relied upon to answer questions and make comments. In fact, we have often noticed in our own classes that when a question is asked or an issue raised the "silent" students will even begin to orient their bodies towards and look at this coterie of talkers with the expectation, presumably, that they will shortly be speaking.

Our concept of the "consolidation of responsibility" is a modification of the ideas put forth by Latane and Darley (1970) in *The Unresponsive Bystander*. In this volume Latane and Darley developed the concept of "the diffusion of responsibility" to explain why strangers are often reluctant to "get involved" in activities where they assist other strangers who may need help. They argue that the delegation of responsibility in such situations is quite unclear and, as a result, responsibility tends to get assigned to no one in particular—the end result being that no assistance at all is forthcoming. In the case of the classroom interaction, however, we are dealing with a situation in which the responsibility for talking gets assigned to a few who can be relied upon to carry the "verbal load"—thus the *consolidation of responsibility*. As a result, the majority of students play a relatively passive role in the classroom and see themselves as recorders of the teacher's information. This expectation is mutually supported by the professor's reluctance to directly call on *specific* students. . . .

While students expect that only a few students will do most of the talking, and while these talkers are relied upon to respond in class, the situation is a bit more complicated than we have indicated to this point. It would appear that while these talkers are "doing their job" by carrying the discussion for the class as a whole, there is still a strong feeling on the part of many students that they ought not to talk *too much*. As noted earlier, more than 60 percent of the students responding to our questionnaire expressed annoyance with students who "talk too much in class." This is interesting to the extent that even those who talk very regularly in class still account for a very small percentage of total class time. While we have no systematic data on time spent talking in class, the comments of the observers indicate that generally a total of less than five minutes of class time (in a fifty-minute period) is accounted for by student talk in class.

A fine balance must be maintained in college classes. Some students are expected to do most of the talking, thus relieving the remainder of the students from the burdens of having to talk in class. At the same time, these talkers must not be "rate-busters." We are suggesting here that students see "intellectual work" in much the same way that factory workers define "piece-work." Talking too much in class, or what might be called "linguistic rate-busting," upsets the normative arrangement of the classroom and, in the students' eyes, increases the probability of raising the professor's expectations vis-à-vis the participation of other students. It may be said, then, that a type of "restriction of verbal output" norm operates in college classrooms, in which those who engage in linguistic rate-busting or exhibit "overinvolvement" in the classroom get defined by other students as "brown-noses" and "apostates" from the student "team." Other students often indicate their annoyance with these "rate-busters" by smiling wryly at their efforts, audibly sighing, rattling their notebooks and, on occasion, openly snickering.

A second factor that ensures in students' minds that it will be safe to refrain from talking is their knowledge that only in rare instances will they be directly called upon by teachers in a college classroom. Our data . . . indicate that of all the interaction occurring in the classes under observation only about 10 percent were due to teachers calling directly upon a specific student. The unwillingness of teachers to call upon students would seem to stem from teachers' beliefs that the classroom situation is fraught with anxiety for students. It is important to note that teachers, unlike students themselves, viewed the possibility that "students might appear unintelligent in the eyes of other students" as a very important factor in keeping students from talking. . . . Unwilling to exacerbate the sense of risk which teachers believe is a part of student consciousness, they refrain from directly calling upon specific students.

The direct result of these two factors is that students feel no obligation or particular necessity for keeping up with reading assignments so as to be able to participate in class. Such a choice is made easier still by the fact that college students are generally tested infrequently. Unlike high school, where homework is the teacher's "daily insurance" that students are prepared for classroom participation, college is a situation in which the student feels quite safe in coming to class without having done the assigned reading and, not having done it, safe in the secure knowledge that one won't be called upon.[2] It is understandable, then, why such items as "not having done the assigned reading" and "the feeling that one does not know enough about the subject matter" would rank so high ... in students' minds as factors keeping them from talking in class.

In sum, we have isolated two factors relative to the way that classrooms actually operate that make it "practically" possible for students not to talk in class. These factors make it possible for the student to pragmatically abide by an early decision to be silent in class. We must now broach the somewhat more complicated question: What are the elements of students' definitions of the college classroom situation that prompt them to be silent in class? To answer this question we must examine how students perceive the teacher as well as their conceptions of what constitutes "intellectual work."

By the time that students have finished high school they have been imbued with the enormously strong belief that teachers are "experts" who possess the "truth." They have adopted, as Freire (1970) has noted, a "banking" model of education. The teacher represents the bank, the huge "fund" of "true" knowledge. As a student it is one's job to make weekly "withdrawals" from the fund, never any "deposits." His teachers, one is led to believe, and often led to believe it by the teachers themselves, are possessors of the truth. Teachers are in the classroom to *teach,* not to *learn.*

If the [aforementioned] contains anything like a reasonable description of the way that students are socialized in secondary school, we should not find it strange or shocking that our students find our requests for criticism of ideas a bit alien. College students still cling to the idea that they are knowledge seekers and that faculty members are knowledge dispensers. Their view of intellectual work leaves little room for the notion that ideas themselves are open to negotiation. It is simply not part of their view of the classroom that ideas are generated out of dialogue, out of persons questioning and taking issue with one another, out of persons being *critical* of each other.

It comes as something of a shock to many of our students when we are willing to give them, at best, a "B" on a paper or exam that is "technically" proficient. When they inquire about their grade (and they do this rarely, believing strongly that our judgment is unquestionable), they want to know what they did "wrong." Intellectual work is for them dichotomous. It is either good or bad, correct or incorrect. They are genuinely surprised when we tell them that nothing is wrong, that they simply have not been critical enough and have not shown enough reflection on the ideas. Some even see such an evaluation as unfair. They claim a kind of incompetence at criticism. They often claim that it would be illegitimate for them to disagree with an author.

Students in class respond as uncritically to the thoughts of their professors as they do to the thoughts of those whom they read. Given this general attitude toward intellectual work, based in large part on students' socialization, and hence their definition of what should go on in classrooms, the notion of using the classroom as a place for generating ideas is a foreign one.

Part of students' conceptions of what they can and ought to do in classrooms is, then, a function of their understanding of how ideas are to be communicated. Students have expressed the idea that if they are to speak in class they ought to be able to articulate their point logically, systematically, and above all completely. The importance of this factor in keeping students from talking is borne out by the very high ranking given to the item ... "the feeling that my ideas are not well enough formulated."

In their view, if their ideas have not been fully formulated in advance, then the idea is not worth relating. They are simply unwilling to talk "off the top of their heads." They feel, particularly in an academic setting such as the college classroom, that there is a high premium placed on being articulate. This feeling is to a large degree prompted by the relative articulateness of the teacher. Students do not, it seems, take into account the fact that the teacher's coherent presentation is typically a function of the time spent preparing his/her ideas. The relative preparedness of the teacher leads to something of a paradox vis-à-vis classroom discussion.

We have had students tell us that one of the reasons they find it difficult to respond in class involves the professor's preparedness; that is, students have told us that because the professor's ideas as presented in lectures are (in their view) so well formulated they could not add anything to those ideas. Herein lies something of a paradox. One might suggest that, to some degree at least, the better prepared a professor is for his/her class, the less likely are students to respond to the elements of his lecture.

We have both found that some of our liveliest classes have centered [on] those occasions when we have talked about research presently in progress. When it is clear to the student that we are ourselves struggling with a particular problem, that we cannot fully make sense of a phenomenon, the greater is the class participation. In most classroom instances, students read the teacher as the "expert,"[3] and once having cast the professor into that role it becomes extremely difficult for students to take issue with or amend his/her ideas.

It must also be noted that students' perceptions about their incapacity to be critical of their own and others' ideas leads to an important source of misunderstanding between college students and their teachers. In an open-ended question we asked students what characteristics they thought made for an "ideal" teacher. An impressionistic reading of these responses indicated that students were overwhelmingly uniform in their answers. They consensually found it important that a teacher "not put them down" and that a teacher "not flaunt his/her superior knowledge." In this regard the college classroom is a setting pregnant with possibil-

ities for mutual misunderstanding. Teachers are working under one set of assumptions about "intellectual work" while students proceed under another. Our experiences as college teachers lead us to believe that teachers tend to value *critical* responses by students and tend to respond critically themselves to the comments and questions of college students. Students tend to perceive these critical comments as in some way an assault on their "selves" and find it difficult to separate a critique of their thoughts from a critique of themselves. Teachers are for the most part unaware of the way in which students interpret their comments.

The result is that when college teachers begin to critically question a student's statement, trying to get the student to be more critical and analytical about his/her assertions, this gets interpreted by students as a "put-down." The overall result is the beginning of a "vicious circle" of sorts. The more that teachers try to instill in students a critical attitude toward one's own ideas, the more students come to see faculty members as condescending, and the greater still becomes their reluctance to make known their "ill-formulated" ideas in class. Like any other social situation where persons are defining the situation differently, there is bound to develop a host of interactional misunderstandings.

Before concluding this section, let us turn to a discussion of the differences in classroom participation rates of male versus female students. Given the fact that men and women students responded quite similarly to the questionnaire items reported here, much of our previous discussion holds for both male and female students. There are some important differences, however, in their *actual behavior* in the college classroom (as revealed by our observational data) that ought to be considered. Foremost among these differences is the fact that the sex of the teacher affects the likelihood of whether male or female students will participate in class. . . . Clearly, male and female teachers in these classes are "giving off expressions" that are being interpreted very differently by male and female students. Male students play a more active role in all observed classes regardless of the teacher's sex, but with female instructors the percentage of female participation sharply increases. Also of interest . . . is the fact that the male instructors are more likely to directly call on male students than on female students (7.1 percent to 3.1 percent), whereas female instructors are just as likely to call on female students as on male students (12.5 percent to 12.8 percent). Possibly female students in female taught classes interpret the instructor's responses as being more egalitarian than those of male professors and thus more sympathetic to the views of female students. With the growing involvement of women faculty and students in feminist "consciousness" groups it may not be unreasonable to assume that female instructors are more sensitive to the problem of female students both inside and outside the college classroom.

With the small percentage of women faculty currently teaching in American universities it may well be that the college classroom is still defined by both male and female students as a setting "naturally" dominated by men. The presence of female professors, however, as our limited data suggest, may bring about some changes in these definitions of "natural" classroom behavior.

IMPLICATIONS

For the reasons suggested in the last few pages, it may be argued that most students opt for noninvolvement in their college classroom. This being the case, and because organizational features of the college classroom allow for noninvolvement (the consolidation of responsibility, the unwillingness of professors to directly call on specific students, the infrequency of testing), the situation allows for a low commitment on the part of students. The college classroom, then, rather than being a situation where persons must be deeply involved, more closely approximates a situation of "anonymity" where persons' obligations are few.

We can now perceive more clearly the source of the dilemma for college instructors who wish to have extensive classroom dialogues with students. To use the terminology generated by Goffman (1963) in *Behavior in Public Places,* we can suggest that instructors are treating the classroom as an instance of "focused" interaction while students define the classroom more as an "unfocused" gathering. Focused gatherings are those where persons come into one another's audial and visual presence and see it as their obligation to interact. These are to be distinguished from unfocused gatherings where persons are also in a face-to-face situation but either feel that they are not privileged to interact or have no obligation to do so.[4]

It may very well be that students more correctly "read" how professors interpret the situation than vice versa. Knowing that the teacher expects involvement, and having made the decision not to be deeply involved, students reach a compromise. Aware that it would be an impropriety to be on a total "away" from the social situation, students engage in what might be called "civil *attention.*" They must *appear* committed enough to not alienate the teacher without at the same time showing so much involvement that the situation becomes risky for them. Students must carefully create a show of interest while maintaining noninvolvement. A show of too great interest might find them more deeply committed to the encounter than they wish to be.

So, students are willing to attend class regularly and they do not hold private conversations while the teacher is talking; they nod their heads intermittently, and maintain enough attention to laugh at the appropriate junctures during a lecture, and so on. Students have become very adept at maintaining the social situation without becoming too involved in it. Teachers interpret these "shows" of attention as indicative of a real involvement (the students' performances have proved highly successful) and are, therefore, at a loss to explain why their involvement is not even greater—why they don't talk very much in class.

CRITICAL-THINKING QUESTIONS

1. Based on this analysis, assess the validity of the commonsense belief that "professors want lots of

discussion in their classes." How do students know if an instructor really seeks class discussion?
2. What did Karp and Yoels conclude about the importance of gender in classroom dynamics?
3. What do the researchers imply about how instructors can increase student involvement in classes? How can students contribute to this goal?

NOTES

1. Some relevant demographic characteristics of the students in the ten classes under observation are as follows: sex: males—52 percent, females—48 percent; year in college: freshmen and sophomores—60 percent, juniors and seniors—40 percent; father's occupation: proprietor—7 percent, management or executive—21 percent, professional—34 percent, clerical and sales—15 percent, skilled worker—16 percent, unskilled worker—7 percent; religious affiliation: Catholic—79 percent, Protestant—7 percent, Other—14 percent. In comparing the students in the observed classes to those students in unobserved classes which were selected at random at the end of the semester, the following differences should be noted: the observed classes contain more women (48 percent) than the unobserved classes (33 percent); there were twice as many freshmen in the observed classes (31 percent) than in the unobserved classes (14 percent); there were twice as many students whose fathers were in clerical and sales occupations in the observed classes (15 percent) than in the unobserved classes (8 percent).

The questionnaire responses of the students in the unobserved classes are not reported here since these were selected only to check on the representativeness of the students in the original ten classes under observation.

2. We have no "hard" data concerning student failure to do the assigned reading other than our own observations of countless instances where we posed questions that went unanswered, when the slightest familiarity with the material would have been sufficient to answer them. We have also employed "pop" quizzes and the student performance on these tests indicated a woefully inadequate acquaintance with the readings assigned for that session. The reader may evaluate our claim by reflecting upon his/her own experience in the college classroom.

3. This attribution of power and authority to the teacher may be particularly exaggerated in the present study due to its setting in a Catholic university with a large number of students entering from Catholic high schools. Whether college students with different religious and socioeconomic characteristics attribute similar degrees of power and authority to professors is a subject worthy of future comparative empirical investigation.

4. If we think of communication patterns in college classrooms as ranging along a continuum from open-discussion formats to lecture arrangements, the classes studied here all fall toward the traditional lecture end of the continuum. Thus, generalizations to other formats, such as the open-discussion ones, may not be warranted by the present data.

REFERENCES

FREIRE, P. 1970. In *Pedagogy of the oppressed,* ed. B. Glaser & A. L. Strauss. New York: Seabury Press.

GOFFMAN, E. 1963. *Behavior in public places.* New York: Free Press.

JACKSON, P. 1968. *Life in classrooms.* New York: Holt, Rinehart and Winston.

LATANE, B., & J. DARLEY. 1970. *The unresponsive bystander: Why doesn't he help?* New York: Appleton-Century-Crofts.

RIESMAN, D. 1950. *The lonely crowd.* New Haven, CT: Yale University Press.

58

Academic Achievement in Southeast Asian Refugee Families

Nathan Caplan, Marcella H. Choy,
and John K. Whitmore

Many analysts pronounce the U.S. educational system in crisis. But are schools to blame for the modest achievement of some children? In this selection, the authors argue that socialization has a greater impact on academic performance than the quality of our schools. Even though most of the Southeast Asian boat people are poor, have had limited exposure to Western culture, know virtually no English, and live in low-income metropolitan areas, their children are excelling in the U.S. school system.

The scholastic success of Asian children is well recognized. Their stunning performance—particularly in the realm of science and mathematics—has prompted American educators to visit Japanese and Taiwanese schools in an effort to unearth the foundations of these achievements. Experts recommend that American schools adopt aspects of their Asian counterparts, such as a longer school year or more rigorous tasks, in order to raise the scholastic level of U.S. students.

Yet there is no need to go abroad to understand why these children do so well. The achievement of Asian-American students indicates that much may be learned about the origins of their triumph within the American school system itself. More specifically, during the late 1970s and early 1980s, devastating political and economic circumstances forced many Vietnamese, Lao and Chinese-Vietnamese families to seek a new life in the U.S. This resettlement of boat people from Indochina offered a rare opportunity to examine the academic achievement of their children.

These young refugees had lost months, even years of formal schooling while living in relocation camps. Like their parents, they suffered disruption and trauma as they escaped from Southeast Asia. Despite their hardships and with little knowledge of English, the children quickly adapted to their new schools and began to excel.

In researching the economic and scholastic accomplishments of 1,400 refugee households in the early 1980s, our group at the University of Michigan studied the forces that shaped the performance of these children. Some of the standard explanations for educational excellence—parental encouragement and dedication to learning—applied to the young students, but other theories proved inadequate.

Although some of our findings are culturally specific, others point overwhelmingly to the pivotal role of the family in the children's academic success. Because this characteristic extends beyond culture, it has implications for educators, social scientists and policymakers as well as for the refugees themselves. It is clear that the U.S. educational system can work—if the requisite familial and social supports are provided for the students outside school.

Our study encompassed many features of resettlement. We gathered survey and other data on 6,750 persons in five urban areas—Orange County, Calif., Seattle, Houston, Chicago, and Boston—and obtained information about their background and home life as well as economic and demographic facts. We discovered that with regard to educational and social status, the refugees proved to be more ordinary than their predecessors who fled Vietnam in 1975 during the fall of Saigon. These newer displaced persons had had limited exposure to Western culture and knew virtually no English when they arrived. Often they came with nothing more than the clothes they wore.

From this larger group, we chose a random sample of 200 nuclear families and their 536 school-age children. Twenty-seven percent of the families had four or more children. At the time of the study, these young refugees had been in the U.S. for an average of three and a half years. We collected information on parents and their children during interviews conducted in their native tongues; we also gained access to school transcripts and other related documents.

All the children attended schools in low-income, metropolitan areas—environs not known for outstanding academic records. The refugees were fairly evenly distributed throughout the school levels: Grades one through eleven each contained about 8 percent of the children in the study; kindergarten and twelfth grade each contained about 5 percent. We converted the students' letter grades into a numerical grade point average (GPA): An A became a four; a D became a one. After calculations, we found that the children's mean GPA was 3.05, or a B average. Twenty-seven percent had an overall GPA in the A range, 52 percent in the B range and 17 percent in the C range. Only 4 percent had a GPA below a C grade.

Even more striking than the overall GPAs were the students' math scores. Almost half of the children earned As in math; another third earned Bs. Thus, four out of five students received either As or Bs. It is not surprising that they would do better in this subject. Their minds could most easily grasp disciplines in which English was not so crucial: math, physics, chemistry and science. As expected, their grades in the liberal arts were lower: In areas where extensive language skills were required, such as English, history or social studies, the combined GPA was 2.64.

To place our local findings in a national context, we turned to standardized achievement test scores, in particular, the California Achievement Test (CAT) results. In this arena as well, we found that the performance of the newly arrived students was exceptional. Their mean overall score on the CAT was in the 54th percentile; that is, they outperformed 54 percent of those taking the test—placing them just above the national average. Interestingly, their scores tended to cluster toward the middle ranges: They showed a more restricted scope of individual differences.

The national tests also reflected an above-average ability in math when the Indochinese children were compared with children taking the exam at equivalent levels. Half of the children studied obtained scores in the top quartile. Even more spectacularly, 27 percent of them scored in the 10th decile—better than 90 percent of the students across the country and almost three times higher than the national norm. The CAT math scores confirmed that the GPAs of these children were not products of local bias but of true mathematical competence.

Again, the lowest scores were found in the language and reading tests. In this case, the mean score was slightly below the national average. For reasons discussed earlier, this finding was expected. It remains remarkable, however, that the students' scores are so close to the national average in language skills.

The GPA and CAT scores show that the refugee children did very well, particularly in light of their background. A history marked by significant physical and emotional trauma as well as a lack of formal education would not seem to predispose them to an easy transition into U.S. schools. Yet even though they had not forgotten their difficult experiences, the children were able to focus on the present and to work toward the future. In so doing, they made striking scholastic progress. Moreover, their achievements held true for the majority, not for just a few whiz kids.

Clearly, these accomplishments are fueled by influences powerful enough to override the impact of a host of geographic and demographic factors. Using various statistical approaches, we sought to understand the forces responsible for this performance. In the process, a unique finding caught our attention, namely, a positive relation between the number of siblings and the children's GPA.

Family size has long been regarded as one of the most reliable predictors of poor achievement. Virtually all studies on the topic show an inverse relation: The greater the number of children in the family, the lower the mean GPA and other measures associated with scholastic performance. Typically, these reports document a 15 percent decline in GPA and other achievement-related scores with the addition of each child to the family. The interpretation of this finding has been subject to disagreement, but there is no conflict about its relation to achievement.

For the Indochinese students, this apparent disadvantage was somehow neutralized or turned into an advantage. We took this finding to be an important clue in elucidating the role of the family in academic performance. We assumed that distinctive family characteristics would explain how these achievements took place so early in resettlement as well as how these children and their parents managed to overcome such adversities as poor English skills, poverty and the often disruptive environment of urban schools.

Because they were newcomers in a strange land, it was reasonable to expect that at least some of the reasons for the children's success rested on their cultural background. While not ignoring the structural forces present here in the U.S.—among them the opportunity for education and advancement—we believed that the values and traditions permeating the lives of these children in Southeast Asia would guide their lives in this country.

Knowledge of one's culture does not occur in a vacuum; it is transmitted through the family. Children often acquire a sense of their heritage as a result of deliberate and concentrated parental effort in the context of family life. This inculcation of values from one generation to another is a universal feature of the conservation of culture.

We sought to determine which values were important to the parents, how well those values had been transmitted to the children and what role values played in promoting their educational achievement. In our interviews we included twenty-six questions about values that were derived from a search of Asian literature and from social science research. Respondents were asked to rate the perceived importance of these values.

We found that parents and children rated the perceived values in a similar fashion, providing empirical testimony that these parents had served their stewardship well. For the most part, the perspectives and values embedded in the cultural heritage of the Indochinese had been carried with them to the U.S. We also determined that cultural values played an important role in the educational achievement of the children. Conserved values constituted a source of motivation and direction as the families dealt with contemporary problems set in a country vastly different from their homeland. The values formed a set of cultural givens with deep roots in the Confucian and Buddhist traditions of East and Southeast Asia.

The family is the central institution in these traditions, within which and through which achievement and knowledge are accomplished. We used factor analyses and other statistical procedures to determine value groupings and their relation to achievement. These analyses showed that parents and children honor mutual, collective obligation to one another and to their relatives. They strive to attain respect, cooperation and harmony within the family.

Nowhere is the family's commitment to accomplishment and education more evident than in time spent on homework. During high school, Indochinese students spend an average of three hours and ten minutes per day; in junior high, an average of two and a half hours; and in grade school, an average of two hours and five minutes. Research in the U.S. shows that American students study about one and a half hours per day at the junior and senior high school levels.

Among the refugee families, then, homework clearly dominates household activities during weeknights. Although the parents' lack of education and facility with English often prevents them from engaging in the content of the exercise, they set standards and goals for the evening and facilitate their children's studies by assuming responsibility for chores and other practical considerations.

After dinner, the table is cleared, and homework begins. The older children, both male and female, help their younger siblings. Indeed, they seem to learn as much from teaching as from being taught. It is reasonable to suppose that a great amount of learning goes on at these times—in terms of skills, habits, attitudes and expectations as well as the content of a subject. The younger children, in particular, are taught not only subject matter but how to learn. Such sibling involvement demonstrates how a large family can encourage and enhance academic success. The familial setting appears to make the children feel at home in school and, consequently, perform well there.

Parental engagement included reading regularly to young children—an activity routinely correlated to academic performance. Almost one half (45 percent) of the parents reported reading aloud. In those families, the children's mean GPA was 3.14 as opposed to 2.97 in households where the parents did not read aloud. (This difference, and all others to follow in which GPAs are compared, is statistically reliable.) It is important to note that the effects of being read to held up statistically whether the children were read to in English or in their native language.

This finding suggests that parental English literacy skills may not play a vital role in determining school performance. Rather, other aspects of the experience—emotional ties between parent and child, cultural validation and wisdom shared in stories read in the child's native language, or value placed on reading and learning—extend to schoolwork. Reading at home obscures the boundary between home and school. In this context, learning is perceived as normal, valuable and fun.

Egalitarianism and role sharing were also found to be associated with high academic performance. In fact, relative equality between the sexes was one of the strongest predictors of GPA. In those homes where the respondents disagreed that a "wife should always do as her husband wishes," the children earned average GPAs of 3.16. But children from homes whose parents agreed with the statement had an average GPA of 2.64. In households where the husband helped with the dishes and laundry, the mean GPA was 3.21; when husbands did not participate in the chores, the mean GPA was 2.79.

This sense of equality was not confined to the parents—it extended to the children, especially in terms of sex-role expectations and school performance. GPAs were higher in households where parents expected both boys and girls to help with chores. Families rejecting the idea that a college education is more important for boys than for girls had children whose average GPA was 3.14; children from families exhibiting a pro-male bias had a mean GPA of 2.83.

Beyond the support and guidance provided by the family, culturally based attributions proved to be important to refugees in their view of scholastic motivation. The "love of learning" category was rated most often by both parents and students as the factor accounting for their academic success. There appeared to be two parts to this sentiment. First, the children experienced intrinsic gratification when they correctly worked a problem through to completion. The pleasure of intellectual growth, based on new knowledge and ideas and combined with increased competence and mastery, was considered highly satisfying. Second, refugee children felt a sense of accomplishment on seeing their younger siblings learn from their own efforts at teaching. Both learning and imparting knowledge were perceived as pleasurable experiences rather than as drudgery.

The gratification accompanying accomplishment was, in turn, founded on a sense of the importance of effort as opposed to ability. The refugees did not trust fate or luck as the determinant of educational outcome; they believed in their potential to master the factors that could influence their destiny. And their culture encompasses a practical approach to accomplishment: setting realistic goals. Without the setting of priorities and standards for work, goals would remain elusive. But anyone endorsing the values of working in a disciplined manner and taking a long-term view could establish priorities and pursue them.

Belief in one's own ability to effect change or attain goals has long been held to be a critical component of achievement and motivation—and our findings support this conclusion. Parents were asked a series of questions relating to their perceived ability to control external events influencing their lives. Those who had a clear sense of personal efficacy had children who attained higher GPAs.

We had some difficulty, however, interpreting the perception of efficacy as an idea generated solely by the individual. Despite a vast social science literature asserting the contrary, we believe that these refugees' sense of control over their lives could be traced to family identity. It seemed to us that the sense of familial efficacy proved critical, as opposed to the more Western concept of personal efficacy.

Other cultural values show us that the refugee family is firmly linked not only to its past and traditions but to the realities of the present and to future possibilities. This aptitude for integrating the past, present and future appears to have imparted a sense of continuity and direction to the lives of these people.

Education was central to this integration and to reestablishment in the U.S. It was and still is the main avenue for refugees in American society to succeed and survive. In contrast, education in Indochina was a restricted privilege. The future of the refugee children, and of their families, is thus inextricably linked to schools and to their own children's performances within them. The emphasis on education as the key to social acceptance and economic success helps us understand why academic achievement is reinforced by such strong parental commitment.

Outside school, the same sense of drive and achievement can be seen in the parents. Having a job and being able to provide for the family is integral to family pride. Shame is felt by Asian families on welfare. Reflecting the same determination and energy that their children manifest in school, Indochinese parents have found employment and climbed out of economic dependency and poverty with dispatch.

Two of the twenty-six values included as a measure of cultural adaptation entailed integration and the acceptance of certain American ways of life: the importance of "seeking fun and excitement" and of "material possessions." These ideas are of particular concern because they address the future of refugee families and mark the potential power and consequence of American life on the refugees and subsequent generations. Not surprisingly, when our subjects were asked to indicate which values best characterized their nonrefugee neighbors, these two items were most frequently cited.

More interesting, however, was our finding that these same two values were correlated with a lower GPA. We found that parents who attributed greater importance to fun and excitement had children who achieved lower GPAs: 2.90 as opposed to 3.14. The results for material possessions were similar: GPAs were 2.66 versus 3.19.

It is not clear why these negative associations exist. Do they reflect less strict parents or families who have integrated so quickly that cultural stability has been lost? We believe it is the latter explanation. Refugees who held that "the past is as important as the future" had children whose GPAs averaged 3.14. Children of those who did not rate the preservation of the past as highly had an average GPA of 2.66. This item was one of the most powerful independent predictors of academic performance. Our findings run contrary to expectations. Rather than adopting American ways and assimilating into the melting pot, the most successful Indochinese families appear to retain their own traditions and values. By this statement we are in no way devaluing the American system. The openness and opportunity it offers have enabled the Indochinese to succeed in the U.S. even while maintaining their own cultural traditions.

Although different in origins, both traditional Indochinese and middle-class American values emphasize education, achievement, hard work, autonomy, perseverance and pride. The difference between the two value systems is one of orientation to achievement. American mores encourage independence and individual achievement, whereas Indochinese values foster interdependence and a family-based orientation to achievement. And in view of the position of these refugees in society during the early phase of resettlement in this country, this approach appears to have worked

well as the best long-term investment. It appears to be the reason why these children are highly responsive to American schools.

The lack of emphasis on fun and excitement also does not indicate misery on the part of these refugee children. Despite evidence that the suicide rate is growing among some Asian-American children, we found that those in our sample were well adjusted. Our interviews revealed no damaging manipulation of their lives by their parents; moreover, their love of learning sustained their academic pursuits.

The Indochinese values that encourage academic rigor and excellence are not culturally unique: earlier studies of other groups have found similar results. The children of Jewish immigrants from Eastern Europe, for example, excelled in the U.S. school system. In 1961 Judith R. Kramer of Brooklyn College and Seymour Leventman of the University of Pennsylvania reported that nearly 90 percent of the third generation attended college, despite the fact that the first generation had little or no education when they arrived in the U.S. Their emphasis on family and culture was held to be instrumental in this success.

In 1948 William Caudill and George DeVos of the University of California at Berkeley found that Japanese students overcame prejudice in U.S. schools immediately after World War II and thrived academically. Their success was attributed to cultural values and to parental involvement. More recently, a study by Reginald Clark of the Claremont Graduate School documented the outstanding achievement of low-income African-American students in Chicago whose parents supported the school and teachers and structured their children's learning environment at home.

These findings, as well as our own, have significance for the current national debate on education. It is clear that the American school system—despite widespread criticism—has retained its capacity to teach, as it has shown with these refugees. We believe that the view of our schools as failing to educate stems from the unrealistic demand that the educational system deal with urgent social service needs. Citizens and politicians expect teachers and schools to keep children off the streets and away from drugs, deal with teenage pregnancy, prevent violence in the schools, promote safe sex and perform myriad other tasks and responsibilities in addition to teaching traditional academic subjects.

As the social needs of our students have moved into the classroom, they have consumed the scarce resources allocated to education and have compromised the schools' academic function. The primary role of teachers has become that of parent by proxy; they are expected to transform the attitude and behavior of children, many of whom come to school ill prepared to learn.

If we are to deal effectively with the crisis in American education, we must start with an accurate definition of the problem. We must separate teaching and its academic purpose from in-school social services. Only then can we assess the true ability of schools to accomplish these two, sometimes opposing, functions—or we can identify and delegate these nonacademic concerns to other institutions.

Throughout this article we have examined the role of the family in the academic performance of Indochinese refugees. We firmly believe that for American schools to succeed, parents and families must become more committed to the education of their children. They must instill a respect for education and create within the home an environment conducive to learning. They must also participate in the process so that their children feel comfortable learning and go to school willing and prepared to study.

Yet we cannot expect the family to provide such support alone. Schools must reach out to families and engage them meaningfully in the education of their children. This involvement must go beyond annual teacher-parent meetings and must include, among other things, the identification of cultural elements that promote achievement.

Similarly, we cannot adopt the complete perspective of an Indochinese or any other culture. It would be ludicrous to impose cultural beliefs and practices on American children, especially on those whose progress in this country has been fraught with blocked access.

We can, however, work to ensure that families believe in the value of an education and, like the refugees, have rational expectations of future rewards for their efforts. Moreover, we can integrate components of the refugees' experience regarding the family's role in education. It is possible to identify culturally compatible values, behaviors and strategies for success that might enhance scholastic achievement. It is in this regard that the example of the Indochinese refugees—as well as the Japanese and Jewish immigrants before them—can shape our priorities and our policies.

CRITICAL-THINKING QUESTIONS

1. How do Indochinese children compare with their U.S. counterparts on such measures of academic performance as grade-point average (GPA), mathematics scores, and the California Achievement Test (CAT)?

2. How do the values of Indochinese and many lower socioeconomic families in the United States differ? How are these differences reflected in children's academic achievement?

3. What remedies do the authors propose for the crisis in U.S. education? What do these proposals demand of our families? Do you think the solutions are realistic?

Classic

59

The Social Structure of Medicine

Talcott Parsons

Talcott Parsons, one of the most influential U.S. sociologists of this century, contributed greatly to the development of structural-functional analysis. In this selection, he examines the significance of health and illness within a social system, with particular attention to the social roles of physicians and patients.

A little reflection will show immediately that the problem of health is intimately involved in the functional prerequisites of the social system. . . . Certainly by almost any definition health is included in the functional needs of the individual member of the society so that from the point of view of functioning of the social system, too low a general level of health, too high an incidence of illness, is dysfunctional. This is in the first instance because illness incapacitates for the effective performance of social roles. It could of course be that this incidence was completely uncontrollable by

SOURCE: *The Social System* by Talcott Parsons. Copyright © 1951, renewed 1979 by Talcott Parsons. Reprinted with permission of The Free Press, Macmillan Publishing Company, a Member of Paramount Publishing.

social action, an independently given condition of social life. But insofar as it is controllable, through rational action or otherwise, it is clear that there is a functional interest of the society in its control, broadly in the minimization of illness. As one special aspect of this, attention may be called to premature death. From a variety of points of view, the birth and rearing of a child constitute a "cost" to the society, through pregnancy, child care, socialization, formal training, and many other channels. Premature death, before the individual has had the opportunity to play out his full quota of social roles, means that only a partial "return" for this cost has been received.

All this would be true were illness purely a "natural phenomenon" in the sense that, like the vagaries of the weather, it was not, to our knowledge, reciprocally involved in the motivated interactions of human beings. In this case illness would be something which merely "happened to" people, which involved consequences which had to be dealt with and conditions which might or might not be controllable but was in no way an expression of motivated behavior.

This is in fact the case for a very important part of illness, but it has become increasingly clear, by no means for all. In a variety of ways motivational factors accessible to analysis in action terms are involved in the etiology of many illnesses, and conversely, though without exact correspondence, many conditions are open to therapeutic influence through motivational channels. To take the simplest kind of case, differential exposure, to injuries or to infection, is certainly motivated, and the role of unconscious wishes to be injured or to fall ill in such cases has been clearly demonstrated. Then there is the whole range of "psychosomatic" illness about which knowledge has been rapidly accumulating in recent years. Finally, there is the field of "mental disease," the symptoms of which occur mainly on the behavioral level. . . .

Summing up, we may say that illness is a state of disturbance in the "normal" functioning of the total human individual, including both the state of the organism as a biological system and of his personal and social adjustments. It is thus partly biologically and partly socially defined. . . .

Medical practice . . . is a "mechanism" in the social system for coping with the illnesses of its members. It involves a set of institutionalized roles. . . . The immediately relevant social structures consist in the patterning of the role of the medical practitioner himself and, though to common sense it may seem superfluous to analyze it, that of the "sick person" himself. . . .

The role of the medical practitioner belongs to the general class of "professional" roles, a subclass of the larger group of occupational roles. Caring for the sick is thus not an incidental activity of other roles though for example mothers do a good deal of it—but has become functionally specialized as a full-time "job." This, of course, is by no

means true of all societies. As an occupational role it is institutionalized about the technical content of the function which is given a high degree of primacy relative to other status-determinants. It is thus inevitable both that incumbency of the role should be achieved and that performance criteria by standards of technical competence should be prominent. Selection for it and the context of its performance are to a high degree segregated from other bases of social status and solidarities. . . . Unlike the role of the businessman, however, it is collectivity-oriented not self-oriented.

The importance of this patterning is, in one context, strongly emphasized by its relation to the cultural tradition. One basis for the division of labor is the specialization of technical competence. The role of physician is far along the continuum of increasingly high levels of technical competence required for performance. Because of the complexity and subtlety of the knowledge and skill required and the consequent length and intensity of training, it is difficult to see how the functions could, under modern conditions, be ascribed to people occupying a prior status as one of their activities in that status, following the pattern by which, to a degree, responsibility for the health of her children is ascribed to the mother-status. There is an intrinsic connection between achieved statuses and the requirements of high technical competence. . . .

High technical competence also implies specificity of function. Such intensive devotion to expertness in matters of health and disease precludes comparable expertness in other fields. The physician is not, by virtue of his modern role, a generalized "wise man" or sage—though there is considerable folklore to that effect—but a specialist whose superiority to his fellows is confined to the specific sphere of his technical training and experience. For example one does not expect the physician as such to have better judgment about foreign policy or tax legislation than any other comparably intelligent and well-educated citizen. There are of course elaborate subdivisions of specialization within the profession. . . . The physician is [also] expected to treat an objective problem in objective, scientifically justifiable terms. For example whether he likes or dislikes the particular patient as a person is supposed to be irrelevant, as indeed it is to most purely objective problems of how to handle a particular disease.

. . . The "ideology" of the profession lays great emphasis on the obligation of the physician to put the "welfare of the patient" above his personal interests, and regards "commercialism" as the most serious and insidious evil with which it has to contend. The line, therefore, is drawn primarily vis-à-vis "business." The "profit motive" is supposed to be drastically excluded from the medical world. This attitude is, of course, shared with the other professions, but it is perhaps more pronounced in the medical case than in any single one except perhaps the clergy. . . .

An increasing proportion of medical practice is now taking place in the context of organization. To a large extent this is necessitated by the technological development of medicine itself, above all the need for technical facilities beyond the reach of the individual practitioner, and the fact that treating the same case often involves the complex cooperation of several different kinds of physicians as well as of auxiliary personnel. This greatly alters the relation of the physician to the rest of the instrumental complex. He tends to be relieved of much responsibility and hence necessarily of freedom, in relation to his patients other than in his technical role. Even if a hospital executive is a physician himself he is not in the usual sense engaged in the "practice of medicine" in performing his functions any more than the president of the Miners' Union is engaged in mining coal.

As was noted, for common sense there may be some question of whether "being sick" constitutes a social role at all—isn't it simply a state of fact, a "condition"? Things are not quite so simple as this. The test is the existence of a set of institutionalized expectations and the corresponding sentiments and sanctions.

There seem to be four aspects of the institutionalized expectation system relative to the sick role. First, is the exemption from normal social role responsibilities, which of course is relative to the nature and severity of the illness. This exemption requires legitimation by and to the various alters involved and the physician often serves as a court of appeal as well as a direct legitimatizing agent. It is noteworthy that like all institutionalized patterns the legitimation of being sick enough to avoid obligations can not only be a right of the sick person but an obligation upon him. People are often resistant to admitting they are sick and it is not uncommon for others to tell them that they *ought* to stay in bed. The word generally has a moral connotation. It goes almost without saying that this legitimation has the social function of protection against "malingering."

The second closely related aspect is the institutionalized definition that the sick person cannot be expected by "pulling himself together" to get well by an act of decision or will. In this sense also he is exempted from responsibility—he is in a condition that must "be taken care of." His "condition" must be changed, not merely his "attitude." Of course the process of recovery may be spontaneous but while the illness lasts he can't "help it." This element in the definition of the state of illness is obviously crucial as a bridge to the acceptance of "help."

The third element is the definition of the state of being ill as itself undesirable with its obligation to want to "get well." The first two elements of legitimation of the sick role thus are conditional in a highly important sense. It is a relative legitimation so long as he is in this unfortunate state which both he and alter hope he can get out of as expeditiously as possible.

Finally, the fourth closely related element is the obligation—in proportion to the severity of the condition, of course—to seek *technically competent* help, namely, in the most usual case, that of a physician and to *cooperate* with him in the process of trying to get well. It is here, of course, that the role of the sick person as patient becomes articulated with that of the physician in a complementary role structure.

It is evident from the above that the role of motivational factors in illness immensely broadens the scope and increases the importance of the institutionalized role aspect of being sick. For then the problem of social control becomes much more than one of ascertaining facts and drawing lines. The privileges and exemptions of the sick role may become objects of a "secondary gain" which the patient is positively motivated, usually unconsciously, to secure or to retain. The problem, therefore, of the balance of motivations to recover, becomes of first importance. In general motivational balances of great functional significance to the social system are institutionally controlled, and it should, therefore, not be surprising that this is no exception.

A few further points may be made about the specific patterning of the sick role and its relation to social structure. It is, in the first place, a "contingent" role into which anyone, regardless of his status in other respects, may come. It is, furthermore, in the type case temporary. One may say that it is in a certain sense a "negatively achieved" role, through failure to "keep well," though, of course, positive motivations also operate, which by that very token must be motivations to deviance. . . .

The orientation of the sick role vis-à-vis the physician is also defined as collectively-oriented. It is true that the patient has a very obvious self-interest in getting well in most cases, though this point may not always be so simple. But once he has called in a physician the attitude is clearly marked, that he has assumed the obligation to cooperate with that physician in what is regarded as a common task. The obverse of the physician's obligation to be guided by the welfare of the patient is the latter's obligation to "do his part" to the best of his ability. This point is clearly brought out, for example, in the attitudes of the profession toward what is called "shopping around." By that is meant the practice of a patient "checking" the advice of one physician against that of another without telling physician A that he intends to consult physician B, or if he comes back to A that he has done so or who B is. The medical view is that if the patient is not satisfied with the advice his physician gives him he may properly do one of two things, first he may request a consultation, even naming the physician he wishes called in, but in that case it is physician A not the patient who must call B in, the patient may not see B independently, and above all not without A's knowledge. The other proper recourse is to terminate the relation with A and become "B's patient." The notable fact here is that a pattern of behavior on the part not only of the physician, but also of the patient, is expected which is in sharp contrast to perfectly legitimate behavior in a commercial relationship. If he is buying a car there is no objection to the customer going to a number of dealers before making up his mind, and there is no obligation for him to inform any one dealer what others he is consulting, to say nothing of approaching the Chevrolet dealer only through the Ford dealer.

The doctor-patient relationship is thus focused on these pattern elements. The patient has a need for technical services because he doesn't—nor do his lay associates, family members, etc.—"know" what is the matter or what to do about it, nor does he control the necessary facilities. The physician is a technical expert who by special training and experience, and by an institutionally validated status, is qualified to "help" the patient in a situation institutionally defined as legitimate in a relative sense but as needing help. . . .

CRITICAL-THINKING QUESTIONS

1. Does Parsons understand illness as a biological condition, that is, "something that happens to people"? What are the social elements in health and illness?

2. According to Parsons, what are the distinctive characteristics of the social role of the physician?

3. What are the major elements of "the sick role"? In what respects does Parsons view the social roles of physicians and patients as complementary? Can you see ways in which they may be in conflict?

HEALTH AND MEDICINE

Contemporary

60

The Health of Black America

Gerald David Jaynes and Robin M. Williams, Jr.*

Although the medical care available to affluent people of the United States is excellent, many others have little means to secure health. As a result, the United States ranks twenty-sixth in infant mortality (behind countries including Greece, Cuba, and Bulgaria). Young African Americans are hit especially hard by poverty, and their health suffers accordingly. This selection from a recent report explains that the health disparity in the United States persists and, in some cases, is increasing.

Who will live and who will die and how much handicap and disability will burden their lives depend in large part on conditions of education, environment, and employment as well as on access to adequate medical services. Health is not only an important "good" in itself, it is also a determinant of life options during the entire life span. For ex-

* Robin M. Williams, Jr. represents the Committee on the Status of Black Americans.

SOURCE: "Black Americans' Health," in *A Common Destiny: Blacks and American Society* by Gerald David Jaynes and Robin M. Williams, Jr. Copyright © 1990 by National Academy of Sciences. Published by National Academy Press, Washington, DC. Reprinted with permission.

ample, lack of prenatal care leads to greater likelihood of infant death, neurological damage, or developmental impairment; childhood illnesses and unhealthy conditions can reduce learning potential; adolescent childbearing, substance abuse, and injuries cause enormous personal, social, and health effects; impaired health or chronic disability in adults contributes to low earning capacity and unemployment; and chronic poor health among older adults can lead to premature retirement and loss of ability for self-care and independent living. Health status is therefore an important indicator of a group's social position as well as of its present and future well-being.

OVERVIEW

This chapter provides data describing trends in black health status and the differential rates of illness, disability, and death that persist between black and white Americans. The discussion focuses on conditions that sustain the continuing health differentials between blacks and whites. We consider biomedical, environmental, and social factors that contribute to the health outcomes for blacks within defined periods of the life span, giving particular attention to poverty and those sociocultural factors that influence access to health services.

Although multiple factors contribute to the persistent health disadvantages of blacks, poverty may be the most profound and pervasive determinant. There has been a consistent finding across communities and nations that persons of the lowest socioeconomic status have higher death rates. In a classic study, Kitagawa and Hauser (1973) found that there was a gradient of mortality rates with steady increases from the highest to the lowest social classes. Mortality rates were higher as socioeconomic status declined for both whites and blacks, whether that status was measured by family income, educational level, or occupation. For people of the lowest status, overall mortality was 80 percent greater than for those at the highest socioeconomic level. In addition to increased mortality, almost every form of disease and disability is more prevalent among the poor.

Because of the relationship between poverty and health, and because poverty has been a persistent problem for blacks in the United States, it is to be expected that blacks' greater poverty is responsible for much of the black-white health disparity. Poverty rates among children cause special concern for their future health status. Poverty in childhood often means lack of proper nutrition, unsafe housing, and poor access to health care or other resources needed for healthy growth and development.

During much of the period covered in this study, there was open segregation of medical facilities in the United States. In the twenty-five-year period before 1965, persistent barriers to access to preventive, primary, and hospital care influenced the quality of life and the patterns of illness observed among blacks.

Organizations such as the Medical Committee on Human Rights, the National Medical Association, and the Student National Medical Association played important roles in efforts to end discrimination in health care facilities and in health professional schools. Following the 1954 *Brown* Supreme Court decision, which declared segregation in public schools unconstitutional, efforts to desegregate health care facilities intensified.

Important events that led to more equal access to medical care for blacks were the Civil Rights Act [of] 1964 and the Medicaid and Medicare legislation [enacted] in 1965. Title VI of the Civil Rights Act prohibited racial discrimination in any institution receiving federal funds, thus giving hospitals a powerful incentive to alter their practices. Hospitals receiving federal funds were forbidden to deny admission to patients, to subject patients to separate treatments, or to deny admitting privileges to medical personnel solely on the basis of race. Access to health care was further increased when litigation in the 1960s explicitly defined the obligation of hospitals using federally provided construction funds to meet their "free care" requirements and to serve those unable to pay.

A second method of addressing blacks' unequal access to health care concerned their underrepresentation in the medical care professions. During the 1960s and 1970s many efforts were mounted to enlarge the representation of blacks and other minorities in the health professions. It was believed that access to health care for poor blacks would improve if there were more black physicians. This belief prompted some medical schools to recruit more black and other minority students and to channel them into primary care specialties.

While the chapter presents facts about past and current health disadvantages of blacks compared with whites, the focus on problem areas should not leave the impression that most black Americans are unhealthy. Over the past fifty years, blacks' health status and life expectancies have improved a great deal. A general overview of this point can be made by considering trends in mortality and life expectancy.

A useful summary index of the effects of differing mortality rates is the average (mean) life expectancy at birth. It is calculated on the basis of age-specific death rates as of a given date, and it estimates the number of years that will be lived on the average by individuals born in a particular year, assuming a constancy of then-current age-specific mortality rates. [Figure 60-1] summarizes trends in black-white differences in life expectancy at birth. In the 1950–1985 time span, death rates fell for both races, particularly for black females, but whites continued to enjoy an advantage over blacks. The difference in life expectancy of black and white men decreased from a gap of about eleven years in 1940 to a six-year difference in 1960 and has shown little improvement since then. Among women, there has been a consistent pattern of relative improvement for blacks, and the racial gap in the mid-1980s was less than one-half its size in 1940. As a result, the advantage in life ex-

pectancy black women enjoy over black men increased during this period. The life expectancy of a black male in 1985 (65.3 years) [was] lower than that already achieved by white males in 1950, 66.5 years (National Center for Health Statistics 1988: 80–81).

Projections of mortality rates into the figure are necessarily uncertain, particularly given the current epidemic of acquired immune deficiency syndrome (AIDS). Nonetheless, we estimate that if the 1950–1985 trends continue, life expectancies for black and white women will converge in the first half of the twenty-first century, but no convergence to white rates can be foreseen for black men (R. Farley 1985).

These summary statements conceal a complex pattern of age-specific and cause-specific changes (Farley and Allen 1987; U.S. Department of Health and Human Services 1985). Among children under age fifteen, there have been consistent and large decreases in the risk of death, but the death rates for black children are 30 percent to 50 percent higher than those for white children. Between 1950 and the late 1960s, mortality rates ac-

FIGURE 60-1 Life Expectancy at Birth, by Race and Sex, 1950–1985.
Source: Data from the National Center for Health Statistics.

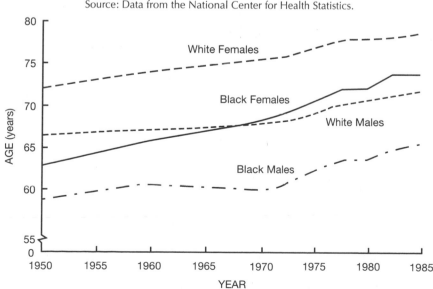

tually rose among adult men, especially black men, and fell at a very slow rate among adult women of both races. The last two decades have been characterized by rapid declines in mortality rates, declines that were not foreseen by health experts. Rates have fallen for almost all race-sex groups, but the decline at the older ages, sixty and above, has been unusually sharp, reflecting, perhaps, improvements in the income level of the elderly and the government's assumption of many health care costs with Medicare (Crimmins 1981). Contagious and infectious diseases were more common causes of death among blacks than among whites in 1940, but that specific cause of disparity has been reduced.

Mortality from heart disease declined slowly between 1940 and the mid-1960s and more rapidly afterward. The pace of change was more rapid for women than men among both races. Improved detection and treatment of hypertension, and changes in smoking, diet, and exercise were factors influencing the reductions. There is still a large disparity and excess of black deaths from heart diseases. Mortality from suicide remains much higher for whites than blacks, while cirrhosis and diabetes death rates, although declining rapidly since the late 1960s, remain higher for blacks (R. Farley 1985).

Two causes of death merit special attention, cancer and homicide. If data from the 1930s and early 1940s are accurate, then blacks formerly had considerably lower cancer mortality rates than whites (Lilienfeld et al. 1972). This has changed in a dramatic manner. Since the 1940s, there have been particularly sharp increases in death rates from lung cancer for both races, but the rise has been greater among blacks, especially black men. Mortality from other types of cancer has held steady or declined among whites in the last two decades but has increased among blacks. Thus, there is now a substantial excess in cancer mortality among blacks. Homicide has a particularly large impact on average life expectancy since its usual victims are young adults. Although recent trends show lower homicide rates among blacks, it remains a leading cause of death for black men.

The U.S. Department of Health and Human Services (HHS) *Report of the Secretary's Task Force on Black and Minority Health* identified six medical conditions for which the gaps in mortality between whites and blacks are the greatest. The six causes of death, taken together, account for about 86 percent of the excess black mortality in relation to the white population: accidents and homicides (35.1 percent), infant mortality (26.9 percent), heart disease and stroke (14.4 percent), cirrhosis (4.9 percent), cancer (3.8 percent), and diabetes (1.0 percent).[1] The report did not attempt to encompass the full dimensions of disparities in health status; while the mortality data for these six conditions are important, they do not capture the full personal and societal costs of deaths from other causes and of chronic or acute illness. In particular, this methodology has omitted important health problems of black children.

In the rest of this chapter we analyze the health status of black Americans across the life span, using the following divisions: pregnancy and infancy; childhood (ages 1–14); adolescents and young adults (ages 15–24); adulthood (ages 25–65); and older adults (over age 65). For each period of life, a few conditions of highest concern have been selected for analysis. In making these choices consideration has been given to magnitude, severity, distribution, and knowledge of contributory factors. We also emphasize the potential for prevention.

The black population has benefited from advances in medicine, but not equally with whites. From birth to advanced old age, blacks at each stage of the life cycle still die at higher rates (except for adult black women since 1970) and suffer disproportionately from a wide range of adverse health conditions. When national health objectives for 1990 were established by the Public Health Service (U.S. Department of Health and Human Services 1980), the black-white disparity in the late 1970s was so great that it did not appear possible to overcome it in the short term. In the areas of infant mortality and deaths by injury, separate and unequal goals for blacks and whites were set. For many of the objectives set by the Public Health Service, the national targets were achieved before

1990 for whites but not for blacks (U.S. Department of Health and Human Services 1986). Based on recent trends, blacks are not projected to achieve equality in health by 1990 or in the near future. . . .

ADULTHOOD

Younger people are expected to be healthier than the elderly, and the differential is usually explained as a result of the aging process. There are some sex differences in mortality. The greater longevity of women has been partly explained by a lesser exposure to environmental hazards and less participation in hazardous life-styles, including use of firearms, speeding, heavy substance abuse, and promiscuity. To the extent that these differences are reduced, there is the prospect that men will approach more closely the life expectancy of women.

Biological differences appear to explain very little of the difference in health status between blacks and whites. There were 58,942 excess deaths for blacks in 1980. Only 379 of these deaths, less than 1 percent, were attributable to hereditary conditions such as sickle cell anemia, for which genetic patterns among blacks have been established (U.S. Department of Health and Human Services 1985e). Instead, the major factors appear to be socioeconomic and physical environments, personal health habits, and life-styles [see Figure 60-2]. In this section we focus on five of the problems that contribute to health disparities between white and black adults—homicide, AIDS, substance abuse, hypertension, and cancer. This list is very different from what it would have been in 1940; tuberculosis and many other infectious diseases are no longer high on the list. But the current problems pose as many challenges today as did infectious diseases in 1940.

MAJOR HEALTH RISKS

Homicide

Intentional injury has only recently been recognized as a public health problem. Intentional injury includes a wide spectrum of assaultive behaviors: child abuse, spouse abuse, rape, suicide, and homicide. Our discussion is focused primarily on homicide because it contributes so heavily to the differential in mortality between blacks and whites during the middle years of life.

FIGURE 60-2 Leading Causes of Death, by Race and Age Group, 1984.
Source: Data from U.S. Department of Health and Human Services.

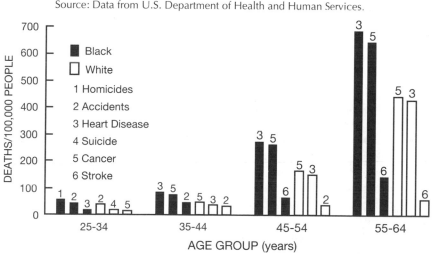

Homicide is the leading cause of death for black males aged 15–34. There are eight thousand black victims of homicide a year. Although blacks were 11.5 percent of the population in 1983, they were 43 percent of the homicide victims. The black-white differentials for homicide are higher than for any other leading cause of death. And because the typical homicide victim is young, every homicide accounts for an average 30.6 years of potential life lost prior to age 65; in comparison, the potential average time of life lost is only 2.1 years for death due to heart disease (Centers for Disease Control 1986a). Although homicide risk is greatest among males in the 25–34 age group, the gap between black and white risks is evident for both sexes in all age groups (see Figure 60-2). In both blacks and whites, most homicides are intraracial and inflicted by young male acquaintances and relatives as a result of a quarrel, not as part of another crime (Jason et al. 1983).

Homicide rates fluctuate a great deal over time, suggesting that societal factors play a significant role. Brenner (1983) reported an association between the homicide rate and unemployment. In recent years, there has been a significant decline in the black homicide rate, and of the five race-specific health objectives stated for 1990, this is the only one which seems likely to be met (U.S. Department of Health and Human Services 1986b). The decline cannot be explained as due to any specific intervention.

The causes of homicide are complex. They are associated with three separate sets of risk factors: biological, psychological, and sociological. Biological risk factors for involvement in homicide as a victim or perpetrator relate to being male and being young. Psychological factors relate to violence that is learned from role models or is the result of disturbed developmental patterns and the failure to develop adequate inhibitions against inappropriate and excessive expression of anger and frustrations. Sociological risk factors relate to American culture and the structure of American society (National Commission on the Causes and Prevention of Violence 1969). For example, it is estimated that about one-half of all homicides in the United States are related to the use of alcohol. Between 10 and 20 percent of homicides nationwide are associated with the use of illegal drugs (U.S. Department of Health and Human Services 1986a: 163).

For attempted homicides, the outcome is influenced by the lethality of the instruments to which the individuals may have access. Access to handguns, used most frequently by people aged 25–34, has been considered to be a major cause of homicide. The evidence for this is not conclusive and indeed is difficult to establish (Wright et al. 1983). Further studies of fatal and nonfatal outcomes may increase understanding of the problem. . . .

At present there are no scientifically proven efficacious interventions that would lead to the reduction of homicide. Under the circumstances, limiting access to handguns and training in conflict resolution have been recommended. But perhaps the most important aspect of the situation is that the subject of violence is now accepted as a legitimate public health concern.

AIDS

AIDS has created an international challenge of enormous proportions for the society in general and the medical profession in particular. Persons at greatest risk are homosexual males, intravenous drug users, recipients of blood transfusions, those who have had heterosexual contact with infected individuals, and children born to women who are infected. Women who are infected with the virus can transmit it during pregnancy to their prospective children. AIDS is a special problem for blacks: 25 percent of all reported cases and more than 50 percent of the children under the age of fifteen who have AIDS are black (Centers for Disease Control 1986b); see [Table 60-1]. Blacks with AIDS are more likely to be IV drug users, most of whom identify themselves as heterosexuals. The epidemiologic patterns of viral transmission in blacks suggest greater incursion into the heterosexual population. The greatest source of new infections is infected persons who presently show no symptoms and do not know they are infected.

The AIDS epidemic can be devastating to peo-

TABLE 60-1   Cumulative Incidence of AIDS and Relative Risk, by Race and Ethnic Groups, Age, and Transmission Category, 1981–1987

Category	White	Black	Hispanic	Other
Adults, total[b]	380.8(1.0)	1,068.1(2.8)[a]	1,036.3(2.7)[a]	141.0(0.4)[a]
Adult men	188.9(1.0)	578.2(3.1)[a]	564.4(3.0)[a]	74.4(0.4)[a]
Adult women	12.2(1.0)	161.1(13.2)[a]	104.6(8.6)[a]	11.1(0.9)
Homosexual men	298.6(1.0)	413.8(1.4)[a]	513.9(1.7)[a]	94.7(0.3)[a]
Bisexual men	46.8(1.0)	177.7(3.8)[a]	126.3(2.7)[a]	24.9(0.5)[a]
Heterosexual IV drug users	10.1(1.0)	201.2(19.9)[a]	195.1(19.3)[a]	4.2(0.3)[a]
Hemophiliacs	2.6(1.0)	1.4(0.6)[a]	2.7(1.0)	1.7(0.7)
Transfusion recipients	5.1(1.0)	7.5(1.5)	6.5(1.3)	5.0(1.0)
Pediatric, total[c]	3.8(1.0)	46.3(12.1)[a]	26.1(6.8)[a]	3.2(0.8)
Mother, IV drug user	0.8(1.0)	21.8(26.4)[a]	13.9(16.9)[a]	1.3(1.6)
Mother's partner, IV drug user	0.2(1.0)	5.5(25.8)[a]	6.2(29.2)[a]	0.0(0.0)
Transfusion-associated	1.1(1.0)	2.7(2.3)[a]	2.1(1.9)	0.0(0.0)
Hemophiliacs	0.6(1.0)	0.7(1.0)	1.3(2.0)	0.6(1.0)

[a] Relative risk significantly different from 1.0 (P < 0.05).

[b] For all men, homosexual men, and bisexual men, the denominator consisted of all men ≥15 years; for all women, the denominator was all women ≥ 15 years; for other adult categories, the denominators included all men and women ≥ 15 years.

[c] For pediatric categories, the denominators consisted of all children < 15 years.

Notes: Cumulative incidence is given per 1 million population. Relative risk is given in parentheses. Relative risk is the ratio of the cumulative incidence in each race or ethnic group to the incidence in whites.

Source: Data from Curran et al. (1988). Reprinted with permission.

ple who face large medical bills without adequate insurance (see section on Provision of Health Care). The financial costs for the care of persons with AIDS are enormous, ranging from $23,000 to $168,000 per patient over a lifetime (Bloom and Carliner 1988). The cost of treatment with azedothymine (AZT), an antiviral agent, can range from $10,000 to $20,000 a year per patient.

Although there is as yet no vaccine and no effective cure, enough is known about methods of transmission of the virus (HIV) that causes AIDS so that almost all future infections with the AIDS virus could theoretically be prevented (Francis and Chin 1987). The use of condoms inhibits the sexual transmission of the virus (Conant et al. 1986), and in the case of intravenous drug users, the use of sterile needles can prevent transmission. The overwhelming need is for public education to change behaviors with respect to safer sex and drug-use practices. A recent report (Turner et al. 1989) detailed how education must be culturally sensitive to blacks and other minorities and initiate comprehensive interventions at various levels of personal and community involvement.

Substance Abuse

Substance abuse includes the excessive use of tobacco, alcohol, or illicit drugs. The abuse of these substances is conceptually linked by the addiction, the compulsion, loss of control, and continued use despite adverse consequences. In general, the use of cigarettes, alcohol, and drugs is learned at an early age (during high school and college) and continued during the adult years, when most of the effects on health and mortality begin to be seen. The National Health Survey (National Center for Health Statistics 1987) indicates that in 1985, among the age group twenty and over, 41 percent of blacks and 32 percent of whites smoked tobacco.

The magnitude of this problem in blacks can be judged by deaths related to substance abuse. The mortality rate per 100,000 people for lung cancer is 95 for black males and 70 for white males. These deaths are largely due to smoking. It is also estimated that cigarette smoking is responsible for 30 percent of cancer deaths and that smoking-related deaths are particularly high among blacks. The mortality from cirrhosis of the liver—which is closely related to alcohol consumption—is 29 for blacks and 15 for whites. Alcohol and drugs are also important factors in many cases of intentional and unintentional injury. It is this combination of circumstances that gives substance abuse its high priority among problems for black adults.

It appears that genetic and social factors play an important role in the case of alcoholism. For example, it has been shown that adopted children with an alcoholic biological parent are at four times higher risk of alcoholism than control subjects (Bohman et al. 1981; Goodwin et al. 1974). Schuckit (1985) has concluded that genetic influences are important in alcoholism and reflect multiple genes interacting with environmental factors.

Apart from genetic influences, children living in a home in which parents use alcohol as a means of coping with problems may learn that model. Ease of access to the various substances also constitutes a considerable risk. Research is needed to clarify the contributions of heredity and environment to all addictive processes and to provide a sound scientific basis for the development of preventive strategies.

Hypertension

It has been recognized for a long time that blacks experience higher rates of hypertension than whites. It has been estimated that hypertensive disease is responsible for more than 5000 excess deaths a year in the black population (National Center for Health Statistics 1987). Hypertension is an important risk factor for stroke, especially stroke due to cerebral hemorrhage. The age-adjusted death rate for stroke among blacks is almost twice that for whites (National Center for Health Statistics 1984). End-stage renal disease is another consequence of hypertension, and it has been estimated that its incidence is three to four times higher among blacks than among whites (Easterling 1977).

Although the cause of hypertension and the racial differences in its incidence are not known, increased awareness of the disease and early diagnosis and treatment have been shown to be effective in reducing hypertension among blacks. Indeed, hypertension control among blacks is one of the success stories of modern public health (see [Table 60-2]).

In the period from 1960 to 1980, the proportion of people with hypertension found in epidemiologic surveys who had had no medical contact for their disease has declined significantly, and the decline among blacks was much greater than the decline among whites. Greater awareness has increased the chances of early diagnosis and prompt treatment (National Center for Health Statistics 1982). Limited use of salt, an adequate supply of foods containing potassium, abstinence from smoking, and weight control are usually recommended as first steps, with medication recommended if these steps are insufficient.

The success of the hypertension program can be attributed not only to individual action but also to a comprehensive national strategy of research and education. There has been the coordinated effort of the National Heart, Lung, and Blood Institute, the American Heart Association, the American Red Cross, the National Black Health Providers' Task Force on Blood Pressure Education and Control, and other organizations. It is an example of how community action combined with individual responsibility can improve individual and public health.

Cancer

Most blacks have learned that hypertension is a problem, but most blacks are believed to be unaware of the magnitude of the problem of cancer in the black population. From 1978 to 1981, the average annual age-adjusted cancer mortality rate per 100,000 population for all sites of cancer was 163.6 for whites and 208.5 for blacks. In 1930, white females had the highest and non-white males the lowest cancer mortality in the United States; by 1970–1975 their relative positions were reversed (Greenberg 1983). There are several possible statistical explanations for the reversal, such as

TABLE 60-2 Prevalence Rates of Hypertension for Persons Aged 25–74 by Treatment History, Race, and Sex, 1960–1980

Hypertension Prevalence	All People[a] %	White Men %	White Women %	Black Men %	Black Women %
In the population					
1960–1962	20.3	16.3	20.4	31.8	39.8
1974–1976	22.1	21.4	19.6	37.1	35.5
1976–1980	22.0	21.2	20.0	28.3	39.8
Hypertension never diagnosed[b]					
1960–1962	51.1	57.6	43.9	70.5	35.1
1974–1976	36.4	42.3	29.7	41.0	28.9
1976–1980	26.6	40.6	25.2	35.7	14.5
On medication					
1960–1962	31.3	22.4	38.2	18.5	48.1
1974–1976	34.2	25.9	48.5	24.0	36.4
1976–1980	56.2	38.3	58.6	40.9	60.6
On medication and controlled[c]					
1960–1962	16.0	11.8	21.9	5.0	20.2
1974–1976	19.6	15.1	28.1	12.7	22.3
1976–1980	36.1	20.9	40.3	16.1	30.9

[a] Includes all other races not shown separately.

[b] Reported that was never told by physician that he or she had high blood pressure or hypertension.

[c] Subset of "on medication" group; those taking antihypertensive medication whose blood pressure was not elevated at the time of the examination.

Notes: Hypertension is defined as elevated blood pressure, that is, a systolic measurement of at least 160 mm Hg or a diastolic measurement of at least 95 mm Hg, or as taking antihypertensive medication. Populations are age adjusted by the direct method to the population at the midpoint of the 1976–1980 National Health and Nutrition Examination Survey.

Source: Data from U.S. Department of Health and Human Services.

increased completeness of diagnosis among blacks and underestimates of the rate among black males because of greater undernumeration of black males in earlier censuses. But even making allowances for these possible errors, the evidence for an increase in the cancer rate for blacks seems indisputable.

Blacks experience higher incidence, higher mortality, and poorer survival from cancer than whites. The overall rate of incidence exceeds that of whites by 10 percent. Much of the difference can be attributed to black males, whose rate of incidence is 25 percent higher than that of white males. Cancers of the lung and prostate account for many of the cancers in males and are largely responsible for the higher rates for blacks. The esophagus is another site at which the black excess is relatively great.

It has been known for a long time that lung cancer is associated with cigarette smoking (U.S. Department of Health, Education, and Welfare 1979). The risk of cancer is related to the duration of tobacco use, the amount of daily smoking, the tar and nicotine content of the tobacco, and the depth of inhalation. Even passive smoking has been shown to be harmful to one's health (Sandler et al. 1985). It has been estimated that 90 percent of the risk of bronchogenic carcinoma can be attributed to smoking. Both tobacco and alcohol are known to contribute to cancer of the esophagus.

Cancer of the cervix is more common in black than in white women. Where diagnosed early, this is a highly treatable form of cancer. The continuing deaths for black women from cervical cancer is a marker of the inadequate prevention and treatment they receive. A number of risk factors have been associated with cervical cancer, but there is still a great deal to be learned about its causes (Hulka 1982; Kessler and Adams 1976). The predominant view is that it is related to sexual behavior and probably precipitated by genital infection with the papilloma virus and herpes virus. Evidence concerning possible causes of prostate cancer other than age is still scanty. Dietary and hormonal factors are thought to be possible contributors.

Socioeconomic factors have been shown to be strongly related to the incidence, survival, and mortality from cancer (Nomura et al. 1981; Page and Kuntz 1980). It is suspected that a significant portion of the higher rates in blacks is due to the higher proportion of persons in the lower socioeconomic positions who are less likely to receive such preventive services such as Pap smears and breast examinations, but a great deal of research is still needed.

Prevention strategies include cessation of smoking, reduction of alcohol use, and periodic Pap smears for early detection of cervical cancer. At the present time, the most important strategy for reducing prostate cancer is to work toward a better understanding of the causes and toward more effective means of early detection. Progress in the reduction of cancer will require more emphasis on prevention research and on education of the black community with respect to the early signs and to the necessary changes in health behavior. . . .

CRITICAL-THINKING QUESTIONS

1. Why do some categories of Americans enjoy better health than others? How much are such differences a matter of public policy?
2. Describe the five major health risks faced by African Americans.
3. If poverty causes poor health, does poor health also cause poverty?

NOTE

1. *Excess death* expresses the difference between the number of deaths actually observed in a minority group and the number of deaths that would have occurred if that group had experienced the same death rates for each age and sex as in the white population.

REFERENCES

BLOOM, D. E., and G. CARLINER. 1988. The economic impact of AIDS in the United States. *Science,* 239:604–9.

BOHMAN, M., S. SIQUAARDSSON, and R. CLONINGER. 1981. Material inheritance of alcohol abuse. *Archives of General Psychiatry,* 38:965–69.

BRENNER, M. H. 1983. Mortality and economic stability: Detailed analysis for Britain and comparative analysis for selected industrialized countries. *International Journal of Health Services,* 13(4):563.

CENTERS FOR DISEASE CONTROL. 1986a. *Morbidity and Mortality Weekly Report,* 35:272.

———. 1986b. Acquired immunodeficiency syndrome (AIDS) among blacks and Hispanics—United States. *Morbidity and Mortality Weekly Report,* 35(42):655–66.

CONANT, M., D. HARDY, J. SORNATINGER, D. SPICER, and J. A. LEVY. 1986. Condoms prevent transmission of AIDS-associated retrovirus. *Journal of the American Medical Association,* 255:1706.

CRIMMINS, E. M. 1981. The changing pattern of American mortality decline, 1940–77, and its implications for the future. *American Journal of Sociology,* 844(6):839–54.

CURRAN, J. W., H. W. JAFFE, A. M. HARDY, W. M. MORGAN, R. M. SELIK, and T. J. DONDERO. 1988. Epidemiology of HIV infection and AIDS in the United States. *Science,* 239(4840):610–16.

EASTERLING, R. E. 1977. Racial factors in the incidence and causation of end-stage renal disease. *Transactions of the American Society for Artificial Internal Organs,* 23:28–33.

FARLEY, R. 1985. An analysis of mortality, 1940 to the present. Paper prepared for the Committee on the Status of Black Americans, National Research Council, Washington, DC.

FARLEY, R., and W. ALLEN. 1987. *The color line and the quality of American life.* New York: Russell Sage Foundation.

FRANCIS, D. P., and J. CHIN. 1987. The prevention of acquired immunodeficiency syndrome in the United States: An objective strategy for medicine, public health, business and the community. *Journal of the American Medical Association,* 257:1357–66.

GOODWIN, D. W., F. SCHULSINGER, and N. MOLLER. 1974. Drinking problems in adopted and nonadopted sons of alcoholics. *Archives of General Psychology,* 31:164–69.

GREENBERG, M. R. 1983. *Urbanization and cancer mortality: The United States experience 1950–1975.* New York: Oxford University Press.

HULKA, B. 1982. Risk factors for cervical cancer. *Journal of Chronic Disease,* 35(1):3–11.

JASON, J., M. FLOCK, and C. W. TYLER, JR. 1983. Epidemiologic characteristics of primary homicides in the United States. *American Journal of Epidemiology,* 117(4):419–28.

KESSLER, J. L., and E. ADAMS. 1976. Human cervical cancer as a venereal disease. *Cancer Research,* 36:783.

KITAGAWA, E. M., and P. M. HAUSER. 1973. *Differential mortality in the United States.* Cambridge: Harvard University Press.

LILIENFELD, A. M., M. L. LEVIN, and I. KESSLER. 1972. *Cancer in the United States.* Cambridge: Harvard University Press.

NATIONAL CENTER FOR HEALTH STATISTICS. 1982. *Blood pressure levels and hypertension in persons aged 6–74. United States 1976–80.* DHHS Pub. No. (PHS) 82-1250. Washington, DC: U.S. Department of Health and Human Services.

———. 1984. *Monthly Vital Statistics Report.* 33(3) Supplement. U.S. Department of Health and Human Services.

———. 1987. *Health United States: 1986.* DHHS Pub. No. (PHS) 87-1232. Washington, DC: U.S. Department of Health and Human Services.

———. 1988. *Health United States: 1987.* DHHS Pub. No. 88-1232. Washington, DC: U. S. Government Printing Office.

NATIONAL COMMISSION ON THE CAUSES AND PREVENTION OF VIOLENCE. 1969. *To establish justice, to insure domestic tranquility, final report.* 13 vols. Washington, DC: U.S. Government Printing Office.

NOMURA, A., L. KOLONEL, W. RELLAHAN, J. LEE, and E. WEGNER. 1981. Racial survival patterns for lung cancer in Hawaii. *Cancer,* 48:1265–71.

PAGE, W. F., and A. J. KUNTZ. 1980. Racial and socioeconomic factors in cancer survival: A comparison of Veterans Administration results with selected studies. *Cancer,* 45:1029–40.

SANDLER D. P., A. J. WILCOX, and R. B. EVERSON. 1985. Cumulative effects of lifetime passive smoking on cancer risks. *Lancet,* 1:312.

SCHUCKIT, M. A. 1985. Genetics and the risk of alcoholism. *Journal of the American Medical Association,* 254:2614–17.

TURNER, C. F., H. G. MILLER, and L. E. MOSES, EDS. 1989. *AIDS: Sexual behavior and intravenous drug use.* Committee on AIDS Research and the Behavioral, Social, and Statistical Sciences, Commission on Behavioral and Social Sciences and Education, National Research Council. Washington, DC: National Academy Press.

U.S. DEPARTMENT OF HEALTH, EDUCATION, AND WELFARE. 1979. *Smoking and health: A report of the Surgeon General.* DHEW Pub. No. (PHS) 79-50066. Washington, DC: U.S. Department of Health, Education, and Welfare.

U.S. DEPARTMENT OF HEALTH AND HUMAN SERVICES. 1980. *Promoting health/preventing disease, objectives for the nation.* Public Health Service, Office of the Assistant Secretary for Health. Washington, DC: U.S. Department of Health and Human Services.

———. 1985. *Secretary's task force on black and minority health.* Office of the Secretary of Health. Washington, DC: U.S. Department of Health and Human Services.

———. 1986a. *Current estimates, 1985.* DHHS Pub. (PHS). Washington, DC: U.S. Department of Health and Human Services.

———. 1986b. *Prevention of disease, disability and death in blacks and other minorities.* Annual Program Review, 1986. Centers for Disease Control, Public Health Service. Washington, DC: U.S. Department of Health and Human Services.

WRIGHT, J. D., P. H. ROSSI, and K. DALY. 1983. *Under the gun: Weapons, crime, and violence in America.* New York: Aldine Publishing Company.

HEALTH AND MEDICINE

61

The AIDS Epidemic in Africa

Loretta Tofani

Half of the 8 to 10 million people worldwide (and three-fourths of the women) infected with human immunodeficiency virus (HIV) live in Africa. Especially in the cities of Zambia, Uganda, and other central African nations, AIDS has become a devastating plague. This selection describes the problem in general terms and offers a heart-wrenching portrait of the stunning human consequences of AIDS to one family in a Zambian village.

The white truck carrying the body pulled into Dundu village, scattering chickens, piglets and dogs. As villagers emerged from their thatched huts, Maxwell Nzemba, twenty-one, got out of the truck and delivered the news to his father: "Henry has died."

Daniel Nzemba, sixty, tall and mustachioed, bowed his head. Now two of his five children had died of AIDS.

A third was dying of the disease in a local hospital. So was one of his nieces.

On a nearby farm, a twenty-three-year-old wife and mother had died of AIDS only the day before. She had already lost her two infants to the disease. The woman's grandfather has AIDS, and both of his wives are infected with the virus.

A few miles down the red-dirt road, a twenty-eight-year-old schoolteacher had died of AIDS a week earlier. The teacher's sister, her father, and one of her father's two wives had already died of the disease.

And now, as Daniel Nzemba watched his son's body being carried into his hut, his family once again had become part of the nightmare that has enveloped Nzemba's village, his country and indeed much of black Africa.

SOURCE: The *Philadelphia Inquirer,* vol. 323, no. 83, March 24, 1991, pp. 1A, 15A. Reprinted with permission.

AIDS is everywhere here.

Of the eight million to ten million people estimated to be infected with the AIDS virus worldwide, at least half live in Africa. About one in fifty adults in sub-Saharan Africa is infected, according to the World Health Organization—eight times the rate for the rest of the world.

In urban areas of Zambia, Uganda, Rwanda, Burundi and Malawi, at least one of every five young adults is believed to be infected.

More striking than mere numbers is the way AIDS has penetrated mainstream African life. Unlike in the United States, where the disease has hit specific groups such as gay men and intravenous drug users, AIDS in Africa is sweeping indiscriminately through the population. It strikes men and women, grandparents and newborns, the educated and the illiterate.

It devastates families and whole villages. In some of the worst-hit countries, an entire generation is threatened. It is, sadly, the generation that is the first to have produced African engineers, teachers, doctors and political leaders born and educated free of colonial rule.

The AIDS virus, which destroys a person's immune system and leaves the person vulnerable to infections and lethal diseases, was once thought to have originated in Africa and spread to humans from monkeys; those theories have been disproved. Today, scientists are more concerned about stopping the virus than with tracing its origins.

There are many reasons for the rapid spread in Africa. But the key reason is resistance to change in these ancient and profoundly traditional cultures. In developing countries such as Kenya and Zambia, the ancient and the modern co-exist—traditional medicine men and physicians, polygamy and monogamy, ancient gods and Christianity. Some of the traditions inadvertently are helping spread the disease.

Herbalists and medicine men use unsterilized instruments that spread blood, and the AIDS virus, from patient to patient. Practices such as polygamy and wife inheritance, in which a widow marries her late husband's brother, spread the virus within families. Especially in rural areas, people generally refuse to use condoms, viewing them as foreign. And there is a reluctance, even among doctors, to tell patients that they have a fatal—and contagious—disease.

Inadequate health care also contributes to the spread. Other sexually transmitted diseases often have gone untreated, leaving many men and women with lesions that now act as easy portals for entry of the fatal human immunodeficiency virus.

All of these things have quickened the epidemic. Three years ago, AIDS in Africa was largely confined to the cities. But contact between rural and urban areas has brought an alarming spread into the villages of Africa.

Henry Nzemba's case was typical.

Nzemba left his village after high school, when he was eighteen. For two years, he lived in Lusaka, Zambia's capital, and then moved here, to the small city of Mazabuka. He found work in a sugar cane factory.

For eight years, before he was married, he had sex with numerous women, he told a health worker here. His wife left him several years ago, before he learned he had AIDS, the health worker said.

Nzemba was diagnosed with AIDS two years ago at the Salvation Army Hospital nearby. At the time, he had infections in his mouth and throat and a skin rash.

"He hoped to marry again," said Roy Mwilu, an AIDS counselor at the hospital. "But he said he'd only marry someone who was HIV-positive" so he wouldn't infect anyone else.

Henry Nzemba, thirty-two, died on the corner cot in the Maayamusuma Clinic at noon on a Friday. Five other patients lay on cots in the same room. Someone covered Henry's body with a blanket.

Four hours later, Nzemba's brother and stepbrother carried the body, feet sticking out from the blanket, into the back of the clinic's white truck for the journey home. The brothers, Maxwell and Bradford, sat next to the body, one on either side. They were silent throughout the two-hour ride.

In the driver's seat was Pookie Evans, forty-six, a white Zambian who scraped together money two years ago to start the rural clinic. Next to him was his wife, Fionia, thirty-five.

"It's heartbreaking Henry's gone," said Fionia, as the truck chugged and bounced over bumpy, red dirt roads. "But he's finished all his pain."

Sitting behind Fionia was Elijah Mweemba, fifty, the clinic administrator. Mweemba's son, Luke, was dying of AIDS in the Salvation Army Hospital in Chikankata, about seven miles from Nzemba's village. After the truck took Henry Nzemba's body home, Mweemba would use it to bring his own son home to die.

As the truck passed wheat fields, jacaranda trees, cows and thatched huts, Fionia Evans reminisced about the dead man behind her.

"Henry stayed with us for about seven months. When he was well, he painted [the clinic] to help earn his keep," she said.

"But last night he had chills and fever," she continued. "He complained that he kept falling asleep and he didn't want to. He must have suspected he was dying.

"The last few days he had no appetite, but I kept making him custard and bringing him strawberries, and he ate a little. I didn't want him to be dehydrated, so we kept giving him Cokes. His brother even brought him Cokes yesterday when he visited."

About 200 people live in Dundu village, which is set back a bit from a wide dirt road. People walk

along that road, and ox carts—and occasional cars—travel along it, usually en route to the Salvation Army Hospital. Dundu is set among grassy hills, each family's compound of huts in a separate small valley.

The day after Henry Nzemba died, his father, brothers and uncles dug his grave a few yards from the family compound of seven huts.

Solemnly, without speaking, they carved a deep hole in the orange dirt, two yards from the mound that was the grave of Marvina Nzemba, Henry's sister, who had died of AIDS the year before.

As they worked, dozens of friends and neighbors streamed into the compound, the women wearing cotton print, ankle-length skirts, carrying in their arms local vegetables—cauliflower, broccoli and rape. On their heads, many women balanced foot-high bags of corn. Babies slept on some of the women's backs, swaddled in print cloth. Other women built fires outside the huts, boiling water in charred pots.

Eventually, about 300 people gathered outside the huts, the men standing with men, the women with women, the women wailing and chanting in notes first high, then low.

The coffin, of reddish wood from the *muplanga* tree, was lowered into the ground. A Salvation Army preacher, Zachary Sibanda, his Bible in hand, read from Ecclesiastes, translating into the tribal language, Citonga.

"All go to the same place," he read. "All come from dust, and to dust all return."

Henry's two daughters, ages six and four, gazed at the coffin and at the wailing women. The preacher said a final prayer. The men pushed soil onto the coffin with their feet, then used poles to pound it down.

"This is very hard for me," said Daniel Nzemba, Henry's father, when it was over. "I had five children, and now I only have two left," he said, anticipating the impending death of his daughter. "I don't know what to do."

The women surrounded Henry's mother, Rodea, sixty, who had tears streaming down her face. Together they resumed wailing and chanting. "Henry, why did you leave us, why did you abandon us and your children?" they chanted in Citonga. "Henry, you are too young to leave us."

A few days later, Henry's mother returned to her vigil at her daughter's bed in the Salvation Army Hospital. Mody Nzemba, twenty-eight, is in the tuberculosis ward, but like half the patients in its twenty beds, she has AIDS.

"Mama, Mama, I'm in pain," Mody moaned, her body skinny and wasted. Her mother, who for the last month had slept at the hospital in a bed next to her daughter, passed a wet white handkerchief over her daughter's forehead and chest, which was bare as a sign of mourning for her brother. Mody continued crying.

Three beds away lay Mody's cousin, Lenty Chinida, thirty-five, also dying of AIDS.

After Mody fell asleep, her mother took a walk outside. Mody, she said, had been a secretary in Mazabuka. She was diagnosed with AIDS last year, after giving birth to a baby boy.

Rodea Nzemba said she was past the point of anguish. She was numb, she said, and robot-like from shock.

"At first I was in pain," she said. "But now I feel like stones have been thrown at me, and I simply must pick them up."

CRITICAL-THINKING QUESTIONS

1. How do patterns of AIDS in Africa differ from those in the United States?
2. What factors account for the high rate of HIV infection in Central Africa?
3. What lessons can people in the United States draw from the African AIDS epidemic?

62

The Metropolis and Mental Life

Georg Simmel

In this, one of his best-known essays, Simmel examines what might be called the "spiritual condition" of the modern world. His focus is the city, in which forces of modernity—including anonymity, a detached sophistication, and a preoccupation with commercial matters—are most clearly evident. Note that Simmel finds reason both to praise this new world and to warn of its ability to destroy our humanity.

The deepest problems of modern life derive from the claim of the individual to preserve the autonomy and individuality of his existence in the face of overwhelming social forces, of historical heritage, of external culture, and of the technique of life. The fight with nature which primitive man has to wage for his *bodily* existence attains in this modern form its latest transformation. The eighteenth century called upon man to free himself of all the historical bonds in the state and in religion, in morals and in economics. Man's nature, originally good and common to all, should develop unhampered. In addition to more liberty, the nineteenth century demanded the functional specialization of man and his work; this specialization makes one individual incomparable to another, and each of them indispensable to the highest possible extent. However, this specialization makes each man the more directly dependent upon the supplementary activities of all others. Nietzsche sees the full development of the individual conditioned by the most

SOURCE: *The Sociology of Georg Simmel,* trans. and ed. Kurt H. Wolff. Copyright © 1950, renewed 1978 by The Free Press. Reprinted with permission of The Free Press, Macmillan Publishing Company, a Member of Paramount Publishing.

ruthless struggle of individuals; socialism believes in the suppression of all competition for the same reason. Be that as it may, in all these positions the same basic motive is at work: The person resists to being leveled down and worn out by a social-technological mechanism. An inquiry into the inner meaning of specifically modern life and its products, into the soul of the cultural body, so to speak, must seek to solve the equation which structures like the metropolis set up between the individual and the superindividual contents of life. Such an inquiry must answer the question of how the personality accommodates itself in the adjustments to external forces. This will be my task today.

The psychological basis of the metropolitan type of individuality consists in the *intensification of nervous stimulation* which results from the swift and uninterrupted change of outer and inner stimuli. Man is a differentiating creature. His mind is stimulated by the difference between a momentary impression and the one which preceded it. Lasting impressions, impressions which differ only slightly from one another, impressions which take a regular and habitual course and show regular and habitual contrasts—all these use up, so to speak, less consciousness than does the rapid crowding of changing images, the sharp discontinuity in the grasp of a single glance, and the unexpectedness of onrushing impressions. These are the psychological conditions which the metropolis creates. With each crossing of the street, with the tempo and multiplicity of economic, occupational and social life, the city sets up a deep contrast with small town and rural life with reference to the sensory foundations of psychic life. The metropolis exacts from man as a discriminating creature a different amount of consciousness than does rural life. Here the rhythm of life and sensory mental imagery flows more slowly, more habitually, and more evenly. Precisely in this connection the sophisticated character of metropolitan psychic life becomes understandable—as over against small town life which rests more upon deeply felt and emotional relationships. These latter are rooted in the more unconscious layers of the psyche and

grow most readily in the steady rhythm of uninterrupted habituations. The intellect, however, has its locus in the transparent, conscious, higher layers of the psyche; it is the most adaptable of our inner forces. In order to accommodate to change and to the contrast of phenomena, the intellect does not require any shocks and inner upheavals; it is only through such upheavals that the more conservative mind could accommodate to the metropolitan rhythm of events. Thus the metropolitan type of man—which, of course, exists in a thousand individual variants—develops an organ protecting him against the threatening currents and discrepancies of his external environment which would uproot him. He reacts with his head instead of his heart. In this an increased awareness assumes the psychic prerogative. Metropolitan life, thus, underlies a heightened awareness and a predominance of intelligence in metropolitan man. The reaction to metropolitan phenomena is shifted to that organ which is least sensitive and quite remote from the depth of the personality. Intellectuality is thus seen to preserve subjective life against the overwhelming power of metropolitan life, and intellectuality branches out in many directions and is integrated with numerous discrete phenomena.

The metropolis has always been the seat of the money economy. Here the multiplicity and concentration of economic exchange gives an importance to the means of exchange which the scantiness of rural commerce would not have allowed. Money economy and the dominance of the intellect are intrinsically connected. They share a matter-of-fact attitude in dealing with men and with things; and, in this attitude, a formal justice is often coupled with an inconsiderate hardness. The intellectually sophisticated person is indifferent to all genuine individuality, because relationships and reactions result from it which cannot be exhausted with logical operations. In the same manner, the individuality of phenomena is not commensurate with the pecuniary principle. Money is concerned only with what is common to all: It asks for the exchange value, it reduces all quality and individuality to the question: How much? All intimate emotional relations between persons are founded in their individuality, whereas in rational relations man is reckoned with like a number, like an element which is in itself indifferent. Only the objective measurable achievement is of interest. Thus metropolitan man reckons with his merchants and customers, his domestic servants and often even with persons with whom he is obliged to have social intercourse. These features of intellectuality contrast with the nature of the small circle in which the inevitable knowledge of individuality as inevitably produces a warmer tone of behavior, a behavior which is beyond a mere objective balancing of service and return. In the sphere of the economic psychology of the small group it is of importance that under primitive conditions production serves the customer who orders the good, so that the producer and the consumer are acquainted. The modern metropolis, however, is supplied almost entirely by production for the market, that is, for entirely unknown purchasers who never personally enter the producer's actual field of vision. Through this anonymity the interests of each party acquire an unmerciful matter-of-factness; and the intellectually calculating economic egoisms of both parties need not fear any deflection because of the imponderables of personal relationships. The money economy dominates the metropolis; it has displaced the last survivals of domestic production and the direct barter of goods; it minimizes, from day to day, the amount of work ordered by customers. The matter-of-fact attitude is obviously so intimately interrelated with the money economy, which is dominant in the metropolis, that nobody can say whether the intellectualistic mentality first promoted the money economy or whether the latter determined the former. The metropolitan way of life is certainly the most fertile soil for this reciprocity, a point which I shall document merely by citing the dictum of the most eminent English constitutional historian: Throughout the whole course of English history, London has never acted as England's heart but often as England's intellect and always as her moneybag!

In certain seemingly insignificant traits, which lie upon the surface of life, the same psychic currents characteristically unite. Modern mind has become more and more calculating. The calculative exactness of practical life which the money economy has brought about corresponds to the ideal of natural science: to transform the world into an arithmetic problem, to fix every part of the world by mathematical formulas. Only money economy has filled the days of so many people with weighing, calculating, with numerical determinations, with a reduction of qualitative values to quantitative ones. Through the calculative nature of money a new precision, a certainty in the definition of identities and differences, an unambiguousness in agreements and arrangements has been brought about in the relations of life-elements—just as externally this precision has been effected by the universal diffusion of pocket watches. However, the conditions of metropolitan life are at once cause and effect of this trait. The relationships and affairs of the typical metropolitan usually are so varied and complex that without the strictest punctuality in promises and services the whole structure would break down into an inextricable chaos. Above all, this necessity is brought about by the aggregation of so many people with such differentiated interests, who must integrate their relations and activities into a highly complex organism. If all clocks and watches in Berlin would suddenly go wrong in different ways, even if only by one hour, all economic life and communication of the city would be disrupted for a long time. In addition an apparently mere external factor: long distances, would make all waiting and broken appointments result in an ill-afforded waste of time. Thus, the technique of metropolitan life is unimaginable without the most punctual integration of all activities and mutual relations into a stable and impersonal time schedule. Here again the general conclusions of this entire task of reflection become obvious, namely, that from each point on the surface of existence—however closely attached to the surface alone—one may drop a sounding into the depth of the psyche so that all the most banal externalities of life finally are connected with the ultimate decisions concerning the meaning and style of life.

Punctuality, calculability, exactness are forced upon life by the complexity and extension of metropolitan existence and are not only most intimately connected with its money economy and intellectualistic character. These traits must also color the contents of life and favor the exclusion of those irrational, instinctive, sovereign traits and impulses which aim at determining the mode of life from within, instead of receiving the general and precisely schematized form of life from without. . . .

The same factors which have thus coalesced into the exactness and minute precision of the form of life have coalesced into a structure of the highest impersonality; on the other hand, they have promoted a highly personal subjectivity. There is perhaps no psychic phenomenon which has been so unconditionally reserved to the metropolis as has the blasé attitude. The blasé attitude results first from the rapidly changing and closely compressed contrasting stimulations of the nerves. From this, the enhancement of metropolitan intellectuality, also, seems originally to stem. Therefore, stupid people who are not intellectually alive in the first place usually are not exactly blasé. A life in boundless pursuit of pleasure makes one blasé because it agitates the nerves to their strongest reactivity for such a long time that they finally cease to react at all. In the same way, through the rapidity and contradictoriness of their changes, more harmless impressions force such violent responses, tearing the nerves so brutally hither and thither that their last reserves of strength are spent; and if one remains in the same milieu they have no time to gather new strength. An incapacity thus emerges to react to new sensations with the appropriate energy. This constitutes that blasé attitude which, in fact, every metropolitan child shows when compared with children of quieter and less changeable milieus.

This physiological source of the metropolitan blasé attitude is joined by another source which flows from the money economy. The essence of the blasé attitude consists in the blunting of discrimination. This does not mean that the objects are not perceived, as is the case with the half-wit, but rather that the meaning and differing values of things, and thereby the things themselves, are experienced as insubstantial. They appear to the blasé person in an evenly flat and gray tone; no one object deserves preference over any other. This mood is the faithful subjective reflection of the completely internalized money economy. By being the equivalent to all the manifold things in one and the same way, money becomes the most frightful leveler. For money expresses all qualitative differences of things in terms of "how much?" Money, with all its colorlessness and indifference, becomes the common denominator of all values; irreparably it hollows out the core of things, their individuality, their specific value, and their incomparability. All things float with equal specific gravity in the constantly moving stream of money. All things lie on the same level and differ from one another only in the size of the area which they cover. In the individual case this coloration, or rather discoloration, of things through their money equivalence may be unnoticeably minute. However, through the relations of the rich to the objects to be had for money, perhaps even through the total character which the mentality of the contemporary public everywhere imparts to these objects, the exclusively pecuniary evaluation of objects has become quite considerable. The large cities, the main seats of the money exchange, bring the purchasability of things to the fore much more impressively than do smaller localities. That is why cities are also the genuine locale of the blasé attitude. In the blasé attitude the concentration of men and things stimulate the nervous system of the individual to its highest achievement so that it attains its peak. Through the mere quantitative intensification of the same conditioning factors this achievement is transformed into its opposite and appears in the peculiar adjustment of the blasé attitude. In this phenomenon the nerves find in the refusal to react to their stimulation the last possibility of accommodating to the contents and forms of metropolitan life. The self-preservation of certain personalities is brought at the price of devaluating the whole objective world, a devaluation which in the end unavoidably drags one's own personality down into a feeling of the same worthlessness.

Whereas the subject of this form of existence has to come to terms with it entirely for himself, his self-preservation in the face of the large city demands from him a no less negative behavior of a social nature. This mental attitude of metropolitans toward one another we may designate, from a formal point of view, as reserve. If so many inner reactions were responses to the continuous external contacts with innumerable people as are those in the small town, where one knows almost everybody one meets and where one has a positive relation to almost everyone, one would be completely atomized internally and come to an unimaginable psychic state. Partly this psychological fact, partly the right to distrust which men have in the face of the touch-and-go elements of metropolitan life, necessitates our reserve. As a result of this reserve we frequently do not even know by sight those who have been our neighbors for years. And it is this reserve which in the eyes of the small-town people makes us appear to be cold and heartless. Indeed, if I do not deceive myself, the inner aspect of this outer reserve is not only indifference but, more often than we are aware, it is a slight aversion, a mutual strangeness and repulsion, which will break into hatred and fight at the moment of a closer contact, however caused. The whole inner organization of such an extensive communicative life rests upon an extremely varied hierarchy of sympathies, indifferences, and aversions of the briefest as well as of the most permanent nature. The sphere of indifference in this hierarchy is not as large as might appear on the surface. Our psychic activity still responds to almost every impression of somebody else with a somewhat distinct feeling. The unconscious, fluid, and changing character of this impression seems to result in a state of indifference. Actually this indifference would be just as unnatural as the diffusion of indiscriminate mutual suggestion would be unbearable. From both these typical dangers of the metropolis, indifference and indiscriminate suggestibility, antipathy protects us. A latent antipathy and the preparatory stage of practical antagonism affect the distances and aversions without which this mode of life could not at all be led. The extent and the mixture of this style of life, the rhythm of its emergence and disappearance, the forms in which it is satisfied—all these, with the unifying motives in the narrower sense, form the inseparable whole of the metropolitan style of life. What appears in the metropolitan style of life directly as dissociation is in reality only one of its elemental forms of socialization.

This reserve with its overtone of hidden aversion appears in turn as the form or the cloak of a more general mental phenomenon of the metropolis: It grants to the individual a kind and an amount of personal freedom which has no analogy whatsoever under other conditions. The metropolis goes back to one of the large developmental tendencies of social life as such, to one of the few tendencies for which an approximately universal formula can be discovered. The earliest phase of social formations found in historical as well as in contemporary social structures is this: a relatively small circle firmly closed against neighboring, strange, or in some way antagonistic circles. However, this circle is closely coherent and allows its individual members only a narrow field for the development of unique qualities and free, self-responsible movements. Political and kinship groups, parties and religious associations begin in this way. The self-preservation of very young associations requires the establishment of strict boundaries and a centripetal unity. Therefore they cannot allow the individual freedom and unique inner and outer development. From this stage social development proceeds at once in two different, yet corresponding, directions. To the extent to which the group grows—numerically, spatially, in significance and in content of life—to the same degree the group's direct, inner unity loosens, and the rigidity of the original demarcation against others is softened through mutual relations and connections. At the same time, the individual gains freedom of movement, far beyond the first jealous delimitation. The individual also gains a specific individuality to which the division of labor in the enlarged group gives both occasion and necessity. . . .

It is not only the immediate size of the area and the number of persons which, because of the universal historical correlation between the enlargement of the circle and the personal inner and outer freedom, has made the metropolis the locale of freedom. It is rather in transcending this visible expanse that any given city becomes the seat of cosmopolitanism. The horizon of the city expands in a manner comparable to the way in which wealth develops; a certain amount of property increases in a quasi-automatical way in ever more rapid progression. As soon as a certain limit has been passed, the economic, personal, and intellectual relations of the citizenry, the sphere of intellectual predominance of the city over its hinterland, grow as in geometrical progression. Every gain in dynamic extension becomes a step, not for an equal, but for a new and larger extension. From every thread spinning out of the city, ever new threads grow as if by themselves, just as within the city the unearned increment of ground rent, through the mere increase in communication, brings the owner automatically increasing profits. At this point, the quantitative aspect of life is transformed directly into qualitative traits of character. The sphere of life of the small town is, in the main, self-contained and autarchic. For it is the decisive nature of the metropolis that its inner life overflows by waves into a far-flung national or international area. . . .

The most profound reason, however, why the metropolis conduces to the urge for the most individual personal existence—no matter whether justified and successful—appears to me to be the following: The development of modern culture is characterized by the preponderance of what one may call the "objective spirit" over the "subjective spirit." This is to say, in language as well as in law, in the technique of production as well as in art, in science as well as in the objects of the domestic environment, there is embodied a sum of spirit. The individual in his intellectual development follows the growth of this spirit very imperfectly and at an ever increasing distance. If, for instance, we view the immense culture which for the last hundred years has been embodied in things and in knowledge, in institutions and in comforts, and if we compare all this with the cultural progress of the individual during the same period—at least in high status groups—a frightful disproportion in growth between the two becomes evident. Indeed, at some points we notice a retrogression in the culture of the individual with reference to spirituality, delicacy, and idealism. This discrepancy results essentially from the growing division of labor. For the division of labor demands from the individual an ever more one-sided accomplishment, and the greatest advance in a one-sided pursuit only too frequently means dearth to the personality of the individual. In any case, he can cope less and less with the overgrowth of objective culture. The individual is reduced to a negligible quantity, perhaps less in his consciousness than in his practice and in the totality of his obscure emotional states that are derived from this practice. The individual has become a mere cog in an enormous organization of things and powers which tear from his hands all progress, spirituality, and value in order to transform them from their subjective form into the form of a purely objective life. It needs merely to be pointed out that the metropolis is the genuine arena of this culture which outgrows all personal life. Here in buildings and educational institutions, in the wonders and comforts of space-conquering technology, in the formations of community life, and in the visible institutions of the state, is offered such an overwhelming fullness of crystallized and impersonalized spirit that the personality, so to speak, cannot maintain itself under its impact. On the one hand, life is made infinitely easy for the personality in that stimulations, interests, uses of time, and consciousness are offered to it from all sides. They carry the person as if in a stream, and one needs hardly to swim for oneself. On the other hand, however, life is composed more and more of these impersonal contents and offerings which tend to displace the genuine personal colorations and incomparabilities. This results in the individual's summoning the utmost in uniqueness and particularization, in order to preserve his most personal core. He has to exaggerate this personal element in order to remain audible even to himself. . . .

CRITICAL-THINKING QUESTIONS

1. *In what respects does the metropolis symbolize modern society?*

2. *What does Simmel mean by suggesting that in modern cities, people experience an "intensification of nervous stimulation"? How do we react "with our heads instead of with our hearts"?*

3. *What does Simmel see as the achievements of modern urban life? What does he think has been lost in the process?*

63

Urbanism As a Way of Life

Louis Wirth

For many decades, sociologists in Europe and the United States have commented on the distinctive qualities of urban social life. In 1938, U.S. sociologist Louis Wirth integrated these various insights into a comprehensive theory of urbanism. Although it has been challenged and reformulated over the years, Wirth's theory remains probably the best-known sociological statement on urbanism.

A SOCIOLOGICAL DEFINITION OF THE CITY

Despite the preponderant significance of the city in our civilization, our knowledge of the nature of urbanism and the process of urbanization is meager, notwithstanding many attempts to isolate the distinguishing characteristics of urban life. Geographers, historians, economists, and political sci-

entists have incorporated the points of view of their respective disciplines into diverse definitions of the city. While in no sense intended to supersede these, the formulation of a sociological approach to the city may incidentally serve to call attention to the interrelations between them by emphasizing the peculiar characteristics of the city as a particular form of human association. A sociologically significant definition of the city seeks to select those elements of urbanism which mark it as a distinctive mode of human group life. . . .

For sociological purposes a city may be defined as a relatively large, dense, and permanent settlement of socially heterogeneous individuals. On the

SOURCE: "Urbanism as a Way of Life," by Louis Wirth in *American Journal of Sociology,* vol. 44, no. 1, July 1938, pp. 1–24.

basis of the postulates which this minimal definition suggests, a theory of urbanism may be formulated in the light of existing knowledge concerning social groups.

A THEORY OF URBANISM

Given a limited number of identifying characteristics of the city, I can better assay the consequences or further characteristics of them in the light of general sociological theory and empirical research. I hope in this manner to arrive at the essential propositions comprising a theory of urbanism. Some of these propositions can be supported by a considerable body of already available research materials; others may be accepted as hypotheses for which a certain amount of presumptive evidence exists, but for which more ample and exact verification would be required. At least such a procedure will, it is hoped, show what in the way of systematic knowledge of the city we now have and what are the crucial and fruitful hypotheses for future research.

The central problem of the sociologist of the city is to discover the forms of social action and organization that typically emerge in relatively permanent, compact settlements of large numbers of heterogeneous individuals. We must also infer that urbanism will assume its most characteristic and extreme form in the measure in which the conditions with which it is congruent are present. Thus the larger, the more densely populated, and the more heterogeneous a community, the more accentuated the characteristics associated with urbanism will be. . . .

Some justification may be in order for the choice of the principal terms comprising our definition of the city, a definition which ought to be as inclusive and at the same time as denotative as possible without unnecessary assumptions. To say that large numbers are necessary to constitute a city means, of course, large numbers in relation to a restricted area or high density of settlement. There are, nevertheless, good reasons for treating large numbers and density as separate factors, because each may be connected with significantly differ-

ent social consequences. Similarly the need for adding heterogeneity to numbers of population as a necessary and distinct criterion of urbanism might be questioned, since we should expect the range of differences to increase with numbers. In defense, it may be said that the city shows a kind and degree of heterogeneity of population which cannot be wholly accounted for by the law of large numbers or adequately represented by means of a normal distribution curve. Because the population of the city does not reproduce itself, it must recruit its migrants from other cities, the countryside, and—in the United States until recently—from other countries. The city has thus historically been the melting-pot of races, peoples, and cultures, and a most favorable breeding-ground of new biological and cultural hybrids. It has not only tolerated but rewarded individual differences. It has brought together people from the ends of the earth *because* they are different and thus useful to one another, rather than because they are homogeneous and like-minded.

A number of sociological propositions concerning the relationship between (a) numbers of population, (b) density of settlement, (c) heterogeneity of inhabitants and group life can be formulated on the basis of observation and research.

Size of the Population Aggregate. Ever since Aristotle's *Politics,* it has been recognized that increasing the number of inhabitants in a settlement beyond a certain limit will affect the relationships between them and the character of the city. Large numbers involve, as has been pointed out, a greater range of individual variation. Furthermore, the greater the number of individuals participating in a process of interaction, the greater is the *potential* differentiation between them. The personal traits, the occupations, the cultural life, and the ideas of the members of an urban community may, therefore, be expected to range between more widely separated poles than those of rural inhabitants.

That such variations should give rise to the spatial segregation of individuals according to color, ethnic heritage, economic and social status, tastes and preferences, may readily be inferred. The bonds of kinship, of neighborliness, and the sentiments arising out of living together for generations under a common folk tradition are likely to be absent or, at best, relatively weak in an aggregate the members of which have such diverse origins and backgrounds. Under such circumstances competition and formal control mechanisms furnish the substitutes for the bonds of solidarity that are relied upon to hold a folk society together.

Increase in the number of inhabitants of a community beyond a few hundred is bound to limit the possibility of each member of the community knowing all the others personally. Max Weber, in recognizing the social significance of this fact, explained that from a sociological point of view large numbers of inhabitants and density of settlement mean a lack of that mutual acquaintanceship which ordinarily inheres between the inhabitants in a neighborhood.[1] The increase in numbers thus involves a changed character of the social relationships. As Georg Simmel points out: "[If] the unceasing external contact of numbers of persons in the city should be met by the same number of inner reactions as in the small town, in which one knows almost every person he meets and to each of whom he has a positive relationship, one would be completely atomized internally and would fall into an unthinkable mental condition."[2] The multiplication of persons in a state of interaction under conditions which make their contact as full personalities impossible produces that segmentalization of human relationships which has sometimes been seized upon by students of the mental life of the cities as an explanation for the "schizoid" character of urban personality. This is not to say that the urban inhabitants have fewer acquaintances than rural inhabitants, for the reverse may actually be true; it means rather that in relation to the number of people whom they see and with whom they rub elbows in the course of daily life, they know a smaller proportion, and of these they have less intensive knowledge.

Characteristically, urbanites meet one another in highly segmental roles. They are, to be sure, dependent upon more people for the satisfactions of their life-needs than are rural people and thus are associated with a greater number of organized groups, but they are less dependent upon particular persons, and their dependence upon others is confined to a highly fractionalized aspect of the other's round of activity. This is essentially what is meant by saying that the city is characterized by secondary rather than primary contacts. The contacts of the city may indeed be face to face, but they are nevertheless impersonal, superficial, transitory, and segmental. The reserve, the indifference, and the blasé outlook which urbanites manifest in their relationships may thus be regarded as devices for immunizing themselves against the personal claims and expectations of others.

The superficiality, the anonymity, and the transitory character of urban social relations make intelligible, also, the sophistication and the rationality generally ascribed to city-dwellers. Our acquaintances tend to stand in a relationship of utility to us in the sense that the role which each one plays in our life is overwhelmingly regarded as a means for the achievement of our own ends. Whereas the individual gains, on the one hand, a certain degree of emancipation or freedom from the personal and emotional controls of intimate groups, he loses, on the other hand, the spontaneous self-expression, the morale, and the sense of participation that comes with living in an integrated society. This constitutes essentially the state of *anomie,* or the social void, to which Durkheim alludes in attempting to account for the various forms of social disorganization in technological society.

The segmental character and utilitarian accent of interpersonal relations in the city find their institutional expression in the proliferation of specialized tasks which we see in their most developed form in the professions. The operations of the pecuniary nexus lead to predatory relationships, which tend to obstruct the efficient functioning of the social order unless checked by professional codes and occupational etiquette. The premium put upon utility and efficiency suggests the adaptability of the corporate device for the organization of enterprises in which individuals can engage only in groups. The advantage that the corporation has over the individual entrepreneur and the partnership in the urban-industrial world derives not only from the possibility it affords of centralizing the resources of thousands of individuals or from the legal privilege of limited liability and perpetual succession, but from the fact that the corporation has no soul.

The specialization of individuals, particularly in their occupations, can proceed only, as Adam Smith pointed out, upon the basis of an enlarged market, which in turn accentuates the division of labor. This enlarged market is only in part supplied by the city's hinterland; in large measure it is found among the large numbers that the city itself contains. The dominance of the city over the surrounding hinterland becomes explicable in terms of the division of labor which urban life occasions and promotes. The extreme degree of interdependence and the unstable equilibrium of urban life are closely associated with the division of labor and the specialization of occupations. This interdependence and this instability are increased by the tendency of each city to specialize in those functions in which it has the greatest advantage.

In a community composed of a larger number of individuals than can know one another intimately and can be assembled in one spot, it becomes necessary to communicate through indirect media and to articulate individual interests by a process of delegation. Typically in the city, interests are made effective through representation. The individual counts for little, but the voice of the representative is heard with a deference roughly proportional to the numbers for whom he speaks.

While this characterization of urbanism, in so far as it derives from large numbers, does not by any means exhaust the sociological inferences that might be drawn from our knowledge of the relationship of the size of a group to the characteristic behavior of the members, for the sake of brevity the assertions made may serve to exemplify the sort of propositions that might be developed.

Density. As in the case of numbers, so in the case of concentration in limited space certain consequences of relevance in sociological analysis of the city emerge. Of these only a few can be indicated.

As Darwin pointed out for flora and fauna and as Durkheim noted in the case of human societies,[3] an increase in numbers when area is held constant (i.e., an increase in density) tends to produce differentiation and specialization, since only in this way can the area support increased numbers. Density thus reinforces the effect of numbers in diversifying men and their activities and in increasing the complexity of the social structure.

On the subjective side, as Simmel has suggested, the close physical contact of numerous individuals necessarily produces a shift in the media through which we orient ourselves to the urban milieu, especially to our fellow-men. Typically, our physical contacts are close but our social contacts are distant. The urban world puts a premium on visual recognition. We see the uniform which denotes the role of the functionaries, and are oblivious to the personal eccentricities hidden behind the uniform. We tend to acquire and develop a sensitivity to a world of artifacts, and become progressively farther removed from the world of nature.

We are exposed to glaring contrasts between splendor and squalor, between riches and poverty, intelligence and ignorance, order and chaos. The competition for space is great, so that each area generally tends to be put to the use which yields the greatest economic return. Place of work tends to become dissociated from place of residence, for the proximity of industrial and commercial establishments makes an area both economically and socially undesirable for residential purposes.

Density, land values, rentals, accessibility, healthfulness, prestige, aesthetic consideration, absence of nuisances such as noise, smoke, and dirt determine the desirability of various areas of the city as places of settlement for different sections of the population. Place and nature of work, income, racial and ethnic characteristics, social status, custom, habit, taste, preference, and prejudice are among the significant factors in accordance with which the urban population is selected and distributed into more or less distinct settlements. Diverse population elements inhabiting a compact settlement thus become segregated from one another in the degree in which their requirements and modes of life are incompatible and in the measure in which they are antagonistic. Similarly, persons of homogeneous status and needs unwittingly drift into, consciously select, or are forced by circumstances into the same area. The different parts of the city acquire specialized functions, and the city consequently comes to resemble a mosaic of social worlds in which the transition from one to the other is abrupt. The juxtaposition of divergent personalities and modes of life tends to produce a relativistic perspective and a sense of toleration of differences which may be regarded as prerequisites for rationality and which lead toward the secularization of life.[4]

The close living together and working together of individuals who have no sentimental and emotional ties foster a spirit of competition, aggrandizement, and mutual exploitation. Formal controls are instituted to counteract irresponsibility and potential disorder. Without rigid adherence to predictable routines a large compact society would scarcely be able to maintain itself. The clock and the traffic signal are symbolic of the basis of our social order in the urban world. Frequent close physical contact, coupled with great social distance, accentuates the reserve of unattached individuals toward one another and, unless compensated by other opportunities for response, gives rise to loneliness. The necessary frequent movement of great numbers of individuals in a congested habitat causes friction and irritation. Nervous tensions which derive from such personal frustrations are increased by the rapid tempo and the complicated technology under which life in dense areas must be lived.

Heterogeneity. The social interaction among such a variety of personality types in the urban milieu tends to break down the rigidity of caste lines and to complicate the class structure; it thus induces a more ramified and differentiated framework of social stratification than is found in more integrated societies. The heightened mobility of the individual, which brings him within the range of stimulation by a great number of diverse individuals and subjects him to fluctuating status in the differentiated social groups that compose the social structure of the city, brings him toward the acceptance of instability and insecurity in the world at large as a norm. This fact helps to account, too, for the sophistication and cosmopolitanism of the urbanite. No single group has the undivided allegiance of the individual. The groups with which he is affiliated do not lend themselves readily to a simple hierarchical arrangement. By virtue of his different interests arising out of different aspects of social life, the individual acquires membership in widely divergent groups, each of which functions only with reference to a single segment of his personality. Nor do these groups easily permit of a concentric arrangement so that the narrower ones fall within the circumference of the more inclusive ones, as is more likely to be the case in the rural community or in primitive societies. Rather the groups with which the person typically is affiliated are tangential to each other or intersect in highly variable fashion.

Partly as a result of the physical footlooseness of the population and partly as a result of their social mobility, the turnover in group membership generally is rapid. Place of residence, place and character of employment, income, and interests fluctuate, and the task of holding organizations together and maintaining and promoting intimate and lasting acquaintanceship between the members is difficult. This applies strikingly to the local areas within the city into which persons become segregated more by virtue of differences in race, language, income, and social status than through choice or positive attraction to people like themselves. Overwhelmingly the city-dweller is not a home-owner, and since a transitory habitat does not generate binding traditions and sentiments, only rarely is he a true neighbor. There is little opportunity for the individual to obtain a conception of the city as a whole or to survey his place in the total scheme. Consequently he finds it difficult to determine what is to his own "best interests" and to decide between the issues and leaders presented to him by the agencies of mass suggestion. Individuals who are thus detached from the organized bodies which integrate society comprise the fluid masses that make collective behavior in the urban community so unpredictable and hence so problematical.

Although the city, through the recruitment of variant types to perform its diverse tasks and the accentuation of their uniqueness through competition and the premium upon eccentricity, novelty, efficient performance, and inventiveness, produces a highly differentiated population, it also exercises a leveling influence. Wherever large numbers of differently constituted individuals congregate, the process of depersonalization also enters. This leveling tendency inheres in part in the economic basis of the city. The development of large cities, at least in the modern age, was largely dependent upon the concentrative force of steam. The rise of the factory made possible mass production for an impersonal market. The fullest exploitation of the possibilities of the division of labor and mass production, however, is possible only with standardization of processes and products. A money economy goes hand in hand with such a system of production. Progressively as cities have developed upon a background of this system of production, the pecuniary nexus which implies the purchasability of services and things has displaced personal relations as the basis of association. Individuality under these circumstances must be replaced by categories. When large numbers have to make common use of facilities and institutions, those facilities and institutions must serve the needs of the average person rather than those of particular individuals. The services of the public utilities, of the recreational, educational, and cultural institutions, must be adjusted to mass requirements. Similarly, the cultural institutions, such as the schools, the movies, the radio, and the newspapers, by virtue of their mass clientele, must necessarily operate as leveling influences. The political process as it appears in urban life could not

be understood unless one examined the mass appeals made through modern propaganda techniques. If the individual would participate at all in the social, political, and economic life of the city, he must subordinate some of his individuality to the demands of the larger community and in that measure immerse himself in mass movements. . . .

On the basis of the three variables, number, density of settlement, and degree of heterogeneity, of the urban population, it appears possible to explain the characteristics of urban life and to account for the differences between cities of various sizes and types. . . .

CRITICAL-THINKING QUESTIONS

1. What basic issue should a sociological theory of urbanism address? Why is Wirth's approach to studying urbanism also termed "ecological"?
2. How does Wirth define a city? How do the three defining factors give rise to an urban way of life?
3. According to Wirth, what are the qualities of social relationships in cities? What moral consequences seem to follow?

NOTES

1. *Wirtschaft und Gesellschaft* (Tübingen, 1925), part I, chap. 8, p. 514.

2. "Die Grossstädte und das Geistesleben," *Die Grossstadt,* ed. Theodor Petermann (Dresden, 1903), pp. 187–206.

3. E. Durkheim, *De la division du travail social* (Paris, 1932), p. 248.

4. The extent to which the segregation of the population into distinct ecological and cultural areas and the resulting social attitude of tolerance, rationality, and secular mentality are functions of density as distinguished from heterogeneity is difficult to determine. Most likely we are dealing here with phenomena which are consequences of the simultaneous operation of both factors.

64

The Urban Real Estate Game: Traditional and Critical Perspectives

Joe R. Feagin and Robert Parker

Feagin and Parker argue that traditional urban sociology has emphasized demographic and technological dimensions of city growth, while accepting the validity of classical economics' market model. Traditionalists explain the growth and change of cities in terms of various demands made by countless urban consumers. A newer, critical perspective sees the process of urban development as dominated by powerful economic interests—industrial executives, developers, and politicians sympathetic to their aims. The authors condemn the traditional model and argue the virtues of the critical approach.

INTRODUCTION

Locating new factories. Relocating offices. Buying hotels. Building office towers. Mortgaging whole streets of houses. Buying and selling utility companies. Bulldozing apartment buildings for office construction. Purchasing large blocks of urban land to secure a land monopoly. Going bankrupt

SOURCE: "Building American Cities: Traditional and Critical Perspectives," by Joe R. Feagin and Robert Parker, in *Building American Cities: The Urban Real Estate Game,* 2d ed., pp. 1–13, 16–17, 22, 23, 30–31. Copyright © 1990 by Prentice Hall, Englewood Cliffs, NJ. Reprinted with permission.

because of overextension in real estate. These actions are part of the real estate game played in every American city. The only place most Americans are able to play anything analogous to this is on the *Monopoly* game board in living-room encounters with their friends. The board game mimics the real world of real estate buying, selling, and development, but the parallels between playing *Monopoly* on the board and playing the real estate game in cities are limited, for in the everyday world of urban development and decline there are real winners and real losers.

In U.S. cities the powerful elites controlling much development—the industrial executives, developers, bankers, and their political allies—have built major development projects, not just the hotels and houses of the *Monopoly* game, but also shopping malls, office towers, and the like. They typically build with little input from local community residents. Executives heading industrial firms and real estate developers have frequently been able to win a string of favorable concessions from city officials: cheap land, industrial parks, tax decreases, and utility services subsidized by rank-and-file taxpayers. In many cities these industrial executives and developers threaten to go elsewhere if these governmental subsidies are not provided. Yet in the 1970s and 1980s some citizen groups . . . tried to change this way of doing city business. Periodically, the voters in cities, from Santa Monica and Berkeley on the West Coast, to Cleveland in the Midwest, to Burlington and Hartford on the East Coast, vote out pro-development political officials in favor of candidates more tuned to slow growth and enhancing the local quality of life. For instance, in the 1980s the residents of Santa Monica, California, voted out a city council allied with landlords, developers, and bankers. They elected in their place a progressive council determined to break with the developer-oriented dominance of city politics. The new council has rejected policies favoring developers and has used a policy called "linked development" to force those developers building new office complexes and shopping centers to take action to meet important local needs. One Santa Monica city council agreement with a developer building a million-square-foot hotel-office complex specified that he must include landscaped park areas, a day-care center, energy conservation measures, and a positive plan for hiring minority workers.[1]

Who Decides on Development?

Some powerful developers, bankers, and other development decision makers are becoming known to the public. There is, for example, Gerald D. Hines, a Houston mechanical engineer whose $200 million estimated net worth was just under the amount necessary to be listed among the nation's 400 richest people by *Forbes* in 1987.[2] Still, Gerald D. Hines Interests of Houston, one of the largest U.S. development firms, controlled buildings worth more than $4.5 billion. In the early 1980s Hines celebrated the laying of the foundation of a Republic Bank office complex in Houston with a lavish $35,000 reception for top business and government leaders; it included a brass ensemble playing fanfares, fine wine and cheeses, and other culinary delights. The massive building itself, red granite in a neo-Gothic style, is just one of more than 360 such office buildings, shopping malls, and other urban projects that have been built by Hines' company in cities from New York to San Francisco.

Residential developers have also shaped U.S. cities in fundamental ways. The famous firm Levitt and Sons is among the 2 percent of developer-builders that have constructed the lion's share of U.S. residential housing since World War II. Using nonunion labor, Levitt and Sons pulled together in one corporation the various aspects of the house manufacturing and marketing process, from controlling the source of nails and lumber to marketing the finished houses. After World War II, Levittowns—names now synonymous with suburbs—were built in cities on the East Coast. One subdivision, Levittown, New Jersey, was carefully planned so that the acreage was within one political jurisdiction. According to Herbert Gans, the company executives had the boundaries of a nearby township changed so that it was not part of the area in which this Levittown would be built, thus giving Levitt and Sons more political control. William Levitt was the key figure in this development firm for decades, and he reportedly built his suburbs with little concern for the expressed tastes of his potential customers; Levitt was not especially "concerned about how to satisfy buyers and meet their aspirations. As the most successful builder in the East . . . he felt he knew what they wanted."[3] Profitability was the basic standard; community-oriented features were accepted when they enhanced profit. No surveys of potential buyers were made to determine consumer preferences, but a great deal of attention was given to advertising, marketing, and selling the houses to consumers. Friendly salespeople were selected and trained by a professional speech teacher. Buyers who were viewed as "disreputable" were excluded; and blacks were excluded until the state government began to enforce a desegregation law.[4]

Developers such as Hines and Levitt and Sons have been a major force in making and remaking the face of American cities. They are key figures in shaping city diversity and decentralization. Since World War II, U.S. cities have exploded horizontally and vertically with thousands of large-scale developments—shopping centers, office towers, business parks, multiple-use projects, convention centers, and residential subdivisions. The "built environments" of our cities have expanded to the point that their growing, and dying, pains have become serious national problems. Trillions of dollars have been invested in tearing down, constructing, and servicing the many and diverse physical structures scattered across hundreds of urban landscapes. For large development projects to be completed in downtown or outlying areas of cities, older buildings are often leveled, even when local citizens oppose such development. The major U.S. developers often see their projects as the "cutting-edge of western civilization." Yet these massive expenditures of capital for large-scale urban development, for lavish towers and the parties celebrating them, are made in cities with severe urban problems—extreme poverty, housing shortages, severe pollution—for whose solution little money allegedly can be found.[5]

Cities are not chance creations; rather, they are human developments. They reflect human choices and decisions. But exactly who decides that our cities should be developed the way they are? Who chooses corporate locations? Who calculates that sprawling suburbs are the best way to house urbanites? Who decides to put workers in glassed-in office towers? Who determines that shopping is best done in centralized shopping centers? Who creates the complex mazes of buildings, highways, and open spaces? There is an old saying that "God

made the country, but man made the town." Cities are indeed human-engineered environments. But which men and women made the cities? And what determines how they shape our cities?

GROWTH AND DECLINE OF CITIES: TRADITIONAL SOCIAL SCIENCE PERSPECTIVES

The Traditional Approach: The Market Knows Best

Examination of urban development and decline has been dominated by a conflict between the market-centered approaches of traditional social scientists and the newer critical analyses developed in recent decades. Traditional social scientists have dominated research and writing about American cities. Beginning in the 1920s and 1930s, there was a major spurt of activity in urban sociology and ecology at the University of Chicago, where researchers such as Robert Park and Ernest W. Burgess drew on the nineteenth-century social philosopher Herbert Spencer to develop their concept of city life, organization, and development; they viewed the individual and group competition in markets in metropolitan areas as resulting in "natural" regularities in land-use patterns and population distributions—and thus in an urban ecological or geographical map of concentric zones of land use, moving out from a central business district zone, with its office buildings, to an outlying commuter zone, with residential subdivisions.[6]

Much urban research between the 1940s and the 1970s established the dominance of the traditional market-centered paradigm in urban sociology, geography, economics, political science, and other social science disciplines. Largely abandoning the concern of the earlier social scientists with urban space and land-use zones, sociological, economic, and geographical researchers have for the most part accented demographic analysis and have typically focused on population trends such as migration flows, suburbanization, and other deconcentration, and on statistical distributions of urban and rural populations in examining modern urban development. Writing in the *Handbook of Sociology,* the urban analysts Kasarda and Frisbie review mainstream research and a small portion of the newer critical research, but they explicitly regard the ecological approach in sociology, geography, and economics as the "dominant (and arguably, the only) general theory of urban form" that has been tested by empirical verification.[7] Books such as Berry and Kasarda's *Contemporary Urban Ecology,* Micklin and Choldin's *Sociological Human Ecology,* and textbooks like Choldin's *Cities and Suburbs* have been influential in establishing a conventional perspective accenting the role of a competitive market in urban development and emphasizing market-centered city growth as beneficial to all urban interest groups. The political scientists in this tradition have also given attention to capitalism-generated growth and the role of the market in city development; they alone have given much attention to the importance of government in urban development. However, their view of government typically accents a pluralism of competing interest groups and an array of government officials acting for the general welfare, a perspective that, as we will discuss, is rather limited.[8]

Consumers and Workers as Dominant

Conventional social scientists have accepted uncritically the workings of the dominant market and the processes of capital accumulation. This perspective on competitive urban markets is grounded in neoclassical economic theory; it sees urban society as the "algebraic sum of the individuals . . . the sum of the interests of individuals."[9] In this view, given a "free-market" system, urban consumers and business firms will freely buy and sell. "If consumers want certain goods they will demand them. Businessmen will sense this demand through the marketplace and seek to satisfy the consumers' wishes. Everyone is happy."[10] Urban sociologist John Kasarda has written of profit-seeking entrepreneurs operating in self-regulating markets as a wise guiding force in city development.[11] Similarly,

economists Bradbury, Downs, and Small, reviewing problems of city decline, argue that "market forces are extremely powerful; so it would be folly to try [governmental] policies that ignored their constructive roles in guiding the form and structure of economic change."[12] From this perspective capitalists follow the profit logic of capital investments that seeks out "good business climates" (low taxes and pro-business governments) in certain cities, such as those in the South. This conventional view implies that whatever exists as the economics and geography of the urban landscape today is fundamentally good for all concerned, if it has resulted from competitive market activity. The rather utopian competitive market idea, Lewis Mumford has suggested, was taken over from earlier theologians: "the belief that a divine providence ruled over economic activity and ensured, so long as man did not presumptuously interfere, the maximum public good through the dispersed and unregulated efforts of every private, self-seeking individual."[13]

Imbedded in this common market assumption is the idea that individual workers and consumers are often more important than corporate decision makers in shaping urban patterns, because the capitalists mostly react to the demands of consumers. A study of the U.S. business creed accented this point: "One way of shedding awkward responsibility is to believe that the consumer is the real boss."[14] Such analysts accept the business view of individual consumers and workers as "voting" in the marketplace with their consumer choices: Cities are viewed as having been created by average Americans whose demands for such things as autos and single-family houses have forced developers, builders, and industrial executives to respond. Consumers are often termed "kings" and "queens" when it comes to urban development. For decades not only urban scholars but also business leaders have argued that through their consumption choices "the masses of Americans have elected Henry Ford. They have elected General Motors. They have elected the General Electric Company, and Woolworth's and all the other great industrial and business leaders of the day."[15]

One assumption in much traditional urban research is that no one individual or small group of individuals has a determinate influence on patterns of urban land uses, building, and development. Mainstream sociologists and land economists such as William Alonso and Richard Muth have argued that urban commercial and residential land markets are determined by free competitive bidding. According to these theories, thousands of consumers, and thousands of firms, are pictured as autonomous atoms competing in a market system, largely without noneconomic (for example, political) relations and conventions, atoms that have a "taste" for commodities such as more space and housing. As their incomes grow, they will seek more space. Conventional analysts offer this as an explanation of why cities grow, expand, or die. Actors in this competitive bidding are recognized as having different interests, even different incomes, which affect the bidding process. However, the fact that a small group of the most powerful decision makers (such as major developers) can do far more to shape the land and building markets than simply outbid their competitors is not seriously analyzed. And the negative consequences of market-generated growth (for example, water pollution from sewer crises) in these same cities are seldom discussed.[16]

David L. Birch, Director of the Massachusetts Institute of Technology's Program on Neighborhood and Regional Change, has offered a worker-driven theory in explaining why many cities have had too much office space. Birch argues that the story of the current high vacancy rates in office buildings in many U.S. cities began decades ago when the "war babies" began to enter the labor force. This movement into the labor force caused a huge increase in employment. Birch argues that both sexes decided they did not want to work in factories. Rather, they "wanted to work in offices. They wanted to join the service economy, wear white shirts, and become managers or clerks."[17] According to this line of reasoning, there was only one thing for developers and builders to do; in order to satisfy this new generation of workers and consumers, "we built them offices." Yet the power of workers and consumers in shaping the urban office landscape has never been as profound as Birch and others describe. Indeed, it is the industrialists, investors, developers, bankers, and their associates who have the capital to invest in job creation and to build office buildings and other workplaces—in places they decide upon and in terms of their corporate restructuring and profit needs.

Accenting Technology and Downplaying Inequality

Traditional social scientists often view the complexity of cities as largely determined by historical changes in transportation and communication technologies, whose economic contexts, histories, and alternatives are not reviewed. Changes in urban form are explained in terms of technological transformation, including shifts in water, rail, and automotive transport systems, without reference to the decisions of powerful decision makers such as investors and top government officials. Waterborne commerce favors port and river cities, while auto, train, and truck technologies facilitate the location of cities apart from water systems. In an opening essay for a 1985 book *The New Urban Reality,* Paul Peterson views technological innovations as independent forces giving "urban development its rate and direction."[18] And in the influential book *Urban Society,* mainstream ecological researcher Amos Hawley looked at the relocation of industry from the industrial heartland to outlying areas and explained this decentralization substantially in terms of technological changes in transport and in communication.[19] Transport and communication technologies are certainly important in urban centralization and decentralization. But the corporate history and capitalistic decision-making *context* that led to the dominance of, for example, automobiles—and not mass transit—in the U.S. transport system should be more carefully examined. . . .

Some Major Omissions

Missing from most traditional research on cities is a major discussion of such major factors in urban development as capital investment decisions, power and resource inequality, class and class conflict, and government subsidy programs. The aforementioned collection, *The New Urban Reality,* has important essays by prominent geographers, economists, political scientists, and sociologists on urban racial demography and the black underclass, but there is no significant discussion of capital investment decisions made by investors and developers and the consequences of these decisions for urban development. Moreover, in the recent summary volume *Sociological Human Ecology,* prominent ecologists and demographers have reviewed the question of how humans survive in changing social environments, including cities, but without discussing inequality, power, conflict, or the role of governments.[20] Traditional urban scholars such as the geographer Berry and the sociologist Kasarda briefly note that in market-directed societies the role of government has been primarily "limited to combating crises that threaten the societal mainstream," that government involvement tends to be incremental, and that state government dealing with the "social consequences of laissez-faire urbanization" are "ineffective in most cases."[21] In his influential urban textbook, *Urban Society,* sociologist Amos Hawley has devoted little space to the government role in city growth and decline. This neglect of the role of government has been most common among mainstream urban sociologists, geographers, and economists. As we will see, the mainstream political scientists among contemporary urban researchers have given more attention to government, but generally with a pluralistic emphasis.[22]

An Important Government Report

However, the federal government has used this traditional urban research for policy purposes. In the 1980s a major federal government report, *Urban America in the Eighties,* publicly articulated the traditional urban perspective for the general public. Prepared by the President's Commission for a National Agenda for the Eighties, this report called on the federal government to refrain from assisting the troubled northern cities. Free-enterprise markets are viewed as driving the basically healthy changes in urban development. And these markets know best. The *Urban America* report's strong conclusions were publicly debated—particularly those suggesting that the federal government should neglect dying northern cities and should, at most, assist workers in leaving Frostbelt cities for the then-booming cities of the Sunbelt. Some northern mayors protested the report's conclusions, but many Sunbelt mayors were enthusiastic. While northern officials were concerned about the report's conclusions, few publicly disputed the report's basic assumptions about how cities grow or die.[23]

This market-knows-best view of the Frostbelt-Sunbelt shift in capital investment and of urban growth more generally drew on the work of traditional urban researchers. Prepared under the direction of prominent business leaders, this report conveys the view of cities found in mainstream urban research: that cities are "less conscious creations" than "accumulations—the products of ongoing change." Again, choices by hundreds of thousands of individual consumers and workers are emphasized as the fundamental determinants of urban landscapes. Changes in cities, such as the then-increasing prosperity of many Sunbelt cities, reflect "nothing more than an aggregate of countless choices by and actions of individuals, families, and firms."[24] The urban land and building market is again viewed as self-regulating; according to this theory the market efficiently allocates land uses and maximizes the benefits for everyone living in the cities. The hidden hand of the market receives heavy emphasis in this conventional accounting. In the policy-oriented conclusions, the authors of *Urban America* pursued this market logic to its obvious conclusion: Those impersonal individuals and firms actively working in cities and shaping urban space know best, and government officials should thus not intervene when impersonal decisions lead to the decline of cities in the North. Growth in, and migration to, booming cities such as those in the Sunbelt should simply be recognized, and, at most, governments should encourage workers to move from dying cities to booming cities.

GROWTH AND DECLINE OF CITIES: THE CRITICAL URBAN PERSPECTIVE

Basic Themes in the New Approach

Since the 1970s the dominance of the mainstream urban research in the United States has been challenged by a critical urban perspective, called by some the "new urban sociology." Both European and American researchers have developed a critical urban paradigm grounded in concepts of capital investment flows, class and inequality, activist governments, and powerful business elites. European researchers such as Henri Lefebvre, Manuel Castells, and David Harvey had developed critiques of the traditional urban approaches by the late 1960s and early 1970s.[25] This European influence was soon felt in U.S. urban studies. By the late 1970s critical urban studies were pursued and published by Michael Peter Smith, Mark Gottdiener, Allen Scott, John Mollenkopf, Norman and Susan Fainstein, Richard Child Hill, Ed Soja, Michael Dear, Richard Walker, Allen Whitt, Todd Swanstrom, and Harvey Molotch, to mention just a few of the growing number of critical social scientists in the United States.[26] The critical urban approach accents issues neglected in most traditional sociological, economic, and political science analysis. While there is still much ferment and debate among contributors to the critical urban perspective, there is some consensus on three fundamental themes.

The first major theme is that city growth and decline, internal city patterns, and city centralization and decentralization are shaped by both economic factors and political factors. Although some critical scholars accent the economic over the political, and others the political over the economic, in this book we will focus on both the economic and political factors. In [Figure 64-1] we show the economic and political influences on cities, as well as the interaction between these economic and political influences. Most Western cities are shaped by capitalistic investments in production, workers, workplaces, land, and buildings. These urban societies are organized along class (also race and gender) lines; and their social institutions are substantially shaped by the commodity production and capital investment processes. Capital investment is centered in corporations calculating profit at the firm level; this can result in major urban social costs associated with the rapid inflow of capital investment and accompanying growth and also with capital outflow (disinvestment) and accompanying urban decline. But [Figure 64-1] indicates that there are governmental (state) factors in urban growth, structuring, and decline as well. Governments protect the right to own and dispose of privately held property as owners see fit. Moreover, governments in capitalistic societies are often linked to business elites and the investment process; various levels of government play a part in fostering corporate profit making. But government officials also react to citizen protests, to class, race, and community-based struggles; as a result, they often try to cope with the costs of capitalist-generated growth and decline. In addition, in cities with relatively independent political organizations (for example, "machines"), politicians may develop interests of their own and work *independently* of individual capitalists and citizen groups to shape and alter cities. In the urban worlds there is much interaction between the political and economic structures and political and economic decision makers.

A second important theme to be found in many

FIGURE 64-1

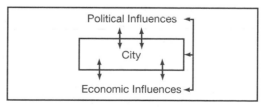

Capital's Global Investment Space

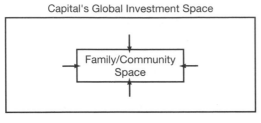

FIGURE 64-2

critical urban arguments has to do with the central role of *space*. Some critical scholars only implicitly touch on spatial issues, while others feature the spatial dimension at the center of their city analysis. As [Figure 64-2] is designed to illustrate, we human beings live not only economic and political lives as workers affected by investments in markets and voters affected by political advertising, but also lives as occupiers of space, in households and families living in the home and neighborhood spaces of our cities. On the one side, we have the group of profit-oriented industrialists, developers, bankers, and landowners who buy, sell, and develop land and buildings just as they do with other for-profit commodities. *Exchange value*, the value (price) of commodities exchanged in markets, is usually the dominant concern in their decisions about buying and selling land and buildings. The investment actions of developers and others seeking to profit off the sale of, and construction on, land are centered in exchange-value considerations. On the other side, we have the group of American tenants and homeowners, low-income and middle-income, black and white, who are usually much more concerned with the *use value* of space, of home and neighborhood, than with the exchange value.

Corporate exchange-value decisions frequently come into conflict with the use-value concerns of many Americans. A concern with use value can mean that the utility of space, land, and building for everyday life, for family life, and for neighborhood life is much more important than land or building profitability. Such use-value concerns are behind the actions of neighborhood residents who

have fought against numerous office buildings, malls, and redevelopment projects in order to keep them from intruding on their home and neighborhood spaces. Some zoning and other government land-use controls have thrown up barriers to the unrestrained expansion of capitalistic investment. Historically, much pressure for land-use regulation has come from worker-homeowners concerned with protecting family spaces and neighborhoods against industrial and commercial encroachment.[27]

Capitalist investors operate today in a worldwide investment space, so they may move factory and office jobs (or real estate capital) quickly from one city or country to another. However, workers and consumers generally spend their lives in more constricted family and home spaces. They often invest their lives in particular communities and cities and cannot move so easily to a city in another region or country, so they suffer when investors relocate quickly to other areas on the globe. Capital accumulation, capital investment, and the capitalistic class structure interact with space to generate urban and rural spatial patterns of production, distribution, and consumption. The aforementioned competition of local urban politicians for capital investments by corporate actors had not only job and construction effects, but also effects on the livability of local urban space. Uneven economic development also means uneven spatial development. Some places, homes and neighborhoods, stay viable and livable, while other urban communities become difficult to live in because of capital flight to other places across the nation or the globe.

A third basic theme in the new critical perspective is that of *structure* and *agency*, which is suggested in [Figure 64-3]. While most critical scholars tend to accent either structure (for example, institutions) or agency (for example, decision makers) in research on urban development, a number of scholars such as Lefebvre, Gottdiener, and Giddens, have called for research giving more attention to *both* dimensions. Some focus on the concrete actors involved in making cities, such as developers and business elites or citizens protesting development, while others prefer to emphasize

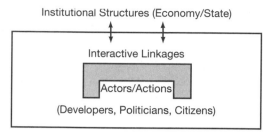

Institutional Structures (Economy/State)

Interactive Linkages

Actors/Actions

(Developers, Politicians, Citizens)

FIGURE 64-3

the complex web of institutions and structures, such as state bureaucracies and capital investment circuits. . . . Economic systems and governments do not develop out of an inevitable and unalterable structural necessity, but rather in a contingent manner; they result from the conscious actions taken by individual decision makers in various class, race, gender, and community-based groups, acting under particular historical circumstances. The most powerful actors have the most influence on how our economic and political institutions develop. Yet they, in turn, are shaped by those institutions.[28]

A Structural Dimension: Private Property

The U.S. legal system, a critical part of our governmental structure, institutionalizes and protects the right to private property. Yet this legal system is critical to the perpetuation of great inequalities in real estate ownership and control. Most Americans own or control little property, other than their homes. Essential to the maintenance of inequality in land decision making is the legal protection of individualized property ownership. The rights of private property give owners, especially the large property owners, a great deal of control over land and buildings. Within broad limits land can be developed, and buildings constructed, as owners desire. This unbridled use of private property has not always been the case in the United States. The early Puritans, for example, had highly planned towns from Maine to Long Island. For two generations Puritan towns were designed by pioneers whose strong religious values influenced the layout of urban areas. The private ownership and control of property were not central; more important communal and collective goals often overrode private property interests. But the Puritan group-centered town planning soon gave way to intensified private landholding, even in New England. Fee-simple (unrestricted transfer) ownership of land became central to the expanding capitalistic system of eighteenth-century America. Early immigrants from Europe were generally hostile to landlords and vigorously sought to own their own land. Ownership of even a small piece of property was a sign of independence from landlords; many immigrants had come to the colonies to escape oppressive European landlords. Land was seen as a civil right by the many small farmers.[29]

Yet this early and heavy commitment to the sacredness of privately held property had a major negative effect on development once the United States was no longer primarily a country of small farmers. By the early decades of the nineteenth century, there were fewer landholders and ever more tenants without land. In many cases, the growing number of Americans with little or no real estate property were seen as unworthy. Yet the strong commitment to private property, on the part of both propertied and landless Americans, has continued to legitimate the private disposal of property by the powerful landowning and development decision makers. As a result, over the last two centuries control over urban land development has become more concentrated in the hands of executives of banks, insurance firms, development corporations, and industrial companies.[30] In addition, there are major social costs for a private property system that gives owners of large amounts of land the right to use the land more or less as they wish. Those who build and develop large projects on central-city land have shown that they can transfer certain social costs onto other people nearby. A good example is the modern skyscraper with its mirrored glass walls, which often generate heat problems for nearby buildings, and with its thousands of workers whose exit in the evenings can create massive traffic jams. Such social costs of skyscraper development are generally not paid for by the developers and owners of the buildings. . . .

POWERFUL AGENTS OF URBAN CHANGE: PRIVATE PRODUCERS

Neglecting Powerful Agents

. . . Mainstream scholars often portray . . . land and building markets as "natural" markets guided by an invisible hand. But they are not natural. In reality, these markets are the creation of the most powerful players on the urban scene—the array of visible real estate decision makers in industry, finance, development, and construction. Over decades of urban development these powerful decision makers have both shaped, and been shaped by, the structures and institutions of urban real estate capitalism. Not only some of the critical analyses, such as the research of Harvey, but also traditional urban analyses, such as Berry and Kasarda's *Contemporary Urban Ecology* and Micklin and Choldin's *Sociological Human Ecology,* have largely ignored the central role of specific capitalistic and political actors in basic decisions about shaping urban land and built environments, the complex array of residential subdivisions, shopping malls, factories, warehouses, and office buildings.[31]

Among the primary decision makers in the urban real estate game are the capitalistic producers. Today real estate capitalism is organized around a complicated network of entrepreneurs and executives heading corporations of varying size. The size and complexity of the urban development industry can be seen in [Table 64-1], which lists major real estate and development decision makers. The categories refer to sets of major decisions that are critical to urban development.[32]

Looking at the private sector, we see that category 1 encompasses those corporate executives whose location decisions (for example, the choice of locating a factory in a northern city or a Sunbelt city) often set the other decision makers into motion. Category 2 covers the developers, land speculators, and landowners who buy, package, and develop land for use by industrial corporations and others.[33] Category 3 encompasses, among others, those bankers and financial corporations that make

TABLE 64-1 Urban Development: Decision Categories and Selected Decision Makers

1. Industrial and commercial location decisions
   Executives of industrial companies
   Executives of commercial companies
2. Development decisions
   Executives of development companies (developers)
   Land speculators and landowners
   Apartment owners and landlords
3. Financial decisions
   Commercial bankers
   Executives of savings and loan associations ("thrifts")
   Executives of insurance companies
   Executives of mortgage companies
   Executives of real estate investment trusts
4. Construction decisions
   Builders and developer-builders
   Executives of architectural and engineering firms
   Construction subcontractors
5. Support decisions
   Chamber of commerce executives
   Real estate brokers
   Executives of leasing companies
   Apartment management firms

the loans for land purchase, construction, and related development. Category 4 includes the various design and construction actors who actually construct urban projects. And category 5 covers a variety of supporting actors, including real estate brokers and chamber of commerce executives.

Today a single corporation may include subsidiaries and other organizational units involved in a variety of decisions across several categories. Within one firm there may be a development subdivision, which not only develops projects but also engages in land speculation; a real estate brokerage subsidiary; and an architectural subsidiary. A major insurance company may have a lending department, as well as its own urban land development subsidiary. Large integrated real estate development companies are often involved in major decisions in more than one category. Frequently, local developers, realtors, and bankers are the major decision makers in local development projects; studies of community decision makers show clearly the role and power of local business people in all types of cities in the North and South.[34] However, major real estate decisions are made not only by local individuals and real estate companies but also by powerful regional and national firms, such as the Hines and Levitt firms cited earlier. There are complex interconnections between influential interests external to cities and those that are part of the internal power structure of a particular city. An example would be a major insurance company, such as the Prudential Life Insurance Company, which, in connection with other local and national companies, finances and owns real estate and development projects in cities across the United States. . . .

GOVERNMENT AND URBAN DEVELOPMENT

Pluralist and Market Politics Analyses

In addition to economic structures and decision makers, we must give substantial attention to political structures and decision makers in understanding city building. Most social scientists have either neglected the role of government in city development or have assumed a pluralist or "market politics" perspective. The pluralist outlook has dominated much political science analysis of U.S. cities: Political decision makers, on the whole, promote the general welfare because their decisions result from responding to and coordinating pressures from a multiplicity of contending pressure groups. Advocates of urban pluralism see a competitive market in the urban political sphere that is analogous to the economic market; there is a political market in which individual voters and an array of diverse interest groups, in ever changing coalitions, compete for influence on local governments within a general value consensus.[35] Yet traditional pluralists have tended to neglect private economic decision making. . . .

Critical Perspectives on Government

In contrast to this market-knows-best perspective on urban economics and politics, critical urban analysts note the overwhelming evidence that certain groups have *far* more power than others to shape both economic and political decisions. Just as markets generally favor powerful capitalist investors over ordinary consumers, the urban political process favors the interests of powerful business and other groups over ordinary voters. Neither U.S. markets nor U.S. political arrangements are neutral. And both economic and political arrangements are dominated by the few. Some critical social scientists emphasize the economic and political decision makers, while others accent economic and governmental structures. But all critical analysts reject the pluralist and market-knows-best perspectives. Certain critical researchers such as Ralph Miliband and G. William Domhoff have accented the importance of specific business decision makers, particularly the capitalists, in state decisions. They view powerful economic decision makers as generally dominant over governmental decision makers and their decisions. Miliband and Domhoff have emphasized the specific ties between the capitalist class and various governments, including the movement of business leaders into and out of key political positions. In the United States, at the federal and local government levels, there is the everyday reality of interpersonal connections between business leaders and governmental officials. Domhoff has demonstrated that in the United States individual capitalists and their close subordinates do in fact rule by serving in critical governmental positions at both the national and the local levels. These governmental actors generally work hard to maintain favorable conditions for capitalists' enterprises and profits.[36]

CONCLUSION: THE NEED FOR PUBLIC BALANCE SHEETS

In this [excerpt] we have examined the traditional social science and governmental perspectives on urban growth and development and have seen them to be substantially grounded in neoclassical economics. These traditional perspectives put heavy emphasis on a "free" land and property market, on allegedly equal individuals competing freely, on private property, on efficient land use, and on the benefits that markets in land are supposed to bring to all urbanites. But the realities are not what these perspectives suggest. As we have seen from examples, there are no free competitive markets in cities, because corporate location, urban land purchase, and urban development are disproportionately controlled, often monopolized, by powerful capitalistic decision makers. The newer critical perspective, also described in this [selection], focuses on these power and inequality realities of city growth and decline.

For the most part, the actions of urban industrialists, developers, bankers, and their political allies are visible and quantifiable. Using the language of the accountant and the economist and calculating profit and loss on their private balance sheets, they are prepared to spell out what they see as the need for and benefits of constant urban growth. Down to the last square foot, they can tell us how much new office space is needed and how much has been created. They inform us of the number of jobs produced by their construction projects, and, once completed, they speculate with great precision about the number of additional employees the employers in their urban monuments will require. They calculate, and often exaggerate, the expected amount of additional tax revenues their large projects will generate, and, using the concept of the multiplier effect, speculate upon the economic benefits of their actions for the city as a whole.

On the other hand, the negative fallout from urban development is noticeably absent from the industrialists' and developers' lexicon. Just as critical, and usually just as obvious, the *social costs* generated by urban growth are less studied and are sometimes more difficult to specify and quantify. For example, why do we not attempt to measure the long-term physical and psychological impact of increasing pedestrian and auto congestion on consumers and workers? How can we eliminate unsafe pollution levels and prevent health damage? How should we measure the psychological impact on urbanites of routinely being deprived of sunlight as high-rise skyscrapers obstruct the sun? And what is the total community cost of the growing numbers of the homeless and those

displaced by the processes of condominium conversion and gentrification in our cities? Finally, how can we calculate the fading sense of community that is produced in many neighborhoods as constant development and redevelopment converge to constitute the modern city?

In the last few years a start on studying social costs has been made. The idea that what is efficient and rational for developers is not necessarily so for workers, consumers, and society as a whole has even been documented in a study of Phoenix, Arizona, by the Center for Business Research at Arizona State University. According to this study the benefits of Phoenix's growth to businesses included more customers, improved market potential, greater availability of labor, and higher profits; the study's research manager stated that "most businesses enjoy a substantial net benefit from urban growth." His evaluation of the net effect of urban growth for ordinary citizens was less favorable. The benefits of expanded job opportunities, a greater selection of goods, and higher incomes for some workers are offset by higher taxes, an increased cost of living, urban sprawl and traffic congestion, water and air pollution, destruction of the natural environment and depletion of resources, waste disposal, a higher crime rate, greater demand for social services, and problems such as homelessness.[37]

Industrial and real estate capitalism does indeed shape the major development projects in cities—the factories, shopping centers, suburbs, business parks, office towers, and apartment complexes. Once the decisions of the powerful are made, smaller scale builders must work around the larger-scale projects, and average workers and their families have to choose within the limits provided. Workers and consumers, especially those with inadequate economic resources, endure the brunt of many social costs of our capitalistic development system. And these costs . . . have been enormous. However, we must not forget that group struggle is at the heart of capitalist cities. Citizens' movements are pressing for the community costs of urban development and decline to be addressed and eliminated.

CRITICAL-THINKING QUESTIONS

1. According to Feagin and Parker, what role do residents have in a city's development? In their view, what role should residents have?

2. What are some of the specific criticisms made of the traditional "market-knows-best" approach?

3. What are the basic assertions of the critical urban perspective? What political values appear to underlie this view? What sort of city would be consistent with these values?

NOTES

1. D. Lindorff, "About-Face in Santa Monica," *Village Voice,* December 2–8, 1981, p. 20.

2. "Who's Gone This Year," *Forbes,* 140 (October 26, 1987), 308. See also H. Banks, "Real Men Don't Need Tax Breaks," *Forbes,* 135 (June 3, 1985), 78, 80.

3. H. Gans, *The Levittowners* (New York: Random House, 1967), p. 6.

4. Ibid., pp. 5–13.

5. "The Master Builder," *Newsweek* (August 31, 1981), p. 45; J. R. Feagin, "Sunbelt Metropolis and Development Capital," in *Sunbelt/Snowbelt: Urban Development and Regional Restructuring,* ed. L. Sawers and W. K. Tabb (New York: Oxford University Press, 1984), pp. 110–11.

6. R. E. Park and E. W. Burgess, *Introduction to the Science of Society* (Chicago: University of Chicago Press, 1924), p. 507.

7. W. P. Frisbie and J. D. Kasarda, "Spatial Processes," in *The Handbook of Sociology,* ed. N. Smelser (Newbury Park, CA: Sage, 1988), pp. 629–66.

8. B. J. L. Berry and J. Kasarda, *Contemporary Urban Ecology* (New York: Macmillan, 1977); M. Micklin and H. M. Choldin, eds., *Sociological Human Ecology* (Boulder: Westview, 1984); Harvey M. Choldin, *Cities and Suburbs: An Introduction to Urban Sociology* (New York: McGraw-Hill, 1985). This paragraph draws on J. R. Feagin, *Free Enterprise City: Houston in Political-Economic Perspective* (New Brunswick, NJ: Rutgers, 1988), pp. 15–21.

9. S. E. Harris, *The Death of Capital* (New York: Pantheon, 1977), p. 64.

10. Ibid., p. 65.

11. J. Kasarda, "The Implications of Contemporary Redistribution Trends for National Urban Policy," *Social Science Quarterly,* 61 (Dec. 1980), 373–400.

12. K. Bradbury, A. Downs, and K. Small, *Urban Decline and the Future of American Cities* (Washington, DC: The Brookings Institution, 1982), p. 296.

13. L. Mumford, *The City in History* (New York: Harcourt, Brace and World, 1961), p. 452.

14. F. X. Sutton et al., *The American Business Creed* (Cambridge: Harvard University Press, 1956), pp. 361–62.

15. E. A. Filene, *Successful Living in the Machine Age* (New York: Simon & Schuster, 1932), p. 98.

16. W. Alonso, *Location and Land Use* (Cambridge: Harvard University Press, 1964); Richard Muth, *Cities and Housing* (Chicago: University of Chicago Press, 1969).

17. D. L. Birch, "Wide Open Spaces," *Inc.,* 9 (Aug. 1987), 28.

18. P. E. Peterson, "Introduction: Technology, Race, and Urban Policy," in *The New Urban Reality* (Washington, DC: Brookings Institution, 1985), pp. 2–12.

19. A. Hawley, *Urban Society,* 2d ed. (New York: Wiley, 1981).

20. Micklin and Choldin, eds., *Sociological Human Ecology.*

21. Berry and Kasarda, *Contemporary Urban Ecology,* pp. 353, 402.

22. Hawley, *Urban Society,* pp. 228–29, 262–63; see also Frisbie and Kasarda, "Spatial Processes."

23. President's Commission for a National Agenda for the Eighties, Panel on Policies and Prospects, *Urban America in the Eighties: Perspectives and Prospects* (Washington, DC: U.S. Government Printing Office, 1980).

24. Ibid., pp. 12, 104.

25. M. Castells, "Is There an Urban Sociology?" in *Urban Sociology,* ed. C. G. Pickvance (London: Tavistock, 1976), pp. 33–57; M. Castells, *The Urban Question* (London: Edward Arnold, 1977); D. Harvey, *The Urbanization of Capital* (Baltimore: Johns Hopkins University Press, 1985); H. Lefebvre, *La Revolution Urbaine* (Paris: Gallimard, 1970).

26. M. P. Smith, *The City and Social Theory* (New York: St. Martin's, 1979); S. Fainstein, N. Fainstein, M. P. Smith, D. Judd, and R. C. Hill, *Restructuring the City* (New York: Longman, 1983); R. C. Hill, "Urban Political Economy," in *Cities in Transformation,* ed. M. P. Smith (Beverly Hills: Sage, 1984), pp. 123–38; J. Allen Whitt, *Urban Elites and Mass Transportation* (Princeton, NJ: Princeton University Press, 1982); M. Gottdiener, *The Social Production of Urban Space* (Austin: University of Texas Press, 1985); G. L. Clark and Michael Dear, *State Apparatus: Structures and Language of Legitimacy* (Boston: Allen and Unwin, 1984), pp. 131–45; J. R. Logan and H. M. Molotch, *Urban Fortunes: The Political Economy of Place* (Berkeley and Los Angeles: University of California Press, 1987).

27. Other pressures for land-use controls have stemmed from local merchants concerned with protecting their business places for profitable marketing uses. In such cases the commitment by local merchants to land is primarily to its use value as a place to make a profit. Thus we actually have three basic interests in land: (1) in the exchange value of the land itself, (2) in the use value of the land for living, family, and neighborhood; (3) in the use value of the land for local commercial or industrial profit making.

28. See M. Gottdiener and J. R. Feagin, "The Paradigm Shift in Urban Sociology," *Urban Affairs Quarterly,* 24 (Dec. 1988), 163–87.

29. Sam Bass Warner, *The Urban Wilderness* (New York: Harper and Row, 1972), pp. 16–17. See also pp. 8–15.

30. Ibid., p. 18.

31. Berry and Kasarda, *Contemporary Urban Ecology;* Micklin and Choldin, eds., *Sociological Human Ecology;* Choldin, *Cities and Suburbs: An Introduction to Urban Sociology.*

32. D. C. McAdams and J. R. Feagin, "A Power Conflict Approach to Urban Land Use," Austin, Texas, University of Texas, unpublished monograph, 1980; and D. Claire McAdams, "Powerful Actors in Public Land Use Decision Making Processes" (Ph.D. diss., University of Texas, 1979), chaps. 1–3.

33. The term "corporation" is used in this [reading] for the various organizational arrangements, including partnerships, that capitalists utilize in profit making, whether or not legally incorporated.

34. J. Walton, "A Systematic Survey of Community Power Research," in *The Structure of Community Power,* ed. M. Aiken and P. Mott (New York: Random House, 1970), pp. 443–64.

35. See R. Dahl, *Who Governs?* (New Haven: Yale University Press, 1961); T. M. Guterbock, "The Political Economy of Urban Revitalization," *Urban Affairs Quarterly,* 15 (Mar. 1980), 429–38.

36. R. Miliband, "State Power and Class Interests," *New Left Review,* 138 (1983), 57–68; R. Miliband, *The State in Capitalist Society* (London: Weidenfeld and Nicolson, 1969); G. W. Domhoff, *Who Rules America?* (Englewood Cliffs, NJ: Prentice-Hall, 1967); this and the next few paragraphs draw on Feagin, *Free Enterprise City: Houston in Political-Economic Perspective,* pp. 34–40.

37. T. R. Rex, "Businesses Enjoy Benefits; Individuals, Society Pay Costs," *Arizona Business,* 34 (Aug. 1987), 3.

65

The Global Population Crisis

David Berreby

Does the earth have the resources to support the rising global population? Or can we rely on human ingenuity to increase productivity (and decrease waste) as a strategy to ensure our future? This selection offers a debate about the state of world population; the two sides are argued by well-known analysts. The fact that each position can point to important evidence suggests that all the arguments are worth careful thought.

In 1968, when Stanford biologist Paul Ehrlich published *The Population Bomb,* there were 3.5 billion human beings. That was more, he warned, than the planet could support. "In the 1970s," he wrote, "the world will undergo famines—hundreds of millions of people are going to starve to death." We now know that didn't happen in the seventies. What did happen was that food production soared worldwide, prices dropped, and growers who could not sell enough of their surplus went bankrupt.

SOURCE: By David Berreby. From *Discover,* April 1990, pp. 42–43, 46–49. Copyright © 1990 by Discover Magazine. Reprinted with permission.

. . . Ehrlich and his wife, Anne, [have now written] *The Population Explosion,* a sequel to the 1968 bestseller. The message is much the same; the timetable, however, is revised. "The human population is now 5.3 billion, and still climbing," they write. "Yet the world has hundreds of billions *fewer* tons of topsoil and hundreds of trillions *fewer* gallons of groundwater with which to grow food crops than it had in 1968." Now, they warn, our excess numbers have overloaded both the environment and human communities. Global warming, acid rain, the hole in the ozone layer, rampant crime, viral epidemics, homelessness—all these problems and more stem from overpopulation. If we don't heed the warning this time, they write, we can look forward to "a billion or more deaths from starvation and disease," and possibly "the dissolution of society as we know it."

The Population Explosion, like the original *Bomb,* is full of statistics to back these claims. Like many sequels, though, this new effort may not get as friendly a reception as the original. These days fear of overpopulation is not what it used to be. Over the past twenty years many social scientists, in particular, have turned skeptical. "A good number of true believers," says Dennis Ahlburg of the University of Minnesota's Center for Population Analysis and Policy, "have become agnostics." They are now framing new hypotheses to explain the world's problems. "We're in a bit of a predicament," says Ahlburg, "because we can't keep saying that population is a horrible thing. The evidence isn't there."

In parts of Asia, Africa, and Latin America, exploding populations are often blamed for poverty, famine, crowding in cities, deforestation, pollution, and practically everything else that goes wrong. But in case after case, says Ahlburg, it's not population that causes the problem: In general the resources exist to support more people—the problem is that societies encourage waste. There are countless ways to do this, from misguided government policies to spectacular blunders like wars. Population growth, Ahlburg argues, is an easy scapegoat for political failures.

Such revisionism is clear in the changing stand of the National Academy of Sciences. In a report issued in 1971 the academy declared rapid population growth a clear danger to the survival of the human race. But in 1986 a new report found that the effects of population growth had been exaggerated in earlier studies. The academy noted that "despite rapid population growth, developing countries have achieved unprecedented levels of income per capita. literacy, and life expectancy." The report concluded that slower population growth is probably desirable in developing countries because it would give them more time to adjust—not because they are breeding themselves into oblivion.

As fear of the teeming billions has subsided, developed nations have reduced spending on contraceptive research. And the United States, in particular, has cut back its funding of international programs aimed at reining in reproduction in the Third World, where up to 90 percent of future population growth is expected.

Meanwhile, in much of the industrial world, birthrates have fallen so low that native populations are leveling off or actually declining. This drop in fertility surprised many planners, and it dramatically changed their projections. In the late sixties the United Nations estimated that the world's population in the year 2000 would be 7.5 billion; the projection now is 6.1 billion.

When a nation's birthrate drops, its population ages: The ratio of old people to young people grows larger. Some governments now worry about supporting growing numbers of retired people, and others fear that languages and cultures may die out. In the French-speaking province of Quebec, where the birthrate is lower than in the rest of Canada, the provincial government started offering cash bonuses this past year for babies. In Singapore, where the number of children born to the average woman dropped from 4.7 in 1965 to 1.4 in 1987, the government started a matchmaking service to coach career-driven nerds (as they are universally known) in the subtle arts of courtship.

Today's apparent lack of alarm over population growth compelled the Ehrlichs to title the first chapter of their new book "Why Isn't Everyone as Scared as We Are?" An important part of the answer to their question is the work of Julian Simon, a professor of business administration at the University of Maryland. For two decades Simon has pushed the idea that "population growth, along with the lengthening of human life, is a moral and material triumph." Although widely reviled in the seventies, Simon, like the Ehrlichs, persevered. His work has dealt the conventional wisdom two severe blows: first, by challenging the widely held assumption that our numbers are driving the planet to the end of its rope; and second, by outlining a theory that gradual population growth not only doesn't harm us and the environment but actually accelerates our progress.

"I find it difficult to understand how they can see some things as only problems when I see them as miracles," says Simon. "The fact we can keep 5 billion people alive now is an incredible accomplishment. We've escaped nature's domination, and all they see is problems. 'Escaped' doesn't mean we've beaten it into submission. It means we've killed the mosquitoes and the smallpox germs."

The Ehrlichs are worse than wrong, says Simon; their efforts to persuade people to have fewer children are morally repugnant. "I'm unhappy about it when I get a letter from a guy saying, 'My wife and I believed, on the basis of what Ehrlich said, that to bring a baby into the world is a negative act against society. So I had myself sterilized and now I can't reverse it.' That makes me sad." He becomes even sadder when a government as powerful as China's campaigns to limit every couple to only one child. "The cost," he says, "is the second child for a hundred million Chinese couples. A hundred million human beings who would never enjoy life as you and I and Ehrlich enjoy it."

Much current thinking on population lies between Simon on one coast and Ehrlich on the other. They heartily despise each other, and each would have you believe that the other is scarcely able to understand, much less contribute to, the population debate. "If you were doing a story on the solar system, would you talk to someone who thinks the Earth is flat?" Ehrlich asks. Meanwhile the index to Simon's most influential work, *The Ultimate Resource*, includes the entry, "Ehrlich, Paul, respect for human life lacking in." Still, they share more than mutual contempt. Each is a gifted polemicist. Each sees himself as an island of sanity in a world that has gone over to the other side. And most important, each considers the other's discipline to be arrogantly wrong in its fundamental assumptions about human populations.

The National Academy of Science's "revisionist" report was prepared entirely by social scientists, says Ehrlich, and thus was "never reviewed by anybody who knew anything about the sub-

ject." Ehrlich belongs to the Club of Earth, which in its own report in 1988 reached a conclusion opposite that of the academy. Every one of those dissenting researchers, Ehrlich points out, also belongs to the academy, but they are all biologists rather than social scientists. As for Simon, he is now working on a paper titled "Why Are Biologists Usually the Most Vocal Doomsayers?"

In the 1960s Ehrlich was a young biology professor at Stanford. He had first noticed the effects of human population growth years before, when as an undergraduate at the University of Pennsylvania he gathered butterflies in New Jersey. "We found out we couldn't raise our butterflies because there was so much pesticide in everything that it killed the caterpillars, and my favorite places to collect were disappearing under Levittowns." In graduate school at the University of Kansas, he met and married Anne, who is now a biological researcher at Stanford. They have only one child—"a contribution you can make toward being socially responsible," he says.

When *The Population Bomb* came out in 1968, headlines were filled with news of Vietnam, protests, and riots. In that apocalyptic year, people were receptive to a book that began, "The battle to feed all of humanity is over." Johnny Carson was certainly receptive; he invited Ehrlich to appear on *The Tonight Show*. Despite a few qualms ("I'd be canceling my ticket with my colleagues"), Ehrlich decided to accept the invitation ("I don't care about glory in science. It's more important that I do this"). He has maintained two careers ever since—as academic scholar and population polemicist.

Ehrlich believes that human populations are subject to the same natural constraints as those of, say, checkerspot butterflies. The absolute limit on any species's success, he says, is the "carrying capacity" of its environment—the maximum number of individuals a habitat can support. "Humanity," Ehrlich argues, "will pay the price for exceeding the carrying capacity of its environment as surely as would a population of checkerspots."

According to Ehrlich, the key limit on the carrying capacity of the planet is photosynthesis—the ability of green plants, algae, and many kinds of bacteria to convert the energy of sunlight into living tissue. Some animals consume those plants and microbes, and bigger animals eat smaller ones. But no matter how high or low on the food chain any species may dine, its numbers are ultimately limited by photosynthesis.

In their new book the Ehrlichs estimate that human beings and their domestic animals now consume 4 percent of the solar energy that photosynthesis captures on land. Adding the amount of this energy we don't directly consume but destroy (such as plants killed when forests are burned) and the amount we prevent from growing (as when we pave productive land) raises the human share to nearly 40 percent. But even 4 percent, in the Ehrlichs' opinion, is a disproportionate share for only one of Earth's 30 million species.

How do the Ehrlichs know we are crowding other species? A population exceeds carrying capacity, they write, when it "can't be maintained without rapidly depleting nonrenewable resources." And by this standard, they declare, "the entire planet and virtually every nation is already vastly overpopulated." Humans are different from butterflies, however, in one important ecological respect: They have more control in choosing what to eat and how to live. This is why the planet's carrying capacity for humans is not a fixed number. The world can support more vegetarian Indians on bicycles than hamburger-eating Americans in cars. Yet the limit on our species, says Ehrlich, is nonetheless real. "And it's beyond my comprehension," he says, "that we should run an experiment to see how many people we can cram on the planet before all its systems collapse."

That concept is essentially the one British economist Thomas Malthus advanced in 1798. In his famous "dismal essay" on the principle of population, Malthus wrote that humans will increase their numbers beyond their means of subsistence until famine, war, and disease wipe out the excess. History may not have worked out the way Malthus expected, but that's only because of what Ehrlich calls a onetime bonanza based on the use of coal and oil to power our industrial civilization. "Malthus," he says, "wasn't wrong."

The problem for this argument—and the foundation of Simon's—is that things haven't yet given way. "Every one of these prophets' dire predictions has failed to come to pass," Simon says. "They've been wrong on food, on energy, on resources, on the environment, on everything."

Simon believes that the most relevant measure of human well-being is life span. Our average life expectancy has increased dramatically, he argues, and this tells you right away that everything we need to sustain us is also increasing. He notes that food production per capita has increased since World War II and says the same holds true for every other resource people worry about.

Global 2000, a projection of global environmental trends to the end of the century, is one of the "doom and gloom" reports that Simon relishes attacking. "The report came out in 1980 saying there was a plateau in world fisheries," he says. "Since then the amount of increase in the world fish catch has been astounding." To refute the report's analysis, Simon refers to statistics compiled by marine biologist John Wise from United Nations reports. In 1979, Wise finds, the world fish catch totaled 78 million tons; in 1987 it was 102 million tons. "Sure, you can say it's because of new methods of extraction," says Simon, "but that doesn't alter the fact that they said it was going to be the other way around."

What such statistics mean, Simon argues, is not that we've been lucky so far. "They mean we're on a permanent roll," he says, "with no limit yet in sight. If the biologists don't see this, it's because they've left something out of their theories."

In 1968, when Ehrlich was taking to the airwaves to promote *The Population Bomb,* Simon was teaching economics at the University of Illinois. Simon's main claim to fame was having written the basic how-to book on running a mail-order business. By 1968 he had already read about the population explosion, become duly concerned, and turned his attention to possible solutions.

One beautiful spring day in 1969, while on the

way to an appointment in Washington, Simon had an epiphany. He described it twelve years later in his book *The Ultimate Resource:* "I thought, Have I gone crazy? What business do I have trying to help arrange it that fewer human beings will be born, each of whom might be a Mozart or a Michelangelo or an Einstein—or simply a joy to his or her family and community, and a person who will enjoy life?" His nagging doubts about the way economic data did not square with the prevailing view of the world's "population crisis" kindled into a crusade to correct the idea.

During the 1970s Simon was denounced as a religious maniac, an emotional wreck, a mere mail-order specialist, and a shabby scholar. At the very first Earth Day in 1970, a fellow faculty member at the university ridiculed him before 2,000 students at a teach-in. (Simon retaliated at a faculty party with three well-aimed gin and tonics.)

But in 1981, the year that Simon published *The Ultimate Resource,* political currents were changing. Ronald Reagan had been elected president in a landslide; vigorous economic development, skepticism of environmentalism, and "family values" were back in style. In the opinion-influencing game of newspaper editorials, seminars, symposia, and government reports, Simon's star began to rise. At the same time, more and more social scientists were becoming convinced by their own data that there was something to his critique of the standard assumptions.

Simon now lives just outside Washington, where he is a figure of some influence. He and his wife, sociologist Rita Simon, have decorated their comfortable, middle-class house with sculptures and framed posters—many of which depict a mother and child. They have three children.

The concept of carrying capacity, Simon argues, shouldn't be applied to human beings at all. Malthus and all who follow in his footsteps pay too little attention to an important fact: Humans are producers as well as consumers. As a resource becomes more difficult to obtain, people find ways to get more of it or to use it more efficiently. Or they develop substitutes. Firewood yields to coal, which yields to oil, which yields to nuclear, solar,

or some other source of power. Simon argues that our resources expand rather than shrink, because we don't really want coal or oil—we want energy. The same holds true even for apparently fixed resources like soil. Farmland isn't just dirt; it's wilderness that was cleared, desert that was irrigated, swamps that were drained. We don't really want dirt—we want nutrition. And humans are the one species that can invent more ways of applying energy (not only the sun's) to materials (not only today's crops and farmland) to get nutrition—as well as all the other things we enjoy in life.

So people are constantly escaping the Malthusian trap. In fact, Simon argues, population growth applies a needed spur. In the short run, new people are a burden: More babies mean more mouths to feed, so the parents work harder and have less of everything for themselves. But in the long run, Simon contends that those babies are the solution to the apparent problem: As adults they add more to our stock of resources than they consume. "It is your mind that matters economically, as much or more so than your mouth or hands," he says.

"Taken in the large," Simon writes, "an increased need for resources usually leaves us with a permanently greater capacity to get them, because we gain knowledge in the process. And there is no meaningful physical limit—even the commonly mentioned weight of the earth—to our capacity to keep growing forever."

This is the economist's vision at its purest. To Simon it is the lesson of the past few centuries. To most any biologist it's beyond strange. "The physical and biological systems are prior," says Ehrlich. "You can change economics, but the laws of nature are out there." Moreover, he argues that Simon's faith in technology is misguided. "It's usually economists or social scientists who expect science to be able to do all these wonderful things. Scientists don't."

That's the sort of argument to the future that gets Simon's goat. He doubts anyone's ability to predict the limits of technology, whether it's genetic engineering or just ordinary farming done more efficiently. In 1968 Ehrlich wrote, "I have yet to meet anyone familiar with the situation who thinks India will be self-sufficient in food by 1971, if ever." Now, despite a population jump from 500 million in 1966 to 835 million today, Simon points out that India has managed to feed itself.

And *that's* the sort of argument from the past that irritates Ehrlich. India's impressive achievement, he says, was bought at the expense of its future. "They managed to up their grain production by throwing away their soil and their groundwater, and that makes the long-term situation worse." The same is true, he argues, for most of the other encouraging statistics. When there are too many people, technology doesn't really solve our problems—it only postpones them. "Electricity was going to be too cheap to meter because of nuclear power, remember. Many technological rabbits that have been pulled out of hats in the past have had nasty droppings."

In short, Ehrlich has not conceded the past. And neither he nor Simon is conceding the present. In their book, the Ehrlichs use every bit of bad news—children starving in Africa, malaria on the rise again in Asia—as ammunition for their claim that our bubble is finally bursting. "We've got 5.3 billion people on the planet now," says Ehrlich. "At least a billion of them are living at a standard that you wouldn't trade for in a million years. The estimates are that at least two hundred million people have died of hunger-related diseases over the past twenty years." Can the Einsteins or Mozarts that Simon is counting on develop their talents, he asks, in utter destitution and misery?

Simon dismisses that distressing information as old news. Some people have always struggled even while the average situation was improving. "Their paradigm," he says of the other side, "is that the present and the future will be unlike the past, that we're at a turning point in history. But you find that sentiment in every generation. There is absolutely no way to tell if we are at a turning point in history."

Accordingly, Simon has made a one-man cottage industry of assaulting alarming reports. He is a relentless sifter of statistics. "When people say, for instance, 'The world is being deforested,'" he says, "I go look for the aggregate data. I found that in fact the world is *not* being deforested; it is being reforested in general. Yes, there are some tropical countries where deforestation is taking place. Is that bad? Is that good? Who knows?"

New Scientist, a British weekly, published Simon's article on deforestation in 1986. He gets a hearing for such contrary views because there are no precise, comprehensive data for many global trends. Current opinion is often based on spot surveys rounded out by estimates, which can be argued up or down. With forests, for instance, not even the record of photographs from satellites shows enough of the globe for enough years to prove whether the loss of a forest in, say, the Philippines has been offset by a gain in Finland.

Researchers debate everything, Ehrlich acknowledges, from the rate of deforestation to the rate of global warming. Nonetheless, he adds, "there isn't a competent scientist who doesn't believe that the world is facing these problems." As long as the data are still coming in, there will always be need for revision. But "you can't wait for absolute proof before acting."

On and on they go, each confident that the other's statistics distort the truth about what our growing population means to our future well-being. Meanwhile, in the most private and secret places, humanity in its billions is deciding for itself how many people to add to the planet, without reference to either Simon or Ehrlich.

CRITICAL-THINKING QUESTIONS

1. What facts lead the Ehrlichs to conclude that the world is facing an immediate and serious problem of overpopulation?

2. What facts underlie Julian Simon's confidence in the world's ability to sustain even greater levels of population?

3. Do you think one side or the other of this debate is more convincing? Which one? Why?

66

Silent Spring

Rachel Carson

Rachel Carson, one of the founders of the modern environmentalist movement, awakened the world to the dangers of chemical pollution. The rate at which we have developed new chemicals for croplands, forests, and even our own lawns has risen dramatically during this century, posing an unprecedented threat to the environment.

There was once a town in the heart of America where all life seemed to live in harmony with its surroundings. The town lay in the midst of a checkerboard of prosperous farms, with fields of grain and hillsides of orchards where, in spring, white clouds of bloom drifted above the green fields. In autumn, oak and maple and birch set up a blaze of color that flamed and flickered across a backdrop of pines. Then foxes barked in the hills and deer silently crossed the fields, half hidden in the mists of the fall mornings.

Along the roads, laurel, viburnum and alder, great ferns and wildflowers delighted the trav-

eler's eye through much of the year. Even in winter the roadsides were places of beauty, where countless birds came to feed on the berries and on the seed heads of the dried weeds rising above the snow. The countryside was, in fact, famous for the abundance and variety of its bird life, and when the flood of migrants was pouring through in spring and fall people traveled from great distances to observe them. Others came to fish the streams, which flowed clear and cold out of the hills and contained shady pools where trout lay. So it had been from the days many years ago when the first settlers raised their houses, sank their wells, and built their barns.

Then a strange blight crept over the area and everything began to change. Some evil spell had settled on the community: Mysterious maladies swept the flocks of chickens; the cattle and sheep sickened and died. Everywhere was a shadow of death. The farmers spoke of much illness among their families. In the town the doctors had become more and more puzzled by new kinds of sickness appearing among their patients. There had been several sudden and unexplained deaths, not only among adults but even among children, who would be stricken suddenly while at play and die within a few hours.

There was a strange stillness. The birds, for example—where had they gone? Many people spoke of them, puzzled and disturbed. The feeding stations in the backyards were deserted. The few birds seen anywhere were moribund; they trembled violently and could not fly. It was a spring without voices. On the mornings that had once throbbed with the dawn chorus of robins, catbirds, doves, jays, wrens, and scores of other bird voices there was now no sound; only silence lay over the fields and woods and marsh.

On the farms the hens brooded, but no chicks hatched. The farmers complained that they were unable to raise any pigs—the litters were small and the young survived only a few days. The apple trees were coming into bloom but no bees droned among the blossoms, so there was no pollination and there would be no fruit.

The roadsides, once so attractive, were now lined with browned and withered vegetation as though swept by fire. These, too, were silent, deserted by all living things. Even the streams were now lifeless. Anglers no longer visited them, for all the fish had died.

In the gutters under the eaves and between the shingles of the roofs, a white granular powder still showed a few patches; some weeks before it had fallen like snow upon the roofs and the lawns, the fields and streams.

No witchcraft, no enemy action had silenced the rebirth of new life in this stricken world. The people had done it themselves.

This town does not actually exist, but it might easily have a thousand counterparts in America or elsewhere in the world. I know of no community that has experienced all the misfortunes I describe. Yet every one of these disasters has actually happened somewhere, and many real communities have already suffered a substantial number of them. A grim specter has crept upon us almost unnoticed, and this imagined tragedy may easily become a stark reality we all shall know.

What has already silenced the voices of spring in countless towns in America? This book is an attempt to explain.

OBLIGATION TO ENDURE

The history of life on earth has been a history of interaction between living things and their surroundings. To a large extent, the physical form and the habits of the earth's vegetation and its animal life have been molded by the environment. Considering the whole span of earthly time, the opposite effect, in which life actually modifies its surroundings, has been relatively slight. Only within the moment of time represented by the present century has one species—man—acquired significant power to alter the nature of his world.

During the past quarter century this power has not only increased to one of disturbing magnitude but it has changed in character. The most alarming of all man's assaults upon the environment is the contamination of air, earth, rivers, and sea with dangerous and even lethal materials. This pollution is for the most part irrecoverable; the chain of evil it initiates not only in the world that must support life but in living tissues is for the most part irreversible. In this now universal contamination of the environment, chemicals are the sinister and little-recognized partners of radiation in changing the very nature of the world—the very nature of its life. Strontium 90, released through nuclear explosions into the air, comes to earth in rain or drifts down as fallout, lodges in soil, enters into the grass or corn or wheat grown there, and in time takes up its abode in the bones of a human being, there to remain until his death. Similarly, chemicals sprayed on croplands or forests or gardens lie long in soil, entering into living organisms, passing from one to another in a chain of poisoning and death. Or they pass mysteriously by underground streams until they emerge and, through the alchemy of air and sunlight, combine into new forms that kill vegetation, sicken cattle, and work unknown harm on those who drink from once pure wells. As Albert Schweitzer has said, "Man can hardly even recognize the devils of his own creation."

It took hundreds of millions of years to produce the life that now inhabits the earth—eons of time in which that developing and evolving and diversifying life reached a state of adjustment and balance with its surroundings. The environment, rigorously shaping and directing the life it supported, contained elements that were hostile as well as supporting. Certain rocks gave out dangerous radiation; even within the light of the sun, from which all life draws its energy, there were short-wave radiations with power to injure. Given time—time not in years but in millennia—life adjusts, and a balance has been reached. For time is the essential ingredient; but in the modern world there is no time.

The rapidity of change and the speed with which new situations are created follow the impetuous and heedless pace of man rather than the deliberate pace of nature. Radiation is no longer merely the background radiation of rocks, the bombardment of cosmic rays, the ultraviolet of the sun that have existed before there was any life on earth; radiation is now the unnatural creation of man's tampering with the atom. The chemicals to which life is asked to make its adjustment are no longer merely the calcium and silica and copper and all the rest of the minerals washed out of the rocks and carried in rivers to the sea; they are the synthetic creations of man's inventive mind, brewed in his laboratories, and having no counterparts in nature.

To adjust to these chemicals would require time on the scale that is nature's; it would require not merely the years of a man's life but the life of generations. And even this, were it by some miracle possible, would be futile, for the new chemicals come from our laboratories in an endless stream;

almost five hundred annually find their way into actual use in the United States alone. The figure is staggering and its implications are not easily grasped—500 new chemicals to which the bodies of men and animals are required somehow to adapt each year, chemicals totally outside the limits of biologic experience.

Among them are many that are used in man's war against nature. Since the mid-1940's over 200 basic chemicals have been created for use in killing insects, weeds, rodents, and other organisms described in the modern vernacular as "pests"; and they are sold under several thousand different brand names.

These sprays, dusts, and aerosols are now applied almost universally to farms, gardens, forests, and homes—nonselective chemicals that have the power to kill every insect, the "good" and the "bad," to still the song of birds and the leaping of fish in the streams, to coat the leaves with a deadly film, and to linger on in soil—all this though the intended target may be only a few weeds or insects. Can anyone believe it is possible to lay down such a barrage of poisons on the surface of the earth without making it unfit for all life? They should not be called "insecticides," but "biocides."

The whole process of spraying seems caught up in an endless spiral. Since DDT was released for civilian use, a process of escalation has been going on in which ever more toxic materials must be found. This has happened because insects, in a triumphant vindication of Darwin's principle of the survival of the fittest, have evolved super races immune to the particular insecticide used, hence a deadlier one has always to be developed—and then a deadlier one than that. It has happened also because, for reasons to be described later, destructive insects often undergo a "flareback," or resurgence, after spraying, in numbers greater than before. Thus the chemical war is never won, and all life is caught in its violent crossfire.

Along with the possibility of the extinction of mankind by nuclear war, the central problem of our age has therefore become the contamination of man's total environment with such substances of incredible potential for harm—substances that accumulate in the tissues of plants and animals and even penetrate the germ cells to shatter or alter the very material of heredity upon which the shape of the future depends.

Some would-be architects of our future look toward a time when it will be possible to alter the human germ plasm by design. But we may easily be doing so now by inadvertence, for many chemicals, like radiation, bring about gene mutations. It is ironic to think that man might determine his own future by something so seemingly trivial as the choice of an insect spray.

All this has been risked—for what? Future historians may well be amazed by our distorted sense of proportion. How could intelligent beings seek to control a few unwanted species by a method that contaminated the entire environment and brought the threat of disease and death even to their own kind?

Yet this is precisely what we have done. We have done it, moreover, for reasons that collapse the moment we examine them. We are told that the enormous and expanding use of pesticides is necessary to maintain farm production. Yet is our real problem not one of *overproduction*? Our farms, despite measures to remove acreages from production and to pay farmers *not* to produce, have yielded such a staggering excess of crops that the American taxpayer in 1962 is paying out more

than one billion dollars a year as the total carrying cost of the surplus-food storage program. And is the situation helped when one branch of the Agriculture Department tries to reduce production while another states, as it did in 1958, "It is believed generally that reduction of crop acreages under provisions of the Soil Bank will stimulate interest in use of chemicals to obtain maximum production on the land retained in crops."

All this is not to say there is no insect problem and no need of control. I am saying, rather, that control must be geared to realities, not to mythical situations, and that the methods employed must be such that they do not destroy us along with the insects.

The problem whose attempted solution has brought such as train of disaster in its wake is an accompaniment of our modern way of life.

CRITICAL-THINKING QUESTIONS

1. What does our society's reliance on so many chemical products say about our way of looking at the natural world?

2. What, according to Carson, is the alternative to our chemical dependency?

3. Do you think problems of pollution in the United States are getting better or worse? Why?

67

The State of the World's Natural Environment

Lester R. Brown

For a decade, the Worldwatch Institute has issued annual reports on the state of the world's natural environment. Their data point to a steady deterioration of the world's natural environment. This troubling trend, they explain, is not simply a technical problem; rather, it results from the ways in which we organize our lives and how we view the planet that supports our existence.

In early 1992, the U.S. National Academy of Sciences and the Royal Society of London issued a report that began: "If current predictions of population growth prove accurate and patterns of human activity on the planet remain unchanged, science and technology may not be able to prevent either irreversible degradation of the environment or continued poverty for much of the world."

It was a remarkable statement, an admission that science and technology can no longer ensure

SOURCE: Excerpts from "A New Era Unfolds" by Lester Brown are reprinted from *State of the World 1993: A Worldwatch Institute Report on Progress Toward a Sustainable Society,* Project Director: Lester R. Brown. By permission of W. W. Norton & Company, Inc. Copyright © by Worldwatch Institute.

a better future unless population growth slows quickly and the economy is restructured. This abandonment of the technological optimism that has permeated so much of the twentieth century by two of the world's leading scientific bodies represents a major shift, but perhaps not a surprising one given the deteriorating state of the planet. That they chose to issue a joint statement, their first ever, reflects the deepening concern about the future among scientists.

This concern is not limited to the scientific community. People everywhere are worried about the planet's continuing deterioration. Attendance at the U.N. Conference on Environment and Development and the parallel nongovernmental events in June in Rio de Janeiro totalled 35,000 people, dwarfing the turnout at the predecessor meetings in Stockholm in 1972. Some 106 heads of state and government participated in the Earth Summit, the largest gathering of national political leaders in history. The 9,000 journalists in Rio for the meetings exceeded the number of total participants in Stockholm.

Despite the intensifying global interest in the planet's future, the U.N. conference fell short of both hopes and expectations. Many of the difficulties centered on the U.S. insistence that goals and timetables for restricting carbon emissions be removed from the climate treaty, leaving it little more than a statement of good intentions. The convention designed to protect biological diversity had some flaws, but perhaps the most serious one was the missing U.S. signature.

The Earth Summit was not a total loss by any means. The climate treaty, which was signed by 154 participating countries, including the United States, recognizes that global warming is a serious issue. And it does provide for setting up an international system for governments to report each year on changes in carbon emissions. This information flow itself will focus attention on the threat of climate change. . . .

[T]he broad indicators showed a continuing wholesale deterioration in the earth's physical condition. During the twenty years since Stockholm, farmers have lost nearly 500 billion tons of topsoil through erosion at a time when they were called on to feed 1.6 billion additional people. Atmospheric concentrations of carbon dioxide (CO_2), the principal greenhouse gas, climbed 9 percent. In Rio, the risks to life on earth posed by the loss of stratospheric ozone and the associated increase of ultraviolet radiation were on everyone's mind; a threat not even imagined in 1972.

The environmental concerns that brought delegates to Rio exist in part because of an economic accounting system that misleads and a biological accounting system that is largely nonexistent. The internationally accepted system of national economic accounting used to calculate gross national product (GNP) rightly subtracts the depreciation

of plant and equipment from the overall output of goods and services. But it takes no account of the depreciation of natural capital, such as the loss of topsoil from erosion, the destruction of forests by acid rain, or the depletion of the protective stratospheric ozone layer. As a result, the economic accounting system now used by governments greatly overstates progress. Failing to reflect reality, it generates environmentally destructive economic policies.

The biological accounting system is fragmentary at best. No one knows how many species of plants and animals are lost each year; indeed, lacking a global inventory of the earth's biological resources, no one even knows how many species there are. Visual evidence, occasional national surveys, and satellite data tell us that forests are disappearing in many countries. Similarly, incomplete data indicate that grasslands are deteriorating. Closely associated with the reduced grass and tree cover is the loss of topsoil. Despite the essential economic role of soil, no global data gathering system measures its gains or losses.

Nor does the biological accounting system warn when carrying capacity thresholds are crossed. We learn that cattle numbers are excessive only when the rangeland begins to deteriorate. We discover that demands on forests are excessive only when they begin to disappear. We find that we have been overfishing only when the catch drops precipitously. Lacking information on sustainable yields, governments have permitted demands on these natural systems to become excessive, leading to their gradual destruction.

The result of this flawed economic accounting system and largely nonexistent biological accounting system is widespread degradation and destruction of the economy's environmental support systems. Industrial firms are allowed to internalize profits while externalizing costs, passing on to society such expenses as those for health care associated with polluted air or those arising from global warming.

An expanding economy based on such an incomplete accounting system would be expected to slowly undermine itself, eventually collapsing as support systems are destroyed. And that is just what is happening. The environmentally destructive activities of recent decades are now showing up in reduced productivity of croplands, forests, grasslands, and fisheries; in the mounting cleanup costs of toxic waste sites; in rising health care costs for cancer, birth defects, allergies, emphysema, asthma, and other respiratory diseases; and in the spread of hunger.

Rapid population growth, environmental degradation, and deepening poverty are reinforcing each other in a downward spiral in many countries. In its *World Development Report 1992,* the World Bank reported that per capita GNP had fallen in forty-nine countries during the eighties. Almost all these nations, containing 846 million people, are low-income, largely agrarian economies experiencing rapid population growth and extensive degradation of their forests, grasslands, and croplands.

As the Royal Society/National Academy statement implies, it may not be possible to reverse this fall in living standards of nearly one sixth of humanity if rapid population growth continues and existing patterns of economic activity are not changed. Just how difficult it will be is only now becoming clear. There is also a real risk that the demographic pressures and environmental deterioration that are replacing progress with decline will spread, enveloping even more of humanity during the nineties.

ENVIRONMENTAL DEGRADATION: THE ECONOMIC COSTS

Many people have long understood, at least intuitively, that continuing environmental degradation would eventually exact a heavy economic toll. Unfortunately, no global economic models incorporate the depletion and destruction of the earth's natural support systems. Only now can we begin to piece together information from several recent independent studies to get a sense of the worldwide economic effects of environmental degradation. Among the most revealing of these are studies on the effects of air pollution and acid rain on

forests in Europe, of land degradation on livestock and crop production in the world's dryland regions, of global warming on the U.S. economy, and of pollution on health in Russia.

These reports and other data show that the five-fold growth in the world economy since 1950 and the increase in population from 2.6 billion to 5.5 billion have begun to outstrip the carrying capacity of biological support systems and the ability of natural systems to absorb waste without being damaged. In country after country, demands for crops and for the products of grasslands, forests, and fisheries are exceeding the sustainable yield of these systems. Once this happens, the resource itself begins to shrink as natural capital is consumed. Overstocking grasslands, overcutting forests, overplowing, and overfishing are now commonplace. Every country is practicing the environmental equivalent of deficit financing in one form or another.

Perhaps the most visible environmental deficit is deforestation, the result of tree cutting and forest clearing that exceeds natural regrowth and tree planting. Each year this imbalance now costs the world some 17 million hectares of tropical forests alone. Over a decade, the destruction of tropical forests clears an area the size of Malaysia, the Philippines Ghana, the Congo, Ecuador, El Salvador, and Nicaragua. Once tropical forests are burned off or clear-cut, the land rapidly loses its fertility, since most of the nutrients in these ecosystems are stored in the vegetation. Although these soils can be farmed for 3–5 years before fertility drops and can be grazed for 5–10 years before becoming wasteland, they typically will not sustain productivity over the long term. Clearing tropical forests is, in effect, the conversion of a highly productive ecosystem into wasteland in exchange for a short-term economic gain.

As timber resources are depleted in the Third World, transforming countries that traditionally exported forest products into importers, logging companies are turning to remote temperate-zone forests. Canada, for example, is now losing 200,000 hectares a year as cutting exceeds regeneration by a wide margin. Similarly, as Japanese and Korean logging firms move into Siberia, the forests there are also beginning to shrink.

It is not only the axe and the chainsaw that threaten forests, but also emissions from power plant smokestacks and automobile exhaust pipes. In Europe, air pollution and acid rain are damaging and destroying the region's traditionally well managed forests. Scientists at the International Institute for Applied Systems Analysis (IIASA) in Austria have estimated the effect on forest productivity of sulfur dioxide emissions from fossil-fuel-burning power plants, factories, and automobiles. They concluded that 75 percent of Europe's forests are now experiencing damaging levels of sulfur deposition Forests in every country on the continent are affected—from Norway and Portugal in the west to the European part, of the former Soviet Union in the east.

The IIASA study estimated that losses associated with the deterioration of Europe's forests total $30.4 billion each year, roughly equal to the annual output of the German steel industry. . . .

Land degradation is also taking a heavy economic toll, particularly in the drylands that account for 41 percent of the earth's land area. In the early stages the costs show up as lower land productivity. But if the process continues unarrested, it eventually creates wasteland, destroying the soil as well as the vegetation. Using data for 1990, a U.N. assessment of the earth's dryland regions estimated that the degradation of irrigated cropland, rainfed cropland, and rangeland now costs the world more than $42 billion a year in lost crop and livestock output, a sum that approximates the value of the U.S. grain harvest. . . .

Excessive demand directly threatens the productivity of oceanic fisheries as well. The U.N. Food and Agriculture Organization (FAO), which monitors oceanic fisheries, indicates that four out of seventeen of the world's fishing zones are now overfished. It also reports that most traditional marine fish stocks have reached full exploitation. Atlantic stocks of the heavily fished bluefin tuna have been cut by a staggering 94 percent. It will take years for such species to recover, even if fishing were to stop altogether.

Dwindling fish stocks are affecting many national economies. In Canada, for example—where the fishing industry traditionally landed roughly 1.5 million tons of fish a year, worth $3.1 billion—depletion of the cod and haddock fisheries off the coast of Nova Scotia has led to shrinking catches and heavy layoffs in the fishing and fish processing industries. In July 1992, in an unprecedented step, Canada banned all cod fishing off the coast of Newfoundland and Labrador for two years in a bid to save the fishery. To cushion the massive layoffs in the industry, the mainstay of Newfoundland's economy, Ottawa authorized a $400-million aid package for unemployment compensation and retraining.

As overfishing of the North Atlantic by U.S., Canadian, and European fleets decimated stocks there during the seventies, the ships turned to the South Atlantic, particularly to the fisheries off the African coast. Unable to control fishing in the 200-mile Exclusive Economic Zones granted by the 1979 Law of the Sea Treaty, some African countries saw their fisheries decimated. Namibia, for instance, watched the catch in its zone fall from nearly 2 million tons in 1980 to less than 100,000 tons a decade later. After banning European ships from its waters in 1990, stocks started to recover.

Inland fisheries are also suffering from environmental mismanagement—water diversion, acidification, and pollution The Aral Sea, located between Kazakstan and Uzbekistan, as recently as 1960 yielded 40 million kilograms of fish per year. Shrinking steadily over the last three decades as the river water feeding it was diverted for irrigation, the sea has become increasingly salty, eventually destroying the fish stock. Today it is effectively dead. A similar situation exists in Pakistan, where Deg Nullah, a small but once highly productive freshwater lake that yielded 400,000 kilograms of fish annually, is now barren—destroyed by pollution. Acidification is also taking a toll. Canada alone now counts 14,000 dead lakes.

In the United States, pollution has severely affected the Chesapeake Bay, one of the world's richest estuaries. Its fabulously productive oyster beds, which yielded 8 million bushels per year a century ago, now produce scarcely a million bushels. Elsewhere, fish have survived, such as in the U.S. Great Lakes and New York's Hudson River, but many species are unsafe for human consumption because of pollution with PCBs and other toxic chemicals. Half the shellfish-growing areas off Nova Scotia in eastern Canada have been closed because of contamination.

The rising atmospheric concentration of greenhouse gases is potentially the most economically disruptive and costly change that has been set in motion by our modern industrial society. William Cline, an economist with the Washington-based Institute for International Economics, has looked at the long-term economic effects of global warming. As part of this study he analyzed the effect of a doubling of greenhouse gases on the U.S. economy, which could come as early as 2025. He estimates that heat, stress and drought would cost U.S. farmers $18 billion in output, that increased electricity for air conditioning would require an additional $11 billion, and that dealing with sea level rise would cost an estimated $7 billion per year. In total, Cline estimates the cost at nearly $60 billion, roughly 1 percent of the 1990 U.S. GNP. . . .

Not all countries would be affected equally. Some island countries, such as the Republic of the Maldives in the Indian Ocean, would become uninhabitable. Low-lying deltas, such as in Egypt and Bangladesh, would be inundated, displacing millions of people. In the end, rising seas in a warming world would be not only economically costly, but politically disruptive as well.

Every society is paying a price for environmental pollution. Contamination of air, water, and soil by toxic chemicals and radioactivity, along with increased ultraviolet radiation, is damaging human health, running up health care costs. An assessment of urban air quality jointly undertaken by the World Health Organization and the United Nations Environment Programme reports that 625 million people are exposed to unhealthy levels of sulfur dioxide from fossil fuel burning. More than a billion people, a fifth of the planet's population, are exposed to potentially health-damaging levels of air pollutants of all kinds. One study for the United States estimates that air pollution may cost the nation as much as $40 billion annually in health care and lost productivity.

In Bulgaria, research that was declassified following democratization showed that those living near heavy industrial complexes had asthma rates nine times higher than people living elsewhere. Skin diseases occurred seven times as often. Liver disease was four times as frequent, and nervous system diseases three times as high.

New data from Russia, Europe's largest country, show all too well the devastating effect of pollution by chemical and organic toxins on human health. At an October 1992 news conference, Vladimir Pokrovsky, head of the Russian Academy of Medical Sciences, shocked the world with his frankness, "We have already doomed ourselves for the next twenty-five years." He added: "The new generation is entering adult life unhealthy. The Soviet economy was developed at the expense of the population's health." Data released by the Academy show 11 percent of Russian infants suffering from birth defects. With half the drinking water and a tenth of the food supply contaminated, 55 percent of school-age children suffer health problems. The Academy reported that the increase in illness and early death among those aged 25–40 was particularly distressing. The bottom line is that Russian life expectancy is now falling.

Another source of higher future health care costs is stratospheric ozone depletion. Epidemiologists at the U.S. Environmental Protection Agency (EPA) estimate that the upward revision in early 1991 of the rate of ozone loss could mean an additional 200,000 skin cancer fatalities in the United States over the next five decades. Worldwide, this translates into millions of deaths. The number of people with cataracts would also increase dramatically in a world where people are exposed to greater doses of ultraviolet radiation than ever recorded. Other associated health care costs include a projected higher incidence of infectious diseases associated with the suppression of immune systems, the economic costs of which are difficult to even estimate.

In addition to the environmental deficits the

world is now experiencing, huge environmental cleanup bills are accumulating. For example, the estimated costs for cleaning up hazardous waste sites in the United States center on $750 billion, roughly three fourths the 1990 U.S. federal budget. And a national survey in Norway has discovered some 7,000 hazardous waste sites, the product of decades of irresponsible dumping. Cleanup is estimated to cost tiny Norway $3–6 billion.

There is no reason to believe that these bills for the United States and Norway are very different from those of other industrial countries. In a world generating more than a million tons of hazardous waste a day, much of it carelessly disposed of, the costs of cleanup are enormous. The alternative to cleaning up these sites is to ignore them and let toxic wastes eventually leak into underground aquifers. One way or another, society will pay—either in cleanup bills or in rising health care costs.

In addition to toxic chemical wastes, damaging nuclear waste is also a threat to human health. National governments in countries with nuclear power plants have failed to design a system for safely disposing of their wastes. At present, radiated fuel at most plants is stored in pools of cooling water at the site itself. No one has yet put a price tag on safely disposing of nuclear waste and decommissioning the nuclear power plants that generate it. Coping with the health problems associated with nuclear waste is, being left to future generations, a part of the nuclear legacy.

Several military powers face the related threat of radiation wastes generated at nuclear weapons manufacturing facilities, which are released into the surrounding areas. In the United States, the cleanup bill for all these sites, including some of the more publicized ones such as Rocky Flats in Colorado and the Savannah River site in South Carolina, is estimated at $200 billion. For the former Soviet Union, where the management of radioactive waste has been even more irresponsible, the costs are likely to be far greater. Again, the question is not whether society will pay the bill for nuclear wastes, but whether it will be in the form of cleanup or in rising health care costs in exposed communities.

The environmental deficits and debts that the world has incurred in recent decades are enormous, often dwarfing the economic debts of nations. Perhaps more important is the often overlooked difference between economic deficits and environmental ones. Economic debts are something we owe each other. For every borrower there is a lender; resources simply change hands. But environmental debts, especially those that lead to irreversible damage or losses of natural capital, can often be repaid only in the deprivation and ill health of future generations.

CRITICAL-THINKING QUESTIONS

1. In what ways are the world's environmental problems social issues?
2. Do you think global gatherings—like the United Nations Conference on Environment and Development held in Rio de Janeiro in 1992—can turn the tide of environmental deterioration?
3. Why do you think the author of this selection stresses the economic costs of environmental problems?

THE NATURAL ENVIRONMENT

Cross-Cultural

68

Supporting Indigenous Peoples

Alan Thein Durning

A particular concern of many environmentalists (and social scientists) is the steady loss of this planet's cultural diversity as thousands of small societies are pushed aside by the relentless march of economic development. This selection describes the problem and points out that protecting indigenous peoples is not just a matter of justice—the well-being of everyone in the world depends on it.

In July of 1992, an aged chief of the Lumad people in the Philippines—a man with a price on his head for his opposition to local energy development—sat at the base of the cloud-covered volcano Mount Apo and made a simple plea. "Our Christian brothers are enjoying their life here in the plains," said eighty-six-year-old Chief Tulalang Maway, sweeping his arm toward the provincial town of Kidapawan and the agricultural lands beyond, lands his tribe long ago ceded to immigrants

SOURCE: Excerpts from "Supporting Indigenous Peoples," by Alan Thein Durning are reprinted from *State of the World 1993: A Worldwatch Institute Report on Progress Toward a Sustainable Society,* Project Director: Lester R. Brown. By permission of W. W. Norton & Company, Inc. Copyright © 1993 by Worldwatch Institute.

from afar. Turning toward the mountain—a Lumad sacred site that he has vowed to defend "to the last drop of blood"—Maway slowly finished his thought, "We only ask them to leave us our last sanctuary."

Chief Maway's words could have been spoken by almost any tribal Filipino, or, for that matter, any Native American, Australian aborigine, African pygmy, or member of one of the world's thousands of other distinct indigenous cultures. All have ancient ties to the land, water, and wildlife of their ancestral domains, and all are endangered by onrushing forces of the outside world. They have been decimated by violence and plagues. Their cultures have been eroded by missionaries and exploited by wily entrepreneurs. Their subsistence economies have been dismantled in the pursuit of national development. And their homelands have been invaded by commercial resource extractors and overrun by landless peasants.

Chief Maway's entreaty, in its essence, is the call of indigenous peoples everywhere: the plea that their lands be spared further abuse, that their birthright be returned to them. It is a petition that the world's dominant cultures have long ignored, believing the passing of native peoples and their antiquated ways was an inevitable, if lamentable, cost of progress. That view, never morally defensible, is now demonstrably untenable.

Indigenous peoples are the sole guardians of vast, little-disturbed habitats in remote parts of every continent. These territories, which together encompass an area larger than Australia, provide important ecological services: They regulate hydrological cycles, maintain local and global climatic stability, and harbor a wealth of biological and genetic diversity. Indeed, indigenous homelands may provide safe haven for more endangered plant and animal species than all the world's nature reserves. Native peoples, moreover, often hold the key to these vaults of biological diversity. They possess a body of ecological knowledge—encoded in their languages, customs, and subsistence practices—that rivals the libraries of modern science.

The human rights enshrined in international law have long demanded that states shield indigenous cultures, but instead these cultures have been dismembered. A more self-interested appeal appears to be in order: Supporting indigenous survival is an objective necessity, even for those callous to the justice of the cause. As a practical matter, the world's dominant cultures cannot sustain the earth's ecological health—a requisite of human advancement—without the aid of the world's endangered cultures. Biological diversity is inextricably linked to cultural diversity.

Around the globe, indigenous peoples are fighting for their ancestral territories. They are struggling in courts and national parliaments, gaining power through new mass movements and international campaigns, and—as on the slopes of Mount Apo—defending their inheritance with their lives. The question is, Who will stand with them?

STATE OF THE NATIONS

Indigenous peoples (or "native" or "tribal" peoples) are found on every continent and in most countries. [See Table 68-1.] The extreme variations in their ways of life and current circumstances defy ready definition. Indeed, many anthropologists insist that indigenous peoples are defined only by the way they define themselves: They think of themselves as members of a distinct people. Still, many indigenous cultures share a number of characteristics that help describe, if not define, them.

They are typically descendants of the original inhabitants of an area taken over by more powerful outsiders. They are distinct from their country's dominant group in language, culture, or religion. Most have a custodial concept of land and other resources, in part defining themselves in relation to the habitat from which they draw their livelihood. They commonly live in or maintain strong ties to a subsistence economy; many are, or are descendants of, hunter-gatherers, fishers, nomadic or seasonal herders, shifting forest farmers, or subsistence peasant cultivators. And their social relations are often tribal, involving collective management of natural resources, thick networks of bonds between individuals, and group decision making, often by consensus among elders.

Measured by spoken languages, the single best indicator of a distinct culture, all the world's people belong to 6,000 cultures; 4,000–5,000 of these are indigenous ones. Of the 5.5 billion humans on the planet, some 190 million to 625 million are indigenous people. (These ranges are wide because of varying definitions of "indigenous." The higher figures include ethnic nations that lack political autonomy, such as Tibetans, Kurds, and Zulus, while the lower figures count only smaller, subnational societies.) In some countries, especially those settled by Europeans in the past five centuries, indigenous populations are fairly easy to

TABLE 68-1 Indigenous Peoples of the World, 1992

Region	*Indigenous Peoples*
Africa and Middle East	Great cultural diversity throughout continent; "indigenous" share hotly contested. Some 25–30 million nomadic herders or pastoralists in East Africa, Sahel, and Arabian peninsula include Bedouin, Dinka, Masai, Turkana. San (Bushmen) of Namibia and Botswana and pygmies of central African rain forest, both traditionally hunter-gatherers, have occupied present homelands for at least 20,000 years. (25–350 million indigenous people overall, depending on definitions; 2,000 languages)
Americas	Native Americans concentrated near centers of ancient civilizations: Aztec in Mexico, Mayan in Central America, and Incan in Andes of Bolivia, Ecuador, and Peru. In Latin America, most Indians farm small plots; in North America, 2 million Indians live in cities and on reservations. (42 million; 900 languages)
Arctic	Inuit (Eskimo) and other Arctic peoples of North America, Greenland, and Siberia traditionally fishers, whalers, and hunters. Sami (Lapp) of northern Scandinavia are traditionally reindeer herders. (2 million; 50 languages)
East Asia	Chinese indigenous peoples, numbering up to 82 million, mostly subsistence farmers such as Bulang of south China or former pastoralists such as ethnic Mongolians of north and west China. Ainu of Japan and aboriginal Taiwanese now largely industrial laborers. (12–84 million; 150 languages)
Oceania	Aborigines of Australia and Maoris of New Zealand, traditionally farmers, fishers, hunters, and gatherers. Many now raise livestock. Islanders of South Pacific continue to fish and harvest marine resources. (3 million; 500 languages)
South Asia	Gond, Bhil, and other adivasis, or tribal peoples, inhabit forest belt of central India. In Bangladesh, adivasis concentrated in Chittagong hills on Burmese border, several million tribal farmers and pastoralists in Afghanistan, Pakistan, Nepal, Iran, and central Asian republics of former Soviet Union. (74–91 million; 700 languages)
Southeast Asia	Tribal Hmong, Karen, and other forest-farming peoples form Asia ethnic mosaic covering uplands. Indigenous population follows distribution of forest: Laos has more forest and tribal peoples, Myanmar and Vietnam have less forest and fewer people, and Thailand and mainland Malaysia have the least. Tribal peoples are concentrated at the extreme ends of the Philippine and Indonesian archipelagos. Island of New Guinea—split politically between Indonesia and Papua New Guinea—populated by indigenous tribes. (32–55 million; 1,950 languages)

SOURCE: Worldwatch Institute.

count. [See Table 68-2.] By contrast, lines between indigenous peoples and ethnic minorities are difficult to draw in Asia and Africa, where cultural diversity remains greatest.

Regardless of where lines are drawn, however, human cultures are disappearing at unprecedented rates. Worldwide, the loss of cultural diversity is keeping pace with the global loss of biological diversity. Anthropologist Jason Clay of Cultural Survival in Cambridge, Massachusetts, writes, "there have been more . . . extinctions of tribal peoples in this century than in any other in history." Brazil alone lost eighty-seven tribes in the first half of the century. One-third of North American languages

TABLE 68-2 Estimated Populations of Indigenous Peoples, Selected Countries, 1992

Country	Population[a]	Share of National Population
	(million)	(percent)
Papua New Guinea	3.0	77
Bolivia	5.6	70
Guatemala	4.6	47
Peru	9.0	40
Ecuador	3.8	38
Myanmar	14.0	33
Laos	1.3	30
Mexico	10.9	12
New Zealand	0.4	12
Chile	1.2	9
Philippines	6.0	9
India	63.0	7
Malaysia	0.8	4
Canada	0.9	4
Australia	0.4	2
Brazil	1.5	1
Bangladesh	1.2	1
Thailand	0.5	1
United States	2.0	1
Former Soviet Union	1.4	>1

[a] Generally excludes those of mixed ancestry.

SOURCE: Worldwatch Institute.

and two-thirds of Australian languages have disappeared since 1800—the overwhelming share of them since 1900.

Cultures are dying out even faster than the peoples who belong to them. University of Alaska linguist Michael Krauss projects that half the world's languages—the storehouses of peoples' intellectual heritages—will disappear within a century. These languages, and arguably the cultures they embody, are no longer passed on to sufficient numbers of children to ensure their survival. Krauss likens such cultures to animal species doomed to extinction because their populations are below the threshold needed for adequate reproduction. Only 5 percent of all languages, moreover, enjoy the relative safety of having at least a half-million speakers.

To trace the history of indigenous peoples' subjugation is simply to recast the story of the rise of the world's dominant cultures: the spread of Han Chinese into Central and Southeast Asia, the as-

cent of Aryan empires on the Indian subcontinent, the southward advance of Bantu cultures across Africa, and the creation of a world economy first through European colonialism and then through industrial development. Surviving indigenous cultures are often but tattered remnants of their predecessors' societies.

When Christopher Columbus reached the New World in 1492, there were perhaps 54 million people in the Americas, almost as many as in Europe at the time; their numbers plummeted, however, as plagues radiated from the landfalls of the conquistadors. Five centuries later, the indigenous peoples of the Americas, numbering some 42 million, have yet to match their earlier population. Similar contractions followed the arrival of Europeans in Australia, New Zealand, and Siberia.

Worldwide, virtually no indigenous peoples remain entirely isolated from national societies. By indoctrination or brute force, nations have assimilated native groups into the cultural mainstream. As a consequence, few follow the ways of their ancestors unchanged. Just one tenth of the Penan hunter-gatherers continue to hunt in the rain forests of Malaysian Borneo. A similar share of the Sami (Lapp) reindeer-herders of northern Scandinavia accompany their herds on the Arctic ranges. Half of North American Indians and many New Zealand Maori dwell in cities.

Tragically, indigenous peoples whose cultures are besieged frequently end up on the bottom of the national economy. They are often the first sent to war for the state, as in Namibia and the Philippines, and the last to go to work: Unemployment in Canadian Indian communities averages 50 percent. They are overrepresented among migrant laborers in India, beggars in Mexico, and uranium miners in the United States. They are often drawn into the shadow economy: They grow drug crops in northern Thailand, run gambling casinos in the United States, and sell their daughters into prostitution in Taiwan. Everywhere, racism against them is rampant. India's adivasis, or tribal people, endure hardships comparable to the "untouchables," the most downtrodden caste.

Native peoples' inferior social status is sometimes codified in national law and perpetuated by institutionalized abuse. Many members of the hill tribes in Thailand are denied citizenship, and until 1988 the Brazilian constitution legally classified Indians as minors and wards of the state. In the extreme, nation-states are simply genocidal: Burmese soldiers systemically raped, murdered, and enslaved thousands of Arakanese villagers in early 1992. Guatemala has exterminated perhaps 100,000 Mayans in its three-decade counterinsurgency. Similar numbers of indigenous people have died in East Timor and Irian Jaya since 1970 at the hands of Indonesian forces intent on solidifying their power.

In much of the world, the oppression that indigenous peoples suffer has indelibly marked their own psyches, manifesting itself in depression and social disintegration. Says Tamara Gliminova of the Khant people of Siberia, "When they spit into your soul for this long, there is little left."

HOMELANDS

Indigenous peoples not yet engulfed in modern societies live mostly in what Mexican anthropologist Gonzalo Aguirre Beltran called "regions of refuge," places so rugged, desolate, or remote that they have been little disturbed by the industrial economy. They remain in these areas for tragic reasons. Peoples in more fertile lands were eradicated outright to make way for settlers and plantations, or they retreated—sometimes at gun point—into these natural havens. Whereas indigenous peoples exercised de facto control over most of the earth's ecosystems as recently as two centuries ago, the territory they now occupy is reduced to an estimated 12–19 percent of the earth's land area—depending, again, on where the line between indigenous peoples and ethnic nations is drawn. And governments recognize their ownership of but a fraction of that area.

Gaining legal protection for the remainder of their subsistence base is most indigenous peoples' highest political priority. If they lose this struggle, their cultures stand little chance of surviving. As the World Council of Indigenous Peoples, a global federation based in Canada, wrote in 1985, "Next to shooting Indigenous Peoples, the surest way to kill us is to separate us from our part of the Earth." Most native peoples are bound to their land through relationships both practical and spiritual, routine and historical. Tribal Filipino Edtami Mansayagan, attempting to communicate the pain he feels at the destruction of the rivers, valleys, meadows, and hillsides of his people's mountain domain, exclaims, "these are the living pages of our unwritten history." The question of who shall control resources in the regions of refuge is the crux of indigenous survival.

Indigenous homelands are important not only to endangered cultures; they are also of exceptional ecological value. Intact indigenous communities and little-disturbed ecosystems overlap with singular regularity, from the coastal swamps of South America to the shifting sands of the Sahara, from the ice floes of the circumpolar north to the coral reefs of the South Pacific. When, for example, a National Geographic Society team in Washington, DC, compiled a map of Indian lands and remaining forest cover in Central America in 1992, they confirmed the personal observation of Geodisio Castillo, a Kuna Indian from Panama: "Where there are forests there are indigenous people, and where there are indigenous people there are forests."

Because populations of both indigenous peoples and unique plant and animal species are numerically concentrated in remnant habitats in the tropics—precisely the regions of refuge that Beltran was referring to—the biosphere's most diverse habitats are usually homes to endangered cultures. The persistence of biological diversity in these regions is no accident. In the Philippines and Thailand, both representative cases, little more than a third of the land officially zoned as forest remains forest-covered; the tracts that do still stand are largely those protected by tribal people.

The relationship between cultural diversity and biological diversity stands out even in global statistics. Just nine countries together account for 60 percent of human languages. Of these nine centers of cultural diversity, six are also on the roster of biological "megadiversity" countries—nations with exceptional numbers of unique plant and animal species. . . . By the same token, two-thirds of all megadiversity countries also rank at the top of the cultural diversity league, with more than 100 languages spoken in each.

Everywhere, the world economy now intrudes on what is left of native lands, as it has for centuries. Writes World Bank anthropologist Shelton Davis: "The creation of a . . . global economy . . . has meant the pillage of native peoples' lands, labor and resources and their enforced acculturation and spiritual conquest. Each cycle of global economic expansion—the search for gold and spices in the sixteenth century, the fur trade and sugar estate economics of the seventeenth and eighteenth centuries, the rise of the great coffee, copra and . . . tropical fruit plantations in the late nineteenth and early twentieth centuries, the modern search for petroleum, strategic minerals, and tropical hardwoods—was based upon the exploitation of natural resources or primary commodities and led to the displacement of indigenous peoples and the undermining of traditional cultures."

The juggernaut of the money economy has not slowed in the late twentieth century; if anything, it has accelerated. Soaring consumer demand among the world's fortunate and burgeoning populations among the unfortunate fuel the economy's drive into native peoples' territories. Loggers, miners, commercial fishers, small farmers, plantation growers, dam builders, oil drillers—all come to seek their fortunes. Governments that equate progress with export earnings aid them, and military establishments bent on controlling far-flung territories back them.

Logging, in particular, is a menace because so many indigenous peoples dwell in woodlands . Japanese builders, for example, are devouring the ancient hardwood forests of tropical Borneo, home of the Penan and other Dayak peoples, for disposable concrete molds. Most mahogany exported from Latin America is now logged illegally on Indian reserves, and most nonplantation teak cut in Asia currently comes from tribal lands in the war-torn hills of Myanmar.

The consequences of mining on native lands are also ruinous. In the late eighties, for instance, tens of thousands of gold prospectors infiltrated the remote northern Brazilian haven of the Yanomami, the last large, isolated group of indigenous peoples in the Americas. The miners turned streams into sewers, contaminated the environment with the 1,000 tons of toxic mercury they used to purify gold, and precipitated an epidemic of malaria that killed more than a thousand children and elders. Just in time, the Brazilian government recognized and began defending the Yanomami homeland in early 1992, a rare and hopeful precedent in the annals of indigenous history. Still, in Brazil overall, mining concessions overlap 34 percent of Indian lands. . . .

Other energy projects, especially large dams, also take their toll on native habitats. In the north of Canada, the provincial electric utility Hydro Quebec completed a massive project called James Bay I in 1985, inundating vast areas of Cree Indian hunting grounds and unexpectedly contaminating fisheries with naturally occurring heavy metals that had previously been locked away in the soil. The Cree and neighboring Inuit tribes have organized against the project's next gigantic phase, James Bay II. The $60-billion project would tame eleven wild rivers, altering a France-sized area to generate 27,000 megawatts of exportable power. As Matthew Coon-Come, Grand Chief of the Cree, says, "The only people who have the right to build dams on our territory are the beavers.". . .

Commercial producers have also taken over indigenous lands for large-scale agriculture. The Barabaig herders of Tanzania have lost more than 400 square kilometers of dry-season range to a mechanized wheat farm. Private ranchers in Botswana have enclosed grazing lands for their own use, and Australian ranchers have usurped aboriginal lands. In peninsular Malaysia, palm and rubber plantations have left the Orang Asli (Original People) with tiny fractions of their ancient tropical forests.

Less dramatic but more pervasive is the ubiquitous invasion of small farmers onto indigenous lands. Sometimes sponsored by the state but ultimately driven by population growth and maldistribution of farmland, poor settlers encroach on native lands everywhere. In Indonesia during the eighties, for example, the government shifted 2 million people from densely populated islands such as Java to 800,000 hectares of newly cleared plots in sparsely populated indigenous provinces such as Irian Jaya, Kalimantan, and Sumatra. Half the area settled was virgin forest—much of it indigenous territory. . . .

Few states recognize indigenous peoples' rights over homelands, and where they do, those rights are often partial, qualified, or of ambiguous legal force. Countries may recognize customary rights in theory, but enforce common or statutory law against those rights whenever there is a conflict; or they may sanction indigenous rights but refuse to enforce them. Through this cloud of legal contradictions a few countries stand out as exceptional. Papua New Guinea and Ecuador acknowledge indigenous title to large shares of national territory, and Canada and Australia recognize rights over extensive areas. . . . Still, across all the earth's climatic and ecological zones—from the Arctic tundra to the temperate and nontropical forests to the savannahs and deserts—native peoples control slim shares of their ancestral domains. . . .

STEWARDS

Sustainable use of local resources is simple self-preservation for people whose way of life is tied to the fertility and natural abundance of the land. Any community that knows its children and grandchildren will live exactly where it does is more apt to take a longer view than a community without attachments to local places.

Moreover, native peoples frequently aim to preserve not just a standard of living but a way of life rooted in the uniqueness of a local place. Colombian anthropologist Martin von Hildebrand notes, "The Indians often tell me that the difference between a colonist [a non-Indian settler] and an Indian is that the colonist wants to leave money for his children and that the Indians want to leave forests for their children."

Indigenous peoples' unmediated dependence on natural abundance has its parallel in their peerless ecological knowledge. Most forest-dwelling tribes display an utter mastery of botany. One typical group, the Shuar people of Ecuador's Amazonian lowlands, uses 800 species of plants for medicine, food, animal fodder, fuel, construction, fishing, and hunting supplies.

Native peoples commonly know as much about ecological processes that affect the availability of natural resources as they do about those resources' diverse uses. South Pacific islanders can predict to the day and hour the beginning of the annual spawning runs of many fish. Whaling peoples of northern Canada have proved to skeptical western marine biologists that bowhead whales migrate under pack ice. Coastal aborigines in Australia distinguish between eighty different tidal conditions.

Specialists trained in western science often fail to recognize indigenous ecological knowledge because of the cultural and religious ways in which indigenous peoples record and transmit that learning. Ways of life that developed over scores of generations could only thrive by encoding ecological sustainability into the body of practice, myth, and taboo that passes from parent to child. . . .

What are the conditions in which traditional systems of ecological management can persist in the modern world? First, indigenous peoples must have secure rights to their subsistence base—rights that are not only recognized but enforced by the state and, ideally, backed by international law. Latin American tribes such as the Shuar of Ecuador, when threatened with losing their land, have cleared their own forests and taken up cattle ranching, because these actions prove ownership in Latin America. Had Ecuador backed up the Shuar's land rights, the ranching would have been unnecessary.

Second, for indigenous ecological stewardship to survive the onslaught of the outside world, indigenous peoples must be organized politically and the state in which they reside must allow democratic initiatives. The Khant and Mansi peoples of Siberia, just as most indigenous people in the former Soviet Union, were nominally autonomous in their customary territories under Soviet law, but political repression precluded the organized defense of that terrain until the end of the eighties. Since then, the peoples of Siberia have begun organizing themselves to turn paper rights into real local control. In neighboring China, in contrast, indigenous homelands remain pure legal fictions because the state crushes all representative organizations.

Third, indigenous communities must have access to information, support, and advice from friendly sources if they are to surmount the obstacles of the outside world. The tribal people of Papua New Guinea know much about their local environments, for example, but they know little about the impacts of large-scale logging and mining. Foreign and domestic investors have often played on this ignorance, assuring remote groups that no lasting harm would result from leasing parts of their land to resource extractors. If the forest peoples of Papua New Guinea could learn from the experience of indigenous peoples elsewhere—through supportive organizations and indigenous peoples' federations—they might be more careful.

A handful of peoples around the world have succeeded in satisfying all three of these conditions. . . .

any movement has its share of internal rivalries, may eventually bring fundamental advances in the status of all endangered cultures. . . .

In a world where almost all nations have publicly committed themselves to the goal of sustainable development and most have signed a global treaty for the protection of biological diversity, the questions of cultural survival and indigenous homelands cannot be avoided much longer. As guardians and stewards of remote and fragile ecosystems, indigenous cultures could play a crucial role in safeguarding humanity's planetary home. But they cannot do it alone. They need the support of international law and national policy, and they need the understanding and aid of the world's more numerous peoples.

Giving native peoples power over their own lives raises issues for the world's dominant culture as well—a consumerist and individualist culture born in Europe and bred in the United States. Indeed, indigenous peoples may offer more than a best-bet alternative for preserving the outlying areas where they live. They may offer living examples of cultural patterns that can help revive ancient values within everyone: devotion to future generations, ethical regard for nature, and commitment to community among people. The question may be, then, Are indigenous peoples the past, or are they the future?

RISING FROM THE FRONTIER

From the smallest tribal settlements to the U.N. General Assembly, indigenous peoples organizations are making themselves felt. Their grassroots movements have spread rapidly since 1970, gaining strength in numbers and through improvement of their political skills. They have pooled their talents in regional, national, and global federations to broaden their influence. This uprising, which like

CRITICAL-THINKING QUESTIONS

1. How many indigenous cultures are there on this planet? What general traits do they have in common?

2. Why are the world's tribal peoples disappearing?

3. The author asserts that sustaining the world's natural environment depends on assuring the future of indigenous peoples. Why is this so?

69

On the Origin of Social Movements

Jo Freeman

According to Jo Freeman, a "spark of life" sometimes transforms a group of like-minded people into a social movement. In this excerpt from her work, Freeman analyzes this process, illustrating her ideas with an account of the civil rights movement and the women's movement in the United States.

Most movements have inconspicuous beginnings. The significant elements of their origins are usually forgotten or distorted by the time a trained observer seeks to trace them out. Perhaps this is why the theoretical literature on social movements usually concentrates on causes (Gurr 1970; Davies 1962; Oberschall 1973) and motivations (Toch 1965; Cantril 1941; Hoffer 1951; Adorno et al. 1950), while the "spark of life" by which the "mass is to cross the threshold of organizational life" (Lowi 1971: 41) has received scant attention. . . .

SOURCE: "On the Origins of Social Movements," by Jo Freeman, in *Social Movements of the Sixties and Seventies,* ed. Jo Freeman, pp. 8–13, 17–30. Copyright © 1983 by Jo Freeman. Reprinted by permission.

From where do the people come who make up the initial, organizing cadre of a movement? How do they come together, and how do they come to share a similar view of the world in circumstances that compel them to political action? In what ways does the nature of the original center affect the future development of the movement?

Before answering these questions, let us first look at data on the origins of [two] social movements prominent in the sixties and seventies: civil rights . . . and women's liberation. These data identify recurrent elements involved in movement formation. The ways in which these elements interact, given a sufficient level of strain, would support the following propositions:

Proposition 1. The need for a *preexisting communications network* or infrastructure within the social base of a movement is a primary prerequisite for "spontaneous" activity. Masses alone do not form movements, however discontented they may be. Groups of previously unorganized individuals may spontaneously form into small local associations—usually along the lines of informal social networks—in response to a specific strain or crisis. If they are not linked in some manner, however, the protest does not become generalized but remains a local irritant or dissolves completely. If a movement is to spread rapidly, the communications network must already exist. If only the rudiments of a network exist, movement formation requires a high input of "organizing" activity.

Proposition 2. Not just any communications network will do. It must be a network that is *cooptable* to the new ideas of the incipient movement.[1] To be cooptable, it must be composed of likeminded people whose backgrounds, experiences, or location in the social structure make them receptive to the ideas of a specific new movement.

Proposition 3. Given the existence of a cooptable communications network, or at least the rudimentary development of a potential one, and a situation of strain, one or more precipitants are required. Here, two distinct patterns emerge that often overlap. In one, a *crisis* galvanizes the network into spontaneous action in a new direction. In the other, one or more persons begin *organizing* a new organization or disseminating a new idea. For spontaneous action to occur, the communications network must be well formed or the initial protest will not survive the incipient stage. If it is not well formed, organizing efforts must occur; that is, one or more persons must specifically attempt to construct a movement. To be successful, organizers must be skilled and must have a fertile field in which to work. If no communications network already exists, there must at least be emerging spontaneous groups that are acutely attuned to the issue, albeit uncoordinated. To sum up, if a cooptable communications network is already established, a crisis is all that is necessary to galvanize it. If it is

rudimentary, an organizing cadre of one or more persons is necessary. Such a cadre is superfluous if the former conditions fully exist, but it is essential if they do not.

THE CIVIL RIGHTS MOVEMENT

The civil rights movement has two origins, although one contributed significantly to the other. The first can be dated from December 7, 1955, when the arrest of Rosa Parks for occupying a "white" seat on a bus stimulated both the Montgomery Bus Boycott and the formation of the Montgomery Improvement Association. The second can be dated either from February 1, 1960, when four freshmen at A & T College in Greensboro, North Carolina, sat-in at a white lunch counter, or from April 15–17, when a conference at Shaw University in Raleigh, North Carolina, resulted in the formation of the Student Non-Violent Co-ordinating Committee. To understand why there were two origins one has to understand the social structure of the southern black community, as an incipient generation gap alone is inadequate to explain it.

Within this community the two most important institutions, often the only institutions, were the church and the black college. They provided the primary networks through which most southern blacks interacted and communicated with one another on a regular basis. In turn, the colleges and churches were linked in a regional communications network. These institutions were also the source of black leadership, for being a "preacher or a teacher" were the main status positions in black society. Of the two, the church was by far the more important; it touched on more people's lives and was the largest and oldest institution in the black community. Even during slavery there had been an "invisible church." After emancipation, "organized religious life became the chief means by which a structured or organized social life came into existence among the Negro masses" (Frazier 1963: 17). Furthermore, preachers were more economically independent of white society than were teachers.

Neither of these institutions represented all the segments of black society, but the segments they did represent eventually formed the main social base for supplying civil rights activists. The church was composed of a male leadership and a largely middle-aged, lower-class female followership. The black colleges were the homes of black intellectuals and middle-class youth, male and female.

Both origins of the civil rights movement resulted in the formation of new organizations, despite the fact that at least three seemingly potential social movement organizations already existed. The wealthiest of these was the Urban League, founded in 1910. It, however, was not only largely restricted to a small portion of the black and white bourgeoisie but, until 1961, felt itself to be "essentially a social service agency" (Clark 1966: 245).

Founded in 1909, the National Association for the Advancement of Colored People (NAACP) pursued channels of legal change until it finally persuaded the Supreme Court to abolish educational segregation in *Brown* v. *Board of Education.* More than any other single event, this decision created the atmosphere of rising expectations that helped precipitate the movement. The NAACP suffered from its own success, however. Having organized itself primarily to support court cases and utilize other "respectable" means, it "either was not able or did not desire to modify its program in response to new demands. It believed it should continue its important work by using those techniques it had already perfected" (Blumer 1951: 199).

The Congress of Racial Equality, like the other two organizations, was founded in the North. It began "in 1942 as the Chicago Committee of Racial Equality, which was composed primarily of students at the University of Chicago. An offshoot of the pacifist Fellowship of Reconciliation, its leaders were middle-class intellectual reformers, less prominent and more alienated from the mainstream of American society than the founders of the NAACP. They regarded the NAACP's legalism as too gradualist and ineffective, and aimed to apply Gandhian techniques of non-violent direct action to the problem of race relations in the United States. A year later, the Chicago Committee joined with a half dozen other groups that had emerged across the country, mostly under the encouragement of the F. O. R. to form a federation known as the Congress of Racial Equality" (Rudwick and Meier 1970: 10).

CORE's activities anticipated many of the main forms of protest of the civil rights movement, and its attitudes certainly seemed to fit CORE for the role of a major civil rights organization. But though it became quite influential, at the time the movement actually began, CORE had declined almost to the point of extinction. Its failure reflects the historical reality that organizations are less likely to create social movements than be created by them. More important, CORE was poorly situated to lead a movement of southern blacks. Northern-based and composed primarily of pacifist intellectuals, it had no roots in any of the existing structures of the black community, and in the North these structures were themselves weak. CORE could be a source of ideas, but not of coordination.

The coordination of a new movement required the creation of a new organization. But that was not apparent until after the Montgomery bus boycott began. That boycott was organized through institutions already existing in the black community of Montgomery.

Rosa Parks's refusal to give up her seat on the bus to a white man was not the first time such defiance of segregation laws had occurred. There had been talk of a boycott the previous time, but after local black leaders had a congenial meeting with the city commissioners, nothing happened—on either side (King 1958: 37–41). When Parks, a former secretary of the local NAACP, was arrested, she immediately called E. D. Nixon, at that time the president of the local chapter. He not only bailed her out but informed a few influential women in the city, most of whom were members of the Women's Political Council. After numerous phone calls between their members, it was the WPC that actually suggested the boycott, and E. D. Nixon who initially organized it (ibid.: 44–45).

The Montgomery Improvement Association

(MIA) was formed at a meeting of eighteen ministers and civic leaders the Monday after Parks's conviction and a day of successful boycotting, to provide ongoing coordination. No one then suspected that coordination would be necessary for over a year, with car pools organized to provide alternative transportation for seventeen thousand riders a day. During this time the MIA grew slowly to a staff of ten in order to handle the voluminous correspondence, as well as to provide rides and keep the movement's momentum going. The organization, and the car pools, were financed by $250,000 in donations that poured in from all over the world in response to heavy press publicity about the boycott. But the organizational framework for the boycott and the MIA was the church. Most, although not all, of the officers were ministers, and Sunday meetings with congregations continued to be the main means of communicating with members of the black community and encouraging them to continue the protest.

The boycott did not end until the federal courts ruled Alabama's bus segregation laws unconstitutional late in 1956—at the same time that state courts ruled the boycott illegal. In the meantime, black leaders throughout the South had visited Montgomery, and out of the discussions came agreement to continue antisegregation protests regularly and systematically under the aegis of a new organization, the Southern Christian Leadership Conference. The NAACP could not lead the protests because, according to an SCLC pamphlet, "during the late fifties, the NAACP had been driven out of some Southern states. Its branches were outlawed as foreign corporations and its lawyers were charged with barratry, that is, persistently inciting litigation."

On January 10, 1957, over one hundred people gathered in Atlanta at a meeting called by four ministers, including Martin Luther King. Bayard Rustin drew up the "working papers." Initially called the Southern Leadership Conference on Transportation and Nonviolent Integration, the SCLC never developed a mass base even when it changed its name. It established numerous "affiliates" but did most of its work through the churches in the communities to which it sent its fieldworkers.

The church was not just the only institution available for a movement to work through; in many ways it was ideal. It performed "the central organizing function in the Negro community" (Halloway 1969: 22), providing both access to large masses of people on a regular basis and a natural leadership. As Wyatt Tee Walker, former executive director of SCLC, commented, "The Church today is central to the movement. If a Negro's going to have a meeting, where's he going to have it? Mostly he doesn't have a Masonic lodge, and he's not going to get the public schools. And the church is the primary means of communication" (Brink and Harris 1964: 103). Thus the church eventually came to be the center of the voter registration drives as well as many of the other activities of the civil rights movement.

Even the young men and women of SNCC had to use the church, though they had trouble doing so because, unlike most of the officers of SCLC, they were not themselves ministers and thus did not have a "fraternal" connection. Instead they tended to draw many of their resources and people from outside the particular town in which they were working by utilizing their natural organizational base, the college.

SNCC did not begin the sit-ins, but came out of them. Once begun, the idea of the sit-in spread initially by means of the mass media. But such sit-ins almost always took place in towns where there were Negro colleges, and groups on these campuses essentially organized the sit-in activities of their communities. Nonetheless, "CORE, with its long emphasis of nonviolent direct action, played an important part, once the sit-ins began, as an educational and organizing agent" (Zinn 1964: 23). CORE had very few staff in the South, but there were enough to at least hold classes and practice sessions in nonviolence.

It was SCLC, however, that was actually responsible for the formation of SNCC; though it might well have organized itself eventually. Ella Baker, then executive secretary of SCLC, thought something should be done to coordinate the rapidly spreading sit-ins in 1960, and many members of SCLC thought it might be appropriate to organize a youth group. With SCLC money, Baker persuaded her alma mater, Shaw University, to provide facilities to contact the groups at centers of sit-in activity. Some two hundred people showed up for the meeting, decided to have no official connection with SCLC beyond a "friendly relationship," and formed the Student Non-Violent Co-ordinating Committee (Zinn 1964: 32–34). It had no members, and its fieldworkers numbered two hundred at their highest point, but it was from the campuses, especially the southern black colleges, that it drew its sustenance and upon which its organizational base rested. . . .

THE WOMEN'S LIBERATION MOVEMENT[2]

Women are not well organized. Historically tied to the family and isolated from their own kind, only in the nineteenth century did women in this country have the opportunity to develop independent associations of their own. These associations took years and years of careful organizational work to build. Eventually they formed the basis for the suffrage movement of the early twentieth century. The associations took less time to die. Today the Women's Trade Union League, the General Federation of Women's Clubs, the Women's Christian Temperance Union, not to mention the powerful National Women's Suffrage Association, are all either dead or a pale shadow of their former selves.

As of 1960, not one organization of women had the potential to become a social movement organization, nor was there any form of "neutral" structure of interaction to provide the base for such an organization. The closest exception to the former was the National Women's Party, which has remained dedicated to feminist concerns since its inception in 1916. However, the NWP has been essentially a lobbying group for the Equal Rights Amendment since 1923. From the beginning, the NWP believed that a small group of women concentrating their efforts in the right places was more

effective than a mass appeal, and so was not appalled by the fact that as late as 1969 even the majority of avowed feminists in this country had never heard of the ERA or the NWP.

The one large women's organization that might have provided a base for a social movement was the 180,000-member Federation of Business and Professional Women's Clubs. Yet, while it has steadily lobbied for legislation of importance to women, as late as "1966 BPW rejected a number of suggestions that it redefine . . . goals and tactics and become a kind of 'NAACP for women' . . . out of fear of being labeled 'feminist' " (Hole and Levine 1971: 89).

Before any social movement could develop among women, there had to be created a structure to bring potential feminist sympathizers together. To be sure, groups such as the BPW, and institutions such as the women's colleges, might be a good source of adherents for such a movement. But they were determined not to be the source of leadership.

What happened in the 1960s was the development of two new communications networks in which women played prominent roles that allowed, even forced, an awakened interest in the old feminist ideas. As a result, the movement actually has two origins, from two different strata of society, with two different styles, orientations, values, and forms of organization. The first of these will be referred to as the "older branch" of the movement, partially because it began first and partially because it was on the older side of the "generation gap" that pervaded the sixties. Its most prominent organization is the National Organization for Women (NOW), which was also the first to be formed. The style of its movement organizations tends to be traditional with elected officers, boards of directors, bylaws, and the other trappings of democratic procedure. Conversely, the "younger branch" consisted of innumerable small groups engaged in a variety of activities whose contact with one another was always tenuous (Freeman 1975: 50).

The forces that led to NOW's formation were set in motion in 1961 when President Kennedy established the President's Commission on the Status of Women at the behest of Esther Petersen, then director of the Women's Bureau. Its 1963 report, *American Women,* and subsequent committee publications documented just how thoroughly women were denied many rights and opportunities. The most significant response to the activity of the President's commission was the establishment of some fifty state commissions to do similar research on a state level. The Presidential and State Commission activity laid the groundwork for the future movement in two significant ways: (1) It unearthed ample evidence of women's unequal status and in the process convinced many previously uninterested women that something should be done; (2) It created a climate of expectations that something would be done. The women of the Presidential and State Commissions who were exposed to these influences exchanged visits, correspondence, and staff, and met with one another at an annual commission convention. They were in a position to share and mutually reinforce their growing awareness and concern over women's issues. These commissions thus provided an embryonic communications network.

During this time, two other events of significance occurred. The first was the publication of Betty Friedan's *The Feminine Mystique* in 1963. A quick best seller, the book stimulated many women to question the *status quo* and some women to suggest to Friedan that an organization be formed to do something about it. The second event was the addition of "sex" to the 1964 Civil Rights Act.

Many thought the "sex" provision was a joke, and the Equal Employment Opportunity Commission treated it as one, refusing to enforce it seriously. But a rapidly growing feminist coterie within the EEOC argued that "sex" would be taken more seriously if there were "some sort of NAACP for women" to put pressure on the government.

On June 30, 1966, these three strands of incipient feminism came together, and NOW was tied from the knot. At that time, government officials running the Third National Conference of Commissions on the Status of Women, ironically titled "Targets for Action," forbade the presentation of a suggested resolution calling for the EEOC to treat sex discrimination with the same consideration as race discrimination. The officials said one government agency could not be allowed to pressure another, despite the fact that the state commissions were not federal agencies. The small group of women who desired such a resolution had met the night before in Friedan's hotel room to discuss the possibility of a civil rights organization for women. Not convinced of its need, they chose instead to propose the resolution. When conference officials vetoed it, they held a whispered conversation over lunch and agreed to form an action organization "to bring women into full participation in the mainstream of American society now, assuming all the privileges and responsibilities thereof in truly equal partnership with men." The name NOW was coined by Friedan who was at the conference doing research on a book. When word leaked out, twenty-eight women paid five dollars each to join before the day was over (Friedan 1967: 4).

By the time the organizing conference was held the following October 29 through 30, over three hundred men and women had become charter members. It is impossible to do a breakdown on the composition of the charter membership, but one of the officers and board is possible. Such a breakdown accurately reflected NOW's origins. Friedan was president, two former EEOC commissioners were vice presidents, a representative of the United Auto Workers Women's Committee was secretary-treasurer, and there were seven past and present members of the State Commissions on the Status of Women on the twenty member board. One hundred twenty-six of the charter members were Wisconsin residents—and Wisconsin had the most active state Commission. Occupationally, the board and officers were primarily from the professions, labor, government, and communications fields. Of these, only those from labor had any experience in organizing, and they resigned a year later in a dispute over support of the Equal Rights Amendment. Instead of organizational experience, what the early NOW members had was experience in working with and in the media, and it was here that their early efforts were aimed.

As a result, NOW often gave the impression of being larger than it was. It was highly successful in getting in the press; much less successful in either bringing about concrete changes or forming an organization. Thus it was not until 1970, when the national press simultaneously did major stories on the women's liberation movement, that NOW's membership increased significantly.

In the meantime, unaware of and unknown to NOW, the EEOC, or the State Commissions, younger women began forming their own movement. Here, too, the groundwork had been laid some years before. The different social action projects of the sixties had attracted many women, who were quickly shunted into traditional roles and faced with the self-evident contradiction of working in a "freedom movement" but not being very free. No single "youth movement" activity or organization is responsible for forming the younger branch of the women's liberation movement, but together they created a "radical community" in which like-minded people continually interacted or were made aware of one another. This community provided the necessary network of communication and its radical ideas the framework of analysis that "explained" the dismal situation in which radical women found themselves.

Papers had been circulated on women and individual temporary women's caucuses had been held as early as 1964 (see Hayden and King 1966). But it was not until 1967 and 1968 that the groups developed a determined, if cautious, continuity and began to consciously expand themselves. At least five groups in five different cities (Chicago, Toronto, Detroit, Seattle, and Gainesville, Florida) formed spontaneously, independently of one another. They came at an auspicious moment, for 1967 was the year in which the blacks kicked the whites out of the civil rights movement, student power was discredited by SDS, and the New Left was on the wane. Only draft resistance activities were on the increase, and this movement more than any other exemplified the social inequities of the sexes. Men could resist the draft. Women could only counsel resistance.

At this point, there were few opportunities available for political work. Some women fit well into the secondary role of draft counseling. Many didn't. For years their complaints of unfair treatment had been forestalled by movement men with the dictum that those things could wait until after the Revolution. Now these political women found time on their hands, but still the men would not listen.

A typical example was the event that precipitated the formation of the Chicago group, the first independent group in this country. At the August 1967 National Conference for New Politics convention a women's caucus met for days, but was told its resolution wasn't significant enough to merit a floor discussion. By threatening to tie up the convention with procedural motions the women succeeded in having their statement tacked to the end of the agenda. It was never discussed. The chair refused to recognize any of the many women standing by the microphone, their hands straining upwards. When he instead called on someone to speak on "the forgotten American, the American Indian," five women rushed the podium to demand an explanation. But the chairman just patted one of them on the head (literally) and told her, "Cool down, little girl. We have more important things to talk about than women's problems."

The "little girl" was Shulamith Firestone, future author of *The Dialectic of Sex,* and she didn't cool down. Instead she joined with another Chicago woman she met there who had unsuccessfully tried to organize a women's group that summer, to call a meeting of the women who had halfheartedly attended those summer meetings. Telling their stories to those women, they stimulated sufficient rage to carry the group for three months, and by that time it was a permanent institution.

Another somewhat similar event occurred in Seattle the following winter. At the University of Washington an SDS organizer was explaining to a large meeting how white college youth established rapport with the poor whites with whom they were working. "He noted that sometimes after analyzing societal ills, the men shared leisure time by 'balling a chick together.' He pointed out that such activities did much to enhance the political consciousness of the poor white youth. A woman in the audience asked, 'And what did it do for the consciousness of the chick?' " (Hole and Levine 1971: 120). After the meeting, a handful of enraged women formed Seattle's first group.

Subsequent groups to the initial five were largely organized rather than formed spontaneously out of recent events. In particular, the Chicago group was responsible for the formation of many new groups in Chicago and in other cities. Unlike NOW, the women in the first groups had had years of experience as trained organizers. They knew how to utilize the infrastructure of the radical community, the underground press, and the free universities to disseminate women's liberation ideas. Chicago, as a center of New Left activity, had the largest number of politically conscious organizers. Many traveled widely to left conferences and demonstrations, and most used the opportunity to talk with other women about the new movement. In spite of public derision by radical men, or perhaps because of it, young women steadily formed new groups around the country.

ANALYSIS

From these data there appear to be four essential elements involved in movement formation: (1) the growth of a preexisting communications network that is (2) cooptable to the ideas of the new movement; (3) a series of crises that galvanize into action people involved in a cooptable network, and/or (4) subsequent organizing effort to weld the spontaneous groups together into a movement. Each of these elements needs to be examined in detail.

COMMUNICATIONS NETWORK

. . . The women's liberation movement . . . illustrates the importance of a network precisely because the conditions for a movement existed *before* a network came into being, but the movement didn't exist until afterward. Analysts of socioeconomic causes have concluded that the

movement could have started anytime within a twenty-year period. Strain for women was as great in 1955 as in 1965 (Ferriss 1971). What changed was the organizational situation. It was not until new networks emerged among women aware of inequities beyond local boundaries that a movement could grow past the point of occasional, spontaneous uprisings. The fact that two distinct movements, with two separate origins, developed from two networks unaware of each other is further evidence of the key role of preexisting communications networks as the fertile soil in which new movements can sprout.

References to the importance of a preexisting communications network appear frequently in case studies of social movements, though the theoretical writers were much slower to recognize their salience. According to Buck (1920: 43–44), the Grange established a degree of organization among American farmers in the nineteenth century that greatly facilitated the spread of future farmers' protests. Lipset has reported that in Saskatchewan, "the rapid acceptance of new ideas and movements . . . can be attributed mainly to the high degree of organization. . . . The role of the social structure of the western wheat belt in facilitating the rise of new movements has never been sufficiently appreciated by historians and sociologists. Repeated challenges and crises forced the western farmers to create many more community institutions (especially co-operatives and economic pressure groups) than are necessary in a more stable area. These groups in turn provided a structural basis for immediate action in critical situations. [Therefore] though it was a new radical party, the C. C. F. did not have to build up an organization from scratch" (1959: 206).

Similarly, Heberle (1951: 232) reports several findings that Nazism was most successful in small, well-integrated communities. As Lipset put it, these findings "sharply challenge the various interpretations of Nazism as the product of the growth of anomie and the general rootlessness of modern urban industrial society" (1959: 146).

Indirect evidence attesting to the essential role of formal and informal communications networks is found in diffusion theory, which emphasizes the importance of personal interaction rather than impersonal media communication in the spread of ideas (Rogers 1962; Lionberger 1960). This personal influence occurs through the organizational patterns of a community (Lionberger 1960: 73). It does not occur through the mass media. The mass media may be a source of information, but they are not a key source of influence.

Their lesser importance in relation to preexisting communications networks was examined in one study on "The Failure of an Incipient Social Movement" (Jackson, Peterson, Bull, Monsen, and Richmond 1960). In 1957 a potential tax protest movement in Los Angeles generated considerable interest and publicity for a little over a month but was dead within a year. According to the authors, this did not reflect a lack of public notice. They concluded that "mass communication alone is probably insufficient without a network of communication specifically linking those interested in the matter. . . . If a movement is to grow rapidly, it cannot rely upon its own network of communication, but must capitalize on networks already in existence" (p. 37).

A major reason it took social scientists so long to acknowledge the importance of communications networks was because the prevailing theories of the post–World War II era emphasized increasing social dislocation and anomie. Mass society theorists, as they were called, hypothesized that significant community institutions that linked individuals to governing elites were breaking down, that society was becoming a mass of isolated individuals. These individuals were seen as increasingly irresponsible and ungovernable, prone to irrational protests because they had no mediating institutions through which to pursue grievances (Kornhauser 1959).

In emphasizing disintegrating vertical connections, mass society theorists passed lightly over the role of horizontal ones, only occasionally acknowledging that "the combination of internal contact and external isolation facilitates the work of the mass agitator" (Kornhauser 1959: 218). This focus changed in the early seventies. Pinard's

study of the Social Credit Party of Quebec (1971) severely criticized mass society theory, arguing instead that "when strains are severe and widespread a new movement is more likely to meet its early success among the more strongly integrated citizens" (Pinard 1971: 192).

This insight was expanded by Oberschall (1973), who created a six-cell table to predict both the occurrence and type of protest. As did the mass society theorists, Oberschall said that even when there are grievances, protest will not occur outside institutional channels by those who are connected, through their own leadership or patron/client relationships, with governing elites. Among those who are segmented from such elites, the type of protest will be determined by whether there is communal, associational, or little organization. In the latter case, discontent is expressed through riots or other short-lived violent uprisings. "It is under conditions of strong . . . ties and segmentation that the possibility of the rapid spread of opposition movements on a continuous basis exists" (p. 123).

The movements we have studied would confirm Oberschall's conclusions, but not as strongly as he makes them. In all these cases a preexisting communications network was a necessary but insufficient condition for movement formation. Yet the newly formed networks among student radicals, welfare recipients, and women can hardly compare with the longstanding ties provided by the southern black churches and colleges. Their ties were tenuous and may not have survived the demise of their movements.

The importance of segmentation, or lack of connection with relevant elites, is less obvious in the sixties' movements. The higher socioeconomic status of incipient feminists and Movement leaders would imply greater access to elites than is true for blacks or welfare recipients. If Oberschall were correct, these closer connections should either have permitted easier and more rapid grievance solutions or more effective social control. They did neither. Indeed, it was the group most closely connected to decision-making elites— women of the Presidential and State Commission—who were among the earliest to see the need of a protest organization. Women of the younger branch of the movement did have their grievances against the men of the New Left effectively suppressed for several years, but even they eventually rejected this kind of elite control, even when it meant rejecting the men.

Conversely, Piven and Cloward show that the establishment of closer ties between leaders of local welfare rights groups and welfare workers through advisory councils and community coordinators led to a curtailment of militance and the institutionalization of grievances (1977: 326–31). They also argue that the development of government-funded community programs effectively coopted many local black movement leaders in the North and that federal channeling of black protest in the South into voter registration projects focused the movement there into traditional electoral politics (ibid.: 253). In short, the evidence about the role of segmentation in movement formation is ambiguous. The effect may be varied considerably by the nature of the political system.

CO-OPTABILITY

A recurrent theme in our studies is that not just any communications network will do. It must be one that is co-optable to the ideas of the new movement. The Business and Professional Women's (BPW) clubs were a network among women, but having rejected feminism, they could not overcome the ideological barrier to new political action until after feminism became established. . . .

On the other hand, the women on the Presidential and State Commissions and the feminist coterie of the EEOC were co-optable largely because their immersion in the facts of female status and the details of sex discrimination cases made them very conscious of the need for change. Likewise, the young women of the "radical community" lived in an atmosphere of questioning, confrontation, and change. They absorbed an ideology of "freedom" and "liberation" far more potent than any latent "antifeminism" might have been. . . .

Exactly what makes a network co-optable is harder to elucidate. Pinard (1971: 186) noted the necessity for groups to "*possess* or *develop* an ideology or simply subjective interests congruent with that of a new movement" for them to "act as mobilizing rather than restraining agents toward that movement," but did not further explore what affected the "primary group climate." More illumination is provided by the diffusion of innovation studies that point out the necessity for new ideas to fit in with already established norms for changes to happen easily. Furthermore, a social system that has as a value "innovativeness" (as the radical community did) will more rapidly adopt ideas than one that looks upon the habitual performance of traditional practices as the ideal (as most organized women's groups did in the fifties). Usually, as Lionberger (1960: 91) points out, "people act in terms of past experience and knowledge." People who have had similar experiences are likely to share similar perceptions of a situation and to mutually reinforce those perceptions as well as their subsequent interpretation. A co-optable network, then, is one whose members have had common experiences that predispose them to be receptive to the particular new ideas of the incipient movement and who are not faced with structural or ideological barriers to action. If the new movement as an "innovation" can interpret these experiences and perceptions in ways that point out channels for social action, then participation in a social movement becomes the logical thing to do.

THE ROLE OF CRISES

As our examples have illustrated, similar perceptions must be translated into action. This is often done by a crisis. For blacks in Montgomery, this was generated by Rosa Parks's refusal to give up her seat on a bus to a white man. For women who formed the older branch of the women's movement, the impetus to organize was the refusal of the EEOC to enforce the sex provision of Title VII, precipitated by the concomitant refusal of federal officials at the conference to allow a supportive resolution. For younger women there were a series of minor crises.

While not all movements are formed by such precipitating events, they are quite common as they serve to crystallize and focus discontent. From their own experiences, directly and concretely, people feel the need for change in a situation that allows for an exchange of feelings with others, mutual validation, and a subsequent reinforcement of innovative interpretation. Perception of an immediate need for change is a major factor in predisposing people to accept new ideas (Rogers 1962: 280). Nothing makes desire for change more acute than a crisis. Such a crisis need not be a major one; it need only embody collective discontent.

ORGANIZING EFFORTS

A crisis will only catalyze a well-formed communications network. If such networks are embryonically developed or only partially co-optable, the potentially active individuals in them must be linked together by someone. . . . As Jackson et al. (1960: 37) stated, "Some protest may persist where the source of trouble is constantly present. But interest ordinarily cannot be maintained unless there is a welding of spontaneous groups into some stable organization." In other words, people must be organized. Social movements do not simply occur.

The role of the organizer in movement formation is another neglected aspect of the theoretical literature. There has been great concern with leadership, but the two roles are distinct and not always performed by the same individual. In the early stages of a movement, it is the organizer much more than any leader who is important, and such an individual or cadre must often operate behind the scenes. The nature and function of these two roles was most clearly evident in the Townsend old-age movement of the thirties. Townsend was the "charismatic" leader, but the movement was organized by his partner, real estate promoter Robert Clements. Townsend himself acknowledges that without Clements' help, the movement

would never have gone beyond the idea stage (Holzman 1963).

The importance of organizers is pervasive in the sixties' movements. Dr. King may have been the public spokesperson of the Montgomery Bus Boycott who caught the eye of the media, but it was E. D. Nixon who organized it. Certainly the "organizing cadre" that young women in the radical community came to be was key to the growth of that branch of the women's liberation movement, despite the fact that no "leaders" were produced (and were actively discouraged). The existence of many leaders but no organizers in the older branch of the women's liberation movement readily explains its subsequent slow development. . . .

The function of the organizer has been explored indirectly by other analysts. Rogers (1962) devotes many pages to the "change agent" who, while he does not necessarily weld a group together or "construct" a movement, does many of the same things for agricultural innovation that an organizer does for political change. Mass society theory makes frequent reference to the "agitator," though not in a truly informative way. Interest groups are often organized by single individuals and some of them evolve into social movements. Salisbury's study of farmers' organizations finds this a recurrent theme. He also discovered that "a considerable number of farm groups were subsidized by other, older, groups. . . . The Farm Bureau was organized and long sustained by subsidies, some from federal and state governments, and some by local businessmen" (Salisbury 1959, p. 13).

These patterns are similar to ones we have found in the formation of social movements. Other organizations, even the government, often serve as training centers for organizers and sources of material support to aid the formation of groups and/or movements. The civil rights movement was the training ground for many an organizer of other movements. . . . The role of the government in the formation of the National Welfare Rights Organization was so significant that it would lead one to wonder if this association should be considered more of an interest group in the traditional sense than a movement "core" organization.

From all this it would appear that training as an organizer or at least as a proselytizer or entrepreneur of some kind is a necessary background for those individuals who act as movement innovators. Even in something as seemingly spontaneous as a social movement, the professional is more valuable than the amateur.

CRITICAL-THINKING QUESTIONS

1. Why has the role of communications networks in the formation of social movements only recently received the attention of researchers?
2. How do leadership roles emerge in social movements? Are "leaders" the same as "organizers"?
3. Cite some similarities and differences in the development of the civil rights movement and the women's movement.

NOTES

1. The only use of this significant word appears rather incidentally in Turner (1964): 123.

2. Data for this section are based on my observations while a founder and participant in the younger branch of the Chicago women's liberation movement from 1967 through 1969 and editor of the first (at that time, only) national newsletter. I was able, through extensive correspondence and interviews, to keep a record of how each group around the country started, where the organizers got the idea from, who they had talked to, what conferences were held and who attended, the political affiliations (or lack of them) of the first members, and so forth. Although I was a member of Chicago NOW, information on the origins of it and the other older branch organizations comes entirely through ex post facto interviews of the principals and examination of early papers in preparation for my dissertation on the women's liberation movement. Most of my informants requested that their contribution remain confidential.

REFERENCES

ADORNO, L. W., et al. 1950. *The authoritarian personality.* New York: Harper & Row.

BLUMER, H. 1951. Social movements. In *New outline of the principles of sociology,* ed. A. M. Lee. New York: Barnes and Noble.

BRINK, W., and L. HARRIS. 1964. *The Negro revolution in America.* New York: Simon & Schuster.

BUCK, S. J. 1920. *The agrarian crusade.* New Haven, CT: Yale University Press.

CANTRIL, H. 1941. *The psychology of social movements.* New York: Wiley.

CLARK, K. B. 1966. The civil rights movement: Momentum and organization. *Daedalus,* Winter.

DAVIS, J. C. 1962. Toward a theory of revolution. *American Sociological Review,* 27(1):5–19.

FERRISS, A. L. 1971. *Indicators of trends in the status of American women.* New York: Russell Sage Foundation.

FIRESTONE, S. 1971. *Dialectics of sex.* New York: Morrow.

FRAZIER, E. F. 1963. *The Negro church in America.* New York: Schocken.

FREEMAN, J. 1975. *The politics of women's liberation.* New York: Longman.

FRIEDAN, B. 1963. *The feminine mystique.* New York: Dell.

————. 1967. NOW: How it began. *Women Speaking,* April.

GURR, T. 1970. *Why men rebel.* Princeton, NJ: Princeton University Press.

HAYDEN, C.,and M. KING. 1966. A kind of memo. *Liberation,* April.

HEBERLE, R. 1951. *Social movements.* New York: Appleton-Century-Crofts.

HOFFER, E. 1951. *The true believer.* New York: Harper & Row.

HOLE, J., and E. LEVINE. 1971. *Rebirth of feminism.* New York: Quadrangle.

HOLLOWAY, H. 1969. *The politics of the Southern Negro.* New York: Random House.

HOLZMAN, A. 1963. *The Townsend movement: A political study.* New York: Bookman.

JACKSON, M., et al. 1960. The failure of an incipient social movement. *Pacific Sociological Review,* 3(1):40.

KING, M. L., JR. 1958. *Stride toward freedom.* New York: Harper & Row.

KORNHAUSER, W. 1959. *The politics of mass society.* Glencoe, IL: Free Press.

LIONBERGER, H. F. 1960. *Adoption of new ideas and practices.* Ames: Iowa State University Press.

LIPSET, S. M. 1959. *Agrarian socialism.* Berkeley: University of California Press.

LOWI, T. J. 1971. *The politics of discord.* New York: Basic Books.

OBERSCHALL, A. 1973. *Social conflict and social movements.* Englewood Cliffs, NJ: Prentice-Hall.

PINARD, M. 1971. *The rise of a third party: A study in crisis politics.* Englewood Cliffs, NJ: Prentice-Hall.

PIVEN, F. F., and R. CLOWARD. 1977. *Poor people's movements: Why they succeed, how they fail.* New York: Pantheon.

ROGERS, E. M. 1962. *Diffusion of innovations.* New York: Free Press.

RUDWICK, E., and A. MEIER. 1970. Organizational structure and goal succession: A comparative analysis of the NAACP and CORE, 1964–1968. *Social Science Quarterly,* 51 (June).

SALISBURY, R. H. 1969. An exchange theory of interest groups. *Midwest Journal of Political Science,* 13(1), (February).

TOCH, H. 1965. *The social psychology of social movements.* Indianapolis, IN: Bobbs-Merrill.

TURNER, R. H. 1964. Collective behavior and conflict: New theoretical frameworks. *Sociological Quarterly.*

ZINN, H. 1964. *SNCC: The new abolitionists.* Boston: Beacon Press.

70

The Who Concert Panic

Norris R. Johnson

In 1979, the media attributed the deaths of eleven people at a Cincinnati rock concert to "panic" as they rushed to enter the building. However, a subsequent investigation by sociologist Norris Johnson turned up little evidence of the kind of panic depicted in the news. He concluded that the idea of a "mob psychology," although widely accepted, may be misleading.

On December 3,1979, eleven young people were killed in a crush entering Riverfront Coliseum in Cincinnati, Ohio for a concert by the British rock group, The Who. The incident was immediately labeled as a "stampede" by the local media, and commentators were quick to condemn the "mob psychology" which precipitated the seemingly selfish, ruthless behavior of participants. Crowd members were thought to have stormed over others in their rush for good seats within the arena,

leading a national columnist (Royko 1979) to refer to the crowd of young people as barbarians who "stomped eleven persons to death [after] having numbed their brains on weeds, chemicals, and Southern Comfort . . . ," and a local editor to write of the "uncaring tread of the surging crowd" (Burleigh 1979). . . .

Those who interpreted the incident in this way and labeled it as a "stampede" recognized that other factors contributed, such as the unreserved seating and the late opening of an inadequate number of doors. The unreserved or "festival" seating prompted many in the crowd to arrive several hours early to compete for the choicest locations within the building. During the hours before the

SOURCE: Norris R. Johnson, "Panic at 'The Who Concert Stampede': An Empirical Assessment." Originally published in *Social Problems,* vol. 34, no. 4, October 1987, pp. 362–73. © 1987 by the Society for the Study of Social Problems. Used with permission.

doors were opened, the large crowd became so tightly packed outside the arena doors that some people who wanted to withdraw could not do so, and policemen patrolling the area could not see the problems that were developing near the doors. In addition, the densely packed crowd was swaying to and fro creating a "wave" effect—people at the edge of the crowd were observed shoving on its fringes just to see the effect begin. . . . This resulted in some people being pushed to the concrete floor of the concourse before the surge for entry began. Nevertheless, police described the crowd at this point as "normal" for a rock concert. Soon after the doors opened, as many as twenty-five people were pushed down into a pile. Eleven died lying on the concourse just a few feet from the entrances, eight others were hospitalized, and several were treated and released at the first aid station. Although the people were not trampled as more dramatic accounts reported, the event did appear to fit the image of panic held by the public and many scholars.

PREVIOUS RESEARCH AND THEORIES OF PANIC

Many social scientists would categorize the crowd behavior described above as a special form of panic—usually termed an "acquisitive panic" (Brown 1965) or "craze" (Smelser 1963). Smelser distinguishes it from the classic panics of escape, e.g., flight from a burning building, in that the latter is a "headlong rush *away* from something" while the craze is a rush "toward something [the participants] believe to be gratifying . . ." (1963: 170; also see Brown 1965). In this form, the competition that arises is not to escape possible entrapment, but to acquire some valued commodity. The special group investigating the event for the city preferred the term "craze" to the "stampede" label affixed by the media (City of Cincinnati 1980).

Although many collective behavior theorists discuss the phenomenon, systematic studies of panic are uncommon. Researchers conducting such studies generally conclude that panic is a rare

form of crowd behavior. Quarantelli and Dynes (1972) report that they have found few instances of panic after years of disaster research. They indicate that even within the famous Cocoanut Grove fire most people did not panic. Smith (1976), a participant observer in a flight from the Tower of London after a 1976 bomb explosion, reported that panic responses were few, and that primary group bonds and roles were crucial in maintaining order in the situation. In fact, primary group ties were important in the minimal panic that did occur. . . .

The core of my analysis is an examination of the Cincinnati Police Division's file on The Who Concert incident. First, I describe the data source and then present a description of the surge based on that evidence. I then use material from the taped transcriptions of interviews with people present at the concert to assess the extent of unregulated competition, breakdown of group ties, and other behaviors characteristic of panic. Finally, I discuss the theoretical implications of this case study.

DATA AND METHODS

My analysis is based on data contained in a file created and kept by the Cincinnati Police Division, supplemented by accounts in daily newspapers. The police file includes forty-six statements taken by officers investigating the event—twenty-two from patrons, thirteen from police officers present, and eleven from Coliseum employees or private security guards. The file also includes ten statements presented by patrons at hearings conducted by a committee of the Cincinnati City Council. My primary data source is transcribed patron interviews and statements that I coded for analysis. I also coded and analyzed six interviews or statements from patrons which appeared in news articles reporting the incident.

I analyzed these materials by developing a questionnaire with which to "interview" each transcript. The questionnaire called for information relevant to theories of panic, particularly evidence of unregulated competition. For example, one question asked whether the "respondent" observed crowd members showing a "lack of concern for others," and another specifically asked, "Did the person report receiving help from others?" Coded responses to the latter question indicated whether, and from whom, help was received. A similar question concerned giving help to others. Other questions pertained to potential control variables such as age and sex of respondent, size and type of group with which the person arrived, time of arrival, and physical location relative to the doors.

I base most of my interpretations on vivid descriptions of the event by those present, particularly those most directly involved, and on the interviews with policemen, security guards, and Coliseum employees. In addition, I present quantitative results from the thirty-eight questionnaires I coded. Of course, these data represent only those persons selected by others for interview (often because they were injured or had accompanied an injured person) or who came forward to write to newspapers or appear before a public hearing.

ANALYSIS

I will focus mainly on the issue of whether the observed behavior involved unregulated competition. I assume that competition in crowds awaiting entry into a concert is regulated by appropriate situational norms. I also assume that such crowds are characterized by a rudimentary social structure, reflecting at least the ties of crowd members to others with whom they arrived. Aveni (1977) has shown that crowd members typically arrive in small, primary groups. Accordingly, all of the persons whose transcripts contain relevant information reported that they arrived at the Coliseum with at least one other person, most often primary group members such as their spouse or other family member. An important research question, then, is whether these elements of social organization constrained behavior. A second question, which emerged during the research, is whether the conventional distinction between panics of escape and of acquisition (i.e., crazes) is a useful one. . . .

Helping Behavior

Since most theoretical explanations of panic focus on unregulated competition, the first research question is whether such competition existed in this case. That many people were killed and injured in a crowd of pushing people is not in dispute; the key issue is whether this was the result of callous competition for a seat at the concert at the expense of the lives of others.

However, evidence from the transcripts does not provide support for the theoretical models of panic and is in clear conflict with interpretations reported in the newspapers. One witness before the City Council committee specifically objected to newspaper accounts of the people as animals or barbarians and asserted:

[T]he people in our area were the most helpful people that I've ever known. . . . Everybody I saw was helping everybody else. At some point in the crowd people could not help them. It's not that they didn't want to. They were physically unable to (Police Division I, YZ).

The coded interview data support this claim. Approximately 40 percent of those interviewed reported helping behavior in each of three coded categories—giving, receiving, and observing help. Of the thirty-eight people interviewed, seventeen reported that they had received some help from others, sixteen reported that they had given help to others, and sixteen reported observing helping behavior by others. Some reported more than one of the categories of helping activities, and when indicators are combined, more than three-fourths of those interviewed (twenty-nine) reported at least one form of pro-social activity.

Helping behavior possibly was even more common than indicated by those results. It is likely that additional respondents observed, but did not report, helping activity since interviewers did not ask a direct question concerning helping. In fact, only seven respondents reported action by others that was coded as showing a lack of concern for others, and six of these also reported helping behavior. Thus, just one of the thirty-eight respondents reported *only* self-interested, competitive behavior. Although we cannot infer from this selective sample that a comparably large proportion of the entire crowd continued to behave in a cooperative manner, this evidence does suggest that many of those centrally located within the crowd, at just the location where persons were in most danger, demonstrated concern for others.

Helping behavior began during the early crush, long before the surge, and continued throughout the episode. People first simply tried to get people to step back and relieve the pressure, but others around them either could not hear or could not move. One young man noticed that the girl next to him could not breathe and "turned to ask people to back up, but soon realized that the only people who could hear me shouting couldn't move either." (Police Division III, M). A small seventeen-year-old girl near the doors away from the worst crush . . . reported having problems nearly an hour before the "stampede." She pleaded with people to let her out, but neither she nor they could move. She told the police detective interviewing her:

I lost my footing an' slowly but surely began going down. People behind me could do nothing to stop the pushing. I was saying "No. No. Please help me . . ." Some of the people around didn't even hear me. . . . So then I grabbed someone's leg an' whoever that was told three other guys about me. They all pushed me up, pulled me up, but it was hard. . . . At about seven o'clock I passed out. The four guys who pulled me off the ground helped me to stay up until we got through the door (Police Division II, V).

A few were successful in extricating themselves and helping others out of the crush. One man reported that he and friends picked up and carried from the crowd two nearly unconscious girls who had fallen (Police Division III, M). These particular young men knew the girls they helped, but many helped others with whom they had no social ties. Thirteen of the seventeen mentioned above as having received help were aided by others they did not know, and twelve of those sixteen giving help gave it to strangers. As one person reported in a letter to a newspaper, "Total strangers probably saved my life" (*Cincinnati Enquirer* 1979). . . .

Although most of the evidence leads to a conclusion that acts of ruthless competition were rare, there *were* such reports. For instance, one patron, who from a position just inside the arena doors was pulling people inside to safety, reported being angry with the mob:

People were climbin' over people ta get in . . . an' at one point I almost started hittin' 'em, because I could not believe the animal, animalistic ways the people, you know, nobody cared (Police Division II, A).

But both the analysis of the coded transcripts and the impressionistic accounts indicate that, even in the face of the throng, most persons tried to help others as long as possible. If a total disregard for others developed—and there is hardly any evidence that it did—it was only after cooperation was no longer possible.

Sex Differences in Helping Behavior

Normative expectations dictate generally that the stronger should help the weaker; specifically, men are expected to help women. The evidence indicates that such sex-role expectations continued to be an important influence on behavior during the event. Nine of the thirteen females received help while only one reported giving help. On the other hand, almost twice as many men gave as received help. A few (three) reported helping their wives or members of their group, but, as noted above, most gave help to those around them, either friends or strangers. Thus, the sex-role norms of men helping women did not collapse when confronted with a threat.

Altruistic behavior, either generally or specifically toward women, was not universal; there *was* selfish competition. For instance, a young woman, interviewed in her hospital room late on the evening of the concert with the horror still fresh in her memory, complained that no one would move back:

They just kept pushin' forward and they would just walk right on top of you, just trample over ya like you were a piece of the ground. They wouldn't even help ya; people were just screamin' "help me" and nobody cared (Police Division II, Mc). . . .

CONCLUSION

We cannot conclude from one study that there are *no* situations in which competition for some valued commodity occurs without regard for social obligations. Perhaps there are situations such as a fire in a crowded theater in which people totally ignore others as they try to escape from danger. However, documented cases of either form of panic are surprisingly scarce in the literature.

One possible reason for the lack of evidence of unregulated competition in The Who concert incident is that the appropriate conditions did not exist. Perhaps the people in this situation did not place such a high value on a preferred location for the concert that they would do harm to others in order to get inside; perhaps those trying to escape the crush did not actually perceive a serious threat to their lives. Kelley et al. (1965) have noted that paniclike responses are less likely when there is variation in perception of the danger; those who define the situation as less urgent are more willing to wait their turns. In this case, those who placed less value on their concert location would be less likely to compete with others. Many did try to leave the crush, giving up their valued locations nearer the entrance. Mann et al. (1976) reached a similar conclusion in their study of the bank run.

But the repeated failure of researchers to find examples of ruthless competition suggests another conclusion. Most crowds are comprised not of unattached individuals but of small, often primary, groups (Aveni 1977; Smith 1976). Group bonds constrain totally selfish behavior, even when the situation seems life threatening; thus, the type of unregulated competition generally labeled as panic occurs very infrequently. More case studies of such infrequent and irregularly occurring social forms must accumulate before general conclusions can be drawn with confidence. However, the evidence from this study is more than sufficient to discount popular interpretations of "The Who Concert Stampede" which focus on the hedonistic attributes of young people and the hypnotic effects of rock music.

CRITICAL-THINKING QUESTIONS

1. Why is there so little research about panic behavior?

2. How does Johnson explain the lack of "callous competition" at the concert? Do you think his conclusions apply to other situations of this kind?

3. In what ways did sex-role expectations affect the events at the concert?

REFERENCES

AVENI, A. 1977. The not-so-lonely crowd: friendship groups in collective behavior. *Sociometry* 49:96–99.

BROWN, R. 1965. *Social psychology.* New York: Free Press.

BURLEIGH, W. R. (1979, Dec. 8) Editors notebook: At death's door. *Cincinnati Post.*

Cincinnati, City of. Task force of Crowd Control and Safety. Report to the City Manager, 1980.

Cincinnati, City of, Police Division. *Final report concerning the eleven deaths which preceded the "Who" rock concert held at Riverfront Coliseum,* Cincinnati; City of Cincinnati.

Enquirer (Cincinnati). (1979, Dec. 10). Readers' views: A dear price has been paid to learn an obvious lesson, 10 A14.

KELLEY, H. H., J. CONDRY, JR., A. DAHLKE, and A. HILL. 1965. Collective behavior in a simulated panic situation. *J. exp. and soc. psych.* 1:20–54.

MANN, L., T. NAGEL, and P. DOWLING. 1976. A study of an economic panic: The "run" on the Hindmarsh Building Society. *Sociometry,* 39:223–35.

QUARANTELLI, E., and R. R. DYNES. 1972. When disaster strikes. *Psych. today,* 5:66–70.

ROYKO, M. (1979, Dec. 4) The new barbarians: A glimpse of the future. *Cincinnati Post.*

SMELSER, N. J. 1963. *Theory of collective behavior.* New York: Free Press.

SMITH, D. 1976. Primary group interaction in panic behavior: A test of theories. Paper presented at the annual meeting of Southern Sociological Society, Miami Beach.

71

Tiananmen Square:
A Personal Chronicle from China

Brian C. Russo

On June 4, 1989, the government brutally quashed a pro democracy movement led primarily by university students in Beijing's Tiananmen Square. Students were killed, beaten, arrested, and tortured during interrogations. In this selection, Brian C. Russo, a U.S. exchange faculty, describes some of the reactions to the movement and its aftermath at the Xi'an Foreign Languages University, one of the institutions of higher education in a northern Chinese province.

Note: Xi'an (pronounced SHEE-ON), a city of 5 million and the capital of north central China's Shaanxi Province, has over twenty institutions of higher education and one of the largest student populations in China. The educational center of China's heartland, Xi'an draws students from Shaanxi, as well as from the less-developed regions of China's vast northwest.

BEFORE JUNE 4

I was finishing my second year as an exchange faculty at the Xi'an Foreign Languages University when the Pro-Democracy movement began. My

first twenty months I had spent as a classroom teacher but in the six weeks before the massacre I became a student, listening, watching and trying to understand. I applauded demonstrators who walked proudly through the streets of Xi'an. As they walked in the heat the students often ate thick square white ice pops. The women wore floppy straw hats to protect their heads. My hand had been shaken numerous times by students and citizens alike. I knew that I as a Westerner represented an

SOURCE: "The Days of Tiananmen: A Personal Chronicle from the Provinces," by Brian C. Russo, in *Prairie Schooner,* vol. 65, no. 2, Summer 1991. Copyright © 1994 by Brian C. Russo. Reprinted with permission.

idea of freedom and this was the reason why my hand had been shaken so often.

One hot afternoon an old man approached me as I stood watching the lines of students. He was short with a shiny bald head and gnarled fingers. He wore the traditional Chinese tunic and baggy trousers and as the students chanted, he pumped my hand while he pointed at them. I gave him the V-sign the students had adopted as their emblematic gesture. He kept shaking my hand. I tried not to get swept up by my thoughts, thoughts about the exhilaration of freedom. I tried not to, but they kept coming even as a traffic policeman dressed in white gestured gruffly for both of us to get back up on the sidewalk. Beaming, the old man watched the demonstrators.

Back at the university a student patiently translated for me the *dazibao,* the big-character posters, that had been pasted all over the walls of the front plaza of our university. The one I remember most clearly was entitled, "Why Am I So Weak?"

Why am I so weak that I cannot speak out for the students? Why am I not brave enough to stop eating, as those in Tiananmen Square have? Why do I just keep silent? Why do my Chinese teachers who have been to the United States, Australia, England now remain silent? Are they afraid they will lose the chance to go abroad again? Why don't they lead us now? When will I stand up?

The vulnerability of that unknown writer who dared to ask but who was somehow ashamed at the same time characterized many of the students I talked to. During the hunger strike I saw this vulnerability when I went with my girlfriend Theresa to visit Chen*, a student of hers who had to be brought back to the school clinic. He was dehydrated and weak yet he insisted that he had failed because he had to be brought back. We tried to reassure him then went out to get him juice, peanuts, and cookies. He refused all when we returned, and we insisted. In the midst of the confusion, problems, and his own pain Chen observed the Chinese formalities: Always refuse several times before accepting any offering. He took the snacks at last and

*All Chinese and Soviet names have been changed to protect the identities of the individuals.

placed them at the foot of his cot. Then no one said anything; it was the silence of hospitals, moments when chat becomes irrelevant in the face of helpless suffering. Yet we knew that Chen was not seriously ill. I wonder now if our silence was not so much for Chen but for that other helpless patient, China.

I at last broke the silence by telling Chen that we were very proud of what he had done. His fasting proved how much he loved his country. Theresa nodded her head in agreement. I felt a lump in my throat as I watched Chen lying there, his jaw set.

And when martial law was declared in Beijing on May 20, I listened as our university loudspeakers blared the news at midnight, again and again. Did I have a choice? Did any of us? When the secret police arrived later that night, complete with black pants, white shirts, and pocket cameras I watched them systematically photograph then scrape off and roll up the *dazibao* that had been glued onto the main building and over the display cases that lined the front gate plaza.

Each night during the television news blackout that followed the martial law declaration students held a meeting at the front gate where they announced the latest "news." The student news promised the imminent fall of the Li Peng government. The students claimed that the mayor of Shanghai had called for Li's ouster, and that governors and generals did not support the Li regime. The announcement that met with the greatest approval was that former Premier Zhou En Lai's wife had said she would resign from the Party if her adopted son, Premier Li, did not.

There was a truth lag, however. If no confirmation came from BBC or the Voice of America by the next day, we assumed each announcement was rumor. The rumors became more outrageous as the days went on. The immolation story was the students' biggest propaganda coup. We heard it first downtown on May 28. A motorcycle with a back cart cruised along the curb. A man stood in the cart with a portable microphone in his hand. We listened as he read from a stack of photocopies: "Two hundred students burned themselves to death in Tiananmen Square." He posted the announcement and the motorcycle drove to the next corner. Everyone in the city was talking about it. Plaintive voices cried out for the dead on the loudspeakers. I remembered how students talked about being willing to die for their cause and how I had mentally dismissed their talk as naive idealism.

Back at the university, we tuned into VOA for confirmation. None came as we waited, hour after hour. At the eleven o'clock meeting, the number of dead was definitely set at two hundred. Then the individual names of the Xi'an dead were announced. The next day a large demonstration took place complete with eight-foot-high funeral wreaths and the wearing of white, the Chinese color of mourning. I refused to go to this demonstration as I did not want to see the hoax perpetrated no matter how good the cause. Students and foreign teachers reported that marchers carrying the wreaths walked in silence down streets lined with the weeping. I believed them.

The nightly meetings went on with our university's two tall wreaths behind the announcers. No one took them away. And in a few days it appeared that the wreaths had only been a little early.

THE MASSACRE

June 4, 1989—Most days come and go with little reflection on actual events. But June 4 was not such a day. It began with a telephone call at four o'clock in the morning. I heard ringing and ringing in the dream before I woke up to answer. It was my older sister calling from the U.S. She cried as she read numbers from the bottom of her television screen: twenty and more dead in Tiananmen Square. She said the pictures were horrible, the tanks, armored personnel carriers, the twisted bicycles. Why wasn't I coming home? She was seeing the pictures, we were in the country where the pictures were taking place but seeing nothing. I told her I didn't know when I was coming home. I assured her that Theresa and I were safe. The soldiers had not come to Xi'an. Everything was go-

ing to be all right. I hung up, put the world of Beijing relayed via the U.S. momentarily away.

I went to another American teacher's house, woke her, listened on her shortwave. We sat, stunned. Everything was suddenly different although it would take us some time to understand how.

On the morning of June 4, 1989, the day of the Beijing massacre, I along with a small group of foreign teachers went on a university-sponsored seven-hour bus trip to the pre-revolutionary village of Hancheng in northern Shaanxi. We did not yet understand that everything we were to do in the coming days—pick up our pay, talk to our students, or go on a trip—would have a different and greater significance than before.

As we drove, Shimaugawa, a Japanese teacher, translated the broadcasts from Radio Japan. We groaned as the death toll rose hourly. We shook our heads then looked out at the picturesque landscape. Northeastern Shaanxi was bright golden in the midst of the wheat harvest. Farmers cut down stalks in the fields while nearer the houses the stalks were beaten and the chaff flew off, a constant dusty screen. An ancient scene, as old as China. The farmers worked as if nothing had happened. And for them, perhaps, nothing had. Did they know? Tiananmen Square was eight hundred miles from them in space. In time?

There were many conversations about what we teachers should do. But we were in the country. I regretted that I had come on this trip. It was a day of dislocations—hearing the telephone voice from the U.S. about the massacre, looking out on tranquil scenery, wanting to get away from Xi'an, wanting to be involved once away. I knew that Americans had little idea of what was happening in China, only what that small-framed dramatized TV screen showed them. And on a minibus out in the middle of China I, too, had little idea. Somehow, there was a larger picture that no one was getting to see.

We saw no pictures of Tiananmen Square on June 4, 1989. We saw Hancheng on a Sunday market day. The streets were jammed with families, buyers, sellers, all out in the afternoon's white heat. We saw many old men and women in baggy black tunics and trousers. Many of the old women hobbled on feet that were bound in another world, crippling them for the world they lived in now. The old men wore thick round glasses, their metal frames elaborately bolted at the nose rest. Looking down the street we saw a sea of stiff, flat straw field hats, their wide brims blocking the sun.

We went down the ancient streets, visited a temple, shopped, bargained, and ate noodles. Were we trying to deny what had come over the phone lines from America, what had come through Shimaugawa's radio? Denial was possible in Hancheng. Freedom? Democracy? We saw only a marketplace and friendly peasants.

At two in the morning we returned to Xi'an. We drove by Xincheng Square, but only a few students were there in front of the capital building. No soldiers along the roads or anywhere on the way. Although the streets were empty, lights were on in many of the apartment buildings.

At our university everyone was awake. At 2:30 I posted a sign announcing a meeting the next afternoon of all foreign teachers and students, about seventy-five people. We couldn't sleep and continued to listen to the news. The numbers of victims ranged from three hundred to seven thousand. No one was certain. Many, it was said, were shot in the back. When I tried to imagine the slaughter a single image recurred: people running hard, breaking free for an instant only to go down as bullets entered their backs. I didn't have other strong mental pictures. My students believed that the demonstrators linked arm in arm and singing the "Internationale" had been mowed down, line after line. We all made our own pictures to understand the words. We wouldn't know which ones were real for weeks. . . .

Soon after the massacre, CCTV began to broadcast nightly the official version of "the counterrevolutionary rebellion." Row upon row of charred tanks and APC's. The bodies of soldiers, the worst with his entrails pulled out and wrapped round his neck. Soldiers hosed down Tiananmen Square's flagstones. A woman in a slinky dress

sang into a microphone for a squadron of soldiers sitting in the Square. Beijing citizens gave food to the troops, others waved to the rolling tanks. I mentioned the TV to Michel, an old Frenchman, who had been in China for ten years. A tall, completely bald man with a gentle smile, he reminded me of a monk. I asked him if he had seen the singer and then the soldiers goose-stepping in the Square.

He nodded his head sadly. "It reminds me so much of the Nazis," he said. "It is exactly the same."

I have never really watched television enough at home or abroad to talk back to the set. But I started to yell one night after watching day after day. I threw a shoe at the screen, but it only bounced off as the tanks rolled on.

The government officially labeled the crackdown a response to "the counterrevolutionary rebellion." So not only was the massacre officially rationalized, but the participants who survived were very directly threatened through the word "counterrevolutionary." There is no single equivalent in English that carries the certainty for personal, professional, and familial ruin that "counterrevolutionary" does for a Chinese. To be branded counterrevolutionary is to lose all possibility for advancement in an already rigid society. The label not only marks the condemned person, it also extends to the family and subsequent generations.

Within three days the battle of Beijing was over. The armies had fallen into line behind Deng, and the citizens for the most part were subdued. The glorious heroes of the People's Liberation Army had been victorious over the counterrevolutionary rebellion. Provincial, city, and university leaders resurfaced in Xi'an after having vanished mysteriously on June 5, 6 and 7.

The evacuation of the universities began in earnest. School leaders sent students home. Most foreigners also left. At our university two-thirds of the foreign staff and all foreign students were gone within a week. Perhaps Ramon was right when he said that most people were afraid. Theresa and I decided to stay. There was a strong feeling of panic as the other foreigners made hasty plans to get out. Mainly I think we reacted against that panic.

We also stayed from paralysis. I kept picturing chaotic scenes at airports and wanted no part of them. I think I might have been in a state of fright that did not cause flight but rather this paralysis. I kept believing we were going to complete our time in China on our terms. But in the back of my mind an image recurred: soldiers waving us somewhere with guns, and I had the sinking feeling it was idiotic to believe we could walk out of this country when it suited us. . . .

RETURN TO CLASSES

By June 17, notification came that the following Monday we were to go back to the classroom. Our university sent out over a thousand telegrams summoning the students back. "Back to their nest," as Enomoto, the Japanese teacher, said. It seemed that with the students regathered, the police would have an easier job making arrests. For those not arrested, the message was clear. Although instruction of any kind had stopped two months before, it was time for everything to return to normal; since it was June, normality meant final exams. After exams, the crackdown would be finalized with weeks of daily "political study sessions," where the movement would be denounced, and students who had demonstrated for democracy would be asked publicly to admit their mistake.

So we went back to our classes, gave our students open-book exams and high grades. I wrote down my address for one of my students who had been heavily involved. During the movement he had called me up, addressed me as Comrade Russo, let me know what the day's activities were to be. He warned me not to write to him, and that he would be in touch when he could. I asked him why Susi, another bright student, had not come for the exam.

"She went to Beijing," he said. "Her brother went there at the beginning of the month and he still hasn't returned."

A few days after classes resumed, the provincial government television crew came to show how life was as normal as ever. Most of the foreign teachers left their rooms and refused to teach when they saw the cameras, but Sakine, the Japanese, did not. He described to me how the school officials watched the filming, poking their heads in the doorway of his room. The first thing Sakine did was to write the Chinese characters for "democracy" on the board. He stood in front of the board and did not move from this background for the rest of his lecture. He spoke in Chinese to his class on the subject of Japanese culture. He explained how important human rights and democracy are to the Japanese. He told me the officials did not look very happy. The cameras, though, were smarter than Sakine. They were far enough away so that the Chinese characters were unclear. A voice-over covered the words of his lecture. But perhaps it was not a total victory for the cameras. They did not return to our university, and the segment was but a few seconds on television.

FIRST PICTURES OF TIANANMEN SQUARE

During the week of June 19, the first pictures of Tiananmen Square became available. There was a black market for them in Xi'an, about $3.00 a photo. The first one I saw was at Sakine's house. It showed a curb littered with twisted bicycles and crushed bodies. Back home I would see this AP photo many times. So who could not agree that China was going forth with its economic reforms? China, after all, was a burgeoning marketplace with government markets, free markets, and black markets. That week the black market had the monopoly on truth—three bucks a shot.

Mail service again began after a three-week stoppage, and we saw other pictures in magazines that arrived from the U.S., Japan, and Hong Kong. We were amazed that these magazines got through, but either the post office was being subversive or just plain inefficient. In any case, the local newspapers continually warned Chinese of the consequences they would suffer if they were discovered with such magazines in their possession.

Besides that first black market photo, two other pictures stood out in my mind. One in stark night light showed a man yelling, and at his feet lay a dead body with a large bloodstain surrounding the body and covering the concrete. The other was of the man who stood in front of the tank. I felt numb as I looked at these pictures again and again. There was no question they were real, but the visceral connection I expected had somehow been severed by all that had happened. As Sakine and I looked at the first pictures, we sat in silence. We stared out the window to the evacuated apartments across the quiet green square that sat between the apartment blocks.

REEDUCATION IN THE CLASSROOM AND ON TELEVISION

Except for the complete absence of tourists at the height of the season, Xi'an, one of China's busiest tourist cities, seemed to return to normal as June blurred into July. It was hard to believe that only a few weeks before, thousands of students had marched down East Street and Changan Avenue every day, that Xincheng Square had been full of hunger strikers, that the Bell Tower at the city's center had been a bottleneck of traffic and marchers, and that commandeered loudspeakers cried out plaintively for the dead students. All of it had vanished, all perhaps but the remains of a ragged flyer with faded characters, something not even the police thought worth taking down.

But reeducation quietly went on, every day of the summer spent on pounding "the truth" into the heads of students and teachers. I saw the results of this psychological battering in the numb and distracted faces of my colleagues, and heard of their anguish as they were forced to sign written statements that agreed with the party's version of the events leading up to the massacre and June 4 itself.

When I casually asked one Chinese colleague whom I hadn't seen for a while how he was, he brushed his hands from side to side, as his eyes darted.

"I did nothing," he insisted. "My brain is pure. White. Clean."

Another, usually highly articulate, was reduced to disjointed statements about "not being worried," lots of nervous laughter, more definite "not worrieds," and finally, a blank gaze into space.

The television droned on every night in July broadcasting the highly edited footage of the "counterrevolutionary rebellion," complete with martial music as the People's Army overcame. Also broadcast were interviews with wounded "heroes" and wailing funerals for the dead soldiers.

New arrests were televised daily. It became a familiar scene. A lineup of students, hands tied behind backs, in jail yards. Individuals brought in for questioning, with soldiers writing down confessions. Often the confession scene was accompanied by footage of the accused, circled in red, at a Tiananmen demonstration.

HOME

In early August, Theresa and I returned to the U.S. via Beijing. Before leaving, we stopped at the U.S. embassy and the press officer showed us on a VCR the Koppel weeklong version of the crackdown. We watched the behind-the-scenes maneuvering of the Central Committee, the troops' arrival, how initially it was going to be a standoff, but then came the garish night light of June 4 in Tiananmen, the tracer bullets, the tanks, the pop of machine gun fire, the bodies with Koppel's steady tone narrating it all. I have never been a great fan of television news and how neatly it packages daily national and international tragedy. But I had to admit it was a relief at last to see something of what had happened. It was also a relief to be going back to the U.S.

We were worried that our bags and all of our papers would be searched, but we were whisked through customs in Beijing. At its gateway, in any case, China had donned the mask of normality. In Shanghai, there was a stopover for passport checks and all passengers deplaned. While waiting, we ran into an American couple who had spent a few days sightseeing in Beijing after having been part of a U.S. citizen reunification delegation in North Korea. The man was burly and he wore a baseball cap. His intense anti-Americanism, his age and the cane that he used to walk told me that perhaps he was a Vietnam vet. When he began to talk about what they had seen in Pyongyang, his companion left for the duty-free shop. He gave glowing reports on the wonderful health care, the building boom, the happy workers, all under the rule of "great leader Kim-Il-Sung." He contrasted what he had seen in North Korea with the horrible situation of the homeless in the United States. He mentioned that an American reporter had asked him in Beijing how he felt about being in China so soon after Tiananmen, and he had responded that China knew best how to handle its problems. I was in no mood to hear about the wisdom of enlightened socialism in East Asia. I kept seeing the face of my terrified colleague as he insisted that his brain was pure and clean. I kept hearing the way the silence

hung over Xi'an after the crackdown. I didn't tell the man with the cane these things, although I wish I had.

CRITICAL-THINKING QUESTIONS

1. The success of a social movement depends, in part, on an effective communication system that mobilizes participants and sympathizers. How informed were the inhabitants of Xi'an (and probably other Chinese cities) of the pro-democracy movement in Beijing?

2. Why do you think the government was effective in destroying the pro-democracy movement within a few days? How did local Chinese governments outside of Beijing discourage further rebellion?

3. What role(s) did Russo play before, during, and after the Tiananmen uprising? Observer? Participant? What role do you think he should have played? Explain your position.

SOCIAL CHANGE AND MODERNITY

Classic

72

Anomy and Modern Life

Emile Durkheim

In this excerpt from his classic study of suicide, Emile Durkheim asserts that human aspiration, which is not bounded by nature as in other creatures, must be framed by limits imposed by society. Modern societies, however, have lost some of their moral power over the individual. The consequence is a societal condition of anomy (or anomie), which people experience as a lack of moral regulation. In the extreme, anomy prompts people to suicide; more generally, an anomic society contains people with weak and vacillating moral values and who have difficulty reining in their own ambitions and desires.

No living being can be happy or even exist unless his needs are sufficiently proportioned to his means. In other words, if his needs require more than can be granted, or even merely something of a different sort, they will be under continual friction and can only function painfully. . . .

In the animal, at least in a normal condition, this equilibrium is established with automatic spontaneity because the animal depends on purely ma-

SOURCE: *Suicide,* by Emile Durkheim, trans. John A. Spaulding and George Simpson. Copyright © 1951, 1979 by The Free Press. Abridged and reprinted with permission of The Free Press, an imprint of Simon & Schuster.

terial conditions. All the organism needs is that the supplies of substance and energy constantly employed in the vital process should be periodically renewed by equivalent quantities; that replacement be equivalent to use. When the void created by existence in its own resources is filled, the animal, satisfied, asks nothing further. Its power of reflection is not sufficiently developed to imagine other ends than those implicit in its physical nature. . . .

This is not the case with man, because most of his needs are not dependent on his body or not to the same degree. . . . But how determine the quantity of well-being, comfort or luxury legitimately to be craved by a human being? Nothing appears in man's organic nor in his psychological constitution which sets a limit to such tendencies. The functioning of individual life does not require them to cease at one point rather than at another; the proof being that they have constantly increased since the beginnings of history, receiving more and more complete satisfaction, yet with no weakening of average health. . . . It is not human nature which can assign the variable limits necessary to our needs. They are thus unlimited so far as they depend on the individual alone. Irrespective of any external regulatory force, our capacity for feeling is in itself an insatiable and bottomless abyss.

But if nothing external can restrain this capacity, it can only be a source of torment to itself. Unlimited desires are insatiable by definition and insatiability is rightly considered a sign of morbidity. Being unlimited, they constantly and infinitely surpass the means at their command; they cannot be quenched. Inextinguishable thirst is constantly renewed torture. It has been claimed, indeed, that human activity naturally aspires beyond assignable limits and sets itself unattainable goals. But how can such an undetermined state be any more reconciled with the conditions of mental life than with the demands of physical life? All man's pleasure in acting, moving and exerting himself implies the sense that his efforts are not in vain and that by walking he has advanced. However, one does not advance when one walks toward no goal, or—which is the same thing—when his goal is infinity. Since the distance between us and it is always the same, whatever road we take, we might as well have made the motions without progress from the spot. Even our glances behind and our feeling of pride at the distance covered can cause only deceptive satisfaction, since the remaining distance is not proportionately reduced. To pursue a goal which is by definition unattainable is to condemn oneself to a state of perpetual unhappiness. Of course, man may hope contrary to all reason, and hope has its pleasures even when unreasonable. It may sustain him for a time; but it cannot survive the repeated disappointments of experi-

ence indefinitely. What more can the future offer him than the past, since he can never reach a tenable condition nor even approach the glimpsed ideal? Thus, the more one has, the more one wants, since satisfactions received only stimulate instead of filling needs. . . .

To achieve any other result, the passions first must be limited. Only then can they be harmonized with the faculties and satisfied. But since the individual has no way of limiting them, this must be done by some force exterior to him. A regulative force must play the same role for moral needs which the organism plays for physical needs. This means that the force can only be moral. The awakening of conscience interrupted the state of equilibrium of the animal's dormant existence; only conscience, therefore, can furnish the means to reestablish it. Physical restraint would be ineffective; hearts cannot be touched by physio-chemical forces. So far as the appetites are not automatically restrained by physiological mechanisms, they can be halted only by a limit that they recognize as just. Men would never consent to restrict their desires if they felt justified in passing the assigned limit. But, for reasons given above, they cannot assign themselves this law of justice. So they must receive it from an authority which they respect, to which they yield spontaneously. Either directly and as a whole, or through the agency of one of its organs, society alone can play this moderating role; for it is the only moral power superior to the individual, the authority of which he accepts. It alone has the power necessary to stipulate law and to set the point beyond which the passions must not go. . . .

. . . Man's characteristic privilege is that the bond he accepts is not physical but moral; that is, social. He is governed not by a material environment brutally imposed on him, but by a conscience superior to his own, the superiority of which he feels. Because the greater, better part of his existence transcends the body, he escapes the body's yoke, but is subject to that of society.

But when society is disturbed by some painful crisis or by beneficent but abrupt transitions, it is momentarily incapable of exercising this influence; thence come the sudden rises in the curve of suicides which we have pointed out above.

In the case of economic disasters, indeed, something like a declassification occurs which suddenly casts certain individuals into a lower state than their previous one. Then they must reduce their requirements, restrain their needs, learn greater self-control. All the advantages of social influence are lost so far as they are concerned; their moral education has to be recommenced. But society cannot adjust them instantaneously to this new life and teach them to practice the increased self-repression to which they are unaccustomed. So they are not adjusted to the condition forced on them, and its very prospect is intolerable; hence the suffering which detaches them from a reduced existence even before they have made trial of it.

It is the same if the source of the crisis is an abrupt growth of power and wealth. Then, truly, as the conditions of life are changed, the standard according to which needs were regulated can no longer remain the same; for it varies with social resources, since it largely determines the share of each class of producers. The scale is upset; but a new scale cannot be immediately improvised. Time is required for the public conscience to reclassify men and things. So long as the social forces thus freed have not regained equilibrium, their respective values are unknown and so all regulation is lacking for a time. The limits are unknown between the possible and the impossible, what is just and what is unjust, legitimate claims and hopes and those which are immoderate. Consequently, there is no restraint upon aspirations. . . . Appetites, not being controlled by a public opinion become disoriented, no longer recognize the limits proper to them. . . . With increased prosperity desires increase. At the very moment when traditional rules have lost their authority, the richer prize offered these appetites stimulates them and makes them more exigent and impatient of control. The state of de-regulation or anomy is thus further heightened by passions being less disciplined, precisely when they need more disciplining. . . .

This explanation is confirmed by the remark-able immunity of poor countries. Poverty protects against suicide because it is a restraint in itself. No matter how one acts, desires have to depend upon resources to some extent; actual possessions are partly the criterion of those aspired to. So the less one has the less he is tempted to extend the range of his needs indefinitely. Lack of power, compelling moderation, accustoms men to it, while nothing excites envy if no one has superfluity. Wealth, on the other hand, by the power it bestows, deceives us into believing that we depend on ourselves only. Reducing the resistance we encounter from objects, it suggests the possibility of unlimited success against them. The less limited one feels, the more intolerable all limitation appears. Not without reason, therefore, have so many religions dwelt on the advantages and moral value of poverty. It is actually the best school for teaching self-restraint. Forcing us to constant self-discipline, it prepares us to accept collective discipline with equanimity, while wealth, exalting the individual, may always arouse the spirit of rebellion which is the very source of immorality. This, of course, is no reason why humanity should not improve its material condition. But though the moral danger involved in every growth of prosperity is not irremediable, it should not be forgotten.

If anomy never appeared except, as in the above instances, in intermittent spurts and acute crisis, it might cause the social suicide-rate to vary from time to time, but it would not be a regular, constant factor. In one sphere of social life, however—the sphere of trade and industry—it is actually in a chronic state.

For a whole century, economic progress has mainly consisted in freeing industrial relations from all regulation. Until very recently, it was the function of a whole system of moral forces to exert this discipline. First, the influence of religion was felt alike by workers and masters, the poor and the rich. It consoled the former and taught them contentment with their lot by informing them of the providential nature of the social order, that the share of each class was assigned by God himself, and by holding out the hope for just compensation in a world to come in return for the inequalities of this world. It governed the latter, recalling that worldly interests are not man's entire lot, that they must be subordinate to other and higher interests, and that they should therefore not be pursued without rule or measure. Temporal power, in turn, restrained the scope of economic functions by its supremacy over them and by the relatively subordinate role it assigned them. Finally, within the business world proper, the occupational groups by regulating salaries, the price of products and production itself, indirectly fixed the average level of income on which needs are partially based by the very force of circumstances. However, we do not mean to propose this organization as a model. Clearly it would be inadequate to existing societies without great changes. What we stress is its existence, the fact of its useful influence, and that nothing today has come to take its place.

Actually, religion has lost most of its power. And government, instead of regulating economic life, has become its tool and servant. The most opposite schools, orthodox economists and extreme socialists, unite to reduce government to the role of a more or less passive intermediary among the various social functions. The former wish to make it simply the guardian of individual contracts; the latter leave it the task of doing the collective bookkeeping, that is, of recording the demands of consumers, transmitting them to producers, inventorying the total revenue and distributing it according to a fixed formula. But both refuse it any power to subordinate other social organs to itself and to make them converge toward one dominant aim. On both sides nations are declared to have the single or chief purpose of achieving industrial prosperity; such is the implication of the dogma of economic materialism, the basis of both apparently opposed systems. And as these theories merely express the state of opinion, industry, instead of being still regarded as a means to an end transcending itself, has become the supreme end of individuals and societies alike. Thereupon the appetites thus excited have become freed of any limiting authority. By sanctifying them, so to speak, this apotheosis of well-being has placed them above all human law. Their restraint seems like a sort of sacrilege. For this reason, even the purely utilitarian regulation of them exercised by the industrial world itself through the medium of occupational groups has been unable to persist. Ultimately, this liberation of desires has been made worse by the very development of industry and the almost infinite extension of the market. So long as the producer could gain his profits only in his immediate neighborhood, the restricted amount of possible gain could not much overexcite ambition. Now that he may assume to have almost the entire world as his customer, how could passions accept their former confinement in the face of such limitless prospects?

Such is the source of the excitement predominating in this part of society, and which has thence extended to the other parts. There the state of crisis and anomy is constant and, so to speak, normal. From top to bottom of the ladder, greed is aroused without knowing where to find ultimate foothold. Nothing can calm it, since its goal is far beyond all it can attain. Reality seems valueless by comparison with the dreams of fevered imaginations; reality is therefore abandoned, but so too is possibility abandoned when it in turn becomes reality. A thirst arises for novelties, unfamiliar pleasures, nameless sensations, all of which lose their savor once known. Henceforth one has no strength to endure the least reverse. The whole fever subsides and the sterility of all the tumult is apparent, and it is seen that all these new sensations in their infinite quantity cannot form a solid foundation of happiness to support one during days of trial. The wise man, knowing how to enjoy achieved results without having constantly to replace them with others, finds in them an attachment to life in the hour of difficulty. But the man who has always pinned all his hopes on the future and lived with his eyes fixed upon it, has nothing in the past as a comfort against the present's afflictions, for the past was nothing to him but a series of hastily experienced stages. What blinded him to himself was his expectation always to find further on the happiness he had so far missed. Now he is stopped in his tracks; from now on nothing remains behind or ahead of him to fix his gaze upon. Weariness alone, moreover, is enough to bring disillusionment, for he cannot in the end escape the futility of an endless pursuit.

We may even wonder if this moral state is not principally what makes economic catastrophes of our day so fertile in suicides. In societies where a man is subjected to a healthy discipline, he submits more readily to the blows of chance. The necessary effort for sustaining a little more discomfort costs him relatively little, since he is used to discomfort and constraint. But when every constraint is hateful in itself, how can closer constraint not seem intolerable? There is no tendency to resignation in the feverish impatience of men's lives. When there is no other aim but to outstrip constantly the point arrived at, how painful to be thrown back! Now this very lack of organization characterizing our economic condition throws the door wide to every sort of adventure. Since imagination is hungry for novelty, and ungoverned, it gropes at random. Setbacks necessarily increase with risks and thus crises multiply, just when they are becoming more destructive.

Yet these dispositions are so inbred that society has grown to accept them and is accustomed to think them normal. It is everlastingly repeated that it is man's nature to be eternally dissatisfied, constantly to advance, without relief or rest, toward an indefinite goal. The longing for infinity is daily represented as a mark of moral distinction, whereas it can only appear within unregulated consciences which elevate to a rule the lack of rule from which they suffer. The doctrine of the most ruthless and swift progress has become an article of faith. But other theories appear parallel with those praising the advantages of instability, which, generalizing the situation that gives them birth, declare life evil, claim that it is richer in grief than in pleasure and that it attracts men only by false claims. Since this disorder is greatest in the economic world, it has most victims there.

Industrial and commercial functions are really among the occupations which furnish the greatest number of suicides. . . . Almost on a level with the liberal professions, they sometimes surpass them; they are especially more afflicted than agriculture, where the old regulative forces still make their appearance felt most and where the fever of business has least penetrated. Here is best recalled what was once the general constitution of the economic order. And the divergence would be yet greater if, among the suicides of industry, employers were distinguished from workmen, for the former are probably most stricken by the state of anomy. The enormous rate of those with independent means (720 per million) sufficiently shows that the possessors of most comfort suffer most. Everything that enforces subordination attenuates the effects of this state. At least the horizon of the lower classes is limited by those above them, and for this same reason their desires are more modest. Those who have only empty space above them are almost inevitably lost in it, if no force restrains them.

CRITICAL-THINKING QUESTIONS

1. How do most creatures restrain their desires? How are human beings distinctive in this way?
2. Why does modern society afford to individuals less moral regulation? Why is this especially true of people (such as rock stars) who experience sudden fame and fortune?
3. How would Durkheim explain the relatively high suicide rate among rock stars and other celebrities?

Classic

73

The Disenchantment of Modern Life

Max Weber

In this excerpt from a speech, "Science as a Vocation," delivered at Munich University in 1918, Weber claims that the rise of science has changed our way of thinking about the world. Where, in the past, humans confronted a world of mystical forces beyond our comprehension, now we assume that all things yield to human comprehension. Thus, Weber concludes, the world has become "disenchanted." Notice, however, that something is lost in the process for, unlike the churches of the past, science can provide no answer to questions of ultimate meaning in life.

Scientific progress is a fraction, the most important fraction, of the process of intellectualization which we have been undergoing for thousands of years and which nowadays is usually judged in such an extremely negative way. Let us first clarify what this intellectualist rationalization, created by science and by scientifically oriented technology, means practically.

Does it mean that we, today, for instance, everyone sitting in this hall, have a greater knowledge

of the conditions of life under which we exist than has an American Indian or a Hottentot? Hardly. Unless he is a physicist, one who rides on the streetcar has no idea how the car happened to get into motion. And he does not need to know. He is satisfied that he may 'count' on the behavior of the streetcar, and he orients his conduct according to this expectation; but he knows nothing about what it takes to produce such a car so that it can move. The savage knows incomparably more about his tools. When we spend money today I bet that even if there are colleagues of political economy here in the hall, almost every one of them will hold a dif-

SOURCE: *From Max Weber: Essays in Sociology,* ed. and trans. H. H. Gerth and C. Wright Mills. Copyright © 1946 by Oxford University Press, Inc., renewed 1973 by H. H. Gerth. Reprinted with permission.

ferent answer in readiness to the question: How does it happen that one can buy something for money—sometimes more and sometimes less? The savage knows what he does in order to get his daily food and which institutions serve him in this pursuit. The increasing intellectualization and rationalization do *not,* therefore, indicate an increased and general knowledge of the conditions under which one lives.

It means something else, namely, the knowledge or belief that if one but wished one *could* learn it at any time. Hence, it means that principally there are no mysterious incalculable forces that come into play, but rather that one can, in principle, master all things by calculation. This means that the world is disenchanted. One need no longer have recourse to magical means in order to master or implore the spirits, as did the savage, for whom such mysterious powers existed. Technical means and calculations perform the service. This above all is what intellectualization means. . . .

Science today is a "vocation" organized in special disciplines in the service of self-clarification and knowledge of interrelated facts. It is not the gift of grace of seers and prophets dispensing sacred values and revelations, nor does it partake of the contemplation of sages and philosophers about the meaning of the universe. This, to be sure, is the inescapable condition of our historical situation. We cannot evade it so long as we remain true to ourselves. And if Tolstoi's question recurs to you: As science does not, who is to answer the question: "What shall we do, and, how shall we arrange our lives?" or, in the words used here tonight: "Which of the warring gods should we serve? Or should we serve perhaps an entirely different god, and who is he?" then one can say that only a prophet or a savior can give the answers. . . .

To the person who cannot bear the fate of the times like a man, one must say: May he rather return silently, without the usual publicity build-up of renegades, but simply and plainly. The arms of the old churches are opened widely and compassionately for him. After all, they do not make it hard for him. One way or another he has to bring

his "intellectual sacrifice"—that is inevitable. If he can really do it, we shall not rebuke him. For such an intellectual sacrifice in favor of an unconditional religious devotion is ethically quite a different matter than the evasion of the plain duty of intellectual integrity, which sets in if one lacks the courage to clarify one's own ultimate standpoint and rather facilitates this duty by feeble relative judgments. In my eyes, such religious return stands higher than the academic prophecy, which does not clearly realize that in the lecture-rooms of the university no other virtue holds but plain intellectual integrity: Integrity, however, compels us to state that for the many who today tarry for new prophets and saviors, the situation is the same as resounds in the beautiful Edomite watchman's song of the period of exile that has been included among Isaiah's oracles:

He calleth to me out of Seir, Watchman, what of the night? The watchman said, The morning cometh, and also the night: if ye will enquire, enquire ye: return, come.

The people to whom this was said has enquired and tarried for more than two millennia, and we are shaken when we realize its fate. From this we want to draw the lesson that nothing is gained by yearning and tarrying alone, and we shall act differently. We shall set to work and meet the "demands of the day," in human relations as well as in our vocation. This, however, is plain and simple, if each finds and obeys the demon who holds the fibers of his very life.

CRITICAL-THINKING QUESTIONS

1. In what sense do members of a traditional society know more about their world than we do? In what sense do we know more?

2. What is "Tolstoi's question"? Why can science not answer it?

3. What does Weber see as the great burden of living in a modern society? In other words, what comforts of the past are less available to modern people?

74

The Search for Meaning
in Modern America

Robert N. Bellah, Richard Madsen, William M. Sullivan, Ann Swidler, and Steven M. Tipton

In the pursuit of their individual dreams, people in the United States seem to have lost the ability to connect with others to form a meaningful human community. In other words, although freed from the grasp of tradition, modern Americans too often seem to be rootless and lonely, unsure of what to believe, and uncommitted to goals beyond their immediate pleasures. This selection from a widely read study of U.S. culture explores the promise—and also the pitfalls—of modern society.

... Much of the thinking about our society and where it should be going is rather narrowly [focused] on our political economy. This focus makes sense in that government and the corporations are the most powerful structures in our society and affect everything else, including our culture and our character. But as an exclusive concern, such a focus is severely limited. Structures are not un-

SOURCE: *Habits of the Heart: Individualism and Commitment in American Life* by Robert N. Bellah, Richard Madsen, William M. Sullivan, Ann Swidler, and Steven Tipton (Berkeley and Los Angeles, CA: University of California Press, 1985), pp. 275–93, 294–96. Copyright © 1985 by the Regents of the University of California. Reprinted with permission.

changing. They are frequently altered by social movements, which grow out of, and also influence, changes in consciousness, climates of opinion, and culture. We have followed Tocqueville and other classical social theorists in [focusing] on the mores—the "habits of the heart"—that include consciousness, culture, and the daily practices of life. It makes sense to study the mores not because they are powerful—in the short run, at least, power belongs to the political and economic structures—but for two other reasons. A study of the mores gives us insight into the state of society, its coherence, and its long-term viability. Secondly, it is in the sphere of the mores, and the climates of opinion they express, that we are apt to discern incipient changes of vision—those new flights of the social imagination that may indicate where society is heading.

A CHANGE OF ERAS?

... John Donne, in 1611, at the very beginning of the modern era, with the prescience that is sometimes given to great poets, vividly described that process:

> 'Tis all in peeces, all cohaerence gone;
> All just supply, and all Relation:
> Prince, Subject, Father, Sonne, are things forgot,
> For every man alone thinkes he hath got
> To be a Phoenix, and that then can bee
> None of that kinde, of which he is, but hee.[1]

Donne lived in a world where the ties of kinship and village and feudal obligation were already loosening, though only a few perceived how radical the consequences would be.

America was colonized by those who had come loose from the older European structures, and so from the beginning we had a head start in the process of modernization. Yet the colonists brought with them ideas of social obligation and group formation that disposed them to recreate in America structures of family, church, and polity that would continue, if in modified form, the texture of older European society. Only gradually did it become clear that every social obligation was vulnerable, every tie between individuals fragile. Only gradually did what we have called ontological individualism, the idea that the individual is the only firm reality, become widespread. Even in our day, when separation and individuation have reached a kind of culmination, their triumph is far from complete. The battles of modernity are still being fought.

But today the battles have become halfhearted. There was a time when, under the battle cry of "freedom," separation and individuation were embraced as the key to a marvelous future of unlimited possibility. It is true that there were always those, like Donne, who viewed the past with nostalgia and the present with apprehension and who warned that we were entering unknown and dangerous waters. It is also true that there are still those who maintain their enthusiasm for modernity, who speak of the third wave or the Aquarian Age or the new paradigm in which a dissociated individuation will reach a final fulfillment. Perhaps most common today, however, is a note of uncertainty, not a desire to turn back to the past but an anxiety about where we seem to be headed. In this view, modernity seems to be a period of enormously rapid change, a transition from something relatively fixed toward something not yet clear. Many might find still applicable Matthew Arnold's assertion that we are

> Wandering between two worlds, one dead,
> The other powerless to be born.[2]

There is a widespread feeling that the promise of the modern era is slipping away from us. A movement of enlightenment and liberation that was to have freed us from superstition and tyranny has led in the twentieth century to a world in which ideological fanaticism and political oppression have reached extremes unknown in previous history. Science, which was to have unlocked the bounties of nature, has given us the power to destroy all life on the earth. Progress, modernity's master idea, seems less compelling when it appears that it may be progress into the abyss. And the globe today is divided between a liberal world so incoherent that it seems to be losing the significance of its own ideals, an oppressive and archaic communist statism, and a poor, and often tyrannical, Third World reaching for the very first rungs of modernity. In the liberal world, the state, which was supposed to be a neutral nightwatchman that would maintain order while individuals pursued their various interests, has become so overgrown and militarized that it threatens to become a universal policeman.

Yet in spite of those daunting considerations, many of those we talked to are still hopeful. They realize that though the processes of separation and individuation were necessary to free us from the tyrannical structures of the past, they must be balanced by a renewal of commitment and community if they are not to end in self-destruction or turn into their opposites. Such a renewal is indeed a world waiting to be born if we only had the courage to see it.

THE CULTURE OF SEPARATION

One of the reasons it is hard to envision a way out of the impasse of modernity is the degree to which modernity conditions our consciousness. If modernity is "the culture of separation," Donne characterized it well when he said " 'Tis all in peeces, all cohaerence gone." When the world comes to us in pieces, in fragments, lacking any overall pattern, it is hard to see how it might be transformed.

A sense of fragmentariness is as characteristic of high intellectual culture as of popular culture. Starting with science, the most respected and influential part of our high culture, we can see at once that it is not a whole, offering a general interpretation of reality, as theology and philosophy once did, but a collection of disciplines each having little to do with the others. . . .

These developments in the realm of high culture have had devastating consequences for education. Here, particularly in higher education, students were traditionally supposed to acquire some general sense of the world and their place in it. In the contemporary multiversity, it is easier to think of education as a cafeteria in which one acquires discrete bodies of information or useful skills. Feeble efforts to reverse these trends periodically convulse the universities, but the latest such convulsion, the effort to establish a "core curriculum," often turns into a battle between disciplines in which the idea of a substantive core is lost. The effort is thus more symptomatic of our cultural fracture than of its cure.

When we turn from intellectual culture to popular culture, particularly the mass media, the situation is, if anything, even more discouraging. Within the disciplinary and subdisciplinary "compartments" of intellectual culture, though there is little integration between them, there is still meaning and intensity in the search for truth. In popular culture, it is hard to say even that much. To take an extreme example, television, it would be difficult to argue that there is any coherent ideology or overall message that it communicates. There is a sense in which the broadcasters' defense of their role—that they are merely mirroring the culture—has a certain plausibility. They do not support any clear set of beliefs or policies, yet they cast doubt on everything. Certainly, they do not glorify "the power structure." Big business is not admirable: Its leaders are frequently power-hungry bullies without any moral restraints (J. R. Ewing, for example). Government is under a cloud of suspicion: Politicians are crooks. Labor is badly tarnished: Labor leaders are mobsters. The debunking that is characteristic of our intellectual culture is also characteristic of the mass media. While television does not preach, it nevertheless presents a picture of reality that influences us more than an overt message could. As Todd Gitlin has described it,

. . . [T]elevision's world is relentlessly upbeat, clean and materialistic. Even more sweepingly, with few exceptions prime time gives us people preoccupied with personal ambition. If not utterly consumed by ambition and the fear of ending up as losers, these characters take both the ambition and the fear for granted. If not surrounded by middle-class arrays of consumer goods, they themselves are glamorous incarnations of desire. The happiness they long for is private, not public; they make few demands on society as a whole, and even when troubled they seem content with the existing institutional order. Personal ambition and consumerism are the driving forces of their lives. The sumptuous and brightly lit settings of most series amount to advertisements for a consumption-centered version of the good life, and this doesn't even take into consideration the incessant commercials, which convey the idea that human aspirations for liberty, pleasure, accomplishment and status can be fulfilled in the realm of consumption. The relentless background hum of prime time is the packaged good life.[3]

Gitlin's description applies best to daytime and prime-time soaps. It does not apply nearly so well to situation comedies, where human relations are generally more benign. Indeed, the situation comedy often portrays people tempted to dishonesty or personal disloyalty by the prospect of some private gain, who finally decide to put family or friends ahead of material aggrandizement. Yet, finally, both soaps and situation comedies are based on the same contrast: human decency versus brutal competitiveness for economic success. Although the soaps show us that the ruthlessly powerful rich are often unhappy and the situation comedies show us that decent "little people" are often happy, they both portray a world dominated by economic competition, where the only haven is a very small circle of warm personal relationships. Thus the "reality" that looms over a narrowed-down version of "traditional morality" is the overwhelming dominance of material ambition.

Of course, in television none of these things is ever really argued. Since images and feelings are better communicated in this medium than ideas, television seeks to hold us, to hook us, by the sheer succession of sensations. One sensation being as good as another, there is the implication that nothing makes any difference. We switch from a quiz show to a situation comedy, to a bloody police drama, to a miniseries about celebrities, and with each click of the dial, nothing remains.

But television operates not only with a complete disconnectedness between successive programs. Even within a single hour or half-hour program, there is extraordinary discontinuity. Commercials regularly break whatever mood has built up with their own, often very different, emotional message. Even aside from commercials, television style is singularly abrupt and jumpy, with many quick cuts to other scenes and other characters. Dialogue is reduced to clipped sentences. No one talks long enough to express anything complex. Depth of feeling, if it exists at all, has to be expressed in a word or a glance.

The form of television is intimately related to the content. Except for the formula situation comedies (and even there, divorce is increasingly common), relationships are as brittle and shifting as the action of the camera. Most people turn out to be unreliable and double-dealing. Where strong commitments are portrayed, as in police dramas, they are only between buddies, and the environing atmosphere, even within the police force, is one of mistrust and suspicion.

If popular culture, particularly television and the other mass media, makes a virtue of lacking all qualitative distinctions, and if the intellectual culture, divided as it is, hesitates to say anything about the larger issues of existence, how does our culture hold together at all? The culture of separation offers two forms of integration—or should we say pseudo-integration?—that turn out, not surprisingly, to be derived from utilitarian and expressive individualism. One is the dream of personal success. As Gitlin has observed, television shows us people who are, above all, consumed by ambition and the fear of ending up losers. That is a drama we can all identify with, at least all of us who have been (and who has not?) exposed to middle-class values. Isolated in our efforts though we are, we can at least recognize our fellows as followers of the same private dream. The second is the portrayal of vivid personal feeling. Television is much more interested in how people feel than in what they think. What they think might separate us, but how they feel draws us together. Successful television personalities and celebrities are thus people able freely to communicate their emotional states. We feel that we "really know them." And the very consumption goods that television so insistently puts before us integrate us by providing symbols of our version of the good life. But a strange sort of integration it is, for the world into which we are integrated is defined only by the spasmodic transition between striving and relaxing and is without qualitative distinctions of time and space, good and evil, meaning and meaninglessness. And however much we may for a moment see something of ourselves in another, we are really, as Matthew Arnold said in 1852, "in the sea of life enisled . . . We mortal millions live *alone.*"[4]

THE CULTURE OF COHERENCE

But that is not the whole story. It could not be the whole story, for the culture of separation, if it ever became completely dominant, would collapse of its own incoherence. Or, even more likely, well before that happened, an authoritarian state would emerge to provide the coherence the culture no longer could. If we are not entirely a mass of interchangeable fragments within an aggregate, if we are in part qualitatively distinct members of a whole, it is because there are still operating among us, with whatever difficulties, traditions that tell us about the nature of the world, about the nature of society, and about who we are as people. Primarily biblical and republican, these traditions are, as we have seen, important for many Americans and significant to some degree for almost all. Somehow families, churches, a variety of cultural associations, and, even if only in the interstices, schools and universities, do manage to communicate a form of life, a *paideia,* in the sense of growing up in a morally and intellectually intelligible world.

. . . [C]ommunities of memory . . . are concerned in a variety of ways to give a qualitative meaning to the living of life, to time and space, to persons and groups. Religious communities, for example, do not experience time in the way the mass media present it—as a continuous flow of qualitatively meaningless sensations. The day, the week, the season, the year are punctuated by an alternation of the sacred and the profane. Prayer breaks into our daily life at the beginning of a meal, at the end of the day, at common worship, reminding us that our utilitarian pursuits are not the whole of life, that a fulfilled life is one in which God and neighbor are remembered first. Many of our religious traditions recognize the significance of silence as a way of breaking the incessant flow of sensations and opening our hearts to the whole-

ness of being. And our republican tradition, too, has ways of giving form to time, reminding us on particular dates of the great events of our past or of the heroes who helped to teach us what we are as a free people. Even our private family life takes on a shared rhythm with a Thanksgiving dinner or a Fourth of July picnic.

In short, we have never been, and still are not, a collection of private individuals who, except for a conscious contract to create a minimal government, have nothing in common. Our lives make sense in a thousand ways, most of which we are unaware of, because of traditions that are centuries, if not millennia, old. It is these traditions that help us to know that it does make a difference who we are and how we treat one another. Even the mass media, with their tendency to homogenize feelings and sensations, cannot entirely avoid transmitting such qualitative distinctions, in however muted a form.

But if we owe the meaning of our lives to biblical and republican traditions of which we seldom consciously think, is there not the danger that the erosion of these traditions may eventually deprive us of that meaning altogether? Are we not caught between the upper millstone of a fragmented intellectual culture and the nether millstone of a fragmented popular culture? The erosion of meaning and coherence in our lives is not something Americans desire. Indeed, the profound yearning for the idealized small town that we found among most of the people we talked to is a yearning for just such meaning and coherence. But although the yearning for the small town is nostalgia for the irretrievably lost, it is worth considering whether the biblical and republican traditions that small town once embodied can be reappropriated in ways that respond to our present need. Indeed, we would argue that if we are ever to enter that new world that so far has been powerless to be born, it will be through reversing modernity's tendency to obliterate all previous culture. We need to learn again from the cultural riches of the human species and to reappropriate and revitalize those riches so that they can speak to our condition today. . . .

SOCIAL ECOLOGY

. . . Without derogating our modern technological achievements, we now see that they have had devastatingly destructive consequences for the natural ecology. We are engaged in an effort to mitigate and reverse the damage and regain an ecological balance whose complete loss could prove fatal. Modernity has had comparable destructive consequences for social ecology. Human beings have treated one another badly for as long as we have any historical evidence, but modernity has given us a capacity for destructiveness on a scale incomparably greater than in previous centuries. And social ecology is damaged not only by war, genocide, and political repression. It is also damaged by the destruction of the subtle ties that bind human beings to one another, leaving them frightened and alone. It has been evident for some time that unless we begin to repair the damage to our social ecology, we will destroy ourselves long before natural ecological disaster has time to be realized.

For several centuries, we have been embarked on a great effort to increase our freedom, wealth, and power. For over a hundred years, a large part of the American people, the middle class, has imagined that the virtual meaning of life lies in the acquisition of ever-increasing status, income, and authority, from which genuine freedom is supposed to come. Our achievements have been enormous. They permit us the aspiration to become a genuinely humane society in a genuinely decent world, and provide many of the means to attain that aspiration. Yet we seem to be hovering on the very brink of disaster, not only from international conflict but from the internal incoherence of our own society. What has gone wrong? How can we reverse the slide toward the abyss?

In thinking about what has gone wrong, we need to see what we can learn from our traditions, as well as from the best currently available knowledge. What has failed at every level—from the society of nations to the national society to the local community to the family—is integration: We have failed to remember "our community as members

of the same body," as John Winthrop put it. We have committed what to the republican founders of our nation was the cardinal sin: We have put our own good, as individuals, as groups, as a nation, ahead of the common good.

The litmus test that both the biblical and republican traditions give us for assaying the health of a society is how it deals with the problem of wealth and poverty. The Hebrew prophets took their stand by the *'anawim,* the poor and oppressed, and condemned the rich and powerful who exploited them. The New Testament shows us a Jesus who lived among the *'anawim* of his day and who recognized the difficulty the rich would have in responding to His call. Both testaments make it clear that societies sharply divided between rich and poor are not in accord with the will of God. Classic republican theory from Aristotle to the American founders rested on the assumption that free institutions could survive in a society only if there were a rough equality of condition, that extremes of wealth and poverty are incompatible with a republic. Jefferson was appalled at the enormous wealth and miserable poverty that he found in France and was sanguine about our future as a free people only because we lacked such extremes. Contemporary social science has documented the consequences of poverty and discrimination, so that most educated Americans know that much of what makes our world and our neighborhoods unsafe arises from economic and racial inequality.[5] Certainly most of the people to whom we talked would rather live in a safe, neighborly world instead of the one we have.

But the solution to our problems remains opaque because of our profound ambivalence. When times are prosperous, we do not mind a modest increase in "welfare." When times are not so prosperous, we think that at least our own successful careers will save us and our families from failure and despair. We are attracted, against our skepticism, to the idea that poverty will be alleviated by the crumbs that fall from the rich man's table, as the neocapitalist ideology tells us. Some of us often feel, and most of us sometimes feel, that we are only someone if we have "made it" and can look down on those who have not. The American dream is often a very private dream of being the star, the uniquely successful and admirable one, the one who stands out from the crowd of ordinary folk who don't know how. And since we have believed in that dream for a long time and worked very hard to make it come true, it is hard for us to give it up, even though it contradicts another dream that we have—that of living in a society that would really be worth living in.

What we fear above all, and what keeps the new world powerless to be born, is that if we give up our dream of private success for a more genuinely integrated societal community, we will be abandoning our separation and individuation, collapsing into dependence and tyranny. What we find hard to see is that it is the extreme fragmentation of the modern world that really threatens our individuation; that what is best in our separation and individuation, our sense of dignity and autonomy as persons, requires a new integration if it is to be sustained.

The notion of a transition to a new level of social integration, a newly vital social ecology, may also be resisted as absurdly utopian, as a project to create a perfect society. But the transformation of which we speak is both necessary and modest. Without it, indeed, there may be very little future to think about at all.

RECONSTITUTING THE SOCIAL WORLD

The transformation of our culture and our society would have to happen at a number of levels. If it occurred only in the minds of individuals (as to some degree it already has), it would be powerless. If it came only from the initiative of the state, it would be tyrannical. Personal transformation among large numbers is essential, and it must not only be a transformation of consciousness but must also involve individual action. But individuals need the nurture of groups that carry a moral tradition reinforcing their own aspirations. Implicitly or explicitly, a number of the communities

of memory . . . hold ethical commitments that require a new social ecology in our present situation. But out of existing groups and organizations, there would also have to develop a social movement dedicated to the idea of such a transformation. We have several times spoken of the civil rights movement as an example. It permanently changed consciousness, in the sense of individual attitudes toward race, and it altered our social life so as to eliminate overt expressions of discrimination. If the civil rights movement failed fundamentally to transform the position of black people in our society, it was because to do that would have required just the change in our social ecology that we are now discussing. So a movement to transform our social ecology would, among other things, be the successor and fulfillment of the civil rights movement. Finally, such a social movement would lead to changes in the relationship between our government and our economy. This would not necessarily mean more direct control of the economy, certainly not nationalization. It would mean changing the climate in which business operates so as to encourage new initiatives in economic democracy and social responsibility, whether from "private" enterprise or autonomous small- and middle-scale public enterprises. In the context of a moral concern to revive our social ecology, the proposals of the proponents of the Administered Society and Economic Democracy . . . could be considered and appropriate ones adopted.[6]

To be truly transformative, such a social movement would not simply subside after achieving some of its goals, leaving the political process much as it found it. One of its most important contributions would be to restore the dignity and legitimacy of democratic politics. We have seen . . . how suspicious Americans are of politics as an area in which arbitrary differences of opinion and interest can be resolved only by power and manipulation. The recovery of our social ecology would allow us to link interests with a conception of the common good. With a more explicit understanding of what we have in common and the goals we seek to attain together, the differences between us that remain would be less threatening. We could move to ameliorate the differences that are patently unfair while respecting differences based on morally intelligible commitments. Of course, a political discourse that could discuss substantive justice and not only procedural rules would have to be embodied in effective political institutions, probably including a revitalized party system.

It is evident that a thin political consensus, limited largely to procedural matters, cannot support a coherent and effective political system. For decades that has become ever clearer. We have been afraid to try for a more substantial consensus for fear that the effort may produce unacceptable levels of conflict. But if we had the courage to face our deepening political and economic difficulties, we might find that there is more basic agreement than we had imagined. Certainly, the only way to find out is to raise the level of public political discourse so that the fundamental problems are addressed rather than obscured.[7]

If we are right in our stress on a revitalized social ecology, then one critically important action that government could take in a new political atmosphere would be, in Christopher Jencks's words, to reduce the "punishments of failure and the rewards of success."[8] Reducing the inordinate rewards of ambition and our inordinate fears of ending up as losers would offer the possibility of a great change in the meaning of work in our society and all that would go with such a change. To make a real difference, such a shift in rewards would have to be a part of reappropriation of the idea of vocation or calling, a return in a new way to the idea of work as a contribution to the good of all and not merely as a means to one's own advancement.

If the extrinsic rewards and punishments associated with work were reduced, it would be possible to make vocational choices more in terms of intrinsic satisfactions. Work that is intrinsically interesting and valuable is one of the central requirements for a revitalized social ecology. For professionals, this would mean a clearer sense that the large institutions most of them work for really contribute to the public good. A bright young lawyer (or a bright old lawyer, for that matter) whose work consists in helping one corporation outwit another is intelligent enough to doubt the social utility of what he or she is doing. The work may be interesting—even challenging and exciting—yet its intrinsic meaninglessness in any larger moral or social context necessarily produces an alienation that is only partly assuaged by the relatively large income of corporate lawyers. Those whose work is not only poorly rewarded but boring, repetitive, and unchallenging are in an even worse situation. Automation that turns millions of our citizens into mere servants of robots is already a form of despotism, for which the pleasures of private life—modest enough for those of minimum skill and minimum wage—cannot compensate. The social wealth that automation brings, if it is not siphoned into the hands of a few, can be used to pay for work that is intrinsically valuable, in the form of a revival of crafts (that already flourish in supplying goods for the wealthy) and in the improvement of human services. Where routine work is essential, its monotony can be mitigated by including workers in fuller participation in their enterprises so that they understand how their work contributes to the ultimate product and have an effective voice in how those enterprises are run.

Undoubtedly, the satisfaction of work well done, indeed "the pursuit of excellence," is a permanent and positive human motive. Where its reward is the approbation of one's fellows more than the accumulation of great private wealth, it can contribute to what the founders of our republic called civic virtue. Indeed, in a revived social ecology, it would be a primary form of civic virtue. And from it would flow a number of positive consequences. For one thing, the split between private and public, work and family, that has grown for over a century, might begin to be mended. If the ethos of work were less brutally competitive and more ecologically harmonious, it would be more consonant with the ethos of private life and, particularly, of family life. A less frantic concern for advancement and a reduction of working hours for both men and women would make it easier for women to be full participants in the workplace without abandoning family life. By the same token, men would be freed to take an equal role at home and in child care. In this way, what seemed at first to be a change only in the nature of work would turn out to have major consequences for family life as well.

Another consequence of the change in the meaning of work from private aggrandizement to public contribution would be to weaken the motive to keep the complexity of our society invisible. It would become part of the ethos of work to be aware of our intricate connectedness and interdependence. There would be no fear of social catastrophe or hope of inordinate reward motivating us to exaggerate our own independence. And with such a change, we might begin to be better able to understand why, though we are all, as human beings, morally deserving of equal respect, some of us begin with familial or cultural advantages or disadvantages that others do not have. Or perhaps, since we would not conceive of life so much in terms of a race in which all the prizes go to the swiftest, we might begin to make moral sense of the fact that there are real cultural differences among us, that we do not all want the same thing, and that it is not a moral defect to find other things in life of interest besides consuming ambition. In short, a restored social ecology might allow us to mitigate the harm that has been done to disadvantaged groups without blaming the victims or trying to turn them into carbon copies of middle-class high achievers.

It should be clear that we are not arguing . . . that a few new twists in the organization of the economy would solve all our problems. It is true that a change in the meaning of work and the relation of work and reward is at the heart of any recovery of our social ecology. But such a change involves a deep cultural, social, and even psychological transformation that is not to be brought about by expert fine-tuning of economic institutions alone. On the contrary, at every point, institutional changes, educational changes, and motivational changes would go hand in hand. For example, part of our task might well involve a recovery of older notions of the corporation. As Alan Trachtenberg has written:

The word [corporation] refers to any association of individuals bound together into a *corpus,* a body sharing a common purpose in a common name. In the past, that purpose had usually been communal or religious; boroughs, guilds, monasteries, and bishoprics were the earliest European manifestations of the corporate form. . . . It was assumed, as it is still in nonprofit corporations, that the incorporated body earned its charter by serving the public good. . . . Until after the Civil War, indeed, the assumption was widespread that a corporate charter was a privilege to be granted only by a special act of a state legislature, and then for purposes clearly in the public interest. Incorporation was not yet thought of as a right available on application by any private enterprise.[9]

As late as 1911 . . . a leading Boston businessman, Henry Lee Higginson, could say, following earlier Protestant notions of stewardship, that corporate property "belongs to the community."

Reasserting the idea that incorporation is a concession of public authority to a private group *in return for* service to the public good, with effective public accountability, would change what is now called the "social responsibility of the corporation" from its present status, where it is often a kind of public relations whipped cream decorating the corporate pudding, to a constitutive structural element in the corporation itself. This, in turn, would involve a fundamental alteration in the role and training of the manager. Management would become a profession in the older sense of the word, involving not merely standards of technical competence but standards of public obligation that could at moments of conflict override obligations to the corporate employer. Such a conception of the professional manager would require a deep change in the ethos of schools of business administration, where "business ethics" would have to become central in the process of professional formation. If the rewards of success in business management were not so inordinate, then choice of this profession could arise from more public-spirited motives. In short, personal, cultural, and structural change all entail one another.

SIGNS OF THE TIMES

Few of those with whom we talked would have described the problems facing our society in exactly the terms we have just used. But few have found a life devoted to "personal ambition and consumerism" satisfactory, and most are seeking in one way or another to transcend the limitations of a self-centered life. If there are vast numbers of a selfish, narcissistic "me generation" in America, we did not find them, but we certainly did find that the language of individualism, the primary American language of self-understanding, limits the ways in which people think.

Many Americans are devoted to serious, even ascetic, cultivation of the self in the form of a number of disciplines, practices, and "trainings," often of great rigor. There is a question as to whether these practices lead to the self-realization or self-fulfillment at which they aim or only to an obsessive self-manipulation that defeats the proclaimed purpose. But it is not uncommon for those who are attempting to find themselves to find in that very process something that transcends them. For example, a Zen student reported: "I started Zen to get something for myself, to stop suffering, to get enlightened. Whatever it was, I was doing it for myself. I had hold of myself and I was reaching for something. Then to do it, I found out I had to give up that hold on myself. Now it has hold of me, whatever 'it' is."[10] What this student found is that the meaning of life is not to be discovered in manipulative control in the service of the self. Rather, through the disciplined practices of a religious way of life, the student found his self more grasped than grasping. It is not surprising that "self-realization" in this case has occurred in the context of a second language, the allusive language of Zen Buddhism, and a community that attempts to put that language into practice.

Many Americans are concerned to find meaning in life not primarily through self-cultivation but through intense relations with others. Romantic love is still idealized in our society. It can, of course, be remarkably self-indulgent, even an excuse to use another for one's own gratification. But it can also be a revelation of the poverty of the self and lead to a genuine humility in the presence of the beloved. We have noted in the early chapters of this book that the therapeutically inclined, jealous though they are of their personal autonomy, nonetheless seek enduring attachments and a community within which those attachments can be nurtured. As in the case of self-cultivation, there is in the desire for intense relationships with others an attempt to move beyond the isolated self, even though the language of individualism makes that sometimes hard to articulate.

Much of what is called "consumerism," and often condemned as such, must be understood in this same ambiguous, ambivalent context. Attempts to create a beautiful place in which to live, to eat well and in a convivial atmosphere, to visit beautiful places where one may enjoy works of art, or simply lie in the sun and swim in the sea, often involve an element of giving to another and find their meaning in a committed relationship.[11] Where the creation of a consumption-oriented lifestyle, which may resemble that of "the beautiful people" or may simply involve a comfortable home and a camper, becomes a form of defense against a dangerous and meaningless world, it probably takes on a greater burden than it can bear. In that case, the effort to move beyond the self has ended too quickly in the "little circle of family and friends" of which Tocqueville spoke, but even so the initial impulse was not simply selfish.

With the weakening of the traditional forms of life that gave aesthetic and moral meaning to everyday living, Americans have been improvising alternatives more or less successfully. They engage, sometimes with intense involvement, in a wide variety of arts, sports, and nature appreciation, sometimes as spectators but often as active participants. Some of these activities involve conscious traditions and demanding practices, such as ballet. Others, such as walking in the country or jogging, may be purely improvisational, though not devoid of some structure of shared meaning. Not infrequently, moments of intense awareness, what are sometimes called "peak experiences," occur in the midst of such activities. At such moments, a profound sense of well-being eclipses the usual utilitarian preoccupations of everyday life. But the capacity of such experiences to provide more than a momentary counterweight to pressures of everyday life is minimal. Where these activities find social expression at all, it is apt to be in the form of what we have called the lifestyle enclave. The groups that form around them are too evanescent, too inherently restricted in membership, and too slight in their hold on their members' loyalty to carry much public weight. Only at rare moments do such largely expressive solidarities create anything like a civic consciousness, as when a local professional sports team wins a national championship and briefly gives rise to a euphoric sense of metropolitan belongingness. . . .

THE POVERTY OF AFFLUENCE

At the very beginning of the modern era, Thomas Hobbes . . . summed up his teaching about human life by arguing that the first "general inclination of mankind" is "a perpetual and restless desire of power after power, that ceaseth only in death."[12] But we are beginning to see now that the race of which he speaks has no winner, and if power is our only end, the death in question may not be merely personal, but civilizational.

Yet we still have the capacity to reconsider the course upon which we are embarked. The morally concerned social movement, informed by republican and biblical sentiments, has stood us in good stead in the past and may still do so again. But we have never before faced a situation that called our deepest assumptions so radically into question. Our problems today are not just political. They are moral and have to do with the meaning of life. We have assumed that as long as economic growth continued, we could leave all else to the private sphere. Now that economic growth is faltering and the moral ecology on which we have tacitly depended is in disarray, we are beginning to understand that our common life requires more than an exclusive concern for material accumulation.

Perhaps life is not a race whose only goal is being foremost. Perhaps true felicity does not lie in continually outgoing the next before. Perhaps the truth lies in what most of the world outside the modern West has always believed, namely that there are practices of life, good in themselves, that are inherently fulfilling. Perhaps work that is intrinsically rewarding is better for human beings than work that is only extrinsically rewarded. Perhaps enduring commitment to those we love and civic friendship toward our fellow citizens are preferable to restless competition and anxious self-defense. Perhaps common worship, in which we express our gratitude and wonder in the face of the mystery of being itself, is the most important thing of all. If so, we will have to change our lives and begin to remember what we have been happier to forget.

We will need to remember that we did not create ourselves, that we owe what we are to the communities that formed us, and to what Paul Tillich called "the structure of grace in history" that made such communities possible. We will need to see the story of our life on this earth not as an unbroken success but as a history of suffering as well as joy. We will need to remember the millions of suffering people in the world today and the millions whose suffering in the past made our present affluence possible.

Above all, we will need to remember our poverty. We have been called a people of plenty, and though our per capita GNP has been surpassed by several other nations, we are still enormously affluent. Yet the truth of our condition is our poverty. We are finally defenseless on this earth. Our material belongings have not brought us happiness. Our military defenses will not avert nuclear destruction. Nor is there any increase in productivity or any new weapons system that will change the truth of our condition.

We have imagined ourselves a special creation, set apart from other humans. In the late twentieth century, we see that our poverty is as absolute as that of the poorest of nations. We have attempted to deny the human condition in our quest for power after power. It would be well for us to rejoin the human race, to accept our essential poverty as a gift, and to share our material wealth with those in need.

Such a vision is neither conservative nor liberal in terms of the truncated spectrum of present American political discourse. It does not seek to return to the harmony of a "traditional" society, though it is open to learning from the wisdom of such societies. It does not reject the modern criticism of all traditions, but it insists in turn on the criticism of criticism, that human life is lived in the balance between faith and doubt. Such a vision arises not only from the theories of intellectuals, but from the practices of life that Americans are already engaged in. Such a vision seeks to combine social concern with ultimate concern in a way that slights the claims of neither. Above all, such a vision seeks the confirmation or correction of discussion and experiment with our friends, our fellow citizens.

CRITICAL-THINKING QUESTIONS

1. In what ways is U.S. culture "individualistic"? What are some of the consequences of living within a "culture of separation"?
2. According to the authors, how is the cultural "fragmentation" of modern life evident in academic life? In the mass media?
3. Explain the authors' notion of the "impasse of modernity." That is, what do the members of modern, industrial societies need to enhance the meaning of life? What suggestions do the authors make toward reconstructing human community?

NOTES

1. John Donne, "An Anatomie of the World: The First Anniversary."

2. Matthew Arnold, "Stanzas from the Grand Chartreuse" (1855).

3. T. Gitlin, *Inside Prime Time* (New York: Pantheon, 1983), pp. 268–69. Conversations with Todd Gitlin and Lisa Heilbronn were helpful in clarifying our views of television.

4. Matthew Arnold, "To Marguerite." Emphasis in original.

5. L. Rainwater, *What Money Buys: Inequality and the Social Meanings of Income* (New York: Basic Books, 1974).

6. On many of these issues, an approach refreshingly free of ideological narrowness is provided by recent Catholic social teaching. See the collection of documents from Vatican II and after: *Renewing the Earth: Catholic Documents on Peace, Justice and Liberation,* ed. D. J. O'Brien and T. A. Shannon (Garden City, NY: Image Books, 1977). See also Pope John Paul II's 1981 encyclical letter *Laborem Exercens,* contained in G. Baum, *The Priority of Labor* (New York: Paulist Press, 1982), which provides a useful commentary. C. K. Wilber and K. P. Jameson use these teachings to reflect about the American economy in their *An Inquiry into the Poverty of Economics* (Notre Dame, IN: University of Notre Dame Press, 1983).

7. On the modern fear of politics and the need to connect politics and vision see S. Wolin, *Politics and Vision: Continuity and Innovation in Western Political Thought* (Boston: Little, Brown, 1960), especially chapter 10. For a helpful consideration of some of these issues see M. Walzer, *Spheres of Justice: A Defense of Pluralism and Equality* (New York: Basic Books, 1983). For a critique of the dangers of too thin a moral consensus see D. Callahan, "Minimalist Ethics," *Hastings Center Report* II (October 1981): 19–25.

8. C. Jencks et al., *Inequality: A Reassessment of the Effect of Family and Schooling in America* (New York: Basic Books, 1972), p. 8. On pp. 230–32 Jencks discusses the various ways, preferably indirect, in which this could be done. Daniel Yankelovich criticizes Jencks for being wildly out of touch with popular American consciousness in making his suggestion about limiting income (*New Rules: Searching for Self-Fulfillment in a World Turned Upside Down* [New York: Random House, 1981], pp. 137–39). But he in no way answers Jencks's argument.

9. A. Trachtenberg, *The Incorporation of America: Culture and Society in the Gilded Age* (New York: Hill and Wang, 1982), pp. 5–6.

10. S. M. Tipton, *Getting Saved From the Sixties* (Berkeley and Los Angeles: University of California Press, 1982), p. 115.

11. The differences between private vacations and public holidays, or holy days, illustrate the moral limits of expressive alternatives to traditional civic and religious forms of enacting our social solidarity. The vacation began its short, century-long history as a stylish middle-class imitation of the aristocrat's seasonal retreat from court and city to country estate. Its character is essentially individualistic and familial: "Everyone plans his own vacation, goes where he wants to go, does what he wants to do," writes Michael Walzer. Vacations are individually chosen, designed, and paid for, regardless of how class-patterned vacation behavior may be or how many vacation spots depend on public funds for their existence. The experience vacations celebrate is freedom—the freedom to break away from the ordinary places and routines of the workaday world and "escape to another world" where every day is "vacant" and all time is "free time." There we have "our own sweet time" to do with as we will and empty days to fill at our own pace with activities of our own choosing. Public holidays, by contrast, were traditionally provided for everyone in the same form and place, at the same time, to celebrate together by taking part in the fixed communal rites, meals, and celebrations

that already filled them. In ancient Rome, the *dies vacantes,* in a telling reversal of meaning, were those ordinary working days devoid of religious festivals or public games. Public holy days such as the Sabbath are the common property of all. "Sabbath rest is more egalitarian than the vacation because it can't be purchased: It is one more thing that money can't buy. It is enjoined for everyone, enjoyed by everyone," Walzer observes. The Sabbath requires a shared sense of obligation and solemnity, backed not only by a shared impulse to celebrate but by a common mechanism of enforcement. God created the Sabbath for everyone and *commanded* all of the faithful to rest although in our society today individuals are free to choose to respect it or not. Nonetheless, the Sabbath signifies a freedom interwoven with civic equality and unity under an ultimate authority that is not merely a man-made social idea (Walzer, *Spheres of Justice,* pp. 190–96).

12. Thomas Hobbes, *Leviathan* (1651), ed. C. B. Mac-Pherson (Harmondsworth, England: Penguin Books, 1968), p. 161.

75

The Price of Modernization: The Case of Brazil's Kaiapo Indians

Marlise Simons

Among the billions of poor people throughout the Third World, few will have a chance for a better life. But this is exactly what has happened to the Kaiapo, people who live deep in Brazil's rain forest. Has affluence been the blessing that the Kaiapo imagined it would be? To at least some of their number, the modernization of the Kaiapo amounts to little more than the systematic destruction of their traditional way of life.

It is getting dark when Chief Kanhonk sits down in the yard outside his home, ready for a long evening of conversation. Night birds are calling from the bush that sparkles with fireflies. Whooping frogs make a racket by the river. No one seems worried by the squadron of bats sweeping low overhead.

It is that important moment of the day when Indians of the Amazon, who use no written language, meet to talk, pass on information, and tell stories.

The night is when they recall ancestral customs, interpret dreams, and comment on changes in nature and other events of the day. But from a nearby home come the sounds of a powerful rival: A television set is screeching cartoons at a group of children. I understand now why, that morning, by way of saying hello, these naked children of the rain forest had shouted things like "He-Man" and "Flintstones."

Three years ago, when money from the sale of gold nuggets and mahogany trees was pouring into Gorotire, Chief Kanhonk agreed to bring in television, or the "big ghost," as it is called here. A shiny satellite dish now stands on the earthen plaza like an alien sculpture, signaling that Gorotire—a

SOURCE: "The Amazon's Savvy Indians," by Marlise Simons, *The New York Times Magazine,* February 26, 1989, pp. 36–37; 48–52. Copyright © 1989 by the New York Times Company. Reprinted with permission.

small settlement of some 800 people on the Fresco River, a tributary of the Amazon—has become one of the wealthiest Indian villages in Brazil.

Yet Chief Kanhonk appears to regret his decision. "I have been saying that people must buy useful things like knives or fishing hooks," he says darkly. "Television does not fill the stomach. It only shows our children and grandchildren white people's things."

The "big ghost" is just one of the changes that have been sweeping over Gorotire, but it seems to be worrying the elders the most. Some believe it is powerful enough to rob them of their culture. Bebtopup, the oldest medicine man in the village, explains his misgivings: "The night is the time the old people teach the young people. Television has stolen the night."

When I discuss this with Eduardo Viveiros, a Brazilian anthropologist who works with a more isolated Amazonian tribe, he seems less worried. "At least they quickly understood the consequences of watching television," he says. "Many people never discover. Now Gorotire can make a choice."

It was the issue of choice that first drew me to the Kaiapo Indians of the lower Amazon Basin. They seemed to be challenging the widely held notion that forest Indians are defenseless in face of the pressures of the competitive and predatory Western world around them. Unlike most of Brazil's 230,000 Indians, they go out into the white world to defend their interests, and it is no longer unusual to see Kaiapo men—in their stunning body paint and feathered headdresses—showing up in Congress in Brasilia, the nation's capital, or lobbying by doing a war dance outside a government office. They have even bought Western gadgets to record and film their festivals.

Once the masters of immense stretches of forest and savannas, the Kaiapo were for hundreds of years among the most skillful farmers and hunters and fiercest warriors of central Brazil. They terrified other tribes with their raids. From the seventeenth to the nineteenth centuries, they not only resisted the slaving raids of the Portuguese invaders but they also attacked white traders and

gold prospectors with such a vengeance that royal orders came from Portugal to destroy the Kaiapo. The white man's wrath and his diseases killed many, yet there are still close to 3600 Kaiapo in more than a dozen different villages near the Xingu River. They have quarreled and regrouped, but their lands, several vast reservations, are more secure than those of many other tribes.

After many years of isolation in the forest, the Kaiapo now have to deal with the growing encroachments of white society. "They are going through a great transition," says Darrell Posey, an American anthropologist who has worked in Gorotire for more than a decade. "Their survival is a miracle in itself. But I worry whether they can go on making the changes on their own terms."

Colombia, Ecuador, Peru, and Venezuela—four of nine nations in the Amazon Basin, which harbors some 800,000 Indians—each have large numbers of tropical-forest Indians. But nowhere are pressures on Indian land as great as they are in Brazil. As the Amazon is opened up, developers bring in highways, settlers, cattle ranchers, mines, and hydroelectric dams. In Brazil alone, more than ninety tribes have disappeared since the beginning of this century.

The clearing of large areas of the rain forest and the fate of the Indians are also rapidly becoming an issue of international concern. Interest in the region has risen as ecological concerns, such as ozone depletion, the greenhouse effect, and other changes in the global environment become political issues. More attention is paid to scientists who are alarmed at the destruction of the rain forest—a vital flywheel in the world's climate and the nursery of at least half of the world's plant and animal species.

This has also prompted an increasing interest in the highly structured world of the forest Indians and their ancient and intricate knowledge of nature that permits them to survive in the tropical jungle without destroying it. (The Hall of South American Peoples, which includes a life-size model of a Kaiapo warrior, recently opened at the Museum of Natural History in New York City.)

As Indians find greater support among environmentalists, they also get more organized in their fight to protect their habitat. The Kaiapo held their first international congress last week in Altamira, in central Brazil, protesting government plans to build several massive dams that would flood Indian land.

In Brazil, Indian tribes occupy 10 percent of the nation's territory, although much of their land has not been demarcated. Brazil's past military regimes elevated Indian affairs to a national-security issue, because many tribes live in large areas of border land. It is official policy to integrate Indians into the larger society, and the National Indian Foundation, with its 4900 employees, is in charge of implementing this.

In my eighteen years in Latin America, I have heard many politicians and anthropologists discuss what is usually called "the Indian problem," what to "do" about cultures that have changed little in thousands of years. One school of thought holds that the remote tribes should be kept isolated and protected until they can slowly make their own choices. Another school accepts that the Indian world is on the wane, and talks about "guiding" the Indians toward inevitable change—a process that should take several generations.

But some anthropologists and politicians, including the Brazilian government, believe in still more rapid integration. When Romeo Jucá was head of the Indian Foundation, he said that it was only right for Indians to exploit their wealth, even if it meant acculturation. "We have to be careful how fast we go," he said, "but being Indian does not mean you have to be poor."

Gerardo Reichel-Dolmatoff is one of Latin America's most respected anthropologists. He insists that the Indians are their own best guides into Western society. An Austrian-born Colombian, Reichel-Dolmatoff has worked in Colombia's forests, at the Amazon's headwaters, for almost fifty years. "We cannot choose for them," he insists. "And we cannot put them into reserves, ghettos, ashokas. They are not museum exhibits. . . . If Indians choose the negative aspects of our civilization, we cannot control that. If there is one basic truth in anthropology, it is that cultures change.

Static cultures do not exist."

The Indians themselves are pleading for more protection and respect for their cultures. Conrad Gorinsky, son of a Guyana Indian mother and himself a chemist in London, recently said: "We don't want the Indians to change because we have them comfortably in the back of our mind like a kind of Shangri-La, something we can turn to even if we work ourselves to death in New York. But we are hounding and maligning them instead of recognizing them as the guardians of the forests, of the world's genetic banks, of our germ plasm and lifelines."

The aboriginal peoples we call Indians are as different from one another as, say, Europeans are. Even the most isolated groups remain separate fiefdoms with widely varying experiences, beliefs, and histories. The degree of contact they have with the outside world is just as varied.

I first met Kaiapo tribesmen three years ago in Belém, a large city at the mouth of the Amazon. I saw them again in Brasilia, the capital. In both places, they demonstrated their political skills and capacity to mobilize, showing up in large numbers to protest measures by the government. They seemed particularly adept at commanding the attention of the press. Their body paint, feathers, and other paraphernalia made them appear warlike, exotic, and photogenic.

Back in Gorotire, as it turns out, they are more "ordinary." Wearing feathers and beads, explains Kubei, a chief's son, is for special occasions. "It's our suit and tie." Besides the satellite dish, the Kaiapo also have their own small airplane. Their new wealth has also given them the luxury of hiring non-Indians to help plant new fields. But they remain ready to attack white intruders; some of the adult men have markings on their chests that record the number of outsiders they have killed.

Two roads fan out from the center of Gorotire. A new sand track leads east on a five-hour drive to the town of Redenção. The other road goes south and, in a sense, it leads into the past. Dipping into the forest, it becomes a path that meanders through open patches where the Kaiapo women grow corn, sweet potatoes, bananas, manioc. On the plain ahead, it joins an ancient trail system that once reached for hundreds of miles into northern and western Brazil.

One morning, Beptopup (medicine man, shaman, connoisseur of nature), the anthropologist Darrell Posey (who speaks the Kaiapo language), and I wander into the bush. Beptopup walks past the plants the way you go down a street where you know everyone. Stopping, nodding, his face lighting up with happy recognition, he sometimes goes into a song—a soft, high-pitch chant for a particular plant.

He picks leaves, each one familiar, each one useful. One serves to remove body hair. Another, he says, can prevent pregnancy. The underside of one leaf is so rough it is used to sandpaper wood and file fingernails. Beptopup collects his plants in the morning, he says, because "that is when they have the most strength."

Stopping at a shrub, we look at the large circle around its stem, where nothing grows. "This and other plants have been sent to a laboratory for analysis," says Posey. "We think this one has a natural weedkiller."

Beptopup holds up a branch of what he calls the "eye of the jaguar." "This was our flashlight," he says, showing how to set it afire and swing it gently so its strong glow will light one's path.

One afternoon, when the heat has crept into everything, the women and children come back from the fields to their village. They stop and sit in a creek to escape the swirling gnats and buzzing bees. Others sit outside their homes, going about their age-old business. One woman plucks the radiant feathers of a dead macaw. Another removes her eyebrows and eyelashes, because the Kaiapo women think they are ugly. (A nurse once told me that this custom might have a hygienic origin—to ward off parasites, for instance.) Kaiapo women also deepen their foreheads by shaving the top of their head in a triangle that reaches the crown—a fearsome sight to the unaccustomed eye.

I envy a mother who is clearly enjoying herself fingerpainting her three children. She draws black designs with genipap juice. On the face and the feet

she puts red dye from the "urucu," or annatto, plant; Indians say it keeps away chiggers and ticks.

Change has come to Gorotire along the other road, the one leading east to Redenção. Recent Kaiapo history is full of "firsts," but a notable turning point came when prospectors struck gold on Gorotire land in 1980. The Kaiapo raided the camp, twenty miles from the village, but failed to drive away the trespassers. Then they made a deal.

Last fall, when I was visiting Gorotire, about 2000 gold diggers were stripping the land to the bone farther upstream, and the River Fresco passed the village the color of mud, its water contaminated with oil and mercury. I heard no one complain about that. Gorotire gets 7 percent of the mine's profits—several pounds of gold a week.

In 1984, a lumber company completed the first road. It signed a contract with the Indian Foundation for Gorotire's mahogany (the Indians are wards of the Brazilian government). Most of the mahogany is gone now, and the government agency split the profits with the Kaiapo. Gorotire chose to spend its gold and timber profits on new water and electricity lines and rows of brick houses. Only about half of the inhabitants now live in traditional palm-frond huts.

The young Kaiapo who earn a salary as supervisors at the gold camp have bought their own gas stoves, radios, sofas, and mattresses. For the community, the four tribal chiefs ordered several boats, trucks, and a small plane that ferries people and goods among nearby Kaiapo villages.

One evening, a truck arriving from Redenção—bringing rice, sugar, bottled gas, oil for the generator—is another reminder of how fast Gorotire is adapting to a Western economy. From being a largely self-sufficient community of hunters and farmers, it is now increasingly dependent on outside goods. In Gorotire, it is clearly money, no longer disease or violence, that has become the greatest catalyst for change. Money has given the Kaiapo the means and the confidence to travel and lobby for their rights. At the same time, it is making them more vulnerable.

I have seen other villages where Indians have received large sums of money—for the passage of a railroad or a powerline, or from a mining company. Such money is usually released in installments, through banks, but its arrival has put new strains on the role of the chiefs. Money and goods have introduced a new, materialistic expression of power in societies that have been egalitarian. Among most Indians, a man's prestige has always depended not on what he acquires but on what he gives away.

In Gorotire, some of the young men complain that the chiefs are not distributing community money and goods equally, that the chiefs' relatives and favorites are getting a bigger share and more privileges.

Darrell Posey, the anthropologist, believes the greatest political change came with the road. With it, he says, "the Kaiapo chiefs lost control of which people and what goods would come in." Previously, the chiefs had been the sole distributors. They had also played the vital roles of keeping the peace and leading the ceremonies. Now, the chiefs hardly know the liturgy of the ceremonies; their main task seems to be to deal with the outside world.

The transition is also changing the role of the medicine man. Bebtopup, for example, has an arsenal of remedies for the common ailments—fevers, diarrheas, snake bites, wounds. But he and his colleagues have lost prestige because they do not know how to deal with the diseases brought to Gorotire by white men, such as the pneumonia that strikes the children and the malaria spreading from the gold miners' camp.

Anthropologists sometimes say that when outsiders visit the Indian world, they often focus on themes central not to Indians but to themselves. This might explain why I was so bothered by the garbage, the flotsam of Western civilization.

Gorotire's setting is Arcadian. It lies on a bluff overlooking the River Fresco, with views of the forests across and the mountains behind. Spring rains bring waterfalls and blossoms. But these days the village is awash with rusting cans, plastic wrappers, tapes sprung from their cassettes, discarded mattresses, and clothes. New domestic animals such as dogs, pigs, and ducks have left a

carpet of droppings. And giant rats, which suddenly appeared some years ago, seem to be everywhere; some have bitten small children.

"Indians have never had garbage that was not biodegradable," says Sandra Machado, a Brazilian researching Kaiapo farming techniques here. "No one wants to take care of it."

It is a mild moonlit evening, and in the men's house many Kaiapo are watching soccer on television. The bank of the river is a quieter place to talk.

"If you look beyond the garbage and the stone houses, this is still a strong and coherent indigenous culture," says Darrell Posey, speaking of the mixed feelings he has about a decade of developments in Gorotire. "Despite everything, the language is alive, the festivals and initiation rights are observed."

Posey says that the Kaiapo in Gorotire and in other villages continue with their age-old natural farming techniques, using plants to fix nitrogen in the soil, chunks of termite nests instead of chemical fertilizers, plant infusions to kill pests, the nests of ferocious ants to protect fruit trees from other ant predators.

Biologists often complain that there have been many studies of exotic rituals, paraphernalia, and kinships of Indians, but that Western science has paid scant attention to the Indians' use of animals and plants.

Like others working in the Amazon region, Posey worries about the gap between the old and the young. "The old chiefs are turning over decisions to the young because they can drive a truck or operate a video machine or go to the bank," he says. "But the young people don't see the relevance of learning the tribal knowledge and it's being lost."

"You can afford to lose one generation," he adds, "because grandparents do the teaching of their grandchildren. But you cannot afford to lose two generations."

Gorotire has a small government school, designed to help Indians integrate into the national society. The teacher, who speaks only Portuguese, has started organizing annual Independence Day parades. On the blackboard is a list of patriotic holidays, including Independence Day and the Day of the Soldier. I ask the children later what a soldier is. "Something of white people," one of them says.

Chief Poropot agrees that everyone must learn Portuguese. "The language of the Kaiapo is very ancient and it will never end," he says. "But the women and the children need to learn Portuguese to defend themselves."

Defend themselves?

"If they go to shop in Redenção, they have to talk," he says. "If they get sick, they cannot tell the doctor what they have."

Thirty miles from Gorotire, in the village of Aukre, another Kaiapo tribe is choosing a different strategy for change. Its best-known member is Paiakan, thirty-seven years old, the son of Chief Tikiri.

Calm and articulate, Paiakan has been named to "keep an eye on the whites" in the state capital of Belém. He acts as a kind of roving ambassador for the Kaiapo, even though each village is autonomous. When Kaiapo interests are threatened, he sends out warnings to the communities.

Paiakan's contacts with the outside world and the many pitfalls it holds for Indians have made him more conservative, he says, more so than in the early days, in the 1970s, when he first left home to work on the Trans-Amazonian Highway. As his father's main adviser, he has insisted that Aukre remain a traditional village.

It is built in the age-old circle of mud-and-thatch huts. There is no television, running water, pigs, or piles of garbage. Paiakan and his father have also banned logging and gold digging. This appears to have saved Aukre from the consumerism—and widespread influenza and malaria—of Gorotire.

"The lumber men have come to us with their bags of money," he says. "And we know we have a lot of gold. But we do not want to bring a lot of money in. The Indian still does not know the value of white man's objects or how to treat them." Paiakan cites clothing as an example. "The Indian wears something until it is stiff with dirt, then he throws it out."

But people now want things from the "world of

the whites," he continues. "Pressure from the white society is so strong, there is no wall that can stop it." It is the task of the chief to measure the change, provide explanations, he says. "If someone wants to get a radio or a tape recorder, the chiefs cannot stop it."

In Aukre, where two aging chiefs are still in charge of buying goods for the community, they say that they will not buy gadgets. "We explain we cannot buy this thing for you because we do not have the batteries you need and we cannot repair it," Paiakan says.

Of late, Paiakan has been invited abroad to campaign for the protection of the rain forest. He knows the problem only too well. Ranchers have moved almost to the reservation's doorstep, felled trees, and set massive forest fires. Because of deforestation, there have been unusual changes in the water level of the Fresco River.

"Our people are getting very disoriented," says Paiakan. "It would be as if people from another planet came to your cities and started to tear down your houses. The forest is our home." With all the destruction going on, he continues, "the breath of life is drifting up and away from us."

At the age of seventy-eight and retired from teaching at the University of California at Los Angeles, the anthropologist Gerardo Reichel-Dolmatoff lives in Bogotá, Colombia, and is still writing. After studying changes in the Amazon for five decades, he is not optimistic about the prospects for the Indians.

"In Colombia, I don't know of a single case where an aboriginal culture has found a strong adaptive mechanism," he says. "Physical survival is possible. But I have not seen the ancient values replaced by a workable value system. I wish I could be more positive. But in fifty years I have seen too many traditions being lost, too many tribes disappear.

"For 500 years we have witnessed the destruction of the Indians. Now we are witnessing the destruction of the habitat. I suggest more field work, and immediate field work, because soon it will be too late."

At a conference on ethnobiology last fall,

Reichel-Dolmatoff urged scientists to insist on spreading the message that Western science has much to learn from Indians, from their well-adapted lives and deeply felt beliefs, their view that whatever man subtracts he must restore by other means.

What suggestions has he made to Indians?

"Indians have to stay in touch with their language—that is absolutely essential," he says. "It embodies their thought patterns, their values, their philosophy." Moreover, he says, talented young Indians should be given a modern academic education, but also the chance to keep in touch with their people. "They come from cultures based on extraordinary realism and imagery. They should not be forced to enter at the lowest level of our society."

One night, I ask the chiefs in Gorotire: What happens if the gold runs out? After all, most of the mahogany is already gone. Young tribesmen have wanted to invest some of the income, and the chiefs have accepted the idea. Gorotire has bought a home in Belém for Kaiapo who travel there, as well as three houses in Redenção. There is talk of buying a farm, a curious thought, perhaps, for a community that lives on 8 million acres of land. But the Kaiapo, so they say, want it so that white farmers can grow rice for them.

And there is talk of planting new mahogany trees. Soon the conversation turns to a bird that a tribesman explains is very important. It is the bird, he says, that spreads the mahogany seeds.

CRITICAL-THINKING QUESTIONS

1. What have been the short-term consequences of the Kaiapo's new wealth? What are their long-term prospects?

2. What arguments can be made in support of continued effort by the Kaiapo to economically develop their resources? What arguments can be made against doing so?

3. In what ways are other countries involved in the changes taking place in the Amazon Basin?